Business Research Methods

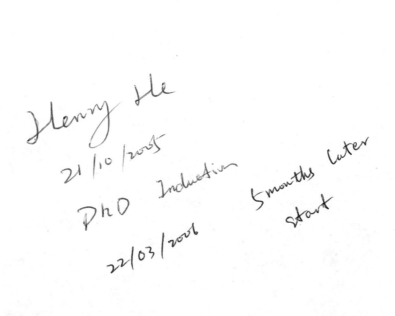

Business Research Methods

ALAN BRYMAN

EMMA BELL

OXFORD
UNIVERSITY PRESS

OXFORD

UNIVERSITY PRESS

Great Clarendon Street, Oxford OX2 6DP

Oxford University Press is a department of the University of Oxford.
It furthers the University's objective of excellence in research, scholarship,
and education by publishing worldwide in

Oxford New York

Auckland Bangkok Buenos Aires Calcutta Cape Town Chennai
Dar es Salaam Delhi Hong Kong Istanbul Karachi Kolkata
Kuala Lumpur Madrid Melbourne Mexico City Mumbai Nairobi
São Paulo Shanghai Taipei Tokyo Toronto
and associated companies in Berlin Ibadan

Oxford is a registered trade mark of Oxford University Press
in the UK and in certain other countries

Published in the United States
by Oxford University Press Inc., New York

British Library Cataloguing in Publication Data

Data available

ISBN–019–925938–0

10 9 8 7 6 5

Typeset by Newgen Imaging Systems (P) Ltd, Chennai, India
Printed in Ashford Colour Press, Gosport, Hampshire

Acknowledgements

This book has benefited from the large number of students who have shared their ideas about, experiences of, and problems encountered in business and management and social science research. These individuals, many of them (unwittingly) have made a significant contribution to the development of the text. Alan Bryman's teaching of research methods at Loughborough University and Emma Bell's experience at Warwick Business School have provided major sources of inspiration in this respect and we would therefore like to express our appreciation for the support provided by both institutions. We would particularly like to acknowledge colleagues Alan Beardsworth, Michael Billig, and Dave Buchanan for their constructive comments on various parts of the book and Dave McHugh for his imaginative contribution in designing the companion web site to accompany the text. In addition, our thanks go to the referees for their close and careful reading of the manuscript. Their criticisms and advice, informed by their substantial experience of teaching research methods to business and management students, have proved invaluable. We are grateful to Sonia Liff for kindly agreeing to let us use photographs from her research. We also wish to thank several people at or connected with Oxford University Press: Patrick Brindle and his editorial team for their support and enthusiasm throughout the project; Laura Hodgson for her firm but fair grip on the book's production; and Hilary Walford for her astute, careful, and tireless copy-editing. However, we have reserved our most important acknowledgements until last. Alan would like to thank Sue and Sarah as usual for their support in putting up with him without a murmur and Emma would like to express her gratitude to Scott, who has provided emotional, practical, and intellectual support, not to mention several examples! Alan would also like to thank Sue for her wonderful work on the proofs for this book. Finally, we take full responsibility for the final text, including its inevitable deficiencies, from which everyone except us must, of course, be absolved.

Contents

Abbreviations

ABTA	Association of British Travel Agents
AES	Annual Employment Survey
ALS	average leadership style
AoM	Academy of Management
ASA	American Sociological Association
BHPS	British Household Panel Study
BMRB	British Market Research Bureau
BSA	British Social Attitudes
BSA	British Sociological Association
CA	conversation analysis
CAPI	computer-assisted personal interviewing
CAQDAS	computer-assisted qualitative data analysis software
CASS	Centre for Applied Social Surveys
CATI	computer-assisted telephone interviewing
CV	curriculum vitae
DA	discourse analysis 張洺. 張港
DEFRA	Department for Environment, Food and Rural Affairs
ECA	ethnographic content analysis
EFS	Expenditure and Food Survey
ESRC	Economic and Social Research Council
FES	Family Expenditure Survey
FTSE	Financial Times (London) Stock Exchange
GHS	General Household Survey
GMID	General Market Information Database
HMO	health maintenance organization
✶ HRM	Human Resource Management
IBSS	International Bibliography of the Social Sciences
ICI	Imperial Chemical Industries
IiP	Investors in People

ISP	Internet Service Provider
ISSP	International Social Survey Programme
JDS	Job Diagnostic Survey
LFS	Labour Force Survey
LPC	least-preferred co-worker
MPS	Motivating Potential Score
MRS	Market Research Society
MUD	multi-user domain
NFS	National Food Survey
OCS	Organizational Culture Scale
OD	organizational development
OECD	Organization for Economic Cooperation and Development
ONS	Office for National Statistics
ORACLE	Observational Research and Classroom Learning Evaluation
PWC	Price Waterhouse Cranfield
REPONSE	Relations Professionnelles et Négociations d'Enterprise
SCELI	Social Change and Economic Life Initiative
SIC	Standard Industrial Classification
SME	small or medium-sized enterprise
SOGI	society, organization, group, and individual
SSCI	Social Sciences Citation Index
SRA	Social Research Association
TDM	Total Design Method
TGI	Target Group Index
TQM	Total Quality Management
VDL	vertical dyadic linkage 二位山. 22值山
WERS	Workplace Employee Relations Survey
WoS	Web of Science
WIRS	Workplace Industrial Relations Survey

The focus of the book

This is a book that will be of use to all students in business schools who have an interest in understanding research methods as they are applied in a business and organizational context. *Business Research Methods* gives students essential guidance on how to carry out their own research projects and introduces readers to the core concepts, methods, and values involved in doing research. The book provides a valuable learning resource through its comprehensive coverage of methods that are used by experienced researchers investigating the world of business as well as introducing some of the philosophical issues and ethical controversies that these researchers face. So, if you want to learn about business research methods, from how to formulate research questions to the process of writing up your research, *Business Research Methods* will provide a clear, easy to follow, and comprehensive introduction.

The book is based on the first-named author's *Social Research Methods*, which was written for students of the social sciences. The success of this book and the interest that it occasioned in business schools led to this book, which has entailed an extensive adaptation for students of business and management studies. This has meant: completely changing the examples that are used in the book; removing the discussion of issues that are not central to the concerns of students of business and management; and including completely new sections on areas that are important to business school students. It has also been comprehensively updated to reflect the growing use of the Internet as a medium for conducting research and also as a source of data, so that there is now an entirely new chapter that deals with these newly emerging research opportunities (Chapter 23).

Because this book is written for a business school audience it is intended to reflect a diverse range of subject areas, including organizational behaviour,

management science, strategy, organization studies, HRM, and marketing. In using the term *Business Research Methods*, we have in mind the kinds of research methods that are employed in these fields, focusing primarily on methods that are used in areas of business and management that have been influenced by the social sciences. Consequently, we do not claim to cover the full gamut of business research methods. Certain areas of business and management research, such as economic research and financial and accounting research, are not included within our purview. Our reason for not including such disciplines is that they are very much self-contained fields with their own traditions and approaches that do not mesh well with the kinds of methods that we deal with in this book.

This book has been written with two groups of readers in mind. First, undergraduates and postgraduates in business and management schools and departments who invariably take at least one module or course in the area of research methods. This book covers a wide range of research methods, approaches to research, and ways of carrying out data analysis, so it is likely to meet the needs of the vast majority of students in this position. Research methods are not tied to a particular nation; many if not most of the principles transcend national boundaries.

The second group, which in most cases overlaps with the first, comprises undergraduates and postgraduates who do a research project as part of the requirement for their degree programmes. This can take many forms, but one of the most common is that a small-scale research project is carried out and a dissertation based on the investigation is presented. In addition, students are often expected to carry out mini-projects in relation to certain modules. The accent in the chapters in Parts Two and Three is on the practice of social research and as such these chapters will be extremely useful in helping students make informed decisions about doing their research. In addition, when each research method is examined, its uses and limitations are explored in order to help students to make these decisions. In Part Four, Chapter 24 provides advice on writing up research. But, most significantly, Chapter 26 has been written specifically for students doing research projects. This chapter thus builds on earlier discussion of research questions in Chapter 2, reinforcing a topic that we see as key to the whole process of doing research.

In addition to providing students with practical advice on doing research, the book also explores the nature of business and management research. This means that it attends to issues relating to fundamental concerns about what doing business and management research entails. For example:

- Is a natural science model of the research process applicable to the study of business and management?

- If not, why not?

- Why do some people feel it is inappropriate to employ such a model?

- If we do use a natural science model, does that mean that we are making certain assumptions about the nature of the world of business and management?

- Equally, do those writers and researchers who reject such a model have an alternative set of assumptions about the nature of the world of business and management?

- What kind or kinds of research findings are regarded as legitimate and acceptable?

- To what extent do values have an impact on the research process?

- Should we worry about the feelings of people outside the research community concerning what we do to people during our investigations?

These and many other issues impinge on research in a variety of ways and will be confronted at different stages throughout the book. While knowing how to do research—how best to design a questionnaire, how to observe, how to analyse documents, and so on—is crucial to an education in research methods,

so too is a broad appreciation of the wider issues that impinge on the practice of business and management research. Thus, so far as we are concerned, the role of an education in research methods is not just to provide the skills that will allow you to do your own research, but also to provide you with the tools for a critical appreciation of how research is done and with what assumptions. One of the most important abilities that an understanding of research methods and methodology provides is an awareness of the need not to take evidence that you come across (in books, journals, and so on) for granted.

The structure of the book

Business and management research has many different traditions, one of the most fundamental of which is the distinction between quantitative and qualitative research. This distinction lies behind the structure of the book and the way in which issues and methods are approached.

The book is divided into four parts.

Part One comprises two scene-setting chapters. It deals with basic ideas about the nature of business and management research.

- Chapter 1 examines such issues as the nature of the relationship between theory and research and the degree to which a natural science approach is an appropriate framework for the study of business and management. It is here that the distinction between quantitative and qualitative research is first encountered. They are presented as different *research strategies* with different ways of conceptualizing how business and management should be studied. It is also shown that there is more to the distinction between them than whether an investigation includes the collection of quantitative data.

- In Chapter 2, the idea of a *research design* is introduced. This chapter allows an introduction to the basic frameworks within which social research is carried out, such as social survey research, case study research, and experimental research. As previously noted, this chapter also includes a discussion of *research questions*—what they are, why they are important, and how they come to be formulated.

These two chapters provide the basic building blocks for the rest of the book.

Part Two contains ten chapters concerned with quantitative research.

- Chapter 3 explores the nature of quantitative research and as such provides a context for the later chapters. The next four chapters are largely concerned with aspects of social survey research.

- Chapter 4 deals with sampling issues—how to select a sample and the considerations that are involved in assessing what can be inferred from different kinds of sample.

- Chapter 5 is concerned with the kind of interviewing that takes place in survey research that is, structured interviewing.

- Chapter 6 covers the design of questionnaires. This involves a discussion of how to devise self-completion questionnaires, such as postal questionnaires.

- Chapter 7 examines the issue of how to ask questions for questionnaires and structured interviews.

- Chapter 8 covers structured observation, which is a method that has been developed for the systematic observation of behaviour. It has been especially influential in the areas of business and management research.

- Chapter 9 presents content analysis, a method that provides a rigorous framework for the analysis of a wide range of documents.

- Chapter 10 deals with the analysis of data collected by other researchers and by official bodies. The emphasis then switches to the ways in which we can analyse quantitative data.

- Chapter 11 presents a range of basic tools for the analysis of quantitative data. The approach taken is non-technical. The emphasis is upon how to choose a method of analysis and how to interpret the findings. No formulae are presented.

- Chapter 12 shows you how to use computer software—in the form of SPSS, the most widely used software for analysing quantitative data—in order to implement the techniques you learned in Chapter 11.

Part Three contains eight chapters on aspects of qualitative research.

- Chapter 13 has the same role in relation to Part Three as Chapter 3 has in relation to Part Two. It provides an overview of the nature of qualitative research and as such supplies the context for the other chapters in this part.

- Chapter 14 is concerned with ethnography and participant observation, which is the source of some of the best-known studies in business and management research. The two terms are often used interchangeably and refer to the immersion of the researcher in a social setting.

- Chapter 15 deals with the kinds of interview that qualitative researchers conduct, which is typically semi-structured interviewing or unstructured interviewing.

- Chapter 16 explores the focus group method, whereby groups of individuals are interviewed on a specific topic.

- Chapter 17 examines two ways in which qualitative researchers analyse language: conversation analysis and discourse analysis.

- Chapter 18 deals with the examination of documents in qualitative research. The emphasis then shifts to the interpretation of documents.

- Chapter 19 explores some approaches to the analysis of qualitative data.

- Chapter 20 shows you how to use computer software—a relatively new development in qualitative research—to assist with your analysis.

It is striking that certain issues recur across Parts Two and Three: interviewing, observation, documents, and data analysis. However, as you will see, quantitative and qualitative research constitute contrasting approaches to such activities.

Part Four contains chapters that go beyond the quantitative/qualitative research contrast.

- Chapter 21 deals with some of the ways in which the distinction between quantitative and qualitative research is less fixed than is sometimes supposed.

- Chapter 22 presents some ways in which quantitative and qualitative research can be combined to produce what is referred to as multi-strategy research.

- Chapter 23 is concerned with the use of the Internet as a context or platform for conducting research.

- Chapter 24 has been included to help with writing up research, an often neglected area of the research process.

- Chapter 25 considers the ways in which ethical issues (impinge) on researchers and the kinds of principles that are involved.

- Chapter 26 takes you through the mains steps that are involved in a research project and offers advice on how to manage this process.

Special features of the book

Several special features have been included in the book to make it more helpful.

- *Examples*. It is often said that the three most important features to look for when buying a house are location, location, location. We think that a parallel for the teaching of research methods is examples, examples, examples. We have always learned a lot by reading research and finding out how others have carried out research and what lessons they seem to have learned. In view of this, the book is full of examples. We have tried to illustrate most of our major points with an example and often more than one. Most of our examples (derive) from published research and it is clearly the case that you will find it difficult to generate research of an equivalent level because of your limited resources, time, and experience. On the other hand, you can get close and it is important to learn about the benchmarks that good practice in published work provide. In your own research, it may be that, to use a well-known term devised by Herbert Simon (1960), you will need to (satisfice.) (Simon devised this term to forge a contrast with the model of rational decision making that was (pervasive) in economics. He argued that, when working in organizations, people satisfice when they make decisions rather than find the most appropriate means

to achieve given ends. Satisficing means that the search for an appropriate course of action is governed by the principle of looking for what is satisfactory, rather than by what is optimal.) The important issue is to know in what ways you are needing to satisfice and what the implications are of doing so.

- *Boxes*. The text is full of boxes. These do a variety of things. Sometimes they provide examples; sometimes they define key terms (What is . . .?); sometimes they list series of important points. They help to break up the text and to provide a focus for definitions and for key examples.

- *Practical tips*. Most chapters have at least one shaded box of practical tips. These draw on our experiences when talking to students about their concerns of special points to think about or to watch out for. In addition, they sometimes reflect our impression that students make certain recurring mistakes that can easily be avoided.

- *Checklists*. Most chapters include checklists of issues that should be borne in mind when engaging in certain activities, like doing a literature review, devising a structured interview schedule, or conducting a focus group. They are meant to alert you to key points you will have encountered in the text so that you can be reminded of what to look out for or consider when doing your own research.

- *Chapter guide*. Each chapter begins with a chapter guide that alerts readers to what they can expect to have learned by the end of each chapter. This is meant to provide a route map of what is to follow.

- *Key points*. At the end of each chapter there is a set of significant points that are particularly crucial for you to take note of. They are meant to alert you to issues that are especially important and to jog your memory about the areas that have been covered.

- *Questions for review*. At the end of each chapter there is also a series of questions to help you to test your understanding of key concepts and ideas.

- *Glossary*. At the end of the book is a glossary of definitions of central terms. Many repeat definitions in the What is . . .? boxes, but they also provide a convenient way of knowing what is meant by key terms.

Companion web site

Business Research Methods is accompanied by an interactive web site, which has been designed and written by Dave McHugh, an experienced management academic and university teacher. You can find and access this website on www.oup.com. The web site has been constructed in such a way as to be closely integrated with the book, and to provide additional teaching and learning material for both lecturers and students. *Oxford+university +press*

The web site contains:

- a lecturer's guide;
- chapter-by-chapter PowerPoint slides;
- real-research style examples of all the main methods outlined in the book;
- up-to-date and updated web links to the best business research web sites;
- summaries of key debates and controversies in business research.

The web site also contains a **Methods and Skills Toolkit**, which is designed to help students use the book to guide them through the dissertation research process. This resource provides a guide to the practicalities and problems that students are faced with when asked to do a dissertation. The toolkit will cover a range of issues, from dealing with your supervisor/tutor to ways of organizing and writing your dissertation for maximum effect. The toolkit will also guide students through the ways in which larger research issues and controversies dealt with in *Business Research Methods* might have some impact upon a student's own experience of doing a small-scale research project.

How to use the book

The book can be used in a number of different ways. However, we would encourage all readers at least to look at the chapter guide at the beginning of each chapter to decide whether or not they in fact need the material covered there and also to gain a sense of the range of issues the book does in fact address.

- *Wider philosophical and methodological issues.* If you do not need to gain an appreciation of the wider philosophical context of enquiry in business and management research, Chapter 1 can largely be ignored. If an emphasis on such issues *is* something you are interested in, Chapter 1 along with Chapter 21 should be a particular focus of attention.

- *Survey research.* Chapters 4 through 7 deal with the kinds of topics that need to be addressed in survey research. In addition, Chapter 11 examines ways of analysing the kinds of data that are generated by survey researchers. Also, sections in Chapter 23 explore issues to do with the conduct of surveys via e-mail or the World Wide Web.

- *Practical issues concerned with doing quantitative research.* This is the province of the whole of Part Two. In addition, you would be advised to read Chapter 2, which maps out the main research designs employed, such as experimental and cross-sectional designs, that are frequently used by quantitative researchers.

- *Practical issues concerned with doing qualitative research.* This is the province of the whole of Part Three. In addition, you would be advised to read Chapter 2, which maps out the main research designs employed, such as the case study, which is frequently employed in qualitative research.

- *Analysing data.* Chapters 11 and 19 explore the analysis of quantitative and qualitative research data respectively, while Chapters 12 and 20 introduce readers to the use of computer software in this connection. It may be that your module on research methods does not get into issues to do with analysis, in which case these chapters would be omitted.

- *Formulating research questions.* As we have already said in this Guide, we see the asking of research questions as fundamental to the research process. Advice on what research questions are, how they are formulated, where they come from, and so on is provided in Part One and is followed through in Chapter 26.

- *Doing your own research project.* We hope that the whole of this book will be relevant to students doing their own research projects or mini-projects, but Chapter 26 is the one where specific advice relating to this issue is located. In addition, we would alert you to the practical tips that have been devised and the checklists of points to remember.

- *Writing.* This issue is very much connected with the last point. It is easy to forget that your research has to be *written up*. This is as much a part of the research process as the collection of data. Chapter 24 discusses a variety of issues to do with writing up research and in Chapter 26 we examine it in connection with doing your own research and writing it up as a dissertation or similar product.

- *Wider responsibilities of researchers.* It is important to bear in mind that as researchers we bear responsibilities to the people and organizations that are the (recipients) of our research activities. Ethical issues are raised at a number of points in this book and Chapter 25 is devoted to a discussion of them. The fact that we have given over an entire chapter to a discussion of ethics is a measure of their importance in terms of the need to ensure that all researchers should be ethically sensitive.

- *The quantitative/qualitative research contrast.* We use the distinction between quantitative and qualitative research in two ways: as a means of organizing the research methods and methods of analysis available to you; and as a way of introducing some wider philosophical issues about business and management research. Chapter 1 outlines the chief areas of difference between quantitative and qualitative research. These are followed up in Chapter 13. We also draw attention to some of the limitations of adhering to an excessively strict demarcation between the two research strategies in Chapter 21, while Chapter 22 explores ways of integrating them. If you do not find it a helpful distinction, these chapters can be avoided or skimmed.

- *The Internet.* The Internet plays an increasingly important role in the research process. At various junctures we provide important web sites where key information can be gleaned. We also discuss in Chapter 26 the use of the Internet as a route for finding references for your *literature review*, itself another important phase of the research process. You will find that many of the references that you find when you do an online search will then themselves be accessible to you in electronic form. Finally, Chapter 23 discusses the use of the Internet as a source of material that can be analysed and as a platform for doing research in the form of such research methods as Web surveys, electronic focus groups, and e-mail surveys.

Part One

recur

Part One of this book is concerned with two ideas that will recur again and again during the course of this book—the idea of research strategy and the idea of research design. Chapter 1 outlines a variety of considerations that impinge on the practice of business and management research and relates these to the issue of research strategy. Two research strategies are identified: quantitative and qualitative research. Chapter 2 identifies the different kinds of research design that are employed.

These chapters provide some basic conceptual building blocks that you will return to at many points in the book. Some of the issues may seem remote from research practice but they are in fact important aspects of how we think about business research.

1

Business research strategies

CHAPTER GUIDE

The chief aim of this chapter is to show that a variety of considerations enter into the process of doing business research. The distinction that is commonly drawn among writers on and practitioners of business research between *quantitative research* and *qualitative research* is explored in relation to these considerations. This chapter explores:

- the nature of the relationship between theory and research, in particular whether theory guides research (known as a *deductive* approach) or whether theory is an outcome of research (known as an *inductive* approach);

- *epistemological* issues—that is, ones to do with what is regarded as appropriate knowledge about the social world; one of the most crucial aspects is the question of whether or not a natural science model of the research process is suitable for the study of the social world;

- *ontological* issues—that is, ones to do with whether the social world is regarded as something external to social actors or as something that people are in the process of fashioning;

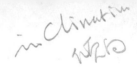

- the ways in which these issues relate to the widely used distinction in the social sciences between two types of *research strategy*: quantitative and qualitative research; there is also a preliminary discussion, which will be followed up in Chapter 21, that suggests that, while

quantitative and qualitative research represent different approaches to business research, we should be wary of driving a wedge between them;

- the ways in which *values* and *practical issues* also impinge on the business research process.

Introduction

This book is about business research. It attempts to equip people who have some knowledge about management and business with an appreciation of how research in this area is conducted and what the research process involves. This latter project involves situating business research in the context of the social science disciplines, such as sociology, psychology, anthropology, and economics, which inform the study of business and its specific fields, which include marketing, human resource management, strategy, organizational behaviour, accounting and finance, industrial relations, and operational research.

Two points are of particular relevance here. First, the methods of management and business research are closely tied to different visions of how organizational reality should be studied. Methods are not simply neutral tools: they are linked to the ways in which social scientists envision the connection between different viewpoints about the nature of social reality and how it should be examined. However, it is possible to overstate this point. While methods are not neutral, they are not entirely suffused with intellectual inclinations either. Secondly, there is the question of how research methods and practice connect with the wider social scientific enterprise. Research data are invariably collected in relation to something. The 'something' is often a pressing organizational problem, such as the effect of mergers and acquisitions on corporate culture or the impact of the introduction of new technology on employee motivation. Another scenario occurs when research is done on a topic when a specific opportunity arises. For example, the NASA space shuttle *Challenger* disaster in 1986 stimulated business and management research into the decision-making processes and group dynamics that had led to the decision to launch the shuttle despite indications that there were

significant safety problems (Shrivasta et al. 1988; Vaughan 1990). Yet another stimulus for research can arise out of personal experiences. Lofland and Lofland (1995) note that many research publications emerge out of the researcher's personal biography. Certainly, Bryman traces his interest in Disney theme parks back to a visit to Disney World in Florida in 1991 (Bryman 1995, 1999), while his interest in the representation of social science research in the mass media (Fenton, Bryman, and Deacon 1998) can almost certainly be attributed to a difficult experience with the press reported in Haslam and Bryman (1994). Similarly, the experience of having been involved in the implementation of a quality management initiative in an NHS hospital trust prompted Bell to explore the meaning of badging in an organizational context (Bell et al. 2002). Finally, research data are also collected in relation to social scientific theory and this raises the issue of the nature of the relationship between theory and research.

The nature of business research

It would be easy to 'cut to the chase' and explore the nature of methods in business research and provide the reader with advice on how best to choose between and implement them. After all, many people might expect a book with the title of the present one to be concerned mainly with the ways in which the different methods in the business researcher's arsenal can be employed. But the practice of business research does not exist in a bubble, hermetically sealed off from the social sciences and the various intellectual allegiances that their practitioners hold. In particular, the diverse nature of management and business scholarship has led to considerable disagreement about how its research claims ought to be

Box 1.1 The difference between research and practice

An interesting point about the relationship between theory and practice in business and management research is made by Gummesson (2000), who sees academic researchers and management consultants as groups of knowledge workers who each place a different emphasis on theory and practice. 'Backed by bits and pieces of theory, the consultant contributes to practice, whereas the scholar contributes to theory supported by fragments of practice' (2000: 9), but fundamentally he sees their roles as closely related. Gummesson sees researchers and consultants as involved in addressing problems that concern management, thereby reinforcing the view that the value of both groups is determined by their ability to convince the business community that their findings are relevant and useful.

evaluated. Hence, some writers have suggested that management research can be understood only as an applied field because it is concerned not only with understanding the nature of organizations but also with solving problems that are related to managerial practice (see Box 1.1). Tranfield and Starkey argue that much management research has lost touch with the concerns and interests of practitioners and that management and business researchers must relearn how to be responsive to them in order for their research to retain a value and a purpose.

However, other writers would suggest that management and business research is too concerned with lengthy 'fact-finding' exercises and is insufficiently guided by theoretical concerns. They would argue that application is not a primary purpose to which management research should be directed (Burrell 1997). For these scholars, making research relevant to managerial practice ought not to be the main aim of academic study (Clegg 2002; Hinings and Greenwood 2002). They believe that research should not be dictated by non-academic interests, such as professional associations and government agencies, who may seek to influence its focus and guide its development in a way that is 'useful' to current practice but susceptible to the whim of current

management fads and fashions. Bell and Bryman (2003) suggest that the applied nature of management and business research has influenced the development of the field in a manner that has made it overly pragmatic and susceptible to users' agendas.

A further debate that has influenced our understanding of the role of management and business research stems from the thesis developed by Gibbons et al. (1994) concerning the way that scientific knowledge is produced. Gibbons et al. suggest that the process of knowledge production in contemporary society falls into two contrasting categories or types, which they describe as 'mode 1' and 'mode 2' knowledge production. These are summarized as follows:

• *Mode 1*. Within this traditional, university-based model, knowledge production is driven primarily by an academic agenda. Discoveries tend to build upon existing knowledge in a linear fashion. The model makes a distinction between theoretically pure and applied knowledge, the latter being where theoretical insights are translated into practice. However, only limited emphasis is placed on the practical dissemination of knowledge because the academic community is defined as the most important audience or consumer of 'mode 1' knowledge.

• *Mode 2*. This model draws attention to the role of *trans-disciplinarity* in research, which it assumes is driven by a process that causes the boundaries of single contributing discipline to be exceeded. Findings are closely related to context and may not easily be replicated, so knowledge production is less of a linear process. Moreover, the production of knowledge is not confined to academic institutions. Instead, it involves academics, policy-makers, and practitioners who apply a broad set of skills and experiences in order to tackle a shared problem. This means that knowledge is disseminated more rapidly and findings are more readily exploited in order to achieve practical advantage.

Although mode 2 research is intended to exist alongside mode 1, rather than to replace it, some researchers have suggested that management and business research is more suited to a 'mode 2' model of knowledge production (Tranfield and Starkey 1998).

eclectical:
折衷的. 折衷学派.

These debates frame a series of questions about the nature and purpose of management and business research, which any new researcher in this field must deal with. For example:

- What is the aim or function of business research?
- Is it conducted primarily in order to find ways of improving organizational performance through increased effectiveness and efficiency?
- Or is it mainly about increasing our understanding of how organizations work their impact on individuals and on society?
- Who are the audiences of business research?
- Is business research conducted primarily for managers and, if not, for whom else in organizations is it conducted?
- Or is it done in order to further the academic development of business and management as a field or even as a discipline?

These questions are the subject of considerable on-going academic debate about the nature and status of business research. Being aware of them is important in understanding what influences your choice of research topic and how you address it. Another means of understanding the nature and status of business research is through the practices of those who engage in it and there are four points that can be made in relation to this.

1. In order to evaluate the quality of management and business research it is necessary to know as much as possible about researchers' *own* role in this process—including how they collected and analysed the data and the theoretical perspective that informed their interpretation of it. This understanding relies on examination of methods used by business researchers, which is why, throughout this book, we have used real examples of published research to illustrate how researchers deal with and justify these methodological choices.

2. This leads to a second point in relation to the use of examples. Business research methods tend on the whole to be more eclectically used and explained in less detail than in some other social sciences such as sociology. Perhaps this is due to the emergent nature of the field or because it draws from such a diverse range of disciplines, but in practice it means that novice researchers can sometimes find it difficult to identify examples of existing research that can be used to inform their own practice. One of the purposes of our use of examples in this book is therefore to draw attention to the range of methodological approaches that business researchers have taken in a way that can be understood by those who are new to this field of study.

3. The third point relates to the kinds of methods used in business research. In some instances, it is hard to identify examples of the use of particular research methods, whilst in others, such as the case study method, there are numerous studies to choose from. We believe, however, that this can provide an opportunity for new researchers to make use of less popular or less commonly used methods in order to gain insight into a research problem. In other words, we hope that, through reading this book, business students will possibly be encouraged to use research methods that are less commonly used, as well as those that have a more established reputation.

4. Finally, despite some of the limitations of business research, in terms of the availability of examples that illustrate the use of various research methods, we have tried to confine our choice of examples to the field of business and management. This is partly because by getting to know how other researchers have approached the study of business it is possible to build up an understanding of how the use of research methods in this field might be improved and developed in the future.

Confine. 替范围

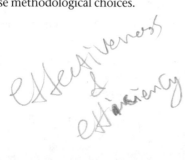

Theory and research

Characterizing the nature of the link between theory and research is by no means a straightforward matter. There are several issues at stake here, but two stand out in particular. First, there is the question of what form of theory one is talking about. Secondly, there is the matter of whether data are collected to test or to build theories.

What type of theory?

The term 'theory' is used in a variety of different ways, but its most common meaning is as an explanation of observed regularities, to explain, for example, why women and ethnic minorities are under-represented in higher-paid managerial positions, or why the degree of alienation caused by the introduction of new technology varies according to the methods of production that are involved. However, such theories do not in themselves constitute a theoretical *perspective*, which is characterized by a higher level of abstraction in relation to research findings. Examples of this kind of theory include structural-functionalism, symbolic interactionism, critical theory, poststructuralism, structuration theory, and so on. What we see here is a distinction between theories of the former type, which are often called *theories of the middle range* (Merton 1967), and *grand theories*, which operate at a more abstract and general level.

According to Merton, grand theories offer few indications to researchers as to how they might guide or influence the collection of empirical evidence. So, if someone wanted to test a theory or to draw an inference from it that could be tested, the level of abstractness is likely to be so great that the researcher would find it difficult to make the necessary links with the real world. For research purposes, then, Merton argued that grand theories are of limited use in connection with social research, although, as the example in Box 1.2 suggests, an abstract theory like structuration theory (Giddens 1984) can have some pay-off in research terms. Instead, middle-range

---

Box 1.2 Grand theory and researching strategy

Giddens's (1984) structuration theory represents an attempt to bridge the gulf between notions of structure and agency in social life and is suggested to have the potential to overcome the dichotomy within organizational studies between the 'structural' perspectives of traditional theories of bureaucracy and the 'interactional' perspectives that emphasize informal processes of talk and action (Ranson, Hinings, and Greenwood 1980). The theory has substantially informed a number of empirical studies of managerial control, agency, and strategy, including Pettigrew's (1985) study of strategic change at ICI, which portrays environmental structures as both enabling and constraining human action. Hence, by combining a focus on the role of executive leadership and managerial action with a concern for the contexts in which managers work, Pettigrew suggests that the actions of managers are framed by the business and economic environment encountered by the organization.

Whittington (1989) also applies structuration theory as a means of understanding the strategic choices made by firms in periods of recession and recovery. Based on comparative case studies of eight British firms within the office furniture and domestic appliance industries, between 1979 and 1985, Whittington suggests that theories of strategic choice have tended to be too deterministic, failing to take sufficient account of the importance of managerial agency. At the same time, however, the inherent duality of structure and agency means that action theory, which prioritizes the role of the agent, goes too far the other way in attributing significance only to what subjects themselves perceive within their environments. To overcome these limitations, Whittington proposes a more critical realist approach (see Box 1.9), in which social structures are portrayed as a precondition for human agency.

theories are 'intermediate to general theories of social systems which are too remote from particular classes of social behavior, organization and change to account for what is observed and to those detailed orderly descriptions of particulars that are not generalized at all' (Merton 1967: 39).

By and large, then, it is not grand theory that typically guides management and business research. Middle-range theories are much more likely to be the focus of empirical enquiry. In fact, Merton formulated the idea as a means of bridging what he saw as a growing gulf between theory (in the sense of grand theory) and empirical findings. This is not to say that there were no middle-range theories before he wrote: there definitely were, but what Merton did was to seek to clarify what is meant by 'theory' when social scientists write about the relationship between theory and research.

Middle-range theories, unlike grand ones, operate in a limited domain. Whether it is a perspective on strategic choice or labour process theory (see Box 1.3), they vary somewhat in the purpose of their application. In other words, they fall somewhere between grand theories and empirical findings. They represent attempts to understand and explain a limited aspect of social life. For example, contingency theory has been used widely in management and business research to explain the interrelationships among subsystems, as well as the relationship between the organization and its environment. The theory relies on a number of assumptions that guide research: first, there is no one best way to organize; secondly, any particular way of organizing is not equally effective under all conditions; and, thirdly, in order to be most effective organizational structures should be appropriate to the type of work and the environmental conditions faced by the organization (Schoonhoven 1981). However, contingency theory has been applied in different ways and for different purposes, by different writers. Some, like Lawrence and Lorsch (1967), have used it descriptively to show that factors within the environment must be taken into account. Others, for example in the field of leadership, have applied the theory in a normative sense, adopting a solution-seeking focus and providing a guide to managerial action based on 'best fit' in a particular situation (e.g. Fiedler 1967). A normative stance suggests that, although factors within the environment should be taken into account, it is up to managers to make decisions about how they respond to these in order to achieve the impact on organizational performance that they want.

However, even the grand/middle-range distinction does not entirely clarify the issues involved in asking the deceptively simple question of 'what is theory?' This is because the term 'theory' is frequently used in a manner that means little more than the background literature in an area of social enquiry. To a certain extent, this point can be taken to apply to contingency theory mentioned above. For example, Schoonhoven (1981) suggests that it is not a theory at all, in the sense of being a well-developed set of interrelated propositions. Willmott (1990) suggests that contingency theory is based on empirical evidence without any acknowledgement of the social theories that affect the political realities of organizations, and so it is unable to deal with complex organizational problems.

Box 1.3 Labour process theory: an example of a middle-range theory

In the sociology of work, labour process theory can be regarded as a middle-range theory. The publication of *Labor and Monopoly Capital* (Braverman 1974) inaugurated a stream of thinking and research around the idea of the labour process and in particular on the degree to which there has been an inexorable trend towards greater and greater control over the manual worker and deskilling of manual labour. A conference volume of much of this work was published as *Labour Process Theory* (Knights and Willmott 1990). P. Thompson (1989) described the theory as having four elements: the principle that the labour process entails the extraction of surplus value; the need for capitalist enterprises constantly to transform production processes; the quest for control over labour; and the essential conflict between capital and labour. Labour process theory has been the focus of considerable empirical research (e.g. Knights and Collinson 1985).

In many cases, the relevant background literature relating to a topic fuels the focus of an article or book and thereby acts as the equivalent of a theory. In Ghobadian and Gallear's (1997) article on Total Quality Management (TQM) and the competitive position of small or medium-sized enterprises (SMEs), there are no, or virtually no, allusions to theories. Instead, the literature informs the generation of research questions in relation to what the authors perceive to be a neglected topic, as the majority of TQM literature tends to focus on large companies. The researchers are then able to seek to resolve inconsistencies between different findings in relation to small and large companies in terms of the impact of TQM on competitive position. Other ways in which background literature influences the focus of research include: the researcher may spot a neglected aspect of a topic; certain ideas may not previously have been tested; the researcher may feel that existing approaches being used for research on a topic are deficient; and so on.

Social scientists are sometimes prone to being somewhat dismissive of research that has no obvious connections with theory—in either the grand or middle-range senses of the term. Such research is often dismissed as naive *empiricism* (see Box 1.4). It would be harsh, not to say inaccurate, to brand as naive empiricism the numerous studies in which the publications-as-theory strategy is employed, simply because their authors have not been preoccupied with theory. Such research is conditioned by and

directed towards research questions that arise out of an interrogation of the literature. The data collection and analysis are subsequently geared to the illumination or resolution of the research issue or problem that has been identified at the outset. The literature acts as a proxy for theory. In many instances, theory is latent or implicit in the literature.

Indeed, research that appears to have the characteristics of the 'fact-finding exercise' should not be prematurely dismissed as naive empiricism either. For example, research in the field of industrial relations that focuses on the detail of current employment practices in a variety of sectors or cultural contexts has sometimes been criticized for its attention to facts over and above the development of theory. However, industrial relations research has been built on a tradition of seeing beneath the formal organization, which has exposed the variety of workplace resistance that often takes place within the employment relationship. At its best, this literature is built on a strong tradition of industrial sociology founded on a theoretically driven understanding of the labour process (Burawoy 1979). However, raising this question invites consideration of another question: in so far as any piece of research is linked to theory, what was the role of that theory? Up to this point, we have tended to write as though theory is something that guides and influences the collection and analysis of data. In other words, research is done in order to answer questions posed by theoretical considerations. But an alternative position is to view theory as something that occurs after the collection and analysis of some or all the data associated with a project. We begin to see here the significance of a second factor in considering the relationship between theory and research—whether we are referring to deductive or inductive theory.

Deductive and inductive theory

Deductive theory represents the commonest view of the nature of the relationship between theory and research. The researcher, on the basis of what is known about in a particular domain and of theoretical considerations in relation to that domain, deduces a hypothesis (or hypotheses) that must then be

---

Box 1.4 ☀ *What is empiricism?*

The term 'empiricism' is used in a number of different ways, but two stand out. First, it is used to denote a general approach to the study of reality that suggests that only knowledge gained through experience and the senses is acceptable. In other words, this position means that ideas must be subjected to the rigours of testing before they can be considered knowledge. The second meaning of the term is related to this and refers to a belief that the accumulation of 'facts' is a legitimate goal in its own right. It is this second meaning that is sometimes referred to as 'naive empiricism'.

subjected to empirical scrutiny. Embedded within the hypothesis will be concepts that will need to be translated into researchable entities. The social scientist must both skilfully deduce a hypothesis and then translate it into operational terms. This means that the social scientist needs to specify how data can be collected in relation to the concepts that make up the hypothesis.

This view of the role of theory in relation to research is very much the kind of role that Merton had in mind in connection with middle-range theory, which, he argued, 'is principally used in sociology to guide empirical inquiry' (Merton 1967: 39). Theory

and the hypothesis deduced from it come first and drive the process of gathering data (see Box 1.5 for an example of a deductive approach to the relationship between theory and data). The sequence can be depicted as one in which the steps outlined in Figure 1.1 take place.

The last step involves a movement that is in the opposite direction from deduction—it involves *induction*, as the researcher infers the implications of his or her findings for the theory that prompted the whole exercise. The findings are fed back into the stock of theory and the research findings associated with a certain domain of enquiry. This can be seen in

---

Box 1.5 An example of a deductive study

In a study that attempted to ascertain the economic value of Total Quality Management (TQM) to the firm, T. C. Powell (1995) critiques existing empirical studies that conclude that TQM produces value, on the grounds that most were conducted by 'consulting firms or quality associations with vested interests in their outcomes, and most did not conform with generally-accepted standards of methodological rigor' (1995: 18). On the basis of a review of the diffusion of innovation literature, Powell posits fifteen hypotheses to test whether TQM produces economic value. These include:

- *Hypothesis 1*: TQM firms outperform non TQM firms;

- *Hypothesis 2*: long-term TQM firms outperform short-term TQM firms.

In addition, because TQM originated from manufacturing environments, and it remains more widely disseminated among manufacturing than service companies, he predicts that:

- *Hypothesis 3*: manufacturing TQM firms outperform service TQM firms.

Powell developed a TQM measurement scale, based on his review of the literature, that covered twelve variables that were identified as significant in the development of a TQM programme. The measures also allowed for firm-level factors, such as organizational climate and structure, which have been shown to have an effect on

performance. The empirical research involved a survey questionnaire sent to a random sample of CEOs of all firms with more than fifty employees in the north-eastern USA generated on the basis of zip/postal codes, whether or not they had adopted TQM. This was followed up by on-site structured interviews with CEOs and quality executives in thirty firms not included in the postal questionnaire survey. Of these, twenty-three had TQM programmes in place.

Findings were shown to support hypothesis 1, and therefore to confirm the underlying assumption that TQM provides economic value to the firm. In relation to hypothesis 2 it was found that 'long-time TQM adopters were more satisfied with their TQM programs than short-time adopters, even though no apparent time-performance correlation existed' (1995: 26). In response to hypothesis 3, Powell finds that manufacturers were significantly more satisfied with their TQM programmes than service firms.

However, at this point Powell departs from a purely deductive approach and starts to draw conclusions from these findings, by relating them back to the literature that stimulated the research in the first place. In particular, he suggests that it may be that long-term TQM firms report greater satisfaction because they have successfully mastered the core TQM techniques. He goes on to conclude that TQM can produce economic value to the firm but it has not done so for all adopters. This is because success relies on intangible factors, rather than just on the application of TQM tools and techniques.

1. Theory
↓
2. Hypothesis
↓
3. Data collection
↓
4. Findings
↓
5. Hypotheses confirmed or rejected
↓
6. Revision of theory

Figure 1.1 The process of deduction

the case of Whittington's (1989) case study research into strategic choice within the domestic appliance and office furniture industries (referred to in Box 1.2). Whittington's approach is primarily deductive, since it is based on the contention that a critical realist approach to strategic choice enables recognition of the importance of (plural and contradictory) social structures for human agency and thus avoids determinism. However, as he points out towards the end of his book, 'after the empirical interlude of the last four chapters, it is time now to return to the theoretical fray' (1989: 244) to assess how well deterministic and realist approaches to strategic choice account for the behaviour within the eight case study firms. At this stage he claims that, although dominant actors within the firms 'began from their structural positions within the capitalist enterprise, this starting point was neither unambiguous or exhaustive' (1989: 282). This finding thus confirms his central proposition that these organizational structures were able to be converted into 'the effective instruments of private agency'.

A further point to bear in mind is that the deductive process appears very linear—one step follows the other in a clear, logical sequence. However, there are many instances where this is not the case. There are several reasons why a researcher's view of the theory or literature may change as a result of the analysis of the collected data:

- new theoretical ideas or findings may be published by others before the researcher has generated his or her findings;
- the relevance of a set of data for a theory may become apparent only *after* the data have been collected;
- the data may not fit with the original hypotheses.

The Hawthorne studies (see Box 2.10), undertaken at the Western Electric Company's Hawthorne plant between 1927 and 1932, aptly illustrate how deductive research can sometimes produce unexpected findings. In the early stages of this research, which explored the human effects of work and working conditions (Roethlisberger and Dickson 1939), the aim was to explore the relationship between conditions of work and the incidence of fatigue and monotony among employees. In order to test this relationship, a series of experiments were undertaken to establish the effects of variables such as lighting, temperature, humidity, and hours of sleep that could be isolated and measured separately. These early experiments involved adjusting the level of artificial illumination in departments at stated intervals in order to see if this had any effect on efficiency of production. However, researchers were not able to make sense of the changes in productivity of workers, which increased and remained high despite manipulation of a range of variables such as temperature and lighting. This led researchers to move away from the 'test room method' and to adopt a more qualitative strategy based on interview and observation. By modifying their approach towards this more inductive position, researchers were able to make sense of the data through generation of an alternative hypothesis that focused on the importance of informal social relationships. Eventually, this led to the development of an alternative method for the study of the informal work group. In the Bank Wiring Observation Room investigators spent a total of six months observing informal social relationships within a group of male operators. The Hawthorne research thus made an important methodological contribution to the study of work organizations by allowing research questions and methods to evolve and change during the course of the investigation (Schwartzman 1993).

Similarly, in a study of the impact of Total Quality Management (TQM) on the competitive position of small and medium-sized enterprises (SMEs), Ghobadian and Gallear (1997) examine the differences between SMEs and large organizations and explore the relationship between organizational size and the implementation of TQM. A series of research questions about this relationship were developed through analysis of the TQM literature. Although Ghobadian and Gallear describe their research as deductive, they also point out that classic hypotheses were not easily formulated, because the variables and issues identified were mainly (contextual) and therefore did not translate into simple constructs. They therefore shift towards a more inductive approach in the later stage of the study, using four case studies to explore the relevance of the research questions and to develop a ten-step framework for the implementation of TQM in SMEs.

This may all seem rather surprising and confusing. There is a certain logic to the idea of developing theories and then testing them. In everyday contexts, we commonly think of theories as things that are quite illuminating but that need to be tested before they can be considered valid or useful. In point of fact, however, while the process of deduction outlined in Figure 1.1 does undoubtedly occur, it is better considered as a general orientation to the link between theory and research. As a general orientation, its broad (contours) may frequently be discernible in business research, but it is also the case that we often find departures from it.

However, in some research *no* attempt is made to follow the sequence outlined in Figure 1.1. Some researchers prefer an approach to the relationship between theory and research that is primarily *inductive*. With an inductive stance, theory is the *outcome* of research. In other words, the process of induction involves drawing generalizable inferences out of observations. To put it crudely, whereas deduction entails a process in which:

theory → observations/findings,

with induction the connection is reversed:

observations/findings → theory.

However, just as deduction entails an element of induction, the inductive process is likely to entail a (modicum of deduction. Once the phase of theoretical reflection on a set of data has been carried out, the researcher may want to collect further data in order to establish the conditions in which a theory will and will not hold. Such a general strategy is often called *iterative*: it involves a weaving back and forth between data and theory. It is particularly evident in *grounded theory*, which will be examined in Chapter 19, but in the meantime the basic point is to note that induction represents an alternative strategy for linking theory and research, although it contains a deductive element too.

However, as with 'theory' in connection with the deductive approach to the relationship between theory and research, we have to be cautious about the use of the term in the context of the inductive strategy too. While some researchers undoubtedly develop theories, it is equally necessary to be aware that very often what one ends up with can (tautologons) be little more than empirical generalizations of the kind Merton (1967) wrote about. Inductive researchers often use a grounded theory approach to the analysis of data and to the generation of theory. This approach, which was first outlined by Glaser and Strauss (1967), is frequently regarded as especially strong in terms of generating theories out of data. This contrasts with the nature of many supposedly inductive studies, which generate interesting and illuminating findings but whose theoretical significance is not entirely clear. They provide insightful empirical generalizations, but little theory. Secondly, in much the same way that the deductive strategy is associated with a quantitative research approach, an inductive strategy of linking data and theory is typically associated with a qualitative research approach. In Box 1.6 is an example of research that can be classified as inductive in the sense that it develops a hypothesis out of interview data about innovation and change and the formation of organizational subcultures. However, the analytic strategy adopted by Sackmann (1992) in Box 1.6 was more complex and multifaceted, combining ethnographic, phenomenological, and clinical methods and relying on qualitative (thematic) content analysis (see Chapter 18). It thus illustrates how research methods can be combined within a broadly inductive approach. In addition, it is not a coincidence that Sackmann's research is based on in-depth, semi-structured interviews that produced qualitative data in the form of respondents' detailed answers to her questions. However, as will be shown below, this characterization of the

Box 1.6 An example of an inductive study

To investigate the existence and formation of organizational subcultures, Sackmann (1992) argues that an inductive approach was needed. 'Rather than hypothesizing about subcultures and their locations a priori, an inductive research methodology was chosen so that unknown groupings could emerge' (1992: 143). This, she suggests, enabled the generation of empirically based knowledge, which provides greater insight into the complexity of culture through identification of the different kinds of cultural knowledge that members of an organization share.

Her 'mid-range methodology' relied on the data collection technique of 'open interviewing' (which is essentially the same as semi-structured interviewing—see Box 5.3) with an 'issue focus' in order '(1) to serve as a stimulus for eliciting culture-specific cognitions, (2) to channel and narrow the potentially broad exploration, and (3) to introduce a reference point for respondents so that the information could be compared' (1992: 143). Three different research sites of a medium-sized US conglomerate were chosen for the study. Focusing on the issue of innovation and change, each interviewee was asked to name the three major innovations/changes that had occurred in the company during the last five years.

As the four-month interview study progressed, Sackmann explains that 'a hypothesis emerged from the data that cultural groupings may form according to functional differentiation' (1992: 147). This hypothesis was subsequently tested by interviewing members of the marketing/sales division of the company, who had not been involved in the earlier part of the study, and it was found that functional subcultures revolved around the specific 'dictionary knowledge' or commonly held descriptions of things and events. Finally, Sackmann suggests that the findings from her inductive research 'may serve as hypotheses for studies of culture using deductive research methodologies' (1992: 154).

inductive strategy as associated with qualitative research is not entirely straightforward: not only does much qualitative research *not* generate theory, but also theory is often used at the very least as a background to qualitative investigations.

It is useful to think of the relationship between theory and research in terms of deductive and inductive strategies. However, as the previous discussion has implied, the issues are not as clear-cut as they are sometimes presented. To a large extent, deductive and inductive strategies are possibly better thought of as tendencies rather than as a hard-and-fast distinction. But these are not the only issues that impinge on the conduct of business research.

Epistemological considerations

An epistemological issue concerns the question of what is (or should be) regarded as acceptable knowledge in a discipline. A particularly central issue in this context is the question of whether the social world can and should be studied according to the same principles, procedures, and ethos as the natural sciences. The position that affirms the importance of imitating the natural sciences is invariably associated with an epistemological position known as *positivism* (see Box 1.7).

A natural science epistemology: positivism

The doctrine of positivism is extremely difficult to pin down and therefore to outline in a precise manner, because it is used in a number of different ways by authors. For some writers, it is a descriptive category—one that describes a philosophical position that can be discerned in research—though there are still disagreements about what it comprises; for

---

Box 1.7 :☼: *What is positivism?*

Positivism is an epistemological position that advocates the application of the methods of the natural sciences to the study of social reality and beyond. But the term stretches beyond this principle, though the constituent elements vary between authors. However, positivism is also taken to entail the following principles.

1 Only phenomena and hence knowledge confirmed by the senses can genuinely be warranted as knowledge (the principle of *phenomenalism*).

2 The purpose of theory is to generate hypotheses that can be tested and that will thereby allow explanations of laws to be assessed (the principle of *deductivism*).

3 Knowledge is arrived at through the gathering of facts that provide the basis for laws (the principle of *inductivism*).

4 Science must (and presumably can) be conducted in a way that is value free (that is, *objective*).

5 There is a clear distinction between scientific statements and normative statements and a belief that the former are the true domain of the scientist.

This last principle is implied by the first because the truth or otherwise of normative statements cannot be confirmed by the senses.

Box 1.8 Positivism in action

In his reflections upon the Aston Programme, Pugh (1983: 45) describes himself as an 'unreconstructed positivist' guided by the belief that organizations exist as concrete entities about which data can be collected. This 'appeal to data' is underpinned by a distinction between facts and values, the former being the goal towards which data collection is directed, leading to the development of a 'conceptual framework' made up of 'analytical constructs' that can be used to analyse the regularities of the data. As a result, conclusions can be drawn about the 'structure and functioning of organizations' and the 'behaviour of groups and individuals within them' (1983: 48), thereby contributing to what Pugh describes as the 'subdiscipline' of organizational behaviour. This results in the generation of scientific knowledge, based on generalizable propositions that can be tested against the facts from which it is possible to discover 'how to organize better'. The main purpose of the Aston studies was therefore to make systematic comparisons across organizations that would enable generalizations about the relationship between organizational size, technology, and structure to be made. The early research was thus an early demonstration of structural contingency theory.

---

others, it is a pejorative term used to describe crude and often superficial data collection.

It is possible to see in the five principles in Box 1.7 a link with some of the points that have already been raised about the relationship between theory and research. For example, positivism entails elements of both a deductive approach (2) and an inductive strategy (3). Also, a fairly sharp distinction is drawn between theory and research. The role of research is to test theories and to provide material for the development of laws. Pugh (1983), for example, describes the research task as entailing the collection of data upon which to base generalizable propositions that can be tested (Box 1.8). But both of these connections between theory and research carries with them the implication that it is possible to collect observations in a manner that is not influenced by pre-existing theories. Moreover, theoretical terms that are not directly amenable to observation are not considered

genuinely scientific; they must be susceptible to the rigours of observation. All this carries with it the implication of greater epistemological status being given to observation than to theory.

It should be noted that it is a mistake to treat positivism as synonymous with science and the scientific. In fact, philosophers of science and of the social sciences differ quite sharply over how best to characterize scientific practice, and since the early 1960s there has been a drift away from viewing it in positivist terms. Thus, when writers complain about the limitations of positivism, it is not entirely clear whether they mean the philosophical term or a scientific approach more generally. *Realism* (in particular, *critical realism*), for example, is another philosophical position that purports to provide an account of the nature of scientific practice (see Box 1.9).

The crux of the epistemological considerations that form the central thrust of this section is the rejection by some writers and traditions of the application of the canons of the natural sciences to the

---

Box 1.9 :☼: *What is realism?*

Realism shares two features with positivism: a belief that the natural and the social sciences can and should apply the same kinds of approach to the collection of data and to explanation, and a commitment to the view that there is an external reality to which scientists direct their attention (in other words, there is a reality that is separate from our descriptions of it). There are two major forms of realism:

- *Empirical realism* simply asserts that, through the use of appropriate methods, reality can be understood. As such, it 'fails to recognise that there are enduring structures and generative mechanisms underlying and producing observable phenomena and events' and is therefore 'superficial' (Bhaskar 1989: 2). This is perhaps the most common meaning of the term. When writers employ the term 'realism' in a general way, it is invariably this meaning to which they are referring.

- *Critical realism* is a specific form of realism whose manifesto is to recognize the reality of the natural order and the events and discourses of the social world and holds that 'we will only be able to understand—and so change—the social world if we identify the structures at work that generate those

events and discourses. . . . These structures are not spontaneously apparent in the observable pattern of events; they can only be identified through the practical and theoretical work of the social sciences' (Bhaskar 1989: 2).

Critical realism implies two things. First, it implies that, whereas positivists take the view that the scientist's conceptualization of reality actually directly reflects that reality, realists argue that the scientist's conceptualization is simply a way of knowing that reality. As Bhaskar (1975: 250) has put it: 'Science, then, is the systematic attempt to express in thought the structures and ways of acting of things that exist and act independently of thought.' Secondly, by implication, critical realists unlike positivists are perfectly content to admit into their explanations theoretical terms that are not directly amenable to observation. As a result, hypothetical entities to account for regularities in the natural or social orders (the 'generative mechanisms' to which Bhaskar refers) are perfectly admissible for realists, but not for positivists. What makes critical realism *critical* is that the identification of generative mechanisms offers the prospect of introducing changes that can transform the status quo.

---

study of social reality. A difficulty here is that it is not easy to disentangle the natural science model from positivism as the butt of their criticisms. In other words, it is not always clear whether they are inveighing against the application of a general natural scientific approach or of positivism in particular. There is a long-standing debate about the appropriateness of the natural science model for the study of society, but, since the account that is offered of that model tends to have largely positivist overtones, it would seem that it is positivism that is the focus of attention rather than other accounts of scientific practice (such as critical realism—see Box 1.9).

Interpretivism

Interpretivism is a term given to a contrasting epistemology to positivism (see Box 1.10). The term

subsumes the views of writers who have been critical of the application of the scientific model to the study of the social world and who have been influenced by different intellectual traditions, which are outlined below. They share a view that the subject matter of the social sciences—people and their institutions—is fundamentally different from that of the natural sciences. The study of the social world therefore requires a different logic of research procedure, one that reflects the distinctiveness of humans as against the natural order. Von Wright (1971) has depicted the epistemological clash as being between positivism and hermeneutics (a term that is drawn from theology and that, when imported into the social sciences, is concerned with the theory and method of the interpretation of human action). This clash reflects a division between an emphasis on the *explanation* of human behaviour that is the chief ingredient of the positivist approach to the social sciences and the *understanding* of human behaviour. The latter is concerned with the empathic understanding of human action rather than with the forces that are deemed to act on it. This contrast reflects long-standing debates that precede the emergence of the modern social sciences but find their expression in such notions as the advocacy by Max Weber (1864–1920) of a *Verstehen* approach. Weber described Sociology as a 'science which attempts the interpretive understanding of social action in order to arrive at a causal explanation of its course and effects' (1947: 88). Weber's definition

seems to embrace both explanation *and* understanding here, but the crucial point is that the task of 'causal explanation' is undertaken with reference to the 'interpretive understanding of social action' rather than to external forces that have no meaning for those involved in that social action. An example of an interpretative understanding of leadership is given in Box 1.11. Grint (2000) claims that the concept of leadership can be understood only through understanding the meaning of the concept for those involved in this form of social action. His approach to this subject is thus broadly interpretative.

One of the main intellectual traditions that has been responsible for the anti-positivist position has been *phenomenology*, a philosophy that is concerned with the question of how individuals make sense of the world around them and how, in particular, the philosopher should bracket out preconceptions in his or her grasp of that world. The initial application of phenomenological ideas to the social sciences is attributed to the work of Alfred Schutz (1899–1959), whose work did not come to the notice of most English-speaking social scientists until the translation from German of his major writings in the 1960s, some twenty or more years after they had been written. His work was profoundly influenced by

---

Box 1.10 *What is interpretivism?*

Interpretivism is taken to denote an alternative to the positivist orthodoxy that has held sway for decades. It is predicated upon the view that a strategy is required that respects the differences between people and the objects of the natural sciences and therefore requires the social scientist to grasp the subjective meaning of social action. Its intellectual heritage includes: Weber's notion of *Verstehen*; the hermeneutic–phenomenological tradition; and symbolic interactionism.

Box 1.11 Interpretivism in action

Grint (2000) challenges much of the positivist thinking that has tended to characterize other studies of leadership, by arguing that effective leadership relies on the management of subjective meaning. Grint claims that the skills of leadership involve shaping the way that organizational problems are defined and persuading others that this definition is correct.

Using the example of Richard Branson, Grint analyses media coverage and biographical accounts of events that are associated with Branson's business ventures. Grint shows how Branson has instilled ideological commitment to a goal, through building a vision of a company where fun rather than rewards is seen as a reason to be associated with the Virgin brand. Branson has also created an image of himself as a plucky daredevil, attacking the establishment in order to protect the interests of the consumer. Much of Branson's success as a leader,

Grint claims, relies on persuasive communication, involving high-profile publicity stunts that help to cement a vision of his leadership in the eyes of employees and consumers. Grint concludes that there is no such thing as 'good' leadership, which can be defined, identified, and measured in terms of the characteristics of the leader. Instead leadership is primarily a social phenomenon that relies on the subjective interpretations of followers, more than the specific actions of individual leaders. The task of leaders is, therefore, to construct an imaginary community that followers can feel a part of. This relies on the construction of an identity and a narrative that can be used to make sense of organizational events—past, present, and future. Grint's argument is thus founded on an essentially interpretivist epistemological position. This enables him to investigate leadership as a construct that is used to make sense of social action.

Box 1.7 💡 What is positivism?

Positivism is an epistemological position that advocates the application of the methods of the natural sciences to the study of social reality and beyond. But the term stretches beyond this principle, though the constituent elements vary between authors. However, positivism is also taken to entail the following principles.

1 Only phenomena and hence knowledge confirmed by the senses can genuinely be warranted as knowledge (the principle of *phenomenalism*).

2 The purpose of theory is to generate hypotheses that can be tested and that will thereby allow explanations of laws to be assessed (the principle of *deductivism*).

3 Knowledge is arrived at through the gathering of facts that provide the basis for laws (the principle of *inductivism*).

4 Science must (and presumably can) be conducted in a way that is value free (that is, *objective*).

5 There is a clear distinction between scientific statements and normative statements and a belief that the former are the true domain of the scientist.

This last principle is implied by the first because the truth or otherwise of normative statements cannot be confirmed by the senses.

Box 1.8 Positivism in action

In his reflections upon the Aston Programme, Pugh (1983: 45) describes himself as an 'unreconstructed positivist' guided by the belief that organizations exist as concrete entities about which data can be collected. This 'appeal to data' is underpinned by a distinction between facts and values, the former being the goal towards which data collection is directed, leading to the development of a 'conceptual framework' made up of 'analytical constructs' that can be used to analyse the regularities of the data. As a result, conclusions can be drawn about the 'structure and functioning of organizations' and the 'behaviour of groups and individuals within them' (1983: 48), thereby contributing to what Pugh describes as the 'subdiscipline' of organizational behaviour. This results in the generation of scientific knowledge, based on generalizable propositions that can be tested against the facts from which it is possible to discover 'how to organize better'. The main purpose of the Aston studies was therefore to make systematic comparisons across organizations that would enable generalizations about the relationship between organizational size, technology, and structure to be made. The early research was thus an early demonstration of structural contingency theory.

others, it is a (pejorative) term used to describe crude and often superficial data collection.

It is possible to see in the five principles in Box 1.7 a link with some of the points that have already been raised about the relationship between theory and research. For example, positivism entails elements of both a deductive approach (2) and an inductive strategy (3). Also, a fairly sharp distinction is drawn between theory and research. The role of research is to test theories and to provide material for the development of laws. Pugh (1983), for example, describes the research task as entailing the collection of data upon which to base generalizable propositions that can be tested (Box 1.8). But both of these connections between theory and research carries with them the implication that it is possible to collect observations in a manner that is not influenced by pre-existing theories. Moreover, theoretical terms that are not directly amenable to observation are not considered

genuinely scientific; they must be susceptible to the rigours of observation. All this carries with it the implication of greater epistemological status being given to observation than to theory.

It should be noted that it is a mistake to treat positivism as synonymous with science and the scientific. In fact, philosophers of science and of the social sciences differ quite sharply over how best to characterize scientific practice, and since the early 1960s there has been a drift away from viewing it in positivist terms. Thus, when writers complain about the limitations of positivism, it is not entirely clear whether they mean the philosophical term or a scientific approach more generally. *Realism* (in particular, *critical realism*), for example, is another philosophical position that purports to provide an account of the nature of scientific practice (see Box 1.9).

The crux of the epistemological considerations that form the central thrust of this section is the rejection by some writers and traditions of the application of the canons of the natural sciences to the

clearcut
活用样本

Box 1.6 An example of an inductive study

混合联合企业

To investigate the existence and formation of organizational subcultures, Sackmann (1992) argues that an inductive approach was needed. 'Rather than hypothesizing about subcultures and their locations a priori, an inductive research methodology was chosen so that unknown groupings could emerge' (1992: 143). This, she suggests, enabled the generation of empirically based knowledge, which provides greater insight into the complexity of culture through identification of the different kinds of cultural knowledge that members of an organization share.

Her 'mid-range methodology' relied on the data collection technique of 'open interviewing' (which is essentially the same as semi-structured interviewing—see Box 5.3) with an 'issue focus' in order '(1) to serve as a stimulus for eliciting culture-specific cognitions, (2) to channel and narrow the potentially broad exploration, and (3) to introduce a reference point for respondents so that the information could be compared' (1992: 143). Three different research sites

of a medium-sized US conglomerate were chosen for the study. Focusing on the issue of innovation and change, each interviewee was asked to name the three major innovations/changes that had occurred in the company during the last five years.

As the four-month interview study progressed, Sackmann explains that 'a hypothesis emerged from the data that cultural groupings may form according to functional differentiation' (1992: 147). This hypothesis was subsequently tested by interviewing members of the marketing/sales division of the company, who had not been involved in the earlier part of the study, and it was found that functional subcultures revolved around the specific 'dictionary knowledge' or commonly held descriptions of things and events. Finally, Sackmann suggests that the findings from her inductive research 'may serve as hypotheses for studies of culture using deductive research methodologies' (1992: 154).

elicit: to draw or bring out 引出或带出.启中

---

inductive strategy as associated with qualitative research is not entirely straightforward: not only does much qualitative research *not* generate theory, but also theory is often used at the very least as a background to qualitative investigations.

It is useful to think of the relationship between theory and research in terms of deductive and inductive strategies. However, as the previous

discussion has implied, the issues are not as clear-cut as they are sometimes presented. To a large extent, deductive and inductive strategies are possibly better thought of as tendencies rather than as a hard-and-fast distinction. But these are not the only issues that impinge on the conduct of business research.

Epistemological considerations

An epistemological issue concerns the question of what is (or should be) regarded as acceptable knowledge in a discipline. A particularly central issue in this context is the question of whether the social world can and should be studied according to the same principles, procedures, and ethos as the natural sciences. The position that affirms the importance of imitating the natural sciences is invariably associated with an epistemological position known as *positivism* (see Box 1.7).

A natural science epistemology: positivism

The doctrine of positivism is extremely difficult to pin down and therefore to outline in a precise manner, because it is used in a number of different ways by authors. For some writers, it is a descriptive category—one that describes a philosophical position that can be discerned in research—though there are still disagreements about what it comprises; for

doctrine

Weber's concept of *Verstehen*, as well as by phenomenological philosophers, like Husserl. Schutz's position is well captured in the following passage, which has been quoted on numerous occasions:

The world of nature as explored by the natural scientist does not 'mean' anything to molecules, atoms and electrons. But the observational field of the social scientist—social reality—has a specific meaning and relevance structure for the beings living, acting, and thinking within it. By a series of common-sense constructs they have pre-selected and pre-interpreted this world which they experience as the reality of their daily lives. It is these thought objects of theirs which determine their behaviour by motivating it. The thought objects constructed by the social scientist, in order to grasp this social reality, have to be founded upon the thought objects constructed by the common-sense thinking of men [and women!], living their daily life within the social world.   (Schutz 1962: 59)

Two points are particularly noteworthy in this quotation. First, it asserts that there is a fundamental difference between the subject matter of the natural sciences and the social sciences and that an epistemology is required that will reflect and capitalize upon that difference. The fundamental difference resides in the fact that social reality has a meaning for human beings and therefore human action is meaningful—that is, it has a meaning for them and they act on the basis of the meanings that they attribute to their acts and to the acts of others. This leads to the second point—namely, that it is the job of the social scientist to gain access to people's 'common-sense thinking' and hence to interpret their actions and their social world from their point of view. It is this particular feature that social scientists claiming allegiance to phenomenology have typically emphasized. In the words of the authors of a research methods text whose approach is described as phenomenological: 'The phenomenologist views human behavior . . . as a product of how people interpret the world. . . . In order to grasp the meanings of a person's behavior, *the phenomenologist attempts to see things from that person's point of view*' (Bogdan and Taylor 1975: 13–14, emphasis in original).

In this exposition of *Verstehen* and phenomenology, it has been necessary to skate over some complex issues. In particular, Weber's examination of *Verstehen* is far more complex than the above commentary

suggests, because the empathetic understanding that seems to be implied above was not the way in which he applied it (Bauman 1978), while the question of what is and is not a genuinely phenomenological approach to the social sciences is a matter of some dispute (Heap and Roth 1973). However, the similarity in the writings of the hermeneutic-phenomenological tradition and of the *Verstehen* approach, with their emphasis upon social action as being meaningful to actors and therefore needing to be interpreted from their point of view, coupled with the rejection of positivism, contributed to a stream of thought often referred to as interpretivism (e.g. Hughes 1990).

Verstehen and the hermeneutic–phenomenological tradition do not exhaust the intellectual influences on interpretivism. The theoretical tradition in sociology known as *symbolic interactionism* has also been regarded by many writers as a further influence. Again, the case is not clear-cut. The implications for empirical research of the ideas of the founders of symbolic interactionism, in particular George Herbert Mead (1863–1931), whose discussion of the way in which our notion of self emerges through an appreciation of how others see us, have been hotly debated. There was a school of research, known as the Iowa school, that has drawn heavily on Mead's concepts and ideas, but has proceeded in a direction that most people would prefer to depict as largely positivist in tone (Meltzer, Petras, and Reynolds 1975). Moreover, some writers have argued that Mead's approach is far more consistent with a natural science approach than has typically been recognized (McPhail and Rexroat 1979). However, the general tendency has been to view symbolic interactionism as occupying similar intellectual space to the hermeneutic–phenomenological tradition and so broadly interpretative in approach. This tendency is largely the product of the writings of Herbert Blumer, a student of Mead's who acted as his mentor's spokesman and interpreter, and his followers (Hammersley 1989; Collins 1994). Not only did Blumer coin the term symbolic interaction; he also provided a gloss on Mead's writings that has decidedly interpretative overtones. Symbolic interactionists argue that interaction takes place in such a way that the individual is continually interpreting the symbolic meaning of his or her environment (which includes the actions of others) and acts on the basis of this imputed meaning. In research terms, according to Blumer (1962: 188), 'the position of symbolic interaction requires the student to catch the process of interpretation through which [actors] construct their actions', a statement that brings out clearly his views of the research implications of symbolic interactionism and of Mead's thought.

It should be appreciated that the parallelism between symbolic interactionism and the hermeneutic–phenomenological tradition should not be exaggerated. The two are united in their antipathy for positivism and have in common an interpretative stance. However, symbolic interactionism is, at least in the hands of Blumer and the many writers and researchers who have followed in his wake, a type of social theory that has distinctive epistemological implications; the hermeneutic–phenomenological tradition, by contrast, is best thought of as a general epistemological approach in its own right. Blumer may have been influenced by the hermeneutic–phenomenological tradition, but there is no concrete evidence of this. There are other intellectual currents that have affinities with the interpretative stance, such as the working-through of the ramifications of the works of the philosopher Ludwig Wittgenstein (Winch 1958), but the hermeneutic–phenomenological, *Verstehen*, and symbolic interactionist traditions can be considered major influences.

Taking an interpretative stance can mean that the researcher may come up with surprising findings, or at least findings that appear surprising if a largely external stance is taken—that is, a position from outside the particular social context being studied. The Hawthorne studies, referred to earlier in this chapter (see also Box 2.10), provide an interesting example of this, particularly as it was the failure of the investigation to come up with answers that related to the original research questions that stimulated the researchers to change their approach and methods and to adopt a more interpretative epistemological position. Of course, when the social scientist adopts an interpretative stance, he or she is not simply laying bare how members of a social group interpret the world around them. The social scientist will almost

---

> **Box 1.12 An example of an inductive study using quantitative data**
>
> Hofstede's (1984) large-scale study of cultural differences between members of a large multinational business organization, which he refers to as the HERMES corporation but is generally known to be IBM, provides an interesting example of inductive investigation based primarily on the analysis of quantitative data. The survey data were collected between 1967 and 1973, from employees in over forty different countries where HERMES had subsidiaries, producing a total of 116,000 self-completion questionnaires. Statistical analysis based on factor analysis formed the basis for Hofstede's development of a theoretical framework consisting of four main dimensions on which country cultures differ. He labelled these as power distance, uncertainty avoidance, individualism, and masculinity. Each dimension was suggested to be statistically independent—that is, a high score on one did not necessarily imply either a high or a low score on the other dimensions. These dimensions were not developed as hypotheses prior to data collection but instead were suggested to have emerged through the process of analysis.

certainly be aiming to place the interpretations that have been elicited into a social scientific frame. As the example in Box 1.11 illustrates, there is a double interpretation going on, whereby the researcher is providing an interpretation of others' interpretations of effective leadership. Indeed, there is a third level of interpretation going on, because the researcher's interpretations have to be further interpreted in terms of the concepts, theories, and literature of a discipline.

The aim of this section has been to outline how epistemological considerations—especially those relating to the question of whether a natural science, and in particular a positivist, approach can supply legitimate knowledge of the social world—are related to research practice. There is a link with the earlier discussion in this chapter about the relationship between theory and research, in that a deductive approach is typically associated with a positivist position. Box 1.7 does try to suggest that inductivism is also a feature of positivism (third principle), but, in the working-through of its implementation in the practice of research, it is the deductive element (second principle) that tends to be emphasized. Similarly, the third level of interpretation that a researcher engaged in interpretative research must bring into operation is very much part of the kind of inductive strategy described in the previous section. However, while such interconnections between epistemological issues and research practice exist, it is important not to overstate them, since they represent tendencies rather than definitive points of correspondence. Thus, particular epistemological principles and research practices do not necessarily go hand in hand in a neat unambiguous manner. For example, although inductive approaches tend to rely on qualitative methods, Hofstede's research study of cultural differences (Box 1.12) provides an example where this is not the case. This point will be made again on several occasions and will be a special focus of Chapter 21.

Ontological considerations

Questions of social ontology are concerned with the nature of social entities. The central point of orientation here is the question of whether social entities can and should be considered objective entities that have a reality external to social actors, or whether they can and should be considered social constructions built up from the perceptions and actions of social actors. These positions are frequently referred to respectively as *objectivism* and *constructionism*. Their differences can be illustrated by reference to two of the most common and central terms in social science—organization and culture.

Objectivism

Objectivism is an ontological position that implies that social phenomena confront us as external facts that are beyond our reach or influence (see Box 1.13). We can discuss organization or *an* organization as a tangible object. It has rules and regulations. It adopts standardized procedures for getting things done. People are appointed to different jobs within a division of labour. There is a hierarchy. It has a mission statement. And so on. The degree to which these features exist from organization to organization is variable, but in thinking in these terms we are tending to the view that an organization has a reality that is external to the individuals who inhabit it. Moreover, the organization represents a social order in that it exerts pressure on individuals to conform to the requirements of the organization. People learn and apply the rules and regulations. They follow the standardized procedures. They do the jobs to which they are appointed. People tell them what to do and they tell others what to do. They learn and apply the values in the mission statement. If they do not do these things, they may be reprimanded or even fired. The organization is therefore a constraining force that acts on and inhibits its members.

The same can be said of culture. Cultures and subcultures can be viewed as repositories of widely shared values and customs into which people are socialized so that they can function as good citizens or as full participants. Cultures and subcultures constrain us because we internalize their beliefs and values. In the case of both organization and culture, the social entity in question comes across as something external to the actor and as having an almost tangible reality of its own. It has the characteristics of an object and hence of having an objective reality. To a very large extent, these are the 'classic' ways of conceptualizing organization and culture.

Box 1.13 *What is objectivism?*

Objectivism is an ontological position that asserts that social phenomena and their meanings have an existence that is independent of social actors. It implies that social phenomena and the categories that we use in everyday discourse have an existence that is independent or separate from actors.

Box 1.14 💡 *What is constructionism?*

Constructionism is an ontological position (often also referred to as constructivism) that asserts that social phenomena and their meanings are continually being accomplished by social actors. It implies that social phenomena and categories are not only produced through social interaction but that they are in a constant state of revision.

In recent years, the term has also come to include the notion that researchers' own accounts of the social world are constructions. In other words, the researcher always presents a specific version of social reality, rather than one that can be regarded as definitive. Knowledge is viewed as indeterminate. The discussion of postmodernism in Chapter 24 further examines this viewpoint. This sense of constructionism is usually allied to the ontological version

of the term. In other words, these are linked meanings. Both meanings are antithetical to *objectivism* (see Box 1.13), but the second meaning is also antithetical to *realism* (see Box 1.9). The first meaning might be thought of usefully as constructionism in relation to the social world; the second as constructionism in relation to the nature of knowledge of the social world (and indeed the natural world).

Increasingly, the notion of constructionism in relation to the nature of knowledge of the social world is being incorporated into notions of constructionism, but in this book we will be using the term in relation to the first meaning, whereby constructionism is presented as an ontological position in relating to social objects and categories—that is, one that views them as socially constructed.

Constructionism

However, we can consider an alternative ontological position—*constructionism* (Box 1.14). This position challenges the suggestion that categories such as organization and culture are pre-given and therefore confront social actors as external realities that they have no role in fashioning.

Let us take organization first. Strauss et al. (1973), drawing on insights from symbolic interactionism, carried out research in a psychiatric hospital and proposed that it was best conceptualized as a 'negotiated order'. Instead of taking the view that order in organizations is a pre-existing characteristic, they argue that it is worked at. Rules were far less extensive and less rigorously imposed than might be supposed from the classic account of organization. Indeed, Strauss et al. prefer to refer to them as 'much less like commands, and much more like general understandings' (1973: 308). Precisely because relatively little of the spheres of action of doctors, nurses, and other personnel was prescribed, the social order of the hospital was an outcome of agreed-upon patterns of action that were themselves the products of negotiations between the different parties involved. The social order is in a constant state of change because the hospital is 'a place where numerous agreements

are continually being terminated or forgotten, but also as continually being established, renewed, reviewed, revoked, revised. . . . In any pragmatic sense, this is the hospital at the moment: this is its social order' (Strauss et al. 1973: 316–17). The authors argue that a preoccupation with the formal properties of organizations (rules, organizational charts, regulations, roles) tends to neglect the degree to which order in organizations has to be accomplished in everyday interaction, though this is not to say that the formal properties have *no* element of constraint on individual action.

Much the same kind of point can be made about the idea of culture. Instead of culture being seen as an external reality that acts on and constrains people, it can be taken to be an emergent reality in a continuous state of construction and reconstruction. Becker (1982: 521), for example, has suggested that 'people create culture continuously. . . . No set of cultural understandings . . . provides a perfectly applicable solution to any problem people have to solve in the course of their day, and they therefore must remake those solutions, adapt their understandings to the new situation in the light of what is different about it.' Like Strauss et al., Becker recognizes that the constructionist position cannot be pushed to the extreme: it is necessary to appreciate that culture has a reality that 'persists and antedates the participation of particular people' and shapes their perspectives, but it is not an inert objective reality that possesses only a sense of constraint: it acts as a point of reference but is always in the process of being formed.

Neither the work of Strauss et al. nor that of Becker pushes the constructionist argument to the extreme. Each admits to the pre-existence of their objects of interest (organization and culture respectively). However, in each case we see an intellectual predilection for stressing the active role of individuals in the social construction of social reality. Not all writers adopting a constructionist position are similarly prepared to acknowledge the existence or at least importance of an objective reality. Walsh, for example, has written that 'we cannot take for granted, as the natural scientist does, the availability of a preconstituted world of phenomena for investigation' and must instead 'examine the processes by which the social world is constructed' (1972: 19). It is precisely this apparent split between viewing the social world as an objective reality and as a subjective reality in a continuous state of flux that Giddens sought to straddle in formulating his idea of structuration (see Box 1.2).

Constructionism also suggests that the categories that people employ in helping them to understand the natural and social world are in fact social products. The categories do not have built-in essences; instead, their meaning is constructed in and through interaction. Thus, a category like 'masculinity' might be treated as a social construction. This notion implies that, rather than being treated as a distinct inert entity, masculinity is construed as something whose meaning is built up during interaction. That meaning is likely to be a highly ephemeral one, in that it will vary according to both time and place. This kind of stance frequently displays a concern with the language that is employed to present categories in particular ways. It suggests that the social world and its categories are not external to us, but are built up and constituted in and through interaction. This tendency can be seen particularly in discourse analysis, which is examined in Chapter 17. As Potter (1996: 98) observes: 'The world . . . is *constituted* in one way or another as people talk it, write it and argue it.' This sense of constructionism is highly antithetical to realism (see Box 1.9). Constructionism frequently results in an interest in the representation of social phenomena. Box 1.15 provides an illustration of this idea in relation to the representation of the position of middle managers during the late 1990s.

Constructionism is also frequently used as a term that reflects the indeterminacy of our knowledge of the social world (see Box 1.14 and the idea of constructionism in relation to the nature of knowledge of the social world). However, in this book, we will be using the term in connection with the notion that social phenomena and categories are social constructions.

Relationship of epistemology and ontology to business research

Questions of social ontology cannot be divorced from issues concerning the conduct of business research. Ontological assumptions and commitments will feed into the ways in which research questions are formulated and research is carried out. If a research question is formulated in such a way as to suggest that organizations and cultures are objective social entities that act on individuals, the researcher is likely to emphasize the formal properties of organizations or the beliefs and values of members of the culture. Alternatively, if the researcher formulates a research problem so that the tenuousness of organization and culture as objective categories is stressed, it is likely that an emphasis will be placed on the active involvement of people in reality construction. In either case, it might be supposed that different approaches to the design of research and the collection of data will be required.

> **Box 1.15 Constructionism in action**
>
> Much research attention has been devoted in recent years to considering the impact of delayering and downsizing on middle management. Some studies have drawn attention to increased job insecurity experienced by middle managers in the late 1990s and the rising levels of stress experienced by those who remain in employment. Others have struck a more optimistic tone, suggesting that managerial work can be transformed through delayering into a more strategic, intrinsically motivating form. These pessimistic and optimistic predictions of the future of middle management have formed the basis for much empirical testing and debate.
>
> However, adopting a social constructionist framework, Thomas and Linstead (2002) suggest an alternative way of thinking about the 'reality' of middle management based on the assumption that the term itself is a social construct. This leads them to a focus on the ways in which middle managers' identity is continually being created and contested through prevailing discourses. In other words, they are interested in understanding how managers make sense of the language and practice that is associated with their changing work roles.
>
> Through the analysis of individual managers' subjective accounts of their work, Thomas and Linstead illustrate how they construct their identity and deal with feelings of insecurity, ambiguity, and confusion that cause them to 'feel that they are losing the plot in their organizations' (2002: 88). Constant changes in terms of their roles and status make it difficult for middle managers to retain a sense of identity. The authors conclude: 'What is apparent . . . is that these middle managers, for a range of reasons, are searching for stability and sense in their reflections on their lives' (2002: 88).
>
> In sum, the social constructionist perspective enables the question of 'what has become of middle management?' to be recast. Instead it asks: 'how are middle managers becoming?'

Competing paradigms

A key influence on understanding the epistemological and ontological foundations of business research has been Burrell and Morgan's (1979) exposition of the four paradigms that they suggest reflect the assumptions that researchers make about the nature of organizations and how we find out about them. Their use of the notion of paradigm draws on the work of Kuhn (1970; see Box 1.16). Burrell and Morgan suggest that each paradigm contains assumptions that can be represented as either:

• *objectivist*—there is an external viewpoint from which it is possible to view the organization, which is comprised of consistently real processes and structures; or,

• *subjectivist*—an organization is a socially constructed product, a label used by individuals to make sense of their social experience, so it can be understood only from the point of view of individuals who are directly involved in its activities.

Each paradigm also makes assumptions about the function and purpose of scientific research in investigating the world of business as either:

• *regulatory*—the purpose of business research is to describe what goes on in organizations, possibly to suggest minor changes that might improve it but not to make any judgement of it; or,

• *radical*—the point of management and business research is to make judgements about the way that organizations ought to be and to make suggestions about how this could be achieved.

Plotting the assumptions of researchers along these two axes provides a framework for the identification of four possible paradigmatic positions for the study of organizations:

• *functionalist*—the dominant framework for the study of organizations, based on problem-solving orientation which leads to rational explanation;

• *interpretative*—questions whether organizations exist in any real sense beyond the conceptions of

Box 1.16 What is a paradigm?

Kuhn's (1970) highly influential use of the term *paradigm* derives from his analysis of revolutions in science. A paradigm is 'a cluster of beliefs and dictates which for scientists in a particular discipline influence what should be studied, how research should be done, [and] how results should be interpreted' (Bryman 1988*a*: 4). Kuhn depicted the natural sciences as going through periods of revolution, whereby normal science (science carried out in terms of the prevailing paradigm) is increasingly challenged by anomalies that are inconsistent with the assumptions and established findings in the discipline at that time. The growth in anomalies eventually gives way to a crisis in the discipline, which in turn occasions a revolution. The period of revolution is resolved when a new paradigm emerges as the ascendant one and a new period of normal science sets in. An important feature of paradigms is that they are *incommensurable*—that is, they are inconsistent with each other because of their divergent assumptions and methods. Disciplines in which no paradigm has emerged as pre-eminent, such as the social sciences, are deemed pre-paradigmatic, in that they feature competing paradigms. One of the problems with the term is that it is not very specific: Masterman (1970) was able to discern twenty-one different uses of it by Kuhn. Nonetheless, its use is widespread in the social sciences (e.g. Ritzer 1975; Guba 1985).

social actors, so understanding must be based on the experience of those who work within them;

- *radical humanist*—sees organization as a social arrangement from which individuals need to be emancipated and research as guided by the need for change;
- *radical structuralist*—views organization as a product of structural power relationships, which result in conflict.

They suggest that each paradigm results in the generation of a quite different type of organizational analysis as each seeks to address specific organizational 'problems' in a different way. Box 1.17 illustrates the different organizational insights that each paradigm can produce.

However, one of the most significant areas of controversy to have arisen in relation to this model relates to the issue of commensurability or otherwise of the four paradigms. Burrell and Morgan were quite specific in arguing that 'a synthesis between paradigms cannot be achieved' (Jackson and Carter 1991: 110), as they are founded upon a commitment to fundamentally opposing beliefs, in other words they are incommensurate with each other. Each paradigm must therefore develop independently of the others. Jackson and Carter argue that paradigm incommensurability is important because it protects the diversity of scientific thought, resisting the hegemony of functionalist approaches, which have tended to dominate business research, particularly in North American-based journals. Reed (1985), on the other hand, suggests that the boundaries between paradigms are not as clear as Burrell and Morgan suggest and that overstatement of the differences between them leads to isolationism and reduces 'the potential for creative theoretical development' (1985: 205). However, Willmott (1993) takes a different tack. He suggests that, although the four-paradigm model challenges the intellectual hegemony of functionalism and opens up possibilities for alternative forms of analysis within management, its central thesis is therefore distinctly double edged. In particular, the division between subjectivist and objectivist forms of analysis leads to a polarization of methodological approaches. Instead he suggests that paradigms arise through critical reflection upon the limitations of competing approaches. For example, labour process theory has sought to incorporate an appreciation of the subjective dimension of work whilst at the same time retaining a commitment to structural analysis of the dynamics involved in capitalist production. Willmott argues that this example draws attention to the 'practical indivisibility' of subjective and objective dimensions of organization.

Whatever view is held in relation to the relative commensurability of the four paradigms, it is clear that this model has significantly influenced business researchers by encouraging them to explore the assumptions that they make about the nature of the social world and the way it can be studied. The paradigm debate thus draws attention to the relationship

Box 1.17 An example of multiple paradigm research

Hassard (1991) uses the multiple paradigm model, developed by Burrell and Morgan (1979), in order to conduct an empirical analysis of work behaviour in the British Fire Service. He shows how different insights into the organization can be gained through using each paradigm as a distinct frame of reference. Because each paradigm community defines its research problems differently, the study was adapted in order to focus on issues of work organization that each paradigm community would consider legitimate. The four main subjects were:

• job motivation (functionalist paradigm);

• work routines (interpretative paradigm);

• management training (radical humanist paradigm);

• employment relations (radical structuralist paradigm).

Although there is no necessary connection between, for example, the study of job motivation and the functionalist paradigm, Hassard states that it was logically and practically difficult to focus on a single issue examined from each of the four perspectives because each paradigm considers particular research problems to be important and not others.

For the functionalist investigation, the aim was to assess how full-time firemen evaluate the motivating potential of their jobs using the Job Diagnostic Survey developed by Hackman and Oldham (1980; see Box 3.4). 110 questionnaires were distributed to a stratified sample of firemen, differentiated by age and length of service, and an 85 per cent response rate was achieved. Analysis of the results using statistical tests showed that, although the fireman's job possesses modest levels of motivation potential, 'this is not in fact a problem for employees whose needs for psychological growth at work are also modest' (Hassard 1991: 285).

For the interpretative part of the study, firemen were asked to describe and explain their daily tasks in order to enable an ethnomethodological study of Fire Service work routines and activities (see Box 13.1 on ethnomethodology). Analysis of conversational data collected over a three-month period highlighted how routine events in the Fire Service are accomplished in a context of uncertainty, which stems from the constant threat of emergency calls. The research suggests that the Fire Service organization 'is a cultural phenomenon which is subject to a continuous process of enactment' (Hassard 1991: 288).

The radical humanist investigation was conducted in the style of critical theory; it describes how management training in the Fire Service contributes towards the reproduction of an ideology that supports and reinforces capitalist values. Data were collected on the training practices used to prepare firemen for promotion to first-line supervision. Analysis of tape recordings of formal classroom sessions and discussions between participants showed how the in-house training programmes allow the organization to retain tight control over the messages delivered, selectively using theories that reinforced the existing authority structure.

Finally, the radical structuralist paradigm was represented through the application of labour process theory, focusing on the development of employment relations and conflicts over working time. Historical analysis of contractual negotiations and strike action showed how, as firemen's working hours were reduced to a level comparable with other manual occupations, 'measures have been taken which at once enhance management's control over the work process whilst yielding greater productivity from the working period' (Hassard 1991: 294).

Hassard thus challenges the notion of paradigm incommensurability, suggesting instead that multiple paradigm research can be used to develop greater variety in organizational research, to challenge the kind of absolutist analysis typical within such journals as *Administrative Science Quarterly*. Yet, according to Johnson and Duberley (2000), the diversity in subject focus between the four investigations merely confirms the fundamental differences between the paradigms and hence their incommensurability. In conclusion, rather than showing how paradigms can be combined, Hassard's study demonstrates how they can be displayed side by side, as competing versions of reality.

between epistemology and ontology in business and management research. It can also reasonably be supposed that the choice of which paradigm to adopt has implications for the design of the research and the data collection approach that will be taken; it is to this question that we will now turn in the following section.

Research strategy: quantitative and qualitative

Many writers on methodological issues find it helpful to distinguish between quantitative and qualitative research. The status of the distinction is ambiguous, because it is almost simultaneously regarded by some writers as a fundamental contrast and by others as no longer useful or even simply as 'false' (Layder 1993: 110). However, there is little evidence to suggest that the use of the distinction is abating and even considerable evidence of its continued, even growing, currency. The quantitative/qualitative distinction will be employed a great deal in this book, because it represents a useful means of classifying different methods of business research and because it is a helpful umbrella for a range of issues concerned with the practice of business research.

On the face of it, there would seem to be little to the quantitative/qualitative distinction other than the fact that quantitative researchers employ measurement and qualitative researchers do not. It is certainly the case that there is a predisposition among researchers along these lines, but many writers have suggested that the differences are deeper than the superficial issue of the presence or absence of quantification. For many writers, quantitative and qualitative research differ with respect to their epistemological foundations and in other respects too. Indeed, if we take the areas that have been the focus of the last three sections—the connection between theory and research, epistemological considerations, and ontological considerations—quantitative and qualitative research can be taken to form two distinctive clusters of *research strategy*. By a research strategy, we simply mean a general orientation to the conduct of business research. Table 1.1 outlines the differences between quantitative and qualitative research in terms of the three areas.

Thus, quantitative research can be construed as a research strategy that emphasizes quantification in the collection and analysis of data and that:

- entails a deductive approach to the relationship between theory and research, in which the accent is placed on the testing of theories;
- has incorporated the practices and norms of the natural scientific model and of positivism in particular; and
- embodies a view of social reality as an external, objective reality.

By contrast, qualitative research can be construed as a research strategy that usually emphasizes words rather than quantification in the collection and analysis of data and that:

- predominantly emphasizes an inductive approach to the relationship between theory and research, in which the emphasis is placed on the generation of theories;
- has rejected the practices and norms of the natural scientific model and of positivism in particular in preference for an emphasis on the ways in which individuals interpret their social world; and
- embodies a view of social reality as a constantly shifting emergent property of individuals' creation.

Table 1.1 Fundamental differences between quantitative and qualitative research strategies

	Quantitative	Qualitative
Principal orientation to the role of theory in relation to research	Deductive; testing of theory	Inductive; generation of theory
Epistemological orientation	Natural science model, in particular positivism	Interpretivism
Ontological orientation	Objectivism	Constructionism

There is, in fact, considerably more to the quantitative/qualitative distinction than this contrast. In Chapters 3 and 13 the nature of quantitative and then qualitative research respectively will be outlined in much greater detail, while in Chapters 21 and 22 the contrasting features will be further explored. In particular, a number of distinguishing features flow from the commitment of the quantitative research strategy to a positivist epistemology and from the rejection of that epistemology by practitioners of the qualitative research strategy. In other words, the three contrasts in Table 1.1 are basic, though fundamental, ones.

However, the interconnections between the different features of quantitative and qualitative research are not as straightforward as Table 1.1 and the last paragraph imply. While it is useful to contrast the two research strategies, it is necessary to be careful about hammering a wedge between them too deeply. It may seem perverse to introduce a basic set of distinctions and then suggest that they are problematic. A recurring theme of this book is that discussing the nature of business research is just as complex as conducting research in the real world. You may discover general tendencies, but they are precisely that—tendencies. In reality, the picture becomes more complicated the more you delve.

For example, it is common to describe qualitative research as concerned with the generation rather than the testing of theories. However, there are examples of studies in which qualitative research has been employed to test rather than to generate theories. For example, Hochschild's (1983) theory of emotion work (see Box 13.2) emerged from a questionnaire study of university students. The theory was subsequently tested to establish its wider significance in employment using two occupational groups, where a wider range of qualitative methods, including interviews and participant observation, were used. This enabled development of the theory to incorporate the idea of emotional labour, which is emotion work that forms part of one's paid employment. This study shows how, although qualitative research is typically associated with generating theories, it can also be employed for testing them. Moreover, it is striking that, although Hochschild's study is broadly interpretivist in epistemological orientation, with its emphasis on how flight attendants view their work role identity, the findings have objectivist, rather than constructionist, overtones. For example, when the author describes the marketing and advertising strategies used by Delta airlines, she explains how, by creating a discrepancy between promise and fact, flight attendants are forced to cope with the disappointed expectations of customers through their emotional labour. She relates the demand for emotional labour to the structural conditions of the airline industry market, thus positing a social world that is 'out there' and as having a formal, objective quality. It is an example of qualitative research in the sense that there is no quantification or very little of it, but it does not have *all* the other features outlined in Table 1.1. As such, it has interpretivist overtones in spite of its use of quantitative research methods.

The point that is being made in this section is that quantitative and qualitative research represent different research strategies and that each carries with it striking differences in terms of the role of theory, epistemological issues, and ontological concerns. However, the distinction is not a hard-and-fast one: studies that have the broad characteristics of one research strategy may have a characteristic of the other. Not only this, but many writers argue that the two can be combined within an overall research project, and Chapter 22 examines precisely this possibility.

Influences on the conduct of business research

We are beginning to get a picture now that business research is influenced by a variety of factors. Figure 1.2 summarizes the influences that have been examined so far, but has added two more—the impact of *values* and of *practical considerations*.

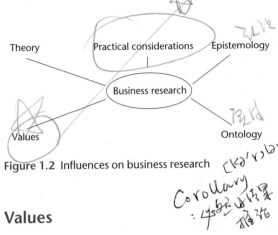

Figure 1.2 Influences on business research

Values

Values reflect either the personal beliefs or the feelings of a researcher. On the face of it, we would expect that social scientists should be value free and objective in their research. After all, one might want to argue that research that simply reflected the personal biases of its practitioners could not be considered valid and scientific because it was bound up with the subjectivities of its practitioners. Such a view is held with less and less frequency among social scientists nowadays. Émile Durkheim (1858–1917) wrote that one of the corollaries of his injunction to treat social facts as things was that all 'preconceptions must be eradicated' (1938: 31). Since values are a form of preconception, his exhortation was at least implicitly to do with suppressing them when conducting research. His position is unlikely to be regarded as credible nowadays, because there is a growing recognition that it is not feasible to keep the values that a researcher holds totally in check. These can intrude at any or all of a number of points in the process of business research:

- choice of research area;
- formulation of research question;
- choice of method;
- formulation of research design and data collection techniques;
- implementation of data collection;
- analysis of data;
- interpretation of data;
- conclusions.

There are, therefore, numerous points at which bias and the intrusion of values can occur. Values can materialize at any point during the course of research. The researcher may develop an affection or sympathy, which was not necessarily present at the outset of an investigation, for the people being studied. It is quite common, for example, for researchers working within a qualitative research strategy, and in particular when they use participant observation or very intensive interviewing, to develop a close affinity with the people that they study to the extent that they find it difficult to disentangle their stance as social scientists from their subjects' perspective. This possibility may be exacerbated by the tendency of some researchers to be very sympathetic to underdog groups. For example, following publication of his classic study of the Ford factory in Dagenham, Beynon (1975) was criticized by the press for having become too emotionally involved in the lives of workers. Equally, social scientists may feel unsympathetic towards the people they study. Although business and management researchers generally tend to emphasize their interest in understanding the problems and issues that affect practitioners, their value systems, particularly if they are working within a radical structuralist paradigm, are very likely to be antithetical to those of many managers working within a profit-making industry.

Another position in relation to the whole question of values and bias is to recognize and acknowledge that research cannot be value free, but to ensure that there is no untrammelled incursion of values into the research process, and to be self-reflective and so exhibit *reflexivity* about the part played by such factors. This view is borne of the assumption that the prior knowledge, experience, and attitudes of the researcher will influence not only how the researcher sees things but also *what* he or she sees. Researchers are increasingly prepared to forewarn readers of their biases and assumptions and how these may have influenced the subsequent findings. There has been a growth since the mid-1970s of collections of inside reports of what doing a piece of research was really like, as against the generalities presented in business research methods textbooks (like this one!). These collections frequently function as 'confessions', an element of which is often the writer's preparedness to be open about his or her personal biases. This point will be taken up further in Chapter 24.

Still another approach is to argue for consciously value-laden research. This is a position taken by some feminist writers who have argued that only research on women that is intendedly *for* women will be consistent with the wider political needs of women. Mies (1993: 68) has argued that in feminist research the 'postulate of *value free research*, of neutrality and indifference towards the research objects, has to be replaced by *conscious partiality*, which is achieved through partial identification with the research objects' (emphases in original).

The significance of feminism in relation to values goes further than this, however. In particular, several feminist researchers around the early 1980s proposed that the principles and practices associated with quantitative research were incompatible with feminist research on women. For writers like Oakley (1981), quantitative research was bound up with male values of control that can be seen in the general orientation of the research strategy—control of the research subject/respondent and control of the research context and situation. Moreover, the research process was seen as one-way traffic, in which researchers extract information from the people being studied and give little or more usually nothing in return. For many feminists, such a strategy bordered on exploitation and was incompatible with feminism's values of sisterhood and non-hierarchical relationships between women. The antipathy towards quantitative research resulted in a preference for qualitative research among feminists. Not only was qualitative research seen as more consistent with the values of feminism; it was seen as more adaptable to those values. Thus, feminist qualitative research came to be associated with an approach in which the investigator eschewed a value-neutral approach and engaged with the people being studied as people and not simply as respondents to research instruments. The stance of feminism in relation to both quantitative and qualitative approaches demonstrates the ways in which values have implications for the process of social investigation. In more recent years, there has been a softening of the attitudes of feminists towards quantitative research. Several writers have acknowledged a viable and acceptable role for quantitative research, particularly when it is employed in conjunction with qualitative research (Jayaratne and Stewart 1991; Oakley 1998). This issue will be picked up in Chapters 13, 21, and 22.

There are, then, different positions that can be taken up in relation to values and value freedom. Far fewer writers overtly subscribe to the position that the principle of objectivity can be put into practice than in the past. Quantitative researchers sometimes seem to be writing in a way that suggests an aura of objectivity (Mies 1993), but we simply do not know how far they subscribe to such a position. There is a greater awareness today of the limits to objectivity, so that some of the highly confident, not to say naive, pronouncements on the subject, like Durkheim's, have fallen into disfavour. A further way in which values are relevant to the conduct of business research is through the following of ethical principles or standards. This issue will be followed up in Chapter 25.

Practical considerations

Nor should we neglect the importance and significance of *practical issues* in decisions about how business research should be carried out. There are a number of different dimensions to this issue. For one thing, choices of research strategy, design, or method have to be dovetailed with the specific research question being investigated. If we are interested in teasing out the relative importance of a number of different causes of a social phenomenon, it is quite likely that a quantitative strategy will fit our needs, because, as will be shown in Chapter 3, the assessment of cause is one of its keynotes. Alternatively, if we are interested in the world views of members of a certain social group, a qualitative research strategy that is sensitive to how participants interpret their social world may be the direction to choose. If a researcher is interested in a topic on which no or virtually no research has been done in the past, the quantitative strategy may be difficult to employ because there is little prior literature from which to draw leads. A more exploratory stance may be preferable and, in this connection, qualitative research may serve the researcher's needs better, since it is typically associated with the generation rather than the testing of theory (see Table 1.1) and with a relatively unstructured approach to the research process (see Chapter 13). Another dimension may have to do with the nature of the topic and of the people being investigated. For example, if the researcher needs to engage with individuals or groups involved in illicit activities, such as industrial sabotage (Sprouse 1992) or pilferage (Ditton 1977), it is unlikely that a social survey would gain the confidence of the subjects involved or achieve the necessary rapport. It is not surprising, therefore, that researchers in these areas have tended to use a qualitative strategy.

While practical considerations may seem rather mundane and uninteresting compared with the lofty realm inhabited by the philosophical debates surrounding such discussions about epistemology and ontology, they are important ones. All business research is a coming-together of the ideal and the feasible. Because of this, there will be many circumstances in which the nature of the topic or of the subjects of an investigation and the constraints on a researcher loom large in decisions about how best to proceed.

K KEY POINTS

- Business research is subject to considerable debate concerning its relevance to practitioners and its fundamental purpose.

- Quantitative and qualitative research constitute different approaches to social investigation and carry with them important epistemological and ontological considerations.

- Theory can be depicted as something that precedes research (as in quantitative research) or as something that emerges out of it (as in qualitative research).

- Epistemological considerations loom large in considerations of research strategy. To a large extent, these revolve around the desirability of employing a natural science model (and in particular positivism) versus interpretivism.

- Ontological considerations, concerning objectivism versus constructionism, also constitute important dimensions of the quantitative/qualitative contrast.

- These considerations have informed the four-paradigm model that has been an important influence on business research.

- Values may impinge on the research process at different times.

- Practical considerations in decisions about research methods are also important.

- Feminist researchers have tended to prefer a qualitative approach, though there is some evidence of a change of viewpoint in this regard.

Q QUESTIONS FOR REVIEW

The nature of business research

- What, in your view, is the function or purpose of business and management research?

- What are the differences between mode 1 and mode 2 forms of knowledge production and why is this distinction important?

Theory and research

- If you had to conduct some business research now, what would the topic be and what factors would have influenced your choice? How important was addressing theory in your consideration?

- Outline, using examples of your own, the difference between grand and middle-range theory.

- What are the differences between inductive and deductive theory and why is the distinction important?

Epistemological considerations

- What is meant by each of the following terms: positivism; realism; and interpretivism? Why is it important to understand each of them?

- What are the implications of epistemological considerations for research practice?

Ontological considerations

- What are the main differences between epistemological and ontological considerations?

- What is meant by objectivism and constructionism?

- Which theoretical ideas have been particularly instrumental in the growth of interest in qualitative research?

- What are the main arguments for and against paradigm commensurability within management and business research?

Relationship of epistemology and ontology to business research

- What are the four main paradigms in business research and how do they influence the insights that are gained?

Research strategy: quantitative and qualitative research

- Outline the main differences between quantitative and qualitative research in terms of: the relationship between theory and data; epistemological considerations; and ontological considerations.

- To what extent is quantitative research solely concerned with testing theories and qualitative research with generating theories?

Influences on the conduct of business research

- What are some of the main influences on business research?

2 Research designs

(handwritten margin notes: trustworthiness · framework · validity · [ˌlɔndʒiˈtjuːdinl] 纵度 · [Lɔndʒitjuːdinl])

CHAPTER GUIDE

In focusing on the different kinds of research design, we are paying attention to the different frameworks for the collection and analysis of data. A research design relates to the criteria that are employed when evaluating business research. It is, therefore, a framework for the generation of evidence that is suited both to a certain set of criteria and to the research question in which the investigator is interested. This chapter is structured as follows.

- Reliability, replication, and validity are presented as criteria for assessing the quality of business research. The latter

entails an assessment in terms of several criteria covered in the chapter: measurement validity; internal validity; external validity; and ecological validity.

- The suggestion that such criteria are mainly relevant to quantitative research is examined, along with the proposition that an alternative set of criteria should be employed in relation to qualitative research. This alternative set of criteria, which is concerned with the issue of trustworthiness, is outlined briefly.

Prominent [handwritten annotation]

- Five prominent research designs are then outlined:
  - experimental and related designs (such as the quasi-experiment);
  - cross-sectional design, the most common form of which is social survey research;
  - longitudinal design and its various forms, such as the panel study and the cohort study;
  - case study design;
  - comparative design.
- Each research design is considered in terms of the criteria for evaluating research findings.

Introduction

In the previous chapter, the idea of research strategy was introduced as a broad orientation to business and management research. The specific context for its introduction was the distinction between quantitative and qualitative research as different research strategies. However, the decision to adopt one or the other strategy will not get you far along the road of doing a piece of research. Two other key decisions will have to be made (along with a host of tactical decisions about the way in which the research will be carried out and the data analysed). These decisions concern choices about research design and research method. On the face of it, these two terms would seem to mean the same thing, but it is crucial to draw a distinction between them (see Boxes 2.1 and 2.2).

Research methods can be and are associated with different kinds of research design. The latter represents a structure that guides the execution of a research method and the analysis of the subsequent data. The two terms are often confused. For example, one of the research designs to be covered in this chapter—the case study—is very often referred to as a method. As we will see, a case study entails the detailed exploration of a specific case, which could be a community, organization, or person. But, once a case has been selected, a research method or research methods are needed to collect data. Simply selecting an organization and deciding to study it intensively are not going to provide data. Do you observe? Do you conduct interviews? Do you examine documents? Do you administer questionnaires? You may in fact use any or all of these research methods, but the crucial point is that deciding to choose a case study approach will not in its own right provide you with

data. This choice is further complicated by the fact that what counts as data is not an entirely straightforward matter. Bartunek, Bobko, and Venkatraman (1993) acknowledge the diversity in the way that

---

Box 2.1 🔆 *What is a research design?*

A research design provides a framework for the collection and analysis of data. A choice of research design reflects decisions about the priority being given to a range of dimensions of the research process. These include the importance attached to:

- expressing causal connections between variables;
- generalizing to larger groups of individuals than those actually forming part of the investigation;
- understanding behaviour and the meaning of that behaviour in its specific social context;
- having a temporal (i.e. over time) appreciation of social phenomena and their interconnections.

Box 2.2 🔆 *What is a research method?*

A research method is simply a technique for collecting data. It can involve a specific instrument, such as a self-completion questionnaire or a structured interview schedule, or participant observation whereby the researcher listens to and watches others.

management researchers define the concept of data to include responses to questionnaire items, transcripts of public inquiry hearings, case studies, and advertisements.

In this chapter, five different research designs will be examined: experimental design and its variants, including quasi-experiments; cross-sectional or social survey design; longitudinal design; case study design; and comparative design. However, before embarking on the nature of and differences between these designs, it is useful to consider some recurring issues in business and management research that cut across some or all of these designs.

Criteria in business research

Three of the most prominent criteria for the evaluation of business and management research are reliability, replication, and validity. All of these terms will be treated in much greater detail in later chapters, but in the meantime a fairly basic treatment of them can be helpful.

Reliability

Reliability is concerned with the question of whether the results of a study are repeatable. The term is commonly used in relation to the question of whether the measures that are devised for concepts in business and management (such as teamworking, employee motivation, organizational effectiveness) are consistent. In Chapter 3, we will be looking at the idea of reliability in greater detail, in particular the different ways in which it can be conceptualized. Reliability is particularly at issue in connection with quantitative research. The quantitative researcher is likely to be concerned with the question of whether a measure is stable or not. After all, if we found that IQ tests, which were designed as measures of intelligence, were found to fluctuate, so that people's IQ scores were often wildly different when administered on two or more occasions, we would be concerned about it as a measure. We would consider it an unreliable measure—we could not have faith in its consistency.

Replication

The idea of reliability is very close to another criterion of research—replication and more especially replicability. It sometimes happens that researchers choose to replicate the findings of others. There may be a host of different reasons for doing so, such as a feeling that the original results do not match other evidence that is relevant to the domain in question. In order for replication to take place, a study must be capable of replication—it must be replicable. This is a very obvious point: if a researcher does not spell out his or her procedures in great detail, replication is impossible. Similarly, in order for us to assess the reliability of a measure of a concept, the procedures that constitute that measure must be replicable by someone else.

Validity

A further and in many ways the most important criterion of research is validity. Validity is concerned with the integrity of the conclusions that are generated from a piece of research. Like reliability, we will be examining the idea of validity in greater detail in later chapters, but in the meantime it is important to be aware of the main types of validity that are typically distinguished:

• *Measurement validity*. This criterion applies primarily to quantitative research and to the search for measures of social scientific concepts. Measurement validity is also often referred to as construct validity. Essentially, it is to do with the question of whether a measure that is devised of a concept really does reflect the concept that it is supposed to be denoting. Does the IQ test really measure variations in intelligence? If we take the study reported in Box 2.7, there are two issue-related concepts that need to be measured in order to test the hypotheses: 'magnitude of consequences' and 'issue framing', and two context-related concepts that also need to be measured: 'perceived social consensus' and 'competitive context'. The question then is: do the measures really represent the concepts they are supposed to be tapping? If they do not, the study's findings will be questionable. It should be appreciated that measurement validity is related to reliability: if a measure of a concept is unstable in that it fluctuates and hence is unreliable, it simply cannot be providing a valid measure of the concept in question. In other words, the assessment of measurement validity presupposes that a measure is reliable.

- *Internal validity.* This form of validity relates mainly to the issue of causality, which will be dealt with in greater detail in Chapter 3. Internal validity is concerned with the question of whether a conclusion that incorporates a causal relationship between two or more variables holds water. If we suggest that *x* causes *y*, can we be sure that it is *x* that is responsible for variation in *y* and not something else that is producing an apparent causal relationship? In the study examined in Box 2.7, the authors conclude that moral awareness is more likely when an individual perceives the issue to have significant harmful consequences, such as putting a competitor out of business ('magnitude of consequences'), and when the individual perceives a social consensus within the organization that the activity in question is ethically problematic ('perceived social consensus'). Internal validity raises the question: can we be sure that 'magnitude of consequences' and 'perceived social consensus' really do cause variation in moral awareness and that this apparent causal relationship is genuine and not produced by something else? In discussing issues of causality, it is common to refer to the factor that has a causal impact as the independent variable and the effect as the dependent variable (see Box 2.3). In the case of the research of Butterfield, Treviño, and Weaver (2000) in Box 2.7, the 'magnitude of consequences' was an independent variable and moral awareness the dependent variable. Thus, internal validity raises the question: how confident can we be that

---

Box 2.3 What is a variable?

A variable is simply an attribute on which cases vary. 'Cases' can obviously be organizations, but they can also include things such as people, offices and shops, production plants, cities, or nations. If an attribute does not vary, it is a constant. If all manufacturing organizations had the same ratio of male to female managers, this attribute of such organizations would be a constant and not a variable. Constants are rarely of interest to business researchers. It is common to distinguish between different types of variable. The most basic distinction is between independent variables and dependent variables. The former are deemed to have a causal influence on the latter.

---

the independent variable really is at least in part responsible for the variation that has been identified in the dependent variable?

- *External validity.* This issue is concerned with the question of whether the results of a study can be generalized beyond the specific research context. It is in this context that the issue of how people or organizations are selected to participate in research becomes crucial. This is why Scase and Goffee (1989) go to such great lengths to detail the process whereby their sample of UK managers was generated (Box 2.16). External validity is one of the main reasons why quantitative researchers are so keen to generate representative samples (see Chapter 4).

- *Ecological validity.* This criterion is concerned with the question of whether social scientific findings are applicable to people's everyday, natural social settings. As Cicourel (1982: 15) has put it: 'Do our instruments capture the daily life conditions, opinions, values, attitudes, and knowledge base of those we study as expressed in their natural habitat?' This criterion is concerned with the question of whether business research sometimes produces findings that may be technically valid but have little to do with what happens in people's everyday lives. If research findings are ecologically invalid, they are in a sense artefacts of the social scientist's arsenal of data collection and analytic tools. The more the social scientist intervenes in natural settings or creates unnatural ones, such as a laboratory or even a special room to carry out interviews, the more likely it is that findings will be ecologically invalid. This was an important finding to have emerged from the Hawthorne studies (see Box 2.10). Furthermore, the conclusions deriving from a study using questionnaires may have measurement validity and a reasonable level of internal validity, and it may be externally valid, in the sense that the findings can be generalized to other samples confronted by the same questionnaire, but the unnaturalness of the fact of having to answer a questionnaire may mean that the findings have limited ecological validity.

Relationship with research strategy

One feature that is striking about most of the discussion so far is that it seems to be geared mainly to quantitative rather than to qualitative research. Both reliability and measurement validity are essentially concerned with the adequacy of measures, which are most obviously a concern in quantitative research. Internal validity is concerned with the soundness of findings that specify a causal connection, an issue that is most commonly of concern to quantitative researchers. External validity may be relevant to qualitative research, but the whole question of representativeness of research subjects with which the issue is concerned has a more obvious application to the realm of quantitative research with its preoccupation with sampling procedures that maximize the opportunity for generating a representative sample. The issue of ecological validity relates to the naturalness of the research approach and seems to have considerable relevance to both qualitative and quantitative research.

Some writers have sought to apply the concepts of reliability and validity to the practice of qualitative research (e.g. LeCompte and Goetz 1982; Kirk and Miller 1986; Peräkylä 1997), but others argue that the grounding of these ideas in quantitative research renders them inapplicable to or inappropriate for qualitative research. Writers like Kirk and Miller (1986) have applied concepts of validity and reliability to qualitative research but have changed the sense in

which the terms are used very slightly. Some qualitative researchers sometimes propose that the studies they produce should be judged or evaluated according to different criteria from those used in relation to quantitative research. Lincoln and Guba (1985) propose that alternative terms and ways of assessing qualitative research are required. For example, they propose trustworthiness as a criterion of how good a qualitative study is. Each aspect of trustworthiness has a parallel with the previous quantitative research criteria.

- *Credibility*, which parallels internal validity—i.e. how believable are the findings?
- *Transferability*, which parallels external validity— i.e. do the findings apply to other contexts?
- *Dependability*, which parallels reliability—i.e. are the findings likely to apply at other times?
- *Confirmability*, which parallels objectivity—i.e. has the investigator allowed his or her values to intrude to a high degree?

These criteria will be returned to in Chapter 13.

Hammersley (1992a) occupies a kind of middle position here in that, while he proposes validity as an important criterion (in the sense that an empirical account must be plausible and credible and should take into account the amount and kind of evidence used in relation to an account), he also proposes relevance as a criterion. Relevance is taken to be assessed from the vantage point of the importance of a topic within its substantive field or the contribution it makes to the literature on that field. The issues in these different views have to do with the different objectives that many qualitative researchers argue are distinctive about their craft. The distinctive features of qualitative research will be examined in later chapters.

However, it should also be borne in mind that one of the criteria previously cited—ecological validity— may have been formulated largely in the context of quantitative research, but is in fact a feature in relation to which qualitative research fares rather well. Qualitative research often involves a naturalistic stance (see Box 2.4). This means that the researcher seeks to collect data in naturally occurring situations

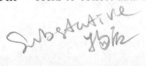

Box 2.4 What is naturalism?

Naturalism is an interesting example of a-mercifully rela- tively rare-instance of a term that not only has different meanings, but also has meanings that can actually be contradictory. It is possible to identify three different meanings.

- *Naturalism means a commitment to adopting the principles of natural scientific method.* This meaning, which has clear affinities with positivism, implies that naturalistic enquiry entails the use of the natural science model for studying the social world (Keat and Urry 1975: 1–2).

- *Naturalism means being true to the nature of the phenomenon being investigated.* According to Matza, naturalism is 'the philosophical view that strives to remain true to the nature of the phenomenon under study' (1969: 5) and 'claims fidelity to the natural world' (1969: 8). This meaning of the term represents a fusion of elements of an interpretivist epistemology and a constructionist ontology, which were examined in Chapter 1. Naturalism is taken to recognize that

people attribute meaning to behaviour and are authors of their social world rather than passive objects.

- *Naturalism is a style of research that seeks to minimize the intrusion of artificial methods of data collection.* This meaning implies that the social world should be as undisturbed as possible when it is being studied (Hammersley and Atkinson 1995: 6).

The second and third meanings overlap considerably, in that it could easily be imagined that, in order to conduct a naturalistic enquiry in the second sense, a research approach that adopted naturalistic principles in the third sense would be required. Both the second and third meanings are incompatible with, and indeed opposed to, the first meaning. Naturalism, in the sense of a tenet of positivism, is invariably viewed by writers drawing on an interpretivist epistemology as not 'true' to the social world, precisely because it entails both the application of natural science methods that ignore the capacity of humans to interpret the social world and to be active agents, and artificial methods of data collection.

and environments, as opposed to fabricated, artificial ones. This characteristic probably applies particul- arly well to ethnographic research, in which particip- ant observation is a prominent element of data collection, but it is sometimes suggested that it applies also to the sort of interview approach typically used by qualitative researchers, which is less directive than the kind used in quantitative research (see Box 1.6). We might expect that much qualitative research is stronger than quantitative investigations in terms of ecological validity.

By and large, these issues in business research have been presented because some of them will emerge in the context of the discussion of research designs in the section on research designs (below), but in a number of ways they also represent background con- siderations for some of the issues to be examined. They will be returned to later in the book.

Research questions

Before considering the nature of the research designs that are employed in business and management research, a crucial issue to discuss is the nature of research questions. Research questions are crucial. No research questions or poorly formulated research questions will lead to poor research. If you do not specify clear research questions, there is a great risk that your research will be unfocused and that you will be unsure about what your research is about and what you are collecting data for. It does not matter how well you design a questionnaire or how skilled an interviewer you are; you must be clear about your research questions. Equally, it does not matter whether your research is for a research contract of £200,000, a doctoral thesis, or a small mini-project. No or poor research questions will cause you problems.

Unfortunately, the process of formulating and assessing research questions is difficult to spell out. We can give only some general thoughts about the process. Research questions are crucial because they will:

- guide your literature search;
- guide your decisions about the kind of research design to employ;
- guide your decisions about what data to collect and from whom;
- guide your analysis of your data;
- guide your writing up of your data;
- stop you from going off in unnecessary directions and tangents.

Research questions in quantitative research are sometimes more specific than in qualitative research. Indeed, some qualitative researchers advocate a very open approach with no research questions. This is a very risky approach and can be a recipe for collecting masses of data without a clear sense of what to observe or what to ask your interviewees. There is a growing tendency for qualitative researchers to advocate a somewhat more focused approach to their craft (e.g. Hammersley and Atkinson 1995: 24–9).

We usually start out with a general research area that interests us. It may derive from any of several sources.

- *Personal interest/experience*. As we pointed out in Chapter 1, Bryman's interests in theme parks can be traced back to a visit to Disney World in Orlando in 1991 (a holiday that was somewhat affected by his showing the first signs of chicken pox on the first night), while Bell's interest in 'Investors in People' stems from her involvement in managing the implementation of this quality standard in an NHS trust hospital.
- *Theory*. Someone might be interested in testing aspects of labour process theory or the contingency perspective on organization structure.
- *The research literature*. Studies relating to a research area like the Japanization of work in British industry could be an example of a literature that might stimulate an interest in the nature of shop-floor work in such a context.

- *Puzzles*. How are team and individual empowerment, both of which have been themes in research on quality initiatives, compatible?
- *New developments in society*. Examples might include the rise of the Internet or the diffusion of new models of organization—e.g. TQM, customer service programmes, call centres.
- *Social problem*. An example might be how staff in call centres should handle consumer rage when consumers are interrupted by unwanted telephone calls.

As these types of source suggest, in research we often start out with a general research area that interests us. This research area has to be narrowed down so that we can develop a tighter focus out of which research questions can be developed. We can depict the process of generating research questions as a series of steps that are suggested in Figure 2.1. The series of stages is meant to suggest that, when developing research questions, the researcher is involved in a process of progressive focusing down, so that we move from a general research area down to specific research questions. In making this movement, we have to recognize the following restrictions.

- We cannot answer all the research questions that occur to us. This is not just to do with issues of time and cost of doing research. It is very much to do with the fact that we must keep a clear focus so that our research questions must relate to each other to form a coherent set of issues.
- We therefore have to select from the possible research questions that we arrive at.
- In making our selection, we should be guided by the principle that the research questions we choose should be related to one another. If they are not, our research will probably lack focus and we may not make as clear a contribution to understanding as would be the case if research questions were connected. Thus, in the example in Figure 2.1, the research questions relating to TQM are closely connected.

Box 2.5 presents some suggestions about the kinds of considerations that should be taken into account when developing your own research questions.

Research area
(TQM)

↓

Select aspect of research area
(Impact of TQM on work)

↓

Research questions
(Does TQM have a positive or negative impact on job satisfaction? Does the effect of TQM on job satisfaction vary by level in the organization? Does TQM disrupt traditional methods of working in firms? Do workers try to resist TQM and if so how far are they successful? Does TQM lead to empowerment or disempowerment? Does the way that TQM is introduced have an influence on the nature of its impact on job satisfaction?)

↓

Select research questions
(Does TQM have a positive or negative impact on job satisfaction? Does the way that TQM is introduced have an influence on the nature of its impact on job satisfaction? Does the effect of TQM on job satisfaction vary by level in the organization?)

Figure 2.1 Steps in selecting research questions

Box 2.5 Considerations when developing research questions

Research questions for a dissertation or project should

- *be clear*. They must be understandable to you and to others.

- *be researchable*. They should be capable of development into a research design, so that data may be collected in relation to them. This means that extremely abstract terms are unlikely to be suitable.

- *connect with established theory and research*. This means that there should be a literature on which you can draw to help illuminate how your research questions should be approached. Even if you find a topic that has been scarcely addressed by social scientists, it is unlikely that there will be no relevant literature (for example, on related or parallel topics). Making connections with theory and research will also allow you to show how your research has made a contribution to knowledge and understanding.

- *be linked to each other*. Unrelated research questions are unlikely to be acceptable, since you should be developing an argument in your dissertation. You could not very readily construct a single argument in relation to unrelated research questions.

- *have potential for making a contribution to knowledge*. They should at the very least hold out the prospect of being able to make a contribution—however small—to the topic.

- *be neither too broad nor too narrow*. The research questions should be neither too large (so that you would need a massive grant to study them) nor too small (so that you cannot make a reasonably significant contribution to your area of study).

If you are stuck about how to formulate research questions (or indeed other phases of your research), it is always a good idea to look at journal articles or research monographs to see how other researchers have formulated them. Also, look at past dissertations for ideas as well.

Box 2.6 provides some considerations that went into Watson's (1994*a*, *b*) exploration of management at ZTC Ryland, a UK-based telecommunications firm. This research is described in more detail in Chapter 14.

One final point to make is that a research question is not the same as a hypothesis. A hypothesis is a specific type of research question. It is an informed speculation, which is set up to be tested, about the

---

Box 2.6 Developing research questions

Watson (1994*b*) gives a very frank account of the process by which he developed his research questions for his participant observation study of ZTC Ryland, 'a plant of three thousand or so employees engaged in developing, making and selling telecommunications products' (Watson 1994*a*: 4). The company was involved in several change initiatives at the time that made it particularly interesting to Watson. His initial aim, therefore, was to improve understanding of how people doing managerial work 'shape' their own lives and identities in the context of organized work efforts (1994*b*). He writes that he 'sharpened' this general area of interest somewhat by reflecting on the impact on managers of the emergence of what were then fairly new developments, such as the rise of cultural change programmes and of HRM principles. In developing this set of interests into research questions,

Watson was influenced by writers and researchers on managerial work who had been critical of existing knowledge in this area. In particular he notes that these critics recommended: greater attention to the terms managers use to reflect on their work; a greater emphasis on explaining why managers engage in the forms of behaviour that have been uncovered; and a greater appreciation of the way in which managerial behaviour is embedded in organizational arrangements. These reflections on the literature on managerial work gave rise to Watson's research questions and led to an emphasis on: the linguistic categories and rhetorical processes involved in managers' constructions of their work and jobs; explaining patterns of bevaviour observed; and exploring the ways in which organizational arrangements have implications for managerial behaviour and indeed are influenced by it.

---

possible relationship between two or more variables. Hypotheses are not as common in quantitative research as is sometimes supposed and in qualitative research they are typically avoided, other than as speculations that arise in the course of fieldwork.

Research designs

In this discussion of research designs, five different types will be examined: experimental design; cross-sectional or social survey design; longitudinal design; case study design; and comparative design. Variations on these designs will be examined in their relevant subsections.

Experimental design

True field experiments are rare in business and management research, mainly because of the problems of achieving the requisite level of control when dealing with organizational behaviour. Why, then, bother to introduce experimental designs at all in the context of a book written for business and management researchers? The chief reason, quite aside from the fact that they are sometimes employed, is that a true experiment is often used as a yardstick against which non-experimental research is assessed. Experimental

research is frequently held up as a touchstone because it engenders considerable confidence in the robustness and trustworthiness of causal findings. In other words, true experiments tend to be very strong in terms of internal validity.

Manipulation

If experiments are so strong in this respect, why then do business researchers not make far greater use of them? The reason is simple: in order to conduct a true experiment, it is necessary to manipulate the independent variable in order to determine whether it does in fact have an influence on the dependent variable. Experimental subjects are likely to be allocated to one of two or more experimental groups, each of which represents different types or levels of the independent variable. It is then possible to establish how far differences between the groups are responsible for variations in the level of the dependent variable.

Manipulation, then, entails intervening in a situation to determine which of two or more things happens to subjects. However, the vast majority of independent variables with which business researchers are concerned cannot be manipulated. If we are interested in the effects of gender on work experiences, we cannot manipulate gender so that some people are made male and others female. If we are interested in the effects of variations in the economic environment on organizational performance, we cannot alter share prices or interest rates. As with the huge majority of such variables, the levels of social engineering that would be required are beyond serious contemplation.

Before moving on to a more complete discussion of experimental design, it is important to introduce a basic distinction between the *laboratory experiment* and the *field experiment*. As its name implies, the laboratory experiment takes place in a laboratory or in a contrived setting, whereas field experiments occur in real-life settings, such as in classrooms and organizations, or as a result of the implementation of reforms or new policies. It is experiments of the latter type that are most likely to touch on areas of interest to business and management researchers. However, in business and management research it is more common to find field experiments in which a scenario is employed as a substitute for a real-life setting, as the example in Box 2.7 illustrates. Furthermore, and somewhat confusingly, researchers will sometimes refer to their research as a field study. This simply means that the research was conducted in a real-life setting; it need not imply that a field experiment was involved.

Classic experimental design

In what is known as the classical experimental design, two groups are established and this forms the basis for experimental manipulation of the independent variable. The *experimental group*, or *treatment group* receives the treatment and it is compared against the *control group*, which does not. The dependent variable is measured before and after the experimental manipulation, so that a before-and-after analysis can be conducted. Moreover, the groups are assigned randomly to their respective groups. This enables the researcher(s) to feel confident that any

difference between the two groups is attributable to manipulation of the independent variable.

In order to capture the essence of this design, the following simple notation is employed:

Obs An **obs**ervation made in relation to the dependent variable; there may well be two or more observations, before (the pre-test) and after (the post-test) the experimental manipulation.

Exp The **exp**erimental treatment (manipulation of the independent variable). **No Exp** refers to the absence of an experimental treatment and represents the experience of the control group.

T The **t**iming of the observations made in relation to the dependent variable.

Thus, the classical experimental design comprises the following elements: random assignment to the experimental and control groups; pre-testing of both groups at T_1; manipulation of the experimental treatment so that the experimental group receives it (Exp) but the control group does not (No Exp); and post testing of the two groups at T_2. The difference between each group's pre- and post-test scores is then computed to establish whether Exp has made a difference.

Classic experimental design and validity

The purpose of the control group in a true experiment is to control (in other words, eliminate) the possible effects of rival explanations of a causal finding. We might then be in a position to take the view that the study is internally valid. The presence of a control group and the random assignment of subjects to the experimental and control groups enable us to eliminate rival explanations and eliminate threats to internal validity. These threats include the following.

- *Testing*. This threat refers to the possibility that subjects may become sensitized to the aims of the experiment (see Box 2.10). The presence of a control group, which presumably also experience the same 'experimenter effect', allows us to discount this possibility if there is no difference between the experimental and control groups.

- *History*. This threat refers to the possibility that events in the experimental environment, unrelated to manipulation of the independent variable, may

Box 2.7 A field experiment in business ethics

In a study of moral awareness in business organizations, Butterfield, Treviño, and Weaver (2000) wanted to understand the factors that influenced whether an individual in an organization was able to recognize the moral nature of an ethically ambiguous situation. They hypothesized that respondents would be influenced by two kinds of factors, those that were:

- *issue related*—the degree of harm that may be caused by an action or decision and the kind of language used to frame the issue;

- *social context related*—the degree of social consensus that exists in the organization about an issue as ethically problematic and the extent to which the business context is characterized by aggressive competition.

The field experiment was conducted on 'competitive intelligence (CI) practitioners', whose job it is to collect information about a business's competitors. They suggest that CI practitioners 'represent a unique, and in some ways ideal, sample for research on moral awareness', because CI is a new field 'in which ethical guidelines, norms concerning ethical and unethical practices and legal guidelines are still emerging' (2000: 992).

A random sample of 1000 practitioners was generated from a membership list of a CI professional association. The researchers constructed scenarios that presented realistic and ethically ambiguous situations that would be relevant to people working in the CI field. Scenario methodology, which is commonly used in business ethics research, was suggested to enable the study of basic cognitive processes and to provide a stimulus to which individuals can respond.

The scenarios formed the basis for a postal questionnaire, which was sent to each individual to be completed anonymously. Two different scenarios were constructed and respondents were randomly assigned to each one. This formed the basis for qualitative and quantitative

analysis of responses to each scenario in order to make comparisons between them. The scenarios were written from the point of view of a protagonist and respondents were encouraged to take on this role. This research strategy, combined with an assurance of anonymity, was designed to ensure against *social desirability bias* (see Chapter 5), which is a particular problem in researching ethical issues.

Immediately after having read the scenario, the respondent was asked to write down a list of issues that the protagonist would view as important in the scenario. The researchers then coded this list according to whether it might reasonably involve ethical concerns. Adding the number of ethical issues together produced a single number, representing the respondent's overall level of moral awareness in response to the scenario, and this was treated as a *dependent* variable.

The scenarios were constructed to manipulate two of the *independent* variables: 'magnitude of consequences' (how much harm may be caused by the decision), and 'issue framing' (the amount of moral language used to describe the issue). The research found that 'magnitude of consequences' was indeed significant in influencing moral awareness, but that 'issue framing' appeared to be significant only in certain scenario conditions. In addition, the social context was also found to influence moral awareness, but not always in the way that was anticipated. The prediction that aggressive competition would be negatively associated with moral awareness was disconfirmed. The authors speculate that working in a highly competitive context may actually make people more, rather than less, sensitive to moral concerns.

Although the authors describe their research as a 'field experiment', and it does involve manipulation of independent variables, this is achieved by way of the scenarios, which act as a substitute for real-life organizational settings, so in this sense the study relies on an artificially created field.

have caused the changes. If there is no control group, we would be less sure that changes to the independent variable are producing the change. If there is a control group, differences between the control and experimental groups can be more confidently attributed to manipulation of the independent variable.

- *Maturation.* Quite simply, people change and the ways in which they change may have implications for the dependent variable. Since maturation should affect the control group subjects as well, the control group allows us to discount the possibility that changes would have occurred anyway, with

or without manipulation of the independent variable.

- *Selection.* If there are differences between the two groups, which would arise if they had been selected by a non-random process, variations between the experimental and control groups could be attributed to pre-existing differences in their membership. However, if a random process of assignment to the experimental and control groups is employed, this possibility can be discounted.

- *Ambiguity about the direction of causal influence.* The very notion of an independent variable and dependent variable presupposes a direction of causality. However, there may be occasions when the temporal sequence is unclear, so that it is not possible to establish which variable affects the other. The existence of a control group can help to make this clear.

These threats are taken from Campbell (1957) and Cook and Campbell (1979), but not all the threats to internal validity they refer to are included. The presence of a control group coupled with random assignment allows us to eliminate these threats. As a result, our confidence in the causal finding is greatly enhanced.

Simply because research is deemed to be internally valid does not mean that it is beyond reproach or that questions cannot be raised about it. When a quantitative research strategy has been employed, other criteria can be applied to evaluate a study. In the case of the Bunce and West (1996) study, for example (Box 2.11), there is a potential question of measurement validity. Even though measures of intrinsic job motivation and intrinsic job satisfaction may appear to exhibit a correspondence with work-related stress—that is, to possess face validity—in the sense that they appear to exhibit a correspondence with what they are measuring, we might feel somewhat uneasy about how far increases in job motivation and satisfaction can be regarded as indicative of improvements in psychological well-being and an individual's ability to manage occupational strain. Does it really measure what it is supposed to measure? The second question relating to measurement validity is whether the experimental manipulation really worked. In other words, did the stress management programme and the innovation promotion programme create the conditions for improvements in psychological well-being and reductions in occupational strain to be examined?

Secondly, is the research externally valid? Campbell (1957) and Cook and Campbell (1979) identify five major threats to the external validity and hence generalizability of an investigation. These can be summarized as follows.

- *Interaction of selection and treatment.* This threat raises the question: to what social and psychological groups can a finding be generalized? Can it be generalized to a wide variety of individuals who might be differentiated by gender, ethnicity, social class, and personality. For instance, many influential studies of leadership, conducted on samples comprising a majority of men, rarely treat gender as a significant variable (Wilson 1995). It is possible that the findings of these studies simply reflect the characteristics of the predominantly male samples and therefore cannot provide a theory of effective leadership that is generalizable across both men and women.

- *Interaction of setting and treatment.* This threat relates to the issue of how confident we can be that the results of a study can be applied to other settings. For example, in T. C. Powell's (1995) research (see Box 1.5), the postal survey was sent to 143 companies in the north-eastern USA. Can his findings about TQM be generalized beyond this geographical area to companies in other countries where TQM programmes are also used? In other words, if this research was not externally valid, it would apply to north-eastern USA and to no other geographical area. If it was externally valid, we would expect it to apply more generally to companies with TQM programmes in other countries and other geographical regions in the USA.

- *Interaction of history and treatment.* This raises the question of whether the findings can be generalized to the past and to the future. The original Aston studies, for example, were conducted over forty years ago. How confident can we be that these findings would apply today?

- *Interaction effects of pre-testing.* As a result of being pre-tested, subjects in an experiment may become sensitized to the experimental treatment.

Consequently, the findings may not be generalizable to groups that have *not* been pre-tested and, of course, in the real world people are rarely tested in this way. The findings may, therefore, be partly determined by the experimental treatment as such and partly by how pre-test sensitization has influenced the way in which subjects respond to the treatment. This may have occurred in Bunce and West's research (Box 2.11).

• *Reactive effects of experimental arrangements.* People are frequently, if not invariably, aware that they are participating in an experiment. Their awareness may influence how they respond to the experimental treatment and therefore affect the generalizability of the findings. This was a major finding of the Hawthorne studies (see Box 2.10).

Thirdly, are the findings ecologically valid? The fact that the research is a field experiment rather than a laboratory experiment seems to enhance this aspect of the Bunce and West (1996) research. The fact that Bunce and West made intensive use of various instruments to measure psychological well-being and job strain might be considered a source of concerns about ecological validity, though this is an area

in which most if not all quantitative research is likely to be implicated.

A fourth issue that we might want to raise relates to the question of replicability. For example, Pugh et al. (1968) lay out very clearly the procedures and measures that were employed in the Aston studies and these have been used by several other researchers seeking to carry out replication of this research, both in business and non-business organizations, including trade unions, churches, schools, and public bureaucracies. Consequently, the research is replicable. However, analysis of the same data by Aldrich (1972) and Hilton (1972) using a different statistical technique showed other possible patterns of relationships between the variables in the Aston studies (see Box 2.8). This failure to replicate casts doubt on the external validity of the original research and suggests that the first three threats referred to above may have played an important part in the differences between the two sets of results.

The laboratory experiment

Many experiments in fields like social psychology are laboratory experiments rather than field experiments. Some of the most well known of these, such as

---

Box 2.8 Establishing the direction of causality

The Aston studies (Pugh et al. 1968) consisted of a highly influential programme of research that derived from an initial survey study of the correlates of organizational structure carried out in forty-six West Midlands organizations during the early 1960s. Whilst the study was guided by the hypothesis that characteristics of an organization's structure would be related to characteristics of its context, there was little in the way of detailed hypothesis formulation on exactly how these characteristics were related. The view taken by the researchers was that, although there was a considerable amount of case study research describing the functioning of organizations, very little in the way of systematic comparison was attempted. Moreover, generalization was made difficult because it was not possible to assess the representativeness of a particular case study. The strategy developed by the Aston researchers was therefore 'to carry out comparative surveys across organizations to establish meaningful stable relationships which would enable the particular idiosyncrasies of case studies to be placed into perspective' (Pugh

1998: p. xv). One of the key assumptions on which the research was based was that 'the nature, structure and functioning of an organization will be influenced by its objectives, context and environment, all of which must be taken into account' (ibid.). The researchers concluded that organizational size and production technology were important potential correlates of organization structure, though their findings implied that size, rather than technology, was the more critical factor. This finding contradicted other studies conducted at the time, such as Woodward (1965), which suggested that technology was a more important causal factor. However, in later analysis of the same data using a different statistical technique, Aldrich (1972) and Hilton (1972) were able to show other possible patterns of relationships between the three variables, which suggested that technology was an important cause of organizational structure, which in turn affected size. From this example we can see some of the difficulties in identifying the causal relationship between variables using survey data.

Milgram's (1974) electric shock experiments or Zimbardo's prison experiments (see Box 25.3), have informed our understanding of how individuals and groups behave within modern work organizations. One of the main advantages of laboratory experiments is that the researcher has far greater influence over the experimental arrangements. For example, it is easier to randomly assign subjects to different experimental conditions in the laboratory than to do the same in an ongoing, real-life organization. The researcher therefore has a higher level of control and this is likely to enhance the internal validity of the study. It is also likely that laboratory experiments will be more straightforward to replicate because they are less bound up with a certain milieu that is difficult to reproduce.

However, laboratory experiments like the one described in Box 2.9 suffer from a number of limitations. First, the external validity is likely to be difficult to establish. There is the interaction of setting and treatment, since the setting of the laboratory is likely to be unrelated to real-world experiences and contexts. Also, there is likely to be an interaction of selection and treatment. In the case of Howell and Frost's (1989) study described in Box 2.9, there are a number of difficulties: the subjects were students who are unlikely to be representative of the general population, so that their responses to the experimental treatment may be distinctive; they were volunteers and it is known that volunteers differ from non-volunteers (Rosnow and Rosenthal 1997: ch. 5); and they were given incentives to participate, which may further demarcate them from others, since not everyone is equally amenable to the blandishments of inducements. There will have been no problem of interaction effects of pre-testing, because, like many experiments, there was no pre-testing. However, it is quite feasible that reactive effects may have been set in motion by the experimental arrangements. As Box 2.10 illustrates, reactive effects associated with an experiment can have a profound effect on the outcomes of the research. Secondly, the ecological validity of the study may be poor because we do not know how well the findings are applicable to the real world and everyday life. However, while the study may lack what is often called mundane realism, it

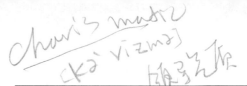

> **Box 2.9** A laboratory experiment on leadership
>
> Howell and Frost (1989) were interested in the possibility that charismatic leadership was a more effective approach within organizations than other types of leadership behaviour. To test this assumption they conducted a laboratory experiment that compared the effectiveness of charismatic leadership as against two alternative approaches—consideration and structuring. A number of hypotheses were generated, including: 'Individuals working under a charismatic leader will have higher task performance than will individuals working under a considerate leader' (1989: 245).
>
> One hundred and forty-four students volunteered for the experiment. Their course grades were enhanced by 3 per cent for agreeing to participate. They were randomly assigned to work under one of the three types of leadership. The work was a simulated business task. All three leadership approaches were performed by two female actresses. In broad conformity with the hypotheses, subjects working under charismatic leaders scored generally higher in terms of measures of task performance than those working under the other leaders, particularly the considerate leader.

Plate 2.1 The Hawthorne Studies. Property of AT & T Archives.
Reprinted with permission of AT & T

Box 2.10 The Hawthorne effect

The effect of the experimenter or occurrence of study on the subject is commonly referred to as the 'Hawthorne effect'. This phrase was coined as a result of the series of interlinked investigations carried out during the late 1920s and early 1930s at the Hawthorne works of the Western Electric Company in the USA (Roethlisberger and Dickson 1939).

One phase of the investigations entailed a group of women carrying out manual tasks being taken away from their department and working in a separate room (see Plate 2.1). The aim of the study was to discover how changes in the number and duration of rest pauses, in length of the working day, in heating and lighting and so on affected productivity. As this quote from the study illustrates:

First, the amount of light was increased regularly day by day, and the girls were asked each day how they liked the change. As the light was increased, the girls told the investigator that they liked the brighter lights. Then for a day or two the investigator allowed the girls to see the electrician come and change the light bulbs. In reality, the electrician merely took out bulbs of a given size and inserted bulbs of the same size, without in any way changing the amount of light. The girls, thinking that the light was still being 'stepped up' day by day, commented favourably about the increase of light. After a few days of this, the experimenter started to decrease the intensity of light, keeping the girls informed of the change and soliciting their reaction. After a period of this day-by-day decrease in illumination, he again allowed the girls to see the electrician change the bulbs without really changing the intensity of illumination. Again the girls gave answers that were to be expected, in that they said the 'lesser' light was not so pleasant to work under as the brighter light. Their production did not change

at any stage of the experiment.   (Roethlisberger and Dickson 1939: 17)

However, as the study went on, it was found that productivity *did* increase, irrespective of the changes that were being introduced. Eventually it was recognized that the women were responding to the positive attention and special treatment they were receiving. The researchers concluded that increases in worker productivity were due not to any changes in the conditions of the working environment, but instead to the favourable circumstances that the experimental arrangements had produced. While this finding did much to stimulate the 'human relations' approach to the study of work, by pointing to the potential advantages of providing people with psycho-social support in the workplace, it also neatly demonstrates that experimental arrangements may induce an effect over and above the intentions of the investigator. This has been referred to, more generally, as the 'experimenter effect', where the researcher creates a bias in the data through participation in the research situation or by inadvertently communicating his or her preferred research outcome.

The Hawthorne effect also draws attention to the way in which researchers themselves represent 'an audience to the actors being studied', and it is therefore likely that the researcher's activities will have an influence on the research setting. This draws attention to the fact that, 'while the researcher attends to the study of other persons and their other activities, these other persons attend to the study of the researcher and his activities' (Van Maanen and Kolb 1985: 6). The results of fieldwork thus depend in part upon the outcomes of the unofficial study that the observed make of the physical nature and psychological character of the observer, as well as the other way around.

may none the less enjoy experimental realism (Aronson and Carlsmith 1968). The latter means that the subjects are very involved in the experiment and take it very seriously.

Quasi-experiments

A number of writers have drawn attention to the possibilities offered by quasi-experiments—that is, studies that have certain characteristics of experimental designs but that do not fulfil all the internal

validity requirements. A large number of different types of quasi-experiments have been identified (Cook and Campbell 1979) and it is not proposed to cover them here. A particularly interesting form of quasi-experiment occurs in the case of 'natural experiments'. These are 'experiments' in the sense of entailing manipulation of a social setting, but as part of a naturally occurring attempt to alter social arrangements. In such circumstances, it is invariably not possible to randomly assign subjects to experimental and control groups. An example is provided in Box 2.11.

The absence of random assignment in the research casts a certain amount of doubt on the study's internal validity, since the groups may not have been equivalent. However, the results of such studies are still compelling, because they are not artificial interventions in social life and because their ecological validity is therefore very strong. Hofstede's study of cultural differences (see Box 1.12) falls into this category, because the research design enabled some degree of control to be maintained over variables—all employees belonged to the same multinational organization, even though the research took place in a natural setting. This meant that corporate culture constituted the dependent variable and differences in national cultures and mentalities of employees constituted independent variables, where Hofstede anticipated the main differences would be seen. In addition, some requirements of internal validity were fulfilled, through replication of the questionnaire survey on two separate occasions, once in 1967–9 and again in 1971–3.

Most writers on quasi-experimentation discount experiments in which there is no control group or basis for comparison (Cook and Campbell 1979). However, some experiments do involve manipulation of the independent variable within experimental groups without a control group as the basis for comparison. For example, in an experimental study of electronic brainstorming, Gallupe et al. (1992) wanted to test the effect of group size on performance. The researchers wanted to find out if electronic brainstorming could more effectively support the generation of ideas within large groups (6 and 12 persons), as well as small groups (2, 4, and 6 persons)—unlike the traditional, verbal brainstorming technique. In this study, both the large and the small groups received the experimental treatment—that is, electronic brainstorming—and both received the control treatment—that is, verbal brainstorming. It was anticipated that large and small groups would show similar levels of productivity in the verbal brainstorming experiment, but that large groups would outperform small groups in the electronic brainstorming experiment. Because there was no

---

Box 2.11 A quasi-experiment

In a study of health-care workers in the UK National Health Service, reported by Bunce and West (1996), a traditional stress management programme was compared with an intervention promoting innovation at work as a form of stress management. It was expected that both types of intervention would improve psychological well-being and reduce strain. In order to test this proposition, the two groups were compared against a control group, which was comprised of health-care workers who were not involved in any kind of workplace stress management initiative. Some of the participants were volunteers, but others were encouraged to take part by their line managers. Bunce and West suggest that this reduced the possibility of self-selection bias.

The groups met on two occasions, a week apart, and were led by qualified facilitators (one of whom was Bunce). A range of questionnaire instruments was used to measure 'psychological well-being', 'psychological strain', 'innovation', and 'session process' amongst participants. Measurements were taken three months prior to the start

of the interventions, three months after they had ended, and again one year later. This meant independent variables were measured before and after the experimental manipulation so that a before-and-after analysis could be conducted. The researchers could therefore be confident that, if they did establish a difference in stress levels between the three groups, it was likely to be due to experimental manipulation.

This study uses a quasi-experimental design, in which a control group is compared to the two treatment groups. It bears some of the hallmarks of a classic experimental design, but there is no random assignment; participants were assigned to the groups according to their work location. Subjects were not randomly assigned to the three groups because of practical constraints such as staff availability. Although the traditional stress management programme and the innovation promotion programme both achieved positive results, it was found that the process of participation was important in achieving these outcomes.

control group, where no manipulation of the independent variable occurs, this study cannot be seen as a classic experimental design. However, the internal validity of the findings was reinforced by the fact that both the experiments were also carried out on small groups, where it was found that electronic brainstorming made no difference to group performance. Comparison between large and small experimental groups helped to reduce threats to the internal validity of the findings. The study thus exhibits some of the characteristics of an experimental design, even though no control group was used.

Finally, experimental designs, and more especially quasi-experimental designs, have been particularly prominent in evaluation research studies (see Box 2.12).

Significance of experimental design

As was stated at the outset, the chief reason for introducing the experiment as a research design is because it is frequently considered to be a yardstick against which quantitative research is judged. This occurs largely because of the fact that a true experiment will allow doubts about internal validity to be allayed and reflects the considerable emphasis placed on the determination of causality in quantitative research.

As we will see in the next section, cross-sectional designs of the kind associated with social survey research are frequently regarded as limited, because of the problems of unambiguously imputing causality when using such designs.

Logic of comparison

However, before exploring such issues, it is important to draw attention to an important general lesson that an examination of experiments teaches us. A central feature of any experiment is the fact that it entails a *comparison*: at the very least it entails a comparison of results obtained by an experimental group with those engendered by a control group. In the case of the Howell and Frost (1989) experiment in Box 2.9 there is no control group: the research entails a comparison of the effects of three different forms of leadership. The advantage of carrying out any kind of comparison like this is that we understand the phenomenon that we are interested in better when we compare it with something else that is similar to it. The case for arguing that charismatic leadership is an effective, performance-enhancing form of leadership is much more persuasive when we view it in relation to other forms of leadership. Thus, while the specific considerations concerning experimental design are typically associated with quantitative

Coalesce

Box 2.12 🔆 *What is evaluation research?*

Evaluation research, as its name implies, is concerned with the evaluation of such occurrences as organizational programmes or interventions. The essential question that is typically asked by such studies is: has the intervention (for example, a new policy initiative or an organizational change) achieved its anticipated goals? A typical design may have one group that is exposed to the treatment— that is, the new initiative—and a control group that is not. Since it is often not feasible or ethical to randomly assign research participants to the two groups, such studies are usually quasi-experimental. The use of the principles of experimental design are fairly entrenched in evaluation research, but other approaches have emerged in recent years. Approaches to evaluation based on qualitative research have emerged. While there are differences of

opinion about how qualitative evaluation should be carried out, the different views typically coalesce around a recognition of the importance of an in-depth understanding of the context in which an intervention occurs and the diverse viewpoints of the stakeholders (Greene 1994, 2000). Pawson and Tilley (1997) advocate an approach that draws on the principles of critical realism (see Box 1.9) and that sees the outcome of an intervention as the result of generative mechanisms and the contexts of those mechanisms. A focus of the former element entails examining the causal factors that inhibit or promote change when an intervention occurs. Pawson and Tilley's approach is supportive of the use of both quantitative and qualitative research methods.

research, the potential of comparison in business research represents a more general lesson that transcends matters of both research strategy and research design. In other words, while the experimental design is typically associated with a quantitative research strategy, the specific logic of comparison provides lessons of broad applicability and relevance. This issue is given more specific attention below in relation to the comparative design.

Cross-sectional design

The cross-sectional design is often called a social survey design, but the idea of the social survey is so closely connected in most people's minds with questionnaires and structured interviewing that the more generic sounding term *cross-sectional design* is preferable. While the research methods associated with social surveys are certainly frequently employed within the context of cross-sectional research, so too are many other research methods, including structured observation, content analysis, official statistics, and diaries. All these research methods will be covered in later chapters, but in the meantime the basic structure of the cross-sectional design will be outlined.

The cross-sectional design is defined in Box 2.13. A number of elements of this definition have been emphasized.

- *More than one case*. Researchers employing a cross-sectional design are interested in variation. That

variation can be in respect of people, organizations, nation states, or whatever. Variation can be established only when more than one case is being examined. Usually, researchers employing this design will select a lot more than two cases for a variety of reasons: they are more likely to encounter variation in all the variables in which they are interested; they can make finer distinctions between cases; and the requirements of sampling procedure are likely to necessitate larger numbers (see Chapter 4).

- *At a single point in time*. In cross-sectional design research, data on the variables of interest are collected more or less simultaneously. When an individual completes a questionnaire, which may contain fifty or more variables, the answers are supplied at essentially the same time. This contrasts with an experimental design. Thus, in the classical experimental design, someone in the experimental group is pre-tested, then exposed to the experimental treatment, and then post-tested. Days, weeks, months, or even years may separate the different phases.

- *Quantitative or quantifiable data*. In order to establish variation between cases (and then to examine associations between variables—see next point), it is necessary to have a systematic and standardized method for gauging variation. One of the most important advantages of quantification is that it provides the researcher with a consistent benchmark. The advantages of quantification and of measurement will be addressed in greater detail in Chapter 3.

- *Patterns of association*. With a cross-sectional design it is only possible to examine relationships between variables. There is no time ordering to the variables, because the data on them are collected more or less simultaneously, and the researcher does not (invariably because he or she cannot) manipulate any of the variables. This creates the problem referred to in Box 2.8 in establishing the direction of causal influence. If the researcher discovers a relationship between two variables, he or she cannot be certain whether this denotes a

---

Box 2.13 🔅 *What is a cross-sectional research design?*

A cross-sectional design entails the collection of data on more than one case (usually quite a lot more than one) and at a single point in time in order to collect a body of quantitative or quantifiable data in connection with two or more variables (usually many more than two), which are then examined to detect patterns of association.

causal relationship, because the features of an experimental design are not present. All that can be said is the variables are related. This is not to say that it is not possible to draw causal inferences from research based on a cross-sectional design. As will be shown in Chapter 11, there are a number of ways in which the researcher is able to draw certain inferences about causality, but these inferences rarely have the credibility of causal findings deriving from an experimental design. As a result, cross-sectional research invariably lacks the internal validity that one finds in most experimental research.

In this book, the term 'survey' will be reserved for research that employs a cross-sectional research design and in which data are collected by questionnaire or by structured interview (see Box 2.14). This will allow us to retain the conventional understanding of what a survey is while recognizing that the cross-sectional research design has a wider relevance—that is, one that is not necessarily associated with the collection of data by questionnaire or by structured interview. An example of a survey that is widely used and cited in the study of UK human resource management and industrial relations is given in Box 2.15.

Reliability, replicability, and validity

How does cross-sectional research measure up in terms of the previously outlined criteria for evaluating quantitative research: reliability, replicability, and validity?

- The issues of *reliability* and *measurement validity* are primarily matters relating to the quality of the measures that are employed to tap the concepts in which the researcher is interested, rather than matters to do with a research design. In order to address questions of the quality of measures, some of the issues outlined in Chapter 3 would have to be considered.

- *Replicability* is likely to be present in most cross-sectional research to the degree that the researcher spells out procedures for: selecting respondents; designing measures of concepts; administration of research instruments (such as structured interview or self-completion questionnaire); and the analysis of data. Most quantitative research based on cross-sectional research designs specifies such procedures to a large degree.

- *Internal validity* is typically weak. As has just been suggested above, it is difficult to establish causal direction from the resulting data. Cross-sectional research designs produce associations rather than findings from which causal inferences can be unambiguously made. However, procedures for making causal inferences from cross-sectional data will be referred to in Chapter 11, though most researchers feel that the resulting causal findings rarely have the internal validity of those deriving from experimental designs.

- *External validity* is strong when, as in the case of research like the Workplace Employee Relations Survey (WERS), formerly the Workplace Industrial Relations Survey (WIRS); (Box 2.15), the sample from which data are collected has been randomly selected. When non-random methods of sampling are employed, external validity becomes questionable. Sampling issues will be specifically addressed in Chapter 4.

- Since much cross-sectional research makes a great deal of use of research instruments, such as self-completion questionnaires and structured observation schedules, *ecological validity* may be jeopardized because the very instruments disrupt

---

Box 2.14 *What is survey research?*

Survey research comprises a cross-sectional design in relation to which data are collected predominantly by questionnaire or by structured interview on more than one case (usually quite a lot more than one) and at a single point in time in order to collect a body of quantitative or quantifiable data in connection with two or more variables (usually many more than two), which are then examined to detect patterns of association.

Box 2.15 An example of survey research: the Workplace Employee Relations Survey (WERS)

The 1998 Workplace Employee Relations Survey (WERS) is the fourth in a series of workplace surveys (formerly Workplace Industrial Relations Survey (WIRS)), the first of which began in 1980, that looks at changing employment relations policies and practices in Britain. The purpose of the survey is to provide 'an extensive and authoritative body of factual information on practice in British workplaces' (Millward, Bryson, and Forth 2000: p. xiv). It is funded by a consortium of government, executive agencies, and research bodies. The principal unit of analysis used in the survey is the 'workplace', which is defined as 'the activities of a single employer at a single set of premises' (Cully et al. 1999: 4).

This definition, which relies on spatial separation, means that a branch of a high-street bank is classed as a workplace, the head office of the bank as another, even though they legally form part of the same organization. A statistically representative random sample is generated using the Inter-Departmental Business Register, which contains details of all private and publicly owned 'going concerns' operating the UK. The sample is stratified by workplace employment size and by industrial activity. High response rates of around 80 per cent were achieved, reinforcing the perceived reliability of the data. The 1998 survey also reduced the size threshold for the survey, from workplaces with twenty-five or more employees to workplaces with ten or more employees.

Managers and worker representatives in more than 3,000 workplaces were interviewed about all aspects of employment relations and almost 30,000 employees completed a questionnaire about their working life. This enabled researchers to build up a picture of employee relations that linked the view of employees with those of managers and workers in the same workplace. A key strength of the survey thus lies in its representation of multiple interests in the workplace, rather than just relying on the account given by a senior manager.

One of the primary interests of the researchers has been in examining changes over time. This was enabled by two specific elements of the survey design: the time-series data set and the panel study. The time series was formed from interviews with the manager in each workplace in each of the four surveys, conducted in 1980, 1984, 1990, and 1998. This provides direct comparison of employment relations practice at four specific points in time over two decades using different, randomly generated samples on each occasion. However, the limitation of time-series analysis derives from the fact that, although it provides a snapshot of practice at a particular point in time, it does not reveal the process whereby change has occurred. For this reason, the researchers incorporated a panel study, comprising workplaces that had taken part in the 1990 survey where the same manager was reinterviewed in 1998. This 'panel' enables greater analysis of the dynamics of change within workplaces that had continued to operate over this eight-year period.

the 'natural habitat', as Cicourel (1982) put it (see quotation on p. 34).

Non-manipulable variables

As was noted at the beginning of the section on Experimental Design, in much, if not most, business research it is not possible to manipulate the variables in which we are interested. This is why most quantitative business research employs a cross-sectional research design rather than an experimental one. Moreover, some of the variables in which social scientists are interested, and which are often viewed as potentially significant independent variables, simply cannot be manipulated, other than by extreme measures. At the individual level of analysis, age, ethnicity, gender, and social backgrounds are 'givens' that are not really amenable to the kind of manipulation that is necessary for a true experimental design. To a lesser extent this also applies at the organizational level of analysis to variables such as size, structure, technology, and culture. On the other hand, the very fact that we can regard certain variables as givens provides us with a clue as to how we can make causal inferences in cross-sectional research. Many of the variables in which we are interested can be *assumed* to be temporally prior to other variables. For example, we can assume that, if we find a relationship between gender and entrepreneurial behaviour, then the former is more likely to be the independent variable because it is likely to be temporally prior to entrepreneurial behaviour. In other words, while we may not be able to manipulate the gender variable, we can draw some causal inferences from cross-sectional data.

Structure of the cross-sectional design

The cross-sectional research design is not easy to depict in terms of the notation previously introduced, but Figure 2.2 captures its main features, except that in this case Obs simply represents an observation made in relation to a variable.

Figure 2.2 implies that a cross-sectional design comprises the collection of data on a series of variables (Obs_1 Obs_2 Obs_3 Obs_4 $Obs_5 \ldots Obs_n$) at a single point in time, T_1. The effect is to create what Marsh (1982) referred to as a 'rectangle' of data that comprises variables Obs_1 to Obs_n and cases $case_1$ to $case_n$, as in Figure 2.3. For each case (which may be a person,

$$T_1$$
$$Obs_1$$
$$Obs_2$$
$$Obs_3$$
$$Obs_4$$
$$Obs_5$$
$$. . .$$
$$Obs_n$$

Figure 2.2 A cross-sectional design

	Obs_1	Obs_2	Obs_3	Obs_4	. . .	Obs_n
$Case_1$						
$Case_2$						
$Case_3$						
$Case_4$						
$Case_5$						
. . .						
$Case_n$						

Figure 2.3 The data rectangle in cross-sectional research

household, city, nation, etc.) data are available for each of the variables, Obs_1 to Obs_n, all of which will have been collected at T_1. Each cell in the matrix will have data in it.

Cross-sectional design and research strategy

This discussion of the cross-sectional design has placed it firmly in the context of quantitative research. Also, the evaluation of the design drew on criteria associated with the quantitative research strategy. It should also be noted, however, that qualitative research often entails a form of cross-sectional design. A fairly typical form of such research is when the researcher employs unstructured interviewing or semi-structured interviewing with a number of people. Box 2.16 provides an illustration of such a study.

Whilst not typical of the qualitative research tradition, the study described in Box 2.16 bears some research design similarities with cross-sectional studies within a predominantly quantitative research tradition, like the WERS (Box 2.15), whilst retaining some research design features more typical of qualitative studies. The research was not directly preoccupied with such criteria of quantitative research as internal and external validity, replicability, measurement validity, and so on, but it is clear that the researchers took considerable care to ensure the representativeness of their sample of managers in relation to the overall population. In fact, it could be argued that the use of interview as a follow-up method after the initial questionnaire survey made the study more ecologically valid than research that just uses more formal instruments of data collection. It is common within business and management research to see such a *triangulated* approach, where attempts are made to cancel out the limitations of one method by the use of another in order to cross-check the findings. Hence, cross-sectional studies in business and management tend not to be so clearly divided into those that use either quantitative or qualitative methods.

Longitudinal design(s)

The longitudinal design represents a distinct form of research design that is typically used to map change

---

Box 2.16 A representative sample?

Scase and Goffee (1989) conducted a survey of 374 managers employed in six large organizations—four of which were privately owned and two of which were in the public sector. A number of issues were taken into account in order to ensure that the sample was representative of a wider population.

1 The sample of 323 men and 51 women chosen for the questionnaire survey was designed to reflect gender proportions within the wider UK management population.

2 The researchers attempted to achieve a broad spread of ages within their sample, to reflect the relative proportions of male and female managers in each group.

3 They also sought to reflect labour market patterns and functional groupings—for example, by including more women in the sample who were engaged in personnel management, training, and industrial relations.

4 They included more men in senior and middle-level management positions to reflect the fact that women are underrepresented in these positions.

5 Finally, the sample was selected to reflect patterns of employment, levels of education, salary levels, and marital status broadly representative of patterns in the wider population.

From the questionnaire survey, a smaller representative group of eighty men and women were selected for in-depth interviews. However, Scase and Goffee make no claim for the statistical representativeness of their sample. Instead they suggest that their findings can be 'regarded as *indicative* of broader trends . . . affecting the work, careers and personal experiences of men and women managers during the closing decades of the twentieth century' (1989: 197).

---

in business and management research. Pettigrew (1990) has emphasized the importance of longitudinal study in understanding organizations as a way of providing data on the mechanisms and processes through which changes are created. Such a 'contextualist' research design involves drawing on 'phenomena at vertical and horizontal levels of analysis and the interconnections between those levels through time' (1990: 269). However, partly because of the time and cost involved, longitudinal design is relatively little used in business and management research. In the form in which it is typically found, it is usually an extension of social survey research based on self-completion questionnaire or structured interview research within a cross-sectional design. Consequently, in terms of reliability, replication, and validity, the longitudinal design is little different from cross-sectional research. However, a longitudinal design can allow some insight into the time order of variables and therefore may be more able to allow causal inferences to be made. This was one of the aims of the WERS series (see Box 2.15).

With a longitudinal design a sample is surveyed and is surveyed again on at least one further occasion. It is common to distinguish two types of longitudinal design: the *panel study* and the *cohort study*. With the former type, a sample, often a randomly selected national one, is the focus of data collection on at least two (and often more) occasions. Data may be collected from different types of case within a panel study framework: individuals, organizations, and so on. An illustration of this kind of study is incorporated into the 1998 WERS (see Box 2.15).

The cohort study selects either an entire cohort of people or a randomly selected sample of them as the focus of data collection. The cohort is made up of people who share a certain characteristic, such as all being born in the same week or having a certain experience, such as being unemployed or getting married on a certain day or in the same week. However, this design is rarely used in business and management research.

Panel and cohort studies share similar features. They have a similar design structure: Figure 2.4

Figure 2.4 The longitudinal design

portrays this structure and implies that data are collected in at least two waves on the same variables on the same people or organizations. They are both concerned with illuminating social change and improving the understanding of causal influences over time. The latter means that longitudinal designs are somewhat better able to deal with the problem of ambiguity about the direction of causal influence that plagues cross-sectional designs. Because certain potentially independent variables can be identified at T_1, the researcher is in a better position to infer that purported effects that are identified at T_2 or later have occurred *after* the independent variables. This does not deal with the entire problem about the ambiguity of causal influence, but it at least addresses the problem of knowing which variable came first. In all other respects, the points made above about cross-sectional designs are the same as those for longitudinal designs.

Panel and cohort studies share similar problems. First, there is the problem of sample attrition through employee job changes, companies going out of business, and so on, and through subjects choosing to withdraw at later stages of the research. The 1998 WERS panel survey, for example, traced a random selection of workplaces from the 1990 survey for re-interview. This yielded a sample of 846 'continuing workplaces', a response rate of 82 per cent, which effectively minimized potential bias through attrition. A continuing workplace was defined as one that employed twenty-five or more people and had continued to operate between 1990 and 1998. However, changes in activity, ownership, or location were not considered critically to impair this concept of continuity. The problem with attrition is largely that those who leave the study may differ in some important respects from those who remain, so that the latter do

not form a representative group. In order to account even more fully for this possibility, the WERS panel survey was accompanied by a short telephone survey of all remaining workplaces from the 1990 cross-section not included in the panel survey. The researchers wanted to know how many of the 1990 cross-section sample workplaces had survived, whether they had expanded, moved premises, changed ownership, or amalgamated with or split from another establishment since the time of the 1990 study. This enabled them to build up a more general picture of the survival status of workplaces, which helped to enhance the internal validity of the panel study. Secondly, there are few guidelines as to when is the best juncture to conduct further waves of data collection. Thirdly, it is often suggested that many longitudinal studies are poorly thought out and that they result in the collection of large amounts of data with little apparent planning. Fourthly, there is evidence that a *panel conditioning* effect can occur whereby continued participation in a longitudinal study affects how respondents behave.

Case study design

The basic case study entails the detailed and intensive analysis of a single case. As Stake (1995) observes, case study research is concerned with the complexity and particular nature of the case in question. Some of the best-known studies in business and management research are based on this kind of design. A case can be:

- *a single organization*, such as Pettigrew's (1985; see Box 2.17) research at Imperial Chemical Industries (ICI), or Joanne Martin's (1992) study of organizational culture at 'OzCo', a high-technology industry company based in California;

- *a single location*, such as a factory, production site, or office building—for example, Pollert's (1981; see Box 14.13) research in a tobacco factory, Linstead's (1985) study of humour in a bakery or Milkman's (1997) investigation of an automobile assembly plant (see Chapter 14);

- *a person*, like in Marshall's (1995; see Box 13.3) study of women managers where each woman

elucidation
澄明

Box 2.17 A longitudinal case study of ICI

Pettigrew (1985) conducted research into the use of organizational development (OD) expertise at Imperial Chemical Industries (ICI). The fieldwork was conducted between 1975 and 1983. He carried out 'long semi-structured interviews' in 1975–7 and again in 1980–2. Some individuals were interviewed more than once and care was taken to ensure that interviews included people from all hierarchical levels in the company and from the different functional and business areas within the firm. The total number of interviews conducted during this period amounted to 175. During the period of the fieldwork Pettigrew also had fairly regular contact with members of the organization through his involvement with the company as a consultant and he had access to archival materials that explained how internal OD consultants were recruited and how external OD consultants were used. He writes: 'The continuous real-time data collection was enriched by retrospective interviewing and archival analysis...' (1985: 40). The study thus covered ten years of 'real-time' analysis, complemented by over twenty years of retrospective data. This longitudinal case study thus spans more than thirty years, although Pettigrew (1990) acknowledges that this is rarely feasible in organizational research.

constitutes a separate case—such studies are characterized as using the life history or biographical approach; or

• *a single event*, such as the Nasa space shuttle *Challenger* disaster in 1986 (Vaughan 1990; see Chapter 18) or the events surrounding a pipeline accident in Canada (Gephart 1993; see Box 18.6).

What is a case?

The most common use of the term associates the case study with a location, such as a workplace or organization. The emphasis tends to be upon an intensive examination of the setting. There is a tendency to associate case studies with qualitative research, but such an identification is not appropriate. It is certainly true that exponents of the case study design often favour qualitative methods, such

as participant observation and unstructured interviewing, because these methods are viewed as particularly helpful in the generation of an intensive, detailed examination of a case. For example, Knights and McCabe (1997) suggest that the case study provides a vehicle through which several qualitative methods can be combined, thereby avoiding too great a reliance on one single approach. In their study of quality management in a UK retail bank, they were able to combine participant observation with semi-structured interviewing and documentary data collection of company reports, TQM management guides, and newsletters. Knights and McCabe suggest that the findings from the case study can be used to identify insights into why so many quality management programmes have failed. However, case studies are frequently sites for the employment of both quantitative and qualitative research, an approach that will receive attention in Chapter 22. Indeed, in some instances, when an investigation is based exclusively upon quantitative research, it can be difficult to determine whether it is better described as a case study or as a cross-sectional research design. The same point can often be made about case studies based upon qualitative research.

With a case study, the case is an object of interest in its own right and the researcher aims to provide an in-depth elucidation of it. Unless a distinction of this or some other kind is drawn, it becomes impossible to distinguish the case study as a special research design, because almost any kind of research can be construed as a case study. However, it also needs to be appreciated that, when specific research illustrations are examined, they can exhibit features of more than one research design. What distinguishes a case study is that the researcher is usually concerned to elucidate the unique features of the case. This is known as an *idiographic* approach. Research designs like the cross-sectional design are known as *nomothetic* in that they are concerned with generating statements that apply regardless of time and place.

With experimental and cross-sectional designs, the typical orientation to the relationship between theory and research is a deductive one. The research design and the collection of data are guided by

idiographic
nomothetic 个人 角度

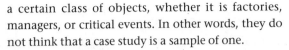
specific research questions that derive from theoretical concerns. However, when a qualitative research strategy is employed within a cross-sectional design, the approach tends to be inductive. In other words, whether a cross-sectional design is inductive or deductive tends to be affected by whether a quantitative or a qualitative research strategy is employed. The same point can be made of case study research. When the predominant research strategy is qualitative, a case study tends to take an inductive approach to the relationship between theory and research; if a predominantly quantitative strategy is taken, it tends to be deductive.

Reliability, replicability, and validity

The question of how well the case study fares in the context of the research design criteria cited early on in this chapter—measurement validity, internal validity, external validity, ecological validity, reliability, and replicability—depends in large part on how far the researcher feels that these are appropriate for the evaluation of case study research. Some writers on case study research, like Yin (1984), consider that they are appropriate criteria and suggest ways in which case study research can be developed to enhance its ability to meet the criteria; for others, like Stake (1995), they are barely mentioned if at all. Writers on case study research whose point of orientation lies primarily with a qualitative research strategy tend to play down or ignore the salience of these factors, whereas those writers who have been strongly influenced by the quantitative research strategy tend to depict them as more significant.

However, one question on which a great deal of discussion has centred concerns the *external validity* or *generalizability* of case study research. How can a single case possibly be representative so that it might yield findings that can be applied more generally to other cases? For example, how could the findings from Pettigrew's (1985) research into ICI (Box 2.17), be generalizable to all large multinational pharmaceutical corporations? The answer, of course, is that they cannot. It is important to appreciate that case study researchers do not delude themselves that it is possible to identify typical cases that can be used to represent a certain class of objects, whether it is factories, managers, or critical events. In other words, they do not think that a case study is a sample of one.

However, although many researchers emphasize that they are interested in the detail of a single case, they do sometimes claim a degree of theoretical generalizability on the basis of it. For example, in her study of Indsco Supply Corporation, Kanter (1977) explains that the case enabled her to generate concepts and give meaning to abstract propositions, which she then sought to test in three other large corporations. It is therefore clear that she is seeking to achieve a degree of theoretical generalizability from this case.

Types of case

Following on from the issue of external validity, it is useful to consider a distinction between different types of case that is sometimes made by writers. Yin (1984) distinguishes three types.

- *The critical case.* Here the researcher has a clearly specified hypothesis, and a case is chosen on the grounds that it will allow a better understanding of the circumstances in which the hypothesis will and will not hold.
- *The unique case.* The unique or extreme case is, as Yin observes, a common focus in clinical studies.
- *The revelatory case.* The basis for the revelatory case exists 'when an investigator has an opportunity to observe and analyse a phenomenon previously inaccessible to scientific investigation' (Yin 1984: 44). While the idea of the revelatory case is interesting, it seems unnecessary to restrict it solely to situations in which something has not previously been studied. Much qualitative case study research that is carried out with a predominantly inductive approach to theory treats single case studies as broadly 'revelatory'.

Exponents of case study research counter suggestions that the evidence they present is limited because it has restricted external validity by arguing that it is not the purpose of this research design to generalize to other cases or to populations beyond the case. This position is very different from that taken by practitioners of survey research. Survey researchers are invariably concerned to be able to generalize their findings to larger populations and frequently use random sampling to enhance the representativeness of the samples on which they conduct their investigations and therefore the external validity of their findings. Case study researchers argue strenuously that this is not the purpose of their craft.

Case study as intensive analysis

Instead, case study researchers tend to argue that they aim to generate an intensive examination of a single case, in relation to which they then engage in a theoretical analysis. The central issue of concern is the quality of the theoretical reasoning in which the case study researcher engages. How well do the data support the theoretical arguments that are generated? Is the theoretical analysis incisive? For example, does it demonstrate connections between different conceptual ideas that are developed out of the data? The crucial question is not whether the findings can be generalized to a wider universe, but how well the researcher generates theory out of the findings (Mitchell 1983; Yin 1984). Such a view places case study research firmly in the inductive tradition of the relationship between theory and research. However, a case study design is not necessarily associated with an inductive approach, as can be seen in the research by Whittington (1989), which was referred to in Chapter 1 (Box 1.2). Thus, case studies can be associated with both theory generation and theory testing.

Longitudinal research and the case study

Case study research frequently includes a longitudinal element. The researcher is often a participant of an organization for many months or years. Alternatively, he or she may conduct interviews with individuals over a lengthy period. Moreover, the researcher may be able to inject an additional longitudinal element by analysing archival information and by retrospective interviewing. Box 2.17 provides an illustration of longitudinal case study research.

Another way in which a longitudinal element occurs is when a case that has been studied is returned to at a later stage. An interesting instance of this is Burawoy's (1979) study of a factory in Chicago, which he claims was the same one as originally studied by Roy in the 1950s. This is a somewhat loose connection, however, as the theoretical focus adopted by the two researchers was markedly different, although their research methods, based on participant observation, were quite similar. A further example of longitudinal research carried out by different researchers is given in Box 2.18. This study is interesting because it relies on social survey methods in addition to preliminary interviews with managers, union officials, and employees. Generally speaking, however, it is difficult for the researcher to establish how far change is the result of real differences over the two time periods or of other factors, such as different people in the organization, different ownership of the company between the two time periods, and the possible influence of the initial study itself.

Comparative design

It is worth distinguishing one further kind of design: comparative design. Put simply, this design entails the study using more or less identical methods of two or more contrasting cases. It embodies the logic of comparison in that it implies that we can understand social phenomena better when they are compared in relation to two or more meaningfully contrasting cases or situations. The comparative design may be realized in the context of either quantitative or qualitative research. Within the former, the data collection strategy will take the form outlined in Figure 2.5. This figure implies that there are at least two cases (which may be organizations, nations, people, etc.) and that data are collected from each usually within a cross-sectional design format.

One of the more obvious forms of such research is in cross-cultural or cross-national research (Box 2.19). In a useful definition, Hantrais (1996) has suggested that such research occurs

when individuals or teams set out to examine particular issues or phenomena in two or more countries with the express intention of comparing their manifestations in different socio-cultural settings (institutions, customs,

Box 2.18 A study of a steelworks spanning fifty years

One way of overcoming some of the difficulties associated with longitudinal study is by revisiting case study organizations that have previously been studied by other researchers in order to explore how they have changed over time. This was the approach taken by Bacon and Blyton (2001) in their case study of a North Wales steelworks. These researchers sought to replicate and extend survey research carried out in the 1950s (Scott et al. 1956), which looked at the social systems of industrial organizations to explain the positive orientation of steelworkers to technical change. Even though the steelworks was not actually named in the original study, information about its size, location, history, and activities meant that it was relatively easy for Blyton and his colleagues to identify it as the Shotton plant.

In 1991, Blyton, Bacon, and Morris (1996) conducted an employee attitude survey at the plant in order to explore the impact of teamworking on employee attitudes and behaviour, focusing on a variety of aspects of job satisfaction,

change, attitudes to management, and industrial relations issues. This survey formed part of a broader study of the role of industrial relations and workplace change in the UK and German steel industries. They found that, despite the massive changes that had affected the plant between the 1950s and the 1990s, the social system of the works continued to influence steelworkers attitudes to work, contributing towards their positive attitude to workplace change. However, at the end of the 1990s, when they returned to the plant to conduct a similar survey, they found that employee attitudes had changed. In particular, the steelworkers, who had been deeply affected by competitive pressures leading to increased job insecurity, were no longer as positively oriented towards change. As the authors note, the 'almost fifty year time span between the first and last surveys provides a unique research setting upon which to base some broader reflections on organisational change, management practices and employee attitudes' (Bacon and Blyton 2001: 224).

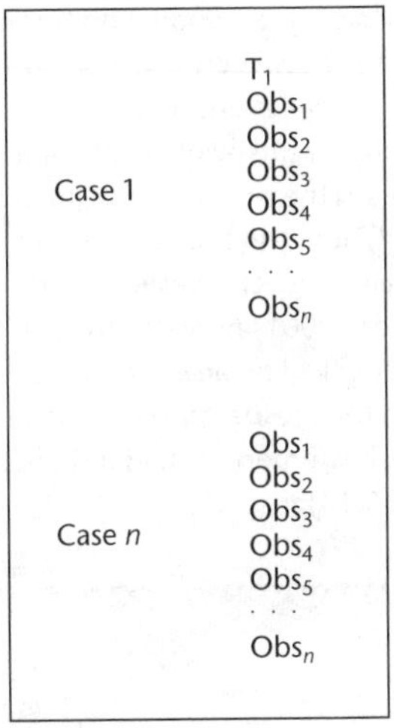

Figure 2.5 A comparative design

traditions, value systems, lifestyles, language, thought patterns), using the same research instruments either to carry out secondary analysis of national data or to conduct new empirical work. The aim may be to seek explanations for similarities and differences or to gain a greater awareness and a deeper understanding of social reality in different national contexts.

Cross-cultural research in business and management tends to presuppose that culture is a major explanatory variable that exerts profound influence on organizational behaviour. In business and management research, there has been a tendency in recent years to question the adaptability of many management theories and practices to other, particularly non-Western, cultural contexts. There has also been mounting criticism of the universalist vision that business and management research has promoted, based predominantly on unacknowledged Anglo-Saxon values. These pressures have led to greater interest in cross-cultural research. Within this overall category, however, there are some important distinctions. International management research concerns itself with how and why companies internationalize, it may focus on a specific country, or make cross-cultural comparisons between several countries. Usunier (1998) distinguishes between:

- *cross-cultural approaches*—which compare national management systems and local business customs in various countries; and

Box 2.19 Cross-cultural and international research

As its name implies, cross-cultural research entails the collection and/or analysis of data from two or more nations. Possible models for the conduct of cross-cultural research are as follows.

1 A researcher, perhaps in conjunction with a research team, collects data in a number of countries. Hofstede's (1984) research on the cultural differences between IBM workers in different countries (see Box 1.12) is an illustration of this model in that he took comparable samples of IBM employees from all hierarchical levels, allowing for a similar representation of gender and age, in sixty-six national subsidiaries of the company. More than forty countries are eventually compared using this method.

2 A central organization coordinates a portion of the work of national organizations or groups. An example is the Global Disney Audiences Project (Wasko, Phillips, and Meehan 2001), whereby a research group in the USA recruited researchers in a variety of countries who were interested in the ways Disney products are viewed, and then coordinated the ways questions were asked in the research. Each nation's research groups were responsible for sampling and other aspects of the interview process.

3 Secondary analysis is carried out using data that are comparable, but where the coordination of their collection is limited or non-existent. This kind of cross-cultural analysis might occur if researchers seek to ask survey questions in their own country that have been asked in another country. The ensuing data may then be analysed cross-culturally. A further form of this model is through the secondary analysis of officially collected data, such as unemployment statistics.

However, this kind of cross-cultural research makes it particularly important to be sure about the accuracy of data, which will probably have been produced by several different agencies, in providing a suitable basis for cross-cultural comparison. For example, Roy, Walters, and Luk (2001) suggest that business researchers have tended to avoid relying on secondary data about China because of concerns about the reliability and representativeness of government sources. Research units associated with local authorities may overstate certain factors to give the impression that the economy is doing better than it really is, statistical approaches and classification schemes may differ from one province to another, and data may have been censored at certain points in time or even lost. Business researchers must therefore be cautious in their use of secondary data for the purpose of cross-cultural analysis.

4 Teams of researchers in participating nations are recruited by a person or body that coordinates the programme. Each researcher or group of researchers has the responsibility of conducting the investigation in his, her, or their own country. The work is coordinated in order to ensure comparability of research questions, survey questions, and procedures for administering the research instruments. This model differs from (2) above in that it usually entails a specific focus on certain research questions. The article by Terence Jackson (2001) provides an example of this model: Jackson relied on academic associates to collect data in their respective countries, using the questionnaire instrument he had designed for this purpose (Box 5.14).

- *intercultural approaches*—which focus on the study of interaction between people and organizations with different national/cultural backgrounds.

Comparative research should not be treated as solely concerned with comparisons between nations. The logic of comparison can be applied to a variety of situations to inform a number of levels of analysis. For example, Hofstede's (1984) research on cultural

differences has informed a generation of studies that have explored cultural differences in organizations other than IBM and the framework has also been applied to understanding specific organizational behaviours, such as ethical decision making.

Cross-cultural research is not without problems such as: managing and gaining the funding for such research (see Box 2.19); ensuring, when existing data, such as official statistics or survey evidence, are submitted to a secondary analysis, that the data are comparable in terms of categories and data-collection methods; and ensuring, when new data are being collected, that the need to translate data-collection instruments (for example, interview schedules) does not undermine genuine comparability. This raises the further difficulty that, even when translation is carried out competently, there is still the potential problem of an insensitivity to specific national and cultural contexts. On the other hand, cross-cultural research helps to reduce the risk of failing to appreciate that social science findings are often, if not invariably, culturally specific. Cross-cultural research also creates particular issues in achieving equivalence—between the samples, variables, and methods that are used (McDonald 2000). For example, in many cases nationality is used as a surrogate for culture; differences may thus be attributed to culture even if they could be more readily attributed to national situation. Equally, people inhabiting a country under the same government may belong to quite different cultures that reflect historical or religious affiliations. Further issues are raised by language differences, which can cause translation problems. Adler (1983) claims that many comparative cross-cultural studies in business and management do not adequately acknowledge these distinctions.

In terms of issues of reliability, validity, replicability, and generalizability, the comparative study is no different from the cross-sectional design. The comparative design is essentially two or more cross-sectional studies carried out at more or less the same point in time.

The comparative design can also be applied in relation to a qualitative research strategy. When this occurs, it takes the form of a multiple-case study (see Box 2.20). Essentially, a multiple-case (or multi-case) study occurs whenever the number of cases examined exceeds one. In business and management multiple-case studies constitute a relatively common research design that usually takes two or more organizations as cases for comparison, but occasionally a number of people are used as cases. For example, Marshall (1984) adopts a multiple-case study

---

Box 2.20 A multiple case study

In their study of the factors that contribute to competitive success among large British companies, Pettigrew and Whipp (1991) adopted a multiple-case study approach. They examined seven organizations, which were made up of a successful and an unsuccessful company in three mature industry and service sectors of the UK economy, these were:

- automobile manufacturing;
- merchant banking;
- book publishing.

An additional company drawn from life insurance was also included in the sample. The objective of the study was to discover why firms operating in the same industry, country, and product markets should record such varying performances. By choosing companies in this way, Pettigrew and Whipp could establish the common and differentiating factors that lay behind the strategic management of change. Sources of data included semi-structured interviews, conducted in each firm and related organizations (including competitors, industry bodies, and government), and primary and secondary documentary evidence. The research was longitudinal, conducted over a period of three years.

---

approach in her study of women managers; she retains a focus on intensive examination of each case but there is qualitative comparison of each woman manager's situation with the others. The main argument in favour of the multiple-case study is that it improves theory building. By comparing two or more cases, the researcher is in a better position to establish the circumstances in which a theory will or will not hold (Yin 1984; Eisenhardt 1989). Moreover, the comparison may itself suggest concepts that are relevant to an emerging theory.

Box 2.20 describes one approach to selecting cases for a multiple-case study. In this illustration, cases were selected on the basis of their representing extreme types—namely, successful and unsuccessful firms, and their operation in certain commercial sectors. With a case selection approach such as this, the findings that are common to the firms can be just as interesting and important as those that differentiate them.

However, not all writers are convinced about the merits of multiple-case study research. Dyer and Wilkins (1991), for example, argue that a multiple-case study approach tends to mean that the researcher pays less attention to the specific context and more to the ways in which the cases can be contrasted. Moreover, the need to forge comparisons tends to mean that the researcher needs to develop an explicit focus at the outset, whereas it may be advantageous to adopt a more open-ended approach in many instances. These concerns about retaining contextual insight and a rather more unstructured research approach are very much associated with the goals of the qualitative research strategy (see Chapter 13).

The key to the comparative design is its ability to allow the distinguishing characteristics of two or more cases to act as a springboard for theoretical reflections about contrasting findings. It is something of a hybrid, in that in quantitative research it is frequently an extension of a cross-sectional design and in qualitative research it is frequently an extension of a case study design. It even exhibits certain features that are similar to experiments and quasi-experiments, which also rely on the capacity to forge a comparison.

Level of analysis

A further consideration for business researchers that applies to the research designs covered in this chapter relates to the concept of level; in other words, what is the primary unit of measurement and analysis? Hence, research might focus on:

- *individuals*—this would include studies that focus on specific kinds of individuals such as managers or shopfloor employees;

- *groups*—this would include research that considered certain types of groupings—for example, HR departments or boards of directors;

- *organizations*—in addition to studies that focused on companies, this would include surveys, such as WERS (see Box 2.15) which treat the workplace as the principal unit of analysis;

- *societies*—the main focus of this kind of analysis would be on the national, political, social, environmental, and economic contexts in which business organizations are located.

Differences in level of analysis are commonly referred to in terms of the SOGI model (societies, organizations, groups, and individuals). However, some research designs draw on samples that combine different levels of analysis—for example, organizations and departments. This begs the question as to whether it is possible to combine data from different levels to produce a meaningful analysis. The complexity of organizational types can make the issue of level particularly difficult to determine. Rousseau (1985) suggests it is important to make explicit the problems of using data derived from one level to represent something at another level in order to avoid misinterpretation. For example, processes of individual and organizational learning may be constructed quite differently at different levels. If researchers make inferences about organizational learning on the basis of data about individuals, they are at risk of making a cross-level misattribution. Since the phenomenon of learning is an essentially human characteristic, as organizations don't behave but people do, this leads to the attribution of human characteristics to a higher-level system. Misattribution can also occur when metaphors are used to interpret organizational behaviour. It is therefore good practice to identify and make clear in your research design the level of analysis that is being used and then to switch to another level only after having made this clear (Rousseau 1985).

Another illustration of mixed-level research cited by Rousseau (1985) is found in the area of leadership studies. The average leadership style (ALS) approach assumes that leaders display the same behavioural style toward all subordinates. Research therefore relies on eliciting subordinate perceptions of the leader, which are averaged and treated as group-level characteristics. In contrast, the vertical dyadic linkage (VDL) model assumes that a leader's style may be different with each subordinate, thereby treating leadership as an individual-level phenomenon rather than a group one. Each model thus conceptualizes leadership at a different level.

Bringing research strategy and research design together

Finally, we can bring together the two research strategies covered in Chapter 1 with the research designs outlined in this chapter. Table 2.1 shows the typical form associated with each combination of research strategy and research design and a number of examples that either have been encountered so far or will be covered in later chapters. Table 2.1 refers also to research methods that will be encountered in later chapters, but which have not been referred to so far.

The Glossary will give you a quick reference to terms used that are not yet familiar to you.

The distinctions are not always perfect. In particular, in some qualitative research it is not obvious whether a study is an example of a longitudinal design or a case study design. Life history studies, research that concentrates on a specific issue over time, and ethnography in which the researcher charts change in a single case are examples of studies that

Table 2.1 Research strategy and research design

Research design	Research strategy Quantitative	Qualitative
Experimental	*Typical form.* Most researchers using an experimental design employ quantitative comparisons between experimental and control groups with regard to the dependent variable. See, for example, Gallupe et al.'s (1992) study of electronic brainstorming mentioned in this chapter, and the study of leadership referred to in Box 2.9.	*No typical form.* However, the Hawthorne experiments (Chapter 1 and Box 2.10) provide an example of experimental research design that gradually moved away from the 'test room method' towards the use of more qualitative methods.
Cross-sectional	*Typical form.* Social survey research or structured observation on a sample at a single point in time. See, for example, the Aston studies (Boxes 1.8 and 2.8) or Powell's research into TQM programmes in firms in the north-eastern USA (Box 1.5). Can also include content analysis on a sample of documents.	*Typical form.* Qualitative interviews or focus groups at a single point in time—for example in Whittington's (1989) study of eight British firms in the office furniture and domestic appliance industries (Box 1.2) and Scase and Goffee's (1989) research into 'reluctant managers' in six large UK organizations (Box 2.16). Can also be based upon qualitative content analysis of a set of documents relating to a single event or specific period in time (Box 18.6).
Longitudinal	*Typical form.* Social survey research on a sample on more than one occasion, as in the Workplace Employee Relations Surveys (WERS) (Box 2.15), or content analysis of documents relating to different time periods.	*Typical form.* Ethnographic research over a long period, qualitative interviewing on more than one occasion, or qualitative content analysis of documents relating to different time periods.

Research design	Research strategy Quantitative	Qualitative
		Such research warrants being dubbed longitudinal when there is a concern to map change, such as in Pettigrew's study of ICI (Box 2.17).
Case study	*Typical form.* Social survey research on a single case with a view to revealing important features about its nature. Examples include Kanter's (1977) study of the Indsco corporation, although it must be noted that this research did use a combination of qualitative and quantitative research methods (Box 22.4).	*Typical form.* The intensive study by ethnography or qualitative interviewing of a single case, which may be an organization—examples include Watson's (1994a) study of 'ZTC Ryland' and Casey's (1995) study of the 'Hephaestus' Corporation (Chapter 14)—or an individual, as in Marshall's (1995) study of women managers (Box 13.3).
Comparative	*Typical form.* Social survey research in which there is a direct comparison between two or more cases, as in cross-cultural research. Examples include Hofstede's (1984) study of cross-cultural differences (Box 1.12).	*Typical form.* Ethnographic or qualitative interview research on two or more cases, such as Pettigrew and Whipp's study of successful and unsuccessful companies in four sectors (Box 2.20) or Ram's (1994) study of three clothing firms in the West Midlands (Box 14.6).

cross the two types. Such studies are perhaps better conceptualized as longitudinal case studies rather than as belonging to one category of research design or another. A further point to note is that there is no typical form in the qualitative research strategy/ experimental research design cell. Qualitative research in the context of true experiments is very unusual. However, as noted in the table, the Hawthorne studies (Roethlisberger and Dickson 1939) provide an interesting example of the way that a quasi-experimental research design can change over time.

Generali zability [handwritten annotation]

K KEY POINTS

- There is an important distinction between a research method and a research design.

- It is necessary to become thoroughly familiar with the meaning of the technical terms used as criteria for evaluating research: reliability; validity; replicability; and the types of validity (measurement, internal, external, ecological).

- It is also necessary to be familiar with the differences between the five major research designs covered (experimental, cross-sectional, longitudinal, case study, and comparative) and to consider the level of analysis (individual, group, organization and market) that research may focus on. In this context, it is important to realize that the term 'experiment', which is often used somewhat loosely in everyday speech, has a specific technical meaning.

- There are various potential threats to validity in non-experimental research.
- Although the case study is often thought to be a single type of research design, it in fact has several forms. It is also important to be aware of the key issues concerned with the nature of case study evidence in relation to issues like external validity (generalizability).

Q QUESTIONS FOR REVIEW

- In terms of the definitions used in this book, what are the chief differences between each of the following: a research method; a research strategy; and a research design?

Criteria in business research

- What are the differences between reliability and validity and why are these important criteria for the evaluation of business research?
- Outline the meaning of each of the following: measurement validity; internal validity; external validity; and ecological validity.
- Why have some qualitative researchers sought to devise alternative criteria from reliability and validity when assessing the quality of investigations?
- What is the 'experimenter effect' and how might it contribute towards bias?
- What is social desirability bias and how might its effects be reduced?

Research questions

- Why are research questions important in the overall research process?
- What are the main characteristics of good research questions?

Research designs

- What are the main research designs that have been outlined in this chapter?
- Why is level of analysis a particular consideration in business and management research?

Experimental design

- 'The main importance of the experimental design for the business researcher is that it represents a model of how to infer causal connections between variables.' Discuss.
- Following on from the last question, if it is so useful and important, why is it not used more?
- What is a quasi-experiment?

Cross-sectional design

- What is meant by a cross-sectional research design?
- In what ways does the social survey exemplify the cross-sectional research design?
- Assess the degree to which the survey researcher can achieve internally valid findings.
- To what extent is the survey design exclusive to quantitative research?

Longitudinal design(s)

- Why might a longitudinal research design be superior to a cross-sectional one?
- What are the main differences between panel and cohort designs in longitudinal research?

Case study design

- What is a case study?
- Is case study research exclusive to qualitative research?
- What are some of the principles by which cases might be selected?

Comparative design

- What are the chief strengths of a comparative research design?
- Why might comparative research yield important insights?

Part Two

Part Two of this book is concerned with quantitative research. Chapter 3 sets the scene by exploring the main features of this research strategy. Chapter 4 discusses the ways in which we sample people on whom we carry out research. Chapter 5 focuses on the structured interview, which is one of the main methods of data collection in quantitative research and in survey research in particular. Chapter 6 is concerned with another prominent method of gathering data through survey research—questionnaires that people complete themselves. Chapter 7 provides guidelines on how to ask questions for structured interviews and questionnaires. Chapter 8 discusses structured observation, a method that provides a systematic approach to the observation of people. Chapter 9 addresses content analysis, which is a distinctive and systematic approach to the analysis of a wide variety of documents. Chapter 10 discusses the possibility of using in your own research data collected by other researchers or official statistics. Chapter 11 presents some of the main tools you will need to conduct quantitative data analysis. Chapter 12 shows you how to use computer software in the form of SPSS—a very widely used package of programs—to implement the techniques learned in Chapter 11.

These chapters will provide you with the essential tools for doing quantitative research. They will take you from the very general issues to do with the generic features of quantitative research to the very practical issues of conducting surveys and analysing your own data.

3

The nature of quantitative research

[handwritten annotation: entail: 需要 to involve or make it necessary]

CHAPTER GUIDE

This chapter is concerned with the characteristics of quantitative research, an approach that has been the dominant strategy for conducting business research, although its influence has waned slightly since the mid-1980s, when qualitative research became more influential. However, quantitative research continues to exert a powerful influence in many quarters. The emphasis in this chapter is very much on what quantitative research typically entails, although at a later point in the chapter the ways in which there are frequent departures from this ideal type are outlined. This chapter explores:

- the main steps of quantitative research, which are presented as a linear succession of stages;

- the importance of concepts in quantitative research and the ways in which measures may be devised for concepts; this discussion includes a discussion of the important idea of an *indicator*, which is devised as a way of measuring a concept for which there is no direct measure;

- the procedures for checking the reliability and validity of the measurement process;

- the main preoccupations of quantitative research, which are described in terms of four features: measurement; causality; generalization; and replication;

- some criticisms that are frequently levelled at quantitative research.

Introduction

In Chapter 1 quantitative research was outlined as a distinctive research strategy. In very broad terms, it was described as entailing the collection of numerical data and as exhibiting a view of the relationship between theory and research as deductive, a predilection for a natural science approach (and of positivism in particular), and as having an objectivist conception of social reality. A number of other features of quantitative research were outlined, but in this chapter we will be examining the strategy in much more detail.

It should be abundantly clear by now that the description of the research strategy as 'quantitative research' should not be taken to mean that quantification of aspects of social life is all that distinguishes it from a qualitative research strategy. The very fact that it has a distinctive epistemological and ontological position suggests that there is a good deal more to it than the mere presence of numbers. In this chapter, the main steps in quantitative research will be outlined. We will also examine some of the principal preoccupations of the strategy and how certain issues of concern among practitioners are addressed, like the concerns about measurement validity.

The main steps in quantitative research

Figure 3.1 outlines the main steps in quantitative research. This is very much an ideal-typical account of the process: it is probably never or rarely found in this pure form, but it represents a useful starting point for getting to grips with the main ingredients of the approach and the links between them. Research is rarely as linear and as straightforward as the figure implies, but its aim is to do no more than capture the main steps and to provide a rough indication of their interconnections.

Some of the chief steps have been covered in the first two chapters. The fact that we start off with theory signifies that a broadly deductive approach to the relationship between theory and research is taken. It is common for outlines of the main steps of quantitative research to suggest that a hypothesis is deduced from the theory and is tested. This notion has been incorporated into Figure 3.1. However, a great deal of quantitative research does not entail the specification of a hypothesis and instead theory acts loosely as a set of concerns in relation to which the business researcher collects data. The specification of hypotheses to be tested is particularly likely to be found in experimental research. Although other research designs sometimes entail the testing of hypotheses, as a general rule, we tend to find that

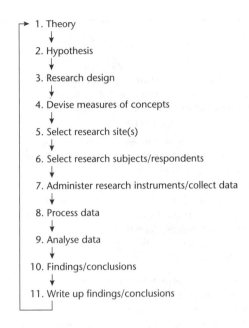

1. Theory
   ↓
2. Hypothesis
   ↓
3. Research design
   ↓
4. Devise measures of concepts
   ↓
5. Select research site(s)
   ↓
6. Select research subjects/respondents
   ↓
7. Administer research instruments/collect data
   ↓
8. Process data
   ↓
9. Analyse data
   ↓
10. Findings/conclusions
   ↓
11. Write up findings/conclusions

Figure 3.1 The process of quantitative research

Step 2 is more likely to be found in experimental research.

The next step entails the selection of a research design, a topic that was explored in Chapter 2. As we have seen, the selection of research design has implications for a variety of issues, such as the external validity of findings and researchers' ability to impute causality to their findings. Step 4 entails devising measures of the concepts in which the researcher is interested. This process is often referred to as *operationalization*, a term that originally derives from physics to refer to the operations by which a concept (such as temperature or velocity) is measured (Bridgman 1927). Aspects of this issue will be explored later on in this chapter.

The next two steps entail the selection of a research site or sites and then the selection of subjects/respondents. (Experimental researchers tend to call the people on whom they conduct research 'subjects', whereas social survey researchers typically call them 'respondents'.) Thus, in social survey research an investigator must first be concerned to establish an appropriate setting for his or her research. A number of decisions may be involved. The *Affluent*

Worker research undertaken by Goldthorpe et al. (1968: 2–5) involved two decisions about a research site or setting. First, the researchers needed a community that would be appropriate for the testing of the 'embourgeoisement' thesis (the idea that affluent workers were becoming more middle class in their attitudes and lifestyles). As a result of this consideration, Luton was selected. Secondly, in order to come up with a sample of 'affluent workers' (Step 6), it was decided that people working for three of Luton's leading employers should be interviewed. Moreover, the researchers wanted the firms selected to cover a range of production technologies, because of evidence at that time that technologies had implications for workers' attitudes and behaviour. As a result of these considerations, the three firms were selected. Industrial workers were then sampled, also in terms of selected criteria that were to do with the researchers' interests in embourgeoisement and in the implications of technology for work attitudes and behaviour. Box 3.1 provides a much more recent example of research that involved similar deliberations about selecting research sites and sampling respondents. In experimental research, these two steps are likely to include the assignment of subjects into control and treatment groups.

Step 7 involves the administration of the research instruments. In experimental research, this is likely to entail pre-testing subjects, manipulating the independent variable for the experimental group and post-testing respondents. In cross-sectional research using social survey research instruments, it will involve interviewing the sample members by structured interview schedule or distributing a self-completion questionnaire. In research using structured observation, this step will mean an observer (or possibly more than one) watching the setting and the behaviour of people and then assigning categories to each element of behaviour.

Step 8 simply refers to the fact that, once information has been collected, it must be transformed into 'data'. In the context of quantitative research, this is likely to mean that it must be prepared so that it can be quantified. With some information this can be done in a relatively straightforward way—for example, for information relating to such things as

Box 3.1 Selecting research sites and sampling respondents: The Social Change and Economic Life Initiative

The Social Change and Economic Life Initiative (SCELI) involved research in six labour markets: Aberdeen, Coventry, Kirkaldy, Northampton, Rochdale, and Swindon. These labour markets were chosen to reflect contrasting patterns of economic change in the early to mid-1980s and in the then recent past. Within each locality, three main surveys were carried out.

- *The Work Attitudes/Histories Survey.* Across the four localities a random sample of 6,111 individuals was interviewed using a structured interview schedule. Each interview comprised questions about the individual's work history and about a range of attitudes.

- *The Household and Community Survey.* A further survey was conducted on roughly one-third of those interviewed for the Work Attitudes/Histories Survey. Respondents and their partners were interviewed by structured interview schedule and each person also completed a self-completion questionnaire. This survey was concerned with such areas as the domestic division of labour, leisure activities, and attitudes to the welfare state.

- *The Baseline Employers Survey.* Each individual in each locality interviewed for the Work Attitudes/Histories Survey was asked to provide details of his or her employer (if appropriate). A sample of these employers was then interviewed by structured interview schedule. The interview schedules covered such areas as the gender distribution of jobs, the introduction of new technologies, and relationships with trade unions.

The bulk of the results was published in a series of volumes, including Penn, Rose, and Rubery (1994) and A. M. Scott (1994). This example shows clearly the ways in which researchers are involved in decisions about selecting both research site(s) and respondents.

people's ages, incomes, number of years spent at school, and so on. For other variables, quantification will entail *coding* the information—that is, transforming it into numbers to facilitate the quantitative analysis of the data, particularly if the analysis is going to be carried out by computer. Codes act as tags that are placed on data about people to allow the information to be processed by the computer. This consideration leads into Step 9—the analysis of the data. In this step, the researcher is concerned to use a number of techniques of quantitative data analysis to reduce the amount of data collected, to test for relationships between variables, to develop ways of presenting the results of the analysis to others, and so on.

On the basis of the analysis of the data, the researcher must interpret the results of the analysis. It is at this stage that the 'findings' will emerge. The researcher will consider the connections between the findings that emerge out of Step 8 and the various preoccupations that acted as the impetus of the research. If there is a hypothesis, is it supported?

What are the implications of the findings for the theoretical ideas that formed the background to the research?

Then the research must be written up. It cannot take on significance beyond satisfying the researcher's personal curiosity until it enters the public domain in some way by being written up as a paper to be read at a conference or as a report to the agency that funded the research or as a book or journal article for academic business researchers. In writing up the findings and conclusions, the researcher is doing more than simply relaying what has been found to others: readers must be convinced that the research conclusions are important and that the findings are robust. Thus, a significant part of the research process entails convincing others of the significance and validity of one's findings.

Once the findings have been published they become part of the stock of knowledge (or 'theory' in the loose sense of the word) in their domain. Thus, there is a feedback loop from Step 11 back up to Step 1. The presence of both an element of deductivism

(Step 2) and inductivism (the feedback loop) is indicative of the positivist foundations of quantitative research. Similarly, the emphasis on the translation of concepts into measures (Step 4) is symptomatic of the principle of phenomenalism (see Box 1.7), which is also a feature of positivism. It is to this important phase of translating concepts into measures that we now turn. As we will see, certain considerations follow on from the stress placed on measurement in quantitative research. By and large, these considerations are to do with the validity and reliability of the measures devised by social scientists. These considerations will figure prominently in the following discussion.

Concepts and their measurement

What is a concept?

Concepts are the building blocks of theory and represent the points around which business research is conducted. Just think of the numerous concepts that have already been mentioned in relation to just some of the research examples cited so far in this book:

structure, agency, deskilling, organizational size, structure, technology, charismatic leadership, followers, TQM, functional subcultures, knowledge, managerial identity, motivation to work, moral awareness, productivity, stress management, employment relations, organizational development, competitive success.

Each represents a label that we give to elements of the social world that seem to have common features and that strike us as significant. As Bulmer succinctly puts it, concepts 'are categories for the organization of ideas and observations' (1984: 43). One item mentioned in Chapter 2 but omitted from the list of concepts above is IQ. It has been omitted because it is not a concept! It is a *measure* of a concept—namely, intelligence. This is a rare case of a social scientific measure that has become so well known that the measure and the concept are almost as synonymous as temperature and the centigrade or Fahrenheit scales, or as length and the metric scale. The concept of intelligence has arisen as a result of noticing that some people are very clever, some are quite clever, and still others are not at all bright. These variations in what we have come to call the concept of 'intelligence' seem important, because we might try to construct theories to explain these variations. We may try to incorporate the concept of intelligence into theories to explain variations in things like job competence or entrepreneurial success. Similarly, with indicators of organizational performance such as productivity or return on investment, we notice that some organizations improve their performance relative to others, others remain static, and others decline in economic value. Out of such considerations, the concept of organizational performance is reached.

If a concept is to be employed in quantitative research, it will have to be measured. Once they are measured, concepts can be in the form of independent or dependent variables. In other words, concepts may provide an explanation of a certain aspect of the social world, or they may stand for things we want to explain. A concept like organizational performance may be used in either capacity: for example, as a possible explanation of culture (are there differences between highly commercially successful organizations and others, in terms of the cultural values, norms, and beliefs held by organizational members?) or as something to be explained (what are the causes of variation in organizational performance?) Equally, we might be interested in evidence of changes in organizational performance over time or in variations between comparable nations in levels of organizational performance. As we start to investigate such issues, we are likely to formulate theories to help us understand why, for example, rates of organizational performance vary between countries or over time. This will in turn generate new concepts, as we try to tackle the explanation of variation in rates.

delineate

Why measure?

There are three main reasons for the preoccupation with measurement in quantitative research.

- Measurement allows us to delineate *fine differences* between people in terms of the characteristic in question. This is very useful, since, although we can often distinguish between people in terms of extreme categories, finer distinctions are much more difficult to recognize. We can detect clear variations in levels of job satisfaction—people who love their jobs and people who hate their jobs—but small differences are much more difficult to detect.

- Measurement gives us a *consistent device* or yardstick for making such distinctions. A measurement device provides a consistent instrument for gauging differences. This consistency relates to two things: our ability to be consistent over time and our ability to be consistent with other researchers. In other words, a measure should be something that is influenced neither by the timing of its administration nor by the person who administers it. Obviously, saying that the measure is not influenced by timing is not meant to indicate that measurement readings do not change: they are bound to be influenced by the process of social change. What it means is that the measure should generate consistent results, other than those that occur as a result of natural changes. Whether a measure actually possesses this quality has to do with the issue of *reliability*, which was introduced in Chapter 2 and which will be examined again below.

- Measurement provides the basis for *more precise estimates of the degree of relationship between concepts* (for example, through correlation analysis, which will be examined in Chapter 11). Thus, if we measure both job satisfaction and the things with which it might be related, such as stress-related illness, we will be able to produce more precise estimates of how closely they are related than if we had not proceeded in this way.

Indicators

In order to provide a measure of a concept (often referred to as an *operational definition*, a term deriving

from the idea of operationalization), it is necessary to have an indicator or indicators that will stand for the concept (see Box 3.2). There are a number of ways in which indicators can be devised:

- through a question (or series of questions) that is part of a structured interview schedule or self-completion questionnaire. The question(s) could be concerned with the respondents' report of an attitude (e.g. job satisfaction) or their employment status (e.g. job title) or a report of their behaviour (e.g. job tasks and responsibilities);

- through the recording of individuals' behaviour using a structured observation schedule (e.g. managerial activity);

- through official statistics, such as the use of WERS survey data (Box 2.15) to measure UK employment policies and practices;

- through an examination of mass media content through content analysis—for example, to determine changes in the salience of an issue, such as courage in managerial decision making (Harris 2001).

Indicators, then, can be derived from a wide variety of different sources and methods. Very often the researcher has to consider whether one indicator of a concept will be sufficient. This consideration is frequently a focus for social survey researchers. Rather than have just a single indicator of a concept, the researcher may feel that it may be preferable to ask a number of questions in the course of a structured interview or a self-completion questionnaire that tap a certain concept (see Boxes 3.3 and 3.4).

Using multiple-indicator measures

What are the advantages of using a multiple-indicator measure of a concept? The main reason for their use is a recognition that there are potential problems with a reliance on just a single indicator:

- It is possible that a single indicator will incorrectly classify many individuals. This may be due to the wording of the question or it may be a product of misunderstanding. But if there are a number of indicators, if people are misclassified through a particular question, it will be possible to offset its effects.

Box 3.2 What is an indicator?

It is worth making two distinctions here. First, there is a distinction between an *indicator* and a *measure*. The latter can be taken to refer to things that can be relatively unambiguously counted. At an individual level measures might include personal salary, age, or years of service, whereas at an organizational level they might include annual turnover or number of employees. Measures in other words are quantities. If we are interested, for example, in some of the correlates of variation in the age of employees in part-time employment, age can be quantified in a reasonably direct way. We use indicators to tap concepts that are less directly quantifiable. If we are interested in the causes of variation in job satisfaction, we will need indicators that will stand for the concept. These indicators will allow job satisfaction to be measured and we can treat the resulting quantitative information as if it were a measure. An indicator, then, is something that is devised or already exists and that is employed *as though it were a measure of a concept*. It is viewed as an indirect measure of a concept, like job satisfaction. An IQ test is a further example, in that it is a battery of indicators of the concept intelligence. We see here a second distinction between *direct* and *indirect* indicators of concepts. Indicators may be direct or indirect in their relationship to the concepts for which they stand. Thus, an indicator of marital status has a much more direct relationship to its concept than an indicator (or set of indicators) relating to job satisfaction. Sets of attitudes always need to be measured by batteries of indirect indicators. So too do many forms of behaviour. When indicators are used that are not true quantities, they will need to be coded to be turned into quantities. Directness and indirectness are not qualities inherent to an indicator: data from a survey question on amount earned per month may be a direct measure of personal income, but, if we treat it as an indicator of social class, it becomes an indirect measure. The issue of indirectness raises the question of where an indirect measure comes from—that is, how does a researcher devise an indicator of something like job satisfaction. Usually, it is based on common-sense understandings of the forms the concept takes or on anecdotal or qualitative evidence relating to that concept.

- One indicator may capture only a portion of the underlying concept or be too general. A single question may need to be of an excessively high level of generality and so may not reflect the true state of affairs for the people replying to it. Alternatively, a question may cover only one aspect of the concept in question. For example, if you were interested in job satisfaction, would it be sufficient to ask people how satisfied they were with their pay? Almost certainly not, because most people would argue that there is more to job satisfaction than just satisfaction with pay. A single indicator such as this would be missing out on such things as satisfaction with conditions, with the work itself, and with other aspects of the work environment. By asking a number of questions the researcher can get access to a wider range of aspects of the concept.

- You can make much finer distinctions. Taking the Terence Jackson (2001) measure as an example (see Box 3.3), if we just took one of the indicators as a measure, we would be able to array people only on a scale of 1 to 5, assuming that answers indicating that a manager believed an item was unethical were assigned 1 and answers indicating a manager believed an item was ethical were assigned 5 and the three other points being scored 2, 3, and 4. However, with a multiple-indicator measure of twelve indicators the range is 12 (12×1) to 60 (12×5).

Dimensions of concepts

One elaboration of the general approach to measurement is to consider the possibility that the concept in which you are interested comprises different dimensions. This view is particularly associated with Lazarsfeld (1958). The idea behind this approach is that, when the researcher is seeking to develop a measure of a concept, the different aspects or components of that concept should be considered. This specification of the dimensions of a concept would be undertaken with reference to theory and research associated with that concept. An example of this kind of approach can be discerned in Hofstede's

discern

Box 3.3 A multiple-indicator measure of a concept

The research on cultural values and management ethics by Terence Jackson (2001) involved a questionnaire survey of part-time MBA and post-experience students in Australia, China, Britain, France, Germany, Hong Kong, Spain, India, Switzerland and the USA. This contained twelve statements, each relating to a specific action, and respondents were asked to judge the extent to which they *personally* believed the action was ethical on a five-point scale, 1 = unethical; 5 = ethical. There was a middle point on the scale that allowed for a neutral response. This approach to investigating a cluster of attitudes is known as a *Likert scale*, though in some cases researchers use a seven-point rather than five-point scale for responses. The twelve statements were as follows:

- accepting gifts/favours in exchange for preferential treatment;
- passing blame for errors to an innocent co-worker;
- divulging confidential information;
- calling in sick to take a day off;
- pilfering organization's materials and supplies;
- giving gifts/favours in exchange for preferential treatment;

- claiming credit for someone else's work;
- doing personal business on organization's time;
- concealing one's errors;
- taking extra personal time (breaks, etc.);
- using organizational services for personal use;
- not reporting others' violations of organizational policies.

Respondents were also asked to judge the extent to which they thought their *peers* believed the action was ethical, using the same scale. Finally, using the same Likert scale, they were asked to evaluate the frequency with which they and their peers act in the way implied by the statement: 1 = infrequently; 5 = frequently. 'Hence, respondents make a judgement as to the extent to which they believe (or they think their colleagues believe) an action is ethical: the higher the score, the higher the belief that the action is ethical' (2001: 1283). The study found that, across all national groups, managers saw their colleagues as less ethical than themselves. The findings also supported the view that ethical attitudes vary according to cultural context.

(1984; see Box 1.12) delineation of four dimensions of cultural difference (power distance, uncertainty avoidance, individualism, and masculinity). Bryman and Cramer (2001) demonstrate the operation of this approach with reference to the concept of 'professionalism'. The idea is that people scoring high on one dimension may not necessarily score high on other dimensions, so that for each respondent you end up with a multidimensional 'profile'. Box 3.4 demonstrates the use of dimensions in connection with the concept of internal motivation to work.

However, in much if not most quantitative research, there is a tendency to rely on a single indicator of concepts. For many purposes this is quite adequate. It would be a mistake to believe that investigations that use a single indicator of core concepts are somehow deficient. In any case, some studies employ both single- and multiple-indicator measures of concepts. What *is* crucial is whether measures are reliable and whether they are valid representations of the concepts they are supposed to be tapping. It is to this issue that we now turn.

Reliability and validity

Although the terms *reliability* and *validity* seem to be almost like synonyms, they have quite different meanings in relation to the evaluation of measures of concepts, as was seen in Chapter 2.

Reliability

As Box 3.5 suggests, reliability is fundamentally concerned with issues of consistency of measures.

Box 3.4 Specifying dimensions of a concept: the case of job characteristics

A key question posed by Hackman and Oldham (1980) was: 'how can work be structured so that employees are internally motivated?' Their answer to this question relied on development of a model identifying five job dimensions that influence employee motivation. At the heart of the model is the suggestion that particular job characteristics ('core job dimensions') affect employees' experience of work ('critical psychological states'), which in turn have a number of outcomes for both the individual and the organization. The three critical psychological states are:

- *experienced meaningfulness*—individual perceives work to be worthwhile in terms of a broader system of values;

- *experienced responsibility*—individual believes him or herself to be personally accountable for the outcome of his or her efforts;

- *knowledge of results*—individual is able to determine on a regular basis whether or not the outcomes of his or her work are satisfactory.

In addition, a particular employee's response to favourable job characteristics is affected by his or her 'growth need strength'—that is, his or her need for personal growth and development. It is expected that favourable work outcomes will occur when workers experience jobs with positive core characteristics; this in turn will stimulate critical psychological states.

In order to measure these factors, Hackman and Oldham devised the Job Diagnostic Survey (JDS), a lengthy questionnaire that can be used to determine the Motivating Potential Score (MPS) of a particular job—that is, the extent to which it possesses characteristics that are

necessary to influence motivation. Below are the five dimensions; in each case an example is given of an item that can be used to measure it.

1 *Skill variety*: 'The job requires me to use a number of complex or high-level skills.'

2 *Task identity*: 'The job provides me with the chance completely to finish the pieces of work I begin.'

3 *Task significance*: 'This job is one where a lot of other people can be affected by how well the work gets done.'

4 *Autonomy*: 'The job gives me considerable opportunity for independence and freedom in how I do the work.'

5 *Feedback*: 'The job itself provides plenty of clues about whether or not I am performing well.'

Respondents are asked to indicate how far they think each statement is accurate, from 1 = very inaccurate, to 7 = very accurate. In Hackman and Oldham's initial study, the JDS was administered to 658 individuals working in sixty-two different jobs across seven organizations. Interpreting an individual's MPS score involves comparison with norms for specific job 'families', which were generated on the basis of this original sample. For example, professional/technical jobs have an average MPS of 154, whereas clerical jobs normally have a score of 106. Understanding the motivational potential of job content thus relies on interpretation of the MPS relative to that of other jobs and in the context of specific job families. Workers who exhibit high growth need strength, adequate knowledge, and skill, and are satisfied with their job context are expected to respond best to jobs with a high MPS.

There are at least three different meanings of the term. These are outlined in Box 3.5 and elaborated upon below.

Stability

The most obvious way of testing for the stability of a measure is the *test–retest* method. This involves administering a test or measure on one occasion and then readministering it to the same sample on

another occasion, i.e.

T_1 T_2
Obs_1 Obs_2

We should expect to find a high correlation between Obs_1 and Obs_2. Correlation is a measure of the strength of the relationship between two variables. This topic will be covered in Chapter 11 in the

---

Box 3.5 ⌇🔆⌇ *What is reliability?*

Reliability refers to the consistency of a measure of a concept. The following are three prominent factors involved when considering whether a measure is reliable.

- *Stability*. This consideration entails asking whether a measure is stable over time, so that we can be confident that the results relating to that measure for a sample of respondents do not fluctuate. This means that, if we administer a measure to a group and then readminister it, there will be little variation over time in the results obtained.

- *Internal reliability*. The key issue is whether the indicators that make up the scale or index are consistent—in other words, whether respondents'

scores on any one indicator tend to be related to their scores on the other indicators.

- *Inter-observer consistency*. When a great deal of subjective judgement is involved in such activities as the recording of observations or the translation of data into categories and where more than one 'observer' is involved in such activities, there is the possibility that there is a lack of consistency in their decisions. This can arise in a number of contexts, for example: in content analysis where decisions have to be made about how to categorize media items; when answers to open-ended questions have to be categorized; or in structured observation when observers have to decide how to classify subjects' behaviour.

---

context of a discussion about quantitative data analysis. Let us imagine that we develop a multiple-indicator measure that is supposed to tap a concept that we might call 'designerism' (a preference for buying goods and especially clothing with 'designer' labels). We would administer the measure to a sample of respondents and readminister it some time later. If the correlation is low, the measure would appear to be unstable, implying that respondents' answers cannot be relied upon.

However, there are a number of problems with this approach to evaluating reliability. Respondents' answers at T_1 may influence how they reply at T_2. This may result in greater consistency between Obs_1 and Obs_2 than is in fact the case. Secondly, events may intervene between T_1 and T_2 that influence the degree of consistency. For example, if a long span of time is involved, changes in the economy or in respondents' personal financial circumstances could influence their views about and predilection for designer goods. There are no obvious solutions to these problems, other than by introducing a complex research design and so turning the investigation of reliability into a major project in its own right. Perhaps for these reasons, many if not most reports of research findings do not appear to carry out tests of stability. Indeed, longitudinal research is often undertaken precisely in order to identify social change and its correlates.

Internal reliability

This meaning of reliability applies to multiple-indicator measures like those examined in Boxes 3.3 and 3.4. When you have a multiple-item measure in which each respondent's answers to each question are aggregated to form an overall score, the possibility is raised that the indicators do not relate to the same thing; in other words, they lack coherence. We need to be sure that all our designerism indicators are related to each other. If they are not, some of the items may actually be unrelated to designerism and therefore indicative of something else.

One way of testing internal reliability is the *split-half* method. We can take the management ethics measure developed by Terence Jackson (2001) as an example (see Box 3.3). The twelve indicators would be divided into two halves with six in each group. The indicators would be allocated on a random or an odd–even basis. The degree of correlation between scores on two halves would then be calculated. In other words, the aim would be to establish whether respondents scoring high on one of the two groups also scored high on the other group of indicators. The calculation of the correlation will yield a figure, known as a coefficient, that varies between 0 (no correlation and therefore no internal consistency) and 1 (perfect correlation and therefore complete internal consistency). It is usually expected that a result of 0.8 and above implies an acceptable level of internal reliability. Do not worry if these figures appear somewhat opaque. The meaning of correlation will be explored in much greater detail later on. The chief point to carry away with you at this stage is that the correlation establishes how closely respondents' scores on the two groups of indicators are related.

Nowadays, most researchers use a test of internal reliability known as *Cronbach's alpha* (see Box 3.6). Its use has grown as a result of its incorporation into computer software for quantitative data analysis.

Inter-observer consistency

The idea of inter-observer consistency is briefly outlined in Box 3.5. The issues involved are rather too advanced to be dealt with at this stage and will be briefly touched on in later chapters. Cramer (1998: ch. 14) provides a very detailed treatment of the issues and appropriate techniques.

Validity

As noted in Chapter 2, the issue of measurement validity has to do with whether a measure of a concept really measures that concept (see Box 3.7). When people argue about whether a person's IQ score really measures or reflects that person's level of intelligence, they are raising questions about the measurement validity of the IQ test in relation to the concept of intelligence. Similarly, one often hears people say that they do not believe that the Retail Price Index really reflects inflation and the rise in the cost of living. Again, a query is being raised in such comments about measurement validity. And whenever students or lecturers debate whether formal examinations provide an accurate measure of academic ability, they too are raising questions about measurement validity.

Writers on measurement validity distinguish between a number of different types of validity. These types really reflect different ways of gauging the validity of a measure of a concept. These different types of validity will now be outlined.

Face validity

At the very minimum, a researcher who develops a new measure should establish that it has *face validity*—that is, that the measure apparently reflects the content of the concept in question. Face validity might be established by asking other people whether the measure seems to be getting at the concept that is the focus of attention. In other words, people, possibly those with experience or expertise in a field, might be asked to act as judges to determine whether on the face of it the measure seems to reflect the concept concerned. Face validity is, therefore, an essentially intuitive process.

Box 3.6 *What is Cronbach's alpha?*

To a large extent we are leaping ahead too much here, but it is important to appreciate the basic features of what this widely used test means. Cronbach's alpha is a commonly used test of internal reliability. It essentially calculates the average of all possible split-half reliability coefficients. A computed alpha coefficient will vary between 1 (denoting perfect internal reliability) and 0 (denoting no internal reliability). The figure 0.80 is typically employed as a rule of thumb to denote an acceptable level of internal reliability, though many writers accept a slightly lower figure. For example, in the case of the burnout scale replicated by Schutte et al. (2000; see Box 3.11), alpha was 0.7, which they suggest, 'as a rule of thumb' is 'considered to be efficient' (2000: 56).

Box 3.7 *What is validity?*

Validity refers to the issue of whether an indicator (or set of indicators) that is devised to gauge a concept really measures that concept. Several ways of establishing validity are explored in the text: face validity; concurrent validity; predictive validity; construct validity; and convergent validity. Here the term is being used as a shorthand for what was referred to as *measurement validity* in Chapter 2. Measurement validity should therefore be distinguished from the other terms introduced in Chapter 2: internal validity; external validity; and ecological validity.

Concurrent validity

The researcher might seek also to gauge the *concurrent validity* of the measure. Here the researcher employs a *criterion* on which cases (for example, people) are known to differ and that is relevant to the concept in question. A new measure of job satisfaction can serve as an example. A criterion might be absenteeism, because some people are more often absent from work (other than through illness) than others. In order to establish the concurrent validity of a measure of job satisfaction, we might see if people who are satisfied with their jobs are less likely than those who are not satisfied to be *absent* from work. If a lack of correspondence was found, such as there being no difference in levels of job satisfaction among frequent absentees, doubt might be cast on whether our measure is really addressing job satisfaction.

Predictive validity

Another possible test for the validity of a new measure is *predictive validity*, whereby the researcher uses a *future* criterion measure, rather than a contemporary one, as in the case of concurrent validity. With predictive validity, the researcher would take future levels of absenteeism as the criterion against which the validity of a new measure of job satisfaction would be examined. The difference from concurrent validity is that a future rather than a simultaneous criterion measure is employed.

Construct validity

Some writers advocate that the researcher should also estimate the *construct validity* of a measure. Here, the researcher is encouraged to deduce hypotheses from a theory that is relevant to the concept. For example, drawing upon ideas about the impact of technology on the experience of work, the researcher might anticipate that people who are satisfied with their jobs are less likely to work on routine jobs; those who are not satisfied are more likely to work on routine jobs. Accordingly, we could investigate this theoretical deduction by examining the relationship between job satisfaction and job routine. However, some caution is required in interpreting the absence of a relationship between job satisfaction and job

routine in this example. First, either the theory or the deduction that is made from it might be misguided. Secondly, the measure of job routine could be an invalid measure of that concept.

Convergent validity

In the view of some methodologists, the validity of a measure ought to be gauged by comparing it to measures of the same concept developed through other methods. For example, if we develop a questionnaire measure of how much time managers spend on various activities (such as attending meetings, touring their organization, informal discussions, and so on), we might examine its validity by tracking a number of managers and using a structured observation schedule to record how much time is spent in various activities and their frequency. An example of convergent validity is described in Box 3.8 and an interesting instance of convergent *in*validity is described in Box 3.9.

Reflections on reliability and validity

There are, then, a number of different ways of investigating the merit of measures that are devised to represent social scientific concepts. However, the discussion of reliability and validity is potentially misleading, because it would be wrong to think that all new measures of concepts are submitted to the rigours described above. In fact, most typically, measurement is undertaken within a stance that Cicourel (1964) described as 'measurement by fiat'. By the term 'fiat', Cicourel was referring not to a well-known Italian car manufacturer but to the notion of 'decree'. He meant that most measures are simply asserted. Fairly straightforward, but minimal steps may be taken to ensure that a measure is reliable and/or valid, such as testing for internal reliability when a multiple-indicator measure has been devised and examining face validity. But in many, if not the majority of cases in which a concept is measured, no further testing takes place. This point will be further elaborated below.

It should also be borne in mind that, although reliability and validity are analytically distinguishable,

Bb

Box 3.8 Job characteristics theory: a case of convergent validity

The job characteristics theory (Hackman and Oldham 1976, 1980; see Box 3.4) has been the subject of extensive empirical examination since it was first published. Much of this research has focused on testing the model through replication of the Job Diagnostic Survey (e.g. Champoux 1991; Saavedra and Kwun 2000). The results are then analysed using a wide range of statistical tests.

However, not all the studies have relied on the same methods as the original study. Orpen (1979), for example, studied seventy-two clerks in three divisions of a local government agency in South Africa. In the first stage of the research, respondents completed a questionnaire based on the JDS. The next stage involved a field experiment in which the clerks were divided into two groups, one group were allocated 'enriched' tasks (with greater skill variety, autonomy, and so on) and the other continued to do the same work they had been doing before; this arrangement was maintained for six months. Finally, employees completed the same questionnaire that had been administered to them at the start of the study. This confirmed that positive job characteristics were associated with higher levels of job satisfaction but less closely with job involvement and intrinsic motivation.

Another study, by Ganster (1980), involved a laboratory experiment conducted on 190 US undergraduate students. After completing a questionnaire designed to measure individual difference and 'growth need strength', the students were asked to work on an electronics assembly task in groups of six. Half of them worked in a way that ensured positive job characteristics were enhanced, while the rest worked on the task without this enrichment. After seventy-five minutes the students completed another questionnaire, to assess their perceptions of the task and

their level of satisfaction with it. Students performing the enhanced task achieved higher satisfaction scores, although there was very little evidence to suggest that this had anything to do with individual differences.

Through their use of experimental methods, both studies were deliberately designed to provide alternatives to the questionnaire instrument devised by Hackman and Oldham (1976) in order to test the original theory through replication. Moreover, their finding that enriched work is associated with job satisfaction provides some convergent validity for the theory. Others, such as Ganster's finding that individual differences have very little impact on task satisfaction associated with enriched work, do not support the theory.

However, the problem with the convergent approach to testing validity is that it is not possible to establish very easily which of the three measures represents the more accurate picture. In the questionnaire survey, data relating to all the variables are collected at the same time. In the field experiment, the researcher intervenes by manipulating the independent variables (core job characteristics) and observing the effects on the dependent variable (job satisfaction). In the laboratory experiment, the independent variable is manipulated for students, rather than 'real' employees. In any case, the 'true' picture with regard to the level of job satisfaction and internal motivation experienced by an individual at any one time is an almost entirely metaphysical notion. While the authors of the experimental study were able to confirm the convergent validity of certain aspects of the job characteristics theory, it would be a mistake to assume that the experimental evidence necessarily represents a definitive and therefore unambiguously valid measure.

---

they are related because validity presumes reliability. This means that, if your measure is not reliable, it cannot be valid. This point can be made with respect to each of the three criteria of reliability that have been discussed. If the measure is not stable over time, it simply cannot be providing a valid measure. The measure could not be tapping the concept it is supposed to be related to if the measure fluctuated. If the measure fluctuates, it may be measuring different things on different occasions. If a measure lacks internal reliability, it means that a multiple-indicator measure is actually measuring two or more different things. Therefore, the measure cannot be valid. Finally, if there is a lack of inter-observer consistency, it means that observers cannot agree on the meaning of what they are observing, which in turn means that a valid measure cannot be in operation.

Box 3.9 The study of strategic HRM: a case of convergent *in*validity?

Researchers in the field of human resource management have sought to develop and test basic hypotheses concerning the impact of strategic human resource management on firm performance. They have set out to measure the extent to which 'high performance work practices' (including comprehensive recruitment and selection procedures, incentive compensation and performance management systems, employee involvement, and training) are related to organizational performance.

In one of the earliest empirical studies of this topic, published in the *Academy of Management Journal*, Arthur (1994) focused on a sample of US steel minimills (relatively small steel-producing facilities) and drew on his previous research in which two types of human resource systems were identified—labelled 'control' and 'commitment'. He explains his approach as follows: 'I developed and tested propositions regarding the utility of this human resource system taxonomy for predicting both manufacturing performance, measured as labor efficiency and scrap rate, and the level of employee turnover' (1994: 671). Based on questionnaire responses from human resource managers at thirty minimills, Arthur concludes that commitment systems were more effective than control systems of human resource management, being associated with lower scrap rates and higher labour efficiency than control. In the following year, Huselid (1995) published

a paper in the same journal claiming that high performance work practices associated with a commitment model of HRM have an economically and statistically significant impact on employee outcomes such as turnover and productivity and on measures of corporate financial performance. Results were based on a sample of nearly 1,000 US firms drawn from a range of industries and data were collected using a postal questionnaire, which was addressed to the senior human resources professional in each firm.

However, this strong tradition of questionnaire-based research is not without its critics. One assumption they tend to make is that HRM effectiveness affects firm performance, but it may be that human resource managers who work in a firm that is performing well tend to think the firm's HRM system must be effective. Moreover, the reliance of these researchers on questionnaire data implies a lack of convergent validity and their tendency to focus on HRM managers as the main or only respondents implies a potential managerial bias. This has been the focus of more recent critiques (Pfeffer 1997) and has led to more qualitative empirical study (e.g. Truss 2001; see Box 22.5) in order to overcome the limitations of earlier work. Some of this research calls into question the validity of the proposed relationship between high performance HR practices and firm performance identified in earlier studies.

The main preoccupations of quantitative researchers

Both quantitative and qualitative research can be viewed as exhibiting a set of distinctive but contrasting preoccupations. These preoccupations reflect epistemologically grounded beliefs about what constitutes acceptable knowledge. In this section, four distinctive preoccupations that can be discerned in quantitative research will be outlined and examined: measurement, causality, generalization, and replication.

Measurement

The most obvious preoccupation is with measurement, a feature that is scarcely surprising in the light of much of the discussion in the present chapter so far. From the position of quantitative research, measurement carries a number of advantages that were previously outlined. It is not surprising, therefore, that issues of reliability and validity are a concern for quantitative researchers, though this is not always manifested in research practice.

Causality

There is a very strong concern in most quantitative research with explanation. Quantitative researchers are rarely concerned merely to describe how things are, but are keen to say why things are the way they are. This emphasis is also often taken to be a feature of the ways in which the natural sciences proceed. Thus, researchers are often not only interested in a phenomenon like motivation to work as something to be described, for example, in terms of how motivated a certain group of employees are, or what proportion of employees in a sample are highly motivated and what proportion are largely lacking in motivation. Rather, they are likely to want to explain it, which means examining its causes. The researcher may seek to explain motivation to work in terms of personal characteristics (such as 'growth need strength', which refers to an individual's need for personal growth and development—see Box 3.4) or in terms of the characteristics of a particular job (such as task interest or degree of supervision). In reports of research you will often come across the idea of 'independent' and 'dependent' variables, which reflect the tendency to think in terms of causes and effects. Motivation to work might be regarded as the dependent variable, which is to be explained, and 'growth need strength' as an independent variable, and which therefore has a causal influence upon motivation.

When an experimental design is being employed, the independent variable is the variable that is manipulated. There is little ambiguity about the direction of causal influence. However, with cross-sectional designs of the kind used in most social survey research, there is ambiguity about the direction of causal influence in that data concerning variables are simultaneously collected. Therefore, we cannot say that an independent variable precedes the dependent one. To refer to independent and dependent variables in the context of cross-sectional designs, we must *infer* that one causes the other, as in the example concerning

'growth need strength' and motivation to work in the previous paragraph. We must draw on common sense or theoretical ideas to infer the likely temporal precedence of variables. However, there is always the risk that the inference will be wrong (see Box 22.7 for an example of this possibility).

The concern about causality is reflected in the preoccupation with internal validity that was referred to in Chapter 2. There it was noted that a criterion of good quantitative research is frequently the extent to which there is confidence in the researcher's causal inferences. Research that exhibits the characteristics of an experimental design is often more highly valued than cross-sectional research, because of the greater confidence that can be enjoyed in the causal findings associated with the former. For their part, quantitative researchers who employ cross-sectional designs are invariably concerned to develop techniques that will allow causal inferences to be made. Moreover, the emergence of longitudinal research like Workplace Employee Relations Survey (WERS; Box 2.15) almost certainly reflects a desire on the part of quantitative researchers to improve their ability to generate findings that permit a causal interpretation.

Generalization

In quantitative research the researcher is usually concerned to be able to say that his or her findings can be generalized beyond the confines of the particular context in which the research was conducted. Thus, if a study of motivation to work is carried out by a questionnaire with a number of people who answer the questions, we often want to say that the results can apply to individuals other than those who responded in the study. This concern reveals itself in survey research in the attention that is often given to the question of how one can create a representative sample. Given that it is rarely feasible to send questionnaires to or interview whole populations (such as all members of a town, or the whole population of a country, or all members of an organization), we have to sample. However, we will want the sample to be as representative as possible in order to be able to say that the results are not unique to

Box 3.10 Generalizability and behaviour: Maslow's (1943) hierarchy of needs

The study of animals has formed an important part of the research design used in several psychological studies of human behaviour (e.g. Skinner 1953). The logic behind this strategy relies on the assumption that non-human behaviour can provide insight into the essential aspects of human nature that have ensured our survival as a species. This has made non-human study particularly attractive in areas such as motivational research, where early studies conducted on mice, rats, pigeons, monkeys, and apes have been used to inform understanding of human behaviour and in particular the relationship between motivation and performance (see Vroom 1964 for a review). However, some writers have cast doubt on the potential generalizability of such findings. In other words, do results from these studies apply equally to humans or should the findings be treated as unique to the particular species upon which the study was conducted?

An interesting illustration of this debate is to be found in Maslow's (1943) hierarchy of needs, which remains one of the most well-known theories of motivation within business and management, even though much subsequent research has cast doubt on the validity of his theory. One of these critics has been Cullen (1997), who has drawn attention to the empirical research on which the theory is based. Cullen draws attention to the fact that Maslow's needs hierarchy was informed by his earlier study of the importance of dominance in explaining primate behaviour. She goes on to explain that differences in the exercise of dominance formed the basis for development of the needs hierarchy founded on the suggestion that

differences in human behaviour were related to differences in individual personality.

However, as Cullen points out, the fundamental problem with motivation theory's use of Maslow's hierarchy is not necessarily the fact that the theory is based on data generated through the study of primates, since several other management theories rely on insights drawn from animal studies. The problem instead relates to the nature of the animal data on which Maslow based his understanding of dominance. In particular, his conclusion that the confidence of some monkeys allowed them to dominate others was based on the study of caged animals that were largely kept isolated from each other: 'If we rely on a theory based on animal data that was collected more than 60 years ago, we are obligated to consider the accuracy and validity of that data' (1997: 368). Cullen suggests that recent studies of free-living primates in their natural habitats have called into question previous understandings of dominance and aggression but 'the experimental methods Maslow used did not permit him to see the social skills involved in establishing and maintaining dominance in non-human primate societies' (1997: 369). This alternative interpretation of dominance 'would seem to have more relevance for complex social settings such as organizations than does Maslow's individualistic interpretation' (1997: 369). Her main argument is that, if we intend to apply insights from the study of primates in order to understand the behaviour of humans in organizations, we cannot afford to ignore current debates and changes in understanding that occur in other research fields.

the particular group upon whom the research was conducted; in other words, we want to be able to generalize the findings beyond the cases (for example, the people) that make up the sample. The preoccupation with generalization can be viewed as an attempt to develop the lawlike findings of the natural sciences. A further issue is raised through the use of animals, such as monkeys, in field or laboratory experiments as the basis for testing theories of human behaviour. This is the basis of some of the criticisms that have been levelled at research by Maslow (1943) and Vroom (1964)—see Box 3.10.

Probability sampling, which will be explored in Chapter 4, is the main way in which researchers seek

to generate a representative sample. This procedure largely eliminates bias from the selection of a sample by using a process of random selection. The use of a random selection process does not guarantee a representative sample, because, as will be seen in Chapter 4, there are factors that operate over and above the selection system used that can jeopardize the representativeness of a sample. A related consideration here is this: even if we did have a representative sample, what would it be representative *of*. The simple answer is that it will be representative of the population from which it was selected. This is certainly the answer that sampling theory gives us. Strictly speaking, we cannot generalize beyond that population.

This means that, if the members of the population from which a sample is taken are all inhabitants of a town, city, or region, or are all members of an organization, we can generalize only to the inhabitants or members of the town, city, region, or organization. But it is very tempting to see the findings as having a more pervasive applicability, so that, even if the sample was selected from a large organization like IBM, the findings are relevant to all similar organizations. We should not make inferences beyond the population from which the sample was selected, but researchers frequently do so. The concern to be able to generalize is often so deeply ingrained that the limits to the generalizability of findings are frequently forgotten or sidestepped.

The concern with generalizability or external validity is particularly strong among quantitative researchers using cross-sectional and longitudinal designs. There is a concern about generalizability among experimental research, as the discussion of external validity in Chapter 2 suggested, but users of this research design usually give greater attention to internal validity issues.

Replication

The natural sciences are often depicted as wishing to reduce to a bare minimum the contaminating influence of the scientist's biases and values. The results of a piece of research should be unaffected by the researcher's special characteristics or expectations. If biases and lack of objectivity were pervasive, the claims of the natural sciences to provide a definitive picture of the world would be seriously undermined. As a check upon the influence of these potentially damaging problems, scientists may seek to replicate—that is, to reproduce—each other's experiments. If there was a failure to replicate, so that a scientist's findings repeatedly could not be reproduced, serious questions would be raised about the validity of his or her findings. Consequently, scientists often attempt to be highly explicit about their procedures so that an experiment is capable of replication. Likewise, quantitative researchers in the social sciences often regard replication, or more precisely the ability to replicate, as an important

ingredient of their activity. It is easy to see why: the possibility of a lack of objectivity and of the intrusion of the researcher's values would appear to be much greater when examining the social world than when the natural scientist investigates the natural order. Consequently, it is often regarded as important that the researcher spells out clearly his or her procedures so that they can be replicated by others, even if the research does not end up being replicated. The study by Schutte et al. (2000) described in Box 3.11 relies on replication of the Maslach Burnout Inventory—General Survey, a psychological measure that has been used by the authors to test for emotional exhaustion, depersonalization, and reduced personal accomplishment across a range of occupational groups and nations.

It has been relatively straightforward and therefore quite common for researchers to replicate the Job Characteristic Model, developed by Hackman and Oldham (1980, see Box 3.4), in order to enhance confidence in the theory and its findings. Several of these have attempted to improve the generalizability of the model through its replication in different occupational settings—for example, on teachers, university staff, nursery school teachers, physical education and sport administrators. However, some criticism has been levelled at the original research for failing to make explicit how the respondent sample was selected, beyond the fact that it involved a diverse variety of manual and non-manual occupations in both manufacturing and service sectors, thus undermining the potential generalizability of the investigation (Bryman 1989a). A further criticism relates to the emphasis that the model places on particular characteristics of a job, such as feedback from supervisors, which may be less of a feature in today's working context than they were in the late 1970s. A final criticism made of subsequent replications of the initial study is that they fail to test the total model, focusing on the core job characteristics rather than incorporating the effects of the mediating psychological states, which Hackman and Oldham suggest are the 'causal core of the model' (1976: 255).

A study by Johns, Xie, and Fang (1992) attempts to address this last criticism by specifically focusing on

Box 3.11 Testing validity through replication: the case of burnout

The Maslach Burnout Inventory relies on the use of a questionnaire to measure the syndrome of burnout, which is characterized by emotional exhaustion, deper-sonalization, and reduced personal accomplishment; it is particularly associated with individuals who do 'people work of some kind'. Findings from the original, North American study (Maslach and Jackson 1981) led the authors to conclude that burnout has certain debilitating effects, resulting ultimately in a loss of professional efficacy.

This particular study by Schutte et al. (2000) attempted to replicate these findings across a number of occupa-tional groups (managers, clerks, foremen, technicians, blue-collar workers) in three different nations—Finland, Sweden and Holland. However, subsequent tests of the Maslach Burnout Inventory scale suggested a need for re-visions that would enable its use as a measure of burnout in occupational groups other than the human services, such as nurses, teachers, and social workers, for whom the original scale was intended. Using this revised, General Survey version, the researchers sought to investigate its *factorial validity*, or the extent to which the dimensions of burnout could be measured using the same questionnaire items in relation to different occupational and cultural groupings than the original study (see p. 87 for a brief explanation of *factor analysis*).

Following Hofstede (1984; see Box 1.12), employees were drawn from the same multinational corporation in different countries, in order to minimize the possibility that findings would reflect 'idiosyncrasies' associated with one company or another. The final sample size of 9,055 reflected a response rate to the questionnaire of 63 per cent.

The inventory comprises three subscales, each meas-ured in terms of a series of items. An example of each is given below:

- *Exhaustion (Ex)*: 'I feel used up at the end of the workday.'
- *Cynicism (Cy)*: 'I have become less enthusiastic about my work.'

- *Professional Efficacy (PE)*: 'In my opinion I am good at my job.'

The individual responds according to a seven-point scale, from 0 = never to 6 = daily. High scores on Ex and Cy and low scores on PE are indicative of burnout. A number of statistical analyses were carried out; for example, the reli-ability of the subscales was assessed using Cronbach's alpha as an indicator of internal consistency, meeting the criterion of 0.70 in virtually all the (sub)samples.

The authors conclude that their present study:

- confirms that burnout is a three-dimensional concept;
- clearly demonstrates the factorial validity of the scale across occupational groups;
- reveals that the three subscales are sufficiently internally consistent.

Furthermore, significant differences were found in the pattern of burnout among white- and blue-collar workers, the former scoring higher on PE and lower on Cy. In interpreting these findings they argue that the higher white-collar PE scores may have arisen because: 'working conditions are more favourable for managers than for workers, offering more autonomy, higher job complexity, meaningful work, and more respect for co-workers' (2000: 64).

Conversely: 'The relatively high scores on Cy for blue-collar workers reflect indifference and a more distant atti-tude towards their jobs. This might be explained by the culture on the shopfloor where distrust, resentment, and scepticism towards management and the organization traditionally prevail' (2000: 64).

Finally, they note that there were significant differences across national samples, the Dutch employees having scores that were consistently lower than their Swedish or Finnish colleagues. The authors conclude that the Maslach Burnout Inventory General Survey is a suitable instrument for measuring burnout in occupational groups other than human services and in nations apart from those that are North American.

the mediating and moderating effects of psychological states on the relationship between job characteristics and outcomes. Basing their research on a random sample of 605 first- and second-level managers in a large utility company (response rate approximately

50 per cent), the authors used a slightly modified version of the JDS questionnaire to determine the relationship between job characteristics, psycho-logical states, and outcome variables. Their results provide some support for the mediating role of

psychological states in determining outcomes based on core job characteristics—however, not always in the way that is specified by the model. In particular, some personal characteristics, such as educational level, were found to affect psychological states in a reverse manner to that which was expected—those with less education responded more favourably to elevated psychological states.

Another significant interest in replication stems from the original Aston studies (see Box 2.7), which stimulated a plethora of replications over a period of more than thirty years following publication of the first generation of research in the early 1960s. Most clearly associated with replication were the 'fourth-generation' Aston researchers, who undertook studies that:

- used a more homogenous sample drawn from a single industry, such as electrical engineering companies, 'to further substantiate the predictive power of the Aston findings' (Grinyer and Yasai-Ardekani 1980: 405) or;
- extended the original findings to other forms of organization, such as churches (e.g. Hinings, Ranson, and Bryman 1976) or educational colleges (Holdaway et al. 1975).

Later proponents of the 'Aston approach' made international comparisons of firms in different countries in order to test the hypothesis that the relationship between the context and the structure of an organization was dependent on the culture of the country in which it operates. Studies conducted in China, Egypt, France, Germany, India, and Japan (e.g. Shenoy 1981) sought to test the proposition that some of the characteristic differences in organizational structure, originally identified by the Aston researchers, remained constant across these diverse national contexts.

However, replication is not a high-status activity in the natural or the social sciences, partly because it is often regarded as a pedestrian and uninspiring pursuit. Moreover, standard replications do not form the basis for attractive articles, so far as many academic journal editors are concerned. Consequently, replications of research appear in print far less frequently than might be supposed. A further reason for the low incidence of published replications is that it is difficult to ensure in business research that the conditions in a replication are precisely the same as those that pertained in an original study. So long as there is some ambiguity about the degree to which the conditions relating to a replication are the same as those in the initial study, any differences in findings may be attributable to the design of the replication rather than to some deficiency in the original study.

Nonetheless, it is often regarded as crucial that the methods taken in generating a set of findings are made explicit, so that it is *possible* to replicate a piece of research. Thus, it is *replicability* that is often regarded as an important quality of quantitative research.

The critique of quantitative research

Over the years, quantitative research along with its epistemological and ontological foundations has been the focus of a great deal of criticism, particularly from exponents and spokespersons of qualitative research. To a very large extent, it is difficult to distinguish between different kinds of criticism when reflecting on the different critical points that have been proffered. These include: criticisms of quantitative research in general as a research strategy; criticisms of the epistemological and ontological foundations of quantitative research; and criticisms of specific methods and research designs with which quantitative research is associated.

Criticisms of quantitative research

To give a flavour of the critique of quantitative research, four criticisms will be covered briefly.

- *Quantitative researchers fail to distinguish people and social institutions from 'the world of nature'.* The phrase 'the world of nature' is from the writings of

Schutz and the specific quotation from which it has been taken can be found in Chapter 1. Schutz and other phenomenologists charge social scientists who employ a natural science model with treating the social world as if it were no different from the natural order. In so doing, they draw attention to one of positivism's central tenets—namely, that the principles of the scientific method can and should be applied to all phenomena that are the focus of investigation. As Schutz argues, this tactic is essentially to imply that this means turning a blind eye to the differences between the social and natural world. More particularly, as was observed in Chapter 1, it therefore means ignoring and riding roughshod over the fact that people interpret the world around them, whereas this capacity for self-reflection cannot be found among the objects of the natural sciences ('molecules, atoms, and electrons', as Schutz put it).

- *The measurement process possesses an artificial and spurious sense of precision and accuracy.* There are a number of aspects to this criticism. For one thing, it has been argued that the connection between the measures developed by social scientists and the concepts they are supposed to be revealing is assumed rather than real; hence, Cicourel's (1964) notion of 'measurement by fiat'. Testing for validity in the manner described in the previous section cannot really address this problem, because the very tests themselves entail measurement by fiat. A further way in which the measurement process is regarded by writers like Cicourel as flawed is that it presumes that when, for example, members of a sample respond to a question on a questionnaire (which is itself taken to be an indicator of a concept), they interpret the key terms in the question similarly. For many writers, respondents simply do not interpret such terms similarly. An often used reaction to this problem is to use questions with fixed-choice answers, but this approach merely provides 'a solution to the problem of meaning by simply ignoring it' (Cicourel 1964: 108).

- *The reliance on instruments and procedures hinders the connection between research and everyday life.* This issue relates to the question of ecological validity that was raised in Chapter 2. Many methods of

quantitative research rely heavily on administering research instruments to subjects (such as structured interviews and self-completion questionnaires) or on controlling situations to determine their effects (such as in experiments). However, as Cicourel (1982) asks, how do we know if survey respondents have the requisite knowledge to answer a question or whether they are similar in their sense of the topic being important to them in their everyday lives? Thus, if respondents answer a set of questions designed to measure motivation to work, can we be sure that they are equally aware of what it is and its manifestations and can we be sure that it is of equal concern to them in the ways in which it connects with their everyday working life? One can go even further and ask how well their answers relate to their everyday lives. People may answer a question designed to measure their motivation to work, but respondents' actual behaviour may be at variance with their answers (LaPiere 1934).

- *The analysis of relationships between variables creates a static view of social life that is independent of people's lives.* Blumer argued that studies that aim to bring out the relationships between variables omit 'the process of interpretation or definition that goes on in human groups' (1956: 685). This means that we do not know how what appears to be a relationship between two or more variables has been produced by the people to whom it applies. This criticism incorporates the first and third criticisms that have been referred to—that the meaning of events to individuals is ignored and that we do not know how such findings connect to everyday contexts—but adds a further element—namely, that it creates a sense of a static social world that is separate from the individuals who make it up. In other words, quantitative research is seen as carrying an objectivist ontology that reifies the social world.

We can see in these criticisms the application of a set of concerns associated with a qualitative research strategy that reveals the combination of an interpretivist epistemological orientation (an emphasis on meaning from the individual's point of view) and a constructionist ontology (an emphasis on viewing the social world as the product of individuals rather than as something beyond them). The criticisms may appear very damning, but, as we will see in Chapter 13, quantitative researchers have a powerful battery of criticisms of qualitative research in their arsenal as well!

Is it always like this?

One of the problems with characterizing any research strategy, research design, or research method is that to a certain extent one is always outlining an ideal-typical approach. In other words, one tends to create something that represents that strategy, design, or method, but that may not be reflected in its entirety in research practice. This gap between the ideal type and actual practice can arise as a result of at least two major considerations. First, it arises because those of us who write about and teach research methods cannot cover every eventuality that can arise in the process of business research, so that we tend to provide accounts of the research process that draw upon common features. Thus, a model of the process of quantitative research, such as that provided in Figure 3.1, should be thought of as a general *tendency* rather than as a definitive description of all quantitative research. A second reason why the gap can arise is that, to a very large extent when writing about and teaching research methods, we are essentially providing an account of *good practice*. The fact of the matter is that these practices are often not followed in the published research that students are likely to encounter in the substantive courses that they will be taking. This failure to follow the procedures associated with good practice is not necessarily due to incompetence on the part of business researchers (though in some cases it can be!), but is much more likely to be associated with matters of time, cost, and feasibility—in other words, the pragmatic concerns that cannot be avoided when one does business research.

Reverse operationism

As an example of the first source of the gap between the ideal type and actual research practice we can take the case of something that Bryman has referred to as 'reverse operationism' (1988*a*: 28). The model of the process of quantitative research in Figure 3.1

implies that concepts are specified and measures are then provided for them. As we have noted, this means that indicators must be devised. This is the basis of the idea of 'operationism' or 'operationalism', a term that derives from physics (Bridgman 1927), and that implies a deductive view of how research should proceed. However, this view of research neglects the fact that measurement can entail much more of an inductive element than Figure 3.1 implies. Sometimes, measures are developed that in turn lead to conceptualization. One way in which this can occur is when a statistical technique known as *factor analysis* is employed. In order to measure the concept of 'charismatic leadership', a term that owes a great deal to Weber's (1947) notion of charismatic authority, Conger and Kanungo (1998) generated twenty-five items to provide a multiple-item measure of the concept. These items derived from their reading of existing theory and research on the subject, particularly in connection with charismatic leadership in organizations. When the items were administered to a sample of respondents and the results were factor analysed, it was found that the items bunched around six factors, each of which to all intents and purposes represents a dimension of the concept of charismatic leadership:

- strategic vision and articulation behaviour;
- sensitivity to the environment;
- unconventional behaviour;
- personal risk;
- sensitivity to organizational members' needs;
- action orientation away from the maintenance of the status quo.

The point to note is that these six dimensions were not specified at the outset: the link between conceptualization and measurement was an inductive one. Nor is this an unusual situation so far as research is concerned (Bryman 1988*a*: 26–8).

Reliability and validity testing

The second reason why the gap between the ideal type and actual research practice can arise is because researchers do not follow some of the recommended practices. A classic case of this tendency is that, while, as in the present chapter, much time and effort are expended on the articulation of the ways in which the reliability and validity of measures should be determined, a great deal of the time these procedures are not followed. There is evidence from analyses of published quantitative research in organization studies (Podsakoff and Dalton 1987) that writers rarely report tests of the stability of their measures and even more rarely report evidence of validity (only 3 per cent of articles provided information about measurement validity). A large proportion of articles used Cronbach's alpha, but, since this device is relevant only to multiple-item measures, because it gauges internal consistency, the stability and validity of many measures that are employed are unknown. This is not to say that this research is necessarily *un*stable and *in*valid, but that we simply do not know. The reasons why the procedures for determining stability and validity are rarely used are almost certainly the cost and time that are likely to be involved. Researchers tend to be concerned with substantive issues and are less than enthusiastic about engaging in the kind of development work that would be required for a thoroughgoing determination of measurement quality. However, what this means is that Cicourel's (1964) previously cited remark about much measurement in sociology being 'measurement by fiat' has considerable weight.

The remarks on the lack of assessment of the quality of measurement should not be taken as a justification for readers to neglect this phase in their work.

Our aim is merely to draw attention to some of the ways in which practices described in this book are not always followed and to suggest some reasons why they are not followed.

Sampling

A similar point can be made in relation to sampling, which will be covered in the next chapter. As we will see, good practice is strongly associated with *random* or *probability sampling*. However, quite a lot of research is based on non-probability samples—that is, samples that have not been selected in terms of the principles of probability sampling to be discussed in Chapter 4. Sometimes the use of non-probability samples will be due to the impossibility or extreme difficulty of obtaining probability samples. Yet another reason is that the time and cost involved in securing a probability sample are too great relative to the level of resources available. And yet a third reason is that sometimes the opportunity to study a certain group presents itself and represents too good an opportunity to miss. Again, such considerations should not be viewed as a justification and hence a set of reasons for ignoring the principles of sampling to be examined in the next chapter, not least because not following the principles of probability sampling carries implications for the kind of statistical analysis that can be employed (see Chapter 11). Instead, our purpose as before is to draw attention to the ways in which gaps between recommendations about good practice and actual research practice can arise.

K **KEY POINTS**

- Quantitative research can be characterized as a linear series of steps moving from theory to conclusions, but the process described in Figure 3.1 is an ideal type from which there are many departures.

- The measurement process in quantitative research entails the search for indicators.

- Establishing the reliability and validity of measures is important for assessing their quality.

- Quantitative research can be characterized as exhibiting certain preoccupations, the most central of which are: measurement; causality; generalization; and replication.

- Quantitative research has been subjected to many criticisms by qualitative researchers. These criticisms tend to revolve around the view that a natural science model is inappropriate for studying the social world.

Q QUESTIONS FOR REVIEW

The main steps in quantitative research

- What are the main steps in quantitative research?

- To what extent do the main steps follow a strict sequence?

- Do the steps suggest a deductive or inductive approach to the relationship between theory and research?

Concepts and their measurement

- Why is measurement important for the quantitative researcher?

- What is the difference between a measure and an indicator?

- Why might multiple-indicator approaches to the measurement of concepts be preferable to those that rely on a single indicator?

Reliability and validity

- What are the main ways of thinking about the reliability of the measurement process? Is one form of reliability the most important?

- 'Whereas validity presupposes reliability, reliability does not presuppose validity.' Discuss.

- What are the main criteria for evaluating measurement validity?

The main preoccupations of quantitative researchers

- Outline the main preoccupations of quantitative researchers. What reasons can you give for their prominence?

- Why might replication be an important preoccupation among quantitative researchers, in spite of the tendency for replications in business research to be fairly rare?

The critique of quantitative research

- 'The crucial problem with quantitative research is the failure of its practitioners to address adequately the issue of meaning.' Discuss.

- How central is the adoption by quantitative researchers of a natural science model of conducting research to the critique by qualitative researchers of quantitative research?

4 Sampling

CHAPTER GUIDE

This chapter and the three that follow it are very much concerned with principles and practices associated with social survey research. Sampling principles are not exclusively concerned with survey research; for example, they are relevant to the selection of documents for content analysis (see Chapter 9). However, in this chapter the emphasis will be on sampling in connection with the selection of people who would be asked questions by interview or questionnaire. The chapter explores:

- the related ideas of generalization (also known as external validity) and of a representative sample; the latter allows the researcher to generalize findings from a sample to a population;

- the idea of a *probability sample*—that is, one in which a random selection process has been employed;

- the main types of probability sample: the simple random sample; the systematic sample; the stratified random sample; and the multi-stage cluster sample;

- the main issues involved in deciding on sample size;

- different types of non-probability sample, including quota sampling, which is widely used in market research and opinion polls;

- potential sources of error in survey research.

Introduction

We imagine that many of the readers of this book will be university or college students. At some point in your stay at your university (we will use this term from now on to include colleges) you may have wondered about the attitudes of your fellow students to various matters, or about their behaviour in certain areas, or something about their backgrounds. If you were to decide to examine any or all of these three areas, you might consider conducting structured interviews or sending out questionnaires in order to find out about their behaviour, attitudes, and backgrounds. You will, of course, have to consider how best to design your interviews or questionnaires, and the issues that are involved in the decisions that need to be made about designing these research instruments and administering them will be the focus of Chapters 5–7. However, before getting to that point, you are likely to be confronted with a problem. Let us say that your university is quite large and has around 9,000 students. It is extremely unlikely that you will have the time and resources to conduct a survey of all these students. It is unlikely that you would be able to send questionnaires to all 9,000 and even more unlikely that you would be able to interview all of them, since conducting survey research by interview is considerably more expensive and time consuming, all things being equal, than by postal questionnaire (see Chapter 6). It is almost certain that you will need to *sample* students from the total population of students in your university.

The need to sample is one that is almost invariably encountered in quantitative research. In this chapter, we will be almost entirely concerned with matters relating to sampling in relation to social survey research involving data collection by structured interview or questionnaire. In social survey research, sampling constitutes a key step in the research process, as illustrated in Figure 4.1. However, other methods of quantitative research also involve sampling considerations, as will be seen in Chapters 8 and 9, when we will examine structured observation and content analysis respectively. The principles of sampling involved are more or less identical in connection with these other methods, but frequently other considerations come to the fore as well.

But will any old sample suffice? Would it be sufficient to locate yourself in a central position on your campus (if it has one) and then interview the students who come past you and whom you are in a position to interview? Alternatively, would it be sufficient to go around your student union asking people to be interviewed? Or again to send questionnaires to everyone on your course?

The answer, of course, depends on whether you want to be able to *generalize* your findings to the entire student body in your university. If you do, it is unlikely that any of the three sampling strategies proposed in the previous paragraph would provide you with a *representative sample* of all students in your university. In order to be able to generalize your findings from your sample to the population from which it was selected, the sample must be representative. See Box 4.1 for an explanation of key terms concerning sampling.

Why might the strategies for sampling students previously outlined be unlikely to produce a representative sample? There are various reasons, of which the following stand out.

- The first two approaches depend heavily upon the availability of students during the time or times that you search them out. Not all students are likely to be equally available at that time, so the sample will not reflect these students.

Decide on topic/area to be researched

↓

Review literature/theories relating to topic/area

↓

Formulate research questions

↓

Consider whether a social survey is appropriate (if not, consider an alternative research design)

↓

Consider what kind of population will be appropriate

↓

Consider what kind of sample design will be employed

↓

Explore whether there is a sampling frame that can be employed

↓

Decide on mode of administration (face to face; telephone; postal; e-mail; Web)

↓

Develop questions (and devise answer alternatives for closed questions)

↓

Review questions and assess face validity

↓

Pilot questions

↓

Revise questions

↓

Finalize questionnaire/schedule

↓

Sample from population

↓

Administer questionnaire/schedule to sample

↓

Transform completed questionnaires/schedules into computer readable data (coding)

↓

Analyse data

↓

Interpret findings

↓

Consider implications of findings for research questions

Figure 4.1 Steps in conducting a social survey

• They also depend on the students going to the locations. Not all students will necessarily pass the point where you locate yourself or go to the student union, or they may vary hugely in the frequency with which they do so. Their movements are likely to reflect such things as where their halls of residence or accommodation are situated, or where their departments are located, or their social habits. Again, to rely on these locations would mean missing out on students who do not frequent them.

- It is possible, not to say likely, that your decisions about which people to approach will be influenced by your judgements about how friendly or cooperative the people concerned are likely to be or by how comfortable you feel about interviewing students of the same (or opposite) gender to yourself, as well as by many other factors.

- The problem with the third strategy is that students on your course by definition take the same subject as each other and therefore will not be representative of all students in the university.

In other words, in the case of all of the three sampling approaches, your decisions about whom to sample are influenced too much by personal judgements, by prospective respondents' availability, or by your implicit criteria for inclusion. Such limitations mean that, in the language of survey sampling, your sample will be *biased*. A biased sample is one that does not represent the population from which the sample was selected. As far as possible, bias should be removed from the selection of your sample. In fact, it is incredibly difficult to remove bias altogether and to derive a truly representative sample. What needs to be done is to ensure that steps are taken to keep bias to an absolute minimum.

Three sources of bias can be identified (see Box 4.1 for an explanation of key terms).

Box 4.1 Basic terms and concepts in sampling

- *Population*—basically, the universe of units from which the sample is to be selected. The term 'units' is employed because it is not necessarily people who are being sampled—the researcher may want to sample from a universe of nations, cities, regions, firms, etc. Thus, 'population' has a much broader meaning than the everyday use of the term, whereby it tends to be associated with a nation's entire population.

- *Sample*—the segment of the population that is selected for investigation. It is a subset of the population. The method of selection may be based on a probability or a non-probability approach (see below).

- *Sampling frame*—the listing of all units in the population from which the sample will be selected.

- *Representative sample*—a sample that reflects the population accurately so that it is a microcosm of the population.

- *Probability sample*—a sample that has been selected using random selection so that each unit in the population has a known chance of being selected. It is generally assumed that a *representative sample* is more likely to be the outcome when this method of selection from the population is employed. The aim of probability sampling is to keep *sampling error* (see below) to a minimum.

- *Non-probability sample*—a sample that has not been selected using a random selection method. Essentially, this implies that some units in the population are more likely to be selected than others.

- *Sampling error*—the difference between a sample and the population from which it is selected, even though a probability sample has been selected.

- *Non-sampling error*—differences between the population and the sample that arise either from deficiencies in the sampling approach, such as an inadequate sampling frame or *non-response* (see below), or from such problems as poor question wording, poor interviewing, or flawed processing of data.

- *Non-response*—a source of non-sampling error that is particularly likely to happen when individuals are being sampled. It occurs whenever some members of the sample refuse to cooperate, cannot be contacted, or for some reason cannot supply the required data (for example, because of mental incapacity).

- *Census*—the enumeration of an entire population. Thus, if data are collected in relation to all units in a population, rather than in relation to a sample of units of that population, the data are treated as census data. The phrase '*the* census' typically refers to the complete enumeration of all members of the population of a nation state—that is, a national census. This form of enumeration occurs once every ten years in the UK. However, in a statistical context, like the term *population*, the idea of a census has a broader meaning than this.

- *If a non-probability or non-random sampling method is used.* If the method used to select the sample is not random, there is a possibility that human judgement will affect the selection process, making some members of the population more likely to be selected than others. This source of bias can be eliminated through the use of probability or random sampling, the procedure for which is described below.

- *If the sampling frame is inadequate.* If the sampling frame is not comprehensive or is inaccurate or suffers from some other kind of similar deficiency, the sample that is derived cannot represent the population, even if a random/probability sampling method is employed.

- *If some sample members refuse to participate or cannot be contacted—in other words, if there is non-response.*

The problem with non-response is that those who agree to participate may differ in various ways from those who do not agree to participate. Some of the differences may be significant to the research question or questions. If the data are available, it may be possible to check how far, when there is non-response, the resulting sample differs from the population. It is often possible to do this in terms of characteristics such as gender or age, or, in the case of something like a sample of university students, whether the sample's characteristics reflect the entire sample in terms of faculty membership. However, it is usually impossible to determine whether differences exist between the population and the sample after non-response in terms of 'deeper' factors, such as attitudes or patterns of behaviour.

Sampling error

In order to appreciate the significance of sampling error for achieving a representative sample, consider Figures 4.2–4.6. Imagine we have a population of 200 employees and we want a sample of 50. Imagine as well that one of the variables of concern to us is whether employees receive regular performance appraisals from their immediate supervisor and that the population is equally divided between those who do and those who do not. This split is represented by the vertical line that divides the population into two halves (Figure 4.2). If the sample is representative we would expect our sample of 50 to be equally split in terms of this variable (Figure 4.3). If there is a small amount of sampling error, so that we have one employee too many who is not appraised and one too few who is, it will look like Figure 4.4. In Figure 4.5 we see a rather more serious degree of over-representation of employees who do not receive appraisals. This time there are three too many who are not appraised and three too few who are. In Figure 4.6 we have a very serious over-representation of employees who do not receive performance appraisals, because there are 35 employees in the sample who are not

appraised, which is much larger than the 25 who should be in the sample.

It is important to appreciate that, as suggested above, probability sampling does not and cannot

Figure 4.2 Having performance appraisals in a population of 200

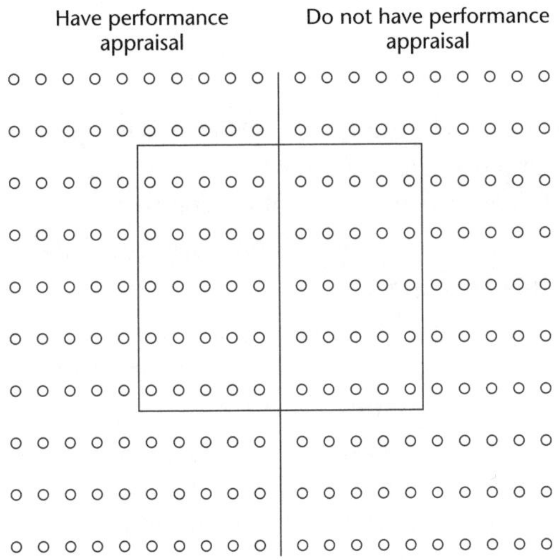

Have performance appraisal | Do not have performance appraisal

Figure 4.3 A sample with no sampling error

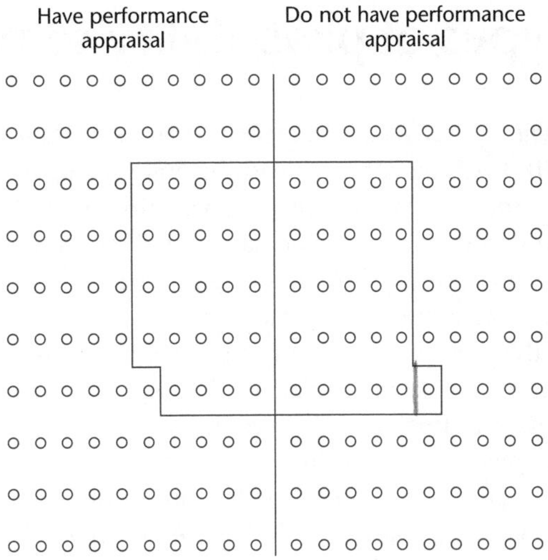

Have performance appraisal | Do not have performance appraisal

Figure 4.4 A sample with very little sampling error

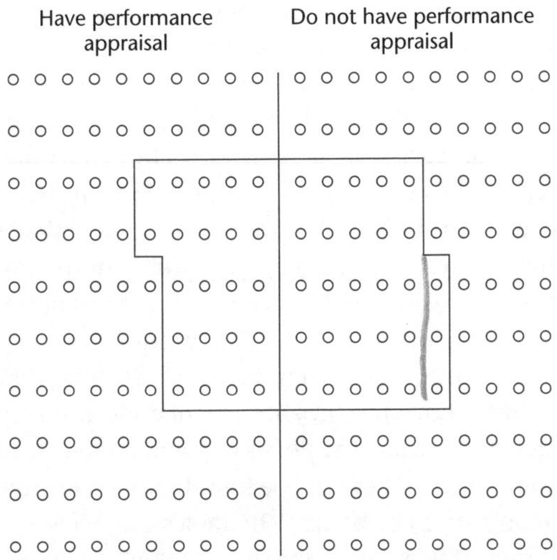

Have performance appraisal | Do not have performance appraisal

Figure 4.5 A sample with some sampling error

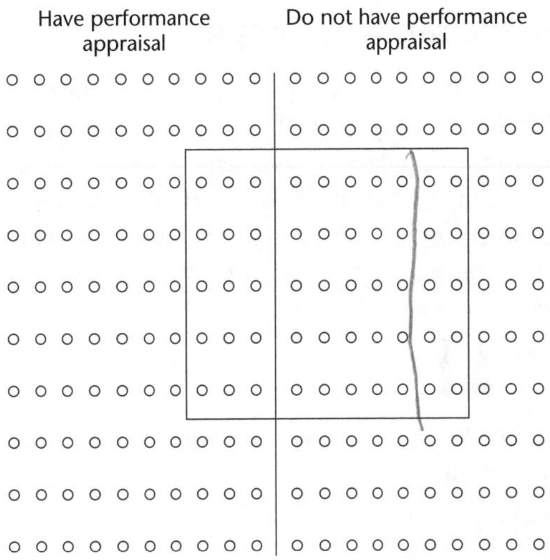

Have performance appraisal | Do not have performance appraisal

Figure 4.6 A sampling with a lot of sampling error

eliminate sampling error. Even with a well-crafted probability sample, a degree of sampling error is likely to creep in. However, probability sampling stands a better chance than non-probability sampling of keeping sampling error in check so that it does not end up looking like the outcome featured in

Figure 4.6. Moreover, probability sampling allows the researcher to employ tests of statistical significance that permit inferences to be made about the sample from which the sample was selected. These will be addressed in Chapter 11.

Types of probability sample

Imagine that we are interested in levels of training, skill development, and learning among employees and the variables that relate to variation in levels of training they have undertaken. We might decide to conduct our research in a single nearby company. This means that our population will all be employees in that company, which in turn will mean that we will be able to generalize our findings only to employees of that company. We simply cannot assume that levels of training and their correlates will be the same in other companies. We might decide that we want our research to be conducted only on full-time employees, so that part-time and subcontracted workers are omitted. Imagine too that there are 9,000 full-time employees in the company.

Simple random sample

The simple random sample is the most basic form of probability sample. With random sampling, each unit of the population has an equal probability of inclusion in the sample. Imagine that we decide that we have enough money to interview 450 employees at the company. This means that the probability of inclusion in the sample is

$$\frac{450}{9,000}, \text{ i.e. 1 in 20}$$

This is known as the *sampling fraction* and is expressed as

$$\frac{n}{N}$$

where n is the sample size and N is the population size.

The key steps in devising our simple random sample can be represented as follows:

1. Define the population. We have decided that this will be all full-time employees at the company. This is our N and in this case is 9,000.

2. Select or devise a comprehensive sampling frame. It is likely that the company's personnel department will keeps records of all employees and that this will enable us to exclude those who do not meet our criteria for inclusion—i.e. part-time employees and those who work on the premises but are not employees of the company.

3. Decide your sample size (n). We have decided that this will be 450.

4. List all the employees in the population and assign them consecutive numbers from 1 to N. In our case, this will be 1 to 9,000.

5. Using a table of random numbers, or a computer program that can generate random numbers, select n (450) different random numbers that lie between 1 and N (9,000).

6. The employees to which the n (450) random numbers refer constitute the sample.

Two points are striking about this process. First, there is almost no opportunity for human bias to manifest itself. Employees would not be selected on such subjective criteria as whether they looked friendly and approachable. The selection of whom to interview is entirely mechanical. Secondly, the process is not dependent on the employees' availability. They do not have to be working in the interviewer's proximity to be included in the sample. The process of selection is done without their knowledge. It is not until they are contacted by an interviewer that they know that they are part of a social survey.

Step 5 mentions the possible use of a table of random numbers. These can be found in the appendices of many statistics books. The tables are made up of columns of five-digit numbers, such as:

09188
90045
73189
75768
54016

08358
28306
53840
91757
89415

The first thing to notice is that, since these are five-digit numbers and the maximum number that we can sample from is 9,000, which is a four-digit number, none of the random numbers seems appropriate, except for 09188 and 08358, although the former is larger than the largest possible number. The answer is that we should take just four digits in each number. Let us take the last four digits. This would yield the following:

9188
0045
3189
5768
4016

8358
8306
3840
1757
9415

However, two of the resulting numbers—9188 and 9415—exceed 9000. We cannot have an employee with either of these numbers assigned to him or her. The solution is simple: we ignore these numbers. This means that the employee who has been assigned the number 45 will be the first to be included inthe sample; the employee who has been assigned the number 3189 will be next; the employee who has been assigned the number 5768 will be next; and so on.

An alternative but very similar strategy to the one that has been described is to write (or get someone to write for you) a simple computer program that will select n random numbers (in our case 450) that lie between 1 and N (in our case 9,000). As with using a table of random numbers, you may be faced with the possibility of some random numbers turning up more than once. Since you will want to interview the person to whom those recurring random numbers refer on only one occasion, you will want to ignore any random number that recurs. This procedure results in a sample known as a simple random sample *without replacement*. More or less all simple random samples will be of this kind in the context of business research and so the qualifier 'without replacement' is invariably omitted.

Systematic sample

A variation on the simple random sample is the systematic sample. With this kind of sample, you select units directly from the sampling frame—that is, without resorting to a table of random numbers.

We know that we are to select 1 employee in 20. With a systematic sample, we would make a random start between 1 and 20 inclusive, possibly by using the last two digits in a table of random numbers. If we did this with the ten random numbers above, the first relevant one would be 54016, since it is the first one where the last two digits yield a number of 20 or below, in this case, 16. This means that the sixteenth employee on our sampling frame is the first to be in our sample. Thereafter, we take every twentieth employee on the list. So the sequence will go:

16, 36, 56, 76, 96, 116, etc.

This approach obviates the need to assign numbers to employees' names and then to look up names of the employees whose numbers have been drawn by the random selection process. It is important to ensure, however, that there is no inherent ordering of the sampling frame, since this may bias the resulting sample. If there is some ordering to the list, the best solution is to rearrange it.

Stratified random sampling

In our imaginary study of company employees, one of the features that we might want our sample to exhibit is a proportional representation of the different departments in which employees work. It might be that the kind of department an employee works in is viewed as relevant to a wide range of attitudinal features that are relevant to the study of skill development and training. Generating a simple random sample or a systematic sample *might* yield such a representation, so that the proportion of employees from the sales and marketing department in the sample is the same as that in the employee population and so on. Thus, if there are 1,800 employees in the sales and marketing department, using our sampling fraction of 1 in 20, we would expect to have

90 employees in our sample from this department of the company. However, because of sampling error, it is unlikely that this will occur and that there will be a difference, so that there may be, say, 85 or 93 from this department.

Because it is very likely that the company will include in its records the department in which employees are based, or indeed may have separate sampling frames for each department, it will be possible to ensure that employees are accurately represented in terms of their departmental membership. In the language of sampling, this means stratifying the population by a criterion (in this case, departmental membership) and selecting either a simple random sample or a systematic sample from each of the resulting strata. In the present example, if there are five departments we would have five strata, with the numbers in each stratum being one-twentieth of the total for each department, as in Table 4.1, which also shows a hypothetical outcome of using a simple random sample, which results in a distribution of employees across departments that does not mirror the population all that well.

The advantage of stratified sampling in a case like this is clear: it ensures that the resulting sample will be distributed in the same way as the population in terms of the stratifying criterion. If you use a simple random or systematic sampling approach, you *may* end up with a distribution like that of the stratified sample, but it is unlikely. Two points are relevant here. First, you can conduct stratified sampling sensibly only when it is relatively easy to identify and allocate units to strata. If it is not possible or it would be very difficult to do so, stratified sampling will not be feasible. Secondly, you can use more than one stratifying criterion. Thus, it may be that you would want to stratify by both department and gender and whether employees are above or below a certain salary level or occupational grade. If it is feasible to identify employees in terms of these stratifying criteria, it is possible to use pairs of criteria or several criteria (such as departmental membership plus gender plus occupational grade).

Stratified sampling is really feasible only when the relevant information is available. In other words, when data are available that allow the ready identification of members of the population in terms of the stratifying criterion (or criteria), it is sensible to employ this sampling method. But it is unlikely to be economical if the identification of population members for stratification purposes entails a great deal of work because there is no available listing in terms of strata.

Multi-stage cluster sampling

In the example we have been dealing with, employees to be interviewed are located in a single company. Interviewers will have to arrange their interviews with the sampled employees, but, because they are all working on the same premises, they will not be involved in a lot of travel. However, imagine that we wanted a *national* sample of employees. It is likely that interviewers would have to travel the length and breadth of the UK to interview the sampled individuals. This would add a great deal to the time and cost of doing the research. This kind of problem occurs whenever

Table 4.1 The advantages of stratified sampling

Department	Population	Stratified sample	Possible simple random or systematic sample
Sales and marketing	1,800	90	85
Finance and accounts	1,200	60	70
Human resource management and training	1,000	50	60
Technical, research, and new-product development	1,800	90	84
Production	3,200	160	151
TOTAL	9,000	450	450

the aim is to interview a sample that is to be drawn from a widely dispersed population, such as a national population, or a large region, or even a large city.

One way in which it is possible to deal with this potential problem is to employ *cluster sampling*. With cluster sampling, the primary sampling unit (the first stage of the sampling procedure) is not the units of the population to be sampled but groupings of those units. It is the latter groupings or aggregations of population units that are known as *clusters*. Imagine that we want a nationally representative sample of 5,000 employees who are working for the 100 largest companies in the UK (this information is publicly available and generated through the FTSE index; size is measured in terms of market capitalization). Using simple random or systematic sampling would yield a widely dispersed sample, which would result in a great deal of travel for interviewers. One solution might be to sample companies and then employees from each of the sampled companies. A probability sampling method would need to be employed at each stage. Thus, we might randomly sample ten companies from the entire population of 100 largest companies in the UK, thus yielding ten clusters, and we would then interview 500 randomly selected employees at each of the ten companies.

This is fine, but there is no guarantee that these ten companies reflect the diverse range of industrial activities that are engaged in by the population as a whole. One solution to this problem would be to group the 100 largest UK companies by Standard Industrial Classification (SIC '92) codes and then to randomly sample companies from each of the major SIC groups (see Box 4.2). We might follow the example of the Workplace Employee Relations Survey (WERS) researchers (see Box 2.15) and exclude the less common SIC groups (agriculture, hunting, forestry and fishing, mining and quarrying—A to C, and private households—P). One company might then be sampled from each of the twelve remaining major SIC code categories (D to O) and then approximately 400 employees from each of the twelve companies would be interviewed. Thus, there are three separate stages:

- group 100 largest UK companies by market capitalization;
- sample one company from each of the twelve major SIC categories;
- sample 400 employees from each of the twelve companies.

In a sense, cluster sampling is always a multi-stage approach, because one always samples clusters first

---

Box 4.2 Using the major SIC '92 codes to stratify a sample

The Standard Industrial Classification (SIC) was first introduced into the UK in 1948 for use in categorizing businesses and other workplaces according to the type of economic activity in which they are engaged. Since then there have been several revisions to the classification to reflect the emergence of new industries and product markets. The most recent major revisions led to UK SIC '92, now the most widely used version of the framework. UK SIC '92 is divided into 17 sections, each denoted by a letter, these are in turn divided into 16 subsections, denoted by a second letter, which are then divided into divisions (60), groups (222), classes (503), and subclasses (253). The 17 main sections are:

A Agriculture, hunting, and forestry
B Fishing
C Mining and quarrying
D Manufacturing

E Electricity, gas, and water supply
F Construction
G Wholesale and retail trade and repair
H Hotels and restaurants
I Transport, storage, and communication
J Financial intermediation (including banking)
K Real estate, renting, and business activities
L Public administration and defence; compulsory social security
M Education
N Health and social work
O Community, social, and personal service activities
P Private households with employees

More information about SIC '92 is available from the UK national statistics web site:
www.statistics.gov.uk/methods_quality/ SIC/contents.asp

Box 4.3 An example of a multi-stage cluster sample

In a survey of skills used at work in modern Britain (1986–2001), the sample used by the researchers aimed to comprise 4,360 interviews with working individuals in Britain aged 20–60. The 2001 Skills Survey followed up on an earlier survey that was conducted in 1997. The sampling process involved several stages based on the selection of households and eligible interviewees. The Postcode Address File (PAF) was used as a sampling frame for the random selection of residential addresses (PAF is considered preferable to the electoral register because it is updated more frequently). This formed the basis for further stratification according to:

- *region*—the sample was then divided into subregions to ensure sample points were spread throughout the country;
- *socio-economic grouping*—each subregion was then further divided into three bands according to the percentage of household heads in non-manual Socio-Economic Groups.

This resulted in the identification of 218 postcode sectors. In each sector, sixty-four addresses were randomly selected.

'Based on the 1997 Skills Survey, it was anticipated that assignments consisting of 64 addresses would each produce just over 20 productive interviews' (Felstead, Gallie, and Green 2002: 86). This formed the basis for selection of:

individuals—the addresses then had to be checked to see if they were eligible in meeting three criteria: (1) residential and currently occupied (2) contained someone aged 20–60 years of age, and (3) contained at least one person in paid work of one hour per week or more. In households where there was more than one eligible interviewee, a further technique for random selection was used.

A total of 4,470 interviews were conducted, suggesting that the researchers' estimation of twenty interviews per sixty-four addresses was slightly conservative; the response rate was thus an improvement on the rate achieved in the 1997 Skills Survey. The result, according to the authors of the report, 'is a high quality, randomly drawn and representative, quality data set' (2002: 23).

---

and then something else—either further clusters or population units—is sampled.

Many examples of multi-stage cluster sampling entail stratification. We might, for example, want further to stratify the companies according to whether their headquarters are located in the UK or abroad. To do this we would group companies according to whether their headquarters were based in the UK or elsewhere and then select one or two companies from each of the two strata per major SIC code.

Box 4.3 provides an example of a multi-stage cluster sample. It entailed three stages: the sampling of subregions within Britain, the sampling of socio-economic groups, and the sampling of individuals.

In a way, there are four stages, because addresses are randomly sampled (using the Postcode Address File) and then, if there was more than one eligible individual at the same address, one person was randomly selected.

The advantage of multi-stage cluster sampling should be clear by now: it allows interviewers to be far more concentrated than would be the case if a simple random or stratified sample was selected. The advantages of stratification can be capitalized upon because the clusters can be stratified in terms of strata. However, even when a rigorous sampling strategy is employed, sampling error cannot be avoided, as the example in Box 4.9 clearly shows.

The qualities of a probability sample

The reason why probability sampling is such an important procedure in social survey research is that it is possible to make inferences from information about a random sample to the population from which it was selected. In other words, we can generalize findings derived from a sample to the population. This is not to say that we treat the population data and the sample data as the same. If we take the example of the level of skill development in our sample of 450 employees, which we will treat as the number of training days completed in the previous twelve months, we will know that the mean number of training days undertaken by the sample ($\bar{x}$) can be used to estimate the population mean (μ) but with known margins of error. The mean, or more properly the arithmetic mean, is the simple average.

In order to address this point it is necessary to use some basic statistical ideas. These are presented in Box 4.4 and can be skipped if just a broad idea of sampling procedures is required.

Sample size

One question about research methods that we are asked by students almost more than any other relates to the size of the sample: 'how large should my sample be?' or 'is my sample large enough?' The decision about sample size is not a straightforward one: it depends on a number of considerations and there is no one definitive answer. This is frequently a source of great disappointment to those who pose such questions. Moreover, most of the time decisions about sample size are affected by considerations of time and cost. Therefore, invariably decisions about sample size represent a compromise between the constraints of time and cost, the need for precision, and a variety of further considerations that will now be addressed.

Absolute and relative sample size

One of the most basic considerations, and one that is possibly the most surprising, is that, contrary to what you might have expected, it is the *absolute* size of a sample that is important not its *relative* size. This means that a national probability sample of 1,000 individuals in the UK has as much validity as a national probability sample of 1,000 individuals in the USA, even though the latter has a much larger population. It also means that increasing the size of a sample increases the precision of a sample. This means that the 95 per cent confidence interval referred to in Box 4.4 narrows. However, a large sample cannot *guarantee* precision, so that it is probably better to say that increasing the size of a sample increases the *likely* precision of a sample. This means that, as sample size increases, sampling error decreases. Therefore, an important component of any decision about sample size should be how much sampling error one is prepared to tolerate. The less sampling error one is prepared to tolerate, the larger a sample will need to be. Fowler (1993) warns against a simple acceptance of this criterion. He argues that in practice researchers do not base their decisions about sample size on a single estimate of a variable. Most survey research is concerned to generate a host of estimates—that is, of the variables that make up the research instrument that is administered. He also observes that it is not normal for survey researchers to be in a position to specify in advance 'a desired level of precision' (Fowler 1993: 34). Moreover, since sampling error will be only one component of any error entailed in an estimate, the notion of using a desired level of precision as a factor in a decision about sample size is not realistic. Instead, to the extent that this notion does enter into decisions about sample size, it usually does so in a general rather than a calculated way.

Time and cost

Time and cost considerations become very relevant in this context. In the previous paragraph it is clearly being suggested that the larger the sample size the greater the precision (because the amount of sampling error will be less). However, by and large up to a sample size of around 1,000, the gains in precision are noticeable as the sample size climbs from low figures of 50, 100, 150, and so on upwards. After a certain point, often in the region of 1,000, the sharp increases in precision become less pronounced, and, although it does not plateau, there is a slowing-down in the extent to which precision increases (and hence the extent to which the sample error of the mean declines). Considerations of sampling size are likely to be profoundly affected by matters of time and cost at such a juncture, since striving for smaller and smaller increments of precision becomes an increasingly uneconomic proposition.

Box 4.4 Generalizing from a random sample to the population

Using our imaginary study of training and skill development in a single nearby company, let us say that the sample mean is 6.7 days of training per employee (the average amount of training received in the previous twelve months in the sample). A crucial consideration here is: how confident can we be that the mean number of 6.7 training days is likely to be found in the population, even when probability sampling has been employed? If we take an infinite number of samples from a population, the sample estimates of the mean of the variable under consideration will vary in relation to the population mean. This variation will take the form of a bell-shaped curve known as a *normal distribution* (see Figure 4.7). The shape of the distribution implies that there is a clustering of sample means at or around the population mean. Half the sample means will be at or below the population mean; the other half will be at or above the population mean. As we move to the left (at or lower than the population mean) or the right (at or higher than the population mean), the curve tails off, implying fewer and fewer samples generating means that depart considerably from the population mean. The variation of sample means around the population mean is the *sampling error* and is measured using a statistic known as the *standard error of the mean*. This is an estimate of the amount that a sample mean is likely to differ from the population mean.

This consideration is important, because sampling theory tells us that 68 per cent of all sample means will lie between + or − one standard error from the population mean and that 95 per cent of all sample means will lie between + or −1.96 standard errors from the population mean. It is this second calculation that is crucial, because it is at least implicitly employed by survey researchers when

they report their statistical findings. They typically employ 1.96 standard errors as the crucial criterion in how confident they can be in their findings. Essentially, the criterion implies that you can be 95 per cent certain that the population mean lies within + or − 1.96 sampling errors from the sample mean.

If a sample has been selected according to probability sampling principles, we know that we can be 95 per cent certain that the population mean will lie between the sample mean + or − 1.96 multiplied by the standard error of the mean. This is known as the *confidence interval*. If the mean number of training days in the previous twelve months in our sample of 450 employees is 6.7 and the standard error of the mean is 1.3, we can be 95 per cent certain that the population mean will lie between

$$6.7 + (1.96 \times 1.3)$$

and

$$6.7 - (1.96 \times 1.3)$$

i.e. between 9.248 and 4.152.

If the standard error was smaller, the range of possible values of the population mean would be narrower; if the standard error was larger, the range of possible values of the population mean would be wider.

If a stratified sample is selected, the standard error of the mean will be smaller, because the variation between strata is essentially eliminated, because the population will be accurately represented in the sample in terms of the stratification criterion or criteria employed. This consideration demonstrates the way in which stratification injects an extra increment of precision into the probability sampling process, since a possible source of sampling error is eliminated.

By contrast, a cluster sample without stratification exhibits a larger standard error of the mean than a comparable simple random sample. This occurs because a possible source of variability between employees (that is, membership of one department rather than another, which may affect levels of training undertaken) is disregarded. If, for example, some departments have a culture of learning in which a large number of employees were involved, and if these departments were not selected because of the procedure for selecting clusters, an important source of variability would have been omitted. It also implies that the sample mean would be on the low side, but that is another matter.

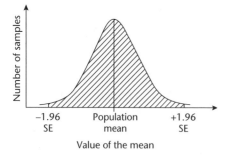

Figure 4.7 The distribution of sample means

Notes: 95 per cent of sample means will lie within the shaded area. SE = standard error of the mean.

Practical Tip 👉 *Sample size and probability sampling*

As we have said in the text, the issue of sample size is the matter that most often concerns students and others. Basically, this is an area where size really does matter (!)—the bigger the sample the more representative it is likely to be (provided the sample is randomly selected), regardless of the size of the population from which it is drawn. However, when doing projects, students clearly need to do their research with very limited resources. You should try to find out from your department or business school whether there are any guidelines about whether samples of a minimum size are expected. If there are no such guidelines, you will need to conduct your mini-survey in such a way as to maximize the number of interviews you can manage or the number of postal questionnaires you can send out given the amount of time and resources available to you. Also, in many if not most cases, a truly random approach to sample selection may not be open to you. The crucial point is to be clear about and to justify what you have done. Explain the difficulties that you would have encountered in generating a random sample. Explain why you really could not include any more in your sample of respondents. But, above all, do not make claims about your sample that are not sustainable. Do not claim that it is representative or that you have a random sample when it is clearly not the case that either of these is true. In other words, be frank about what you have done. People will be much more inclined to accept an awareness of the limits of your sample design than claims about a sample that are patently false. Also, it may be that there are lots of good features about your sample—the range of people included, the good response rate, the high level of cooperation you received from the firm. Make sure you play up these positive features at the same time as being honest about its limitations.

Non-response

However, considerations about sampling error do not end here. The problem of *non-response* should be borne in mind. Most sample surveys attract a certain amount of non-response. Thus, it is likely that only some of our sample will agree to participate in the research. If it is our aim to ensure as far as possible that 450 employees are interviewed and if we think that there may be a 20 per cent rate of non-response, it may be advisable to sample 540–550 individuals, on the grounds that approximately ninety will be non-respondents. For example, of the 143 survey questionnaires posted to companies in T. C. Powell's (1995) research (referred to in Box 1.5), only forty were returned and of these thirty-six were usable, making a response rate of 25 per cent. This raises the question of whether this sample is significant enough to represent companies in the geographical area of the north-eastern USA that the study claims to represent (see Chapter 6 for a further discussion of acceptable response rates). The issue of non-response, and in particular of refusal to participate, is of particular significance, because it has been suggested by some researchers that response rates (see Box 4.5) to surveys are declining in many countries. This implies that there is a growing tendency towards people refusing to participate in survey research. In 1973, an article in the American magazine *Business Week* carried an article ominously entitled 'The Public Clams up on Survey Takers'. The magazine asked survey companies about their experiences and found considerable concern about declining response rates. Similarly, in Britain, a report from a working party on the Market Research Society's Research and Development Committee in 1975 pointed to similar concerns among market research companies. However, an analysis of this issue by T. W. Smith (1995) suggests that, contrary to popular belief, there is no consistent evidence of such a decline. Moreover, Smith shows that it is difficult to disentangle general trends in response rates from such variables as the subject matter of the research, the type of respondent, and the level of effort

---

Box 4.5 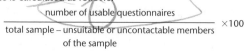 *What is a response rate?*

The notion of a response rate is a common one in social survey research. When a social survey is conducted, whether by structured interview or by self-completion questionnaire, it is invariably the case that some people who are in the sample refuse to participate. The response rate is, therefore, the percentage of a sample that does, in fact, agree to participate. However, the calculation of a response rate is a little more complicated than this. First, not everyone who replies will be included: if a large number of questions are not answered by a respondent or if there are clear indications that he or she has not taken the interview or questionnaire seriously, it is better to employ only the number of *usable* interviews or questionnaires as the numerator. Similarly, it also tends to occur that not everyone in a sample turns out to be a suitable or appropriate respondent or can be contacted. Thus the response rate is calculated as follows:

$$\frac{\text{number of usable questionnaires}}{\text{total sample} - \text{unsuitable or uncontactable members of the sample}} \times 100$$

---

expended on improving the number of respondents to individual surveys. The strategies that can improve responses to survey instruments such as structured interviews and postal questionnaires will be examined in Chapter 5.

Heterogeneity of the population

Yet another consideration is the homogeneity and heterogeneity of the population from which the sample is to be taken. When a sample is very heterogeneous, like a sample of a whole country or city, the population is likely to be highly varied. When it is relatively homogeneous, such as members of a company or of an occupation, the amount of variation is less. The implication of this is that, the greater the heterogeneity of a population, the larger a sample will need to be.

Kind of analysis

Finally, researchers should bear in mind the *kind of analysis* they intend to undertake. A case in point

here is the contingency table. A contingency table shows the relationship between two variables in tabular form. It shows how variation in one variable relates to variation in another variable. To understand this point, consider our example of employee skill development and learning in the 100 largest UK companies. A contingency table would show how far the 5,000 employees that comprise the sample vary in terms of skill and learning, measured in terms of training received during the previous twelve months. In addition the table would also need to reflect differences between companies that represent the seventeen main SIC code sections. However, it is unlikely that the initial criterion of selecting the 100 largest companies would enable all the SIC sections, such as education, community activities, or fishing, to be represented; therefore some of the cells of the table would remain empty. In order to overcome this problem, the sample would have to be designed to reflect a much wider range of public and private organizational activity, perhaps by removing the criterion of size of company from the study. This would have a bearing on the number of employees who would be sampled from each company.

Types of non-probability sampling

The term *non-probability sampling* is essentially an umbrella term to capture all forms of sampling that are not conducted according to the canons of probability sampling outlined above. It is not surprising, therefore, that the term covers a wide range of different types of sampling strategy, at least one of which—the quota sample—is claimed by some practitioners to be almost as good as a probability sample.

In this section we will cover three main types of non-probability sample: the convenience sample; the snowball sample; and the quota sample.

Convenience sampling

A convenience sample is one that is simply available to the researcher by virtue of its accessibility. Imagine that a researcher who teaches at a university business school is interested in the way that managers deal with ethical issues when making business decisions. The researcher might administer a questionnaire to several classes of students, all of whom are managers taking a part-time MBA degree. The chances are that the researcher will receive all or almost all the questionnaires back, so that there will be a good response rate. The findings may prove quite interesting, but the problem with such a sampling strategy is that it is impossible to generalize the findings, because we do not know of what population this sample is representative. They are simply a group of managers who are available to the researcher. They are almost certainly not representative of managers as a whole—the very fact they are taking this degree programme marks them off as different from managers in general.

This is not to suggest that convenience samples should never be used. Let us say that our lecturer/researcher is developing a battery of questions that are designed to measure the ethical decision-making processes used by managers. It is highly desirable to pilot such a research instrument before using it in an investigation, and administering it to a group who are not a part of the main study may be a legitimate way of carrying out some preliminary analysis of such issues as whether respondents tend to answer in identical ways to a question, or whether one question is often omitted when managers respond to it. In other words, for this kind of purpose, a convenience sample may be acceptable though not ideal. A second kind of context in which it may be at least fairly acceptable to use a convenience sample is when the chance presents itself to gather data from a convenience sample and it represents too good an opportunity to miss. The data will not allow definitive findings to be generated, because of the problem of generalization, but it could provide a springboard for further research or allow links to be forged with existing findings in an area.

It also perhaps ought to be recognized that convenience sampling probably plays a more prominent role than is sometimes supposed. Certainly, in the field of business and management, convenience samples are very common and indeed are more prominent than are samples based on probability sampling (Bryman 1989*a*: 113–14). Boxes 4.6 and 4.7 provide examples of the use of convenience samples in leadership research and in a study of university students. Probability sampling involves a lot of preparation so that it is frequently avoided because of the difficulty and costs involved.

Snowball sampling

In certain respects, snowball sampling is a form of convenience sample, but it is worth distinguishing because it has attracted quite a lot of attention over the years. With this approach to sampling, the researcher makes initial contact with a small group of people who are relevant to the research topic and then uses these to establish contacts with others. Bryman used an approach like this to create a sample of British visitors to Disney theme parks (Bryman 1999). Another example of snowball sampling is given in Franwick et al.'s (1994) study of strategic decision making (see Box 4.8) where this sampling technique was used to identify members of the organization who had been involved in the decision-making network associated with the introduction of a core technology.

A snowball sample is in no sense random, because there is no way of knowing the precise extent of the population from which it would have to be drawn. In other words, there is no accessible sampling frame for the population from which the sample is to be taken, and the difficulty of creating such a sampling frame means that such an approach is the only feasible one. Moreover, even if one could create a sampling frame of strategic decision-makers or of British visitors to Disney theme parks, it would almost certainly be inaccurate straight away, because this is a shifting population. People will constantly be becoming and ceasing to be associated with the decision-making network, while new theme park visitors are arriving all the time. The problem with snowball sampling is that it is very unlikely that the sample

Box 4.6 A convenience sample

Hall, Workman, and Marchioro (1998) were interested in whether or not leadership perceptions are dependent on an individual's sex and behavioural flexibility, as well as the sex type of the group task. Their convenience sample comprised undergraduate and graduate students at the University of Akron, where all three of the researchers were employed. More than 200 potential participants were pre-screened and a sample of 112 was selected on the basis of their responses to a questionnaire that was designed to measure behavioural flexibility—that is, the extent to which individuals are able and willing to adapt their responses to fit their social context.

This stratified sample of socially adaptable and socially inflexible participants was then subdivided into experimental groups of sixteen people made up of four four-person groups. Each four-person group consisted of two males and two females, one pair being adaptable and the other inflexible. High attendance at the experimental session was ensured by the fact that the students received course credit for their participation.

The laboratory experiment involved two group tasks, each lasting around twenty minutes. The first was a manufacturing game, which the authors expected would be congruent with a masculine sex role; the second was a brainstorming task related to children's health, which the authors expected would be more gender neutral. After completing the task, the participants rated the other group members according to their leadership impressions, on such questions as 'to what degree did this person fit your image of a leader?' Response options ranged from 5 = very much to 1 = not at all, on a five-point Likert scale.

The results showed that males emerged as leaders in 71 per cent of groups in relation to the first task and in 68 per cent of groups for the second task. The researchers had expected women to be perceived as more leader-like in the second task than the first. However, the effect of the task on leadership perception was not statistically significant. Finally, the study did find that both men and women who are more behaviourally flexible are perceived as more leader-like than those who are less behaviourally flexible.

The researchers claim that their use of student subjects instead of working adults was driven by their experimental research design, which 'would have been difficult, if not impossible to implement in an organizational setting' (1998: 27). That said, the fact that their sample involved persons who had not worked together before, may not have known each other, and were not in paid employment means that the ability of the research to detect the cumulative effects of disparity between the sexes on leader perceptions in an organizational setting is somewhat limited.

Box 4.7 Another convenience sample

Lucas (1997) describes a study of university students that was undertaken to find out about the extent and kinds of part-time employment among the students. Data were collected in spring 1995 from students in five of the seven faculties at Manchester Metropolitan University, where the author of the report was a lecturer. The specific degree programmes chosen were first degrees in: chemistry, combined studies, electrical engineering, history, hotel and catering management, illustration, law, psychology, and social science. Self-completion questionnaires were given out to students in the first, final, and either second or third years of their degrees (depending on whether the course lasted three or four years). The choice of subjects was designed to maximize the amount of variety in the type of degree programme and to provide similar numbers of males and females (since one gender frequently predominates in particular degree programmes). The questionnaire 'was issued, completed and collected at the end of class contact time by one of the researchers, or by a member of teaching staff' (1997: 600–1). These procedures represent a very good attempt to generate a varied sample. It is a convenience sample, because the choice of degree programmes was selected purposively rather than randomly and because absentees from classes were unavailable to answer the questionnaires. On the other hand, because of the way questionnaires were administered, there was a very high rate of response among those students to whom the questionnaires were administered. An interesting question is whether absence from classes might be connected in some way to part-time working; in other words, might absence be due to students working at the time of the class or to students perhaps being too tired to go to the class because of their part-time work?

Box 4.8 A snowball sample

In a study of strategic decision making in a *Fortune* 500 high-technology company, Franwick et al. (1994) explore a strategic decision, involving the development of a core technology, that would have a major impact on the firm's competitive strategy. They focused on the Techno project—a small team of managers led by an executive with a technical background with responsibility for 'brain-storming' potential technology that could be used to improve the firm's competitive position. A snowball sampling technique was used to identify organizational members who were involved in the Techno project. 'This technique identifies members of a network of decision participants by asking each actor to identify others with whom he or she communicated regarding a specific decision situation' (1994: 99). To be considered part of the decision-making

network, a manager must be identified as a decision participant by at least three other people.

Following this procedure, the researchers generated a potential sample of 42 managers who were members of the network. An actual sample of 39 managers was generated on the basis of this list, and open-ended telephone interviews were conducted with these managers. In the interview, respondents were asked to describe the Techno project and then asked to state what they thought were the pros and cons regarding the project and why. They were also asked to identify other managers with whom they communicated regularly regarding the project. From this information the researchers were able to identify the decision-making network and each manager's position in it.

will be representative of the population, though, as we have just suggested, the very notion of a population may be problematic in some circumstances. However, by and large, snowball sampling is used not within a quantitative research strategy, but within a qualitative one: both Franwick's and Bryman's study were carried out within a predominantly qualitative research framework. Concerns about external validity and the ability to generalize do not loom as large within a qualitative research strategy as they do in a quantitative research one (see Chapters 3 and 13). In qualitative research, the orientation to sampling is more likely to be guided by a preference for *theoretical sampling* than with the kind of statistical sampling that has been the focus of this chapter (see Box 14.9). There is a much better 'fit' between snowball sampling and the theoretical sampling strategy of qualitative research than with the statistical sampling approach of quantitative research. This is not to suggest that snowball sampling is entirely irrelevant to quantitative research: when the researcher needs to focus upon or to reflect relationships between people, tracing connections through snowball sampling may be a better approach than conventional probability sampling (J. S. Coleman 1958).

Quota sampling

Quota sampling is used intensively in commercial research, such as market research and political opinion polling. The aim of quota sampling is to produce a sample that reflects a population in terms of the relative proportions of people in different categories, such as gender, ethnicity, age groups, socioeconomic groups, and region of residence, and in combinations of these categories. However, unlike a stratified sample, the sampling of individuals is not carried out randomly, since the final selection of people is left up to the interviewer. Information about the stratification of the UK population or about certain regions can be obtained from sources like the Census and from surveys based on probability samples such as the WERS (Box 2.15) or the UK Skills Survey (Box 4.3).

Once the categories and the number of people to be interviewed within each category (known as *quotas*) have been decided upon, it is then the job of interviewers to select people who fit these categories. The quotas will typically be interrelated. In a manner similar to stratified sampling, the population may be divided into strata in terms of, for example, gender, social class, age, and ethnicity. Census data might be used to identify the number of people who should be in each subgroup. The numbers to be interviewed in each subgroup will reflect the population. Each interviewer will probably seek out individuals who fit several subgroup quotas. Accordingly, an interviewer may know that among the various subgroups of people he or she must find, and interview, five Asian, 25–34-year-old, lower-middle-class females in the area in which the interviewer has been asked to work (say, the Wirral). The interviewer usually asks people who are available to him or her about their characteristics (though gender will presumably be self-evident) in order to determine their suitability for a particular subgroup. Once a subgroup quota (or a combination of subgroup quotas) has been achieved, the interviewer will no longer be concerned to locate individuals for that subgroup.

The choice of respondents is left to the interviewer, subject to the requirement of all quotas being filled, usually within a certain time period. Those of you who have ever been approached on the street by a person toting a clipboard and interview schedule and have been asked about your age, occupation, and so on, before being asked a series of questions about a product or whatever, have almost certainly encountered an interviewer with a quota sample to fill. Sometimes, he or she will decide not to interview you because you do not meet the criteria required to fill a quota. This may be due to a quota already having been filled or to the criteria for exclusion meaning that a person with a certain characteristic you possess is not required.

A number of criticisms are frequently levelled at quota samples.

- Because the choice of respondent is left to the interviewer, the proponents of probability sampling argue that a quota sample cannot be representative. It may accurately reflect the population in terms of superficial characteristics, as defined by the quotas. However, in their choice of people to approach, interviewers may be unduly influenced by their perceptions of how friendly people are or by whether the people make eye contact with the interviewer (unlike most of us who look at the ground and shuffle past as quickly as possible because we do not want to be bothered in our leisure time).

- People who are in an interviewer's vicinity at the times he or she conducts interviews, and are therefore available to be approached, may not be typical. There is a risk, for example, that people in full-time paid work may be under-represented and that those who are included in the sample are not typical.

- The interviewer is likely to make judgements about certain characteristics in deciding whether to approach a person, in particular, judgements about age. Those judgements will sometimes be incorrect—for example, when someone who is eligible to be interviewed, because a quota that he or she fits is unfilled, is not approached because the interviewer makes an incorrect judgement (for example, that the person is older than he or she looks). In such a case, a possible element of bias is being introduced.

- It has also been argued that the widespread use of social class as a quota control can introduce difficulties, because of the problem of ensuring that interviewees are properly assigned to class groupings (Moser and Kalton 1971).

- It is not permissible to calculate a standard error of the mean from a quota sample, because the non-random method of selection makes it impossible to calculate the range of possible values of a population.

All of this makes the quota sample look a poor bet and there is no doubt that it is not favoured by academic researchers. It does have some arguments in its favour, however.

- It is undoubtedly cheaper and quicker than an interview survey on a comparable probability sample. For example, interviewers do not have to spend a lot of time travelling between interviews.

- Interviewers do not have to keep calling back on people who were not available at the time they were first approached.

- Because calling back is not required, a quota sample is easier to manage. It is not necessary to keep track of people who need to be recontacted or to keep track of refusals. Refusals occur, of course, but it is not necessary (and indeed it is not possible) to keep a record of which respondents declined to participate.

- When speed is of the essence, a quota sample is invaluable when compared to the more cumbersome probability sample. Newspapers frequently need to know how a national sample of voters feel about a certain topic or how they intend to vote at that time. Alternatively, if there is a sudden major news event, such as the terrorist attack on the World Trade Centre in New York, the news media may seek a more or less instant picture of the nation's views or responses. Again, a quota sample will be much faster.

- As with convenience sampling, it is useful for conducting development work on new measures or on research instruments. It can also be usefully employed in relation to exploratory work from which new theoretical ideas might be generated.

- Although the standard error of the mean should not be computed for a quota sample, it frequently is. As Moser and Kalton (1971) observe, some writers argue that the use of a non-random method in quota sampling should not act as a barrier to such a computation because its significance as a source of error is small when compared to other errors that may arise in surveys (see Figure 4.8). However, they go on to argue that at least with random sampling the researcher can calculate the amount of sampling error and does not have to be concerned about its potential impact.

There is some evidence to suggest that, when compared to random samples, quota samples often result in biases. They under-represent people in lower social strata, people who work in the private sector and manufacturing, and people at the extremes of income, and they over-represent women in households with children and people from larger households (Marsh and Scarbrough 1990; Butcher 1994). On the other hand, it has to be acknowledged that probability samples are often biased too.

Limits to generalization

One point that is often not fully appreciated is that, even when a sample has been selected using probability sampling, any findings can be generalized only to the population from which that sample was taken. This is an obvious point, but it is easy to think that findings from a study have some kind of broader applicability. If we take our imaginary study of training and skill development among employees of a company, any findings could be generalized only to that company. In other words, you should be very cautious about generalizing to employees at other companies. There are many factors that may imply that the level of training and skill development is higher (or lower) than among company employees as a whole. There may be a higher (or lower) level of skill required in order to do the jobs that the company requires its employees to do, there may be more

(or less) money in the company's training budget, there may be more (or less) of a culture of learning at this company, or the company may recruit a higher (or lower) proportion of employees who are already skilled. There may be many other factors too.

Similarly, we should be cautious of overgeneralizing in terms of locality. Hence a frequent criticism made in relation to research on employee motivation relates to the extent to which it can be assumed to be generalizable beyond the confines of the national culture on which the study is based. For example, Herzberg, Mausner, and Snyderman (1959) conducted semi-structured interviews with 203 engineers and accountants in the Pittsburgh area in the USA. Most of the companies that constituted sites for the study were involved in heavy industry, such as steel making or shipbuilding. The population from which the sample was selected consisted of all accountants and engineers who worked for these companies. Respondents were chosen randomly according to certain criteria for stratification, including age, job title, level in the company, and length of service. It is interesting that there is no mention of gender in the study, although we can fairly safely assume that, given that this was a study of accountants and engineers in the late 1950s, there is likely to be a male bias to the study. The maximum number of individuals selected for interview in each company was approximately fifty. As the authors acknowledge, 'the fact that this work was done within a thirty-mile radius around Pittsburgh will inevitably raise questions about the degree to which the findings are applicable in other areas of the country' (1959: 31). The findings may also reflect the values of high-individualism, self-interest, and high masculinity that have been identified as characteristic of American culture (Hofstede 1984). This is part of the reason there have been so many attempts to replicate the study on other occupational groups and in other localities including different cultures and nationalities.

However, there could even be a further limit to generalization that is implied by the Herzberg et al. sample. The main study was conducted in the late 1950s. One issue that is rarely discussed in this context, and that is almost impossible to assess, is whether there is a time limit on the findings that are generated. Quite aside from the fact that we need to appreciate that the findings cannot (or at least should not) be generalized beyond the Pittsburgh area, is there a point at which we have to say, 'well, those findings applied to the Pittsburgh area then but things have changed and we can no longer assume that they apply to that or any other locality'? We are, after all, used to thinking that things have changed when there has been some kind of prominent change. To take a simple example: no one would be prepared to assume that the findings of a study in 1980 of university students' budgeting and personal finance habits would apply to students in the early twenty-first century. Quite aside from changes that might have occurred naturally, the erosion and virtual dismantling of the student grant system has changed the ways students finance their education, including perhaps a greater reliance on part-time work (Lucas 1997), a greater reliance on parents, and use of loans. But, even when there is no definable or recognizable source of relevant change of this kind, there is none the less the possibility (or even likelihood) that findings are temporally specific. Such an issue is impossible to resolve without further research (Bryman 1989b).

Error in survey research

We can think of 'error', a term that has been employed on a number of occasions, as being made up of four main factors (Figure 4.8).

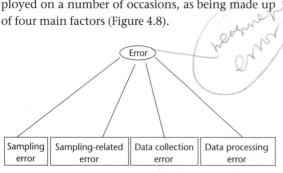

Figure 4.8 Four sources of error in social survey research

• *Sampling error.* See Box 4.1 for a definition. This kind of error arises because it is extremely unlikely that one will end up with a truly representative sample, even when probability sampling is employed.

• We can distinguish what might be thought of as *sampling-related error*. This is error that is subsumed under the category *non-sampling error* (see Box 4.1) but that arises from activities or events that are related to the sampling process and that are connected with the issue of generalizability or external validity of findings. Examples are an inaccurate sampling frame and non-response.

- There is also error that is connected with the implementation of the research process. We might call this *data collection error*. This source of error includes such factors as: poor question wording in self-completion questionnaires or structured interviews; poor interviewing techniques; and flaws in the administration of research instruments.

- Finally, there is *data processing error*. This arises from faulty management of data, in particular, errors in the *coding* of answers.

Box 4.9 Sources of sampling and non-sampling error in a survey of the effects of privatization

In a study of the effects of privatization on corporate culture and employee wellbeing, Cunha and Cooper (2002) describe, first, the difficulties they experienced in obtaining access to companies in Portugal that were going through privatization and, secondly, the impact of a high non-response rate on their research design. Commenting on the first issue, the authors explain, 'we faced a very strong resistance on the part of top management of the companies we contacted, which is understandable considering the "sensitive" [sic] political and human resource decisions that were being taken' (2002: 27). In relation to the second point, samples were selected by the human resource managers, forming the basis for the questionnaire survey, which was sent directly by the researchers to the employees' home address. The three companies, the samples, and non-response rates were as follows:

- The first was a cement company. It employed approximately 2,500 employees and a stratified sample of 750 employees was chosen—in managerial, technical/professional, clerical and manual jobs; 133 valid responses were obtained (18 per cent response rate);

- The second was a smaller cement company. From a population of 500 a stratified sample of 125 employees was chosen, but no manual workers were included in the sample owing to the low literacy levels amongst workers. Thirty-five valid responses were received (28 per cent response rate). By occupational level this sample consisted of 22 managers, 11 technical/professional, and 2 clerical employees;

- The third was a paper pulp company with 2,800 employees. A stratified sample of 1,244 employees was chosen. In this case a longitudinal element was built into the survey—questionnaires were sent in 1994 (before partial privatization) and again in 1996 (after partial privatization). However, the number of employees who responded to both of these surveys was quite small ($n = 45$), so the researchers had to select different kinds of sample that focused on subgroups that were involved in privatization.

This study raises a number of questions in relation to possible sources of sampling error. The fact that samples were chosen by the HR manager in the company means that they were non-random and thus may have reflected a bias on the part of the individual who was making these choices. The researchers' original aim—to conduct a longitudinal analysis based on surveying employees before and after privatization had to be modified, owing to insufficient access. This meant that the researchers were limited in the extent to which they were able to suggest that changes in corporate culture were caused by privatization.

A further possible source of bias associated with the sampling frame related to the exclusion of manual workers from the survey in the second company, owing to their low levels of literacy. However, it is worth noting that this problem could potentially have been overcome through the use of a structured interview approach instead of a self-administered questionnaire. In addition, we can see from the profile of responses in this company (22 managers, 11 technical/professional, and 2 clerical employees) that this sample consists of significantly more managers than other kinds of employees. It is, therefore, extremely likely that the sample does not reflect the actual population. Finally, the high non-response rate in the third company introduced a further source of sample bias (this forced the researchers to find other ways of breaking down the sample in ways that were more statistically meaningful).

The example shows how various sources of sampling and non-sampling error are sometimes closely interrelated. In particular, it illustrates how non-response rates and sampling frames can be affected by the sensitivity of the issue that is being investigated and the consequent willingness of companies and employees to participate in the research.

The third and fourth sources of error relate to factors that are not associated with sampling and instead relate much more closely to concerns about the validity of measurement, which was addressed in Chapter 3. An example of the way that non-response can impact upon the external validity and generalizability of findings is shown in Box 4.9. However, the kinds of steps that need to be taken to keep these sources of error to a minimum in the context of social survey research will be addressed in the next three chapters.

K KEY POINTS

- Probability sampling is a mechanism for reducing bias in the selection of samples.

- Ensure you become familiar with key technical terms in the literature on sampling such as: representative sample; random sample; non-response; population; sampling error; etc.

- Randomly selected samples are important because they permit generalizations to the population and because they have certain known qualities.

- Sampling error decreases as sample size increases.

- Quota samples can provide reasonable alternatives to random samples, but they suffer from some deficiencies.

- Convenience samples may provide interesting data, but it is crucial to be aware of their limitations in terms of generalizability.

- Sampling and sampling-related error are just two sources of error in social survey research.

Q QUESTIONS FOR REVIEW

- What do each of the following terms mean: population; probability sampling; non-probability sampling; sampling frame; representative sample; and sampling and non-sampling error?

- What are the goals of sampling?

- What are the main areas of potential bias in sampling?

Sampling error

- What is the significance of sampling error for achieving a representative sample?

Types of probability sample

- What is probability sampling and why is it important?

- What are the main types of probability sample?

- How far does a stratified random sample offer greater precision than a simple random or systematic sample?

- If you were conducting an interview survey of around 500 people in Manchester, what type of probability sample would you choose and why?
- A researcher positions herself on a street corner and asks 1 person in 5 who walks by to be interviewed: she continues doing this until she has a sample of 250. How likely is she to achieve a representative sample?

The qualities of a probability sample

- A researcher is interested in levels of job satisfaction among manual workers in a firm that is undergoing change. The firm has 1,200 manual workers. The researcher selects a simple random sample of 10 per cent of the population. He measures job satisfaction on a Likert scale comprising ten items. A high level of satisfaction is scored 5 and a low level is scored 1. The mean job satisfaction score is 34.3. The standard error of the mean is 8.57. What is the 95 per cent confidence interval?

$$34.3 \pm 1.96 \times 8.57$$

Sample size

- What factors would you take into account in deciding how large your sample should be when devising a probability sample?
- What is non-response and why is it important to the question of whether you will end up with a representative sample?

Types of non-probability sample

- Are non-probability samples useless?
- In what circumstances might you employ snowball sampling?
- 'Quota samples are not true random samples, but in terms of generating a representative sample there is little difference between them, and this accounts for their widespread use in market research and opinion polling.' Discuss.

Limits to generalization

- 'The problem of generalization to a population is not just to do with the matter of getting a representative sample.' Discuss.

Error in survey research

- 'Non-sampling error, as its name implies, is concerned with sources of error that are not part of the sampling process.' Discuss.

5

Structured interviewing

CHAPTER GUIDE

Once sampling issues have been taken into consideration, the next stage of the survey research process (see Figure 4.1) involves considering whether to administer the questionnaire face to face or to rely on self-completion. This chapter deals with the first option, the structured interview, whilst the following chapter addresses issues relating to self-completion. A further option to consider is whether to administer the questionnaire by e-mail or using the Web; this possibility will be covered later on in Chapter 23.

The structured interview is one of a variety of forms of research interview, but it is the one that is most commonly employed in survey research. The goal of the structured interview is for the interviewing of respondents to be standardized so that differences between interviews in any research project are minimized. As a result, there are many guidelines about how structured interviewing should be carried out so that variation in the conduct of interviews is small. This chapter explores:

- the reasons why the structured interview is a prominent research method in survey research; this issue

entails a consideration of the importance of standardization to the process of measurement;

- the different contexts of interviewing, such as the use of more than one interviewer and whether the administration of the interview is in person or by telephone;

- various prerequisites of structured interviewing, including: establishing rapport with the interviewee; asking questions as they appear on the interview schedule; recording exactly what is said by interviewees; ensuring there are clear instructions on the interview schedule concerning question sequencing and the recording of answers; and keeping to the question order as it appears on the schedule;

- problems with structured interviewing, including: the influence of the interviewer on respondents and the possibility of systematic bias in answers (known as *response sets*); the feminist critique of structured interview, which raises a distinctive cluster of problems with the method, is also examined.

Introduction

The interview is a common occurrence in social life, because there are many different forms of interview. There are job interviews, media interviews, social work interviews, police interviews, appraisal interviews. And then there are research interviews, which represent the kind of interview that will be covered in this and other chapters (such as Chapters 15 and 16). These different kinds of interview share some common features, such as the eliciting of information by the interviewer from the interviewee and the operation of rules of varying degrees of formality or explicitness concerning the conduct of the interview.

In the business research interview, the aim is for the interviewer to elicit from the interviewee or *respondent*, as he or she is frequently called in survey research, all manner of information: interviewees' own behaviour or that of others, attitudes, norms, beliefs, and values. There are many different types or styles of research interview, but the kind that is primarily employed in survey research is the structured interview, which is the focus of this chapter. Other kinds of interview will be briefly mentioned in this chapter but will be discussed in greater detail in later chapters.

The structured interview

The research interview is a prominent data collection strategy in both quantitative and qualitative research. The social survey is probably the chief

context within which business researchers employ the structured interview (see Box 5.1) in connection with quantitative research and it is this form of the

aggregated

Box 5.1 🔅 *What is a structured interview?*

A structured interview, sometimes called a *standardized interview*, entails the administration of an interview schedule by an interviewer. The aim is for all interviewees to be given exactly the same context of questioning. This means that each respondent receives exactly the same interview stimulus as any other. The goal of this style of interviewing is to ensure that interviewees' replies can be aggregated and this can be achieved reliably only if those replies are in response to identical cues. Interviewers are supposed to read out questions exactly and in the same order as they are printed on the schedule. Questions are usually very specific and very often offer the interviewee a fixed range of answers (this type of question is often called *closed, closed ended, precoded,* or *fixed choice*). The structured interview is the typical form of interview in social survey research.

Variation

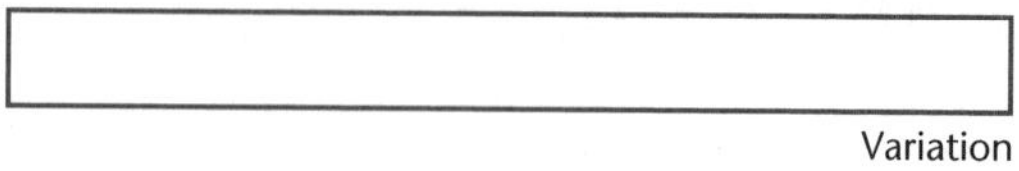

Figure 5.1 A variable

Box 5.2 Some prominent sources of error in survey research

There are many sources of error in survey research, in addition to those associated with sampling. This is a list of the principal sources of error:

1 a poorly worded question;

2 the way the question is asked by the interviewer;

3 misunderstanding on the part of the interviewee;

4 memory problems on the part of the interviewee;

5 the way the information is recorded by the interviewer;

6 the way the information is processed, either when answers are coded or when data are entered into the computer.

interview that will be emphasized in this chapter. The reason why survey researchers typically prefer this kind of interview is that it promotes standardization of *both* the asking of questions *and* the recording of answers. This feature has two closely related virtues from the perspective of quantitative research.

Reducing error due to interviewer variability

The standardization of both the asking of questions and the recording of answers means that, if it is properly executed, variation in people's replies will be due to 'true' or 'real' variation and not due to the interview context. To take a simple illustration, when we ask a question that is supposed to be an indicator of a concept, we want to keep error to a minimum, an issue that was touched on at the end of Chapter 4. We can think of the answers to a question as constituting the values that a variable takes. These values, of course, exhibit variation. This could be the question on skill development and training among employees that was a focus of Chapter 4 at certain points. Employees will vary in the number of training

days they receive (see Figure 5.1). However, some respondents may be inaccurately classified in terms of the variable. There are a number of possible reasons for this (see Box 5.2).

Most variables will contain an element of error, so that it is helpful to think of variation as made up of two components: true variation and error. In other words:

variation = true variation + variation due to error.

The aim is to keep the error component to a minimum (see Figure 5.2), since error has an adverse effect on the validity of a measure. If the error component is quite high (see Figure 5.3), validity will be jeopardized. The significance for error of standardization in the structured interview is that two sources of variation due to error—the second and fifth in Box 5.2—are likely to be less pronounced, since the opportunity for variation in interviewer behaviour in these two areas (asking questions and recording answers) is reduced.

The significance of standardization and of thereby reducing interviewer variability is this: assuming

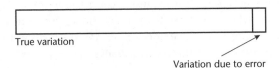

Figure 5.2 A variable with little error

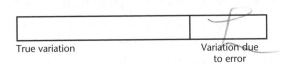

Figure 5.3 A variable with considerable error

that there is no problem with an interview question due to such things as confusing terms or ambiguity (an issue that will be examined in Chapter 7), we want to be able to say as far as possible that the variation that we find is connected with true variation between interviewees and not to variation in the way a question was asked or the answers recorded in the course of the administration of a survey by structured interview. Variability can occur in either of two ways. First, *intra-interviewer variability*, whereby an interviewer is not consistent in the way he or she asks questions and/or records answers. Secondly, when there is more than one interviewer, there may be *inter-interviewer variability*, whereby interviewers are not consistent with each other in the ways they ask questions and/or record answers. Needless to say, these two sources of variability are not mutually exclusive; they can coexist, compounding the problem even further. In view of the significance of standardization, it is hardly surprising that some writers prefer to call the structured interview a *standardized interview* (e.g. Oppenheim 1992) or *standardized survey interview* (e.g. Fowler and Mangione 1990).

Accuracy and ease of data processing

Like self-completion questionnaires, most structured interviews contain mainly questions that are variously referred to as *closed, closed ended, pre-coded,* or *fixed choice*. This issue will be covered in detail in Chapter 7. However, this type of question has considerable relevance to the current discussion. With the closed question, the respondent is given a limited choice of possible answers. In other words, the interviewer provides respondents with two or more possible answers and asks them to select which one or ones apply. Ideally, this procedure will simply entail the interviewer placing a tick in a box by the answer(s) selected by a respondent or circling the selected answer or using a similar procedure. The advantage of this practice is that the potential for interviewer variability is reduced: there is no problem of whether the interviewer writes down everything that the respondent says or of misinterpretation of the reply given. If an *open* or *open-ended* question is asked, the interviewer may not write down everything said, may embellish what is said, or may misinterpret what is said.

However, the advantages of this type of question in the context of survey research go further than this, as we will see in Chapter 7. One advantage that is particularly significant in the context of the present discussion is that closed questions greatly facilitate the processing of data. When an open question is asked, the answers need to be sifted and *coded* in order for the data to be analysed quantitatively. Not only is this a laborious procedure, particularly if there is a large number of open questions and/or of respondents; it also introduces the potential for another source of error, which is the sixth in Box 5.2: it is quite likely that error will be introduced as a result of variability in the coding of answers. When open questions are asked, the interviewer is supposed to write down as much of what is said as possible. Answers can, therefore, be in the form of several sentences. These answers have to be examined and then categorized, so that each person's answer can be aggregated with other respondents' answers to a certain question. A number will then be allocated to each category of answer so that the answers can then be entered into a computer database and analysed quantitatively. This general process is known as coding and will be examined in greater detail in Chapter 7.

Coding introduces yet another source of error. First, if the rules for assigning answers to categories, collectively known as the *coding frame*, are flawed, the variation that is observed will not reflect the true variation in interviewees' replies. Secondly, there may be variability in the ways in which answers are categorized. As with interviewing, there can be two sources: *intra-coder variability*, whereby the coder varies over time in the way in which the rules for assigning answers to categories are implemented, and *inter-coder variability*, whereby coders differ from each other in the way in which the rules for assigning answers to categories are implemented. If either (or both) source(s) of variability occur, at least part of the variation in interviewees' replies will not reflect true variation and instead will be caused by error.

The closed question sidesteps this problem neatly, because respondents' allocate *themselves* to categories. The coding process is then a simple matter of attaching a different number to each category of answer and of entering the numbers into a computer database. It is not surprising, therefore, that this type of question is often referred to as pre-coded, because decisions about the coding of answers are typically undertaken as part of the design of the schedule—that is, before any respondents have actually been asked questions. There is very little opportunity for interviewers or coders to vary in the recording or the coding of answers. Of course, if some respondents misunderstand any terms in the alternative answers with which they are presented, or if the answers do not adequately cover the appropriate range of possibilities, the question will not provide a valid measure. However, that is a separate issue and one that will be returned to in Chapter 7. The chief point to register about closed questions for the moment is that, when compared to open questions, they reduce one potential source of error *and* are much easier to process for quantitative data analysis.

Relationship of the structured interview to other types of interview

The structured interview is by no means the only type of interview, but it is certainly the main type that is likely to be encountered in survey research and in quantitative research generally. Unfortunately, a host of different terms have been employed by writers on research methodology to distinguish the diverse forms of research interview. Box 5.3 represents an attempt to capture some of the major terms and types.

All of the forms of interview outlined in Box 5.3, with the exception of the *structured interview* and the *standardized interview*, are primarily used in connection with qualitative research and it is in that context that they will be encountered again later in this book. They are rarely used in connection with quantitative research, and survey research in particular, because the absence of standardization in the asking of questions and recording of answers makes respondents' replies difficult to aggregate and to process. This is not to say that they have no role at all. For example, as we will see in Chapter 7, the unstructured interview can have a useful role in relation to developing the fixed-choice alternatives with which respondents are provided in the kind of closed question that is typical of the structured interview.

Interview contexts

In an archetypal interview, an interviewer stands or sits in front of the respondent asking the latter a series of questions and writing down the answers. However, there are several possible departures from it, although this archetype is the most usual context for an interview.

More than one interviewee

In the case of group interviews or focus groups, there is more than one, and usually quite a few more than one, respondent or interviewee. Nor is this the only context in which more than one person is interviewed. Bell, Taylor, and Thorpe (2001) carried out

Box 5.3 Major types of interview

- *Structured interview.* See Box 5.1.

- *Standardized interview.* See Box 5.1.

- *Semi-structured interview.* This is a term that covers a wide range of instances. It typically refers to a context in which the interviewer has a series of questions that are in the general form of an interview schedule but is able to vary the sequence of questions. The questions are frequently somewhat more general in their frame of reference than that typically found in a structured interview schedule. Also, the interviewer usually has some latitude to ask further questions in response to what are seen as significant replies.

- *Unstructured interview.* The interviewer typically has only a list of topics or issues, often called an *interview guide* or *aide mémoire*, that are typically covered. The style of questioning is usually informal. The phrasing and sequencing of questions will vary from interview to interview.

- *Intensive interview.* This term is employed by Lofland and Lofland (1995) as an alternative term to the *unstructured interview*. Spradley (1979) uses the term *ethnographic interview* to describe a form of interview that is also more or less synonymous with the *unstructured interview*.

- *Qualitative interview.* For some writers, this term seems to denote an *unstructured interview* (e.g. Mason 1996), but more frequently it is a general term that embraces interviews of both the semi-structured and unstructured kind (e.g. Rubin and Rubin 1995).

- *In-depth interview.* Like the term *qualitative interview*, this one sometimes refers to an *unstructured interview* but more often refers to both semi-structured and unstructured interviewing.

- *Focused interview.* This is a term devised by Merton, Fiske, and Kendall (1956) to refer to an interview using predominantly open questions to ask interviewees questions about a specific situation or event that is relevant to them and of interest to the researcher.

- *Focus group.* This is the same as the *focused interview*, but interviewees discuss the specific issue in groups. See Box 16.1 for a more detailed definition.

- *Group interview.* Some writers see this term as synonymous with the *focus group*, but a distinction may be made between the latter and a situation in which members of a group discuss a variety of matters that may be only partially related.

- *Oral history interview.* This is an *unstructured* or *semi-structured interview* in which the respondent is asked to recall events from his or her past and to reflect on them (see also Box 15.4). There is usually a cluster of fairly specific research concerns to do with a particular epoch or event, so there is some resemblance to a *focused interview*.

- *Life history interview.* This is similar to the *oral history interview*, but the aim of this type of *unstructured interview* is to glean information on the entire biography of each respondent (see also Box 15.4).

---

interviews with two managers in the same company, both of whom had been involved in the implementation of the people-management initiative, Investors in People. The managers, who had often had different roles in relation to the initiative or been involved with it at different stages of its development, were together able to build a chronological understanding of its implementation. Similarly, in Bryman's research on visitors to Disney theme parks, not just couples but often their children took part in the interview as well (Bryman 1999). However, it is very unusual for structured interviews to be used in connection with this kind of questioning. In survey research, it is almost always a specific individual who is the object of questioning. Indeed, in survey

interviews it is very advisable to discourage as far as possible the presence and intrusion of others during the course of the interview. Investigations in which more than one person is being interviewed tend to be exercises in qualitative research, though this is not always the case: Wiersma's (1994; see Box 5.10) study of work–home role conflict employed a critical incident method and relied on interviewing couples and then husbands and wives separately.

More than one interviewer

This is a very unusual situation in business research, because of the considerable cost that is involved in dispatching two (or indeed more than two) people to interview someone. Bechhofer, Elliott, and McCrone (1984) describe research in which two people interviewed individuals in a wide range of occupations. However, while their approach achieved a number of benefits for them, their interviewing style was of the unstructured kind that is typically employed in qualitative research, and they argue that the presence of a second interviewer is unlikely to achieve any added value in the context of structured interviewing.

In person or by telephone?

A third way in which the archetype may not be realized is that interviews may be conducted by telephone rather than face to face. While telephone interviewing is quite common in fields like market research, it is less common in business research. (See Box 4.8, however, for an interesting example of the use of telephone interviewing in combination with a snowball sampling technique.)

There are several advantages of telephone over personal interviews.

- On a like-for-like basis, they are far cheaper and also quicker to administer. This arises because, for personal interviews, interviewers have to spend a great deal of time and money travelling between respondents. This factor will be even more pronounced when a sample is geographically dispersed, a problem that is only partially mitigated for personal interview surveys by strategies like cluster sampling. Of course, telephone interviews take time and hired interviewers have to be paid, but the cost of conducting a telephone interview will still be lower than a comparable personal one.

- The telephone interview is easier to supervise than the personal interview. This is a particular advantage when there are several interviewers, since it becomes easier to check on interviewers' transgressions in the asking of questions, such as rephrasing questions or the inappropriate use of probes by the interviewer.

- Telephone interviewing has a further advantage that is to do with evidence (which is not as clear-cut as one might want) that suggests that, in personal

interviews, respondents' replies are sometimes affected by characteristics of the interviewer (for example, class or ethnicity) and indeed by his or her mere presence (implying that the interviewees may reply in ways they feel will be deemed desirable by interviewers). The remoteness of the interviewer in telephone interviewing removes this potential source of bias to a significant extent. The interviewer's personal characteristics cannot be seen and the fact that he or she is not physically present may offset the likelihood of respondents' answers being affected by the interviewer.

Telephone interviewing suffers from certain limitations when compared to the personal interview.

- People who do not own or who are not contactable by telephone obviously cannot be interviewed by telephone. In business research, this characteristic is most likely to be a feature of lower-status employees and, therefore, the potential for sampling bias exists. Lower-income households are more likely not to own a telephone; also, many people choose to be ex-directory—that is, they have taken action for their telephone numbers not to appear in a telephone directory. Again, these people cannot be interviewed by telephone. One likely solution to this last difficulty is *random digit dialling*. With this technique, the computer randomly selects telephone numbers within a predefined geographical area. Not only is this a random process that conforms to the rules about probability sampling examined in Chapter 4, it also stands a chance of getting at ex-directory households, though it cannot, of course, gain access to those without a telephone at all. The question of whether response rates (see Box 4.5) are lower with surveys by telephone interview than with surveys by personal interview is unclear, in that there is little consistent evidence on this question, but generally it is believed that telephone surveys achieve lower rates (see Table 23.1).

- Telephone interviewers cannot engage in observation. This means that they are not in a position to respond to signs of puzzlement or unease on the faces of respondents when they are asked a question. In a personal interview, the interviewer may respond to such signs by restating the question or attempting to clarify the meaning of the question, though this has to be handled in a standardized way as far as possible. A further issue relating to the inability of the interviewer to observe is that, sometimes, interviewers may be asked to collect subsidiary information in connection with their visits (for example, whether or not health and safety procedures are made evident at a business premises). Such information cannot be collected when telephone interviews are employed.

- It is frequently the case that specific individuals in households or firms are the targets of an interview. In other words, simply anybody will not do. This requirement is likely to arise from the specifications of the population to be sampled, which means that people in a certain role or position or with particular characteristics are to be interviewed. It is probably more difficult to ascertain by telephone interview whether the correct person is replying.

- The telephone interviewer cannot readily employ visual aids such as show cards (see below) from which respondents might be asked to select their replies or to use diagrams or photographs.

Computer-assisted interviewing

In recent years, increasing use has been made of computers in the interviewing process. A large percentage of telephone interviews are conducted with the aid of personal computers, but the reason for their growing use has been that the portability and affordability of 'laptop' computers provide greater opportunity for them to be used in connection with personal interviews. With computer-assisted interviewing

(sometimes referred to as computer-assisted personal interviewing (CAPI)), the questions that comprise an interview schedule appear on the screen. As interviewers ask each question, they 'key in' the appropriate reply using a mouse and proceed to the next question. Moreover, this process has the great advantage that, when *filter questions* (see Box 5.5) are asked, so that certain answers may be skipped as a result of a person's reply, the computer can be programmed to 'jump' to the next relevant question. This removes the possibility of interviewers inadvertently asking inappropriate questions or failing to ask ones that should be asked. If the interviewer is out in an organization all day, he or she can either take a disk with the saved data to the research office or send the data down a telephone line with the aid of a modem. It is possible that technophobic respondents may be a bit alarmed by their use, but, by and large, the use of computer-assisted interviewing seems destined to grow. One of us has had personal experience of this technique as a respondent in a market research survey: in this instance the laptop started to beep part of the way through the interview because the battery was about to expire and needed to be replaced with a back-up. An incident such as this could be disruptive to the flow of an interview and be alarming for technophobic respondents.

Finally, the Internet and e-mail communications have introduced a number of further possibilities in terms of the use of computers to facilitate data collection using methods such as interviewing. This issue will be taken up in more detail in Chapter 23, where a detailed comparison of the advantages and disadvantages of face-to-face interviewing, versus other modes of questionnaire delivery, is provided (see Table 23.1).

Conducting interviews

Issues concerning the conduct of interviews are examined here in a very general way. In addition to the matters considered here, there is clearly the important issue of how to word the interview questions

themselves. This area will be explored in Chapter 7, since many of the rules of question asking relate to self-completion questionnaire techniques like postal questionnaires as well as to structured interviews.

One further general point to make here is that the advice concerning the conduct of interviews provided in this chapter relates to structured interviews. The framework for conducting the kinds of interviewing conducted in qualitative research (such as unstructured and semi-structured interviewing and focus groups) will be handled in later chapters.

Know the schedule

Before interviewing anybody, an interviewer should be fully conversant with the schedule. Even if you are the only person conducting interviews, make sure you know it inside out. Interviewing can be stressful for interviewers and it is possible that under duress standard interview procedures like filter questions (see Box 5.5) can cause interviewers to get flustered and miss questions out or ask the wrong questions. If two or more interviewers are involved, they need to be fully trained to know what is required of them and to know their way around the schedule. Training is especially important in order to reduce the likelihood of interviewer variability in the asking of questions, which is a source of error.

Introducing the research

Prospective respondents have to be provided with a credible rationale for the research in which they are being asked to participate and for giving up their valuable time. This aspect of conducting interview research is of particular significance at a time when response rates to social survey research appear to be declining, though, as noted in Chapter 4, the evidence on this issue is the focus of some disagreement. The introductory rationale may be either spoken by the interviewer or written down. In many cases, respondents may be presented with both modes. It comes in spoken form in such situations as when interviewers make contact with respondents on the street or when they 'cold call' respondents in their homes or at their place of work, in person or by telephone. A written rationale will be required to alert respondents that someone will be contacting them in person or on the telephone to request an interview. Respondents will frequently encounter both

forms—for example, when they are sent a letter and then ask the interviewer who turns up to interview them what the research is all about. An example of how respondents were contacted for the Workplace Employee Relations Survey (WERS) is given in Box 5.9. It is important for the rationale given by telephone to be consistent with the one given by letter, as if respondents pick up inconsistencies they may well be less likely to participate in the survey.

Introductions to research should typically contain the bits of information outlined in Box 5.4. Since interviewers represent the interface between the research and the respondent, they have an important role in maximizing the response rate for the survey. In addition to the advice given in Box 5.4, the following points should be borne in mind.

- Interviewers should be prepared to keep calling back if interviewees are out or unavailable. This will require taking into account people's likely work and leisure habits—for example, there is no point in calling at home on people who work during the day. In addition, first thing in the morning may not be the best time to contact a busy manager who is likely to be briefing colleagues and responding to queries.

- Be self-assured in that you may get a better response if you presume that people will agree to be interviewed rather than that they will refuse.

- Reassure people that you are not a salesperson. Because of the tactics of certain organizations whose representatives say they are doing market or business research, many people have become very suspicious of people saying they would just like to ask you a few questions.

- Dress in a way that will be acceptable to a wide spectrum of people.

- Make it clear that you will be happy to find a time to suit the respondent.

Rapport

It is frequently suggested that it is important for the interviewer to achieve *rapport* with the respondent. This means that very quickly a relationship must be

---

Box 5.4 Topics and issues to include in an introductory statement

There are several issues to include in an introductory statement to a prospective interviewee. The following list comprises the principal considerations.

- Make clear the identity of the person who is contacting the respondent.

- Identify the auspices under which the research is being conducted—for example, a university, a market research agency.

- Mention any research funder, or, if you are a student doing an undergraduate or postgraduate dissertation or doing research for a thesis, make this clear.

- Indicate what the research is about in broad terms and why it is important, and give an indication of the kind of information to be collected.

- Indicate why the respondent has been selected—e.g. selected by a random process.

- Provide reassurance about the confidentiality of any information provided.

- Make it clear that participation is voluntary.

- Reassure the respondent that he or she will not be identified or be identifiable in any way. This can usually be achieved by pointing out that data are anonymized when they are entered into the computer and that analysis will be conducted at an aggregate level.

- Provide the respondent with the opportunity to ask any questions—e.g. provide a contact telephone number if the introduction is in the form of a written statement, or, if in person, simply ask if the respondent has any questions.

These suggestions are also relevant to the covering letter that accompanies mail questionnaires, except that researchers using this method need to remember to include a stamped addressed envelope!

---

established that encourages the respondent to want (or at least be prepared) to participate in and persist with the interview. Unless an element of rapport can be established, some respondents may initially agree to be interviewed but then decide to terminate their participation because of the length of time the interview is taking or perhaps because of the nature of the questions being asked. While this injunction essentially invites the interviewer to be friendly with respondents and to put them at ease, it is important that this quality is not stretched too far. Too much rapport may result in the interview going on too long and the respondent suddenly deciding that too much time is being spent on the activity. Also, the mood of friendliness may result in the respondent answering questions in a way that is designed to please the interviewer. The achievement of rapport between interviewer and respondent is therefore a delicate balancing act. Moreover, it is probably somewhat easier to achieve in the context of the face-to-face interview rather than the telephone interview, since in the latter the interviewer is unable to offer obvious visual cues of friendliness like smiling or maintaining good eye contact, which is also

frequently regarded as conducive to gaining and maintaining rapport.

Asking questions

It was earlier suggested that one of the aims of the structured interview is to ensure that each respondent is asked exactly the same questions. Recall that in Box 5.2 it was pointed out that variation in the ways a question is asked is a potential source of error in survey research. The structured interview is meant to reduce the likelihood of this occurring, but it cannot guarantee that this will not occur, because there is always the possibility that interviewers will embellish or otherwise change a question when it is asked. There is considerable evidence that this occurs, even among centres of social research that have a solid reputation for being rigorous in following correct methodological protocol (Bradburn and Sudman 1979). The problem with such variation in the asking of questions was outlined above: it is likely to engender variation in replies that does not reflect 'true' variation—in other words, error. Consequently, it is important for interviewers to appreciate the importance of keeping exactly to the wording of the questions they are charged with asking.

You might say: 'does it really matter?' In other words, surely small variations to wording cannot make a significant difference to people's replies? While the impact of variation in wording obviously differs from context to context and is in any case difficult to quantify exactly, experiments in question wording suggest that even small variations in wording can exert an impact on replies (Schuman and Presser 1981). Three experiments in England conducted by Social and Community Planning Research concluded that a considerable number of interview questions are affected by interviewer variability. The researchers estimated that, for about two-thirds of the questions that were considered, interviewers contributed to less than 2 per cent of the total variation in each question (M. Collins 1997). On the face of it, this is a small amount of error, but the researchers regarded it as a cause for concern.

The key point to emerge, then, is the importance of getting across to interviewers the importance of asking questions as they are written. There are many reasons why interviewers may vary question wording, such as reluctance to ask certain questions, perhaps because of embarrassment (M. Collins 1997), but the general admonition to keep to the wording of the question needs to be constantly reinforced when interviewers are being trained. It also needs to be borne in mind for your own research.

Recording answers

An identical warning for identical reasons can be registered in connection with the recording of answers by interviewers, who should write down respondents' replies as exactly as possible. Not to do so can result in interviewers distorting respondents' answers and hence introducing error. Such errors are less likely to occur when the interviewer has merely to allocate respondents' replies to a category, as in a closed question. This process can require a certain amount of interpretation on the part of the interviewer, but the error that is introduced is far less than when answers to open questions are being written down (Fowler and Mangione 1990).

Clear instructions

In addition to instructions about the asking of questions and the recording of answers, interviewers need instructions about their progress through an interview schedule. An example of the kind of context in which this is likely to occur is in relation to *filter questions*. Filter questions require the interviewer to ask questions of some respondents but not others. For example, the question

How many days of on-the-job training have you received in the past twelve months?

presumes that the respondent is in employment. This option can be reflected in the fixed-choice answers that are provided, so that one of these is a 'not-in-employment' alternative. However, a better solution is not to presume anything about respondents' work behaviour but to ask them whether they are currently in employment and then to filter out those who are not. A further consideration in relation to this filter question is how many hours or days they are employed for. For example, in the Skills Survey (Box 4.3) the researchers were interested in anyone who was employed for one hour per week or more. In this case, there was no point in asking those who were not in paid work about the training opportunities they had received as part of their employment. Box 5.5 provides a simple example in connection with an imaginary study of feedback and job performance. The chief point to register about this example is that it requires clear instructions for the interviewer. If such instructions are not provided, there is the risk that either respondents will be asked inappropriate questions (which can be irritating for them) or the interviewer will inadvertently fail to ask a question (which results in missing information).

Question order

In addition to warning interviewers about the importance of not varying the asking of questions and the recording of answers, they should be alerted to the importance of keeping to the order of asking questions. For one thing, varying the question order can result in certain questions being accidentally omitted,

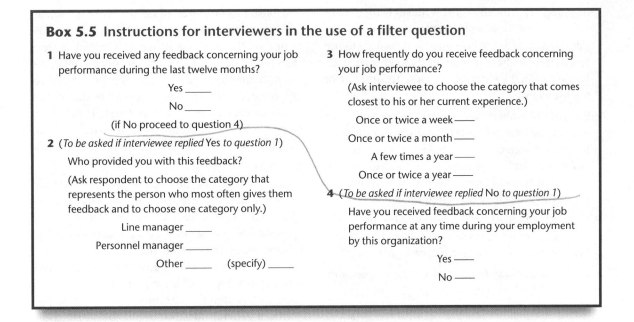

Box 5.5 Instructions for interviewers in the use of a filter question

1 Have you received any feedback concerning your job performance during the last twelve months?

Yes _____

No _____

(if No proceed to question 4)

2 (*To be asked if interviewee replied* Yes *to question 1*)

Who provided you with this feedback?

(Ask respondent to choose the category that represents the person who most often gives them feedback and to choose one category only.)

Line manager _____

Personnel manager _____

Other _____ (specify) _____

3 How frequently do you receive feedback concerning your job performance?

(Ask interviewee to choose the category that comes closest to his or her current experience.)

Once or twice a week ____

Once or twice a month ____

A few times a year ____

Once or twice a year ____

4 (*To be asked if interviewee replied* No *to question 1*)

Have you received feedback concerning your job performance at any time during your employment by this organization?

Yes ____

No ____

because the interviewer may forget to ask those that have been leapfrogged during the interview. Also, variation in question order may have an impact on replies: if some respondents have been previously asked a question that they should have been asked whereas others have not, a source of variability in the asking of questions will have been introduced and therefore a potential source of error.

Quite a lot of research has been carried out on the general question of question order, but few if any consistent effects on people's responses that derive from asking questions at different points in a questionnaire or interview schedule have been unveiled. Different effects have been demonstrated on various occasions. A study in the USA found that people were less likely to say that their taxes were too high when they had been previously asked whether government spending ought to be increased in a number of areas (Schuman and Presser 1981: 32). Apparently, some people perceived an inconsistency between wanting more spending and lower taxes, and adjusted their answers accordingly. However, it is difficult to draw general lessons from such research, at least in part because experiments in question order do not always reveal clear-cut effects of varying the order in which questions are asked, even in cases where effects

might legitimately have been expected. There are two general lessons.

- Within a survey, question order should not be varied (unless, of course, question order is the subject of the study!)
- Researchers should be sensitive to the possible implications of the effect of early questions on answers to subsequent questions.

The following rules about question order are sometimes proposed.

- Early questions should be directly related to the topic of the research, about which the respondent has been informed. This removes the possibility that the respondent will be wondering at an early stage in the interview why he or she is being asked apparently irrelevant questions. This injunction means that personal questions about age, social background, and so on should *not* be asked at the beginning of an interview.
- As far as possible, questions that are more likely to be salient to respondents should be asked early in the interview schedule, so that their interest and attention are more likely to be secured. This suggestion may conflict with the previous one, in that

de mutualization

questions specifically on the research topic may not be obviously salient to respondents, but it implies that as far as possible questions relating to the research topic that are more likely to grab their attention should be asked at or close to the start of the interview.

- Potentially embarrassing questions or ones that may be a source of anxiety should be left till later. In fact, research should be designed to ensure that as far as possible respondents are not discomfited, but it has to be acknowledged that with certain topics this effect may be unavoidable.

- With a long schedule or questionnaire, questions should be grouped into sections, since this allows a better flow than skipping from one topic to another.

- Within each group of questions, general questions should precede specific ones. Box 5.6 provides an illustration of such a sequence, which follows the recommendations of Gallup (1947, cited in Foddy 1993: 61–2). The example is concerned to demonstrate how the approach might operate in connection with building society demutualization, the process whereby several British mutual building societies turned themselves into banks and hence into public companies quoted on the Stock Exchange. The question order sequence is designed with a number of features in mind. It is designed to

establish people's levels of knowledge of demutualization before asking questions about it and to distinguish those who feel strongly about it from those who do not. According to Foddy (1993), the second question is always open ended, so that respondents' frames of references can be established with respect to the topic at hand. However, it seems likely that, if sufficient pilot research has been carried out, a closed question could be envisaged, a point that applies equally to question 4.

- A further aspect of the rule that general questions should precede specific ones is that it has been argued that, when a specific question comes before a general one, the aspect of the general question that is covered by the specific one is discounted in the minds of respondents because they feel they have already covered it. Thus, if a question about how people feel about the amount they are paid precedes a general question about job satisfaction, there are grounds for thinking that respondents will discount the issue of pay when responding about job satisfaction.

- During the course of an interview, it sometimes happens that a respondent provides an answer to a question that is to be asked later in the interview. Because of the possibility of a question order effect, when the interviewer arrives at the question that appears already to have been answered, it should be repeated.

However, question order effects remain one of the more frustrating areas of structured interview and questionnaire design, because of the inconsistent evidence that is found and because it is difficult to formulate generalizations or rules from the evidence that does point to their operation.

Probing

Probing is a highly problematic area for researchers employing a structured interview method. It frequently happens in interviews that respondents need help with their answers. One obvious case is where it is evident that they do not understand the question—they may either ask for further information or it is clear from what they say that they are struggling

---

Box 5.6 A sequence of questions on the topic of building society demutualization

1 Have you heard of demutualization?

Yes —— No ——

2 What are your views about demutualization?

3 Do you favour or not favour demutualization?

Favour —— Not favour ——

4 Why do you favour (not favour) demutualization?

5 How strongly do you feel about this?

Very strongly ——

Fairly strongly ——

Not at all strongly ——

to understand the question or to provide an adequate answer. The second kind of situation the interviewer faces is when the respondent does not provide a sufficiently complete answer and has to be probed for more information. The problem in either situation is obvious: the interviewer's intervention may influence the respondent and the nature of interviewers' interventions may differ. A potential source of variability in respondents' replies that does not reflect 'true' variation is introduced—that is, error.

Some general tactics with regard to probes are as follows.

- If further information is required, usually in the context of an open-ended question, standardized probes can be employed, such as 'Could you say a little more about that?' or 'Are there any other reasons why you think that?' or simply 'mmmm...?'

- If the problem is that when presented with a closed question the respondent replies in a way that does not allow the interviewee to select one of the predesigned answers, the interviewer should repeat the fixed-choice alternatives and make it apparent that the answer needs to be chosen from the ones that have been provided.

- If the interviewer needs to know about something that requires quantification, such as the number of visits to building societies in the last four weeks or the number of building societies in which the respondent has accounts, but the respondent resists this by answering in general terms ('quite often' or 'I usually go to the building society every week'), the interviewer needs to persist with securing a number from the respondent. This will usually entail repeating the question. The interviewer should not try to second guess a figure on the basis of the respondent's reply and then suggest that figure to him or her, since the latter may be unwilling to demur from the interviewer's suggested figure.

Prompting

Prompting occurs when the interviewer suggests a possible answer to a question to the respondent. The key prerequisite here is that all respondents receive the same prompts. All closed questions entail standardized prompting, because the respondent is provided with a list of possible answers from which to choose. An unacceptable approach to prompting would be to ask an open question and to suggest possible answers only to some respondents, such as those who appear to be struggling to think of an appropriate reply.

During the course of a face-to-face interview, there are several circumstances in which it will be better for the interviewer to use 'show cards' rather than rely on reading out a series of fixed-choice alternatives. Show cards (sometimes called 'flash cards') display all the answers from which the respondent is to choose and are handed to the respondent at different points of the interview. Three kinds of context in which it might be preferable to employ show cards rather than to read out the entire set of possible answers are as follows.

- There may be a very long list of possible answers. For example, respondents may be asked which daily newspaper they each read most frequently. To read out a list of newspapers would be tedious and it is probably better to hand the respondent a list of newspapers from which to choose.

- Sometimes, during the course of interviews, respondents are presented with a group of questions to which the same possible answers are attached. An example of this approach is Likert scaling, which is an approach to attitude measurement. A typical strategy entails providing respondents with a series of statements and asking them how far they agree or disagree with the statements (see Chapter 3). These are often referred to as *items* rather than as *questions*, since strictly speaking the respondent is not being asked a question. An example was provided in Box 3.3. It would be excruciatingly dull to read out all seven possible answers ten times. Also, it may be expecting too much of respondents to read out the answers once and then require them to keep the possible answers in their heads for the entire batch of questions to which they apply. A show card that can be used for the entire batch and to which respondents can constantly refer is an obvious solution. As was mentioned in Box 3.3, most Likert scales of this kind comprise five levels of agreement/disagreement

excruciate
折磨人

Box 5.7 A show card

Card 6
Strongly agree
Agree
Undecided
Disagree
Strongly disagree

Box 5.8 Another show card

Card 11

(*a*) Below 20

(*b*) 20–29

(*c*) 30–39

(*d*) 40–49

(*e*) 50–59

(*f*) 60–69

(*g*) 70 and over

---

and it is this more conventional approach that is illustrated in the show card in Box 5.7.

- Some people are not keen to divulge personal details such as their age or their income. One way of neutralizing the impact of such questioning is to present respondents with age or income bands with a letter or number attached to each band. They can then be asked to say which letter applies to them (see Box 5.8). This procedure will obviously not be appropriate if the research requires *exact* ages or incomes.

Leaving the interview

Do not forget common courtesies like thanking respondents for giving up their time. But the period immediately after the interview is one in which some care is necessary in that sometimes respondents try to engage the interviewer in a discussion about the purpose of the interview. Interviewers should resist elaboration beyond their standard statement, because respondents may communicate what they are told to others, which may bias the findings.

Training and supervision

On several occasions, reference has been made to the need for interviewers to be trained. The standard texts on survey research and on interviewing practice tend to be replete with advice on how best to train interviewers. Such advice is typically directed at contexts in which a researcher hires an interviewer to conduct a large amount or even all the interviews. It also has considerable importance in research in which several interviewers (who may be either collaborators or hired interviewers) are involved in a study, since the risk of interviewer variability in the asking of questions needs to be avoided.

For many readers of this book who are planning to do research, such situations are unlikely to be relevant because they will be 'lone' researchers. You may be doing an undergraduate dissertation, or an exercise for a research methods course, or you may be a postgraduate conducting research for a Master's dissertation or for a Ph.D. thesis. Most people in such a situation will not have the luxury of being able to hire a researcher to do any interviewing (though you may be able to find someone to help you a little). When interviewing on your own, you must train yourself to follow the procedures and advice provided above. This is a very different situation from a large research institute or market research agency, which relies on an army of hired interviewers who carry out the interviews. Whenever people other than the lead researcher are involved in interviewing, they will need training and supervision in the following areas:

- contacting prospective respondents and providing an introduction to the study;
- reading out questions as written and following instructions in the interview schedule (for example, in connection with filter questions);
- appropriate styles of probing;
- recording exactly what is said;
- maintaining an interview style that does not bias respondents' answers.

Box 5.9 An example of research involving multiple interviewers

This example is taken from the Workplace Employee Relations Survey (WERS, formerly the Workplace Industrial Relations Survey (WIRS); see also Box 2.15), which is jointly sponsored by the Department for Trade and Industry (DTI), ACAS, the Economic and Social Research Council, and the Policy Studies Institute. The research team, put together under the auspices of the DTI, consisted of a number of UK and international employment relations experts and academics. However, it was the National Centre for Social Research that was responsible for actually conducting the fieldwork in each of the four surveys in the series.

The research design has remained broadly the same throughout the series. Fieldwork for the 1998 survey commenced in the middle of October 1997. Prior to this, each of the 156 interviewers working on the survey took part in a two-day training course, which, in addition to covering issues related to administering the survey and the use of computer-assisted personal interviewing, also sought to familiarize interviewers with introductory concepts in employment relations. Many of the interviewers who worked on the 1998 survey had also been involved with the earlier surveys.

An innovative feature of the survey involved the establishment of a free-phone facility so that any potential respondents who had a query about it could contact the research team directly. This provided support to the interviewers, who were primarily responsible for negotiating participation of respondents. This involved:

1 telephoning the workplace to ascertain the name and job title of the appropriate management respondent;

2 sending an official letter of introduction from the DTI explaining the nature of the survey and asking for their cooperation;

3 telephoning again to arrange an interview.

In addition, some reluctant participants were contacted by the DTI research team and encouraged to reconsider their unwillingness to participate in the survey. All this contributed to the overall success of the fieldwork and the high overall response rate (Box 4.5) achieved in the survey of 80 per cent.

Fowler (1993) cites evidence that suggests that training of less than one full day rarely creates good interviewers.

Supervision of interviewers in relation to these issues can be achieved by:

- checking individual interviewers' response rates;

- tape recording at least a sample of interviews;

- examining completed schedules to determine whether any questions are being left out or if they are being completed properly;

- call-backs on a sample of respondents (usually around 10 per cent) to determine whether they were interviewed and to ask about interviewers' conduct.

Box 5.9 provides an example of some of the considerations involved when doing research involving multiple interviewers.

Other approaches to structured interviewing

There are a number of other techniques that are used in business and management research to supplement the structured interview and determine the focus of the analysis. Four of these—critical incident method, projective techniques, verbal protocol approach, and repertory grid technique—will be discussed in this section. We have grouped these four techniques together here because they are often used in a way that forms part of the structured or semi-structured interview. Therefore, similar guidance to that which we have given in previous sections of this chapter also applies, although it should be remembered that they are sometimes used as an alternative to interviewing. A further use of these techniques is to check findings from more conventional quantitative approaches such as structured interviews or questionnaire surveys.

Critical incident method

This technique for structured interviewing involves asking respondents to describe *critical incidents*, which are defined very broadly by Flanagan (1954) as any observable human activity where the consequences are sufficiently clear as to leave the observer with a definite idea as to their likely effects. The term is derived from the analysis of near disaster situations, where a version of the technique can be used to build up a picture of the events that contribute to a potential disaster and to develop a plan of action for dealing with them. The most common use of critical incident method involves interviewing respondents about particular types of event or behaviour in order to develop an understanding of their sequence and their significance to the individual.

One of the earliest and most well-known illustrations of the technique in management research is the study by Herzberg, Mausner, and Snyderman (1959), which was mentioned in Chapter 4. The authors explain: 'We decided to ask people to tell us stories about times when they felt exceptionally good or bad about their jobs. We decided that from these stories we could discover the kinds of situations leading to negative or positive attitudes toward the job and the effects of these attitudes' (1959: 17). Their initial interview strategy was followed up by a series of probe questions that filled in missing information in the spontaneously told accounts. Content analysis (see Chapter 9) was then used to focus on exploring the essential features of the critical incident in order to reveal the values that they reflected. A more recent example of the use of critical incident method is to be found in the study of work–home role conflict by Wiersma (1994; see Box 5.10).

Finally, although we have introduced critical incident method in Part Two of the book, which deals with quantitative research, we should point out that the technique can also be employed in relation to a more qualitative research strategy. An example of this is the study of small business owner-managers by Curran and Blackburn (1994; see Box 15.5). In this instance, respondents were asked to recall a situation that had arisen in the previous two years in which they had lost a major customer and to explain what had happened and how they had coped with it. Curran and Blackburn's analysis of the data was primarily qualitative, relying on the use of themes

---

Box 5.10 An example of the use of critical incident method

The purpose of Wiersma's (1994) study was to identify the behavioural strategies used by dual-career couples to solve work–home role conflicts. Interviews were conducted with a sample of nine males and fifteen females from twenty-four different dual-career couples in the north-west USA. The research was based on an adaptation of the critical incident method in relation to seven broad issues in work–home role conflict: domestic chores, maintaining social relations, role cycling, job relocations, sex-role socialization, social pressure, and direct competition between spouses.

The participant was asked to tell a story in which he or she described the circumstances surrounding an incident, the behavioural solution used to solve the problem, and the consequences of the action that was taken. A total of 130 critical incidents were generated through these interviews and they were categorized according to the seven areas of role conflict that had been identified in the literature review.

Findings indicated that couples must cope with two kinds of work–home role conflict, the first relating to time-based issues and the second relating to role quality. Wiersma claims that couples use multiple-coping strategies in sequence. For example, a working mother 'initially denies that she is losing the superwoman race, then seeks support from friends, after which she negotiates with family members to distribute the housework more equitably, only finally to ignore rude comments from outsiders when they see her husband doing the ironing' (1994: 220). By seeking to elicit multiple examples of coping from each participant, Wiersma suggests he was able to build up a more complex impression of how couples cope with work–home role conflict than other, more deductive studies had done.

illustrated by the inclusion of direct quotes from respondents.

Projective techniques

These involve the presentation of ambiguous stimuli to individuals, which are interpreted by the researcher to reveal underlying characteristics of the individual concerned. A common example is the Rorschach inkblot test, where respondents are asked to describe random inkblots. Analysis relies on expert psychological interpretation of the way that respondents have described the inkblots and this is suggested to be indicative of their dominant channels of thinking. Another form of projective analysis involves the 'sentence-completion test', where the individual is asked to complete a number of unfinished sentences; this technique has been used in the context of recruitment and selection, often as an assessment centre exercise.

However, one of the best-known examples of the use of projective techniques in management and business research is the study by McClelland (1961) of leadership and the need for individual achievement. Informed by experimental psychology and the psychoanalytic insights of Freud, McClelland's study first involved stimulating the achievement motive in a group of subjects. He then sought to elicit their 'spontaneous thoughts' and fantasies in order to determine the effect of achievement motivation. The subjects were male college students who were told that they were going to be tested to determine their intelligence and leadership ability; it was assumed that this would arouse a desire in the subjects to do well. After the 'tests' were completed, subjects were asked to write short, five-minute stories suggested by pictures that flashed onto a screen for a few seconds. 'The pictures represented a variety of life situations centering particularly around work' (1961: 40). The stories were compared with those that had been written by a control group under normal conditions. The experimental group was found to refer more often in their stories to ideas related to achievement. From this, McClelland concluded that, if someone 'in writing his stories consistently uses achievement-related ideas of the same kind as those elicited in

everyone under achievement "pressure", then he would appear to be someone with a "bias", a "concern", or a "need" for achievement' (1961: 43). This led him to develop a score for the need for Achievement, defined as the number of achievement-related ideas in stories written by an individual under normal conditions.

Some interesting recent examples of projective techniques can also be found in advertising research (Box 5.11). Using collage, storytelling, sentence completion, word associations, and other projective techniques, the authors sought to investigate the nature of consumer desire among students in three countries. This example is a particularly good illustration of the diverse range of projective research techniques.

Verbal protocol approach

This technique builds on the work of Newell and Simon (1972) in the area of human problem solving and has since been used in relation to a number of topics that are relevant to business and management researchers. The approach involves asking respondents to 'think aloud' while they are performing a task. The idea is to elicit the respondent's thought processes while they are making a decision or judgement or solving a problem. The subject's account of what they are doing and why is usually tape-recorded and transcribed and then content analysed using a coding scheme that is used to discern different categories of thinking. An interesting example of the use of verbal protocol analysis can be found in a study by Cable and Graham (2000), who wanted to explore the factors that job-seekers consider when evaluating employers' reputations (Box 5.12).

Repertory grid technique

Repertory grid technique is based on G. A. Kelly's (1955) personal construct theory and it is used to identify the interpretative processes whereby an individual constructs meaning in relation to his or her social context. The theory portrays the individual as a scientist, striving to make sense of his or her

Collage [kɔ-laˑ3]

[Synonym]

Box 5.11 The use of projective techniques in consumer research

In a cross-cultural study of consumer desire, Belk, Ger, and Askegaard (1997) wanted to explore the cultural differences in consumer desire among students in the USA ($n = 38$), Turkey ($n = 29$), and Denmark ($n = 17$).

Desire is defined by the authors as belief-based passions that involve longing or wishing for something. Hence 'we may speak of hungering for, lusting after, or craving certain consumer goods as if they were delicious foods, alluring sexual mates, or addictive drugs' (1997: 24). Research informants were graduate and undergraduate students at the three universities where each of the three authors was employed. The projective methods used included:

- *collage*—using popular magazines, informants were asked to create a collage to express their understanding of desire;

- *associations*—informants were asked to imagine swimming in a sea of things (objects, experiences, people) that bring them pleasure and to describe them;

- *sketches*—they were told to imagine themselves as artists commissioned to create artworks called 'desire' and 'not desire';

- *synonyms*—they were asked to name an object, experience, or person (X) that they desired and to list as many words or phrases that might be used in the sentence, 'I — X';

- *synonym examples and feelings*—informants were asked to name things a person might strongly desire and to describe the feelings a person might have (1) before he or she gets it, (2) at the moment he or she gets it, and (3) after he or she gets it.

Perhaps unsurprisingly, the study found that men and women tended to focus on different objects of desire: objects that emerged with greater frequency for men included luxury cars; for women they included food, and especially chocolates. Although both sexes focused on people as objects of desire, women were more likely to specify relationships as the interpersonal objects of their desire whereas men were more likely to desire women as objects. American and Turkish women were more likely than Danish women to see desire as sinful. The authors conclude that desire is a positive emotional state that is at the same time interpersonal, whether in a competitive sense of wanting more or better things than others, or in the sense of wanting approval and love from others.

---

environment in order to predict and cope with future events. Kelly claimed that sense making occurs through an individual's personal construct system, which provides an order for dealing with incoming information. This system is composed of a series of interlinked and hierarchically related constructs, which are the bipolar sorting mechanisms that distinguish between similarity and dissimilarity for a given event. In order to make sense of an event, the individual must assign information to either one pole of the construct or the other. The researcher's task therefore involves identifying the *constructs* that people use to make sense of their world and seeking to understand the way in which a person's thought processes are conditioned by events that they anticipate.

The first stage in developing of a repertory grid involves the researcher, sometimes together with the participant, identifying a number of (usually between six and twelve) *elements*, which are terms or categories that are deemed relevant to the subject of study—they may be persons, events, or objects. These elements are then written on cards and presented to the respondent, typically in groups of three. The researcher then asks questions that encourage respondents to express how they see the relationship between these elements, such as: 'In what way are two similar?' or 'How does one differ?' The process is then repeated with another three cards, until eventually a picture is built up about how the person construes his or her particular context. This procedure, which is known as the *sequential triadic method*, enables the elements to be sorted. These data can then be entered into the grid, which relates elements to the constructs that underlie the individual's rationale for sorting decisions and the respondent is asked to rank each element in relation to each construct, using a five- or seven-point scale, as shown in Figure 5.4.

Box 5.12 The use of verbal protocol method to enable experimental testing

Cable and Graham (2000) were interested in the factors affecting graduate job-seekers' assessment of employers' reputations. Their sample consisted of fourteen under-graduate students at two large state universities in the USA. Half of the students were on engineering degree programmes and the other half were doing management degrees. The subjects were given a task that involved eval-uating the reputations of three employers. They were given a management trainee job description, which was the same for all three organizations, and recruitment brochures from the three companies—General Electric, WalMart, and Broadview Associates. In making their decision, the subjects were told that they should speak all their thoughts aloud. The 'thinking-aloud' process was tape-recorded and content analysis was conducted on the transcripts using categories that were drawn from the recruitment and job search literatures. Frequently men-tioned categories included 'opportunities for growth' and 'organizational culture'. Typical of the former was the comment 'they have a vast array of opportunities no matter what you do your major in or what you want to do'; a comment typical of the latter was: 'It talks about integrity which is high on my list. I don't want to work for a company that doesn't value integrity and morals.'

The second stage of the research was designed to improve confidence in the findings generated from the first part of the study. It relied on an experimental design involving sixty-six undergraduate job-seekers, who were asked to read a series of scenarios that described an organization. After reading the scenarios they reported their perceptions of each company's reputation.

The third stage of the research involved the use of an experimental design to examine the effects of some of the attributes of organizational reputation that had been identified through the verbal protocol analysis. The field experiment involved 126 undergraduate and postgraduate job-seekers who were asked to complete a questionnaire survey about six organizations with diverse reputations that recruited at the two universities they attended. The survey was repeated three weeks later, in order to limit potential survey biases such as mood effects.

Using these three methods—verbal protocol analysis, an experiment based on scenarios, and a questionnaire survey—the theory of organizational reputation that was developed inductively from the first part of the study using verbal protocol method can then be subjected to further empirical testing using other methods.

Construct—emergent pole (1)	Elements					Construct—contrast pole (5)
	Present job	Disliked past job	Liked past job	Neutral past job	Ideal job	
1. Career opportunities*	4	5	2	3	1	No career opportunities
2. Close supervision	4	2	4	3	5	Discretionary*
3. Changeable*	2	5	2	4	1	Fixed
4. Challenging*	1	5	2	4	1	Not challenging
5. Innovative*	2	4	2	3	2	Repetitive
6. Deskbound	5	1	5	4	5	Mobile*
7. No leadership responsibility	4	5	4	2	4	Leadership responsibilities*
8. Administrative work	4	1	4	3	5	Planning work*
9. Enjoyed variety*	2	5	1	3	1	Monotonous/repetitive
10. 'Standing still'	2	2	5	3	5	Career development*

Figure 5.4 An example of a repertory grid designed to elicit an applicant's perceptions of preferred job tasks

* Denotes preferred pole

Source: adapted from N. Anderson (1990)

Repertory grids have been used in the study of strategic management and decision making and in studies of recruitment, personnel management, and other areas of organizational behaviour. For example, a study conducted by Neil Anderson (1990) explored how the technique could be used in employee selection to assess the task reactions of applicants in a recruitment situation. In this study, it was used to focus on the job–person match for a marketing manager vacancy. An example of a completed grid for a marketing manager applicant, which has been adapted and simplified for our purposes of illustration, is provided in Figure 5.4. The grid illustrates ten elicited constructs relating to five elements, which in this case are 'present job', 'disliked past job', 'liked past job', 'neutral past job', and 'ideal job'. The participant was presented with these elements in triads and asked to identify two that were alike and to explain what differentiated them from the third element. This process resulted in the generation of a series of constructs, such as 'career opportunities', which the participant used to relate one kind of job to another. The participant was then asked to indicate the preferred pole for each of the constructs he or she had identified, so 'career opportunities' was identified as preferred to 'no career opportunities'. Finally, the applicant was asked to assess each

element against each construct using a five-point scale with 1 = 'emergent pole' and 5 = 'contrast pole'. As Figure 5.4 illustrates, this managerial applicant has ranked the elements 'ideal job' and 'disliked past job' at opposite ends of these poles, as might be expected. Once the grid is completed, analysis can be either interpretative or statistical in nature. Anderson's use of the technique involved feedback of the results of the analysis to each participant as a basis for counselling and discussion. However, as you will probably by now have gathered, one of the difficulties with using repertory grids is that the technique is quite complex, both for the researcher to use and for the respondent to complete. Some researchers therefore suggest that the primary value of repertory grid technique derives from its use as a tool for enabling in-depth discussion and thinking about a topic.

A qualitative application of the repertory grid technique can be found in the study of recruiters' perceptions of job applicants conducted by Kristof-Brown (2000; see Box 5.13). In this study, semi-structured

---

Box 5.13 An example of the use of repertory grid technique

Kristof-Brown (2000) carried out a study using repertory grid technique to assess whether recruiters form perceptions of an applicant based on:

- the match between the person and the requirements of a specific job, or;
- the match between the applicant and the broader organizational attributes.

In the first part of the study, thirty-one recruiters from four consulting organizations participated in the study. The repertory grid method was chosen because it allowed recruiters to articulate their own criteria for evaluating applicants. The recruiters watched a video recording showing a series of short mock interviews with job applicants, who were also MBA students, and then they reviewed the applicants' curriculum vitae. This allowed recruiters to view applicants' verbal and non-verbal behaviour, appearance, and interpersonal skills in a realistic setting. After they had watched the video, individual interviews were carried out with each recruiter. Each person was presented with the details of three randomly selected applicants and questions were asked about the degree to

which each one matched (a) the job and (b) the organization. For example, the researcher might ask: 'comparing applicants four, five, and two, which of these people is the best fit with your company?'

After having identified the best-fitting applicant in terms of the person and the job, recruiters were then asked to describe the characteristics of the applicant that had led them to make this choice. The process of presenting three applicants at a time to recruiters was repeated until all applicants had been evaluated and this information could be represented in the form of a repertory grid.

The researchers then coded the data from the interviews to generate a list of 119 characteristics of applicants, which were judged by five independent raters for similarity, resulting in the eventual generation of sixty-two applicant characteristics. The coders then analysed the responses from each interview to generate frequency data, including the number and type of characteristics that were reported by each recruiter. The study thus combined qualitative data collection with quantitative analysis of data that were generated using the repertory grid technique.

interviews were used to determine what the recruiters thought about each applicant, but the data generated were analysed quantitatively in order to gain an impression of the relative importance of each characteristic. This study illustrates a further important aspect of the technique, which is that it requires that participants base their responses on a common set of stimuli. The use of videotaped interviews in this study of recruiters' selection of job applicants meant that all participants were basing their responses on exactly the same set of interviews.

In sum, the repertory grid technique has been used as a supplement and as an alternative to structured interviewing, both as a basis for qualitative exploration and analysis and as a device for generating data that can be statistically analysed using quantitative methods. For an illustration of some of the potential applications of the repertory grid interview in management and business you might want to consult the following website:

www.enquirewithin.co.nz

Problems with structured interviewing

While the structured interview is a commonly used method of business research, certain problems associated with it have been identified over the years. These problems are not necessarily unique to the structured interview, in that they can sometimes be attributed to kindred methods, such as the self-completion questionnaire in survey research or even semi-structured interviewing in qualitative research. However, it is common for the structured interview to be a seen as a focus for the identification of certain limitations that are briefly examined below.

Characteristics of interviewers

There is evidence that interviewers' attributes can have an impact on respondents' replies, but, unfortunately, the literature on this issue does not lend itself to definitive generalizations. In large part, this ambiguity in the broader implications of experiments relating to the effects of interviewer characteristics is due to several problems, such as: the problem of disentangling the effects of interviewers' different attributes from each other ('race', gender, socio-economic status); the interaction between the characteristics of interviewers and the characteristics of respondents; and the interaction between any effects observed and the topic of the interview. Nonetheless, there is undoubtedly some evidence that effects due to characteristics of interviewers can be discerned.

The ethnicity of interviewers is one area that has attracted some attention. Schuman and Presser (1981) cite a study that asked respondents to nominate two or three of their favourite actors or entertainers. Respondents were much more likely to mention black actors or entertainers when interviewed by black interviewers than when interviewed by white ones. Schuman and Converse (1971) interviewed 619 black Detroiters shortly after Martin Luther King's assassination in 1968. The researchers found significant differences between black and white interviewers in around one-quarter of the questions asked.

Although this proportion is quite disturbing, the fact that the majority of questions appear to have been largely unaffected does not give rise to a great deal of confidence that a consistent biasing factor is being uncovered. Similarly inconclusive findings tend to occur in relation to experiments with other sets of characteristics of interviewers. These remarks are not meant to play down the potential significance of interviewers' characteristics for measurement error, but to draw attention to the limitations of drawing conclusive inferences about the evidence. All that needs to be registered at this juncture is that almost certainly the characteristics of interviewers do have an impact on respondents' replies but that the extent and nature of the impact are not clear and are likely to vary from context to context.

Response sets

Some writers have suggested that the structured interview is particularly prone to the operation among respondents of what Webb et al. call 'response sets', which they define as 'irrelevant but lawful sources of variance' (Webb et al. 1966: 19). This form of response bias is especially relevant to multiple-indicator measures (see Chapter 3), where respondents reply to a battery of related questions or items, of the kind found in a Likert scale (see Box 3.3). The idea of a response set implies that people respond to the series of questions in a consistent way but one that is irrelevant to the concept being measured. Two of the most prominent types of response set are known as the 'acquiescence' (also known as 'yeasaying' and 'naysaying' effect) and the 'social desirability' effect.

Acquiescence

Acquiescence refers to a tendency for some people consistently to agree or disagree with a set of questions or items. Imagine respondents who replied to all the items in Box 3.3 stating that they believed they were all unethical (scale = 5) and judging that

they and their peers acted in the way implied by the statement infrequently (scale = 1). The problem with this multiple-item measure is that none of the item measure statements is written in a way that implies an opposite stance. In other words, there are no items that are ethical or likely to be engaged in frequently by many ethically responsible people. This could be seen as a potential source of bias in this multiple-item measure. A wording that would imply an opposite stance might be 'being prepared to take responsibility for errors' or 'refusing to accept gifts/favours in exchange for preferential treatment'. This would help to weed out those respondents who were replying within the framework of an acquiescence response set.

Social desirability

The social desirability effect refers to evidence that some respondents' answers to questions are related to their perception of the social desirability of those answers. An answer that is perceived to be socially desirable is more likely to be endorsed than one that is not. This phenomenon has been demonstrated in studies of ethical behaviour and managerial decision making (see Box 5.14). In order to try to prevent

---

Box 5.14 Reducing social desirability bias

Terence Jackson (2001) wanted to understand the effect of underlying cultural values on ethical attitudes towards management decision making. He proposed that national differences could be attributed to differences in underlying cultural values. His research design therefore relied upon exploration of Hofstede's cultural dimensions of 'individualism-collectivism' and 'uncertainty avoidance' (see Box 1.12), which Jackson took to be important in determining ethical attitudes.

The study involved 425 managers across ten nations and four continents that were chosen to reflect diverse positions along the two cultural dimensions. In each country a postal questionnaire survey was carried out using samples drawn from university business schools, of part-time MBA participants, most of whom were middle-ranking managers. Although the study was based on postal questionnaires (which will be covered in Chapter 6), it raises issues concerning the management of bias that are also very relevant to the conduct of structured

interviewing. In an attempt to reduce social desirability response bias, managers were asked to respond to each questionnaire item according to:

1 'what I believe; what I would do', i.e. as a 'participant';

2 'what my peers believe; what my peers would do', i.e. as an 'observer'.

However, an almost universal finding to emerge from the study was that managers appeared to see others as less ethical than themselves. In this case, did the former represent a biased response and the latter a 'true' response, as other researchers had suggested? This would be to imply that the 'observer' response was actually a projection of the respondents' own attitudes, rather than a reflection of how they perceived the attitudes of others. However, the finding may indicate that managers really do judge their colleagues to be less ethical than they are in an absolute sense. The conclusions drawn thus depend ultimately on how one interprets this data.

social desirability bias, Terence Jackson (2001) framed the questions in a way that was intended to enable the respondents to distance themselves from their responses, by imagining what a peer might do rather than having to state what they would do. It was expected that this would reduce the likelihood that individuals would respond in a way that they anticipate will be more acceptable.

In so far as these forms of response error go undetected, they represent sources of error in the measurement of concepts. However, while some writers have proposed outright condemnation of social research on the basis of evidence of response sets (e.g. Phillips 1973), it is important not to get carried away with such findings. We cannot be sure how prevalent these effects are, and to some extent awareness of them has led to measures to limit their impact on data (for example, by weeding out cases obviously affected by them) or by instructing interviewers to limit the possible impact of the social desirability effect by not becoming overly friendly with respondents and by not being judgemental about their replies.

The problem of meaning

A critique of survey interview data and findings gleaned from similar techniques was developed by social scientists influenced by phenomenological and other interpretivist ideas of the kinds touched on in Chapter 1 (Cicourel 1964, 1982; Filmer et al. 1972; Briggs 1986; Mishler 1986). This critique revolves around what is often referred to in a shorthand way as the 'problem of meaning'. The kernel of the argument is that when humans communicate they do so in a way that not only draws on commonly held meanings but also simultaneously creates meanings. 'Meaning' in this sense is something that is worked at and achieved—it is not simply pre-given. Allusions to the problem of meaning in structured interviewing draw attention to the notion that survey researchers presume that interviewer and respondent share the same meanings of terms employed in the interview questions and answers. In fact, the problem of meaning implies that the possibility that interviewer and respondent may not be sharing the same meaning systems and hence imply different things in their use of words is simply sidestepped in structured interview

research. The problem of meaning is resolved by ignoring it.

The feminist critique

The feminist critique of structured interviewing is difficult to disentangle from the critique launched against quantitative research in general, which was briefly outlined in Chapter 1. However, for many feminist social researchers the structured interview symbolized more readily than other methods the limitations of quantitative research, partly because of its prevalence but also partly because of its nature. By 'its nature' is meant the fact that the structured interview epitomizes the asymmetrical relationship between researcher and subject that is seen as an ingredient of quantitative research: the researcher extracts information from the research subject and gives nothing in return. For example, standard textbook advice of the kind provided in this chapter implies that *rapport* is useful to the interviewer but he or she should guard against becoming too familiar. This means that questions asked by respondents (for example, about the research or about the topic of the research) should be politely but firmly rebuffed on the grounds that too much familiarity should be avoided and because the respondents' subsequent answers may be biased.

This is perfectly valid and appropriate advice from the vantage point of the canons of structured interviewing with its quest for standardization and for valid and reliable data. However, from the perspective of feminism, when women interview women, a wedge is hammered between them that, in conjunction with the implication of a hierarchical relationship between the interviewer and respondent, is incompatible with its values. An impression of exploitation is created, but exploitation of women is precisely what feminist social science seeks to fight against. Hence Cotterill (1992) claims the methods that feminists adopt are crucially important in developing an understanding of women that relies on breaking down the artificial split between researcher and researched. According to Oakley (1981), this entails the interviewer investing her own personal identity in the research relationship, by answering questions, giving support, and sharing knowledge and experience in a way that can lead to long-term friendships with interviewees. Oakley's point is that to act according to the canons of textbook practice would be impossible for a feminist in such a situation. It was this kind of critique of structured interviewing and indeed of quantitative research in general that ushered in a period in which a great many feminist social researchers found qualitative research more compatible with their goals and norms. In terms of interviewing, this trend resulted in a preference for forms of interviewing such as unstructured and semi-structured interviewing and focus groups. These will be the focus of later chapters. However, as noted in Chapter 1, there has been some softening of attitudes towards the role of quantitative research among feminist researchers, although there is still a tendency for qualitative research to remain the preferred research strategy.

K KEY POINTS

- The structured interview is a research instrument that is used to standardize the asking and often the recording of answers in order to keep interviewer-related error to a minimum.

- It can be administered in person or over the telephone.

- It is important to keep to the wording and order of questions when conducting social survey research by structured interview.

- While there is some evidence that interviewers' characteristics can influence respondents' replies, the findings of experiments on this issue are somewhat equivocal.

- Response sets can be damaging to data derived from structured interviews and steps need to be taken to identify respondents exhibiting them.

- The structured interview symbolizes the characteristics of quantitative research that feminist researchers find distasteful: in particular, the lack of reciprocity and the taint of exploitation.

Q QUESTIONS FOR REVIEW

The structured interview

- Why is it important in interviewing for survey research to keep interviewer variability to a minimum?

- How successful is the structured interview in reducing interviewer variability?

- Why might a survey researcher prefer to use a structured rather than an unstructured interview approach for gathering data?

- Why do structured interview schedules typically include mainly closed questions?

Interview contexts

- Are there any circumstances in which it might be preferable to conduct structured interviews with more than one interviewer?
- 'Given the lower cost of telephone interviews as against personal interviews, the former are generally preferable.' Discuss.

Conducting interviews

- Prepare an opening statement for a study of manual workers in a firm, in which access has already been achieved.
- To what extent is rapport an important ingredient of structured interviewing?
- How strong is the evidence that question order can significantly affect answers?
- How strong is the evidence that interviewers' characteristics can significantly affect answers?
- What is the difference between probing and prompting? How important are they and what dangers are lurking with their use?

Other approaches to structured interviewing

- What is the critical incident method and how has it been applied in business and management research?
- Make a list of the projective techniques that could be used in a study of organizational culture and consider how they might be applied.
- How might repertory grids be used in qualitative analysis?

Problems with structured interviewing

- What are response sets and why are they potentially important?
- What are the main issues that lie behind the critique of structured interviewing by feminist researchers?

6

Self-completion questionnaires

CHAPTER GUIDE

Questionnaires that are completed by respondents themselves are one of the main instruments for gathering data using a social survey design, along with the structured interview that was covered in the previous chapter. Probably the most common form is the mail or postal questionnaire. The term *self-completion questionnaire* is often used because it is somewhat more inclusive than *postal questionnaire*. This chapter explores:

- the advantages and disadvantages of the questionnaire in comparison to the structured interview;

- how to address the potential problem of poor response rates, which is often a feature of the postal questionnaire;

- how questionnaires should be designed in order to make answering easier for respondents and less prone to error;

- the use of diaries as a form of self-completion questionnaire.

Introduction

In a very real sense, the bulk of the previous chapter was about questionnaires. The structured interview is in many, if not most respects a questionnaire that is administered by an interviewer. However, there is a tendency, which borders on a convention, to reserve the term 'questionnaire' for contexts in which a battery of usually closed questions is completed by respondents themselves.

Self-completion questionnaire or postal questionnaire?

The *self-completion questionnaire* is sometimes referred to as a *self-administered questionnaire*. The former term will be followed in this book. With a self-completion questionnaire, respondents answer questions by completing the questionnaire themselves. As a method, the self-completion questionnaire can come in several different forms. Probably the most prominent of these forms is the *mail* or *postal questionnaire*, whereby, as its name implies, a questionnaire is sent through the post to the respondent. The latter, following completion of the instrument, is usually asked to return it by post; an alternative form of return is when respondents are requested to deposit their completed questionnaires in a certain location, such as a box in a supervisor's office in a firm or on the top of a cashier's desk in a restaurant or shop. The self-completion questionnaire also covers forms of administration, such as when a researcher hands out questionnaires to all students in a class and collects them back after they have been completed. 'Self-completion questionnaire' is, therefore, a more inclusive term than 'postal questionnaire', though it is probably true to say that the latter is the most prominent form of the self-completion questionnaire.

In the discussion that follows, when points apply to more or less all forms of self-completion questionnaire, this term will be employed. When points apply specifically or exclusively to questionnaires sent through the post, the term 'postal questionnaire' will be used.

Evaluating the self-completion questionnaire in relation to the structured interview

In many ways, the self-completion questionnaire and the structured interview are very similar methods of business research. The obvious difference between them is that, with the self-completion questionnaire, there is no interviewer to ask the questions; instead, respondents must read each question themselves and answer the questions themselves. Beyond this obvious, but central, difference, they are remarkably similar. However, because there is no interviewer in the administration of the self-completion questionnaire, the research instrument has to be especially easy to follow and its questions have to be particularly easy to answer. After all, respondents cannot be trained in the way interviewers can be; nor do they know their ways around a research instrument in the way a 'lone researcher' might.

As a result, self-completion questionnaires, as compared to structured interviews, tend to:

- have fewer open questions, since closed ones tend to be easier to answer;

- have easy-to-follow designs to minimize the risk that the respondent will fail to follow filter questions or will inadvertently omit a question;

- be shorter to reduce the risk of 'respondent fatigue', since it is manifestly easier for a respondent who becomes tired of answering questions in a long questionnaire to consign it to a waste paper bin than to terminate an interview.

Advantages of the self-completion questionnaire over the structured interview

Cheaper to administer

Interviewing can be expensive. The cheapness of the self-completion questionnaire is especially advantageous if you have a sample that is geographically widely dispersed. When this is the case, a postal questionnaire will be much cheaper, because of the time and cost of travel for interviewers. This advantage is obviously less pronounced in connection with telephone interviews, because of the lower costs of telephone charges relative to travel and time spent travelling. But, even in comparison to telephone interviewing, the postal questionnaire enjoys cost advantages.

Quicker to administer

Self-completion questionnaires can be sent out by post or otherwise distributed in very large quantities at the same time. A thousand questionnaires can be sent out by post in one batch, but, even with a team of interviewers, it would take a long time to conduct personal interviews with a sample of that size. However, it is important to bear in mind that the questionnaires do not all come back immediately and that they may take several weeks to be returned. Also, there is invariably a need to send out follow-up letters and/or questionnaires to those who fail to return them initially, an issue that will be returned to below.

Absence of interviewer effects

It was noted in Chapter 5 that various studies have demonstrated that characteristics of interviewers (and respondents) may affect the answers that people give. While the findings from this research are somewhat equivocal in their implications, it has been suggested that such characteristics as ethnicity, gender, and the social background of interviewers may combine to bias the answers that respondents provide. Obviously, since there is no interviewer present when a self-completion questionnaire is being completed, interviewer effects are eliminated. However, this advantage probably has to be regarded fairly cautiously, since few consistent patterns have emerged over the years from research to suggest what kinds of interviewer characteristics bias answers. Probably of greater importance to the presence of an interviewer is the tendency for people to be more likely to exhibit social desirability bias when an interviewer is present. Research by Sudman and Bradburn (1982) suggests that postal questionnaires work better than personal interviews when a question carries the possibility of such bias. There is also evidence to suggest that respondents are less likely to under-report activities that induce anxiety or about which they feel sensitive in self-completion questionnaires than in structured interviews (Tourangeau and Smith 1996).

No interviewer variability

Self-completion questionnaires do not suffer from the problem of interviewers asking questions in a different order or in different ways.

Convenience for respondents

Self-completion questionnaires are more convenient for respondents, because they can complete a questionnaire when they want and at the speed that they want to go.

Disadvantages of the self-completion questionnaire in comparison to the structured interview

Cannot prompt

There is no one present to help respondents if they are having difficulty answering a question. It is always important to ensure that the questions that are asked are clear and unambiguous, but this is especially so with the self-completion questionnaire, since there is no interviewer to help respondents with questions they find difficult to understand and hence to answer. Also, great attention must be paid to ensure that the questionnaire is easy to complete; otherwise questions will be inadvertently omitted if instructions are unclear.

Cannot probe

There is no opportunity to probe respondents to elaborate an answer. Probing can be very important when open-ended questions are being asked. Interviewers are often trained to get more from respondents. However, this problem largely applies to open questions, which are not used a great deal in self-completion questionnaire research.

Cannot ask many questions that are not salient to respondents

Respondents are more likely than in interviews to become tired of answering questions that are not very salient to them, and which they are likely to perceive as boring. Because of the risk of a questionnaire being consigned to a waste paper bin, it is important to avoid including many non-salient questions in a self-completion questionnaire. However, this point suggests that, when a research issue *is* salient to the respondent, a high response rate is feasible (Altschuld and Lower 1984). This means that, when questions are salient, the self-completion questionnaire may be a good choice for researchers, especially when the much lower cost is borne in mind.

Difficulty of asking other kinds of question

In addition to the problem of asking many questions that are not salient to respondents, as previously suggested, it is also important to avoid asking more than a very small number of open questions (because respondents frequently do not want to write a lot). Questions with complex structures, such as filters, should be avoided as far as possible (because respondents often find them difficult to follow).

Questionnaire can be read as a whole

Respondents are able to read the whole questionnaire before answering the first question. When this occurs, none of the questions asked is truly independent of the others. It also means that you cannot be sure that questions have been answered in the correct order. It also means that the problems of question order effects, of the kind discussed in Chapter 5, may occur.

Do not know who answers

With postal questionnaires, you can never be sure whether the right person has answered the questionnaire. If a questionnaire is sent to a certain person in a household, it may be that someone else in that household completes the questionnaire. It is also impossible to have any control over the intrusion of non-respondents (such as other members of a household) in the answering of questions. Similarly, if a questionnaire is sent to a manager in a firm, the task may simply be delegated to someone else. This advantage of the structured interview over the postal questionnaire does not apply when the former is administered by telephone, since the same problem applies.

Cannot collect additional data

With an interview, interviewers might be asked to collect snippets of information about the workplace, firm, manager, or whatever. This is not going to be possible in connection with a postal questionnaire, but if self-completion questionnaires are handed out in an organization, it is more feasible to collect such additional data.

Difficult to ask a lot of questions

As signalled above, because of the possibility of 'respondent fatigue', long questionnaires are rarely feasible. They may even result in a greater tendency for questionnaires not to be answered in the first place, since they can be offputting.

Not appropriate for some kinds of respondent

Respondents whose literacy is limited or whose facility with English is restricted will not be able to answer the questionnaire, as the example in Box 4.9, of the exclusion of manual workers in a cement factory from a questionnaire survey owing to low levels of literacy illustrates. The second of these difficulties cannot be entirely overcome when interviews are being employed, but the difficulties are likely to be greater with postal questionnaires.

Greater risk of missing data

Partially answered questionnaires are more likely, because of a lack of prompting or supervision, than is possible in interviews. It is also easier for respondents actively to decide not to answer a question when on their own than when being asked by an interviewer. For example, questions that appear boring or irrelevant to the respondent may be especially likely to be skipped. If questions are not answered, this creates a problem of *missing data* for the variables that are created.

Lower response rates

One of the most damaging limitations is that surveys by postal questionnaire typically result in lower response rates (see Box 4.5) than comparable interview-based studies. The significance of a response rate is that, unless it can be proven that those who do not participate do not differ from those that do, there is likely to be the risk of bias. In other words, if, as is likely, there are differences between participants and refusals, it is probable that the findings relating to the sample will be affected. If a response rate is low, it seems likely that the risk of bias in the findings will be greater.

The problem of low response rates seems to apply particularly to postal questionnaires. This explains why some researchers who use postal questionnaires as a data collection method tend to employ a multi-strategy research design (see Chapter 22 for a discussion of this kind of research) that includes other methods. This is because they anticipate the likelihood of a low response rate to the questionnaire survey and therefore seek to increase the validity of their research through *triangulation* (see Box 22.1) with other methods. However, there are strategies that can be employed by researchers to improve self-completion questionnaire response rates. These can sometimes include the provision of a small financial incentive. Alternatively, researchers may choose to

administer self-completion questionnaires to samples drawn from a population that is more within their control—for example, by sampling from a group of practising managers who are part-time students at the university where the researcher also works. Box 4.7 describes a survey by self-completion questionnaire that was answered by all students to whom it was administered; the only non-respondents were those who were absent from the lecture. When a self-completion questionnaire is employed in this kind of context, it seems less vulnerable to the problem of a low response rate.

Mangione (1995: 60–1) has provided the following classification of bands of response rate to postal questionnaires:

over 85% excellent

70–85% very good

60–70% acceptable

50–60% barely acceptable

below 50% not acceptable.

Steps to improve response rates to postal questionnaires

Because of the tendency for postal questionnaire surveys to generate lower response rates than comparable structured interview surveys (and the implications this has for the validity of findings), a great deal of thought and research has gone into ways of improving survey response. The following steps are frequently suggested.

- Write a good covering letter explaining the reasons for the research, why it is important, and why the recipient has been selected; mention sponsorship if any, and provide guarantees of confidentiality. The advice provided in Box 5.4 in connection with the kind of letter that might go out in advance of a respondent being asked to be interviewed can be followed to good effect.

- Postal questionnaires should always be accompanied by a stamped addressed envelope or, at the very least, return postage.

- Follow up individuals who do not reply at first, possibly with two or three further mailings. The

---

Practical Tip 👉 *response rates*

As we have explained, response rates are important because, the lower a response rate, the more questions are likely to be raised about the representativeness of the achieved sample. This is likely, however, to be an issue only with randomly selected samples. With samples that are not selected on the basis of a probability sampling method, it could be argued that the response rate is less of an issue, because the sample would not be representative of a population even if everyone participated! Postal questionnaire surveys in particular are often associated with low response rates and, as Mangione's classification illustrates, according to some authorities a response rate of below 50 per cent is not acceptable. On the other hand, many published articles report the results of studies that are well below this level. In an examination of published studies in the field of organizational research in the years 1979–83, Terence Mitchell (1985) found a range of response rates of 30–94 per cent. Bryman (1989*a*: 44) points to two articles in the early 1980s that achieved response rates of 21 per cent and 25 per cent. Moreover,

these articles were published in two of the most highly regarded journals in the field: *Academy of Management Journal* and *Strategic Management Journal*. One of the surveys reported by Cunha and Cooper (2002; see Box 4.9) achieved a sample of just 18 per cent. The point we are making is that, if you achieve a low response rate, do not despair. Although writers like Mangione (1995) may regard response rates of 18 per cent, 21 per cent, and 25 per cent as unacceptable (and he may be right about this judgement), a great deal of published research also achieves low response rates. The key point is to recognize and acknowledge the implications of the possible limitations of a low response rate. On the other hand, if your research is based on a convenience sample, ironically it could be argued that a low response rate is less significant. Many students find postal and other forms of self-completion questionnaire attractive because of their low cost and quick administration. The point of this discussion is that you should not be put off using such techniques because of the prospect of a low response rate.

---

importance of reminders cannot be overstated—they do work. Our preferred and recommended approach is to send out a reminder letter to non-respondents two weeks after the initial mailing, reasserting the nature and aims of the survey and suggesting that the person should contact either the researcher or someone else in the research team to obtain a replacement copy of the questionnaire if the initial mailing has been mislaid or lost. Then, two weeks after that, all further non-respondents should be sent another letter along with a further copy of the questionnaire. These reminders have a demonstrable effect on the response rate. Some writers argue for further mailings of reminder letters to non-respondents. If a response rate is worryingly low, such further mailings would certainly be desirable.

- Unsurprisingly, shorter questionnaires tend to achieve better response rates than longer ones. However, this is not a clear-cut principle, because it is difficult to specify when a questionnaire becomes 'too long'. Also, the evidence suggests that the effect

of the length of questionnaires on response rates cannot be separated very easily from the salience of the topic(s) of the research for respondents and from the nature of the sample. Respondents may be highly tolerant of questionnaires that contain many questions on topics that interest them.

- Clear instructions and an attractive layout improve postal questionnaire response rates. Dillman (1983), as part of what he calls the Total Design Method (TDM) for postal questionnaire research, recommends lower case for questions and upper case for closed-ended answers. However, with the growing use of e-mail and the associated rise of 'netiquette', upper case is increasingly associated with shouting, so that this recommendation may become less desirable as this medium of communication spreads.

- Do not allow the questionnaire to appear unnecessarily bulky. Dillman (1983) recommends a booklet format for the questionnaire and using the photocopier to reduce the size of the questionnaire to fit the booklet format. This approach also gives the impression of a more professional approach.

- As with structured interviewing (see Chapter 5), begin with questions that are more likely to be of interest to the respondent. This advice is linked to the issue of salience (see above) but has particular significance in the context of research that may have limited salience for the respondent.

- There is some controversy about how significant for response rates it is to personalize covering letters, by including the respondent's name and address (Baumgartner and Heberlein 1984). However, one of the features of the TDM approach advocated by Dillman (1983) is that these details are supplied on covering letters and each is individually signed.

- We are inclined to the view that, in general, postal questionnaires should comprise as few open questions as possible, since people are often deterred by the prospect of having to write a lot. In fact, many writers on the subject recommend that open questions are used as little as possible in self-completion questionnaires.

- Providing monetary incentives can be an effective way of increasing the response rate, although it is very unlikely to be an option for most students undertaking project work or research for their dissertation. Incentives are more effective if the money comes with the questionnaire rather than if it is promised once the questionnaire has been returned. Apparently, respondents typically do not cynically take the money and discard the questionnaire! The evidence also suggests that quite small amounts of money have a positive impact on the response rate, but that larger amounts do not necessarily improve the response rate any further.

Several of the steps taken by the Workplace Employee Relations Survey (WERS) research team, mentioned in Box 5.9 (see also Box 2.15), follow the recommendations that we have outlined; this was suggested by the researchers to have improved response rates in both the structured interview and the postal questionnaire surveys. Some advantages and disadvantages of the self-completion questionnaire, as compared to the structured interview, are illustrated by the example provided in Box 6.1. The WERS study employed a research design that combined both of these methods in order to overcome some of the limitations of each and to represent the perspectives of managers, worker representatives, and employees on a range of employment relations issues. Table 6.1 illustrates their combined use of these methods and provides details of the response rates obtained in each case. The main advantage with this triangulated approach is that it enabled a much larger and more diverse sample to be represented within the financial and temporal constraints of the study.

In a sense, the choice between structured interviews or self-administered questionnaires as a method of data collection is an issue that is primarily about mode of administration. The advantages and disadvantages of postal questionnaires versus other modes of questionnaire administration, including telephone interviewing, e-mail, and web-based surveys, are summarized in Table 23.1.

Designing the self-completion questionnaire

Do not cramp the presentation

Because of the well-known problem of low response rates to the postal questionnaire in particular, it is sometimes considered preferable to make the instrument appear as short as possible in order for it to be less likely to deter prospective respondents from answering. However, this is almost always a mistake. As Dillman (1983) observes, an attractive layout is likely to enhance response rates, whereas the kinds of tactics that are sometimes employed to make a questionnaire appear shorter than it really is—such as reducing margins and the space between questions—make it look cramped and thereby unattractive. Also, if questions are too close together, there is a risk that they will be inadvertently omitted.

This is not to say that you should be ridiculously liberal in your use of space, as this does not necessarily

Box 6.1 Combining the use of structured interviews with self-completion questionnaires

Structured interviews can be used in conjunction with self-completion questionnaires to gain understanding of the perspectives of different groups of participants. The Workplace Employee Relations Survey (WERS; formerly known as the Workplace Industrial Relations Survey (WIRS)) (see Boxes 2.15 and 5.9) is an example of a project that has been concerned to use different research methods to reach different categories of respondent.

- The principal method of data collection used is a structured face-to-face interview with the senior member of management at each workplace who deals with industrial relations, employee relations, or personnel matters. These interviews are based on a pre-piloted questionnaire and cover a range of issues such as trade union membership and recognition, patterns of flexible working, training and development, working hours and payment systems, and employee communication. Although the approach is quite structured, the interviewer, who is formally trained, is encouraged to follow up any inconsistent responses within the interview.

- The second group of respondents included in the cross-sectional survey is worker representatives. They are interviewed about the state of employment relations at their workplaces. The researchers explain that, although the majority of questions covered by

the survey are factual, the reason for inclusion of worker representatives is because of differences in frames of reference. 'For example, a manager may state that the workplace operates a staff suggestion scheme, but a worker representative may think it dormant or non-existent if no-one has made a suggestion for several years' (Cully et al. 1999: 7).

- The third group of respondents is employees; in the 1998 survey up to 25 employees were randomly selected from each workplace. This new element to the survey was introduced partly because of a decline in worker representation evident from the 1990 survey. A postal questionnaire was sent to each of these employees. The aim of this part of the study was to understand how employees themselves see the employment relationship and to build up a picture of their experience based on their access to training, their participation in workplace decision making, and their interpretation of the psychological contract.

The WERS survey is designed to combine the views of different groups of participants in order to overcome the limitations and partiality of any one group of respondents. The combined use of structured interviews and self-completion questionnaires enables this aim to be achieved, despite the vast scale of the project.

Table 6.1 Outcomes from the WERS fieldwork 1998 cross-section survey

	Total responses (Number)	Response rate (%)	Average duration (Minutes)
Management (structured interview)	2,191	80	108
Worker representative (structured interview)	947	82	47
Employee (postal questionnaire)	28,237	64	—

Source: adapted from Cully et al. (1999).

provide for an attractive format either and may run the risk of making the questionnaire look bulky. As with so many other issues in business research, a steady course needs to be steered between possible extremes.

Clear presentation

Far more important than making a self-completion questionnaire appear shorter than is the case is to make sure that it has a layout that is easy on the eye, as Dillman emphasizes, and that it facilitates the answering of all questions that are relevant to the respondent. Dillman's recommendation of lower case for questions and upper case for closed answers is an example of one consideration, but at the very least a variety of print styles (for example, different fonts, print sizes, bold, italics, and capitals) can enhance the appearance *but must be used in a consistent manner.* This last point means that you should ensure that you use one style for general instructions, one for headings, perhaps one for specific instructions (e.g., 'Go to question 7'), one for questions, and one for closed-ended answers. Mixing print styles, so that one style is sometimes used for both general instructions and questions, can be very confusing for respondents.

Vertical or horizontal closed answers?

Bearing in mind that most questions in a self-completion questionnaire are likely to be of the closed kind, one consideration is whether to arrange the fixed answers vertically or horizontally. Very often, the nature of the answers will dictate a vertical arrangement because of their sheer length. Many writers prefer a vertical format whenever possible, because, in some cases where either arrangement is feasible, confusion can arise when a horizontal one is employed (Sudman and Bradburn 1982). Consider the following:

What do you think of the CEO's performance in his job since he took over the running of this company? (*Please tick the appropriate response*)

Very ____ Good ____ Fair ____ Poor ____ Very ____
good   poor

There is a risk that, if the questionnaire is being answered in haste, the required tick will be placed in the wrong space—for example, indicating Good when Fair was the intended response. Also, a vertical format more clearly distinguishes questions from answers. To some extent, these potential problems can be obviated through the judicious use of spacing and print variation, but they represent significant considerations. A further reason why vertical alignments can be superior is that they are probably easier to code, especially when pre-codes appear on the questionnaire. Very often, self-completion questionnaires are arranged so that to the right of each question are two columns: one for the column in which data

relating to the question will appear in a data matrix; the other for all the pre-codes. The latter allows the appropriate code to be assigned to a respondent's answer by circling it for later entry into the computer. Thus, the choice would be between the formats presented in Boxes 6.2*a* and 6.2*b*. In the second case, not only is there less ambiguity about where a tick is to be placed; the task of coding is easier. However, when there is to be a battery of questions with identical answer formats, as in a Likert scale, a vertical format will take up too much space. One way of dealing with this kind of questioning is to use abbreviations with an accompanying explanation. An example can be found in Box 6.3. The four items presented in Box 6.3 are taken from an eighteen-item Likert scale designed to measure job satisfaction (Brayfield and Rothe 1951).

Identifying response sets in a Likert scale

One of the advantages of using closed questions is that they can be pre-coded, thus turning the processing of data for computer analysis into a fairly simple

---

Box 6.2*a* Closed question with a horizontal format

What do you think of the CEO's performance in his job since he took over the running of this company? (*Please tick the appropriate response*)

Very __ Good __ Fair __ Poor __ Very __   5 4 3 2 1
good   poor

Box 6.2*b* Closed question with a vertical format

What do you think of the CEO's performance in his job since he took over the running of this company? (*Please tick the appropriate response*)

Very good	____	5
Good	____	4
Fair	____	3
Poor	____	2
Very poor	____	1

Box 6.3 Formatting a Likert scale

In the next set of questions, you are presented with a statement. You are being asked to indicate your level of agreement or disagreement with each statement by indicating whether you: Strongly Agree (SA), Agree (A), are Undecided (U), Disagree (D), or Strongly Disagree (SD).

Please indicate your level of agreement by circling the appropriate response.

23. My job is like a hobby to me.

    SA   A   U   D   SD

24. My job is usually interesting enough to keep me from getting bored.

    SA   A   U   D   SD

25. It seems that my friends are more interested in their jobs.

    SA   A   U   D   SD

26. I enjoy my work more than my leisure time.

    SA   A   U   D   SD

---

task (see Chapter 7 for more on this). However, some thought has to go into the scoring of the items of the kind presented in Box 6.3. We might for example score question 23 as follows:

Strongly agree = 5

Agree = 4

Undecided = 3

Disagree = 2

Strongly disagree = 1

Accordingly, a high score for the item (5 or 4) indicates satisfaction with the job and a low score (1 or 2) indicates low job satisfaction. The same applies to question 24. However, when we come to question 25, the picture is different. Here, agreement indicates a *lack* of job satisfaction. It is disagreement that is indicative of job satisfaction. We would have to reverse the coding of this item, so that:

Strongly agree = 1

Agree = 2

Undecided = 3

Disagree = 4

Strongly disagree = 5

The point of including such items is to identify people who exhibit response sets, like acquiescence (see Chapter 5). If someone were to agree with all eighteen items, when some of them indicated *lack* of job satisfaction, it is likely that the respondent was affected by a response set and the answers are unlikely to provide a valid assessment of job satisfaction for that person.

Clear instructions about how to respond

Always be clear about how you want respondents to indicate their replies when answering closed questions. Are they supposed to place a tick by or circle or underline the appropriate answer, or are they supposed to delete inappropriate answers? Also, in many cases it is feasible for the respondent to choose more than one answer—is this acceptable to you? If it is not, you should indicate this in your instructions, for example:

(Please choose the ONE answer that best represents your views by placing a tick in the appropriate box).

If you do not make this clear and if some respondents choose more than one answer, you will have to treat their replies as if they had not answered. This possibility increases the risk of missing data from some respondents.

If it is acceptable to you for more than one category to be chosen you need to make this clear, for example:

(Please choose all answers that represent your views by placing a tick in the appropriate boxes).

It is a common error for such instructions to be omitted and for respondents either to be unsure about how to reply or to make inappropriate selections.

Keep question and answers together

This is a simple and obvious, though often transgressed, requirement—namely, that you should never split up a question so that it appears on two separate pages. A common error is to have some space left at the bottom of a page into which the question can be slotted but for the closed answers to appear on the next page. Doing so carries the risk of the respondent forgetting to answer the question or providing an answer in the wrong group of closed answers (a problem that is especially likely when a series of questions with a common answer format is being used, as with a Likert scale).

Diaries as a form of self-completion questionnaire

When the researcher is specifically interested in pre-cise estimates of different kinds of behaviour, the diary warrants serious consideration, though it is still a relatively underused method. Unfortunately, the term 'diary' has somewhat different meanings in business research (see Box 6.4). It is the first of the three meanings—what H. Elliott (1997) calls the *re-searcher-driven diary*—that is the focus of attention here, especially in the context of its use in relation to quantitative research. When employed in this way, the researcher-driven diary functions in a similar way to the self-completion questionnaire. Equally, it could be said that the researcher-driven diary is an al-ternative method of data collection to observation. It can be thought of as the equivalent of structured ob-servation (see Chapter 8) in the context of research questions that are framed in terms of quantitative re-search, or of ethnography (see Chapter 14) in the context of research questions in terms of qualitative research.

Corti (1993) distinguishes between 'structured di-aries' and 'free text diaries'. Either may be employed by quantitative researchers. The research on man-agers and their jobs by Stewart (1967) is an illustra-tion of the structured kind of diary (see Box 6.5). The diary has the general appearance of a questionnaire with largely closed questions. The kind of diary employed in this research is often referred to as a

---

Box 6.4 The diary in business research

There are three major ways in which the term 'diary' has been employed in the context of business research.

- *The diary as a method of data collection.* Here the researcher devises a structure for the diary and then asks a sample of diarists to complete the instruments so that they record what they do more or less contemporaneously with their activities. H. Elliott (1997) refers to this kind of use of the diary as *researcher-driven diaries*. Such diaries can be employed for the collection of data within the context of both quantitative and qualitative research. Sometimes, the collection of data in this manner is supplemented by a personal interview in which the diarist is asked questions about such things as what he or she meant by certain remarks. This *diary-interview*, as it is often referred to (Zimmerman and Wieder 1977), is usually employed when diarists record their behaviour in prose form rather than simply indicating the amount of time spent on different kinds of activity.

- *The diary as a document.* The diary in this context is written spontaneously by the diarist and not at the behest of a researcher. Diaries in this sense are often used by historians but have some potential for business researchers working on issues that are of social scientific significance. As John Scott (1990) observes, the diary in this sense often shades into autobiography. Diaries as documents will be further addressed in Chapter 18.

- *The diary as a log of the researcher's activities.* Researchers sometimes keep a record of what they do at different stages as an *aide mémoire*. For example, the famous social anthropologist Malinowski (1967) kept an infamous log of his activities ('infamous' because it revealed his distaste for the people he studied and his inappropriate involvement with females). This kind of diary often shades into the writing of field notes by ethnographers, about which more is written in Chapter 14.

Box 6.5 A diary study of managers and their jobs

Stewart's (1967) now classic study of managerial time use focused on:

- the amount of time managers spent on particular activities;
- the frequency with which they undertook particular tasks.

'The diary method was chosen instead of observation because the research aimed to study more than 100 managers in a large number of companies. This aim could not be achieved by observation without a large team of observers' (1967: 7). In addition to recording the nature of the task that was being undertaken (such as paperwork, telephone calls, discussions, and so on) managers were asked to record in their diary:

1 the duration of the incident (hours and minutes);

2 where the work was done (own office, travelling, etc.);

3 who else was involved (boss, secretary, colleagues, etc.)

The diary entry took the form of a grid, which was filled in by ticking the appropriate boxes, which were subsequently coded. A distinction was made between episodes of work lasting five minutes or more, and 'fleeting contacts' of less than five minutes. The latter were recorded separately from the main section of the diary so managers could record as many of these short incidents as possible. Each day, the managers completed in addition to the main diary entry a form asking them to describe the three activities that had taken up the most work time. Each week, the managers filled in a form designed to check how well they had kept the diary, asking for example 'how often did you fill in the diary?' One hundred and sixty managers kept diaries for a period of four weeks, a time period which Stewart considered was long enough to gain an impression of variations in the job but not so long that managers would lose interest in the exercise.

'time-use' diary, in that it is designed so that diarists can record more or less contemporaneously the amount of time engaged in certain activities, such as time spent travelling, doing paperwork, in committee meetings, and so on. Estimates of the amount of time spent in different activities are often regarded as more accurate, because the events are less subject to memory problems or to the tendency to round up or down. Structured diaries are also regarded as more accurate in tracking events as they occur, as the example in Box 6.5 illustrates. However, the diary method is more intrusive than answering a questionnaire and it could be argued that it causes changes in behaviour or behavioural awareness of an issue. For example, in their study of psychological contract breach, Conway and Briner (2002; see Box 6.6) note that their research design may have encouraged respondents to report very minor breaches of the psychological contract that they perhaps otherwise would not have regarded as significant. They thus conclude that 'it is a matter of debate as to what can be considered as lying inside or outside a psychological contract' (2002: 299).

An example of a free-text diary is provided by Bowey and Thorpe's (1986; see Box 18.2) study of coal miners' attitudes to incentive schemes. Respondents were asked to keep a daily written record of their work and work relationships and to explain how the incentive bonus scheme affected them. The diary method allowed Bowey and Thorpe to collect a variety of information from the written prose relating to the coal miners' work activity over a three-month period. The diary method was used in conjunction with several other methods of data collection as part of an overall triangulated approach, including a questionnaire survey of managers, employees, and employee representatives in sixty-three firms. One of several advantages of the diary method for this research was that it provided contextual information about factors that had an impact on the bonus scheme, such as machinery faults that caused delay and affected productivity. This kind of information would probably have been much more difficult to glean from questionnaires or even from the semi-structured interviews that also formed part of the study.

Box 6.6 A diary study of responses to psychological contract breach

Conway and Briner (2002) suggest that one of the limitations of existing studies of psychological contract breach—when an organization breaks a promise made to the employee—stems from the methods that are used for study—that is, questionnaire surveys. In particular, 'breaches of an employee's psychological contract are *events* that happen at work or in relation to work. For accurate measurement they therefore need to be assessed soon after they occur' (2002: 288).

This led the researchers to conduct a daily diary study in order to develop a better understanding of the psychological contract. The sample comprised:

- 21 managers who worked for a UK bank, and;
- a convenience sample of 24 participants who were part-time M.Sc. students at Birkbeck College, where both of the researchers were employed.

All 45 participants were in employment, mostly in professional occupations. The researchers anticipated that exceeded promises would be construed positively whereas broken promises would be construed negatively.

The diary was completed over ten consecutive working days. Participants were posted their diary booklets and asked to complete their daily diary schedules immediately at the end of each working day. The first three pages of the daily diary booklet provided instructions on how to complete the diary. (2002: 291)

On each occasion, participants were first asked how they had felt overall at work on that particular day; items were assessed on a 6-point scale from 'not at all' to 'all of the time'. They were then asked (*a*) whether the organization had broken any promises to them on that day and (*b*) if the organization had exceeded any promises during the day. If a promise had either been broken or exceeded, they were asked to provide written details of the event and to complete emotion checklists by responding to a list of adjectives that represented possible reactions, such as 'resentment' (reaction to broken promise) and 'excitement' (reaction to exceeded promise).

The research suggests a far greater incidence of psychological contract breach than previous survey studies had suggested. This, suggest the authors, may be in part attributable to the method used, in particular the sensitivity of the diary method in picking up events as they occur on a day-to-day basis.

Using free-text recording of behaviour carries the same kinds of problems as those associated with coding answers to structured interview open questions—namely, the time-consuming nature of the exercise and the increased risks associated with the coding of answers. However, the free-text approach is less likely to be problematic when, as in the case of Bowey and Thorpe's research, diarists can be instructed about what information is required and the kinds of behaviour being studied are specific, such as that relating to the operation of an incentive bonus scheme. It would be much more difficult to code free-text entries relating to a more general arena of types of behaviour of the kind studied by Conway and Briner (2002).

Corti (1993) recommends that the person preparing the diary should:

- provide explicit instructions for diarists;
- be clear about the time periods within which behaviour is to be recorded—i.e. day, twenty-four hours, week;

- provide a model of a completed section of a diary;
- provide checklists of 'items, events, or behaviour' that can jog people's memory—but the list should not become too daunting in length or complexity;
- include fixed blocks of time or columns showing when the designated activities start and finish (for example, diaries of the kind used by Stewart (1967), which show how managers spend their time).

Advantages and disadvantages of the diary as a method of data collection

The two studies that have been used to illustrate the use of diaries also suggest its potential advantages.

- When fairly precise estimates of the frequency and/or amount of time spent in different forms of behaviour are required, the diary may provide more valid and reliable data than questionnaire data.

- When information about the sequencing of different types of behaviour is required, it is likely to perform better than questionnaires or interviews.
- The first two advantages could be used to suggest that structured observation would be just as feasible, but structured observation is probably less appropriate for producing data on behaviour that is personally sensitive, such as sexual behaviour. Moreover, although data on such behaviour can be collected by structured interview, it is likely that respondents will be less willing to divulge personal details. If such information were collected by questionnaire, there is greater risk of recall and rounding problems (see the first point in this list).

On the other hand, diaries may suffer from the following problems.

- They tend to be more expensive than personal interviews (because of the costs associated with recruiting diarists and of checking that diaries are being properly completed).
- Diaries can suffer from a process of attrition, as people decide they have had enough of the task of completing a diary.
- This last point raises the possibility that diarists become less diligent over time about their record keeping.
- There is sometimes failure to record details sufficiently quickly, so that memory recall problems set in.

However, diary researchers argue that the resulting data are more accurate than the equivalent data based on interviews or questionnaires.

K KEY POINTS

- Many of the recommendations relating to the self-completion questionnaire apply equally or almost equally to the structured interview, as has been mentioned on several occasions.
- Closed questions tend to be used in survey research rather than open ones. Coding is a particular problem when dealing with answers to open questions.
- Structured interviews and self-completion questionnaires both have their respective advantages and disadvantages, but a particular problem with questionnaires sent by post is that they frequently produce a low response rate. However, steps can be taken to boost response rates for postal questionnaires.
- Presentation of closed questions and the general layout constitute important considerations for the self-completion questionnaire.
- The researcher-driven diary was also introduced as a possible alternative to using questionnaires and interviews when the research questions are very specifically concerned with aspects of people's behaviour.

Q **QUESTIONS FOR REVIEW**

Self-completion questionnaire or postal questionnaire?

• Are the self-completion questionnaire and the postal questionnaire the same thing?

Evaluating the self-completion questionnaire in relation to the structured interview

• 'The low response rates frequently achieved in research with postal questionnaires mean that the structured interview is invariably a more suitable choice.' Discuss.

• What steps can be taken to boost postal questionnaire response rates?

Designing the self-completion questionnaire

• Why are self-completion questionnaires usually made up mainly of closed questions?

• Why might a vertical format for presenting closed questions be preferable to a horizontal format?

Diaries as a form of self-completion questionnaire

• What are the main kinds of diary used in the collection of business research data?

• Are there any circumstances when the diary approach might be preferable to the use of a self-completion questionnaire?

Asking questions

[handwritten annotation: vignette 方法三、场景]

CHAPTER GUIDE

This chapter is concerned with the considerations that are involved in asking questions that are used in structured interviews and questionnaires of the kinds discussed in the two previous chapters. As such, it continues the focus upon survey research that began in Chapter 4 and moves on to the next stage in the process that we outlined in Figure 4.1. The chapter explores:

• the issues involved in deciding whether or when to use open or closed questions;

• the different kinds of question that can be asked in structured interviews and questionnaires;

• rules to bear in mind when designing questions;

• vignette questions in which respondents are presented with a scenario and are asked to reflect on the scenario;

• the importance of piloting questions;

• the possibility of using questions that have been used in previous survey research.

Introduction

To many people, how to ask questions represents the crux of considerations surrounding the use of survey instruments such as the structured interview or the self-completion questionnaire. As the previous two chapters have sought to suggest, there is much more to the design and administration of such research instruments than how best to phrase questions. However, there is no doubt that the issue of how questions should be asked is a crucial concern for the survey researcher and it is not surprising that this aspect of designing survey instruments has been a major focus of attention over the years and preoccupies many practising researchers.

Open or closed questions?

One of the most significant considerations for many researchers is whether to ask a question in an open or closed format. This distinction was first introduced in Chapter 5. The issue of whether to ask a question in an open or closed format is relevant to the design of both structured interview and self-administered questionnaire research.

With an open question respondents are asked a question and can reply however they wish. With a closed question they are presented with a set of fixed alternatives from which they have to choose an appropriate answer. All of the questions in Box 5.5 are of the closed kind. So too are the Likert-scale items in Boxes 3.3, 3.4, 6.2*a*, and 6.2*b*; these form a particular kind of closed question. What, then, are some of the advantages and limitations of these two types of question format?

Open questions

Open questions present both advantages and disadvantages to the survey researcher, though, as the following discussion suggests, the problems associated with the processing of answers to open questions tend to mean that closed questions are more likely to be used.

Advantages

Although survey researchers typically prefer to use closed questions, open questions do have certain advantages over closed ones, as outlined in the list below.

- Respondents can answer in their own terms. They are not forced to answer in the same terms as those foisted on them by the closed answers.

- They allow unusual responses to be derived. Replies that the survey researcher may not have contemplated (and that would therefore not form the basis for fixed-choice alternatives) are possible.

- The questions do not suggest certain kinds of answer to respondents. Therefore, respondents' levels of knowledge and understanding of issues can be tapped. The salience of issues for respondents can also be explored.

- They are useful for exploring new areas or ones in which the researcher has limited knowledge.

- They are useful for generating fixed-choice format answers. This is a point that will be returned to below.

Disadvantages

However, open questions present problems for the survey researcher, as the following list reveals.

- They are time-consuming for interviewers to administer. Interviewees are likely to talk for longer than is usually the case with a comparable closed question.

- Answers have to be 'coded'. This is very time-consuming. For each open question it entails reading through answers, deriving themes that can be employed to form the basis for codes, and then going through the answers again so that the answers can be coded for entry into a computer spreadsheet. The process is essentially identical to that involved in *content analysis* and is sometimes called *post-coding* to distinguish it from *pre-coding*, whereby the researcher designs a coding frame in advance of administering a survey instrument and often includes the pre-codes in the questionnaire (as in Box 7.2). However, in addition to being time-consuming, post-coding can be an unreliable process, because it can introduce the possibility of variability in the coding of answers and therefore of measurement error (and hence lack of validity). This is a form of data processing error (see Figure 4.8). Box 7.1 deals with aspects of the coding of open questions.

- They require greater effort from respondents. Respondents are likely to talk for longer than would be the case for a comparable closed question, or, in the case of a self-completion questionnaire, would need to write for much longer. Therefore, it is often suggested that open questions have limited utility in the context of self-completion questionnaires. Because of the greater effort involved, many prospective respondents are likely to be put off by the prospect of having to write extensively, which may exacerbate the problem of low response

rates with postal questionnaires in particular (see Chapter 6).

- There is the possibility in research based on structured interviews of variability between interviewers in the recording of answers. This possibility is likely to arise as a result of the difficulty of writing down verbatim what respondents say to interviewers. The obvious solution is to use a tape recorder; however, this may not be practicable, for example, in a noisy environment. Also, the transcription of answers to tape-recorded open questions is immensely time-consuming and adds additional costs to a survey. The problem of transcription is one continually faced by qualitative researchers using semi-structured and unstructured interviews (see Chapter 15).

Closed questions

The advantages and disadvantages of closed questions are in many respects implied in some of the considerations relating to open questions.

Advantages

Closed questions offer the following advantages to researchers.

Box 7.1 Coding a very open question

Coding an open question usually entails reading and rereading transcripts of respondents' replies and formulating distinct themes in their replies. A *coding frame* then needs to be designed that identifies the types of answer associated with each question and their respective codes (i.e. numbers). A coding schedule may also be necessary to keep a record of rules to be followed in the identification of certain kinds of answer in terms of a theme. The numbers allocated to each answer can then be used in the computer processing of the data.

Foddy (1993) reports the results of an exercise in which he asked a small sample of his students 'Your father's occupation is (was)...?' and requested three details: nature of business; size of business; and whether owner or employee. In answer to the size of business issue, the

replies were particularly variable in kind, including: 'big', 'small', 'very large', '3,000 acres', 'family', 'multinational', '200 people', and 'Philips'. The problem here is obvious: you simply cannot compare and therefore aggregate people's replies. In a sense, the problem is only partly to do with the difficulty of coding an open question. It is also due to a lack of specificity in the question. If, instead, Foddy had asked 'How many employees are (were) there in your father's organization?', a more comparable set of answers should have been forthcoming. Whether his students would have known this information is, of course, yet another issue. However, the exercise does illustrate the potential problems of asking an open question, particularly one like this that lacks a clear reference point for gauging size.

- It is easy to process answers. For example, the respondent in a self-completion questionnaire or the interviewer using a structured interview schedule will place a tick or circle an answer for the appropriate response. The appropriate code can then be almost mechanically derived from the selected answer, since the pre-codes are placed to the side of the fixed-choice answers. See Box 7.2 for an example based on Box 6.2b.

- Closed questions enhance the comparability of answers, making it easier to show the relationship between variables and to make comparisons between respondents or types of respondents. For example, in the research described in Box 7.3, Guest and Dewe were able to generate a contingency table on the basis of their pre-coding of respondents' answers. Although contingency tables can also be generated by post-coding respondents' answers to open questions, with post-coding there is always a problem of knowing how far respondents' answers that receive a certain code are genuinely comparable. As previously noted, the assignment of codes to people's answers may be unreliable (see the sixth point in Box 5.2). Checks are necessary to ensure that there is a good deal of agreement between coders and that coders do not change their coding conventions over time. Closed questions essentially circumvent this problem.

- Closed questions may clarify the meaning of a question for respondents. Sometimes, respondents may not be clear about what a question is getting at and the availability of answers may help to clarify the situation for them.

- Closed questions are easy for interviewers and/or respondents to complete. Precisely because interviewers and respondents are not expected to write extensively and instead have to place ticks or circle answers, closed questions are easier and quicker to complete.

- In interviews, closed questions reduce the possibility of variability in the recording of answers in structured interviewing. As noted in Chapter 5, if interviewers do not write down exactly what respondents say to them when answering questions, a source of bias and hence of invalidity is in prospect. Closed questions reduce this possibility, though there is still the potential problem that interviewers may have to *interpret* what is said to them in order to assign answers to a category.

Box 7.2 Processing a closed question

What do you think of the CEO's performance in his job since he took over the running of this company?

(*Please tick the appropriate response*)

Very good	——	5
Good	✓	④
Fair	——	3
Poor	——	2
Very poor	——	1

Table 7.1 A contingency table to show employee identity

	Union members (%)	Non-unionists (%)	Total sample (%)
Dual identity	16.9	2.5	9.7
Union identity	27.1	1.2	14.2
Management identity	11.1	35.7	23.4
No identity	44.9	60.6	52.8
Of which: Alienated	*8.0*	*22.1*	*15.1*

Source: adapted from Guest and Dewe (1991).

Box 7.3 Coding closed questions to create a contingency table

In order to establish whether employees were more strongly committed to their company or their union, Guest and Dewe (1991) selected a sample of 716 workers at random from three electronics plants in the South-east of England as the basis for a self-completion questionnaire survey. Just under half of the sample belonged to a trade union. The questions were developed and piloted specifically for the survey and covered a broad range of issues, including:

> *management role*—'How well do the decisions of local management on this site reflect your opinions?' Responses were on a five-point scale from 'very well' to 'I do not expect anything from the management';

union role—'How far are the unions successful in properly representing the interests of employees at plant *X*?' Responses were on a five-point scale from 1 = very successful to 5 = unsuccessful'.

The results were used to construct a *contingency table* (Table 7.1). This included, on the one hand, employees who perceived both management and unions to represent their interests very well or fairly well (dual identity), and, at the other extreme, employees who perceived that neither management nor unions represented their interests at all (alienated). This showed that the majority of employees did not identify either with the union or with the company.

Disadvantages

However, closed questions exhibit certain disadvantages.

- There is a loss of spontaneity in respondents' answers. There is always the possibility that they might come up with interesting replies that are not covered by the fixed answers that are provided. One solution to this possible problem is to ensure that an open question is used to generate the categories (see Box 7.4). Also, there may be a good case for including a possible response category of 'Other' and to allow respondents to indicate what they mean by this category.

- It can be difficult to make forced-choice answers mutually exclusive. The fixed answers with which respondents are provided should not overlap. If they do overlap, respondents will not know which one to choose and so will arbitrarily select one or the other or alternatively may tick both answers. If a respondent were to tick two or more answers when one is required, it would mean that you would have to treat the respondent's answer as missing data, since you would not know which of the ticked answers represented the true one. One of the most frequently encountered forms

of this problem can be seen in the following age bands:

18–30
30–40
40–50
50–60
60 and over.

In which band would a 40-year-old position him- or herself?

- It is difficult to make forced-choice answers exhaustive. All possible answers should really be catered for, although in practice this may be difficult to achieve, since this rule may result in excessively long lists of possible answers. Again, a category of 'Other' may be desirable to provide a wide range of answers.

- There may be variation among respondents in the interpretation of forced-choice answers. There is always a problem when asking a question that certain terms may be interpreted differently by respondents. If this is the case, then validity will be jeopardized. The presence of forced-choice answers can exacerbate this possible problem, because there may be variation in the understanding of key terms in the answers.

disparity

Box 7.4 A comparison of results for a closed and an open question

Schuman and Presser (1981) conducted an experiment to determine how far responses to closed questions can be improved by asking the questions first as open questions and then developing categories of reply from respondents' answers. They asked a question about what people look for in work in both open and closed format. Different samples were used. They found considerable disparities between the two sets of answers (40 per cent of the open format categories were not capable of being subsumed by the closed format answers). They then revised the closed categories to reflect the answers they had received from people's open-ended answers. They readministered the open question and the revised closed question to two large samples of Americans. The question and the answers they received are as follows.

This next question is on the subject of work. People look for different things in a job. Which one of the following five things do you most prefer in a job? [closed question]. What would you most prefer in a job? [open question]

Closed format		Open format	
Answer	**%**	**Answer**	**%**
Work that pays well	13.2	Pay	16.7
Work that gives a feeling of accomplishment	31.0	Feeling of accomplishment	14.5
Work where there is not too much supervision and you make most decisions yourself	11.7	Control of work	4.6
Work that is pleasant and people are nice to work with	19.8	Pleasant work	14.5
Work that is steady + little chance of being laid off	20.3	Security	7.6
	96% of sample		*57.9% of sample*
		Opportunity for promotion	1.0
		Short hours/lots of free time	1.6
		Working conditions	3.1
		Benefits	2.3
		Satisfaction/liking a job	15.6
Other/DK/NA	4.0	Other responses	18.3

With the revised form for the closed question, Schuman and Presser were able to find a much higher proportion of the sample whose answers to the open question corresponded to the closed one. They argue that the new closed question was superior to its predecessor and is also superior to the open question. However, it is still disconcerting that only 58 per cent of respondents answering the open question could be subsumed under the same categories as those answering the closed one. Also, the distributions are somewhat different: for example, twice as many respondents answer in terms of a feeling of accomplishment with the closed format than with the open one. Nonetheless, the experiment demonstrates the desirability of generating forced-choice answers from open questions.

- Closed questions may be irritating to respondents when they are not able to find a category that they feel applies to them.

- In interviews, a large number of closed questions may make it difficult to establish rapport, because the respondent and interviewer are less likely to engage with each other in a conversation. The interview is more likely to have an impersonal feel to it. However, because it is difficult to determine the extent to which rapport is a desirable attribute of structured interviewing (see Chapter 5), this is not necessarily too much of a problem.

Types of question

It is worth bearing in mind that, when you are employing a structured interview or self-completion questionnaire, you will probably be asking several different types of question. There are various ways of classifying these, but here are some prominent types of question.

- *Personal factual questions*. These are questions that ask the respondent to provide *personal information*, such as age, gender, education, employment status, income, and so on. This kind of question also includes questions about *behaviour*. Such factual questions may have to rely on the respondents' memories, as when they are asked about such things as frequency of individual performance appraisal meetings, how often they visit certain shops, or when they last had any time off work. For example, in the study by Deery, Iverson, and Walsch (2002; see Box 7.8), in addition to being asked to provide demographic details, telephone call centre workers were asked about the number of calls they took on an average day and the average length of calls taken.

- *Factual questions about others*. Like the previous type of question, this one asks for personal information about others, sometimes in combination with the respondent. An example of such a question would be one about team performance, which would require respondents to consider their own productivity (measured in terms of such things as daily work rate, frequency of lateness for work, and so on) in conjunction with the productivity of fellow team members. However, a criticism of such research is precisely that it relies on the possibly distorted views of respondents concerning their own and others' behaviour. Like personal factual questions, an element of reliance on memory recall is likely to be present.

- *Informant factual questions*. Sometimes, we place people who are interviewed or who complete a questionnaire in the position of informants rather than as respondents answering questions about themselves. This kind of question can also be found in such contexts as when people are asked about such things as the size of the firm for which they work, who owns it, whether it employs certain technologies, and whether it has certain specialist functions. Such questions are essentially about characteristics of an entity of which they have knowledge, in this case, a firm. However, informant factual questions may also be concerned with behaviour; for example, in the study by Deery, Iverson, and Walsch (2002; see Box 7.8), telephone call centre employees were asked about the demands placed upon them by customers and priorities of the call centre management.

- *Questions about attitudes*. Questions about attitudes are very common in both structured interview and self-completion questionnaire research. The Likert scale is one of the most frequently encountered formats for measuring attitudes. Box 7.5 provides a number of different ways of presenting response formats for Likert scales and other types of scales.

- *Questions about beliefs*. Respondents are frequently asked about their beliefs. Another form of asking questions about beliefs is when respondents are asked whether they believe that certain matters are true or false—for example, a question asking whether the respondent believes the UK is better off as a result of being a member of the European Community. Or a survey about workplace stress might ask respondents to indicate whether they believe that the incidence of stress-related absence from work is increasing.

- *Questions about normative standards and values*. Respondents may be asked to indicate what principles of behaviour influence them or they hold dear. The elicitation of such norms of behaviour is likely to have considerable overlap with questions about attitudes and beliefs, since norms and values can be construed as having elements of both.

- *Questions about knowledge*. Questions can sometimes be employed to 'test' respondents' knowledge in an area. For example, a study of health and safety in

Semantic

Box 7.5 Response formats for scales

There are several different ways of presenting the response formats for the individual items that make up a scale like a Likert scale. The kind used in Box 6.3 is an example of a verbal format (see below).

Binary response format:

My job is usually interesting enough to keep me from getting bored

        Agree _____   Disagree _____

(This format is sometimes elaborated to include a 'don't know' response)

Numerical response format:

My job is usually interesting enough to keep me from getting bored

        5   4   3   2   1

(where 5 means Strongly agree and 1 means Strongly disagree)

Verbal format:

My job is usually interesting enough to keep me from getting bored

Strongly __ Agree __ Undecided __ Disagree __ Strongly __
agree   disagree

Bipolar numerical response format:

 I love my job   7   6   5   4   3   2   1   I hate my job

Frequency format:

My job is usually interesting enough to keep me from getting bored

All of ___ Often ___ Fairly ___ Occasionally ___ None ___
the   often   of the
time   time

The bipolar numerical response format is used in connection with *semantic differential* scales. With such scales, the respondent is given lists of pairs of adjectives. Each pair represent adjectival opposites (for example, masculine/feminine). A well-known example is the Fielder (1967) least-preferred co-worker (LPC) scale. With this scale, each leader in a sample of leaders is given a set of between sixteen and twenty-five pairs of adjectives and is asked to describe with whom he or she has least preferred co-working. Examples of the pairs are:

Pleasant	8	7	6	5	4	3	2	1	Unpleasant
Friendly	8	7	6	5	4	3	2	1	Unfriendly
Rejecting	1	2	3	4	5	6	7	8	Accepting
Distant	1	2	3	4	5	6	7	8	Close

Each leader's score on each pair is aggregated to give a total score for that leader. Fiedler argued that leaders who describe their least-preferred co-workers in largely positive terms (pleasant, friendly, accepting, close) were predominantly relationship-oriented; those who described their least-preferred co-workers in largely negative terms (unpleasant, unfriendly, rejecting, distant) were predominantly task-oriented.

---

the workplace might ask questions about the legal requirements that companies must comply with, in order to test respondents' awareness of these issues.

Most structured interview schedules and self-completion questionnaires will comprise more than one, and often several, of these types of question. It is important to bear in mind the distinction between different types of question.

There are a number of reasons for this.

• It is useful to keep the distinctions in mind because they force you to clarify in your own mind what you are asking about, albeit in rather general terms.

• It will help to guard against asking questions in an inappropriate format. For example, a Likert scale is entirely unsuitable for asking factual questions about behaviour.

• When building scales like a Likert scale, it is best not to mix different types of question. For example, attitudes and beliefs sound similar and you may be tempted to use the same format for mixing questions about them. However, it is best not to do this and instead to have separate scales for attitudes and beliefs. If you mix them, the questions cannot really be measuring the same thing, so that measurement validity is threatened.

Rules for designing questions

Over the years, numerous rules (and rules of thumb) have been devised in connection with the dos and don'ts of asking questions. In spite of this, it is one of the easiest areas for making mistakes. There are three simple rules of thumb as a starting point; beyond that the rules specified below act as a means of avoiding further pitfalls.

General rules of thumb

Always bear in mind your research questions

The questions that you will ask in your self-completion questionnaire or structured interview should always be geared to answering your research questions. This first rule of thumb has at least two implications. First, it means that you should make sure that you ask questions that relate to your research questions. Ensure, in other words, that the questionnaire questions you ask will allow your research questions to be addressed. You will definitely not want to find out at a late stage that you forgot to include some crucial questions. Secondly, it means that there is little point in asking questions that do not relate to your research questions. It is also not fair to waste your respondents' time answering questions that are of little value.

What do you want to know?

Rule of thumb number two is decide exactly what it is you want to know. Consider the seemingly harmless question:

Do you have a car?

What is it that the question is seeking to tap? Is it car ownership? If it is car ownership, the question is inadequate, largely because of the ambiguity of the word 'have'. The question can be interpreted as: personally owning a car; having access to a car in a household; and 'having' a company car or a car for business use. Thus, an answer of 'yes' may or may not be indicative of car ownership. If you want to know whether your respondent owns a car, ask him or her

directly about this matter. Similarly, there is nothing wrong with the question:

How many people does your company employ?

However, this question does not clarify whether you are interested in the workplace, the company, or in the business as a whole—which may include a number of subsidiary companies. In addition, it does not distinguish between full- and part-time workers, or temporary and permanent employees. Hence, if you are interested in knowing how many full-time or full-time equivalent employees there are, then you need to specify this. Similarly, if you are interested only in people who are employed directly by the firm (rather than temporary or contract staff who work on the premises), you need to make this clear in your question.

How would *you* answer it?

Rule of thumb number three is put yourself in the position of the respondent. Ask yourself the question and try to work out how you would reply. If you do this, there is at least the possibility that the ambiguity that is inherent in the 'Do you have a car?' question will manifest itself and its inability to tap car ownership would become apparent. Let us say as well that there is a follow-up question to the previous one:

Have you driven the car this week?

Again, this looks harmless, but if you put yourself in the role of a respondent, it will be apparent that the phrase 'this week' is vague. Does it mean the last seven days or does it mean the week in which the questioning takes place, which will, of course, be affected by such things as whether the question is being asked on a Monday or a Friday? In part, this issue arises because the question designer has not decided what the question is about. Equally, however, a moment's reflection in which you put yourself in the position of the respondent might reveal the difficulty of answering this question.

Taking account of these rules of thumb and the following rules about asking questions may help you to avoid the more obvious pitfalls.

Specific rules when designing questions

Avoid ambiguous terms in questions

Avoid terms such as 'often' and 'regularly' as measures of frequency. They are very ambiguous, because respondents will operate with different frames of reference when employing them. Sometimes their use is unavoidable, but when there is an alternative that allows actual frequency to be measured, this will nearly always be preferable. So, a question like

How often do you usually visit the cinema?

Very often ——
Quite often ——
Not very often ——
Not at all ——

suffers from the problem that, with the exception of 'not at all', the terms in the response categories are ambiguous. Instead, try to ask about actual frequency, such as:

How frequently do you usually visit the cinema? (*Please tick whichever category comes closest to the number of times you visit the cinema.*)
More than once a week ——
Once a week ——
2 or 3 times a month ——
Once a month ——
A few times a year ——
Once a year ——
Less than once a year ——

Alternatively, you might simply ask respondents about the number of times they have visited the cinema in the previous four weeks.

Words like 'colleagues' or 'management' are also ambiguous, because people will have different notions of who their colleagues are or who makes up the management. As previously noted, words like 'have' can also be sources of ambiguity.

It is also important to bear in mind that certain common words, such as 'quality' and 'customer', mean different things to different people. For some, quality is dependent on the purpose of the product, whereas for others it is an absolute measure of the standard of the product. Similarly, some people refer to colleagues from different departments as customers, whereas others take the word to mean those external to the organization who consume the products or services that the firm provides. In such cases, it will be necessary to define what you mean by such terms.

Avoid long questions

It is commonly believed that long questions are undesirable. In a structured interview the interviewee can lose the thread of the question and in a self-completion questionnaire the respondent may be tempted to omit such questions or to skim them and therefore not give them sufficient attention. However, Sudman and Bradburn (1982) have suggested that this advice applies better to attitude questions than to ones that ask about behaviour. They argue that, when the focus is on behaviour, longer questions have certain positive features in interviews—for example, they are more likely to provide memory cues and they facilitate recall because of the time taken to complete the question. However, by and large, the general advice to keep questions short is the main piece of advice to be followed.

Avoid double-barrelled questions

Double-barrelled questions are ones that in fact ask about two things. The problem with this kind of question is that it leaves respondents unsure about how best to respond. Take the question:

How satisfied are you with pay and conditions in your job?

The problem here is obvious: the respondent may be satisfied with one but not the other. Not only will the respondent be unclear about how to reply, but any answer that is given is unlikely to be a good reflection of the level of satisfaction with pay *and* conditions. Similarly,

How frequently does your boss give you information concerning your daily work schedule and new developments within the company?

double — barrelled

suffers from the same problem. A boss may provide extensive information about the daily work schedule but be totally uninformative about what is going on in the company more generally, so any stipulation of frequency of information is going to be ambiguous and will create uncertainty for respondents.

The same rule applies to fixed-choice answers. In Box 7.4, one of Schuman and Presser's (1981) answers is:

Work that is pleasant and people are nice to work with.

While there is likely to be a symmetry between the two ideas in this answer—pleasant work and nice people—there is no *necessary* correspondence between them. Pleasant work may be important for someone, but he or she may be relatively indifferent to the issue of how pleasant their co-workers are. Further instances of double-barrelled questions are provided in Box 7.6.

Avoid very general questions

It is easy to ask a very general question when in fact what is wanted is a response to a specific issue. The problem with questions that are very general is that they lack a frame of reference. Thus,

How satisfied are you with your job?

seems harmless but it lacks specificity. Does it refer to pay, conditions, the nature of the work, or all of these? If there is the possibility of such diverse interpretations, respondents are likely to vary in their interpretations too, and this will be a source of error. One of our favourite general questions comes from Karl Marx's *Enquête Ouvrière*, a questionnaire that was sent to 25,000 French socialists and others (though there is apparently no record of any being returned). The final (one-hundredth) question reads:

What is the general, physical, intellectual, and moral condition of men and women employed in your trade? (Bottomore and Rubel 1963: 218)

Avoid leading questions

Leading or loaded questions are ones that appear to lead the respondent in a particular direction. Questions of the kind 'Do you agree with the view that…?' fall into this class of question. The obvious

problem with such a question is that it is suggesting a particular reply to respondents, although invariably they do have the ability to rebut any implied answer. However, it is the fact that they might feel pushed in a certain direction that they do not naturally incline towards. Such a question as,

Do you think that UK corporate directors receive excessive financial compensation?

is likely to make it difficult for some people to answer in a way that indicates they do not believe that UK corporate directors are overpaid for what they do. But once again, Marx is the source of a favourite leading question:

If you are paid piece rates, is the quality of the article made a pretext for fraudulent deductions from wages? (Bottomore and Rubel 1963: 215)

Avoid questions that are actually asking two questions

The double-barrelled question is a clear instance of the transgression of this rule, but in addition there is the case of a question like:

When did you last discuss your training needs with your supervisor/line manager?

What if the respondent has never discussed his or her training needs with the line manager? It is better to ask two separate questions:

Have you ever discussed your training needs with your supervisor/line manager?
Yes ——
No ——
If YES, when did your most recent discussion take place?

Another way in which more than one question can be asked is with a question like:

How effective have your different job search strategies been?
Very effective ——
Fairly effective ——
Not very effective ——
Not at all effective ——

The obvious difficulty is that, if the respondent has used more than one job search strategy, his or her estimation of effectiveness will vary for each strategy. A mechanism is needed for assessing the success of each strategy rather than forcing respondents to average out their sense of how successful the various strategies were.

Avoid questions that include negatives

The problem with questions with 'not' or similar formulations in them is that it is easy for the respondent to miss the word out when completing a self-completion questionnaire or to miss it when being interviewed. If this occurs, a respondent is likely to answer in the opposite way from the one intended. There are occasions when it is impossible to avoid negatives, but a question like the following should be avoided as far as possible:

> Do you agree with the view that students should not have to take out loans to finance higher education?

Instead, the question should be asked in a positive format. Questions with double negatives should be totally avoided, because it is difficult to know how to respond to them. Oppenheim (1966) gives the following as an example of this kind of question:

> Would you rather not use a non-medicated shampoo?

It is quite difficult to establish what an answer of 'yes' or 'no' would actually mean in response to this question.

One context in which it is difficult to avoid using questions with negatives is when designing Likert scale items. Since you are likely to want to identify respondents who exhibit response sets and will therefore want to reverse the direction of your question asking (see Chapter 6), the use of negatives will be difficult to avoid.

Box 7.6 Matching question and answers in closed questions (and some double-barrelled questions too)

You can sometimes find examples of badly designed questions in situations that you encounter in your everyday life. A recent example we have come across is of a feedback questionnaire produced by a publisher and inserted into the pages of a novel that one of us was reading. At one point in the questionnaire there was a series of Likert-style items regarding the book's quality. In each case, the respondent is asked to indicate whether the attribute being asked about is: poor; acceptable; average; good; or excellent. However, in each case, the items are presented as questions, for example:

> Was the writing elegant, seamless, imaginative?

The problem here is that an answer to this question is 'yes' or 'no'. At most, we might have gradations of yes and no, such as: definitely; to a large extent; to some extent; not at all. However, 'poor' or 'excellent' cannot be answers to this question. The problem is that the questions should have been presented as statements, such as:

> Please indicate the quality of the book in terms of each of the following criteria:
>
> The elegance of the writing:
>
> Poor __ Acceptable __ Average __ Good __ Excellent __

Of course, we have changed the sense slightly here, because, as it was stated, a further problem with the question is that it is a double-barrelled question. In fact, it is 'treble-barrelled', because it actually asks about three attributes of the writing in one. The reader's views about the three qualities may vary. A similar question asked:

> Did the plot offer conflict, twists, and a resolution?

Again, not only does the question imply a 'yes' or 'no', it actually asks about three attributes. How would you answer if you had different views about each of the three criteria?

It might be argued that the issue is a nit-picking one: someone reading the question obviously knows that he or she is being asked to rate the quality of the book in terms of each attribute. The problem is that we simply do not know what the impact might be of a disjunction between question and answer, so you may as well get the connection between question and answers right (and do not ask double- or treble-barrelled questions either!).

Practical Tip common mistakes when asking questions

Over the years, we have read many projects and dissertations based on structured interviews and self-completion questionnaires. We have noticed that a small number of mistakes recur. Here is a list of some of them.

1 An excessive use of open questions. Students sometimes include too many open questions. While a resistance to closed questions may be understandable, although not something we would agree with, open questions are likely to reduce your response rate and will cause you analysis problems. Keep the number to an absolute minimum.

2 An excessive use of yes/no questions. Sometimes students include lots of questions that provide just a yes/no form of response. This is usually the result of lazy thinking and preparation. The world rarely fits into this kind of response. Take a question like:

> Are you satisfied with opportunities for promotion in the firm?
>
> Yes ____   No ____

This does not provide for the possibility that respondents will vary in their satisfaction. So why not rephrase it as:

How satisfied are you with opportunities for promotion in the firm?

Very satisfied	____
Satisfied	____
Neither satisfied nor dissatisfied	____
Dissatisfied	____
Very dissatisfied	____

3 Students often fail to give clear instructions on self-completion questionnaires about how the questions should be answered. Make sure whether you want a tick, something to be circled or deleted, or whatever. If only one response is required, make sure you say so—for example, 'tick the answer that comes closest to your view'.

4 Be careful about letting respondents choose more than one answer. Sometimes it is unavoidable, but questions that allow more than one reply are often a pain to analyse.

5 In spite of the fact that we always warn about the problems of overlapping categories, students still formulate closed answers that are not mutually exclusive. In addition, some categories may be omitted. For example:

How many times per week do you consult with your line manager?

1–3 times __ 3–6 times __ 6–9 times __ More than __
                                              10 times

Not only does the respondent not know where to answer if his or her answer might be 3 or 6; there is no answer for someone who would want to answer 10.

6 Students sometimes do not ensure the answers correspond to the question. For example:

Do you regularly meet with your appraiser for an appraisal interview?

Never	――
Once a year	――
Twice a year	――
More than twice a year	――

The problem here is that the answer to the question is logically either 'yes' or 'no'. However, the student quite sensibly wants to gain some idea of frequency (something that we would agree with in the light of our second point in this list!). The problem is that the question and the response categories are out of kilter. The question should be:

How frequently do you meet with your appraiser in any year (January to December)?

Never	____
Once a year	____
Twice a year	____
More than twice a year	____

If you never committed any of these 'sins', you would be well on the way to producing a questionnaire that would stand out from the rest, provided you took into account the other advice we give in this chapter as well!

Avoid technical terms

Use simple, plain language and avoid jargon. Do not ask a question like,

> Do you sometimes feel alienated from work?

The problem here is that many respondents will not know what is meant by 'alienated', and furthermore they are likely to have different views of what it means, even if it is a remotely meaningful term to them.
    Consider the following question:

> The influence of the TUC on management–worker relations has declined in recent years.
> Strongly __ Agree __ Undecided __Disagree__ Strongly __
> agree   disagree

The use of acronyms like TUC can be a problem, because some people may be unfamiliar with what they stand for.

Does the respondent have the requisite knowledge?

There is little point in asking respondents lots of questions about matters of which they have no knowledge. It is very doubtful whether meaningful data about computer use could be extracted from respondents who have never used or come into direct contact with one.

Make sure that there is a symmetry between a closed question and its answers

A common mistake is for a question and its answers to be out of phase with each other. Box 7.6 describes such an instance.

Memory problems

Do not rely too much on stretching people's memories to the extent that the answers for many of them are likely to be inaccurate. It would be nice to have accurate replies to a question about the number of times respondents have visited the cinema in the previous twelve months, but it is highly unlikely that most will in fact recall events accurately over such a long space of time (other perhaps than those who have not gone at all or only once or twice in the preceding twelve months). It was for this reason that, in the question on cinema visiting above, the time frame was predominantly just one month.

Vignette questions

A form of asking mainly closed questions that has been used in connection with the examination of people's normative standards is the vignette technique. The technique essentially comprises presenting respondents with one or more scenarios and then asking them how they would respond when confronted with the circumstances of that scenario. Box 7.7 describes a vignette that was employed in the context of a study of the ethical behaviour of marketing professionals in different situations. The study focused on marketing professionals because, of all the functional areas of business, marketing has been the one most frequently charged with unethical practices.

    Four different vignettes were used in this study to tease out respondents' responses to ethical dilemmas of different kinds. Of the two dilemmas presented in Box 7.7, the first is concerned with a conflict of interest (this is where an individual has more than one interest, which, if both are pursued, may lead to personal gain at the expense of the firm); the second dilemma is concerned with a case of false advertising aimed at deception and falsehood. Each dilemma deals with a different aspect of the marketing mix, such as price or promotion. For each vignette, respondents are asked how they would act and responses are recorded on a five-point scale, from 1 = definitely would, to 5 = definitely would not. Many aspects of the issues being tapped by the vignette questions could be accessed through attitude items, such as:

> If a senior marketing professional has private business interests that are also related to the business of the firm, he has a duty to declare these interests to other senior executives immediately they arise.
>
> Strongly __ Agree __Undecided __ Disagree __ Strongly __
> agree   disagree

Box 7.7 Two vignette questions about ethical behaviour

The following vignettes were used by Lund (2000) in a study of marketing professionals. Each of the vignettes reflects a different aspect of the marketing mix (place, promotion, price, and product) and each poses a different kind of ethical dilemma. These vignettes were developed for an earlier study of marketing professionals conducted by Fritzsche (1988); the fact that they have been pretested gives us greater confidence in the validity of their use as a measure of ethical behaviour. Two of the four vignettes are presented below.

Vignette 1 [Price]: conflict of interest

Jack Brown is vice-president of marketing for Tangy Spices, a large spice manufacturer. Brown recently joined in a private business venture with Tangy's director of purchasing to import black pepper from India. Brown's private venture is about to sign a five-year contract with Tangy to supply its black pepper needs, but the contract is set at a price of 3 cents per pound above contracts available from other spice importers that provide comparable service and quality. If you were Brown, what are the chances that you would sign the contract?

Definitely would ( )
Probably would ( )
Neither would nor would not ( )
Probably would not ( )
Definitely would not ( )

Vignette 2 [Promotion]: deceit and falsehood

Dave Smith is developing an advertisement for a new housing development his firm is about to start. The development is located in a low area which has flooded in the past. The company has recently done some work to reduce the danger of flooding in the future. In the preliminary advertisement, Smith has included a statement indicating that the firm has solved the flooding problem. The fact is that if a flood occurs, the homes are still likely to be flooded with up to five feet of water. If you were Smith, what are the chances that you would include the statement in the advertisement?

Definitely would ( )
Probably would ( )
Neither would nor would not ( )
Probably would not ( )
Definitely would not ( )

Source: Lund (2000: 334).

The advantage of the vignette over such an attitude question is that it anchors the choice in a situation and as such reduces the possibility of an unreflective reply. In addition, when the subject matter is a sensitive area (in this case, dealing with ethical behaviour), there is the possibility that the questions may be seen as threatening by respondents. Respondents may feel that they are being judged by their replies. If the questions are about other people (and imaginary ones at that), this permits a certain amount of distance between the questioning and the respondent and results in a less threatening context. However, it is hard to believe that respondents will not feel that their replies will at least in part be seen as reflecting on them, even if the questions are not about them as such.

One obvious requirement of the vignette technique is that the scenarios must be believable, so that

considerable effort needs to go into the construction of credible situations. Finch (1987) points out two further considerations in relation to this style of questioning. First, it is more or less impossible to establish how far assumptions are being made about the characters in the scenario (such as their ethnicity) and what the significance of those assumptions might be for the validity and comparability of people's replies. Secondly, it is also difficult to establish how far people's answers reflect their own normative views or indeed how they themselves would act when confronted with the kinds of choices revealed in the scenarios. However, in spite of these reservations, the vignette technique warrants serious consideration when the research focus is concerned with an area that lends itself to this style of questioning.

to detect any tendency for respondents
interests to be lost at certain
junctures

Piloting and pre-testing questions

It is always desirable, if at all possible, to conduct a pilot study before administering a self-completion questionnaire or structured interview schedule to your sample. In fact, the desirability of piloting such instruments is not solely to do with trying to ensure that survey questions operate well; piloting also has a role in ensuring that the research instrument as a whole functions well. Pilot studies may be particularly crucial in relation to research based on the self-completion questionnaire, since there will not be an interviewer present to clear up any confusion. Also, with interviews, persistent problems may emerge after a few interviews have been carried out and these can then be addressed. However, with self-completion questionnaires, since they are sent or handed out in large numbers, considerable wastage may occur prior to any problems becoming apparent.

Here are some uses of pilot studies in survey research.

- If the main study is going to employ mainly closed questions, open questions can be asked in the pilot to generate the fixed-choice answers. Glock (1988), for example, extols the virtues of conducting qualitative interviews in preparation for a survey for precisely this kind of reason.

- Piloting an interview schedule can provide interviewers with some experience of using it and can infuse them with a greater sense of confidence.

- If everyone (or virtually everyone) who answers a question replies in the same way, the resulting data are unlikely to be of interest because they do not form a variable. A pilot study allows such a question to be identified.

- In interview surveys, it may be possible to identify questions that make respondents feel uncomfortable and to detect any tendency for respondents' interest to be lost at certain junctures.

- Questions that seem not to be understood (more likely to be realized in an interview than in a self-completion questionnaire context) or questions that are often not answered should become apparent. The latter problem of questions being skipped may be due to confusing or threatening phrasing, poorly worded instructions, or confusing positioning in the interview schedule or questionnaire. Whatever the cause might be, such missing data are undesirable and a pilot study may be instrumental in identifying the problem.

- Pilot studies allow the researcher to determine the adequacy of instructions to interviewers, or to respondents completing a self-completion questionnaire.

- It may be possible to consider how well the questions flow and whether it is necessary to move some of them around to improve this feature.

The pilot should not be carried out on people who might have been members of the sample that would be employed in the full study. One reason for this is that, if you are seeking to employ probability sampling, the selecting-out of a number of members of the population or sample may affect the representativeness of any subsequent sample. If possible, it is best to find a small set of respondents who are comparable to members of the population from which the sample for the full study will be taken.

Using existing questions

One final observation regarding the asking of questions is that you should also consider using questions that have been employed by other researchers for at least part of your questionnaire or interview schedule. This may seem like stealing and you would be advised to contact the researchers concerned regarding the use of questions they have devised. However, employing existing questions allows you to use questions that have in a sense been piloted for you. If any reliability and validity testing has taken place, you will know about the measurement qualities of the existing questions you use. A further advantage of using existing questions is that they allow you to draw comparisons with other research. This might allow you to indicate whether change has occurred or whether place makes a difference to findings. At the very least, examining questions used by others might give you some ideas about how best to approach your own questions, even if you decide not to make use of them as they stand. An example of how questions developed by other researchers were used in a study of telephone call centre operators is given in Box 7.8.

The process of finding questions has been made a great deal easier by the creation of 'question banks', which act as repositories of questions employed in surveys and elsewhere. The Centre for Applied Social Surveys (CASS), which aims to improve standards in UK survey research, has a very good question bank providing access to questionnaires from major surveys (including the Census) and associated commentary to assist survey design. It is freely available and can be found at the following site: **www://qb.soc.surrey.ac.uk**

Box 7.8 Using scales developed by other researchers in a survey of telephone call centre operators

In a study of call centre operators working in the telecommunications industry in Australia, Deery, Iverson, and Walsch (2002) were interested in the possible negative effects of this form of work on the psychological well-being of employees. Specifically, they sought to:

1 identify the factors leading to feelings of emotional exhaustion among operators; and

2 analyse the effects of emotional exhaustion on employee absence.

Emotional exhaustion was defined as the extent to which individuals feel emotionally drained from their work. It was predicted that emotional exhaustion would be higher amongst employees who felt they had a high workload and amongst those who felt they lacked the skills needed to do the job.

In designing the questionnaire used to test these relationships, Deery et al. used scales that had been devised by other researchers in earlier studies. These included:

- a five-item scale taken from Wharton (1993) used to measure emotional exhaustion, item statements included: 'I feel emotionally drained from my work';

- emotional expressivity measured by four items adapted from Kring (1994), including 'I can't hide the way I'm feeling when talking to customers';

- workload and role overload measured by items taken from Caplan et al. (1975), including 'my job requires me to work very fast';

- team leader and team member support measured using items adapted from House (1981), such as 'my team members are willing to listen to my job-related problems'.

Deery et al. supplemented these scales with items they developed themselves to measure other variables in the study, such as:

- *customer interactions*—with the statement 'I now have more abusive customer calls than I used to have'; and

- *management focus on quality*—using item statements such as 'I believe senior management are more concerned about the quantity rather than the quality of work'.

The study illustrates how item scales developed by other researchers can be combined with those developed by those conducting the present study to create a questionnaire instrument that is sensitive to the context and relevant to the questions that the research is seeking to address.

Practical Tip 👉 *getting help in designing questions*

When designing questions, as we suggested earlier, try to put yourself in the position of someone who has been asked to answer the questions. This can be difficult, because some (if not all) the questions may not apply to you—for example, if you are a student doing a survey of managers. However, try to think about how you would reply. This means concentrating not just on the questions themselves but also on the links between the questions. For example, do filter questions work in the way you expect them to? Then try the questions out on some people you know, as in a pilot study. Ask them to be critical and to consider how well the questions connect to each other. Also, do look at the questionnaires and structured interview schedules that experienced researchers have devised. They may not have asked questions on your topic, but the way they have asked the questions and the flow of the questions should give you an idea of what to do and what to avoid when designing such instruments.

Checklist of issues to consider for your structured interview schedule or self-completion questionnaire

✓ Have you devised a clear and comprehensive way of introducing the research to interviewees or questionnaire respondents?

✓ Have you considered whether there are any existing questions used by other researchers to investigate this topic that could meet your needs?

✓ Do the questions allow you to answer all your research questions?

✓ Could any questions that are not strictly relevant to your research questions be dropped?

✓ Have you tried to put yourself in the position of answering as many of the questions as possible?

✓ Have you piloted the questionnaire with some appropriate respondents?

✓ If it is a structured interview schedule, have you made sure that the instructions to yourself and to anyone else involved in interviewing are clear (e.g. which questions should be answered next with filter questions)?

✓ If it is a self-completion questionnaire, have you made sure that the instructions to yourself and to anyone else involved in interviewing are clear (e.g. which questions should be answered next with filter questions)?

✓ Are instructions about how to record responses clear (e.g. whether to tick or circle; whether more than one response is allowable)?

✓ Have you included as few open questions as possible?

✓ Have you allowed respondents to indicate levels of intensity in their replies, so that they are not forced into 'yes' or 'no' answers where intensity of feeling may be more appropriate?

✓ Have you ensured that questions and their answers do not span more than one page?

✓ Have socio-demographic questions been left until the end of the questionnaire? *Why*

✓ Are questions relating to the research topic at or very close to the beginning?

✓ Have you taken steps to ensure that the questions you are asking really do supply you with the information you need?

✓ Have you taken steps to ensure that there are no:

✓ ambiguous terms in questions or closed answers?

✓ long questions?

✓ double-barrelled questions?

✓ very general questions?

✓ leading questions?

✓ questions that are asking about two or more things?

☑ questions that include negatives

☑ questions using technical terms?

☑ Have you made sure that your respondents will have the requisite knowledge to answer your questions?

☑ Is there an appropriate match between your questions and your closed answers?

☑ Do any of your questions rely too much on your respondents' memory?

☑ If you are using a Likert scale approach:

☑ Have you included some items that can be reverse scored in order to minimize response sets?

☑ Have you made sure that the items really do relate to the same underlying cluster of attitudes so that they can be aggregated?

☑ Have you ensured that your closed answers are exhaustive?

☑ Have you ensured that your closed answers do not overlap?

☑ Have you ensured that there is a category of 'other' (or similar category such as 'unsure' or 'either agree nor disagree') so that respondents are not forced to answer in a way that is not indicative of what they think or do?

K KEY POINTS

- While open questions undoubtedly have certain advantages, closed questions are typically preferable for a survey, because of the ease of asking questions and recording and processing answers.

- This point applies particularly to the self-completion questionnaire.

- Open questions of the kind used in qualitative interviewing have a useful role in relation to the formulation of fixed-choice answers and piloting.

- It is crucial to learn the rules of question asking to avoid some of the more obvious pitfalls.

- Remember always to put yourself in the position of the respondent when asking questions and to make sure you will generate data appropriate to your research questions.

- Piloting or pre-testing may clear up problems in question formulation.

Q QUESTIONS FOR REVIEW

Open or closed questions?

- What difficulties do open questions present in survey research?

- Why are closed questions frequently preferred to open questions in survey research?

- What are the limitations of closed questions?

- How can closed questions be improved?

V.gnette

Types of question

- What are the main types of question that are likely to be used in a structured interview or self-administered questionnaire?

Rules for designing questions

- What is wrong with each of the following questions?

  What is your annual salary?
  - Below £10,000
  - £10,000–15,000
  - £15,000–20,000
  - £20,000–25,000
  - £25,000–30,000
  - £30,000–35,000
  - £35,000 and over.

  week
  month

  Do you ever feel alienated from your work?
  - All the time
  - Often
  - Occasionally
  - Never.

  How satisfied are you with the customer services and products provided by this company?
  - Very satisfied
  - Fairly satisfied
  - Neither satisfied nor dissatisfied
  - Fairly dissatisfied
  - Very dissatisfied.

Vignette questions

- In what circumstances are vignette questions appropriate?

Piloting and pre-testing questions

- Why is it important to pilot questions?

Using existing questions

- Why might it be useful to use questions devised by others?

8 Structured observation

CHAPTER GUIDE

Structured observation attracted a good deal of attention in business and management research during the 1970s and early 1980s. However, in more recent years it has been less commonly employed as a research method. It entails the direct observation of behaviour and the recording of that behaviour in terms of categories that have been devised prior to the start of data collection. This chapter explores:

- the limitations of survey research for the study of behaviour;

- the different forms of observation in business research;

- the potential of structured observation for the study of behaviour;

- how to devise an observation schedule;

- different strategies for observing behaviour in structured observation;

- sampling issues in structured observation research; with this method, the issue of sampling is to do not

just with people but also with the sampling of time and contexts;
- issues of reliability and validity in structured observation;
- field stimulations, whereby the researcher actively intervenes in social life and records what happens as a consequence of the intervention, as a form of structured observation;
- some criticisms of structured observation.

Introduction

Structured observation is a method for systematically observing the behaviour of individuals in terms of a schedule of categories. It is a technique in which the researcher employs explicitly formulated rules for the observation and recording of behaviour. One of its main advantages is that it allows behaviour to be observed directly, unlike in survey research, which only allows behaviour to be inferred. In survey research, respondents frequently report their behaviour, but there are good reasons for thinking that such reports may not be entirely accurate. Structured observation constitutes a possible solution in that it entails the direct observation of behaviour. Interest in structured observation within business and management stemmed initially from the fact that it was seen as having the potential to provide researchers with far greater insight into the issue of what managers actually do. In this respect it was seen by many as providing an alternative to the diary study method (see Chapter 6) used by Stewart (1967).

Problems with survey research on behaviour

Chapters 4–7 have dealt with several different aspects of survey research. In the course of outlining procedures associated with the social survey, certain problems with the techniques with which it is typically associated have been identified. For example, in the field of leadership research, which relies a great deal on questionnaire measures, researchers have relied heavily on the responses of subordinates and what they *say* leaders do, rather than what leaders actually do (the two are often used interchangeably). To some extent the deficiencies associated with the survey are recognized by researchers, who have developed ways of dealing with them or at least of offsetting their impact to some degree. When survey techniques such

Box 8.1 Problems with using social survey research to investigate behaviour

- *Problem of meaning*. People may vary in their interpretations of key terms in a question.
- *Problem of omission*. When answering the question, respondents may inadvertently omit key terms in the question.
- *Problem of memory*. They may misremember aspects of the occurrence of certain forms of behaviour.
- *Social desirability effect*. They may exhibit a tendency towards replying in ways that are meant to be consistent with their perceptions of the desirability of certain kinds of answer.
- *Question threat*. Some questions may appear threatening and result in a failure to provide an honest reply.
- *Interviewer characteristics*. Aspects of the interviewer may influence the answers provided.
- *Gap between stated and actual behaviour*. How people say they are likely to behave and how they actually behave may be inconsistent.

as the structured interview or the self-completion questionnaire are employed in connection with the study of respondents' *behaviour*, certain characteristic difficulties are encountered, some of which have been touched on in earlier chapters. Box 8.1 identifies some of the difficulties entailed in using survey methods to research behaviour. The list is by no means exhaustive but it does capture some of the main elements.

So why not observe behaviour?

An obvious solution to the problems identified is to observe people's behaviour directly rather than to rely on research instruments like questionnaires to elicit such information. In this chapter, we are going to outline a method called *structured observation* (see Box 8.2), also often called *systematic observation*.

Much like the interview (see Box 5.3), there are many different forms of the observation approach in business research. Box 8.3 outlines some major ways of conducting observation studies in business research.

It has been implied that structured observation can be viewed as an alternative to survey methods of research. After all, in view of the various problems identified in Box 8.1, it would seem an obvious solution to observe people instead. However, structured observation has not attracted a large following and instead tends to be in use in certain specific research areas, such as in educational research, where it is used to study the behaviour of school teachers and pupils and the interaction between them.

Central to any structured observation study will be the *observation schedule* or *coding scheme*. This specifies the categories of behaviour that are to be observed and how behaviour should be allocated to those categories. It is best to illustrate what this involves by looking at examples. One of the best-known studies to have used structured observation is Mintzberg's (1973) study of managerial work. Mintzberg studied five chief executives, each for one week, as they went about their normal business day, took phone calls, attended scheduled and unscheduled meetings, scanned mail, received visitors, and walked around buildings. The detailed nature of his investigation restricted the amount of quantitative data that could be generated but it also enabled more detailed analysis of the kind of work that managers do. The activity categories used in the study were: desk work, tours,

---

Box 8.2 **What is structured observation?**

Structured observation, often also called *systematic observation*, is a technique in which the researcher employs explicitly formulated rules for the observation and recording of behaviour. The rules inform observers about what they should look for and how they should record behaviour. Each person who is part of the research (we will call these people 'participants') is observed for a predetermined period of time using the same rules. These rules are articulated in what is usually referred to as an *observation schedule*, which bears many similarities to a structured interview schedule with closed questions. The aim of the observation schedule is to ensure that each participant's behaviour is systematically recorded so that it is possible to aggregate the behaviour of all those in the sample in respect of each type of behaviour being recorded. The rules that constitute the observation schedule are as specific as possible in order to direct observers to exactly what aspects of behaviour they are supposed to be looking for. The resulting data resemble questionnaire data considerably, in that the procedure generates information on different aspects of behaviour that can be treated as variables. Moreover, structured observation research is typically underpinned by a cross-sectional research design (see Box 2.13 and Figures 2.2 and 2.3).

[handwritten: Immersion 沉浸]

[handwritten: Contrived 设计的]

Box 8.3 Major types of observation research

- *Structured observation.* See Box 8.2.

- *Systematic observation.* See Box 8.2.

- *Participant observation.* This is one of the best-known methods of data collection in business and management research. It is primarily associated with qualitative research and entails the relatively prolonged immersion of the observer in a social setting in which he or she seeks to observe the behaviour of members of that setting (group, organization, community, etc.) and to elicit the meanings they attribute to their environment and behaviour. Participant observers vary considerably in how much they participate in the social settings in which they locate themselves. See Box 14.1 and Chapter 14 generally for a more detailed treatment.

- *Non-participant observation.* This is a term that is used to describe a situation in which the observer observes but does not participate in what is going on in the social setting. Structured observers are usually non-participants in that they are in the social setting being observed but rarely participate in what is

happening. The term can also be used in connection with unstructured observation.

- *Unstructured observation.* As its name implies, unstructured observation does not entail the use of an observation schedule for the recording of behaviour. Instead, the aim is to record in as much detail as possible the behaviour of participants with the aim of developing a narrative account of that behaviour. In a sense, most participant observation is unstructured but the term unstructured observation is usually employed in conjunction with non-participant observation.

- *Simple observation* and *contrived observation.* Webb et al. (1966) write about forms of observation in which the observer is unobtrusive and is not observed by those being observed. With simple observation, the observer has no influence over the situation being observed; in the case of contrived observation, the observer actively alters the situation to observe the effects of an intervention. These two types of observation are invariably forms of non-participant observation and can entail either structured or unstructured observation.

Box 8.4 Mintzberg's categories of basic activities involved in managerial work

Mintzberg (1973) identified five categories into which the activities of managerial work could be placed. They are listed below.

- *Scheduled meeting.* A prearranged face-to-face meeting involving the manager and one or more other participants is defined as scheduled.

- *Unscheduled meeting.* A meeting is defined as unscheduled if it is arranged hastily, as when someone just 'drops in'.

- *Desk work.* This refers to the time the manager spends at his or her desk, processing mail, scheduling activities, writing letters, or communicating with the secretary.

- *Call.* This category refers to telephone calls.

- *Tour.* This refers to a chance meeting in the hall, or to the 'promenades' taken by the manager to observe activity and to deliver information.

[handwritten: Promenade (ˌprɒməˈnɑːd) 散步]

unscheduled meetings, scheduled meetings, and telephone calls (see Box 8.4).

Structured data were collected using three records:

- *chronology record*—described activity patterns, noting the time, nature and duration of the activity;

- *mail record*—described each piece of incoming/outgoing mail and the action that was taken in order to respond to it;

- *contact record*—described each verbal contact, noting the participants and where it took place.

In Mintzberg's coding scheme, time and activities were coded separately, so that the distribution of clock time might overlap an activity or vice versa. For example, 'tours' of the work site and 'desk work' included time spent talking. Almost 40 per cent of activities were meetings; this accounted for 70 per cent of the managers' work time. From such data a number of features could be derived. Mintzberg's main conclusions were that managerial work is highly fragmented, varied, and brief, and that managers have a need for instant communication, on which to base further verbal contact and action. These findings ran contrary to the traditional view that was dominant at the time, which suggested that managerial activity was planned and rational. Mintzberg's research was highly influential and it generated a number of other observational studies of managers that used similar or identical schemes in order to replicate or extend his work in various ways (for an example see Box 8.5).

It is interesting to think about how a scheme like this might be employed in connection with higher education teaching and in particular in tutorials and seminars. In the following imaginary scheme, the focus is on the tutor. The categories might be:

Tutor:

1. asking question addressed to group;
2. asking question addressed to individual;
3. responding to question asked by member of group;

4. responding to comment by member of group;
5. discussing topic;
6. making arrangements;
7. silence.

Student(s):

8. asking question;
9. responding to question from tutor;
10. responding to comment from tutor;
11. responding to question from another student;
12. responding to comment from another student;
13. talking about arrangements.

We might want to code what is happening every five seconds. The coding sheet for a five-minute period in the tutorial might look like Figure 8.1. We might try to relate the amount of time that the tutor is engaged in particular activities to such things as: number of students in the group; layout of the room; subject discipline; gender of tutor; age of tutor; and so on.

Box 8.5 Structured observation of managerial work

In this study, Martinko and Gardner (1990) sought to investigate the relationship between managerial behaviour and performance through structured observation of managerial work. The study involved replication of Mintzberg's (1973) earlier observational study of what managers actually do in their day-to-day work.

The sample consisted of forty-one school principals. These managers were selected because they have a relatively high level of autonomy in their work (and therefore an ability to influence organizational performance). Also, because they are a relatively homogenous group, their performance levels can be more easily compared.

The observations were conducted mainly by doctoral students who attended a two-day training session in which they were taught the principles of structured observation. Minute-by-minute observation led to the production of written protocols that recorded managerial events, the time they started and ended, and their purpose. The mean number of observations was 6.7 days per principal.

The sample was stratified into high- and moderate-performing managers, based on the assumption that the performance of the principal would be reflected by the performance of the school. Although the research confirmed Mintzberg's earlier finding that managerial work is brief, varied, fragmented, and interpersonal, there was no evidence to suggest that managerial behaviour was related to performance level. In other words, there was no significant difference in the behaviours of highly effective and less effective managers in terms of how they organized their daily activities.

It is interesting to note that the researchers deliberately excluded low-performing managers from their sample because they had anticipated difficulties in securing the cooperation of individuals who had been labelled as low performers. However, it may have been that a comparison of high- and low-performing managers would have revealed greater differences between principals in terms of the time spent on events and the number of events that were associated with certain activities.

3	3	3	3	10	10	10	10	10	10	10	10
10	10	10	10	10	10	7	7	7	8	8	8
8	8	8	8	8	8	8	8	11	11	11	11
11	11	11	11	11	11	11	11	11	11	11	11
7	7	7	7	7	4	4	4	4	4	4	1

Figure 8.1 Coding sheet for imaginary study of university tutors

Note: Each cell represents a five-second interval and each row is one minute.

The observation schedule

Devising a schedule for the recording of observations is clearly a crucial step in the structured observation project. The considerations that go into this phase are very similar to those involved in producing a structured interview schedule. The following considerations are worth taking into account.

- A clear focus is necessary. There are two aspects to this point. First, it should be clear to the observer exactly who or what (and possibly both) is to be observed. For example, if people are the focus of attention, the observer needs to know precisely who is to be observed. Also, the observer needs to know which if any aspects of the setting are to be observed and hence recorded. The second sense in which a clear focus is necessary is that the research problem needs to be clearly stated so that the observer knows which of the many things going on in any setting are to be recorded.

- As with the production of a closed question for a structured interview schedule or self-completion questionnaire, the forms taken by any category of behaviour must be both mutually exclusive (i.e. not overlap) and inclusive. Taking the earlier example of coding behaviour in a university tutorial, we might conceivably run into a problem of the twelve categories not being exhaustive if a student knocks on the tutor's door and quickly asks him or her a question (perhaps about the tutorial topic if the student is from another of the tutor's groups). An observer unfamiliar with the ways of university

life might well be unsure about whether this behaviour needs to be coded in terms of the twelve categories or whether the coding should be temporarily suspended. Perhaps the best approach would be to have another category of behaviour to be coded that we might term 'interruption'. It is often desirable for a certain amount of unstructured observation to take place prior to the construction of the observation schedule and for there to be some piloting of it so that possible problems associated with a lack of inclusiveness can be anticipated.

- The recording system must be easy to operate. Complex systems with large numbers of types of behaviour will be undesirable. In a similar way to interviewers using a structured interview schedule, observers need to be trained, but even so it is easy for an observer to become flustered or confused if faced with too many options.

- One possible problem with some observation schedules is that they sometimes require a certain amount of interpretation on the part of the observer. For example, it might be difficult to distinguish in any meaningful sense between an unscheduled meeting and a discussion with two or three colleagues that takes place in a corridor, apart from the fact that in the first instance the participants are more likely to be seated! To the extent that it may be difficult to distinguish between the two, a certain amount of interpretation on the part

---

Box 8.6 Observing jobs

Jenkins et al. (1975) report the results of an exploratory study employed to measure the nature of jobs. The research focused on several different types of job in a number of different types of organization. An observation schedule was devised to assess the nature of twenty aspects (dimensions) of the jobs in question. Most of the dimensions were measured through more than one indicator, each of which took the form of a question that observers had to answer on a six- or seven-point scale. These were then aggregated for each dimension. While the research has a predominantly psychological slant, many of the twenty dimensions relate to issues that have been raised in the sociology of work by labour process theorists and others (e.g. Braverman 1974). One dimension relates to 'Worker pace control' and comprises three observational indicators such as:

How much control does the employee have in setting the pace of his/her work?

Another dimension was 'Autonomy', which comprised four items, such as:

The job allows the individual to make a lot of decisions on his/her own.

Most of the observers were university students. The procedure for conducting the observations was as follows:

'Each respondent was observed twice for an hour. The observations were scheduled so that the two different observations were separated by at least 2 days, were usually made at different times of the day, and were always made by two different observers' (Jenkins et al. 1975: 173).

---

of the observer may be required. If such interpretation is required, there would need to be clear guidelines for the observer and considerable experience would be required (see Box 8.6 for an illustration of a study in which a good deal of interpretation seems to have been necessary).

Strategies for observing behaviour

There are different ways of conceptualizing how behaviour should be recorded.

- We can record in terms of *incidents*. This means waiting for something to happen and then recording what follows from it. Essentially, this is what Mintzberg (1973) did, as the following account of his method illustrates: 'The researcher observes the manager as he performs his work. Each observed event (a verbal contact or a piece of incoming or outgoing mail) is categorized by the researcher in a number of ways (for example, duration, participants, purpose). . .' (1973: 231). In this study, the categories, or activity codes, are developed either during the observation or shortly after it takes place, rather than beforehand. Only after the observation has taken place did Mintzberg begin to draw connections between the activities in order to develop his final activity codes. Similarly, a newspaper story several years ago reported that someone placed a ladder over a pavement and then observed whether people preferred to go under the ladder or to risk life and limb in the face of oncoming traffic. A considerable number preferred the latter option, confirming the persistence of superstitious beliefs in an apparently secular society. Once again, an incident (someone approaching the ladder) triggered the observation. Webb et al. (1966) would regard this as an example of *contrived observation*, because the researchers fabricated the situation. The discussion later in this chapter of *field stimulations* provides further illustrations of this kind of research.

- We can observe and record in terms of short periods of time, observing one individual for a couple of minutes but returning at structured intervals to conduct further observations. This can help to ensure the generalizability of what goes on in the setting. For example, if a manager holds regular meetings each day at 4 p.m., three observations, each lasting twenty minutes, conducted in the morning, at lunchtime, and in the afternoon, will ensure a more representative sample of activities than would an observation lasting an hour at 4–5 p.m.

- We can observe and record observations for quite *long periods* of time. The observer watches and records more or less continuously. For example, the study of job characteristics by Jenkins et al. (1975), which entailed the observation of each worker on two occasions but for an hour on each occasion (see Box 8.6): 'The observation hour was structured so that the observer spent 10 min becoming oriented to the job, 30 min observing specific job actions, and 20 min rating the job in situ. The observers then typically spent an additional 15 min away from the job completing the observation instrument' (Jenkins et al. 1975: 174). This last study is an example of what Martin and Bateson (1986) refer to as 'continuous recording', whereby the observer observes for extended periods, thus allowing the frequency and duration of forms of behaviour to be measured. They contrast this approach with time sampling.

- *Time sampling* is a further approach to the observation of behaviour. An example here would be a study of schools known as the ORACLE (Observational Research and Classroom Learning Evaluation) project (Galton, Simon, and Croll 1980). In this research, eight children (four of each gender) in each class in which observation took place were observed for around four minutes but on ten separate occasions. A mechanical device made a noise every twenty-five seconds and on each occasion this occurred the observer made a note of what the teacher or pupils were doing in terms of the observation schedule. The sampling of time periods was random.

Sampling

Just like survey research, structured observation necessitates decisions about sampling. Mintzberg's study was somewhat unusual in that it relied on a very small sample of only five individuals—a decision that he explains was forced partly by practical constraints, as the research was done for his doctoral dissertation. This meant that 'the time of only one researcher was available, and that for only 12 months or so' (Mintzberg 1973: 237). However, with structured observation it is more usual not only to sample a larger number of people, but also to incorporate several other sampling issues as well.

Sampling people

When people are being sampled, considerations very similar to those encountered in Chapter 4 in respect of probability sampling come to the fore. This means that the observer will ideally want to sample on a random basis. In the study of job characteristics (Box 8.6), the individuals who were observed at work were randomly selected (Jenkins et al. 1975).

Sampling in terms of time

As implied by the idea of time sampling (see above), it is often necessary to ensure that, if certain individuals are sampled on more than one occasion, they are not always observed at the same time of the day. This means that, if particular individuals are selected randomly for observation on several different occasions for short periods, it is desirable for the observation periods to be randomly selected. For example, it would not be desirable for a certain manager working in his office always to be observed at the end of the day. He or she may be tired and this will give a false impression of that manager's behaviour.

Further sampling considerations

The sampling procedures mentioned so far conform to probability sampling principles, because it is feasible to construct a sampling frame for individuals. However, this is not always possible for different kinds of reason. Studies in public areas, like the research on

ad libitum

superstition mentioned above, do not permit random sampling, because we cannot very easily construct a sampling frame of people walking along a street. Similarly, it is not feasible to construct a sampling frame of interactions—for example, of meetings between managers and their subordinates. The problem with doing structured observation research on such a topic is that it does not lend itself to the specification of a sampling frame and therefore the researcher's ability to generate a probability sample is curtailed.

As suggested in Chapter 4, considerations relating to probability sampling derive largely from concerns surrounding the external validity of findings. Such concerns are not necessarily totally addressed by resorting to probability sampling, however. For example, if a structured observation study is conducted over a relatively short span of time, issues of the representativeness of findings are likely to arise. If the research was conducted in estate agents' offices, observations conducted over the summer, when most people are on holiday and the housing market is quite quiet, may affect the results obtained compared to observations at a different point in the year. Consequently, consideration has to be given to the question of the timing of observation. Furthermore, how are the sites in which structured observation is to take place selected? Can we presume that they are themselves representative? Clearly, a random sampling procedure for the selection of organizations

may assuage any worries in this connection. However, in view of the difficulty of securing access to settings such as schools and business organizations, it is likely that the organizations to which access is secured may not be representative of the population of appropriate ones.

A further set of distinctions between types of sampling in structured observation have been drawn by Martin and Bateson (1986) between:

- 'ad libitum sampling', whereby the observer records whatever is happening at the time;

- 'focal sampling', in which a specific individual is observed for a set period of time; the observer records all examples of whatever forms of behaviour are of interest in terms of a schedule;

- 'scan sampling', whereby an entire group of individuals is scanned at regular intervals and the behaviour of all of them is recorded at that time. This sampling strategy allows only one or two types of behaviour to be observed and recorded; and

- 'behaviour sampling', whereby an entire group is watched and the observer records who was involved in a particular kind of behaviour.

Most structured observation research seems to employ focal sampling, such as Mintzberg's (1973) study, and the research by Martinko and Gardner (1990; Box 8.5) and Jenkins et al. (1975; Box 8.6).

Issues of reliability and validity

One writer has concluded that, when compared to interviews and questionnaires, structured observation: 'Provides (a) more reliable information about events; (b) greater precision regarding their timing, duration, and frequency; (c) greater accuracy in the time ordering of variables; and (d) more accurate and economical reconstructions of large-scale social episodes' (McCall 1984: 277). This is a very strong endorsement for structured observation, but, as McCall notes, there are several issues of reliability and validity that confront practitioners of the

method. Some of these issues are similar to those faced by researchers when seeking to develop measures in business research in general (see Chapter 3) and by survey research in particular. However, certain concerns are specific to structured observation.

Reliability

Practitioners of structured observation have been concerned with the degree of inter-observer consistency. Essentially, this issue entails considering

Box 8.7 Cohen's kappa

Cohen's kappa is a measure of the degree of agreement over the coding of items by two people. As such, it could be applied to the coding of any textual information, as in the content analysis of newspaper articles or of answers to open interview questions, as well as to the coding of observation. Much like Cronbach's alpha (see Box 3.6), you will end up with a coefficient that will vary between 0 and 1. The closer the coefficient is to 1, the higher the agreement and the better the inter-observer consistency. A coefficient of 0.75 or above is considered very good; between 0.6 and 0.75, it is considered good; and between 0.4 and 0.6, it is regarded as fair. The meaning of kappa is

that it measures the degree of agreement between observers beyond that which would occur by chance. Croll (1986) refers to a very similar statistic, the Scott coefficient of agreement, which can be interpreted in an identical way.

The values of kappa in the study of job characteristics referred to in Box 8.6 were mainly in the 'fair' category. The two items referred to in Box 8.6 achieved kappa values of 0.43 and 0.54 respectively (Jenkins et al. 1975). These are not very encouraging and suggest that the coding of job characteristics was not very reliable.

the degree to which two or more observers of the same behaviour agree in terms of their coding of that behaviour on the observation schedule—that is, *inter-observer consistency*. The chief mechanism for assessing this component of reliability is a statistic called *Kappa* (see Box 8.7; *this box can be ignored if you feel unsure about addressing more complex statistical issues at this stage*).

A second consideration in relation to reliability is the degree of consistency of the application of the observation schedule over time—that is, *intra-observer consistency*. This is clearly a difficult notion, because of the capacity for and often necessity for people to behave in different ways on different occasions and in different contexts. Assessing the consistency of observation ratings across all possibilities is clearly a difficult undertaking. The procedures for assessing this aspect of reliability are broadly similar to those applied to the issue of inter-observer consistency. The Jenkins et al. (1975) research addressed the issue of inter-observer consistency over time and found that the measures fared even worse in this respect.

It is clearly not an easy matter to achieve reliability in structured observation. This is a point of some significance in view of the fact that validity presupposes reliability (see Chapter 3). Reliability may be difficult to achieve on occasions, because of the effects of such factors as observer fatigue and lapses in attention. However, this point should not be exaggerated,

because some studies have been able to achieve high levels of reliability for many of their measures, and indeed two critics of structured observation have written that 'there is no doubt that observers can be trained to use complex coding schedules with considerable reliability' (Delamont and Hamilton 1984: 32).

Validity

Measurement validity relates to the question of whether a measure is measuring what it is supposed to measure. The validity of any measure will be affected by,

- whether the measure reflects the concept it has been designed to measure (see Chapter 3), and

- error that arises from the implementation of the measure in the research process (see Chapter 5).

The first of these issues simply means that in structured observation it is necessary to attend to the same kinds of issues concerning the checking of validity (assessing face validity, concurrent validity, and so on) that are encountered in research based on interviews and questionnaires. The second aspect of validity—error in implementation—relates to two matters in particular.

- Is the observation instrument administered as it is supposed to be? This is the equivalent of ensuring that interviewers using a structured interview schedule follow the research instrument and its instructions exactly as they are supposed to. If there is variability between observers or over time, the measure will be unreliable and therefore cannot be valid. Ensuring that observers have as complete an understanding as possible of how the observation schedule should be implemented is therefore crucial.

• Do people change their behaviour because they know they are being observed? This is an instance of what is known as the 'reactive effect' (Box 8.8)—after all, if people adjust the way they behave because they know they are being observed (perhaps because they want to be viewed in a favourable way by the observer), their behaviour would have to

be considered atypical. As a result, we could hardly regard the results of structured observation research as indicative of what happens in reality. As McCall (1984) notes, there is evidence that a reactive effect occurs in structured observation, but that by and large research participants become accustomed to being observed, so that the researcher essentially becomes less intrusive the longer he or she is present. Moreover, it should be borne in mind that frequently people's awareness of the observer's presence is offset by other factors. For example, managers have many tasks to accomplish that reflect the demands of the organization, so that the observer's ability to make a big impact on behaviour may be curtailed by the requirements of the situation.

Box 8.8 Reactive effect

Webb et al. wrote about the 'reactive measurement effect', by which they meant that 'the research subject's knowledge that he is participating in a scholarly search may confound the investigator's data' (1966: 13). They distinguished four components of this effect.

• *The guinea pig effect—awareness of being tested.* Examples of the kind of concern that Webb et al. were writing about are such effects as the research participant wanting to create a good impression or feeling prompted to behave in ways (or express attitudes) that would not normally be exhibited.

• *Role selection*. Webb et al. argue that participants are often tempted to adopt a particular kind of role in research. An example is that there is a well-known effect in experimental research (but which may have a broader applicability) whereby some individuals seek out cues about the aims of the research and adjust what they say and do in line with their perceptions (which may of course be false) of those aims (this is also known as the Hawthorne effect—see Box 2.10).

• *Measurement as a change agent*. The very fact of a researcher being in a context in which no researcher is normally present may itself cause things to be

different. For example, the fact that there is an observer sitting in on a management meeting means that there is space and a chair being used that otherwise would be unoccupied. This very fact may influence behaviour.

• *Response sets*. This is an issue that primarily relates to questionnaire and interview research and occurs when the respondent replies to a set of questions in a consistent but clearly inappropriate manner. Examples of this kind of effect are measurement problems like the social desirability effect and yea-saying and nay-saying (consistently answering yes or no to questions or consistently agreeing or disagreeing with items regardless of the meaning of the question or item).

Reactive effects are likely to occur in any research in which participants know they are the focus of investigation. Webb et al. called for greater use of what they call *unobtrusive measures* or *non-reactive methods*, which do not entail participants' knowledge of their involvement in research (see Box 10.11 for a more complete explanation). The Hawthorne effect, mentioned in Chapter 2, is a form of reactive effect, but Webb et al's categories provide a more inclusive summary of this term.

Checklist for structured observation research

✓ Have you clearly defined your research questions?

✓ Is the sample to be observed relevant to your research questions?

✓ Can you justify your sampling approach?

✓ Does your observation schedule indicate precisely which kinds of behaviour are to be observed?

✓ Have your observation categories been designed so that there is no need for the observer to interpret what is going on?

✓ Have you made sure that the categories of behaviour do not overlap?

✓ Do all the different categories of behaviour allow you to answer your research questions?

✓ Have you piloted your observation schedule?

✓ Are the coding instructions clear?

✓ Are the categories of behaviour inclusive?

✓ Is it easy to log the behaviour as it is happening?

Other forms of structured observation

Field stimulation

Salancik (1979) has used the term 'field stimulation' to describe a form of observation research that shares many of structured observation's characteristics. Although he classifies field stimulations as a qualitative method, they are in fact better thought of as operating with a quantitative research strategy, since the researcher typically seeks to quantify the outcomes of his or her interventions. In terms of the classification offered in Box 8.3, it is in fact 'contrived observation'. A field stimulation is a study in which the researcher directly intervenes in and/or manipulates a natural setting in order to observe what happens as a consequence of that intervention. However, unlike most structured observation, in a field stimulation participants do not know they are being studied, which makes it a form of unobtrusive measure as defined by Webb (1966; see Box 10.11). In business and management, consumer researchers use field stimulations to study the behaviour of retail front-line staff using the 'mystery shopper' technique (see Box 8.9). An example of the use of this

---

Box 8.9 Field stimulation and the mystery shopper

A popular technique used in consumer research to evaluate the effectiveness of retail staff is the 'mystery shopper' technique. This typically involves sending people into a shop to buy products. After the interaction, the shoppers typically fill out a rating sheet detailing the nature of the interaction and service they received. This information is then fed back via the consumer research organization to the firm concerned so that it can make any necessary improvements to front-line service. More recent developments have included supplying mystery shoppers with wireless hidden cameras that can be concealed in their cap, button, or cellphone in order to record the transactions and interaction between the customer and the assistant.

The mystery shopper technique is a type of field simulation, because it involves the researcher entering the shop (a natural setting) and intervening in order to see what happens. In addition, the retail staff are not aware that they are being studied. However, because this involves observing people without their informed consent, the mystery shopper technique does raise ethical issues (see Chapter 25), particularly if the encounter is recorded in some way, as this has even greater potential to violate their privacy, also thereby potentially raising legal considerations.

Box 8.10 A mystery shopper investigation into the selling behaviour of travel agents

In a study designed to assess the influence of travel agency recommendations on UK consumers who were choosing a holiday, Hudson et al. (2001) conducted research that combined focus groups, semi-structured interviews, and 'mystery shoppers'.

Travel agents have come under scrutiny for directional selling, placing pressure on consumers to purchase package holidays that are linked to their parent companies. The researchers wanted to investigate the extent to which this bias influenced consumer choice. They wanted to gain an insight into the interaction that occurs between travel agent and customer when the latter books a holiday. The focus groups and interviews provided the researchers with an insight into the process whereby consumers choose a holiday and this formed the basis for the construction of scenarios that were used in the second stage of data collection, which relied on the mystery shopper technique.

Fifty-two agencies from the three largest UK travel agency chains: Lunn Poly (owned by Thomson), Going Places (owned by Airtours, now renamed MyTravel), and Thomas Cook/Carlson (owned by Thomas Cook) were selected using a quota sampling technique. A list of travel agents obtained from the Association of British Travel Agents (ABTA) constituted the sampling frame from which the travel agencies were selected.

Thirty-six visits and 120 telephone calls were made by the mystery shoppers to travel agents in the London area. The 'shoppers' were trained, using role plays, to ensure that they adopted a neutral rather than an aggressive or defensive approach in the encounter with agents. None of the respondents was aware that he or she was being studied. The mystery shoppers were given one of four different scenarios.

- *Scenario 1.* The customer has a specific holiday from one brochure/operator in mind. (It was hypothesized that, in this situation, the agent would not attempt to influence the customer but would book the holiday as requested.)
- *Scenario 2.* The customer has a number of alternatives chosen from different brochures. (In this situation it

was suggested that the agent would attempt to influence the customer's choice, attempting to sell the holiday of the parent company.)

- *Scenario 3.* The customer has a certain amount of money in mind (£2,000) as well as a destination (Spain). (Here it was speculated that the travel agent would strongly influence the customer's choice, recommending the holiday of the parent company.)
- *Scenario 4.* The customer is looking for a last-minute holiday and calls the agent to see what is available. (In this circumstance it was predicted that the travel agent would exert strong influence over the customer's eventual decision.)

Each face-to-face interview lasted on average thirty minutes, while telephone encounters lasted an average of fifteen minutes. Following the interaction, 'shoppers' completed a report form, detailing for example, how forcibly the agent used directional selling tactics (i.e. did the agent try to guide the shopper towards purchasing a holiday offered by their parent company?) using a five-point scale.

Findings from the study showed that in the first scenario none of the agents made an attempt to guide the customer towards an alternative holiday, but in the third scenario all the agencies employed directional selling tactics. The study also found that the agencies owned by Airtours (MyTravel) and Thomas Cook gave more biased advice than those owned by Thomson. Of Going Places agencies, 90 per cent pushed the Airtours brand, while 75 per cent of agencies owned by Thomas Cook tried to sell their own brands, the largest being JMC holidays.

The use of the mystery shopper technique produced findings that appear to confirm the view of smaller agents and operators—that directional selling tactics are much more widespread than the larger operators or the Monopolies and Mergers Commission would like to admit. Moreover, given the publicity and interest in this issue, it is unlikely that the agents would have used directional selling tactics to such an extent if they had known that they were being studied.

technique in the study of travel agents' recommendations is given in Box 8.10.

While such research provides some quite striking findings and gets around the problem of reactivity by

not alerting research participants to the fact that they are being observed, ethical concerns are sometimes raised, such as the use of deception. Moreover, the extent to which an observation schedule can be

---

Box 8.11 Looking Glass Inc.: an organizational simulation

Looking Glass Inc. is a simulation developed by the Centre for Creative Leadership (McCall and Lombardo 1982), which requires participants to act as managers in a hypothetical glass-manufacturing organization. Unlike many other simulations, which tend to be developed for training, Looking Glass was based on research, involving interviews with executives, site visits, and the collection of data from business publications. The simulation lasts approximately six hours. Twenty participants are assigned to twenty top management roles ranging from President to Plant Manager and spanning three divisions. Their task is to run the company for a day in any way they want.

The simulation begins the evening before, with events that are designed to familiarize participants with the company, including a slide show explaining the structure of the company. Participants are assigned roles and spend some time in their offices; job descriptions and annual reports are distributed. The following morning, the simulation of a business day commences. 'Each participant spends the first 45 minutes at his or her desk reviewing an in-basket containing today's mail . . . After 45 minutes the telephone system is turned on and the managers are free to call meetings, send memos, place phone calls, etc. Using memo or phone participants can contact anyone inside or outside the company' (1982: 535).

The simulation includes a wide range of management problems and issues that participants must deal with (or ignore if they see fit). These cover a range of functional areas and include:

- an opportunity to acquire a new plant;
- a lawsuit with a major customer;
- technological innovation and obsolescence.

The three divisions within the company face different external environments:

- *Advanced Products*—makes products for electronics and communications industries and exists in a highly uncertain and rapidly changing business environment;
- *Commercial Glass*—makes light bulb casings and flat glass and faces a relatively predictable, stable market;
- *Industrial Glass*—faces a mixed environment because of the wide variety of products it makes, from auto glass (stable) to spacecraft windows (unstable).

The simulation enables a variety of data collection methods to be used, including the possibility of structured observation. Observers can be assigned to observe specific roles or to time sample all the roles on a scheduled basis. Memos sent by participants and telephone calls made provide a further unobtrusive source of data. However, McCall and Lombardo claim that, 'in many respects, studying Looking Glass presents the same challenges as studying a real organization' (1982: 540), because it is impossible to control the variables involved.

---

employed is inevitably limited (unless the researcher is carrying a hidden camera, as some 'mystery shoppers' have done), because excessive use will blow the observer's cover. All that can usually be done is to engage in limited coding at the time of the interaction, paying particular attention to the nature of the effect of the intervention, or to document the interaction immediately after the observation has taken place, as the Hudson et al. (2001) research in Box 8.10 did.

Organizational simulation

An alternative method for observing behaviour in which participants are made aware of the fact that they are being studied involves the organizational simulation. A simulation involves representing a situation by creating an artificial setting in which individual or group behaviour can be observed. An example of an organizational simulation is provided in Box 8.11. In a sense, a simulation is similar to a laboratory experiment (see Chapter 2), except that it does not seek to control participants' activities as much as in an experimental research design. Simulations can thus give participants much greater freedom to act according to their judgement and to make decisions and their actions become the focus of observation. McEnery and Blanchard (1999) used an adapted version of the Looking Glass simulation (see Box 8.11) to examine the reliability and validity of assessor, peer, and self-ratings of management skills. The sample comprised 261 business undergraduate students in a university in the midwestern USA. The 'president' of Looking Glass was elected by class vote after a nomination speech. The president then collaborated with other participants to determine who would play which role. Once this was decided, participants were each provided with an annual report and various memos and reports to accompany individual roles.

The simulations were conducted in university laboratories that were intended to resemble organizational conference rooms and students were expected to dress as though they were business professionals. The students were assessed by graduate students and faculty volunteers, who observed and rated them according to a behavioural checklist, which included items such as 'delegating: matches tasks with people effectively' and 'listening: gives feedback, does not interrupt, used a variety of listening skills and techniques'. After the simulation, students completed a self-rating checklist to rate their own managerial skills. Each student was also assessed by a peer who had been working with him or her. The study found that the highest evaluation of managerial skill was made by peers, whereas the lowest was made by assessors. They suggest this was due to the fact that assessors were more likely to be objective because they did not know the students and because they had received more training.

Simulations create large amounts of data in a relatively short period of time, thereby overcoming some of the difficulties of cost and access that are often associated with business and management research. They also enable access to issues that may not be amenable to observation in real life, such as problem solving or decision making. Moreover, simulation enables the researcher to create and alter the situation in order to examine the effect of an intervention; if the effects of such interventions are studied in 'real' organizations, research is likely to take a considerable length of time. However, simulations are subject to the charge of artificiality. For example, by ensuring that participants dress as business professionals, as McEnery and Blanchard (1999) did in their study, there is no certainty that they will see themselves as business professionals (rather than undergraduate students) and act accordingly.

Criticisms of structured observation

Although it is not very extensively used in business and management research, structured observation has, in the past, been quite controversial. Certain criticisms have been implied in some of the previous discussion of reliability and validity issues, as well as in connection with the issue of generalizability. However, certain other areas of criticism warrant further discussion.

- There is a risk of imposing a potentially inappropriate or irrelevant framework on the setting being observed. This point is similar to the problem of the closed question in questionnaires. This risk is especially great if the setting is one about which little is known. One solution is for the structured observation to be preceded by a period of unstructured observation, so that appropriate variables and categories can be specified.

- Because it concentrates upon directly observable behaviour, structured observation is rarely able to get at intentions behind behaviour. Sometimes, when intentions are of concern, they are imputed by observers. Thus, in Mintzberg's basic activity categories of managerial behaviour it is not entirely clear what the difference is between an 'unscheduled meeting' and a 'tour' that involves a chance meeting. Essentially, the problem is that structured observation does not readily allow the observer to get a grasp of the meaning of behaviour.

- There is a tendency for structured observation to generate lots of bits of data. The problem here can be one of trying to piece them together to produce an overall picture, or one of trying to find general themes that link the fragments of data together. It becomes difficult, in other words, to see a bigger picture that lies behind the segments of behaviour that structured observation typically uncovers. It has been suggested, for example, that the tendency for structured observation studies of managers at work to find little evidence of planning in their everyday work (e.g. Mintzberg 1973) is due to the tendency for the method to fragment a manager's activities into discrete parts. As a result, something like planning, which may be an element in many managerial activities, becomes obscured from view (Snyder and Glueck 1980).

- It is often suggested that structured observation neglects the context within which behaviour takes place. For example, Martinko and Gardner (1990) found that some of Mintzberg's categories of basic activity were represented differently amongst school principals, rather than general managers, and, in particular, the amount of time spent on unscheduled meetings was much greater. Of course, were data about the context in which behaviour takes place collected, this criticism would have little weight, but the tendency of structured observation researchers to concentrate on overt behaviour tends to engender this kind of criticism.

On the other hand...

It is clear from the previous section that there are undeniable limitations to structured observation. However, it also has to be remembered that, when overt behaviour is the focus of analysis and perhaps issues of meaning are less salient, structured observation is almost certainly more accurate and effective than getting people to report on their behaviour through questionnaires. It may also be that structured observation is a method that works best when accompanied by other methods. Since it can rarely provide reasons for observed patterns of behaviour, if it is accompanied by another method that can probe reasons, it is of greater utility.

In laboratory experiments in fields like social psychology and medical research, observation with varying degrees of structure is quite commonplace, but in business and management research, with the exception of Mintzberg's classic study, structured observation has not been that frequently used. Perhaps one major reason is that, although interviews and questionnaires are limited in terms of their capacity to tap behaviour accurately, as noted above, they do offer the opportunity to reveal information about both behaviour *and* attitudes and social backgrounds. In other words, they are more flexible and offer the prospect of being able to uncover a variety of correlates of behaviour (albeit reported behaviour), such as social background factors. They can also ask questions about attitudes and investigate explanations that people proffer for their behaviour. As a result, researchers using questionnaires are able to gain information about some factors that may lie behind the patterns of behaviour they uncover. Also, not all forms of behaviour are liable to be accessible to structured observation and it is likely that survey research or researcher-driven diaries (see Box 6.4) are the only likely means of gaining access to them. However, greater use of structured observation may result in greater facility with the method, so that reliable measures might emerge.

K KEY POINTS

- Structured observation is an approach to the study of behaviour that is an alternative to survey-based measures.

- It comprises explicit rules for the recording of behaviour.

- Structured observation has tended to be used in relation to a rather narrow range of forms of behaviour, such as that of managers.

- It shares with survey research many common problems concerning reliability, validity, and generalizability.

- Reactive effects have to be taken into account but should not be exaggerated.

- Field stimulations represent a form of structured observation but suffer from difficulties concerning ethics.

- Problems with structured observation revolve around the difficulty of imputing meaning and ensuring that a relevant framework for recording behaviour is being employed.

Q QUESTIONS FOR REVIEW

Problems with survey research on social behaviour

- What are the chief limitations of survey research with regard to the study of behaviour?

So why not observe behaviour?

- What are the chief characteristics of structured observation?

- To what extent does it provide a superior approach to the study of behaviour than questionnaires or structured interviews?

The observation schedule

- What is an observation schedule?

- 'An observation schedule is much like a self-completion questionnaire or structured interview except that it does not entail asking questions.' Discuss.

- Devise an observation schedule of your own for observing an area of social interaction in which you are regularly involved. Ask people with whom you normally interact in those situations how well they think it fits what goes on. Have you missed anything out?

Strategies for observing behaviour

- What are the main ways in which behaviour can be recorded in structured observation?

Sampling

- Identify some of the main sampling strategies in structured observation.

Issues of reliability and validity

- How far do considerations of reliability and validity in structured observation mirror those encountered in relation to the asking of questions in structured interviews and self-completion questionnaires?

- What is the reactive effect and why might it be important in relation to structured observation research?

Other forms of structured observation

- What are field stimulations and what ethical concerns are posed by them?

- What are the advantages and disadvantages of simulation as a form of structured observation?

Criticisms of structured observation

- 'The chief problem with structured observation is that it does not allow us access to the intentions that lie behind behaviour.' Discuss.

- How far do you agree with the view that structured observation works best when used in conjunction with other research methods?

the intention → lie behind
& motivation behaviour

Structured observation

9 Content analysis

CHAPTER GUIDE

Content analysis is an approach to the analysis of documents and texts (which may be printed or visual) that seeks to quantify content in terms of predetermined categories and in a systematic and replicable manner. It is a very flexible method that can be applied to a variety of different media. In a sense, it is not a research method, in that it is an approach to the analysis of documents and texts rather than a means of generating data. However, it is usually treated as a research method because of its distinctive approach to analysis. This chapter explores:

- the kinds of research question to which content analysis is suited;

- how to approach the sampling of documents to be analysed;

- what kinds of features of documents or texts are counted;

- how to go about *coding*, which is probably the central and most distinctive stage of doing a content analysis;

- the advantages and disadvantages of content analysis.

Introduction

Imagine that you are interested in the amount and nature of the interest shown by the mass media, such as newspapers, in a business news item such as the collapse of Enron and WorldCom and the impact this has had on corporate accountability and ethical behaviour. You might ask such questions as:

• When did news items on this topic first begin to appear?

• Which newspapers were fastest in generating an interest in the topic?

• Which newspapers have shown the greatest interest in the topic?

• At what point did media interest begin to wane?

• Have journalists' stances on the topic changed, for example, in terms of their support for business accountants and consultants, such as Arthur Anderson, or in calling for increased government regulation of corporate behaviour?

If you want to know the answers to research questions such as these, you are likely to need to use content analysis to answer them.

Probably the best-known definition of content analysis is as follows:

Content analysis is a research technique for the objective, systematic and quantitative description of the manifest content of communication.   (Berelson 1952: 18)

Another well-known and apparently similar definition is:

Content analysis is any technique for making inferences by objectively and systematically identifying specified characteristics of messages.   (Holsti 1969: 14)

It is striking that both of these definitions contain a reference to two qualities: objectivity and being systematic. The former quality means that, as with something like an observation schedule (Chapter 8), rules are clearly specified in advance for the assignment of the raw material (such as newspaper stories) to categories. Objectivity in this sense resides in the fact that there is transparency in the procedures for assigning the raw material to categories so that the analyst's personal biases intrude as little as possible in the process. The content analyst is simply applying the rules in question. The quality of being systematic means that the application of the rules is done in a consistent manner so that bias is again suppressed. As a result of these two qualities, anyone could employ the rules and (hopefully) come up with the same results. The process of analysis is one that means that the results are not an extension of the analyst and his or her personal biases. The rules in question may, of course, reflect the researcher's interests and concerns and therefore these might be a product of subjective bias, but the key point is that, once formulated, the rules can be (or should be capable of being) applied without the intrusion of bias.

Berelson's definition also makes reference to 'quantitative description'. Content analysis is firmly rooted in the quantitative research strategy, in that the aim is to produce quantitative accounts of the raw material in terms of the categories specified by the rules. The feature of quantification adds to the general sense of the systematic and objective application of neutral rules, so that it becomes possible to say with some certainty and in a systematic way that, for example, broadsheet newspapers carried far more coverage of a particular issue than tabloid newspapers.

Two other elements in Berelson's definition are striking, especially when juxtaposed against Holsti's. First, Berelson refers to 'manifest content'. This means that content analysis is concerned with uncovering the apparent content of the item in question: what it is clearly about. Holsti makes no such reference, alluding only to 'specified characteristics'. The latter essentially opens the door to conducting an analysis in terms of what we might term 'latent content'—that is, with meanings that lie beneath the superficial indicators of content. Uncovering such latent content means interpreting meanings that lie beneath the surface, such as whether the impression is given that the author construes the Enron scandal as an issue solely of concern to US shareholders and accountancy practices, or as having a broader set of implications for business practice and corporate accountability across the globe. A related distinction is sometimes made between an emphasis on the linguistic structure of the text (in particular, counting certain words) and an emphasis on themes within the text, which entails searching for certain ideas within the text (Beardsworth 1980).

A second element in Berelson's definition not found in Holsti's is the reference to 'communication'. Berelson's (1952) book was concerned with communication research, a field that has been especially concerned with newspapers, television, and other mass media. Holsti refers somewhat more generally to 'messages', which raises the prospect of a quite wide applicability of content analysis beyond the specific boundaries of the mass media and mass communications. Content analysis becomes applicable to many different forms of unstructured information, such as transcripts of semi- and unstructured interviews (e.g. Bryman, Stephens, and A Campo 1996) and even qualitative case studies of organizations (e.g. Hodson 1996). Nor is it necessary for the medium being analysed to be in a written form. Research has been conducted on:

- the visual images (as well as the text) of company annual reports to explore how these reflect organizational beliefs about customers (Dougherty and Kunda 1990; see Box 18.4);

- motivational videos featuring management guru Frederick Herzberg giving a live lecture to managers (Jackson and Carter 1998);

- the pictures drawn by managers to express their views about organizational change (Broussine and Vince 1996).

However, there is little doubt that the main use of content analysis has been to examine mass media items as well as texts and documents that are either produced by the organization, such as annual reports, or written about it, such as articles in the business press. For example, Bettman and Weitz (1983) examined letters to stockholders from the annual reports of 181 companies in four industries. A good year (1972) and a bad year (1974) were compared, based on GNP and stock market performance. In this regard, content analysis is one of a number of approaches to the examination of texts that have been developed over the years (see Box 9.1). Insch, Moore, and Murphy (1997) suggest that one of the reasons content analysis has not been very popular in business and management is because researchers are unsure how to use it. They advocate a step-by-step

---

Box 9.1 :Ö: *What is content analysis?*

- *Content analysis*. An approach to the analysis of documents and texts that seeks to quantify content in terms of predetermined categories and in a systematic and replicable manner.

Content analysis can usefully be contrasted with two other approaches to the analysis of the content of communication:

- *Semiotics*. The study/science of signs. An approach to the analysis of documents and other phenomena that emphasizes the importance of seeking out the deeper meaning of those phenomena. A semiotic approach is concerned to uncover the processes of meaning production and how signs are designed to have an effect upon actual and prospective consumers of those signs. This approach will be explored in Chapter 18.

- *Ethnographic content analysis*. A term employed by Aitheide (1996) to refer to an approach to documents that emphasizes the role of the investigator in the construction of the meaning of and in texts. It is sometimes also referred to as *qualitative content analysis*. As with most approaches that are described as ethnographic, there is an emphasis on allowing categories to emerge out of data and on recognizing the significance for understanding meaning in the context in which an item being analysed (and the categories derived from it) appeared. This approach will be explored in Chapter 18.

When the term 'content analysis' is employed in this chapter, it will be referring to quantitative content analysis—that is, the first of the three forms of analysis referred to in this list and which is the kind of analysis to which Berelson (1952) and Holsti (1969) refer.

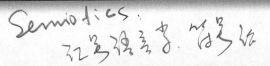

process whereby the researcher reviews the literature to develop understanding of the construct of interest and then identifies texts that are likely to capture it.

It is the intention of this chapter to provide a framework through which systematic content analysis can be conducted.

What are the research questions?

As with most quantitative research, it is necessary to specify the research questions precisely, as these will guide both the selection of the media to be content analysed and the coding schedule. If the research questions are not clearly articulated, there is a risk that inappropriate media will be analysed or that the coding schedule will miss out key dimensions. Most content analysis is likely to entail several research questions. For example, the aim of Harris's (2001) study was to investigate the way the word 'courage' was used in the business community. In itself this is not very specific and hardly directs you to a clear specification of the media to be examined or the development of a coding schedule. However, to achieve this aim Harris sought to content analyse stories in broadsheet newspapers that were about courage in order to compare a definition of courage derived from the literature with the way the word 'courage' is used in the community (especially in business, commerce, and government). This gave rise to other, more specific research questions, including:

- Is it possible to categorize the types of courage event described in the newspaper stories?

- What tools, if any, are said to have helped people show courage?

- Are obstacles identified in accounts of courage, and, if so, what are they?

- Are aspects of the accounts linked to specific professions or sectors of activity?

- Is courage used to describe dispositions, actions, or a virtue?

Such questions seem to revolve around the questions of: *who* (gets reported); *what* (gets reported); *where* (does the issue get reported); *location* (of coverage within the items analysed); *how much* (gets reported); and *why* (does the issue get reported).

As with much content analysis, the researchers were just as interested in omissions in coverage as in what *does* get reported. For example, details about the profession, qualifications, and beliefs of the courageous person were frequently omitted. Such omissions are in themselves potentially interesting, as they may reveal what is and is not important to reporters and their editors.

Another kind of issue that is frequently encountered in content analysis is:

How far does the amount of coverage of the issue change over time?

This kind of research question or problem is particularly asked by researchers who are keen to note trends in coverage to demonstrate ebbs and flows in interest. An example of this kind of research is a study by Barley, Meyer, and Gash (1988), who used content analysis to assess whether members of two distinct subcultures, business and management academics and practitioners, have influenced each other's interpretations. Content analysis focused on 192 articles published on the subject of organizational culture between 1975 and 1984. This time span was chosen to reflect changes in discussion of organizational culture at a time when understanding of this topic in the business and management field was still emerging. Content analysis focused on changes in the language used by the two groups to frame this particular issue. The research showed that, although in the mid-1970s academics and practitioners conceptualized organizational culture quite differently, by the mid-1980s academics had moved towards greater appreciation of the practitioners' point of view whilst practitioners' interpretations were little influenced by academics.

Selecting a sample

There are several phases in the selection of a sample for content analysis. Because it is a method that can be applied to many different kinds of document, the case of applying it to the mass media will be explored here. However, the basic principles have a broader relevance to a wide range of applications of content analysis.

Sampling media

Many studies of the mass media entail the specification of a research problem in the form of 'the representation of X in the mass media'. The X may be trade unions, courage in managerial decision making, or women and leadership. But which mass media might one choose to focus upon? Will it be newspapers or television or radio or magazines, or whatever? And, if newspapers, will it be all newspapers or tabloids or broadsheets? And, if both tabloids and broadsheets, will it be all of them and will it include Sunday papers? If it will be a sample of newspapers, including Sunday ones, will these be national or local or both? And will it include free newspapers? And if newspapers, will all news items be candidates

for analysis—for example, would feature articles and letters to the editor be included? And if newspapers, will newspapers from more than one country be included?

Typically, researchers will opt for one or possibly two of the mass media and may sample within that type or types. In the research described in Box 9.2, Harris (2001) chose to focus on just four broadsheet newspapers over one year, 1996, which is just as well since the author was able to locate a large number of appropriate items (news items containing one or more of the words 'courage', 'courageous', or 'courageously')—610 in total. However, the study also incorporated a cross-cultural element by sampling one newspaper from Australia, the UK, the USA, and China. However, other media that typically have a smaller more carefully selected audience can also form the focus for content analysis. For example, Barley, Meyer, and Gash (1988) conducted content analysis on items from business and management journals. Although these periodicals cannot be classified as mass media in the conventional sense, as the average peer-reviewed journal article is read by only a handful of people, these journals do represent

---

Box 9.2 A content analysis of courage and managerial decision-making

The aim of Harris's (2001) study was to investigate the way the word 'courage' was used in the business community and to compare this with a theoretical definition of the construct defined prior to data collection based on a selective review of the literature. The content analysis procedure that followed relied on searching through the 1996 editions of four daily newspapers—the *Australian Financial Review*, the *Guardian* (UK), the *Los Angeles Times*, and the *South China Morning Post*. These newspapers were selected because they all had substantial coverage of business and commerce, they covered a wide geographical spread, and they could provide information about the way that courage was perceived in the business community.

Using a searchable database, Harris included items where the word 'courage', or derivatives such as 'courageous', appeared in the text. This gave him a total population of 610 items. Each of the items was coded by the researcher using a specially designed form that allowed for inclusion of information about the nature of the article, the characteristics of the individual who was described as courageous, and the features of the courage that was being described. A coding 'dictionary' was devised that showed the coding rules, so that more than one coder could be involved in the classification and thereby increase validity. Findings showed that the newspaper stories about courage confirmed the theoretical definition of the construct that had been developed during the first stage of the study.

a highly influential medium for the subcultural groups that Barley and his colleagues were concerned to investigate.

Sampling dates

Sometimes, the decision about dates is more or less dictated by the occurrence of a phenomenon. For example, the timing of representation of the Enron scandal will have been more or less dictated by the speed of the US government investigation into the company's downfall and its accounting practices. One could hardly examine the issue fully prior to this investigation, though there may be an important consideration in deciding at what point the content analysis should cease, since discussions about Enron and what it means for other businesses could continue for some time after the cessation of the investigation and may entail a reappraisal as a result of subsequent events, such as the demise of Anderson Consulting.

With a research question that entails an ongoing general phenomenon, such as the representation of courage in managerial decision making or the cultural values of companies, the matter of dates is more open. The principles of probability sampling

---

Box 9.3 A computer-aided content analysis of organizational values

Kabanoff, Wardersee, and Cohen (1995) studied eighty-eight large, well-known Australian organizations, which comprised the sample based on content analysis of four kinds of organizational documents:

- annual reports;
- company-wide internal magazines;
- mission or corporate values statements;
- other documents produced for distribution to employees (e.g. newsletters).

The organizations all provided documents of this type (or as many as they could) for the years 1986–90. Over 1,000 documents were analysed using computer-aided content analysis against the words specified in a content dictionary that was created by the researchers to identify value structures. The researchers claim that computer-aided content analysis provides a number of advantages over manual content analysis, not least that it offers perfect reliability in the classification of text, unlike human coders, and it is labour saving in terms of time and effort. In dealing with the criticisms associated with computer-aided methods, the researchers suggest that the apparent advantage of manual coding—that human coders can better judge the meaning of a word in context—are less apparent than has previously been supposed. Because the research was concerned with organizational values rather than with individually held values, documents such as annual reports were seen as likely to represent the value consensus among senior managers within the firm.

Sections of the documents that referred to organizational goals and values were analysed, in addition to 'any "human interest" stories that made mention of "what it means to work for this organization" ' (1995: 1081). The documents were coded according to nine categories of organizational values, including authority, leadership, teamwork, participation, commitment, performance, and reward. The authors noted the frequency of occurrence of each type of organizational value within each organization and for each document type.

On the basis of this measurement of values, the organizations were measured against four prototypical value structures and categorized as:

- elite;
- meritocratic;
- leadership;
- collegial.

Using this classification, the next step of the research involved exploration of the way that change was portrayed by each of the four types of organizations. The study found that descriptions of organizational change were consistent with the organization's value structure. For example, elite organizations tended to view change as a top-down process driven by the needs of the organization, whereas meritocratic organizations tended to emphasize the need to motivate employees to play a constructive role in the process. The authors conclude that the study supports the view that a key aspect of managing organizational change involves recognition of an organization's value structure.

outlined in Chapter 4 can readily be adapted for sampling dates—for example, generating a systematic sample of dates by randomly selecting one day of the week and then selecting every *n*th day thereafter. Alternatively, Monday newspapers could provide the first set of newspapers for inclusion, followed by Tuesday the following week, Wednesday the week after, and so on.

One important factor is whether the focus will be on an issue that entails keeping track of representation as it happens, in which case the researcher may begin at any time and the key decision becomes when to stop, or whether it is necessary to go backwards in time to select media from one or more time periods in the past. For example, if Kabanoff, Waldersee, and Cohen (1995) had wanted to examine whether there had been a marked change in the way that companies represent their cultural values through annual reports and other documents (see Box 9.3), they would obviously have needed to examine the reports, magazines, and newsletters of years

prior to 1986. They might have taken comparable samples from ten and twenty years earlier, had the companies been in existence for this long, and perhaps even beyond. Similarly, because the topic of organizational culture had attracted 'only sporadic interest before the late 1970s', Barley, Meyer, and Gash (1988: 32) stipulated that content analysis should be carried out only on articles, written in English, that appeared in periodicals or collections of readings published after January 1975. The researchers' own informed judgement of interest in this topic thus determined their decision as to how far back to go in their sampling of the journals. Moreover, content analysis of texts was seen by the authors to be a more favourable method for studying the way that concepts of organizational culture have changed over time because journal articles are preserved at the point in time when they were written. This makes them less prone to retrospective construction than other, observational methods that could have been used to capture the author's point of view.

What is to be counted?

Obviously, decisions about what should be counted in the course of a content analysis are bound to be profoundly affected by the nature of the research questions under consideration. Content analysis offers the prospect of different kinds of 'units of analysis' being considered. The following kinds of units of analysis are frequently encountered and can be used as guides to the kinds of objects that might be the focus of attention. However, what you would actually *want* or *need* to count will be significantly dictated by your research question.

Significant actors

Particularly in the context of mass media news reporting, the main figures in any news item and their characteristics are often important items to code. These considerations are likely to result in such persons as the following being recorded in the course of a content analysis.

- What kind of person has produced the item (e.g. general or specialist news reporter)?
- Who is or are the main focus of the item (e.g. senior executive of an organization, manager, politician, or employee representative)?
- Who provides alternative voices (e.g. consumer representative, official from a professional association or employee)?
- What was the context for the item (e.g. publication of financial results, major organizational event or disaster)?

In the case of the content analysis of managerial courage (see Box 9.2), the significant actors included:

- the courage event or events described in the newspaper story;
- the type of newspaper item (e.g. long or short general article, biography or obituary, book review etc.) in which the courage event was reported;

- the details of the actor associated with the courageous act or action in the item (e.g. personal details, status, and the kinds of obstacles he or she faced and the tools he or she used to help him or her to take courageous action).

The chief objective in recording such details is to map the main protagonists in news reporting in an area and to begin to reveal some of the mechanics involved in the production of information for public consumption.

Words

While it may seem a dull activity, counting the frequency with which certain words occur is sometimes undertaken in content analysis. Deciding what the unit of analysis will be, whether word, phrase, or sentence, is an important consideration in content analysis research. In Kabanoff, Waldersee, and Cohen's (1995) study, for example (see Box 9.3), the focus was on the sentence, and a total of 40,593 sentences were analysed. Such a large sample would be difficult to contemplate using manual analysis and the scale of this study to some extent justifies the authors' use of computer-aided content analysis. Gephart (see Box 18.6) also used data analysis software to assist his qualitative study of accounts of a pipeline disaster, taking the phrase, rather than the word, to be the unit of analysis. Similarly, in Bettman and Weitz's (1983) study of corporate annual reports, the unit of analysis was defined as a phrase or sentence in which there is some sort of causal reasoning about a performance outcome. The use of some words rather than others can often be of some significance because they have the potential to reveal the interpretative frameworks used by different subcultural groupings. For example, Barley, Meyer, and Gash (1988) posited that practitioner-oriented papers on organizational culture would use words that were associated with rational organizing strategies. In order to test this proposition, they calculated the percentage of a paper's paragraphs that contained words associated with bureaucracy, such as 'hierarchy', and words associated with structural differentiation, such as 'departments' or 'divisions'. Similarly,

they suggested that practitioner-oriented papers would also make more references to external forces and environmental uncertainty that posed a threat to corporate performance. Words associated with this discourse included 'changing technology', 'foreign competition', 'fluctuating interests', and 'Japanese management'.

Subjects and themes

Frequently in a content analysis the researcher will want to code text in terms of certain subjects and themes. Essentially, what is being sought is a categorization of the phenomenon or phenomena of interest. In the study by Barley, Meyer, and Gash (1988), the researchers further posited that academically oriented articles would exhibit a number of key themes. In addition, words associated with the causal framework employed in the papers that were written for a practitioner audience would be 'conspicuously absent'. While categorizations of specific words are often relatively straightforward, when the process of coding is thematic, a more interpretative approach needs to be taken. At this point, the analyst is searching not just for manifest content but latent content as well. It becomes necessary to probe beneath the surface in order to ask deeper questions about what is happening. One theme that cut across all the papers was the justification of organizational culture as an alternative paradigm for understanding organizational phenomena. Hence they found that, 'although the precise nature of the alternative varied from article to article, the perception that culture offered a radical departure from traditional organizational theory was nearly invariant' (1988: 44). Like the practitioner-oriented articles, academic articles also viewed organizational culture as a source of social integration, but, unlike the articles aimed at practitioners, they did not seek to portray culture as a force for social control. The researchers therefore sought to classify academically oriented articles according to the percentage of paragraphs that contained sentences which expressed gain or loss of control through culture. They speculated that articles written for an academic audience from a functionalist perspective would see culture as a means of gaining control but that very few of the articles would see culture as leading to loss of control because this would not fit with the academics' anthropologically informed paradigm. To test the model, the three researchers therefore coded all 192 of the articles according to these indicators and arrived at a final score that comprised a percentage average of the three individual ratings. Their analysis showed that, although practitioners and academics initially saw culture quite differently, over time academics changed their understanding of organizational culture to incorporate the practitioner's point of view, even though practitioners' understanding of culture was little influenced by the academic viewpoint.

Dispositions

A further level of interpretation is likely to be entailed when the researcher seeks to demonstrate a disposition in the texts being analysed. For example, it may be that the researcher wants to establish whether the journalists, in the reporting of an issue in the news media, are favourably inclined or hostile towards an aspect of it, such as their stances on the practice of paying chief executives large financial bonuses. Alternatively, the researcher may be interested in the views of a news article reader, rather than the writer. For example, in the case of the study by Chen and Meindl (1991), the authors wanted to discern the image formed by news article readers about the owner of the airline People Express, entrepreneur Donald Burr. Each item was coded in terms of whether the reader had interpreted the editorial commentary on the leader's image in a way that was positive or negative. In many cases, it was necessary to infer whether the editorial commentary was implicitly positive or negative on the basis of image themes. For example, positive image themes were defined by the authors to include 'motivation'—that is, Burr as an individual who is motivated, ambitious, and energetic—whereas the theme 'overdone' was interpreted by the authors as a negative image, characterized by descriptions of the leader as overzealous, idealistic, and lacking in realism. Such an analysis entails establishing whether a judgemental stance can be discerned in the items being coded and, if so, what the nature of the judgement is.

Coding

As much of the foregoing discussion has implied, coding is a crucial stage in the process of doing a content analysis. There are two main elements to a content analysis coding scheme: designing a coding schedule and designing a coding manual. To illustrate its use, imagine a student who is interested in newspaper reports of employment tribunal hearings dealing with sex, race, or disability discrimination in the workplace and reported in a national daily newspaper over a three-month period. The student chooses to focus on the reporting of the employment tribunal hearing and the outcomes of the hearing. To simplify the issue, the following variables might be considered:

1. nature of the claim (e.g. denial of promotion);
2. gender of the complainant;
3. ethnicity of the complainant;
4. occupation of complainant;
5. age of complainant;
6. marital status of complainant;
7. nature of the employer's business;
8. number of employees;
9. outcome of tribunal (case sustained/not sustained; nature of award);
10. position of the news item;
11. number of words in the item.

Analysis would enable the student to record information about the kinds of sex, race, or disability discrimination issues that employment tribunals deal with and also to look for patterns in the characteristics of complainants and employers. The content analysis could thereby provide valuable insight—for example, into the way that gendered managerial structures, cultures, and organizational practices are reproduced (Collinson and Hearn 1996). Content analysts would normally be interested in a much larger number of variables than this, but a simple illustration like this can be helpful to show the kinds of variables that might be considered.

Coding schedule

The coding schedule is a form into which all the data relating to an item being coded will be entered. Figure 9.1 provides an example of a coding schedule based on the study of managerial courage and decision-making described in Box 9.2. The schedule is very much a simplification in order to facilitate the discussion of the principles of coding in content analysis and of the construction of a coding schedule in particular.

Each of the roman numerals in Figure 9.1 relates to a specific dimension that is being coded—for example, 'iii' relates to the dimension 'qualifications' of the actor. The blank cells on the coding form are the places where codes are written. A new coding schedule form would be used for each media item coded. The codes can then be transferred to a computer data file for analysis with a software package like SPSS (see Chapter 12).

Coding manual

On the face of it, the coding schedule in Figure 9.1 seems very bare and does not appear to provide much information about what is to be done or where. This is where the coding manual comes in. The coding manual, sometimes referred to as the content analysis dictionary, is a statement of instructions to coders that specifies the categories that will be used to classify the text based on a set of written rules that define how the text will be classified. It provides: a list of all the dimensions; the different categories subsumed under each dimension; the letters or numbers (i.e. *codes*) that correspond to each category; and guidance on what each dimension is concerned with, the definitions or rules to be used in assigning words to categories, and any factors that should be taken into account in deciding how to allocate any particular code to each dimension. The coding manual enables the message content to be coded in a consistent manner. The coding categories for each dimension need to be mutually exclusive and exhaustive so that there is no sense of overlap. There are a number of off-the-shelf content analysis dictionaries (e.g. Harvard VI Psychosocial Dictionaries) that are often used as a starting point from which the researcher him- or

No.	Information about the actor	Code	No.	Features of courage displayed, sought, or observed	Code
i.	Gender of actor		viii.	Word used to describe courage	
ii.	Age of actor		ix.	Tools mentioned	
iii.	Qualifications		x.	Obstacles mentioned	
iv.	Profession		xi.	Involves choice between personal values and corporate values	
v.	Place		xii.	Involves defence of corporate/ organizational values or vision	
vi.	Rank		xiii.	Involves choice between personal advantage and corporate/community good	
vii.	Evidence of being a risk-taker		xiv.	Courage refers to the action or to disposition of actor or to a virtue	

Figure 9.1 Coding schedule
Source: adapted from Harris (2001).

Information about the actor	Features of courage displayed, sought, or observed
i. Gender of actor Male (1); Female (2); Unknown (3)	**viii. Word used to describe courage** Courage/ous/ly (1); Moral courage (2); Brave/ry (3); Dare/ing (4); Moral fibre (5); Strong will (6); Persevere/nce (7)
ii. Age of actor (at the time the event occurred) Record age in years (0 if unknown)	**ix. Tools mentioned (activities, circumstances, or events that facilitated the courage)** Bind (1) = made a public statement so as to make it harder to avoid the intended action Devil's Advocate (2) = a person specifically designated to put contrary views Example (3) = e.g. 'seeing what A did gave me courage' Horror (4) = can't allow it to continue, sheer enormity (to the actor) of what is proposed/happening meant that major obstacles had to be overcome Others (5) = support expressed by others who may not necessarily be being courageous themselves Vision (6) = clear focus Faith (7) = inspiration or belief in a higher force
iii. Qualifications (only include if unambiguous) Degree/professional (1); Trade (2); Unknown (3)	**x. Obstacles mentioned (something faced or overcome, a difficulty, concern, temptation, or hurdle)** Easy path (1) = temptation to avoid the hard work Name calling (2) = personal abuse directed at the actor Physical threat (3) = violence or threat of violence to actor, family, etc. Commercial risk (4) = includes potential financial consequences Unpopular (5) = what is planned is unpleasant or trenchantly opposed
iv. Profession (only include if unambigious) Law (1); Medicine (2); Engineering (3); Accounting (4); Journalism (5); Other (6); Not clear or combined (7)	**xi. Involves choice between personal values and corporate values** Yes, personal values chosen (1); Yes, corporate and community values chosen (2); Unknown (3)
v. Place in which the event occurred Use 2-letter ISO country code (see Box 9.4 for some examples); if many, code as World (–1)	**xii. Involves defence of corporate/organizational values or vision** Yes (1); No (2)
vi. Rank (only include if unambiguous) Minister and ranking opposition, US senator (1); Member of Parliament (2); Manager (3); Company owner (4); Board member (5); Self-employed (6); Corporate professional, e.g. engineer or lawyer (7); other (8)	**xiii. Involves choice between personal advantage and corporate/community good** Yes, personal advantage chosen (1); Yes, corporate and community good chosen (2); Unknown (3)
vii. Evidence of being a risk-taker (evidence in the item apart from courage event of the actor being a risk-taker) Yes (1); No (2)	**xiv. Courage refers to the action or to disposition of actor or to a virtue** The word 'courage' is used to describe an act or action, or some other outcome—*a courageous act, acted courageously, acted with courage* (1); Courage is attributed to the actor in relation to the act(s)—*to show courage, to be courageous* (2); Courage is mentioned without attribution to either act or person *e.g. reference to a disembodied virtue* (3)

Figure 9.2 Coding manual

Source: adapted from Harris (2001).

herself constructs a coding manual that relates to the particular research project.

For example, in his study of managerial courage and managerial decision making Harris (2001) constructed a coding manual to define the features of courage that he was looking for in the newspaper stories. Figure 9.2 provides a simplified version of the coding manual that corresponds to the coding schedule developed by Harris in this study (see Figure 9.1). The coding manual includes all the dimensions that would be employed in the coding process, indications of guidance for coders, and the lists of categories that were created for each dimension. The coding manual includes instructions for classification of information about the actor in addition to categories for various features of the courage referred to in the newspaper article, how it was displayed, sought, or observed. The coding schedule and manual permit only one obstacle or tool to be recorded in relation to a particular phrase or sentence in a newspaper article. However, if a phrase contains two or more obstacles or tools, the coder may break down the phrase and code a single word or a few words at a time.

The coding manual is crucial, because it provides coders with complete listings of all categories for each dimension they are coding and guidance about how to interpret the dimensions. At this stage decisions must be made regarding the treatment of words that have more than one meaning. For example, Harris (2001) had to filter out items that were referring to 'Courage' as a brand of beer or its brewer from those that were dealing with courage as a quality or personal trait. It is on the basis of these lists and guidance that a coding schedule of the kind presented in Figure 9.1 will be completed. Even if you are a lone researcher, such as a student conducting a content analysis for a dissertation or thesis, it is important to spend a lot of time providing yourself with instructions about how to code. While you may not face the problem of inter-coder reliability, the issue of intra-coder reliability is still significant for you and you will probably need to use the coding manual to keep reminding yourself of your rules for coding the data.

Figure 9.3 illustrates how a fictitious example of a news item that presents an act of courage might be coded according to Harris' coding manual. The news story, published in the UK newspaper the *Guardian*, focuses on a 35-year-old female entrepreneur and small business-owner who is described as having acted courageously in taking the decision to turn down a contract with a major distributor and retailer because of concerns, which were subsequently proved correct, about the tactics being used to undermine the competition. The coding of the incident would then appear as in Figure 9.3 and the data

---

Box 9.4 Some of the ISO country codes used in Harris's (2001) study

The International Organization for Standardization (ISO) produces codes for the representation of names of countries and their subdivisions, some of which are listed below. Each one is also allocated a number to facilitate SPSS data entry.

AR Argentina (1)
AU Australia (2)
BR Brazil (3)
CH Switzerland (4)
CN China (5)
DK Denmark (6)
FI Finland (7)
JP Japan (8)
LK Sri Lanka (9)

MZ Mozambique (10)
PT Portugal (11)
RU Russian Federation (12)
TW Taiwan (13)
UK United Kingdom (14)
ZA South Africa (15)

This forms part of the organization's broader mission to produce documentary agreements, such as the ISO 9000 series, which are designed to enable international trade through establishing criteria that can be used consistently as rules, guidelines, or definitions. What this means in terms of coding is that their work could provide a basis for the development and definition of categories, as Harris (2001) has done (see Fig. 9.2).

No.	Information about the actor	Code	No.	Features of courage displayed, sought, or observed	Code
i.	Gender of actor	2	viii.	Word used to describe courage	1
ii.	Age of actor	35	ix.	Tools mentioned	4
iii.	Qualifications	1	x.	Obstacles mentioned	4
iv.	Profession	6	xi.	Involves choice between personal values and corporate values	3
v.	Place	14	xii.	Involves defence of corporate/organizational values or vision	1
vi.	Rank	4	xiii.	Involves choice between personal advantage and corporate/community good	2
vii.	Evidence of being a risk-taker	2	xiv.	Courage refers to the action or to disposition of actor or to a virtue	1

Figure 9.3 Completed coding schedule

Source: adapted from Harris (2001).

would be entered into a computer program like SPSS as follows:

2   35   1   6   14   4   2   1   4   4   3   1   2   1

Each newspaper item that mentions the word 'courage' would create a row of data with an identical structure.

Potential pitfalls in devising coding schemes

There are several potential dangers in devising a content analysis coding scheme and they are very similar to the kinds of consideration that are involved in the design of structured interview and structured observation schedules.

- *Discrete dimensions.* Make sure that your dimensions are entirely separate; in other words, there should be no conceptual or empirical overlap between them. For example, coding manual rules may be needed to distinguish the noun 'management' (referring to administrators of a firm) from the verb 'management' (e.g. the management of innovation).

- *Mutually exclusive categories.* Make sure that there is no overlap in the categories supplied for each dimension. If the categories are not mutually exclusive, coders will be unsure about how to code each item.

- *Exhaustive.* For each dimension, all possible categories should be available to coders.

- *Clear instructions.* Coders should be clear about how to interpret what each dimension is about and what factors to take into account when assigning codes to each category. Sometimes, these will have to be very elaborate. Coders should have little or no discretion in how to allocate codes to units of analysis.

- *Be clear about the unit of analysis.* For example, in Harris's (2001) study of courage and managerial decision making, more than one courage event per media item can be recorded. The coding schedule needs to be clear in distinguishing between the media item (for example, a newspaper article) and the event being coded. In practice, a researcher is interested in both but needs to keep the distinction in mind.

In order to be able to enhance the quality of a coding scheme, it is highly advisable to pilot early versions of

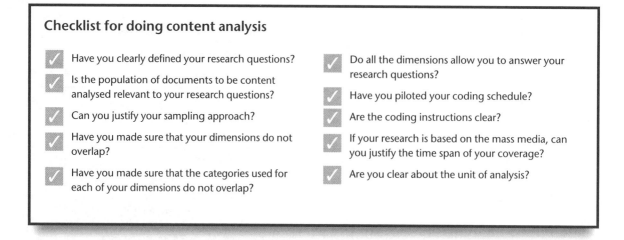

Checklist for doing content analysis

- ☑ Have you clearly defined your research questions?
- ☑ Is the population of documents to be content analysed relevant to your research questions?
- ☑ Can you justify your sampling approach?
- ☑ Have you made sure that your dimensions do not overlap?
- ☑ Have you made sure that the categories used for each of your dimensions do not overlap?
- ☑ Do all the dimensions allow you to answer your research questions?
- ☑ Have you piloted your coding schedule?
- ☑ Are the coding instructions clear?
- ☑ If your research is based on the mass media, can you justify the time span of your coverage?
- ☑ Are you clear about the unit of analysis?

the scheme. Piloting will help to identify difficulties in applying the coding scheme, such as uncertainty about which category to employ when considering a certain dimension or discovering that no code was available to cover a particular case. Piloting will also help to identify any evidence that one category of a dimension tends to subsume an extremely large percentage of items. If this occurs, it may be necessary to consider breaking that category down so that it allows greater discrimination between the items being analysed.

The reliability of coding is a further potential area of concern. Coding must be done in a consistent manner. As with structured observation, coding must be consistent between coders (*inter-coder reliability*) and each coder must be consistent over time (*intra-coder reliability*). An important part of piloting the coding scheme will be testing for consistency between coders and, if time permits, intra-coder reliability. The process of gauging reliability is more or less identical to that briefly covered in the context of structured observation in Box 8.7.

Advantages of content analysis

Kabanoff, Waldersee, and Cohen (1995) suggest that content analysis offers an important method for the cultural study of organizations because it enables researchers to analyse organizational values, traces of which can be observed in organizational documents. Moreover, by measuring the frequency with which values occur, researchers are able to discern their importance. Content analysis has several further advantages, which are outlined below.

- Content analysis is a very transparent research method. The coding scheme and the sampling procedures can be clearly set out so that replications and follow-up studies are feasible. It is this transparency that often causes content analysis to be referred to as an objective method of analysis.

- It can allow a certain amount of longitudinal analysis with relative ease. Several of the studies referred to above allow the researcher to track changes in frequency over time (Barley, Meyer, and Gash 1988; Chen and Meindl 1991; Kabanoff, Waldersee, and Cohen 1995). For example, Kabanoff et al.'s research entailed an analysis of organizational values over a four-year time period. Similarly, in the example of employment tribunal hearings concerning sex, 'race' or disability discrimination, a temporal analysis could be introduced through comparison of employment tribunal reporting in newspapers during two different time periods, such as the 1960s and the 1990s. Changes in emphasis could thus be examined.

unobtrusive 不引人注目的 . 谦虚的

- Content analysis is often referred to favourably as an *unobtrusive method*, a term devised by Webb et al. (1966) to refer to a method that does not entail participants in a study having to take the researcher into account (see Box 10.11). It is therefore a *non-reactive method* (see Box 8.8). However, this point has to be treated with a little caution. It is certainly the case that, when the focus of a content analysis is upon things such as newspaper articles or television programmes, there is no reactive effect. Newspaper articles are obviously not written in the knowledge that a content analysis may one day be carried out on them. Hence Harris (2001) suggests that the content analysis of secondary data such as newspaper articles is particularly useful when researching sensitive issues such as the ethical behaviour of managers, because the method overcomes the problematic tendency of individuals to deny socially undesirable traits and only to admit to socially desirable ones (see Chapter 5 on social desirability as a source of error). On the other hand, if the content analysis is being conducted on documents, such as interview transcripts or ethnographies (e.g. Hodson 1996; see Box 9.5), while the process of content analysis does not itself introduce a reactive effect, the documents may have at least partly been influenced by such an effect.

- It is a highly flexible method. It can be applied to a wide variety of different kinds of unstructured information. While content analysis in the social sciences is primarily associated with the analysis of mass media outputs, in business and management research it has a much broader applicability than this. Box 9.5 presents an illustration of a rather unusual but none the less interesting application of content analysis.

- Content analysis can allow information to be generated about social groups that are difficult to gain access to. For example, most of our knowledge of

---

Box 9.5 A content analysis of qualitative research on the workplace

Hodson reports the results of a content analysis of 'book-length ethnographic studies based on sustained periods of direct observation' (1996: 724). The idea of ethnography will be explored in detail in Chapter 14. As a method, ethnography entails a long period of participant observation in order to understand the culture of a social group. Hodson's content analysis concentrated on ethnographic studies of workplaces that had been published in book form (that is, published articles were excluded because they rarely included sufficient detail). Thousands of case studies were assessed for possible inclusion in the sample, but in the end 86 ethnographies were selected, which meant that 106 cases were analysed (several published ethnographies were of more than one case). The sample was made up of studies from different countries and included some well-known British ones (Beynon 1975; Nichols and Beynon 1977; Pollert 1981; Cavendish 1982). Each case was coded in terms of one of five types of workplace organization (craft, direct supervision, assembly line, bureaucratic, and worker participation). This was the independent variable. Various dependent variables and 'control' variables (variables deemed to have an impact on the relationships between independent and dependent variables) were also coded. Here are two of the variables and their codes:

Job satisfaction

1 = very low; 2 = moderately low; 3 = average; 4 = high; 5 = very high

Autonomy

1 = none (the workers' tasks are completely determined by others, by machinery or by organizational rules); 2 = little (workers occasionally have the chance to select among procedures or priorities); 3 = average (regular opportunities to select procedures or set priorities within definite limits); 4 = high (significant latitude in determining procedures and setting priorities); 5 = very high (significant interpretation is needed to reach broadly specified goals). (Hodson 1996: 728)

Hodson's findings suggest that some pessimistic accounts of worker participation schemes (for example, that they do not genuinely permit participation and do not necessarily have a beneficial impact on the worker) are incomplete. A more detailed treatment of this research can be found in Hodson (1999).

the social backgrounds of elite groups, such as company directors, derives from content analyses of such publications as *Who's Who* and *Burke's Peerage* (Bryman 1974).

Disadvantages of content analysis

Like all research techniques, content analysis suffers from certain limitations, which are described below.

- A content analysis can only be as good as the documents on which the practitioner works. John Scott (1990) recommends assessing documents in terms of such criteria as: authenticity (that the document is what it purports to be); credibility (whether there are grounds for thinking that the contents of the document have been or are distorted in some way); and representativeness (whether the documents examined are representative of all possible relevant documents, as if certain kinds of document are unavailable or no longer exist generalizability will be jeopardized). These kinds of consideration will be especially important to bear in mind when a content analysis is being conducted on documents like company reports or internal memoranda. These issues will be explored in further detail in Chapter 18.

- It is almost impossible to devise coding manuals that do not entail some interpretation on the part of coders. Coders must draw upon their everyday knowledge as participants in a common culture in order to be able to code the material with which they are confronted (Cicourel 1964; Garfinkel 1967). To the extent that this occurs, it is questionable whether it is justifiable to assume a correspondence of interpretation between the persons responsible for producing the documents being analysed and the coders (Beardsworth 1980).

- Particular problems are likely to arise when the aim is to impute latent rather than manifest content. In searching for traditional markers of organizational leadership, as in Chen and Meindl's study (1991), or inferring organizational values (Box 9.3), the potential for invalid inference being made is magnified.

- It is difficult to ascertain the answers to 'why?' questions through content analysis. For example, Barley, Meyer, and Gash (1988) found that over the course of nearly a decade academically oriented papers on the subject of organizational culture gradually adopted or accommodated practitioners' concerns. Why? Although the authors provide a number of speculative answers to these questions, content analysis alone cannot provide the answers. As they claim, 'the convergence may have resulted because academics were subtly influenced to adopt a more managerial agenda in order to secure valued resources and a larger audience for their work, but given the nature of the data, other explanations are equally plausible' (1988: 55). Hence, the authors claim that to establish the motives for the convergence would require interviewing the paper authors 'and studying networks of citations to determine who influenced whom' (1988: 55).

- Content analytic studies are sometimes accused of being atheoretical. It is easy to see why an atheoretical approach might arise. The emphasis in content analysis on measurement can easily and unwittingly result in an accent being placed on what is measurable rather than on what is theoretically significant or important. However, content analysis is not necessarily atheoretical. For example, Barley et al. place their findings about academic and practitioner subcultures in the context of a political perspective of knowledge creation and diffusion, suggesting that the research interests of academics are ultimately defined by the interests of practitioners who influence the research process, through exercising constraints on funds, sites, and objectives. Similarly, Hodson's (1996) content analysis of workplace ethnographies was underpinned by theoretical ideas deriving from the work of influential writers such as Blauner (1964) and Edwards (1979) concerning developments in modes of workplace organization and their impacts on workers' experiences.

K KEY POINTS

- Content analysis is very much located within the quantitative research tradition of emphasizing measurement and the specification of clear rules that exhibit reliability.

- While traditionally associated with the analysis of mass media content, it is in fact a very flexible method that can be applied to a wide range of phenomena.

- It is crucial to be clear about your research questions in order to be certain about your units of analysis and what exactly is to be analysed.

- You also need to be clear about what is to be counted.

- The coding schedule and coding manual are crucial stages in the preparation for a content analysis.

- Content analysis becomes particularly controversial when it is used to seek out latent meaning and themes.

Latent   Controversial

Q QUESTIONS FOR REVIEW

- To what kinds of documents and media can content analysis be applied?
- What is the difference between manifest and latent content? What are the implications of the distinction for content analysis?

What are the research questions?

- Why are precise research questions especially crucial in content analysis?
- With what general kinds of research questions is content analysis concerned?

Selecting a sample

- What special sampling issues does content analysis pose?

What is to be counted?

- What kinds of things might be counted in the course of doing a content analysis?
- To what extent do you need to infer latent content when you go beyond counting words?

Coding

Coding

- Why is coding so crucial in content analysis?
- What is the difference between a coding schedule and a coding manual?
- What potential pitfalls need to be guarded against when devising coding schedules and manuals?

Advantages of content analysis

- 'One of the most significant virtues of content analysis is its immense flexibility in that it can be applied to a wide variety of documents.' Discuss.

Disadvantages of content analysis

- To what extent does the need for coders to interpret meaning undermine content analysis?

- How far are content analysis studies atheoretical?

10

Secondary analysis and official statistics

CHAPTER GUIDE

This chapter explores the possibilities associated with the analysis of data that have been collected by others. There are two main types discussed in this chapter:

- the secondary analysis of data collected, either for commercial or academic purposes, by other researchers;
- the secondary analysis of official statistics—that is, statistics collected by government departments in the course of their work or specifically for statistical purposes.

This chapter explores :

- the advantages and disadvantages of carrying out secondary analysis of data collected by other researchers, particularly in view of many data sets being based on

large, high-quality investigations that are invariably beyond the means of students;

- how to obtain such data sets;
- the potential of official statistics in terms of their reliability and validity;
- the growing recognition of the potential of official statistics after a period of neglect as a result of criticisms levelled at them;
- the notion that official statistics are a form of *unobtrusive method*—that is, a method that is not prone to a reaction on the part of those being studied to the fact that they are research participants.

Introduction

Many of the techniques we have covered so far—survey research by questionnaire or structured interview, structured observation, and content analysis—can be extremely time-consuming and expensive to conduct. Students in particular may have neither the time nor the financial resources to conduct very extensive research. Yet we know that large amounts of quantitative data about business and management are collected by social scientists, market intelligence firms, professional associations, and others. Some of this information, such as that produced by market research organizations, can be expensive. However, many organizations, most notably government departments and their various representatives, collect data that are presented in statistical form and that may be usable without charge by students and university researchers. Would it not be a good idea to analyse such data rather than collect new data? It would have the additional advantage for managers and employees that they would not be bothered by interviewers and by questionnaires popping through their letter boxes.

This is where *secondary analysis* comes in. Secondary analysis offers this kind of opportunity. Box 10.1 contains a brief definition of secondary analysis and raises one or two basic points about what it involves. As the opening paragraph suggests, we will in this chapter be concerned with two kinds of issue:

- the secondary analysis of data that have been collected by other researchers;
- the secondary analysis of data that have been collected by various institutions in the course of their business.

In business and management, secondary analysis is of increasing interest to researchers. Traditionally, it has been the province of economists to analyse secondary data and draw conclusions about how it relates to the world of business. However, since the 1960s, more researchers, particularly those from an industrial relations background, have begun to take

greater interest in the analysis of large-scale workplace survey data. Part of the reason for this relates to the success of the Workplace Employee Relations Survey (WERS; formerly the Workplace Industrial Relations Survey (WIRS); see Boxes 2.15 and 5.9), which considerably opened up the potential for secondary analysis of work-related issues, largely because of its breadth and scope. The success of the WERS has encouraged these researchers to explore other secondary data sets, such as the Labour Force Survey (LFS), and to engage in greater cross-national, comparative analysis. Moreover, their experience of designing survey research has informed the way that these data were collected and used, by bringing insights from a more qualitative case-study-based tradition to bear on the design and development of large-scale surveys and ensuring that the right kinds of question continue to be asked (Marginson 1998).

Box 10.1 *What is secondary analysis?*

Secondary analysis is the analysis of data by researchers who will probably not have been involved in the collection of those data, for purposes that in all likelihood were not envisaged by those responsible for the data collection. Secondary analysis may entail the analysis of either quantitative data (Dale, Arber, and Proctor 1988) or qualitative data (Corti, Foster, and Thompson 1995), but it is with the former that we will be concerned in this chapter. To some extent, it is difficult to know where primary and secondary analysis start and finish. If a researcher is involved in the collection of survey interview data and analyses some of the data, resulting in some publications, but then some time later decides to rework the data, it is not entirely clear how far the latter is primary or secondary analysis. Typically, secondary analysis entails the analysis of data that others have collected, but, as this simple scenario suggests, this need not necessarily be the case.

Other researchers' data

There are several reasons why secondary analysis should be considered a serious alternative to collecting new data. These advantages of secondary analysis have been covered by Dale, Arber, and Proctor (1988), from which we have borrowed most of the following observations. In considering the various advantages of secondary analysis, we have in mind the particular needs of the lone student conducting a small research project as an undergraduate or a more substantial piece of work as a postgraduate. However, this emphasis should definitely not be taken to imply that secondary analysis is really appropriate or relevant only to students. Quite the contrary: secondary analysis should be considered by all business researchers, and, indeed, the Economic and Social Research Council (ESRC) requires applicants for research grants who are proposing to collect new data to demonstrate that relevant data are not already available in the UK Data Archive (see below). Our reason for emphasizing the prospects of secondary analysis for students is simply based on our personal experience that they tend to assume that any research they carry out has to entail the collection of primary data.

Advantages of secondary analysis

Secondary analysis offers numerous benefits to students carrying out a research project. These are outlined below.

- *Cost and time.* As noted at the outset, secondary analysis offers the prospect of having access to good quality data, such as that available from the UK Data Archive (see section on Accessing the UK Data Archive below), for a tiny fraction of the resources involved in carrying out a data collection exercise yourself.
- *High-quality data.* Many of the data sets that are employed most frequently for secondary analysis are of extremely high quality. By this we mean several things. First, the sampling procedures have

been rigorous, in most cases resulting in samples that are as close to being representative as one is likely to achieve. While the organizations responsible for these studies suffer the same problems of survey non-response as anybody else, well-established procedures are usually in place for following up non-respondents and thereby keeping this problem to a minimum. Secondly, the samples are often national samples or at least cover a wide variety of regions of Great Britain or the UK. In addition, some data sets enable cross-national comparison (see Box 10.2). The degree of geographical spread and the sample size of such data sets are invariably attained only in research that attracts quite substantial resources. It is certainly inconceivable that student projects could even get close to the coverage that such data sets attain. Thirdly, many data sets have been generated by highly experienced researchers and, in the case of some of the large data sets, like the WERS (see Boxes 2.15 and 5.9), the UK Skills Survey (Box 4.3), and the LFS (see Box 10.6), the data have been gathered by research organizations that have developed structures and control procedures to check on the quality of the emerging data (see Table 10.1).

- *Opportunity for longitudinal analysis.* Partly linked to the last point is the fact that secondary analysis can offer the opportunity for longitudinal research, which, as noted in Chapter 2, is rather rare in business and management research because of the time and cost involved. Sometimes, as with the WERS, a panel design has been employed and it is possible to chart trends and connections over time. Such data are sometimes analyzed cross-sectionally, but there are obviously opportunities for longitudinal analysis as well. Also, with data sets such as the LFS, where similar data are collected over time, usually because certain interview questions are recycled each year, trends (such as changes in working time or shifting patterns of employment) can be identified over time. With such data sets, respondents differ from year to

Box 10.2 Cross-national comparison of work orientations: an example of a secondary data set

The International Social Survey Programme (ISSP) has conducted two surveys focusing on the topic of work orientations, first in 1989 and again in 1997. Participating countries in the 1997 survey included Bangladesh, Bulgaria, Canada, Cyprus, the Czech Republic, Denmark, France, Germany, Great Britain, Hungary, Israel, Italy, Japan, the Netherlands, New Zealand, Norway, the Philippines, Poland, Portugal, Russia, Slovenia, Spain, Sweden, Switzerland, and the USA. As in 1989, the survey, which uses oral interviews and self-completion questionnaires, focused on respondents' general attitudes towards work and leisure, work organization, and work content. Opinions were elicited on such issues as: respondents' preferences for more work or more leisure time, the value of work in general, and the relative importance to respondents of factors such as job security, high income, opportunities for advancement, job interest, independence, and value to others. Other questions focused on what factors should determine how to pay two people doing the same kind of work, the effects the introduction of new technologies (computers, robots, etc.) would have on the workplace, attitudes about self-employment, size of the workplace, public- versus private-sector employment, and full-time versus part-time work. Respondents were also asked how easy or difficult it would be to find an acceptable job, how they felt about their present job, and how they viewed their working conditions (for example, if they came home exhausted from work, the amount of stress and possible danger on the job, working hours, place of work, whether their status was temporary or permanent, how their present job made use of their skills, and how they acquired these skills). Additional questions elicited information on relations in the workplace between management and employees and between workmates, how satisfied respondents were with their job, how they felt about their organization, how many days they had been absent (excluding vacation) from work in the last six months, how likely it was that they would try to find a new job within the next twelve months, and how much they worried about the possibility of losing their job. A special group of questions focused on respondents who were not currently employed. Demographic variables include age, sex, education, marital status, personal and family income, employment status, household size and composition, occupation, religion and church attendance, social class, union membership, political party, voting history, size of community, region, and ethnicity. The data set can be accessed via the UK Data Archive at the University of Essex.

year, so that causal inferences over time cannot be readily established, but nonetheless it is still possible to gauge trends. For example, although the study by Knight and Latreille (2000) was confined to use of the 1998 WERS data (see Box 10.3) the authors made frequent comparison with analyses from the 1990 WERS data to show that there had been relatively little change in patterns and rates of disciplinary sanctions and dismissals, and complaints to employment tribunals during this time period. Similarly, a study by Addison and Belfield (2000) used data from the 1998 WERS to replicate research done by other researchers who had used data from the 1990 WERS in order to test whether efforts to boost employee participation have had any effect.

• *Subgroup or subset analysis.* When large samples are the source of data (as in the WERS and the British Household Panel Survey (BHPS)), there is the opportunity to study what can often be quite sizeable subgroups of individuals or subsets of questions. Very often, in order to study specialized categories of individuals, small, localized studies are the only feasible way forward because of costs. However, large data sets can frequently yield quite large nationally representative samples of specialized categories of individuals, such as workers in a particular industry or occupation, or with a particular set of personal characteristics. These can form the basis for representative sampling of individuals. Similarly, when a large-scale survey covers several topic areas, analysis may involve focusing on a smaller subset of questions that are covered by the survey. For example, Addison and Belfield (2000) were interested in the effects of European works councils on organizational performance and

Table 10.1 Large UK and European data sets suitable for secondary analysis

Title	Data set details	Topics covered
Annual Employment Survey; formerly Census of Employment	Since 1971, Census of Employment conducted every two years. Provides a picture of the level and distribution of employment in Great Britain consisting of sample censuses (300,000 businesses) and full census in 1993 covering 1.25 million businesses. Since 1995, the Census of Employment has been replaced by the Annual Employment Survey (AES), a much smaller annual survey covering approximately 130,000 businesses, the results of which are published more rapidly. Sponsored by the Office for National Statistics: **www.statistics.gov.uk**	Data are collected on the number of jobs by geographical location, detailed industrial activity (SIC code), and whether full or part-time.
British Household Panel Survey (BHPS)	Began in 1991 and conducted annually by interview and questionnaire with a national representative sample of some 5,500 households and 10,300 individuals. It is interesting in that it follows the same representative sample of individuals—i.e. the panel—over a period of years and it is household based, interviewing every adult member of sampled households. Data deposited in the UK Data Archive. BHPS also has a homepage: **www.iser.essex.ac.uk/bhps**	Household organization; labour market behaviour; income and wealth; housing; health; and socio-economic values.
British Social Attitudes survey (BSA)	Traces the nation's social values during the 1980s and 1990s. Each annual survey consists of an hour-long interview and a self-completion questionnaire on a sample of 3,500 randomly selected adults. Sponsored by the National Centre for Social Research and held by the UK Data Archive. See: **www.natcen.ac.uk**	Covers wide range of areas of social attitudes and behaviour. The survey focuses mainly on people's attitudes, but also collects details of their behaviour patterns, household circumstances, and work.
Company Level Industrial Relations Survey	Conducted in 1985 and 1992. Sample comprises large UK organizations—with 1000+ employees on two or more sites. Sponsored by the Economic and Social Research Council (ESRC) and the Department of Trade and Industry (DTI). Face-to-face interviews were carried out with two senior managers in each company, one with the HR director, the other with a finance executive. Data deposited at UK Data Archive.	Covers a wide range of employee relations issues. The main difference between this survey and WERS is the level of analysis; instead of focusing on the workplace as the principal unit of analysis, this survey concentrates on obtaining company-level data.
European Community Studies and Eurobarometer	Since the early 1970s, public opinion surveys conducted on behalf of the European Commission at least twice a year in all member states of the European Union. The Eurobarometer series began in 1974. It comprises individual face-to-face interviews with national samples and is conducted biannually, in spring and autumn. Can be accessed via UK Data Archive.	Cross-national comparison of wide range of social and political issues, including European integration; life satisfaction; social goals; currency issues; working conditions; and travel.
Expenditure and Food Survey (EFS)	The Expenditure and Food Survey took over from the Family Expenditure Survey (FES) and the National Food Survey (NFS) in April 2001. The new EFS is therefore an amalgamation of the two surveys. It is similar in design and has kept the majority of questions from the FES. Each year around 12,000	Information on household expenditure, income, and food consumption.

Title	Data set details	Topics covered
	addresses are sampled and households are asked to keep diary records of expenditure and income over a two-week period. Face to face interviews are also conducted using computer-assisted personal interviewing (CAPI). Results are to be published by the Office for National Statistics (ONS) and by the Department for Environment, Food and Rural Affairs (DEFRA). For more information see: **www.statistics.gov.uk**	
General Household Survey (GHS)	Annual interviews since 1971 with members aged over 16 in over 8,000 randomly sampled households. Data deposited in UK Data Archive.	Has tended to cover standard issues such as education and health about which questions are asked each year, plus additional items that vary annually. Huge variety of questions relating to social behaviour and attitudes.
International Social Survey Programme (ISSP)	Annual programme, since 1983 of cross-national collaboration covering survey topics important for social science research. Brings together pre-existing projects, thereby adding a cross-national, cross-cultural perspective to the individual national studies. Coordinated by the University of Cologne, accessible via UK Data Archive.	Attitudes towards legal systems and the economy. Covers special topics including work orientations (see Box 10.4); the environment; and national identity.
Labour Force Survey (LFS)	Biennial interviews, 1973–83, annual interviews, 1984–91, comprising a quarterly survey of around 15,000 addresses per quarter and an additional survey in March–May; since 1991, quarterly survey of around 60,000 addresses. Since 1998, core questions are also administered in member states of the European Union. Results are held by UK Data Archive.	Covers hours worked, job search methods, training, and personal details, such as nationality and gender.
Office for National Statistics (ONS) Omnibus Survey	Survey carried out eight times a year since 1990 using face-to-face structured interviews on a sample of just under 2,000 people. Uses short, simple sets of questions to gain an impression of public attitudes concerning topics that change frequently. Accessible via UK Data Archive.	Covers core demographic questions about respondents plus questions that change from month to month about topics that change frequently—e.g. food safety, eating behaviour, personal finance, sports participation, Internet access, human rights, AIDS awareness.
Population Census (UK)	A simple questionnaire survey of the United Kingdom population held every ten years since 1801. The last Census was held in 2001 and the one before that in 1991. It can be accessed via UK Data Archive's Census Registration Service at: **www.census.ac.uk**	Contains information about households and individuals covering topics as diverse as age, gender, occupation, qualifications, ethnicity, social class, employment, family structure, amenities, and tenure.
UK New Earnings Survey	Since 1970, annual sample survey of the earnings of employees in Great Britain sponsored by the Office for National Statistics (ONS). Reports are free to view or download from the National Statistics website at: **www.statistics.gov.uk**	Looks at levels, composition, and distribution of earnings and details of hours worked, broken down by industry, occupation, age group, and gender.
Workplace Employee Relations Survey (WERS); formerly Workplace Industrial Relations Survey (WIRS)	This survey has been carried out in 1980, 1984, 1990 (as WIRS), and under its new name, WERS, in 1998. Workplaces of ten or more employees are sampled, and interviews carried out with managers, worker representatives, and employees. Accessible through UK Data Archive.	Wide range of areas covered, including: pay determination; recruitment and training; equal opportunities; workplace change; work attitudes; management organization; and employee representation.

Box 10.3 Unfair dismissal complaints and employment tribunals: an example of secondary analysis using the WERS data

Knight and Latreille (2000) used the 1998 Workplace Employee Relations Survey (WERS) data to investigate the incidence of disciplinary sanctions, dismissals, and unfair dismissal complaints made to UK employment tribunals. Using the management respondent data set, their analysis is based on analysis of the following dependent variables:

1 the disciplinary sanction rate per 100 employees;

2 the dismissal rate per 100 employees; and

3 the incidence of claims for unfair dismissal during the twelve months preceding the survey.

In a consideration of disciplinary sanction rates, analysis of the WERS data revealed that the rate of disciplinary sanction is lower amongst part-time and female workers. This confirms findings of other researchers (P. Edwards 1995), which suggested that women and part-time workers are more compliant to work discipline because of shorter tenure and lower pay. Knight and Latreille's findings show that the probability of dismissal is highest in workplaces with higher proportions of manual workers who are employed in routine and unskilled jobs. They also found that rates of dismissal are higher in workplaces where a greater proportion of younger workers is employed. These findings also confirm the findings of other researchers, which suggest that discipline and dismissal rates will be higher in workplaces where there is a high proportion of manual and less skilled workers because the costs of hiring and firing are lower compared with skilled employees. Finally, in workplaces where union membership is high, there is a significantly lower rate of dismissals, suggesting that unions protect their members from discipline and dismissal. In terms of the incidence of employment tribunal applications for unfair dismissal, the researchers found similar patterns: that the incidence of tribunal applications is higher in workplaces where there is a higher proportion of manual workers and in larger workplaces. The reasons for this latter finding, however, may relate to a number of factors, not least that there are likely to be more dismissals in larger workplaces and therefore more occasions on which employees are likely to feel sufficiently aggrieved to make an application to an employment tribunal. This highlights some of the limitations of the WERS data, from which it is not possible to establish the number of unfair dismissal claims brought at each workplace.

employee attitudes. They therefore analysed the responses from just *one* question in the 1998 WERS, which related to the status of these new institutional arrangements.

• *Opportunity for cross-cultural analysis*. Cross-cultural research has considerable appeal at a time when social scientists are more attuned to the processes associated with globalization and to cultural differences. It is easy to forget that many findings should not be taken to apply to countries other than that in which the research was conducted. However, cross-cultural research presents barriers to the social scientist. There are obvious barriers to do with the cost and practical difficulties of doing research in a different country, especially when language and cultural differences are likely to be significant. The secondary analysis of comparable data from two or more countries provides one possible model for conducting cross-cultural

research. The International Social Survey Programme (ISSP) is explicitly concerned with bringing together findings from existing social science surveys from different countries and contexts. An example of the kind of cross-cultural analysis the programme has produced is given in Box 10.2. Another example to illustrate how data from more than one country can be compared is a study by Coutrot (1998), in which he compared the industrial relations systems of France and Britain through statistical analysis of two broadly similar data sets—WIRS 1990 and Relations Professionnelles et Negotiations d'Entreprise (REPONSE) 1992 (a large-scale survey that covers similar issues to WIRS and is based on interviews with managers and employee representatives in France). However, in order for a cross-cultural analysis to be conducted, some coordination is necessary so that the questions asked are comparable. Differences between countries in the definitions used and the criteria for inclusion can make this difficult, as the example relating to the use of official statistics, given by J. Davies (2001; see Box 10.9), illustrates.

- *More time for data analysis*. Precisely because data collection is time-consuming, the analysis of data is often squeezed. It is easy to perceive the data collection as the difficult phase and to take the view that the analysis of data is relatively straightforward. This is not the case. Working out what to make of your data is no easy matter and requires considerable thought and often a preparedness to consider learning about unfamiliar techniques of data analysis. While secondary analysis invariably entails a lot of data management—partly so that you can get to know the data and partly so that you can get it into a form that you need (see below)—and this phase should not be underestimated—the fact that you are freed from having to collect fresh data means that your approach to the analysis of data can be more considered than perhaps it might otherwise have been.

- *Reanalysis may offer new interpretations*. It is easy to take the view that, once a set of data has been analysed, the data have in some sense been drained of further insight. What, in other words, could possibly be gained by going over the same data that someone else has analysed? In fact, data can be analysed in so many different ways that it is very unusual for the range of possible analyses to be exhausted. Several possibilities can be envisaged. A secondary analyst may decide to consider the impact of a certain variable on the relationships between variables of interest. Such a possibility may not have been envisaged by the initial researchers. Secondly, the arrival of new theoretical ideas may suggest analyses that could not have been conceived of by the original researchers. In other words, the arrival of such new theoretical directions may prompt a reconsideration of the relevance of the data. Thirdly, an alternative method of quantitative data analysis may be employed and offer the prospect of a rather different interpretation of

the data. Fourthly (and related to the last point), new methods of quantitative data analysis are continuously emerging. One of these is meta-analysis (see Box 10.4), which involves summarizing the results of a large number of quantitative studies and conducting various analytical tests to show whether or not a particular variable has an effect. An example of a meta-analytical study of team-working effectiveness is provided in Box 10.5. As awareness of such techniques spreads, and their potential relevance is recognized, researchers become interested in applying them to new data sets.

- *The wider obligations of the business researcher*. For all types of business research, research participants give up some of their time, usually for no reward. It is not unreasonable that the participants should expect that the data that they participate in generating should be mined to its fullest extent. However, much business research is chronically underanalysed. Primary researchers may feel they want to analyse only data relating to central research questions or lose interest as a new set of research

---

Box 10.4 *What is meta-analysis?*

Meta-analysis provides a means whereby the results of large numbers of quantitative studies of a particular topic can be summarized and compared. The aim of this approach is to establish whether or not a particular variable has a certain effect by comparing the results of different studies. Meta-analysis thus involves pooling the results from various studies in order to estimate an overall effect by correcting the various sampling and non-sampling errors that may arise in relation to a particular study. In a sense, a meta-analysis lies between two kinds of activity covered in this book: conducting a secondary analysis of other reseachers' data (the focus of this chapter) and doing a literature review of existing studies in an area in which you are interested (see the section on 'Searching the existing literature' in Chapter 26). However, the technique relies on all the relevant information being available for each of the studies examined. Since not all the same information relating to methods of study and sample size is included in published papers, meta-analysis is not always feasible.

questions interpose themselves into their imagination. Making data available for secondary analysis enhances the possibility that fuller use will be made of data.

Limitations of secondary analysis

The foregoing list of benefits of secondary analysis sounds almost too good to be true. In fact, there are not very many limitations, but the following warrant some attention.

- *Lack of familiarity with data.* When you collect your own data, when the data set is generated, it is hardly surprising that you are very familiar with the structure and contours of your data. However, with data collected by others, a period of familiarization is necessary. You have to get to grips with the range of variables, the ways in which the variables have been coded, and various aspects of the organization of the data. The period of familiarization can be quite substantial with large complex data sets and should not be underestimated.

- *Complexity of the data.* Some of the best-known data sets that are employed for secondary analysis, such as the WERS and the General Household Survey (GHS), are very large in the sense of having large numbers of both respondents and variables. Sometimes, the sheer volume of data can present problems with the management of the information at hand, and, again, a period of acclimatization may be required. Also, some of the most prominent data sets that have been employed for secondary analysis are known as *hierarchical* data sets, such as the WERS. The difficulty here is that the data are collected and presented at the level of both the organization and the individual, as well as other levels. The secondary analyst must decide which level of analysis is going to be employed. If the decision is to analyse individual-level data, the individual-level data must then be extracted from the data set. Different data will apply to each level. Thus, at the organizational level, the WERS provides data on such variables as number of employees and level of ownership, while, at the individual level, data on age, qualifications, and salary level can be

---

Box 10.5 A meta-analysis of the effectiveness of teamwork

A meta-analysis conducted by Gully et al. (2002) sought to test the proposition that team *efficacy*, a team's belief that it can successfully perform a particular task, and team *potency*, a team's general belief in its capabilities across tasks and contexts, are positively related to team performance. They also wanted to examine the impact of *interdependence* (defined as the task, goal, and outcome interconnections between team members) on this relationship. They hypothesized that team efficacy would be more strongly related to performance when interdependence within a team was high.

Studies were identified using computer and manual searches of management-related journals and abstracting and indexing databases. Gully and his colleagues also contacted researchers working in the field to find out about projects that they were currently involved with and they searched conference proceedings for relevant papers. Sixty-seven studies were identified as suitable for meta-analysis. Each was read and coded according to

the size of the effect relating team efficacy or potency to performance and was rated for aspects of interdependence. The researchers explored the reliability of the measurement instruments that had been used and took the sample size into account in their analysis of the studies.

Results of the analysis indicated that team efficacy and potency are related positively to performance. In addition, although interdependence was found to moderate the relationship between team efficacy and performance, interdependence was not found to affect the relationship between team potency and performance. These findings led the authors to conclude that the characteristics of the task environment are an important influence on the relationship between team efficacy and performance. In particular, when there is a high degree of interdependence—that is, coordination, communication, and cooperation among team members—team efficacy is more strongly related to performance.

found. For example, Hoque (2003) was interested in the impact of Investors in People (IiP) accreditation on workplace training practice. He used data from the 1998 WERS managers survey to extract organization-level data to build up a profile of workplaces that have IiP accreditation. However, in order to evaluate the impact of IiP accreditation on training practice, Hoque relied on individual-level data, in the form of data about training activity taken from the survey of employees. These included questions about the number of days spent on training that were paid for or organized by the employer and whether or not the employee had, in the previous twelve months, discussed their training needs with their supervisor. He used these data to draw conclusions at the level of the organization, and to make comparisons of the effectiveness of training practice in accredited versus non-accredited workplaces.

• *No control over data quality*. The point has been made on several occasions that secondary analysis offers the opportunity for students and others to examine data of far higher quality than they could collect themselves. However, this point applies mainly to data sets from a regulated source such as the UK Data Archive (see Table 10.1). These tend to be commissioned by a government department and conducted by researchers who are regarded as independent or at least somewhat distanced from the issues that are being investigated, such as academics working for a university research unit. While the quality of data should never be taken for granted, in the case of such data sets it is reasonably assured, though that is not to say that the data will necessarily meet all a prospective secondary analyst's needs, since they may not have been collected on an aspect of a topic that would have been of considerable interest. As an example of this last point, see the use by Felstead et al. (2001) of the LFS (see Box 10.6). With other data sets, somewhat more caution may be necessary in connection with assessment of data quality. This may be of particular concern when using data that are the result of commercially commissioned research, as is the case in market research or when using surveys that have been conducted in-house by a company that

wants, for example, to measure the effectiveness of its human resource management strategy.

• *Absence of key variables*. Because secondary analysis entails the analysis of data collected by others for their own purposes, it may be that one or more key variables may not be present. You may, for example, want to examine whether a relationship between two variables holds even when one or more *other* variables are taken into account. Such an analysis is known as *multivariate analysis*, an area that will be touched on in the next chapter. The inability to examine the significance or otherwise of a theoretically important variable can be frustrating and can arise when, for example, a theoretical approach that has emerged since the collection of the data suggests its importance. This is also a drawback in meta-analysis, sometimes making it difficult for researchers to generate unambiguous conclusions as a result of the analysis (see Box 10.7). Obviously, when researchers collect primary data themselves, the prospect of this happening should be less pronounced.

Accessing the UK Data Archive

The UK Data Archive at the University of Essex is likely to be your main source of quantitative data for secondary analysis. This national resource centre houses over 4,000 data sets and is thus the largest collection of accessible digital data in the social sciences and humanities in the UK. It is particularly useful for obtaining data on social and economic topics. Data are acquired from academic, commercial and government sources and preserved and made available for further analysis by the research community. The Archive has a very good web site, which can be searched in a variety of ways, such as keywords (see below).

Access to the Archive's holdings is provided to all researchers and teachers unless restrictions have been placed on the dataset by the owners. In addition to British cross-sectoral studies from academic, government, and commercial sources, the Archive holds time series data, major longitudinal studies, panel surveys, and major cross-sectional studies.

Box 10.6 Working at home: an example of secondary analysis using the Labour Force Survey

The aim of Felstead et al.'s (2001) research was to obtain 'a reliable statistical portrait of people who work at home' (2001:216) through analysis of a national data set. Having identified a number of drawbacks associated with UK census data—notably the lack of currency of the data, which are collected only once every ten years, and the imprecision of the census in establishing exactly where work is conducted—they decided to carry out an analysis using Labour Force Survey (LFS) data instead. The data enabled specification of three separate groups:

- those who work *mainly* at home;

- those who work *partially* at home (at least one day a week); and

- those who work *sometimes* at home.

Their analysis suggests that, although the incidence of working at home is increasing, as popular commentaries on the future of work suggest, most of the people who work at home do so on a fairly irregular, infrequent basis. Even though the number of people working mainly at home has increased from 1.5 per cent to 2.5 per cent over the 1991–8 period, this remains a very small proportion of the employed workforce.

In terms of characteristics, analysis showed that the image of people who work at home as predominantly comprising women with young children, the under-qualified, and members of ethnic minorities was somewhat of an oversimplification. The results showed that, among those working mainly at home, women outnumber men but the opposite is true among those who work at home partially and sometimes. Moreover, when the category of those who work mainly at home is disaggregated to show manual and non-manual workers, it reveals that 88.2 per cent of manual employees who work mainly at home are women. In terms of the impact of dependent children, the researchers found that the proportion of women with pre-school children is higher among those working mainly at home (15.8 per cent) than women in employment (10.2 per cent), but the reverse is true for men. In terms of qualifications, those who work mainly from home have qualification levels similar to those of the employed population, but those who work at home partially or sometimes are significantly more likely to be educated to degree level than the rest of the employed population. Finally, they suggest that ethnic minorities are generally under-represented among those who work at home. However, they are over-represented amongst those working mainly at home in manual occupations and are amongst the worst paid. The analysis reveals that 'the social relations of those who work at home are not homogeneous but rather comprise a fragmented and diverse mosaic' in which the 'cross-cutting divisions of gender, ethnicity, occupation and employment status' are prominent (2001: 229).

Data holdings include: UK Census data; General Household Survey (GHS); Family Expenditure Survey (FES); Office for National Statistics (ONS) Omnibus Survey; Labour Force Survey (LPS); British Crime Survey; British Social Attitudes (BSA). Data are made available over the network, on CD-ROM, and on other media, depending on the user's needs. The archive can also be used to locate and acquire data from other archives within Europe and worldwide, using a series of reciprocal agreements with the individual institutions. The Data Archive publishes a regular newsletter called *DAtabytes,* which provides information about new developments and data sets that are deposited in the archive. Back copies are readily available from most academic libraries. However, by far the most straightforward route to finding out whether the Archive contains data on a topic in which you are interested is via the Archive's online catalogue. Access to this catalogue can be obtained by going to the Archive's home page at:

www.data-archive.ac.uk

This will bring up the catalogue home page (see Plate 10.1). Resources can be found either by searching the catalogue or by browsing selected data series; it is also possible to search by geographical area. In this instance, however, we are interested in searching the catalogue by keyword. Clicking on the **Finding**

Box 10.7 A meta-analysis of the relationship between rewards and intrinsic motivation

Deci, Koestner, and Ryan (2001) conducted a meta-analysis of reward effects on intrinsic motivation in educational settings such as classrooms. They began by calculating the effects of rewards—whether verbal or tangible—on the intrinsic motivation of students in educational settings. The authors examined 128 experiments published between 1971 and 1996. Their concept of reward included verbal rewards or positive feedback as well as tangible rewards, such as money or prizes that are given to students to reinforce their motivation to learn. The researchers speculated that rewards could be used to affect student motivation in a way that was either informational or controlling. The meta-analysis tested the following hypotheses:

1 controlling positive feedback would lead to less intrinsic motivation than informational positive feedback;

2 tangible rewards will decrease intrinsic motivation.

The results were analysed in two separate meta-analyses by separating studies into those that examined verbal versus those that examined tangible rewards. The tangible reward studies were further subdivided into four groups according to whether they were:

• contingent on working on a task;

• *not* contingent on working on a task;

• contingent on finishing a task;

• contingent on a specified level of task performance.

The research found that verbal rewards tend to have an enhancing effect on intrinsic motivation, although they are more likely to have a negative effect if the interpersonal context within which they are administered is controlling rather than informational. On the other hand, the meta-analysis showed that tangible rewards significantly undermined intrinsic motivation, particularly amongst children. This led them to conclude that rewards substantially undermine intrinsic interest.

This contradicted the finding from an earlier meta-analytic study on the same subject (Cameron and Pierce 1994), which found that negative effects of reward occur only under certain conditions, and, when appropriately arranged, rewards could actually be used to enhance intrinsic motivation and performance. These competing meta-analyses have thus become the focus of fierce intellectual debate, critics comparing their analysis to 'putting a beautiful dessert (peaches and ice cream drizzled with raspberry sauce and a dollop of whipped cream) into an industrial blender and liquefying the entire concoction' (in Cameron 2001: 31). Much of the debate relates to the way that studies are categorized so their findings can be meaningfully compared. Criticisms are also levelled at the way studies are selected for inclusion in the analysis, for example: how long is the period of time for the meta-analysis and are only published studies considered or does the analysis include unpublished studies, such as doctoral dissertations?

A further reason for the fierceness of the debate relates to the relationship between educational research and policy. One of the aims of this meta-analysis was to produce a definitive statement about the relationship between rewards and intrinsic motivation that could be used to inform current educational practice. Hence, Deci et al. relate their findings to a wider agenda by stating 'it is an injustice to the integrity of our teachers and students to simply advocate that educators focus on the use of rewards to control behaviour rather than grapple with the deeper issues of (a) why many students are not interested in learning within our educational system and (b) how intrinsic motivation and self regulation can be promoted among these students' (2001: 50). Similar issues about the role of meta-analysis in creating such a link between research and practice apply in the field of management and business.

tab takes us to the **Finding Data** page and we chose **Search Catalogue**. The UKDA's catalogue can be searched via a free-text search on 'All of study description', or a more focused search can be conducted on a specific field, such as 'title' or 'time period', selected from the drop-down list. In this case we asked for studies with the keyword 'profit sharing' anywhere in the study description, which includes the abstract and the methodology. Clicking on the 'go' button resulted in 53 studies being found. We selected Study Number SN 4511 and requested **Study Description/Online Documentation** (see Plate 10.2). The information provided gave a description of the study, along with a variety of particulars: sponsors; sampling details; method of data collection; main topics of the survey; and information

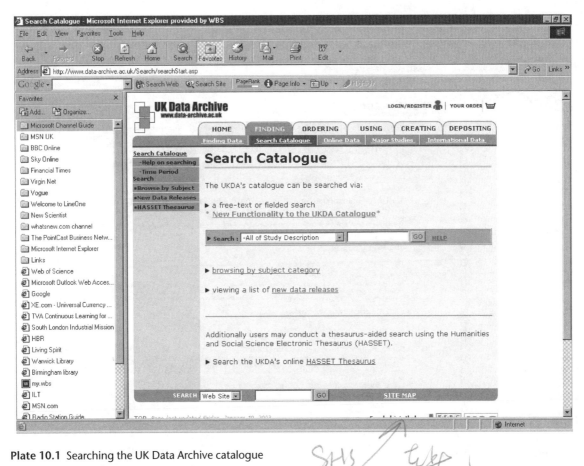

Plate 10.1 Searching the UK Data Archive catalogue

about publications deriving from the study. It also informs you whether there are special conditions relating to access. With the one we specified, we are told that there are no access restrictions and that the data series is available in downloadable form to registered users. To register, users must sign an access agreement. You will need to find out if there is an administrative charge for receiving the data, but it is likely that if you are a student at or a member of staff in a UK institution of higher education, there will be no charge. Information about charges and access can be found at the **Ordering/Downloading Data** page.

Information about searching for qualitative data for the purpose of conducting a secondary analysis can be found in Chapter 19. Qualitative data can be searched for through **Qualidata**, which is a specialist unit housed within the UK Data Archive; it can be accessed via:

www.qualidata.essex.ac.uk

Qualidata's focus is now on acquiring data collections created during the course of research projects from ESRC Research Programmes, both from multi-strategy research (see Chapter 22 for a definition) and from UK-based classic studies such as *The Affluent Worker* by Goldthorpe et al. (1968).

A web site that has been designed to increase the use of secondary analysis and that provides a variety of hyperlinks to useful sites is:

http://tramss.data-archive.ac.uk

Table 10.1 lists several large data sets that are accessible to students and would repay further investigation

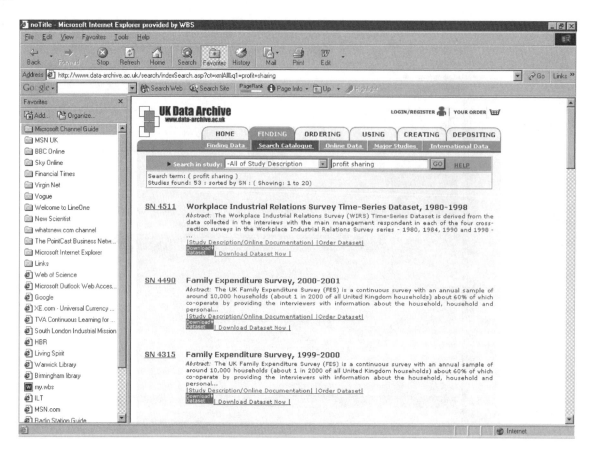

Plate 10.2 Choosing a study

in terms of their potential use in the context of research questions in which you might be interested. Further information about these data sets can be found via the UK Data Archive unless otherwise specified in Table 10.1.

Finally, in addition to the government-sponsored data sets available via the UK Data Archive, there are also several commercially sponsored sources of business information. For example, Target Group Index (TGI) is one of the largest commercially produced continuous consumer surveys conducted in Great Britain. The survey covers the ownership, level, and frequency of purchase and expenditure on most consumer products and services. It also covers information on respondents' media habits—that is, what they read, listen to, or watch. An annual survey is carried out amongst 25,000 adults, nationwide. Data

are available in two formats—hard copy (thirty-four volumes of data categorized by product group) and online through the British Market Research Bureau (BMRB). Similarly, The Price Waterhouse Cranfield (PWC) Survey of European Human Resource Management is an international comparative survey of human resource policies and practices carried out in 1990, 1991, and 1992 in more than fourteen European countries. The questionnaire, which was administered to personnel specialists, relates to changes in the employment relationship, recruitment, training, remuneration, and employee relations. However, although some of the older TGI survey data can be accessed from libraries and some of the PWC survey data have been published in raw form (see e.g. Brewster and Hegwisch 1994), as we have already mentioned, accessing this kind of data

---

Box 10.8 Doing secondary analysis of secondary materials

It is often assumed that secondary analysis is always of primary data—that is, original data collected by another researcher. However, this need not always be the case. One of the authors has a long-standing interest in the early animation industry in the USA. The history of animation is a field where a considerable number of academic historians and animation enthusiasts have written some fascinating histories of both the industry as a whole and of individual studios and directors. Bryman (1997) used these materials in relation to the debate, which has raged in marketing circles, about whether it is better to be a pioneer ('first mover') or a late entrant in an industry. Interestingly, this is a debate in which there is both quantitative and qualitative research: the former tends to show that it is better to be a pioneer, whereas the qualitative case study studies tend to demonstrate that late entrants fare better. Bryman's examination of the animation industry came down firmly on the superiority of being a late entrant, since the early entrants floundered, while the later entrants were able to build upon the experiences and

mistakes of the pioneers. A later article (Bryman 2000) examined the industry in relation to various theories about technology and its relationship to the organization of work. The study shows, among other things, that the early pioneers of animation drew on norms about the design of technology and about the organization of work that were in tune with their times. Later entrants adopted similar approaches to the design of technology and of work in order to gain a sense of legitimacy in what was at the time a fledgling industry. These findings are interpreted in terms of institutional theory, which proposes that organizations are propelled to incorporate 'the practices and procedures defined by prevailing rationalized concepts of organizational work and institutionalized in society' (Meyer and Rowan 1977: 340). The two publications point to the potential that historical analysis has for the understanding of business and management and to the possibilities that can be opened up by an analysis of secondary materials like these histories of animation and studios.

---

is likely to prove prohibitively expensive for a lone researcher. Moreover, it need not necessarily be the case that secondary analysis entails the analysis of primary data collected by other researchers, as the example of Bryman's secondary analysis using historical accounts of the US animation industry (see Box 10.8) illustrates.

Official statistics

The use and analysis of official statistics for purposes of business research have been subject to controversy for many years. Agencies of the state, in the course of their business, are required to keep a running record of their areas of activity. When these records are aggregated, they form the official statistics in an area of activity. Thus, in Great Britain, the Employment Service collects data that form the basis for the level of unemployment (also known as the 'claimant count'). This is just one, as it happens high-profile, set of statistics that can be subsumed under the general category of 'official statistics'. Such statistics are frequently the cause of headlines in the mass media—for example, if there has been a sharp

increase in the level of unemployment. But they would also seem to offer considerable potential for business and management researchers. We could imagine such official statistics offering the researcher certain advantages over some other forms of quantitative data, such as data based on surveys.

- The data have already been collected. Therefore, as with other kinds of secondary analysis of data (see above), considerable time and expense may be saved. Also, the data may not be based on samples, so that a complete picture can be obtained.

- Since the people who are the source of the data are not being asked questions that are part of a research project, the problem of *reactivity* will be much less pronounced than when data are collected by interview or questionnaire.

- There is the prospect of analysing the data both cross-sectionally and longitudinally. When analysing the data cross-sectionally, we could examine employment rates (in addition to unemployment rates) in terms of such standard variables as social class, income, ethnicity, age, gender, and region. Such analyses allow us to search for the factors that are associated with employment. Also, we can analyse the data over time. Precisely because the data are compiled over many years, it is possible to chart trends over time and perhaps to relate these to wider social changes.

- There is the prospect as well of cross-cultural analysis, since the official statistics from different nation states can be compared for a specific area of activity.

However, readers who recall the discussion of convergent validity introduced in Chapter 3 will already be on their guard. The official statistics concerned with an area of social life like employment can be very misleading, because they record only those individuals who are processed by the agencies that have the responsibility for compiling the statistics. In addition, the process whereby official statistics are generated involves an element of interpretation. As the example in Box 10.9 illustrates, government agencies will vary in terms of how they record information. In the case of labour disputes, this means that a substantial number of disputes are likely to go unrecorded as a result either of not being reported or of not being recognized as a labour dispute according to the criteria used by the agency. This level of unrecorded activity is sometimes referred to in relation to the field of crime (which has been one of the main areas for discussions about the uses and limitations of official statistics) as 'the dark figure' (Coleman and Moynihan 1996). Nor can the example of labour disputes be regarded as alone in this connection. To push the point even further, the deficiencies of official statistics also extend to the recording of levels of employment and unemployment. For example, the 'claimant count', which is used to gain a picture each month of the level

of unemployment, may misrepresent the 'real' level of unemployment: people who are unemployed but who do not claim benefits or whose claim is disallowed will not be counted in the statistics, while those who form part of the claimant count but who work in part of what is known as the 'black' or 'informal' economy (and who therefore are not really unemployed) *will* be included in the unemployment statistics.

A great deal of national and cross-national official statistical information can be obtained via Internet sources. **National Statistics Online** is the UK web site of official statistics, reflecting the economy, population, and society at national and local level, publishing summary stories and detailed data releases free of charge. Similarly, **UKonline**, the UK government's information gateway, provides a useful access point for information relating to the Census of Employment. Reports such as *Labour Market Trends* and *Social Trends* provide aggregated results based on this type of large-scale survey data. The web-site addresses for these gateways are given below:

www.ukonline.gov.uk
www.statistics.gov.uk

Finally, **Europa**, the portal site of the European Union, provides an additional useful source of official documents and statistics relating to European Union affairs and European integration. The web site can be found at:

http://europa.eu.int

Reliability and validity

Issues of reliability and validity seem to loom large in these considerations. Reliability seems to be jeopardized because definitions and policies regarding the phenomena to be counted vary over time, as the example of the different definitions of labour disputes used by Organization for Economic Cooperation and Development (OECD) nations given by Jackie Davies (2001) effectively illustrates (see Box 10.9). The problem for the reliability of such statistics is that variations over time in levels of labour dispute may be due not to variations in the level of workplace conflict but to variations in the propensity to expend

---

Box 10.9 Difficulties in making cross-cultural comparisons using official statistics

Jackie Davies (2001) carried out an international comparison of labour disputes and stoppages through strike action in twenty-three OECD countries between 1990 and 1999 using statistical data collected at a national level. However, the article is careful to point out the limitations of such an analysis for the following reasons:

- *Voluntary notification.* In most of the countries governments rely on employers notifying them of any disputes, which they are then able to confirm through media reports.

- *Fail to measure full effects.* None of the countries records the full effects of stoppages at work—for example, measured, in terms of lost working time in companies that are not involved in the dispute but are unable to work because of a shortage of materials caused by the strike.

- *Different thresholds for inclusion.* The countries differ in the criteria they used to determine when a stoppage is entered into the statistics. In the UK, for example, disputes involving fewer than ten employees or lasting less than one day are excluded from the recorded figures. In some countries, the thresholds for inclusion are particularly high. For example, in the USA, records include only disputes involving more than 1,000 workers. This can make comparison of strike rates between countries particularly problematic.

- *Exclusion of certain industrial sectors.* Some of the countries exclude the effects of disputes in certain sectors—for example, Portugal omits public-sector and general strikes.

- *Changes in the way figures are recorded.* For example, France has changed the way it records lost working days, thus making it difficult to make comparison over time.

- *Indirectly involved workers.* There are differences between the countries in their attempts to record those workers who are indirectly involved in a stoppage but who are unable to work because others at their workplace are on strike. Half of the countries, including France, the Netherlands, and New Zealand, attempt to include these workers in the statistics, but the other half, including Italy and Japan, do not.

- *Dispute rates affected by small number of very large strikes.* Some countries can appear to have very high labour dispute rates in one particular year because of one strike involving a large number of workers. In France, for example, there was a strike in 1995 involving the whole public sector. Some of these difficulties can be overcome by making comparisons over several years.

These differences lead some countries, such as the USA or Japan, to record a lower number of working days lost through labour disputes than say the UK or Germany simply because of the different methods used for compiling statistics in the individual countries. This means that cross-cultural comparisons using nationally collected statistics need to be made with a degree of caution.

---

resources in recording these events. Also, there may be changes over time in the definitions of labour dispute or in the propensity of employers to report disputes to government. Such changes will clearly affect the degree to which fluctuations in the rate of occurrence of labour disputes reflect 'real' fluctuations in the rate of incidence. To the extent that such factors operate, the reliability of the data will be adversely affected and, as a result, validity will be similarly impaired.

Also, the problems with official statistics extend to the examination of the variables with which the rate of occurrence is associated. For example, it might be assumed that, if an examination of differences in labour disputes demonstrates that the rate varies by sector—for example, with industries such as manufacturing and transport having consistently high strike rates whereas sectors like agriculture have very low ones—this implies that the industrial sector is related to labour militancy leading to strike action. There are two problems with drawing such an inference. First, there is an analytic difficulty known as *the ecological fallacy* (see Box 10.10). Secondly, even if we could ignore the problem of the ecological fallacy (which we cannot, of course), we would still be faced with an issue that is related to the matter of validity. Variations between industrial sectors may be a product of factors other than the difference in their

Box 10.10 ⌲ *What is the ecological fallacy?*

The ecological fallacy is the error of assuming that inferences about individuals or organizations can be made from findings relating to aggregate data. For example, official statistics might demonstrate a positive relationship between size of firm and the number of labour disputes involving strike action. Such a finding could be taken to imply that employees in larger firms are more likely than those in small firms to take strike action. However, it would be wrong to draw such an inference about individual firms or groups of employees from aggregate data. A particular large firm may show quite low levels of strike activity, while a particular small firm might show a high level. The fallacy can arise for several reasons, the reason highlighted in this case being that it may not be the size of the firm that is responsible for the level of strike activity.

propensity to take strike action. Instead, the variations may be due to such factors as: variations in the average rates of pay and the terms and conditions of employment in different industrial sectors; likelihood of employers in different industrial sectors to report a dispute; differences in the number of employees working in these sectors; variation in the average number of people employed by organizations in different sectors; differences in the level of union membership and union activity; and variations in the effectiveness of formal communication systems.

Condemning and resurrecting official statistics

Criticism of the use of various kinds of official statistics in the social sciences has drawn attention to these problems. Instead, it was recommended that researchers should turn their attention to the investigation of the organizational processes that produce the various deficiencies identified by the various writers. The effect of this view was to consign official statistics to the sidelines of business research so that it became an object of research interest rather than a

potential source of data, although research based on official statistics continued in certain quarters. It would also be wrong to think that critique was the sole reason for the neglect of official statistics during this period. The fact that official statistics, because they are a sideline for many state agencies, are invariably not tailored to the needs of business and management researchers can be considered a further limitation. In other words, it may be that the definitions of apparently similar or identical terms (such as labour disputes or working at home) employed by those responsible for compiling official statistics may not be commensurate with the definitions employed by business and management researchers. However, others have argued that the flaws in many of the official statistics are probably no worse than the errors that occur in much measurement deriving from methods like social surveys based on questionnaires and structured interviews (Bulmer 1980). Indeed, some forms of official statistics are probably very accurate by almost any set of criteria, such as population census data.

A further criticism of the rejection of various forms of official statistics is that it seems to imply that quantitative data compiled by business researchers are somehow error free or at least superior. However, as we have seen in previous chapters, while business and management researchers do their best to reduce the amount of error in their measurement of key concepts (such as through the standardization of the asking of questions and the recording of answers in survey research), it is not the case that the various measures that are derived are free of error. All social measurement is prone to error; what is crucial is taking steps to keep that error to a minimum. Therefore, to reject official statistics because they contain errors is misleading if in fact all measurement in business research contains errors. It is clear that the wholesale rejection of official statistics by many researchers has been tempered. While there is widespread recognition and acknowledgement that problems remain with certain forms of official statistics, each set of statistics has to be evaluated for the purposes of business and management research on its own merits.

Official statistics as a form of unobtrusive method

One of the most compelling and frequently cited cases for the continued use of official statistics is that they can be considered a form of unobtrusive measure, although nowadays many writers prefer to use the term 'unobtrusive method' (Lee 2000). This term is derived from the notion of 'unobtrusive measure' coined by Webb et al. (1966). In a highly influential book, Webb et al. argued that social researchers are excessively reliant on measures of social phenomena deriving from methods of data collection that are prone to *reactivity* (see Boxes 2.10 and 8.8, where this idea is introduced). This means that, whenever

---

Box 10.11 🔅 *What are unobtrusive measures?*

An unobtrusive measure is 'any method of observation that directly removes the observer from the set of interactions or events being studied' (Denzin 1970). Webb et al. (1966) distinguished four main types.

1 *Physical traces*. These are the 'signs left behind by a group' and include such things as graffiti and rubbish.

2 *Archive materials*. This category includes statistics collected by governmental and non-governmental organizations, diaries, the mass media, and historical records.

3 *Simple observation*. This refers to 'situations in which the observer has no control over the behavior or sign in question, and plays an unobserved, passive, and nonintrusive role in the research situation' (Webb et al. 1966: 112).

4 *Contrived observation*. This is the same as simple observation, but the observer either actively varies the setting in some way (but without jeopardizing the unobtrusive quality of the observation) or employs hidden hardware to record observations, such as video cameras.

Official statistics would be subsumed under Category 2, as would content analysis of media content of the kind described in Chapter 9. However, a content analysis like that described in Box 9.5 would not be considered an example of an unobtrusive measure, because the material being content analysed (workplace ethnographies) derives from studies in which the data were generated in an obtrusive fashion. Structured observation of the kind covered in Chapter 8 will typically not fall into Categories 3 and 4, because the observer is usually known to those being observed. However, field stimulations, such as the mystery shopper example described in Box 8.10, are an example of contrived observation. In this case, the mystery shoppers were not known by travel agents to be researchers

and they actively varied the situation through communication of their specific holiday requirements in order to elicit travel agents' recommendations.

It is important to realize that Webb et al. (1966) were not intending that unobtrusive methods should supplant conventional methods. Instead, they argued that the problem they were identifying was the almost exclusive reliance upon methods that were likely to be affected by reactivity. Webb et al. argued for greater 'triangulation' (see Box 13.4) in social research, whereby conventional (reactive) and unobtrusive (non-reactive) methods would be employed in conjunction. For example, they wrote that they were providing an inventory of unobtrusive methods, 'because they demonstrate ways in which the investigator may shore up reactive infirmities of the interview and questionnaire' (1966: 174).

It is worth noting that unobtrusive methods or measures encapsulate at least two kinds of ways of thinking about the process of capturing data. First, many so-called unobtrusive measures are in fact *sources* of data, such as graffiti, diaries, media articles, and official statistics. Such sources require analysis in order to be rendered interesting to a business school audience. Secondly, it includes *methods* of data collection, such as simple and contrived observation. While the data generated by such methods of data collection also require analysis, the data have to be produced by the methods. The data are not simply out there awaiting analysis in the way in which diaries or newspaper articles are (although, of course, a great deal of detective work is often necessary to unearth such sources). This means that neither of the terms 'unobtrusive methods' or 'unobtrusive measures' captures the variety of forms terribly well. A further disadvantage of the term 'unobtrusive measure' is that it seems to imply a connection to quantitative research alone, whereas certain approaches employed by qualitative researchers may qualify as unobtrusive methods.

Contrived observation
操控之操之也 2種差

people know that they are participating in a study (which is invariably the case with methods of data collection such as structured interviewing, self-completion questionnaire, and structured observation), a component of their replies or behaviour is likely to be influenced by their knowledge that they are being investigated. In other words, their answers to questions or the behaviour they exhibit may be untypical.

Official statistics fit fairly squarely in the second of the four types of unobtrusive measures outlined in

Box 10.11. As noted in the box, this second grouping covers a very wide range of sources of data, which includes statistics generated by organizations that are not agencies of the state. This is a useful reminder that potentially interesting statistical data are frequently compiled by a wide range of organizations, such as market research agencies. There may be greater potential for searching out and mining statistical data produced by organizations that are relatively independent of the state.

K   KEY POINTS

- Secondary analysis of existing data offers the prospect of being able to explore research questions of interest to you without having to go through the process of collecting the data yourself.

- Very often, secondary analysis offers the opportunity of being able to employ high-quality data sets that are based on large reasonably representative samples.

- Secondary analysis presents few disadvantages.

- The analysis of official statistics may be thought of as a special form of secondary analysis but one that is more controversial because of the unease about the reliability and validity of certain types of official data, especially those relating to unemployment and labour disputes.

- Some forms of official statistics are much less prone to errors, but there remains the possible problem of divergences of definition between compilers of such data and business researchers.

- Official statistics represent a form of unobtrusive method and enjoy certain advantages (especially lack of reactivity) because of that.

Q   QUESTIONS FOR REVIEW

- What is secondary analysis?

Other researchers' data

- Outline the main advantages and limitations of secondary analysis of other researchers' data.

- Does the possibility of conducting a secondary analysis apply only to quantitative data produced by other researchers?

- What is meta-analysis and why is it of particular interest to researchers in business and management?

Official statistics

- Why have many business researchers been sceptical about the use of official statistics for research purposes?

- How justified is their scepticism?

- What reliability and validity issues do official statistics pose?

- What are unobtrusive methods or measures? What is the chief advantage of such methods?

11

Quantitative data analysis

CHAPTER GUIDE

In this chapter, some of the basic, but nonetheless most frequently used methods for analysing quantitative data analysis will be presented. In order to illustrate the use of the methods of data analysis, a small imaginary set of data based on attendance at a gym is used. It is the kind of small research project that would be feasible for most students doing undergraduate research projects for a dissertation or similar exercise.

The chapter explores:

- the importance of *not* leaving considerations of how you will analyse your quantitative data until after you have collected all your data; you should be aware of the ways in which you would like to analyse your data from the earliest stage of your research;

- the distinctions between the different kinds of variable that can be generated in quantitative research; knowing how to distinguish types of variables is crucial so that you appreciate which methods of analysis can be applied when you examine variables and relationships between them;

- methods for analysing a single variable at a time (*univariate analysis*);

- methods for analysing relationships between variables (*bivariate analysis*);

- the analysis of relationships between three variables (*multivariate analysis*).

Introduction

In this chapter, some very basic techniques for analysing quantitative data will be examined. In the next chapter, the ways in which these techniques can be implemented using sophisticated computer software (SPSS for Windows) will be introduced. The formulae that underpin the techniques to be discussed will not be presented, since the necessary calculations can easily be carried out by using SPSS for Windows. Two chapters cannot do justice to these topics and readers are advised to move as soon as possible on to books that provide more detailed and advanced treatments (e.g. Bryman and Cramer 2001).

Before beginning this exposition of techniques, we would like to give you advance warning of one of the biggest mistakes that people make about quantitative data analysis:

I don't have to concern myself with how I'm going to analyse my survey data until after I've collected my data. I'll leave thinking about it till then, because it doesn't impinge on how I collect my data.

This is a common error that arises because quantitative data analysis looks like a distinct phase that occurs after the data have been collected (see for example Figure 3.1, in which the analysis of quantitative data is depicted as a late step—number 9—in

quantitative research). Quantitative data analysis is indeed something that occurs typically at a late stage in the overall process and is also a distinct stage.

However, that does not mean that you should not be considering how you will analyse your data until then. In fact, you should be fully aware of what techniques you will apply at a fairly early stage—for example, when you are designing your questionnaire, observation schedule, coding frame, or whatever. The two main reasons for this are as follows.

- You cannot apply just any technique to any variable. Techniques have to be appropriately matched to the types of variables that you have created through your research. This means that you must be fully conversant with the ways in which different types of variable are classified.

- The size and nature of your sample are likely to impose limitations on the kinds of techniques you can use (see the discussion in Chapter 4 of the issue of 'Kind of analysis').

In other words, you need to be aware that decisions that you make at quite an early stage in the research process, such as the kinds of data you collect and the size of your sample, will have implications for the sorts of analysis that you will be able to conduct.

A small research project

The discussion of quantitative data analysis will be based upon an imaginary piece of research carried out by an undergraduate marketing student for a dissertation. The student in question is interested in the role of the sport and leisure industry and in particular, because of her own enthusiasm for leisure clubs and gyms, with the ways in which such venues are used and people's reasons for joining them. She has read an article that suggests that participant involvement in adult fitness programmes is associated with their attitudinal loyalty, comprising investment of time and money, social pressure from significant others, and internalization or commitment to the fitness regime (Park 1996). She intends to use this theory as a framework for her findings. The student is also interested in issues relating to gender and body image and she suspects that men and women will differ in their reasons for going to a gym and the kinds of activities in which they engage in the gym. Her final issue of interest relates to the importance of age in determining gym involvement. In particular, she has discovered that previous research has shown that older people tend to show higher levels of attitudinal loyalty to recreational activities more generally and she wants to find out if this finding also applies to involvement in leisure clubs and gyms.

She secures the agreement of a gym close to her home to contact a sample of its members by post. The gym has 1,200 members and she decides to take a simple random sample of 10 per cent of the membership (i.e. 120 members). She sends out postal questionnaires to members of the sample with a covering letter testifying to the gym's support of her research. One thing she wants to know is how much time people spend on each of the three main classes of activity in the gym: cardiovascular equipment, weights equipment, and exercises. She defines each of these carefully in the covering letter and asks members of the sample to keep a note of how long they spend on each of the three activities on their next visit. They are then requested to return the questionnaires to her in a pre-paid reply envelope.

She ends up with a sample of 90 questionnaires—a response rate of 75 per cent.

Part of the questionnaire is presented in Box 11.1. The entire questionnaire runs to four pages. Twelve of the questions are provided in Box 11.1. Many of the questions (1, 3, 4, 5, 6, 7, 8, and 9) are pre-coded and the student simply has to circle the code to the far right of the question under the column 'code'. With the remainder of the questions, specific figures are requested and she simply transfers the relevant figure to the code column. An example of a questionnaire that has been completed by a respondent and coded by the student is presented in Box 11.2.

Missing data

The data for all 90 respondents are presented in Box 11.3. Each of the twelve questions is known for the time being as a variable number (var00001, etc.) Each variable number corresponds to the question number in Box 11.1 (i.e. var00001 is question 1, var00002 is question 2, etc.) An important issue arises in the management of data as to how to handle 'missing data'. Missing data arise when respondents fail to reply to a question—either by accident or because they do not want to answer the question. Thus, respondent 24 has failed to answer question 2, which is concerned with age. This has been coded as a zero (0) and it will be important to ensure that the computer software is notified of this fact, since it needs to be taken into account during the analysis. Also, question 9 has a large number of zeros, because many people did not answer it, because they have been filtered out by the previous question (i.e. they do not have other sources of regular exercise). These have also been coded as zero to denote missing data, though strictly speaking their failure to reply is more indicative of the question not being applicable to them. Note also, that there are zeros for var00010, var00011, and var00012. However, these do *not* denote missing data but that the respondent spends zero minutes on the activity in question. Everyone

Box 11.1 Part of a questionnaire used in research on use of a gym

Questionnaire

Code

1. Are you male or female (please tick)?

   Male _____ Female _____   1 2

2. How old are you?

   _____ years

3. Which of the following best describes your *main* reason for going to the gym? (please tick *one* only)

Relaxation	_____	1
Maintain or improve fitness	_____	2
Lose weight	_____	3
Meet others	_____	4
Build strength	_____	5
Other (please specify)	_____	6

4. When you go to the gym, how often do you use the cardiovascular equipment (jogger, step machine, bike, rower)? (please tick)

Always	_____	1
Usually	_____	2
Rarely	_____	3
Never	_____	4

5. When you go to the gym, how often do you use the weights machines (including free weights)? (please tick)

Always	_____	1
Usually	_____	2
Rarely	_____	3
Never	_____	4

6. How frequently do you usually go to the gym? (please tick)

Every day	_____	1
4–6 days a week	_____	2
2 or 3 days a week	_____	3
Once a week	_____	4
2 or 3 times a month	_____	5
Once a month	_____	6
Less than once a month	_____	7

7. Are you usually accompanied when you go to the gym or do you usually go on your own? (please tick *one* only)

On my own	_____	1
With a friend	_____	2
With a partner/spouse	_____	3

8. Do you have sources of regular exercise other than the gym?

   Yes _____   No _____   1 2

   *If you have answered **No** to this question, please proceed to question 10*

9. If you have replied **Yes** to question 9, please indicate the *main* source of regular exercise in the last six months from this list. (please tick *one* only)

Sport	___	1
Cycling on the road	___	2
Jogging	___	3
Long walks	___	4
Other (please specify)	___	5

10. During your last visit to the gym, how many minutes did you spend on the cardiovascular equipment (jogger, step machine, bike, rower)?

_____ minutes

11. During your last visit to the gym, how many minutes did you spend on the weights machines (including free weights)?

_____ minutes

12. During your last visit to the gym, how many minutes did you spend on other activities (e.g. stretching exercises)?

_____ minutes

Box 11.2 A completed and processed questionnaire

Questionnaire

Code

1. Are you male or female (please tick)?

Male __✓__ Female ____   ①2

2. How old are you?

__21__ years   21

3. Which of the following best describes your *main* reason for going to the gym? (please tick *one* only)

Relaxation	___	1
Maintain or improve fitness	✓	②
Lose weight	___	3
Meet others	___	4
Build strength	___	5
Other (please specify)	___	6

4. When you go to the gym, how often do you use the cardiovascular equipment (jogger, step machine, bike, rower)? (please tick)

Always	✓	①
Usually	___	2
Rarely	___	3
Never	___	4

5. When you go to the gym, how often do you use the weights machines (including free weights)? (please tick)

Always	✓	①
Usually	___	2
Rarely	___	3
Never	___	4

6. How frequently do you usually go to the gym? (please tick)

Every day	___	1
4–6 days a week	___	2
2 or 3 days a week	✓	③
Once a week	___	4
2 or 3 times a month	___	5
Once a month	___	6
Less than once a month	___	7

7. Are you usually accompanied when you go to the gym or do you usually go on your own? (please tick *one* only)

On my own	✓	①
With a friend	___	2
With a partner/spouse	___	3

8. Do you have sources of regular exercise other than the gym?

   Yes ____ No ✓   1②

   *If you have answered **No** to this question, please proceed to question 10*

9. If you have replied **Yes** to question 9, please indicate the *main* source of regular exercise in the last six months from this list. (please tick *one* only)   ○

Sport	___	1
Cycling on the road	___	2
Jogging	___	3
Long walks	___	4
Other (please specify)	___	5

10. During your last visit to the gym, how many minutes did you spend on the cardiovascular equipment (jogger, step machine, bike, rower)?

    <u>33</u> minutes   33

11. During your last visit to the gym, how many minutes did you spend on the weights machines (including free weights)?

    <u>17</u> minutes   17

12. During your last visit to the gym, how many minutes did you spend on other activities (e.g. stretching exercises)?

    <u>5</u> minutes   5

has answered questions 10, 11, and 12, so there are in fact no missing data for these variables. If there had been missing data, it would be necessary to code missing data with a number that could not also be a true figure. For example, nobody has spent 99 minutes on these activities, so this might be an appropriate number as it is easy to remember and could not be read by the computer as anything other than missing data.

Box 11.3 Gym survey data

var00001	var00002	var00003	var00004	var00005	var00006	var00007	var00008	var00009	var00010	var00011	var00012
1	21	2	1	1	3	1	2	0	33	17	5
2	44	1	3	1	4	3	1	2	10	23	10
2	19	3	1	2	2	1	1	1	27	18	12
2	27	3	2	1	2	1	2	0	30	17	3
1	57	2	1	3	2	3	1	4	22	0	15
2	27	3	1	1	3	1	1	3	34	17	0
1	39	5	2	1	5	1	1	5	17	48	10
2	36	3	1	2	2	2	1	1	25	18	7
1	37	2	1	1	3	1	2	0	34	15	0
2	51	2	2	2	4	3	2	0	16	18	11
1	24	5	2	1	3	1	1	1	0	42	16
2	29	2	1	2	3	1	2	0	34	22	12
1	20	5	1	1	2	1	2	0	22	31	7
2	22	2	1	3	4	2	1	3	37	14	12
2	46	3	1	1	5	2	2	0	26	9	4
2	41	3	1	2	2	3	1	4	22	7	10
1	25	5	1	1	3	1	1	1	21	29	4
2	46	3	1	2	4	2	1	4	18	8	11
1	30	3	1	1	5	1	2	0	23	9	6
1	25	5	2	1	3	1	1	1	23	19	0
2	24	2	1	1	3	2	1	2	20	7	6
2	39	1	2	3	5	1	2	0	17	0	9
1	44	3	1	1	3	2	1	2	22	8	5
1	0	1	2	2	4	2	1	4	15	10	4
2	18	3	1	2	3	1	2	1	18	7	10
1	41	3	1	1	3	1	2	0	34	10	4
2	38	2	1	2	5	3	1	2	24	14	10
1	25	2	1	1	2	1	2	0	48	22	7
1	41	5	2	1	3	1	1	2	17	27	0
2	30	3	1	1	2	2	2	0	32	13	10
2	29	3	1	3	2	1	2	0	31	0	7
2	42	1	2	2	4	2	1	4	17	14	6
1	31	2	1	1	2	1	2	0	49	21	2
2	25	3	1	1	2	3	2	0	30	17	15
1	46	3	1	1	3	1	1	3	32	10	5
1	24	5	2	1	4	1	1	2	0	36	11
2	34	3	1	1	3	2	1	4	27	14	12
2	50	2	1	2	2	3	2	0	28	8	6
1	28	5	1	1	3	2	1	1	26	22	8
2	30	3	1	1	2	1	1	4	21	9	12
1	27	2	1	1	2	1	1	3	64	15	8
2	27	2	1	2	4	2	1	4	22	10	7
1	36	5	1	1	3	2	2	0	21	24	0
2	43	3	1	1	4	1	2	0	25	13	8
1	34	2	1	1	3	2	1	1	45	15	6
2	27	3	1	1	2	1	1	4	33	10	9
2	38	2	1	3	4	2	2	0	23	0	16
1	28	2	1	1	3	3	1	2	38	13	5
1	44	5	1	1	2	1	2	0	27	19	7
2	31	3	1	2	3	2	2	0	32	11	5
2	23	2	1	1	4	2	1	1	33	18	8
1	45	3	1	1	3	1	1	2	26	10	7
2	34	3	1	2	2	3	2	0	36	8	12
1	27	3	1	1	2	3	1	3	42	13	6
2	40	3	1	1	2	2	1	4	26	9	10
2	24	2	1	1	2	1	1	2	22	10	9

var00001	var00002	var00003	var00004	var00005	var00006	var00007	var00008	var00009	var00010	var00011	var00012
1	37	2	1	1	5	2	2	0	21	11	0
1	22	5	1	1	4	1	1	1	23	17	6
2	31	3	1	2	3	1	1	4	40	16	12
1	37	2	1	1	2	3	2	0	54	12	3
2	33	1	2	2	4	2	2	0	17	10	5
1	23	5	1	1	3	1	1	1	41	27	8
1	28	3	1	1	3	3	2	0	27	11	8
2	29	2	1	2	5	2	1	2	24	9	9
2	43	3	1	1	2	1	2	0	36	17	12
1	28	5	1	1	3	1	1	1	22	15	4
1	48	2	1	1	5	1	1	4	25	11	7
2	32	2	2	2	4	2	2	0	27	13	11
1	28	5	1	1	2	2	2	0	15	23	7
2	23	2	1	1	5	1	1	4	14	11	5
2	43	2	1	2	5	1	2	0	18	7	3
1	28	2	1	1	4	3	1	2	34	18	8
2	23	3	1	1	2	1	2	0	37	17	17
2	36	1	2	2	4	2	1	4	18	12	4
1	50	2	1	1	3	1	1	2	28	14	3
1	37	3	1	1	2	2	2	0	26	14	9
2	41	3	1	1	2	1	1	4	24	11	4
1	26	5	2	1	5	1	1	1	23	19	8
2	28	3	1	1	4	1	2	0	27	12	4
2	35	2	1	1	3	1	1	1	28	14	0
1	28	5	1	1	2	1	1	2	20	24	12
2	36	2	1	1	3	2	2	0	26	9	14
2	29	3	1	1	4	1	1	4	23	13	4
1	34	1	2	2	4	2	1	0	24	12	3
1	53	2	1	1	3	3	1	1	32	17	6
2	30	3	1	1	4	1	2	0	24	10	9
1	43	2	1	1	2	1	1	2	24	14	10
2	26	5	2	1	4	1	1	1	16	23	7
2	44	1	1	1	4	2	2	0	27	18	6
1	45	1	2	2	3	3	2	0	20	14	5

Types of variable

One of the things that might strike you when you look at the questions is that the kinds of information that you receive varies by question. Some of the questions call for answers in terms of real numbers: questions 2, 10, 11, and 12. Questions 1 and 8 yield either/or answers and are therefore in the form of dichotomies. The rest of the questions take the form of lists of categories, but there are differences between these too. Some of the questions are in terms of answers that are rank ordered: questions 4, 5, and 6. Thus we can say in the case of question 6 that the category 'every day' implies greater frequency than '4–6 days a week', which in turn implies greater frequency than '2 or 3 days a week', and so on. However, in the case of questions 3, 7, and 9, the categories are *not* capable of being rank ordered. We cannot say in the case of question 3 that 'relaxation' is more of something than 'maintain or improve fitness' or 'lose weight'.

These considerations lead to a classification of the different types of variable that are generated in the course of research. The four main types are:

- *Interval/ratio variables*. These are variables where the distances between the categories are identical across the range of categories. In the case of variables var00010 to var00011, the distance between the categories is one minute. Thus, a person may spend 32 minutes on cardiovascular equipment, which is one minute more than someone who spends 31 minutes on this equipment. That difference is the same as the difference between someone who spends 8 minutes and another who spends 9 minutes on the equipment. This is the highest level of measurement and a very wide range of techniques of analysis can be applied to interval/ratio variables. There is, in fact, a distinction between interval and ratio variables, in that the latter are interval variables with a fixed zero point. However, since most ratio variables exhibit this quality in business research (e.g. income, age, number of employees, revenue), they are not being distinguished here.

- *Ordinal variables*. These are variables whose categories can be rank ordered (as in the case of interval/ratio variables) but the distances between the categories are not equal across the range. Thus, in the case of question 6, the difference between the category 'every day' and '4–6 days a week' is not the same as the difference between '4–6 days a week' and '2 or 3 days a week', and so on. Nonetheless, we can say that 'every day' is more frequent than '4–6 days a week', which is more frequent than '2 or 3 days a week', etc. You should also bear in mind that, if you subsequently group an interval/ratio variable like var00002, which refers to people's ages, into categories (e.g. 20 and under; 21–30; 31–40; 41–50; 51 and over), you are transforming it into an ordinal variable.

- *Nominal variables*. These variables, also known as *categorical variables*, comprise categories that cannot be rank ordered. As noted previously, we cannot say in the case of question 3 that 'relaxation' is more of something than 'maintain or improve fitness' or 'lose weight'.

- *Dichotomous variables*. These variables contain data that have only two categories (e.g. gender). Their position in relation to the other types is slightly ambiguous, as they have only one interval. They therefore can be considered as having attributes of the other three types of variable. They look as though they are nominal variables, but because they have only one interval they are sometimes treated as ordinal variables. However, it is probably safest to treat them for most purposes as if they were ordinary nominal variables.

The four main types of variable and illustrations of them from the gym survey are provided in Table 11.1.

Multiple-indicator (or multiple-item) measures of concepts, like Likert scales (see Box 3.3), produce strictly speaking ordinal variables. However, many writers argue that they can be treated as though they produce interval/ratio variables, because of the relatively large number of categories they generate. For a brief discussion of this issue, see Bryman and Cramer, who distinguish between 'true' interval/ratio variables and those produced by multiple-indicator measures (2001: 58–9).

Figure 11.1 provides guidance about how to identify variables of each type.

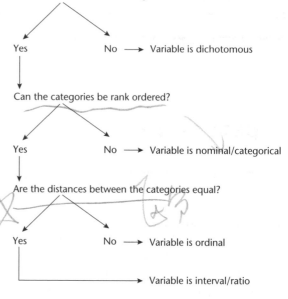

Figure 11.1 Deciding how to categorize a variable

Table 11.1 Types of variable

Type	Description	Examples in gym study	Variable Name in SPSS (see Chapter 12)
Interval/ratio	Variables where the distances between the categories are identical across the range	var00002 var00010 var00011 var00012	age cardmins weimins othmins
Ordinal	Variables whose categories can be rank ordered but the distances between the categories are not equal across the range	var00004 var00005 var00006	carduse weiuse frequent
Nominal	Variables whose categories cannot be rank ordered; also known as *categorical*	var00003 var00007 var00009	reasons accomp exercise
Dichotomous	Variables containing data that have only two categories	var00001 var00008	gender othsourc

Univariate analysis

Univariate analysis refers to the analysis of one variable at a time. In this section, the commonest approaches will be outlined.

Frequency tables

A frequency table provides the number of people and the percentage belonging to each of the categories for the variable in question. It can be used in relation to all of the different types of variable. An example of a frequency table is provided for var00003 in Table 11.2. Notice that nobody chose two of the possible choices of answer—'meet others' and 'other'—so these are not included in the table. The table shows, for example, that 33 members of the sample go the gym to lose weight and that they represent 37 per cent (percentages are often rounded up and down in frequency tables) of the entire sample. The procedure for generating a frequency table with SPSS is described on page 265.

If an interval/ratio variable (like people's ages) is to be presented in a frequency table format, it is invariably the case that the categories will need to be grouped. When grouping in this way, take care to ensure that the categories you create do not overlap (for example, like this: 20–30, 30–40, 40–50, etc.). An example of a frequency table for an interval/ratio variable is shown in Table 11.3, which provides a frequency table for var00002, which is concerned with the ages of those visiting the gym. If we do not group people in terms of age ranges, there would be thirty-four different categories, which is too many to take in. By creating five categories, the distribution of ages is easier to comprehend. Notice that the sample totals 89 and that the percentages are based on a total

Table 11.2 Frequency table showing reasons for visiting the gym

Reason	*n*	per cent
Relaxation	9	10
Maintain or improve fitness	31	34
Lose weight	33	37
Build strength	17	19
TOTAL	90	100

Table 11.3 Frequency table showing ages of gym members

Age	n	per cent
20 and under	3	3
21–30	39	44
31–40	23	26
41–50	21	24
51 and over	3	3
TOTAL	89	100

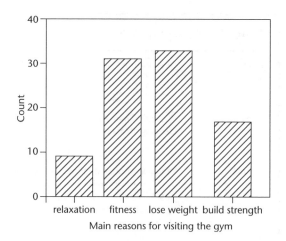

Figure 11.2 Bar chart showing main reasons for visiting the gym (SPSS output)

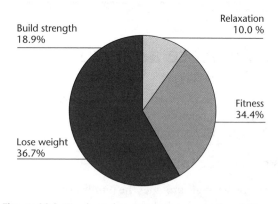

Figure 11.3 Pie chart showing main reasons for visiting the gym (SPSS output)

of 89 rather than 90. This is because this variable contains one missing value (respondent 24). The procedure for grouping respondents with SPSS is described on pages 263–4.

Diagrams

Diagrams are among the most frequently used methods of displaying quantitative data. Their chief advantage is that they are relatively easy to interpret and understand. If you are working with nominal or ordinal variables, the *bar chart* and the *pie chart* are two of the easiest methods to use. A bar chart of the same data presented in Table 11.2 is presented in Figure 11.2. Each bar represents the number of people falling in each category. This figure was produced with SPSS for Windows. The procedure for generating a bar chart with SPSS is described on page 265.

Another way of displaying the same data is through a pie chart, like the one in Figure 11.3. This also shows the relative size of the different categories but brings out as well the size of each slice relative to the total sample. The percentage that each slice represents of the whole sample is also given in this diagram, which was also produced with SPSS for Windows. The procedure for generating a pie chart with SPSS is described on pages 266–7.

If you are displaying an interval/ratio variable, like var00002, a *histogram* is likely to be employed. Figure 11.4, which was also generated by SPSS for Windows, uses the same data and categories as Table 11.3. As with the bar chart, the bars represent

the relative size of each of the age bands. However, note that, with the histogram, there is no space between the bars, whereas there is a space between the bars of a bar chart. Histograms are produced for interval/ratio variables, whereas bar charts are produced for nominal and ordinal variables. The procedure for generating a histogram with SPSS is described on pages 267–8.

Measures of central tendency

Measures of central tendency encapsulate in one figure a value that is typical for a distribution of values. In effect, we are seeking out an average for a

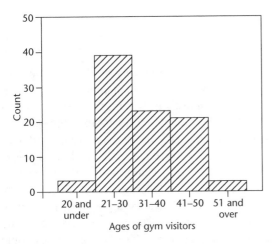

Figure 11.4 Histogram showing the ages of gym visitors (SPSS output)

distribution, but, in quantitative data analysis, three different forms of average are recognized.

- *Arithmetic mean.* This is the average as we understand it in everyday use—that is, we sum all the values in a distribution and then divide by the number of values. Thus, the arithmetic mean (or more simply the *mean*) for var00002 is 33.6, meaning that the average age of gym visitors is nearly 34 years of age. The mean should be employed only in relation to interval/ratio variables, though it is not uncommon to see it being used for ordinal variables as well.
- *Median.* This is the mid-point in a distribution of values. Whereas the mean is vulnerable to *outliers* (extreme values at either end of the distribution), which will exert considerable upwards or downwards pressure on the mean, by taking the mid-point of a distribution the median is not affected in this way. The median is derived by arraying all the values in a distribution from the smallest to the largest and then finding the middle point. If there is an even number of values, the median is calculated by taking the mean of the two middle numbers of the distribution. In the case of var00002, the median is 31. This is slightly lower than the mean in part because some considerably older members (especially respondents 5 and 10) inflate the mean slightly. The median can be

employed in relation to both interval/ratio and ordinal variables.

- *Mode.* This is the value that occurs most frequently in a distribution. The mode for var00002 is 28. The mode can be employed in relation to all types of variable.

The procedure for generating the mean, median, and mode with SPSS is described on page 268.

Measures of dispersion

The amount of variation in a sample can be just as interesting as providing estimates of the typical value of a distribution. For one thing, it becomes possible to draw contrasts between comparable distributions of values. For example, is there more or less variability in the amount of time spent on cardiovascular equipment as compared to weights machines?

The most obvious way of measuring dispersion is by the *range*. This is simply the difference between the maximum and the minimum value in a distribution of values associated with an interval/ratio variable. We find that the range for the two types of equipment is 64 minutes for the cardiovascular equipment and 48 minutes for the weights machines. This suggests that there is more variability in the amount of time spent on the former. However, like the mean, the range is influenced by outliers, such as respondent 60 in the case of var00010.

Another measure of dispersion is the *standard deviation*, which is essentially the average amount of variation around the mean. Although the calculation is somewhat more complicated than this, the standard deviation is calculated by taking the difference between each value in a distribution and the mean and then dividing the total of the differences by the number of values. The standard deviation for var00010 is 9.9 minutes and for var00011 it is 8 minutes. Thus, not only is the average amount of time spent on the cardiovascular equipment higher than for the weights equipment; the standard deviation is greater too. The standard deviation is also affected by outliers, but, unlike the range, their impact is offset by dividing by the number of values in the distribution. The procedure for generating the standard deviation with SPSS is described on page 268.

Bivariate analysis

Bivariate analysis is concerned with the analysis of two variables at a time in order to uncover whether the two variables are related. Exploring relationships between variables means searching for evidence that the variation in one variable coincides with variation in another variable. A variety of techniques are available for examining relationships, but their use depends on the nature of the two variables being analysed. Figure 11.5 attempts to portray the main types of bivariate analysis according to the types of variable involved.

Relationships not causality

An important point to bear in mind about all of the methods for analysing relationships between variables is that it is precisely *relationships* that they uncover. As was noted in Chapter 2 in relation to cross-sectional designs, this means that you cannot infer that one variable causes another. Indeed, there are cases when what appears to be a causal influence working in one direction actually works in the other way. An interesting example of this problem of causal direction will be presented much later in the book in Chapter 22. The example shows that Sutton and Rafaeli (1988) expected to find a relationship between the display of positive emotions (for example, smiling, or friendliness on the part of checkout staff) in retail outlets and sales in those outlets. In other words, the display of positive emotions was deemed to have a causal influence on levels of retail sales. In fact, the relationship was found to be the other way

	Nominal	Ordinal	Interval/ratio	Dichotomous
Nominal	Contingency table + chi-square (χ^2) + Cramér's V	Contingency table + chi-square (χ^2) + Cramér's V	Contingency table + chi-square (χ^2) + Cramér's V. If the interval/ratio variable can be identified as the dependent variable, compare means + eta	Contingency table + chi-square (χ^2) + Cramér's V
Ordinal	Contingency table + chi-square (χ^2) + Cramér's V	Spearman's rho (ρ)	Spearman's rho (ρ)	Spearman's rho (ρ)
Interval/ratio	Contingency table + chi-square (χ^2) + Cramér's V. If the interval/ratio variable can be identified as the dependent variable, compare means + eta	Spearman's rho (ρ)	Pearson's r	Spearman's rho (ρ)
Dichotomous	Contingency table + chi-square (χ^2) + Cramér's V	Spearman's rho (ρ)	Spearman's rho (ρ)	phi (ϕ)

Figure 11.5 Methods of bivariate analysis

round: levels of retail sales exerted a causal influence on the display of emotions (see Box 22.7 for more detailed explanation of this study).

Sometimes, we may feel confident that we can infer a causal direction when a relationship between two variables is discerned—for example, if we find that age and voting behaviour are related. It is impossible for the way people vote to influence their age, so, if we do find the two variables to be related, we can infer with complete confidence that age is the independent variable. It is not uncommon for researchers, when analysing their data, to draw inferences about causal direction based on their assumptions about the likely causal direction among related variables, as Sutton and Rafaeli (1988) did in their study. Although such inferences may be based on sound reasoning, they can only be inferences and there is the possibility that the real pattern of causal direction is the opposite of that which is anticipated.

Contingency tables

Contingency tables are probably the most flexible of all methods of analysing relationships in that they can be employed in relation to any pair of variables, though they are not the most efficient method for some pairs, which is the reason why the method is not recommended in all of the cells in Figure 11.5.

Table 11.4 Contingency table showing the relationship between gender and reasons for visiting the gym

Reasons	Gender			
	Male		Female	
	No.	%	No.	%
Relaxation	3	7	6	13
Fitness	15	36	16	33
Lose weight	8	19	25	52
Build strength	16	38	1	2
TOTAL	42		48	

Note: $\chi^2 = 22.726 \ p < 0.0001$.

A contingency table is like a frequency table but it allows two variables to be simultaneously analysed so that relationships between the two variables can be examined. It is normal for contingency tables to include percentages, since these make the tables easier to interpret. Table 11.4 examines the relationship between two variables from the gym survey: gender and reasons for visiting the gym. The percentages are *column percentages*—that is, they calculate the number in each cell as a percentage of the total number in that column. Thus, to take the top left-hand cell, the 3 men who go to the gym for relaxation are 7 per cent of all 42 men in the sample. Users of contingency tables often present the presumed independent variable (if one can in fact be presumed) as the column variable and the presumed dependent variable as the rows variable. In this case, we are presuming that gender influences reasons for going to the gym. In fact, we know that going to the gym cannot influence gender. In such circumstances, it is column rather than row percentages that will be required. The procedure for generating a contingency table with SPSS is described on pages 268–71.

Contingency tables are generated so that patterns of association can be searched for. In this case, we can see clear gender differences in reasons for visiting the gym. As our student anticipated, females are much more likely than men to go to the gym to lose weight. They are also somewhat more likely to go the gym for relaxation. By contrast, men are much more likely to go to the gym to build strength. There is little difference between the two genders in terms of fitness as a reason.

Pearson's *r*

Pearson's *r* is a method for examining relationships between interval/ratio variables. The chief features of this method are as follows:

- the coefficient will almost certainly lie between 0 (zero or no relationship between the two variables) and 1 (a perfect relationship)—this indicates the *strength* of a relationship;
- the closer the coefficient is to 1, the stronger the relationship; the closer it is to zero, the weaker the relationship;

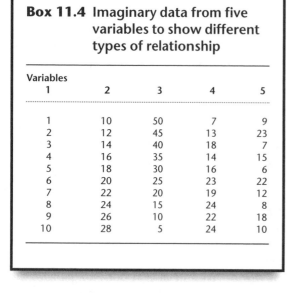

Box 11.4 Imaginary data from five variables to show different types of relationship

Variables				
1	2	3	4	5
1	10	50	7	9
2	12	45	13	23
3	14	40	18	7
4	16	35	14	15
5	18	30	16	6
6	20	25	23	22
7	22	20	19	12
8	24	15	24	8
9	26	10	22	18
10	28	5	24	10

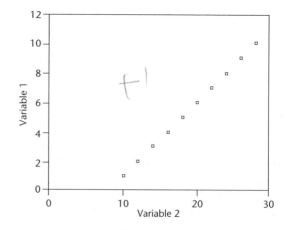

Figure 11.6 Scatter diagram showing a perfect positive relationship

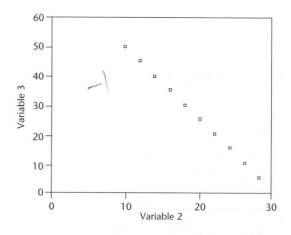

Figure 11.7 Scatter diagram showing a perfect negative relationship

• the coefficient will be either positive or negative—this indicates the *direction* of a relationship.

To illustrate these features consider Box 11.4, which gives imaginary data for five variables, and the scatter diagrams in Figures 11.6–11.9, which look at the relationship between pairs of interval/ratio variables. The scatter diagram for variables 1 and 2 is presented in Figure 11.6 and shows a perfect positive relationship, which would have a Pearson's *r* correlation of +1. This means that, as one variable increases, the other variable increases by the same amount and that no other variable is related to either of them. If the correlation was below 1, it would mean that variable 1 is related to at least one other variable as well as variable 2.

The scatter diagram for variables 2 and 3 (Figure 11.7) shows a perfect negative relationship, which would have a Pearson's *r* correlation of −1. This means that, as one variable increases, the other variable decreases and that no other variable is related to either of them.

If there was no or virtually no correlation between the variables, there would be no apparent pattern to the markers in the scatter diagram. This is the case with the relationship between variables 2 and 5. The correlation is virtually zero at −0.041. This means that the variation in each variable is associated with

other variables than the ones present in this analysis. Figure 11.8 shows the appropriate scatter diagram.

If a relationship is strong, a clear patterning to the variables will be evident. This is the case with variables 2 and 4, whose scatter diagram appears in Figure 11.9. There is clearly a positive relationship and in fact the Pearson's *r* value is +0.88 (usually, positive correlations are presented without the + sign). This means that the variation in the two variables is very closely connected, but that there is some influence of other variables in the extent to which they vary.

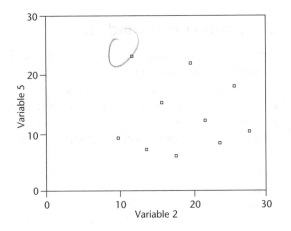

Figure 11.8 Scatter diagram showing two variables that are not related

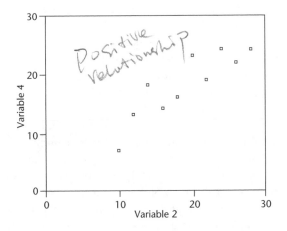

Figure 11.9 Scatter diagram showing a strong positive relationship

Going back to the gym survey, we find that the correlation between age (var00002) and the amount of time spent on weights equipment (var00011) is −0.27, implying a weak negative relationship. This suggests that there is a tendency such that, the older a person is, the less likely he or she is to spend much time on such equipment, but that other variables clearly influence the amount of time spent on this activity.

In order to be able to use Pearson's r, the relationship between the two variables must be broadly *linear*—that is, when plotted on a scatter diagram,

the values of the two variables approximate to a straight line (even though they may be scattered, as in Figure 11.9) and do not curve. Therefore, plotting a scatter diagram before using Pearson's r is important, in order to determine that the nature of the relationship between a pair of variables does not violate the assumptions being made when this method of correlation is employed.

If you square a value of Pearson's r, you can derive a further useful statistic—namely the *coefficient of determination*, which expresses how much of the variation in one variable is due to the other variable. Thus, if r is −0.27, r^2 is 0.0729. We can then express this as a percentage by multiplying r^2 by 100. The product of this exercise is 7 per cent. This means that just 7 per cent of the variation in the use of cardiovascular equipment is accounted for by age. The coefficient of determination is a useful adjunct to the interpretation of correlation information.

The procedure for generating Pearson's r with SPSS is described on page 271 and the procedure for generating scatter diagrams with SPSS is described on page 271.

Spearman's rho

Spearman's rho, which is often represented with the Greek letter ρ, is designed for the use of pairs of ordinal variables, but is also used, as suggested by Figure 11.5, when one variable is ordinal and the other is interval/ratio. It is exactly the same as Pearson's r in terms of the outcome of calculating it, in that the computed value of rho will be either positive or negative and will vary between 0 and 1. If we look at the gym study, there are three ordinal variables: var00004, var00005, and var00006 (see Table 11.1). If we use Spearman's rho to calculate the correlation between the first two variables, we find that the correlation between var00004 and var00005—frequency of use of the cardiovascular and weights equipment—is low at 0.2. A slightly stronger relationship is found between var00006 (frequency of going to the gym) and var00010 (amount of time spent on the cardiovascular equipment), which is 0.4. Note that the latter variable is an interval/ratio variable. When confronted with a situation in which we want to calculate the correlation between an ordinal and an interval/ratio variable, we cannot use Pearson's *r*, because both variables must be at the interval/ratio level of measurement. Instead, we must use Spearman's rho (see Figure 11.5). The procedure for generating Spearman's rho with SPSS is described on page 271.

Phi and Cramér's *V*

Phi (ϕ) and Cramér's *V* are two closely related statistics. The phi coefficient is used for the analysis of the relationship between two dichotomous variables. Like Pearson's *r*, it results in a computed statistic that varies between 0 and + or −1. The correlation between var00001 (gender) and var00008 (other sources of regular exercise) is 0.24, implying that males are somewhat more likely than females to have other sources of regular exercise, though the relationship is weak.

Cramér's *V* uses a similar formula to phi and can be employed with nominal variables (see Figure 11.5). However, this statistic can take on only a positive value, so that it can give an indication only of the strength of the relationship between two variables, not of the direction. The value of Cramér's *V* associated with the analysis presented in Table 11.4 is 0.50. This suggests a moderate relationship between the two variables. Cramér's *V* is usually reported along with a contingency table and a chi-square test (see below). It is not normally presented on its own. The procedure for generating phi and Cramér's *V* with SPSS is described on pages 268–71.

Comparing means and eta

If you need to examine the relationship between an interval/ratio variable and a nominal variable, and if the latter can be relatively unambiguously identified as the independent variable, a potentially fruitful approach is to compare the means of the interval/ratio variable for each subgroup of the nominal variable. As an example, consider Table 11.5, which presents the mean number of minutes spent on cardiovascular equipment (var00010) for each of the four categories of reasons for going to the gym (var00003). The means suggest that people who go to the gym for fitness or to lose weight spend considerably more time on this equipment than people who go to the gym to relax or to build strength.

This procedure is often accompanied by a test of association between variables called *eta*. This statistic expresses the level of association between the two variables and, like Cramér's *V*, will always be positive. The level of eta for the data in Table 11.5 is 0.48. This suggests a moderate relationship between the two variables. Eta-squared expresses the amount of variation in the interval/ratio variable that is due to the nominal variable. In the case of this example, eta-squared is 22 per cent. Eta is a very flexible method for exploring the relationship between two variables, because it can be employed when one variable is nominal and the other interval/ratio. Also, it does not make the assumption that the relationship between variables is linear. The procedure for comparing means and for generating eta with SPSS is described on page 271.

Table 11.5 Comparing subgroup means: time spent on cardiovascular equipment by reasons for going to the gym

Time	Reasons				
	Relaxation	Fitness	Lose weight	Build strength	Total
Mean number of minutes spent on cardiovascular equipment	18.33	30.55	28.36	19.65	26.47
n	9	31	33	17	90

Multivariate analysis

Mutivariate analysis entails the simultaneous analysis of three or more variables. This is quite an advanced topic and it is recommended that readers examine a textbook on quantitative data analysis for an exposition of techniques (e.g. Bryman and Cramer 2001). There are three main contexts within which multivariate analysis might be employed.

Could the relationship be spurious?

In order for a relationship between two variables to be established, not only must there be evidence that there is a relationship but the relationship must be shown to be *non-spurious*. A spurious relationship exists when there appears to be a relationship between two variables, but the relationship is not real: it is being produced because each variable is itself related to a third variable. For example, if we find a relationship in a firm between employees' levels of organizational commitment and job satisfaction, we might ask: could the relationship be an artefact of the leadership style of respondents' immediate managers (see Figure 11.10)? The more committed people are to their organization, the more job satisfaction they are likely to exhibit. However, whether leaders are considerate to their subordinates or not is likely to influence both organizational commitment *and* job satisfaction. If leadership style were found to be producing the apparent relationship between organizational commitment and job satisfaction, we would conclude that the relationship is spurious. An interesting possible case of a spurious relationship was highlighted in a very short report in *The Times* (1 October 1999: 2) of some medical findings. The article noted that there is evidence to suggest that women on hormone replacement therapy (HRT) have lower levels of heart disease than those not on this form of therapy. The article cites Swedish findings that suggest that the relationship may be due to the fact that women who choose to start the therapy are 'thinner, richer and healthier' than those who do not. These background factors would seem to affect both the likelihood of taking HRT *and* the likelihood of getting heart disease. A further illustration in connection with a health-related issue comes from another *Times* article (Hawkes 2003) which reports a relationship among men between frequency of shaving and likelihood of a heart attack or stroke. The reason appears to be that each of the variables (frequency of shaving and vulnerability to a heart attack or stroke) is affected by lifestyle and hormonal factors.

Could there be an intervening variable?

Let us say that we do not find that the relationship is spurious, we might ask *why* there is a relationship between two variables. For example, there have been several studies that have explored the relationship between an organization's market orientation and its business performance. However, the mixed nature of the findings to have emerged from these studies led Piercy, Haris, and Lane (2002) to suggest that there is a more complex relationship between these two variables than previous studies have assumed. In particular, they speculated that higher levels of market orientation are associated with higher levels of employee motivation, satisfaction, and commitment, which in turn leads to enhanced organizational performance. Employee attitudes are thus an *intervening variable*:

market orientation	→	employee attitudes	→	organizational performance

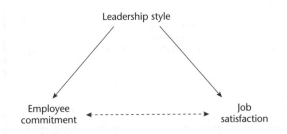

Figure 11.10 A spurious relationship

An intervening variable allows us to answer questions about the bivariate relationship between variables. It suggests that the relationship between the two variables is not a direct one, since the impact of market orientation on organizational performance is viewed as occurring via employee attitudes.

Could a third variable moderate the relationship?

We might ask a question like: does the relationship between two variables hold for men but not for women? If it does, the relationship is said to be moderated by gender. We might ask in the gym study, for example, whether the relationship between age and whether visitors have other sources of regular exercise (var00008) is moderated by gender. This would imply that, if we find a pattern relating age to other sources of exercise, that pattern will vary by gender.

Table 11.6 shows the relationship between age and other sources of exercise. In this table, age has been broken down into just three age bands to make the table easier to read. The table suggests that the 31–40 age group are less likely to have other sources of regular exercise than the 30 and under and 41 and over age groups. However, Table 11.7, which breaks the relationship down by gender, suggests that the pattern for males and females is somewhat different. Among males, the pattern shown in Table 11.6 is very pronounced, but for females the likelihood of having other sources of exercise declines with gender. It would seem that the relationship between age and other sources of exercise is moderated by gender. This example illustrates the way in which contingency tables can be employed for multivariate analysis. However, there is a wide variety of other techniques (Bryman and Cramer 2001: ch. 10). The procedure for conducting such an analysis with SPSS is described on page 271.

Table 11.6 Contingency table showing the relationship between age and whether gym visitors have other sources of regular exercise (percentages)

Other source of exercise	Age		
	30 and under	31–40	41 and over
Other source	64	43	58
No other source	36	57	42
n	42	23	24

Table 11.7 Contingency table showing the relationship between age and whether gym visitors have other sources of regular exercise for males and females (percentages)

Other source of exercise	Gender					
	Male			Female		
	30 and under	31–40	41 and over	30 and under	31–40	41 and over
Other source	70	33	75	59	50	42
No other source	30	67	25	41	50	58
n	20	9	12	22	14	12

Statistical significance

One difficulty with working on data deriving from a sample is that there is often the lingering worry that, even though you have employed a probability sampling procedure (as in the gym survey), your findings will not be generalizable to the population from which the sample was drawn. As we saw in Chapter 4, there is always the possibility that *sampling error* (difference between the population and the sample that you have selected) has occurred, even when probability sampling procedures have been followed. If this happens, the sample will be unrepresentative of the wider population and therefore any findings will be invalid. To make matters worse, there is no feasible way of finding out whether they do in fact apply to the population! What you can do is to provide an indication of how confident you can be in your findings. This is where statistical significance and the various tests of statistical significance come in.

We need to know how confident we can be that our findings can be generalized to the population from which that sample was selected. Since we cannot be absolutely certain that a finding based on a sample will also be found in the population, we need a technique that allows us to establish how confident we can be that the finding exists in the population and what risk we are taking in inferring that the finding exists in the population. These two elements—confidence and risk—lie at the heart of tests of statistical significance (see Box 11.5). However, it is

important to appreciate that tests of statistical significance can be employed only in relation to samples that have been drawn using probability sampling.

In Chapter 4 (see Box 4.4), in the context of the discussion of the standard error of the mean, we began to get an appreciation of the ideas behind statistical significance. For example, we know that the mean age of the gym sample is 33.6. Using the concept of the standard error of the mean, we can calculate that we can be 95 per cent confident that the population mean lies between 31.72 and 35.47. This suggests that we can determine in broad outline the degree of confidence that we can have in a sample mean.

In the rest of this section, we will look at the tests that are available for determining the degree of confidence we can have in our findings when we explore relationships between variables. All of the tests have a common structure.

Not guilt unless you can prove it

- *Set up a null hypothesis*. This stipulates that two variables are not related in the population—for example, that there is *no* relationship between gender and visiting the gym in the population from which the sample was selected.

- *Establish the level of statistical significance that you find acceptable*. This is essentially a measure of the degree of risk that you might reject the null hypothesis (implying that there *is* a relationship in the population) when you should support it

---

Box 11.5 💡 *What is a test of statistical significance?*

A test of statistical significance allows the analyst to estimate how confident he or she can be that the results deriving from a study based on a randomly selected sample are generalizable to the population from which the sample was drawn. When examining statistical significance in relation to the relationship between two variables, it also tells us about the risk of concluding that there is in fact a relationship in the population when there is no

such relationship in the population. If an analysis reveals a statistically significant finding, this does not mean that that finding is intrinsically significant or important. The word 'significant' seems to imply importance. However, statistical significance is solely concerned with the confidence researchers can have in their findings. It does not mean that a statistically significant finding is substantively significant.

on average   *+ Criminal*   *no low Population Sample*

no Guilt   (0.01)   1 in 100 → Reject

assume Yes Guilty   (0.1)   1 in 10 → accept

(implying that there is no relationship in the population). Levels of statistical significance are expressed as probability levels—that is, the probability of rejecting the null hypothesis when you should be confirming it. See Box 11.6 on this issue. The convention among most business researchers is that the maximum level of statistical significance that is acceptable is $p < 0.05$, which implies that there are fewer than five chances in 100 that you could have a sample that shows a relationship when there is not one in the population.

- *Determine the statistical significance of your findings* (i.e. use a statistical test like chi-square—see below).

- If your findings are statistically significant at the 0.05 level—so that the risk of getting a relationship as strong as the one you have found, when there is *no* relationship in the population, is no higher than 5 in 100—you would *reject* the null hypothesis. Therefore, you are implying that the results are unlikely to have occurred by *chance*.

Prob < 0.05

There are in fact two types of error that can be made when inferring statistical significance. These errors are known as Type I and Type II errors (see Figure 11.11). A Type I error occurs when you reject the null hypothesis when it should in fact be confirmed. This means that your results have arisen by chance and you are falsely concluding that there is a relationship in the population when there is not one. Using a $p < 0.05$ level of significance means that we are more likely to make a Type I error than when using a $p < 0.01$ level of significance. This is because with 0.01 there is less chance of falsely rejecting the null hypothesis. However, in doing so, you increase the chance of making a Type II error (accepting the

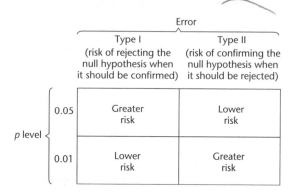

Figure 11.11 Type I and Type II errors

Box 11.6   What is the level of statistical significance?

The level of statistical significance is the level of risk that you are prepared to take that you are inferring that there is a relationship between two variables in the population from which the sample was taken when in fact no such relationship exists. The maximum level of risk that is conventionally taken in business and managerial research is to say that there are up to 5 chances in 100 that we might be falsely concluding that there is a relationship when there is not one in the population from which the sample was taken. This means that, if we drew 100 samples, we are recognizing that as many as 5 of them might exhibit a relationship when there is not one in the population. Our sample might be one of those five, but the risk is fairly small. This significance level is denoted by $p < 0.05$ (p means probability). If we accepted a significance level of $p < 0.1$, we would be accepting the possibility that as many as 10 in 100 samples might show a relationship where none exists in the population. In this case, there is a greater risk than with $p < 0.05$ that we might have a sample that implies a relationship when there is not one in the population, since the probability of our having such a sample is greater when the risk is 1 in 10 (10 out of 100 when $p < 0.1$) than when the risk is 1 in 20 (5 out of 100 when $p < 0.05$). Therefore, we would have greater confidence when the risk of falsely inferring that there is a relationship between 2 variables is 1 in 20, as against 1 in 10. But, if you want a more stringent test, perhaps because you are worried about the use that might be made of your results, you might choose the $p < 0.01$ level. This means that you are prepared to accept as your level of risk a probability of only 1 in 100 that the results could have arisen by chance (that is, due to sampling error). Therefore, if the results, following administration of a test, show that the results are statistically significant at the $p < 0.05$ level, but *not* the $p < 0.01$ level, you would have to confirm the null hypothesis.

null hypothesis when you should reject it). This is because you are more likely to confirm the null hypothesis when the significance level is 0.01 (1 in 100) than when it is 0.05 (1 in 20).

The chi-square test

The chi-square (χ^2) test is applied to contingency tables like Table 11.4. It allows us to establish how confident we can be that there is a relationship between the two variables in the population. The test works by calculating for each cell in the table an expected frequency or value—that is, one that would occur on the basis of chance alone. The chi-square value, which in Table 11.4 is 22.726, is calculated by calculating the differences between the actual and expected values for each cell in the table and then summing those differences (it is slightly more complicated than this, but the details need not concern us here). The chi-square value means nothing on its own and can be meaningfully interpreted only in relation to its associated level of statistical significance, which in this case is $p < 0.0001$. This means that there is only one chance in 10,000 of rejecting the null hypothesis (that is, inferring that there *is* a relationship in the population when there is no such relationship in the population). You could be extremely confident that there is a relationship between gender and reasons for visiting the gym among all gym members, since the chance that you have obtained a sample that shows a relationship when there is no relationship among all gym members is 1 in 10,000.

Whether a chi-square value achieves statistical significance depends not just on its magnitude but also on the number of categories of the two variables being analysed. This latter issue is governed by what is known as the 'degrees of freedom' associated with the table. The number of degrees of freedom is governed by the simple formula:

Number of degrees of freedom =
(number of columns − 1)(number of rows − 1).

In the case of Table 11.5, this will be $(2 - 1)(4 - 1)$, that is, 3. In other words, the chi-square value that is arrived at is affected by the size of the table, and this is taken into account when deciding whether the chi-square value is statistically significant or not. The procedure for chi-square in conjunction with a contingency table with SPSS is described on page 268.

Correlation and statistical significance

Examining the statistical significance of a computed correlation coefficient, which is based on a randomly selected sample, provides information about the likelihood that the coefficient will be found in the population from which the sample was taken. Thus, if we find a correlation of −0.62, what is the likelihood that a relationship of at least that size exists in the population? This tells us whether the relationship could have arisen by chance.

If the correlation coefficient r is −0.62 and the significance level is $p < 0.05$, we can reject the null hypothesis that there is no relationship in the population. We can infer that there are only five chances in 100 that a correlation of at least −0.62 could have arisen by chance alone. You *could* have one of the five samples in 100 that shows a relationship when there is not one in the population, but the degree of risk is reasonably small. If, say, it was found that $r = -0.62$ and $p < 0.1$, there could be as many as ten chances in 100 that there is no correlation in the population. This would *not* be an acceptable level of risk for most purposes. It would mean that in as many as one sample in 10 we might find a correlation of −0.62 or above when there is not a correlation in the population. If $r = -0.62$ and $p < 0.001$, there is only one chance in 1,000 that no correlation exists in the population. There would be a very low level of risk if you inferred that the correlation had not arisen by chance.

Whether a correlation coefficient is statistically significant or not will be affected by two factors:

• the size of the computed coefficient, and

• the size of the sample.

This second factor may appear surprising. Basically, the larger a sample, the more likely it is that a computed correlation coefficient will be found to be statistically significant. Thus, even though the correlation between age and the amount of time spent on weights machines in the gym survey was found to be just −0.27, which is a fairly weak relationship, it is statistically significant at the $p < 0.01$ level. This means that there is only one chance in 100 that there is no relationship in the population. Because the question of whether a correlation coefficient is statistically significant depends so much on the sample size, it is important to realize that you should always examine *both* the correlation coefficient *and* the significance level. You should not examine one at the expense of the other.

This treatment of correlation and statistical significance applies to both Pearson's *r* and Spearman's rho. A similar interpretation can also be applied to phi and Cramér's *V*. SPSS automatically produces information regarding statistical significance when Pearson's *r*, Spearman's rho, phi, and Cramér's *V* are generated.

Table 11.5. This procedure entails treating the total amount of variation in the dependent variable—amount of time spent on cardiovascular equipment—as made up of two types: variation *within* the four subgroups that make up the independent variable and variation *between* them. The latter is often called the *explained variance* and the former the *error variance*. A test of statistical significance for the comparison of means entails relating the two types of variance to form what is known as the *F* statistic. This statistic expresses the amount of explained variance in relation to the amount of error variance. In the case of the data in Table 11.5, the resulting *F* statistic is statistically significant at the $p < 0.001$ level. This finding suggests that there is only one chance in 1,000 that there is no relationship between the two variables among all gym members. SPSS produces information regarding the *F* statistic and its statistical significance if the procedures described on p. 254 are followed.

Comparing means and statistical significance

A test of statistical significance can also be applied to the comparison of means that was carried out in

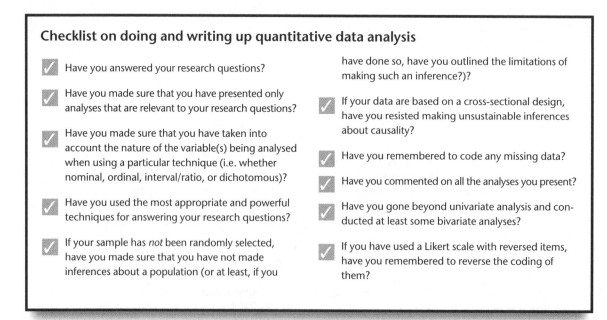

Checklist on doing and writing up quantitative data analysis

✓ Have you answered your research questions?

✓ Have you made sure that you have presented only analyses that are relevant to your research questions?

✓ Have you made sure that you have taken into account the nature of the variable(s) being analysed when using a particular technique (i.e. whether nominal, ordinal, interval/ratio, or dichotomous)?

✓ Have you used the most appropriate and powerful techniques for answering your research questions?

✓ If your sample has *not* been randomly selected, have you made sure that you have not made inferences about a population (or at least, if you have done so, have you outlined the limitations of making such an inference?)?

✓ If your data are based on a cross-sectional design, have you resisted making unsustainable inferences about causality?

✓ Have you remembered to code any missing data?

✓ Have you commented on all the analyses you present?

✓ Have you gone beyond univariate analysis and conducted at least some bivariate analyses?

✓ If you have used a Likert scale with reversed items, have you remembered to reverse the coding of them?

tempting

- You need to think about your data analysis before you begin designing your research instruments.

- Techniques of data analysis are applicable to some types of variable and not others. You need to know the difference between nominal, ordinal, interval/ratio, and dichotomous variables.

  Scale

- You need to think about the kinds of data you are collecting and the implications your decisions will have for the sorts of techniques you will be able to employ.

- Become familiar with computer software like SPSS before you begin designing your research instruments, because it is advisable to be aware at an early stage of difficulties you might have in presenting your data in SPSS.

- Make sure you are thoroughly familiar with the techniques introduced in this chapter and when you can and cannot use them.

- The basic message, then, is not to leave these considerations until your data have been collected, tempting though it may be.

- Do not confuse statistical significance with substantive significance.

- At what stage should you begin to think about the kinds of data analysis you need to conduct?

- What are missing data and why do they arise?

Types of variable

- What are the differences between the four types of variable outlined in this chapter: interval/ratio; ordinal; nominal; and dichotomous?

interval

- Why is it important to be able to distinguish between the four types of variable?

- Imagine the kinds of answers you would receive if you administered the following four questions in an interview survey. What kind of variable would each question generate: dichotomous; nominal; ordinal; or interval/ratio?

  1 Do you enjoy going shopping?

  Yes   ——

  No   ——

  2 How many times have you shopped in the last month? Please write in the number of occasions below.

  ——

3 For which kinds of items do you most enjoy shopping? Please tick one only.

Clothes (including shoes) ——

Food ——

Things for the house ——

Presents ——

Entertainment (CDs, videos, etc.) ——

4 How important is it to you to buy clothes with designer labels?

Very important ——

Fairly important ——

Not very important ——

Not at all important ——

Univariate analysis

- What is an outlier and why might one have an adverse effect on the mean and the range?

- In conjunction with which measure of central tendency would you expect to report the standard deviation: the mean; the median; or the mode?

Bivariate analysis

- Can you infer causality from bivariate analysis?

- Why are percentages crucial when presenting contingency tables?

- In what circumstances would you use each of the following: Pearson's r; Spearman's rho; phi; Cramér's V; eta?.

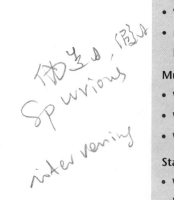

Multivariate analysis

- What is a spurious relationship?

- What is an intervening variable?

- What does it mean to say that a relationship is moderated?

Statistical significance

- What does statistical significance mean and how does it differ from substantive significance?

- What is a significance level?

- What does the chi-square test achieve?

- What does it mean to say that a correlation of 0.42 is statistically significant at $p < 0.05$?

CHAPTER GUIDE

In order to implement the techniques that you learned in Chapter 11, you would need to do either of two things: learn the underlying formula for each technique and apply your data to it, or use computer software to analyse your data. The latter is the approach chosen in this book for two main reasons.

- It is closer to the way in which quantitative data analysis is carried out in real research nowadays.

- It helps to equip you with a useful transferable skill.

You will be learning SPSS for Windows, which is the most widely used package of computer software for doing this kind of analysis. It is relatively straightforward to use. We will be continuing to refer to the techniques introduced in Chapter 11 and will continue to use the gym survey as an example.

This chapter largely operates in parallel to Chapter 11, so that you can see the links between the techniques learned there and the use of SPSS to implement them.

Introduction

This chapter aims to provide a familiarity with some basic aspects of SPSS for Windows, which is possibly the most widely used computer software for the analysis of quantitative data for social scientists. SPSS, which originally was short for Statistical Package for the Social Sciences, has been in existence since the mid-1960s and over the years has undergone many revisions, particularly since the arrival of personal computers. The version that was used in preparing this section was Release 11. From this point on, when referring to SPSS for Windows in the text, it will be called simply SPSS. The gym survey used in Chapter 11 will be employed to illustrate SPSS operations and methods of analysis. The aim here is to introduce ways of using SPSS to implement the methods of analysis discussed in Chapter 11.

SPSS operations will be presented in **bold**, for example, **Variable Name:** and **Analyze**. Names given to variables in the course of using SPSS will be presented in **_bold italics_**, e.g. **_gender_** and **_reasons_**. Labels given to values or to variables are also in bold but in a different font, e.g. **reasons for visiting** and **male**. Box 12.1 presents a list of basic operations in SPPS. One further element in the presentation is that a right-pointing arrow— → —will be used to denote 'click once with the left-hand button of your mouse'. This action is employed to make selections and similar activities.

Getting started in SPSS

Beginning SPSS

To start SPSS, double click on the **spsswin** icon on your computer screen. If there is no icon, → the **Start** button in the bottom left-hand corner of your screen. From the menu of programs, → **SPSS for Windows**. A follow-on menu will appear, from which you should select **SPSS 11.0 for Windows**. When SPSS loads, you _may_ be faced with an opening dialog box with the title 'What do you want to do?' and a list of options. Many users prefer to disable this opening box. It is not important in relation to the following exposition, so → **Cancel**. You will then be faced with the **SPSS Data Editor**. This is made up of two components: **Data View** and **Variable View**. In the following discussion, these two screens are referred to as the **Data Viewer** and the **Variable Viewer**. You move between these two viewers by selecting the appropriate tab at the bottom of the screen. The **Data Viewer** is in the form of a spreadsheet

grid into which you enter your data. The columns represent _variables_—in other words, information about characteristics of each person in the gym study sample. Until data are entered, each column simply has **var** as its heading. The rows represent _cases_, which can be people (as in the example you will be working through) or any unit of analysis. Each block in the grid is referred to as a 'cell'. Note also that when the data are in the SPSS spreadsheet, they will look different, for example, 1 will be 1.00.

Entering data in the Data Viewer

To input the data into the **Data Viewer**, make sure that the top left-hand cell in the grid is highlighted (Plate 12.1). If it is not highlighted, simply click once in that cell. Then, type the appropriate figure for that cell—that is, 1. This number goes directly into that cell and into the box beneath the toolbar. As an alternative to using the mouse, many people find it

Box 12.1 Basic operations in SPSS for Windows

- The **SPSS Data Editor**. This is the sphere of SPSS into which data are entered and subsequently edited and defined. It is made up of two screens: the **Data Viewer** and the **Variable Viewer**. You move between these two viewers by selecting the appropriate tab at the bottom of the screen.

- The **Data Viewer**. This is the spreadsheet into which your data are entered. When you start up SPSS, the **Data Viewer** will be facing you.

- The **Variable Viewer**. This is another spreadsheet, but this one displays information about each of the variables and allows you to change that information. It is the platform from which you provide for each variable such information as: the variable name; a variable label; and value labels (see below).

- The **Output**. When you perform an analysis or produce a diagram (called a 'chart' in SPSS), your output will be deposited here. The **Output Viewer** superimposes itself over the **Data Editor** after an analysis has been performed or a chart generated.

- A **Variable Name**. This is the name that you give to a variable, e.g. *gender*. The name must be no more than eight characters. Until you give a variable a name, it will be referred to as *var00001*, etc. When the variable has been given a name, it will appear in the column for that variable in the **Data View** window. It is generated from the **Variable Viewer**.

- A **Variable Label**. This is a label that you can give to a variable but which is not restricted to eight characters. Spaces can be used, e.g. **reasons for visiting**. The Label will appear in any output you generate. It is generated from the **Variable Viewer**.

- A **Value Label**. This is a label that you can attach to a code that has been used when entering data for all types of variables other than interval/ratio variables. Thus, for var00001, we would attach the label **male** to 1 and **female** to 2. When you generate output, such as a frequency table or chart, the labels for each value will be presented. This makes the interpretation of output easier. It is generated from the **Variable Viewer**.

- **Missing Values . . . .** When you do not have data for a particular variable when entering data for a case, you must specify how you are denoting missing values for that variable. Missing values are generated from the **Variable Viewer**.

- **Recode**. A procedure that allows codes or numbers to be changed. It is especially helpful when you need to combine groups of people—for example, when producing age bands.

- **Compute . . . .** A procedure that allows you to combine two or more variables to form a new variable.

- **Analyze**. This is the point on the menu bar above the **Data Editor** from which you choose (via a drop-down menu) which method of analysis you want to select. Note that, whenever an item on a menu appears with a right-pointing arrowhead after it, this means that, if you select that option, a further menu will follow on.

- **Graphs**. This is the point on the menu bar above the **Data Editor** from which you choose (via a drop-down menu) which chart you want to select.

- **Chart Editor**. When you produce a graph, you can edit it with the **Chart Editor**. To activate this editor, double-click anywhere in the graph. A small chart editor window will appear and your main graph will appear opaque until you exit the Editor. From the Editor, you can make various changes and enhancements to your graph.

---

easier to use the arrow keys on their keyboard to move from cell to cell. If you make a mistake at any point, simply click once in the cell in question, type in the correct value, and click once more in that cell. When you have finished, you should end up in the bottom right-hand cell of what will be a perfect rectangle of data. Plate 12.2 shows the **Data Viewer** with the data from the gym survey entered (though only part of the set of data is visible, in that only the first twenty-two respondents and ten of the twelve variables are visible). The first row of data contains the coded answers from the completed questionnaire in Box 11.2.

In order to proceed further, you will find that SPSS works in the following typical sequence for defining variables and analysing your data.

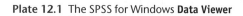

Plate 12.1 The SPSS for Windows **Data Viewer**

	var00001	var00002	var00003	var00004	var00005	var00006	var00007	var00008	var00009	var00010
1	1.00	21.00	2.00	1.00	1.00	3.00	1.00	2.00	.00	33.00
2	2.00	44.00	1.00	3.00	1.00	4.00	3.00	1.00	2.00	10.00
3	2.00	19.00	3.00	1.00	2.00	2.00	1.00	1.00	1.00	27.00
4	2.00	27.00	3.00	2.00	1.00	2.00	1.00	2.00	.00	30.00
5	1.00	57.00	2.00	1.00	3.00	2.00	3.00	1.00	4.00	22.00
6	2.00	27.00	3.00	1.00	1.00	3.00	1.00	1.00	3.00	34.00
7	1.00	39.00	5.00	2.00	1.00	5.00	1.00	1.00	5.00	17.00
8	2.00	36.00	3.00	1.00	2.00	2.00	2.00	1.00	1.00	25.00
9	1.00	37.00	2.00	1.00	1.00	3.00	1.00	2.00	.00	34.00
10	2.00	51.00	2.00	2.00	2.00	4.00	3.00	2.00	.00	16.00
11	1.00	24.00	5.00	2.00	1.00	3.00	1.00	1.00	1.00	.00
12	2.00	29.00	2.00	1.00	2.00	3.00	1.00	2.00	.00	34.00
13	1.00	20.00	5.00	1.00	1.00	2.00	1.00	2.00	.00	22.00
14	2.00	22.00	2.00	1.00	3.00	4.00	2.00	1.00	3.00	37.00
15	2.00	46.00	3.00	1.00	1.00	5.00	2.00	2.00	.00	26.00
16	2.00	41.00	3.00	1.00	2.00	2.00	3.00	1.00	4.00	22.00
17	1.00	25.00	5.00	1.00	1.00	3.00	1.00	1.00	1.00	21.00
18	2.00	46.00	3.00	1.00	2.00	4.00	2.00	1.00	4.00	18.00
19	1.00	30.00	3.00	1.00	1.00	5.00	1.00	2.00	.00	23.00
20	1.00	25.00	5.00	2.00	1.00	3.00	1.00	1.00	1.00	23.00
21	2.00	24.00	2.00	1.00	1.00	3.00	2.00	1.00	2.00	20.00
22	2.00	39.00	1.00	2.00	3.00	5.00	1.00	2.00	.00	17.00

Plate 12.2 The **Data Viewer** with 'gym study' data entered

1. You make a selection from the menu bar at the top of the screen, e.g. → **Analyze**.

2. From the menu that will appear, make a selection, e.g. → **Descriptive Statistics**.

3. This will bring up a *dialog box* into which you will usually inform SPSS of what you are trying to do—e.g. which variables are to be analysed.

4. Very often, you then need to convey further information and to do this you have to → a button that will bring up what is called, following Bryman and Cramer (2001), a *sub-dialog box*.

5. You then provide the information in the sub-dialog box and then go back to the dialog box. Sometimes, you will need to bring up a further sub-dialog box and then go back to the dialog box.

When you have finished going through the entire procedure, → **OK**. The toolbar beneath the menu bar allows shortcut access to certain SPSS operations.

Defining variables: variable names, missing values, variable labels, and value labels

Once you have finished entering your data, you need to define your variables. The following steps will allow you to do this:

1. → the **Variable View** tab at the bottom of the **Data Viewer** (opens the **Variable Viewer** shown in Plate 12.3).

2. To provide a variable name, click on the current variable name (e.g. *var00003*) and type the name of the name you want to give it (e.g. *reasons*). Remember that this name must be no more than eight characters and you can*not* use spaces.

3. You can then give your variable a more detailed name, known in SPSS as a variable label. To do this, → cell in the **Label** column relating to the

	Name	Type	Width	Decimals	Label	Values	Missing	Columns	
1	var00001	Numeric	8	2		None	None	8	Rigl
2	var00002	Numeric	8	2		None	None	8	Rigl
3	var00003	Numeric	8	2		None	None	8	Rigl
4	var00004	Numeric	8	2		None	None	8	Rigl
5	var00005	Numeric	8	2		None	None	8	Rigl
6	var00006	Numeric	8	2		None	None	8	Rigl
7	var00007	Numeric	8	2		None	None	8	Rigl
8	var00008	Numeric	8	2		None	None	8	Rigl
9	var00009	Numeric	8	2		None	None	8	Rigl
10	var00010	Numeric	8	2		None	None	8	Rigl
11	var00011	Numeric	8	2		None	None	8	Rigl
12	var00012	Numeric	8	2		None	None	8	Rigl

Plate 12.3 The **Variable Viewer**

variable for which you want to supply a variable label. Then, simply type in the variable label (i.e. **reasons for visiting**).

4. Then you will need to provide 'value labels' for variables that have been given codes. The procedure generally applies to variables that are not interval/ratio variables. The latter, which are numeric variables, do not need to be coded (unless you are grouping them in some way). To assign value labels, → in the **Values** column relating to the variable you are working on. A small button with three dots on it will appear. → the button. The **Value Labels** dialog box will appear (Plate 12.4). → the box to the right of **Value** and begin to define the value labels. To do this, enter the value (e.g. **1**) in the area to the right of **Value** and then the value label (e.g. **relaxation**)

in the area to the right of **Value Label**. Then → **Add**. Do this for each value. When you have finished → **OK**

5. You will then need to inform SPSS of the value that you have nominated for each variable to indicate a missing value. In the case of *reasons*, the value is 0 (zero). To assign the missing value, → the cell for this variable in the **Missing** column. Again, → the button that will appear with three dots on it. This will generate the **Missing Values** dialog box (Plate 12.5). In the **Missing Values** dialog box, enter the missing value (**0**) below **Discrete missing value:** and then → **OK**

In order to simplify the following presentation, *reasons* will be the only variable for which a variable label will be defined.

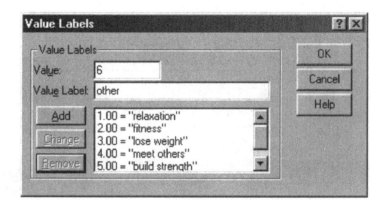

Plate 12.4 The **Value Labels** dialog box

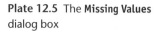

Plate 12.5 The **Missing Values** dialog box

Recoding variables

Sometimes you need to recode variables—for example, when you want to group people. You would need to do this in order to produce a table like Table 11.3 for an interval/ratio variable like **var00002**, which we will give the variable name *age*. SPSS offers two choices: you can recode *age* so that it will be changed in the **Data Viewer**, or you can keep *age* as it is and create a new variable. This latter option is desirable whenever you want to preserve the variable in question as well as create a new one. Since we may want to carry out analyses involving *age* as an interval/ratio variable, we will recode it so that a new variable, which we will call *agegp*, for *age* groups, will be created. The aim of the following operations is to create a new variable—*agegp*—which will comprise five age bands, as in Table 11.3.

1. → **Transform** → **Recode** → **Into Different Variables** [opens **Recode into Different Variables** dialog box shown in Plate 12.6]

2. → *age* → ▶ button [puts *age* in **Numeric Variable->Output Variable:** box] → box beneath **Output Variable Name:** and type *agegp* → **Change** [puts *agegp* in the **Numeric Variable->Output**

Variable: box] → **Old and New Values . . .** [opens **Recode into Different Variables: Old and New Values** sub-dialog box shown in Plate 12.7]

3. → the circle by **System- or user-missing** and by **System-missing** under **New Value**, if you have missing values for a variable, which is the case for this variable

4. → circle by **Range: Lowest Through** and type **20** in the box → box by **Value** in **New Value** and type **1** → **Add** [the new value will appear in the **Old**-- >**New:** box]

5. → first box by **Range:** and type **21** and in box after **through** type **30** → box by **Value** in **New Value** and type **2** → **Add**

6. → first box by **Range:** and type **31** and in box after **through** type **40** → box by **Value** in **New Value** and type **3** → **Add**

7. → first box by **Range:** and type **41** and in box after **through** type **50** → box by **Value** in **New Value** and type **4** → **Add**

8. → circle by **Range: through highest** and type **51** in the box → box by **Value** in **New Value** and type **5** → **Add** → **Continue** [closes the **Recode into Different Variables: Old and New Values** sub-dialog box shown in Plate 12.7 and returns

Plate 12.6 The **Recode into Different Variables** dialog box

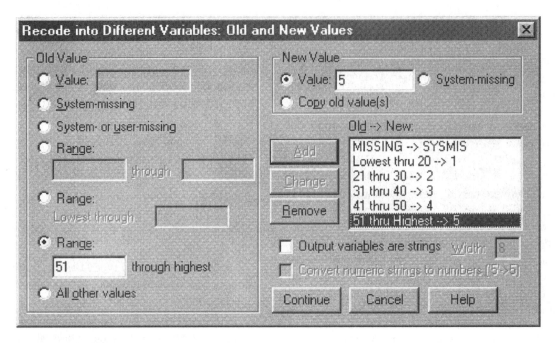

Plate 12.7 The **Recode into Different Variables: Old and New Values** sub-dialog box

you to the **Recode into Different Variables** shown in Plate 12.6]

9. → **OK**

The new variable *agegp* will be created and will appear in the **Data Viewer**. You would then need to generate **value labels** for the five age bands and possibly a **variable label** using the approach described above.

Computing a new variable

A person's total amount of time spent in the gym is made up of three variables: *cardmins, weimins,* and *othmins*. If we add these up, we should arrive at the total number of minutes spent on activities in the gym. In so doing, we will create a new variable *totalmin*. To do this, this procedure should

be followed:

1. → **Transform** → **Compute** ... [opens the **Compute Variable** dialog box shown in Plate 12.8]

2. under **Target Variable:** type *totalmin*

3. select **SUM[numexpr, numexpr, . . .]** from the list underneath **Functions:** and click on the button with an upward-pointing arrowhead to send it into the box underneath **Numeric Expression:**

4. from the list of variables at the left, → *cardmins* → ► button [puts *cardmins* in box after **SUM**]; → *weimins* → ► button [puts *weimins* in box after **,cardmins**]; → *othmins* → ► button [puts *othmins* in box after **,weimins**]

5. → OK

The new variable *totalmin* will be created and will appear in the **Data Editor**.

Now at last, we can begin to analyse the data!

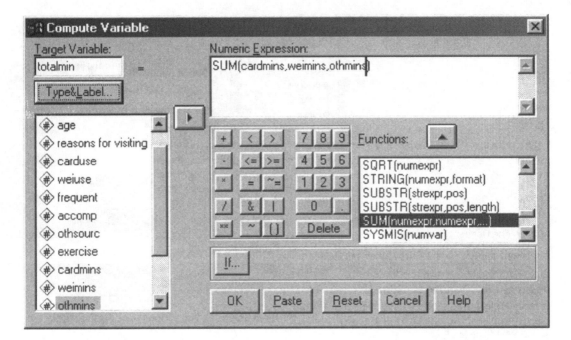

Plate 12.8 The **Compute Variable** dialog box

Data analysis with SPSS

Generating a frequency table

To produce a frequency table like the one in Table 11.2:

1. → **A̱nalyze** → **Ḏescriptive Statistics** → **F̱requencies** . . . [opens the **Frequencies** dialog box shown in Plate 12.9]
2. → **reasons for visiting** → ▶ button [puts **reasons for visiting** in **Variable[s]:** box]
3. → **OK**

The table will appear in the **Output Viewer** (see Plate 12.10)

Note that in the **Frequencies** dialog box, variables that have been assigned labels will appear in terms of their variable labels, but those that have not been assigned labels will appear in terms of their variable names. This is a feature of all dialog boxes produced via **A̱nalyze** and **G̱raphs** (see below).

Generating a bar chart

To produce a bar chart like the one in Figure 11.2:

1. → **G̱raphs** → **Ḇar** . . . [opens **Bar Charts** dialog box]
2. → **Simple** → **Summaries for groups of c̱ases** → **Define** [opens **Define Simple Bar: Summaries for Groups of Cases** sub-dialog box shown in Plate 12.11]
3. → **reasons for visiting** → ▶ button by **Category Ax̱is** → [**reasons for visiting** will appear in the box] → **Ṉ of cases** beneath **Bars Represent** [*if* this has not already been selected, otherwise continue without doing this]
4. → **OK**

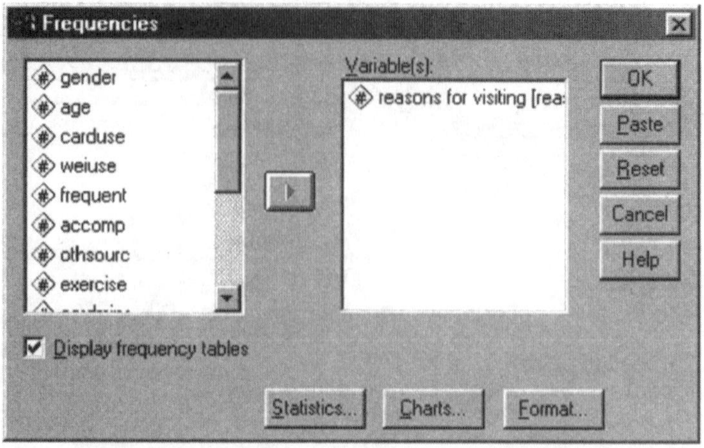

Plate 12.9 The **Frequencies** dialog box

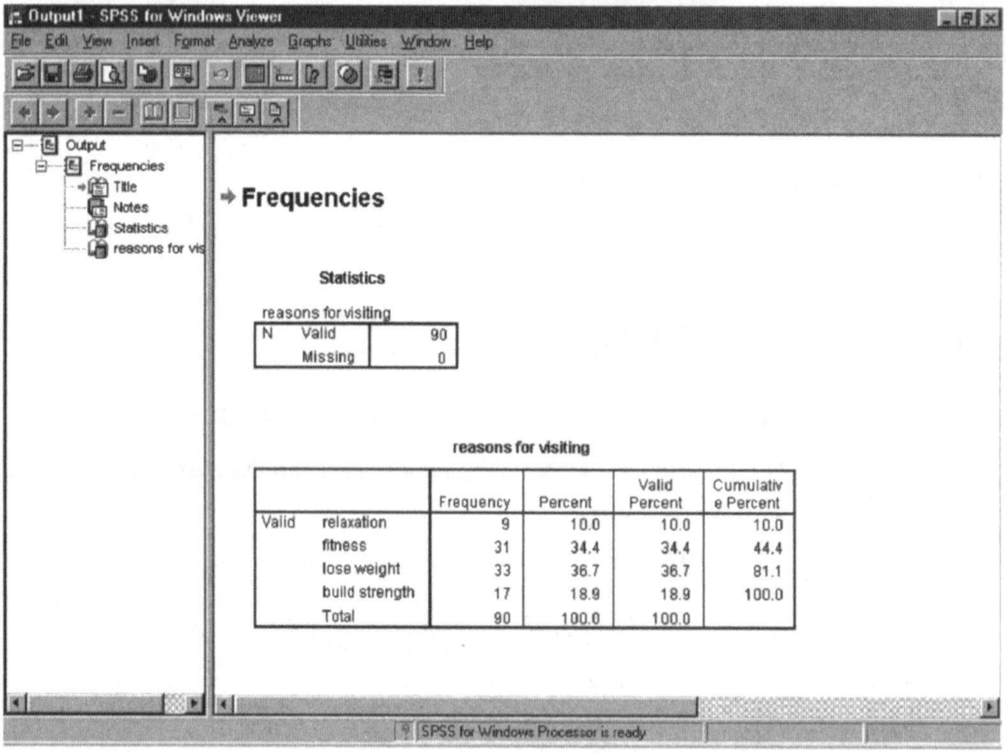

Plate 12.10 The **Output Viewer**

Generating a pie chart

To produce a pie chart like the one in Figure 11.3:

1. → **Graphs** → **Pie** . . . [opens the **Pie Charts** dialog box] → **Summaries for groups of cases** → **Define**

[opens the **Define Pie: Summaries for Groups of Cases** sub-dialog box]

2. → **reasons for visiting** → ▶ button by **Define slices by** [reasons for visiting will appear in the box] → **N of cases** beneath **Slices Represent:** [if

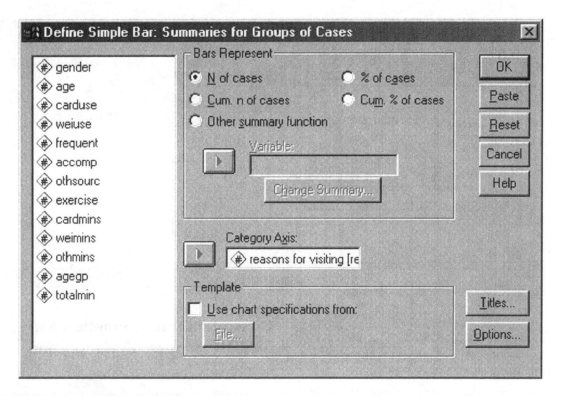

Plate 12.11 The **Define Simple Bar: Summaries for Groups of Cases**

this has *not* already been selected, otherwise continue without doing this]

3. → **OK**

In order to include percentages, as in Figure 11.3, *double-click* anywhere in the chart in order to bring up the **Chart Editor**. The chart will appear in the **Chart Editor** and the main figure will become opaque. Then → **Chart** and then → **Options . . .** and then place a tick by **Percents** [there should also be a tick by **Text**].

Your chart will be in colour, but, if you only have access to a monochrome printer, you can change your pie chart into patterns, which allows the slices to be clearer. At the end of the next section, there is a description of how to do this.

Generating a histogram

Producing a histogram like the one in Figure 11.4 is somewhat more complicated. The standard procedure

for generating a histogram is → **Graphs** → **Histogram** and then selecting the relevant variable. This procedure will generate a very good histogram but SPSS will define the age bands. If you want to define the bars yourself, you should follow the steps for the one produced for Figure 11.4, which involved following the steps entailed in generating a bar chart:

1. → **Graphs** → **Bar . . .** [opens **Bar Charts** dialog box]

2. → **Simple** → **Summaries for groups of cases** → **Define** [opens **Define Simple Bar: Summaries for Groups of Cases** sub-dialog box shown in Plate 12.11]

3. → *agegp* → ▶ button by **Category Axis** [*agegp* will appear in the box] → **N of cases** beneath **Bars Represent** [*if* this has not already been selected, otherwise continue without doing this] → **OK**

4. after the bar chart appears in the **SPSS for Windows** viewer, double-click anywhere in the body of the figure; this will bring up the **SPSS for**

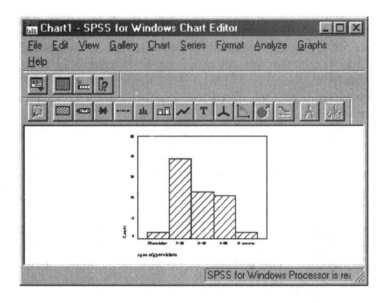

Plate 12.12 The **Chart Editor**

Windows **Chart Editor** shown in Plate 12.12 →
Chart → **Bar Spacing** . . . [opens the **Bar Spacing**
sub-dialog box]

5. in the small box to the right of **Inter-Bar Spacing**
   replace the figure in the box with **0** → **OK** [closes
   the **Bar Spacing** sub-dialog box and returns you to
   the **SPSS for Windows Chart Editor** shown in Plate
   12.12]

6. → **File** → **Close**

A new bar chart will appear in the **SPSS for Windows
Chart Editor**, which will be the same as the one
produced in Figure 11.4. This procedure
essentially entails producing a bar chart but with the
spaces between bars removed so that a histogram is
generated. This procedure allows you to define your
own bars.

When the **SPSS for Windows Chart Editor** is open, all
figures can be edited, so that, for example, colours
can be changed or patterns inserted. This can be very
useful if you do not have access to a colour printer.
Figures 11.2, 11.3, and 11.4 were produced by changing the bars or slices to white and then
introducing patterns. When in the **SPSS for Windows
Chart Editor**, you can experiment by → **Format** and
then selecting from the choices there. This procedure
applies to all charts.

Generating the arithmetic mean, median, standard deviation, and range

To produce the mean, median, standard deviation
and the range for an interval/ratio variable like *age*,
the following steps should be followed:

1. → **Analyze** → **Descriptive Statistics** → **Explore** . . .
   [opens the **Explore** dialog box]

2. → *age* → ▶ button to the left of **Dependent List:**
   [puts *age* in the **Dependent List:** box] → **Statistics**
   under **Display** → **OK**

The output will also include the 95 per cent confidence interval for the mean, which is based on the
standard error of the mean. The output can be found
in Table 12.1.

Generating a contingency table, chi-square, and Cramér's *V*

In order to generate a contingency table, like that in
Table 11.4, along with a chi-square test and Cramér's
V, the following procedure should be followed:

1. → **Analyze** → **Descriptive Statistics** → **Crosstabs**
   . . . [opens the **Crosstabs** dialog box shown in
   Plate 12.13]

Table 12.1 Explore output for *age* (SPSS output)

Explore

Case Processing Summary

	Cases					
	Valid		Missing		Total	
	N	Percent	N	Percent	N	Percent
AGE	89	98.9%	1	1.1%	90	100.0%

Descriptives

			Statistic	Std. Error
AGE	Mean		33.5955	.9420
	95% Confidence	Lower bound	31.7235	
	Interval for mean	Upper bound	35.4675	
	5% Trimmed mean		33.3159	
	Median		31.0000	
	Variance		78.971	
	Std. Deviation		8.8866	
	Minimum		18.00	
	Maximum		57.00	
	Range		39.00	
	Interquartile Range		14.0000	
	Skewness		.446	.255
	Kurtosis		−.645	.506

Plate 12.13 The **Crosstabs** dialog box

2. → **reasons for visiting** → ▶ button by **R**o**w[s]** [**reasons for visiting** will appear in the **R**o**w[s]:** box] → *gender* → ▶ button by **C**o**lumn[s]:** [*gender* will appear in the **C**o**lumn[s]:** box] → **C**e**lls** [opens **Crosstabs: Cell Display** sub-dialog box shown in Plate 12.14]

3. Make sure **O**b**served** in the **Counts** box has been selected. Make sure **C**o**lumn** under **Percentages** has been selected. If either of these has not been selected, simply click at the relevant point.

→ **Continue** [closes **Crosstabs: Cell Display** sub-dialog box and returns you to the **Crosstabs** dialog box shown in Plate 12.13]

4. → **S**t**atistics . . .** [opens the **Crosstabs: Statistics** sub-dialog box shown in Plate 12.15]

5. → **Ch**i**-square** → **P**h**i and Cramér's V** → **Continue** [closes **Crosstabs: Statistics** sub-dialog box and returns you to the **Crosstabs** dialog box shown in Plate 12.13]

6. → **OK**

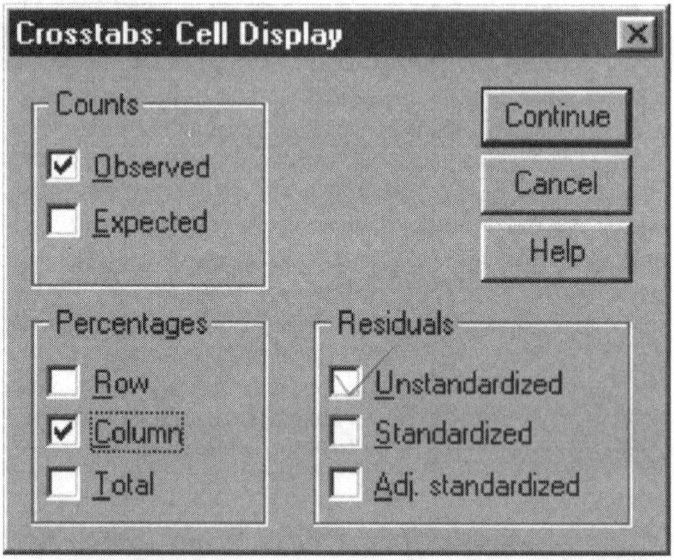

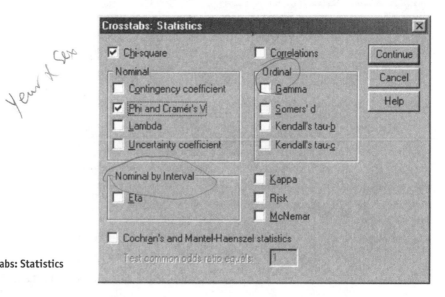

Plate 12.14 The **Crosstabs: Cell Display** sub-dialog box

Plate 12.15 The **Crosstabs: Statistics** sub-dialog box

The resulting output can be found in Table 12.2.

If you have a table with two dichotomous variables, you would use the same sequence of steps to produce phi.

Generating Pearson's *r* and Spearman's rho

To produce Pearson's *r* in order to find the correlations between *age*, *cardmins*, and *weimins*, follow these steps:

1. → **Analyze** → **Correlate** → **Bivariate** . . . [opens **Bivariate Correlations** dialog box shown in Plate 12.16]

2. → *age* → ▶ button → *cardmins* → ▶ button → *weimins* → ▶ button [*age, cardmins,* and *weimins* should now be in the **Variables:** box] → **Pearson** [*if* not already selected] → **OK**

The resulting output is in Table 12.3.

To produce correlations with Spearman's rho, follow the same procedure but instead of selecting **Pearson**, you should → **Spearman** instead.

Generating scatter diagrams

Scatter diagrams, known as *scatterplots* in SPSS, are produced in the following way. Let us say that we want to plot the relationship between *age* and *cardmins*. There is a convention that, if one variable can be identified as likely to be the independent variable, it should be placed on the *x* axis, that is, the horizontal axis. Since *age* is bound to be the independent variable, we would follow these steps:

1. → **Graphs** → **Scatter** . . . [opens the **Scatter Plot** dialog box]

2. → **Simple** [usually this has been automatically selected] → **Define** [opens the **Simple Scatterplot** sub-dialog box shown in Plate 12.17]

3. → *cardmins* → ▶ button by **Y** Axis: → *age* → ▶ button by **X** Axis: → **OK**

The scatter diagram can then be edited by bringing up the **SPSS for Windows Chart Editor.** For example, the type and size of the markers can be changed by clicking anywhere in the chart in the **Chart Editor** and then → **Format** and then → **Marker** . . .

Comparing means and eta

To produce a table like Table 11.5, these steps should be followed:

1. → **Analyze** → **Compare Means** → **Means** . . . [opens the **Means** dialog box shown in Plate 12.18]

2. → *cardmins* → ▶ button to the left of **Dependent List:** → **reasons for visiting** → ▶ button to the left of **Independent List:** → **Options** [opens the **Means: Options** sub-dialog box]

3. → **Anova table and eta** underneath **Statistics for First Layer** → **Continue** [closes the **Means: Options** sub-dialog box and returns you to the **Means** dialog box shown in Plate 12.18] → **OK**

Generating a contingency table with three variables

To create a table like that in Table 11.7, you would need to follow these steps:

1. → **Analyze** → **Descriptive Statistics** → **Crosstabs** . . . [opens the **Crosstabs** dialog box shown in Plate 12.13]

2. → *othsourc* → ▶ button by **Row[s]** [*othsourc* will appear in the **Row[s]:** box]

3. → *age3* [this is the name we gave when we created a new variable with *age* recoded into three categories] → ▶ button by **Column[s]:** [*age3* will appear in the **Column[s]:** box] → *gender* → ▶ button beneath **Previous** [*gender* will appear in the box underneath **Layer 1 of 1**] → **Cells** [opens **Crosstabs: Cell Display** sub-dialog box shown in Plate 12.14]

4. Make sure **Observed** in the **Counts** box has been selected. Make sure **Column** under **Percentages** has been selected. If either of these has not been selected, simply click at the relevant point. → **Continue** [closes **Crosstabs: Cell Display** sub-dialog box and returns you to the **Crosstabs** dialog box shown in Plate 12.13]

5. → **OK**

The resulting table will look somewhat different from Table 11.7 in that *gender* will appear as a row rather than as a column variable.

Table 12.2 Contingency table for **reasons for visiting** by *age* (SPSS output)

Crosstabs

Case Processing Summary

	Cases					
	Valid		Missing		Total	
	N	Percent	N	Percent	N	Percent
reasons for visiting * GENDER	90	100.0%	0	.0%	90	100.0%

reasons for visiting * GENDER Crosstabulation

			GENDER		
			1.00	2.00	Total
reasons for visiting	relaxation	Count	3	6	9
		% within GENDER	7.1%	12.5%	10.0%
	fitness	Count	15	16	31
		% within GENDER	35.7%	33.3%	34.4%
	lose weight	Count	8	25	33
		% within GENDER	19.0%	52.1%	36.7%
	build strength	Count	16	1	17
		% within GENDER	38.1%	2.1%	18.9%
Total		Count	42	48	90
		% within GENDER	100.0%	100.0%	100.0%

Chi-Square Tests

	Value	df	Asymp. Sig. (2-sided)
Pearson Chi-Square	22.726[a]	3	.000
Likelihood Ratio	25.805	3	.000
Linear-by-Linear Association	9.716	1	.002
N of Valid Cases	90		

[a] 2 cells (25.0%) have expected count less than 5. The minimum expected count is 4.20.

Symmetric Measures

		Value	Approx. Sig
Nominal by Nominal	Phi	.503	.000
	Cramer's V	.503	.000
N of Valid Cases		90	

[a] Not assuming the null hypothesis.
[b] Using the asymptotic standard error assuming the null hypotheses.

Table 12.3 Correlations output for *age*, *weimins*, and *cardmins* (SPSS output)

Correlations

Correlations

		AGE	WEIMINS	CARDMINS
AGE	Pearson Correlation Sig. (2-tailed) N	1.000 . 89	−.273 ** .010 89	−.109 .311 89
WEIMINS	Pearson Correlation Sig. (2-tailed) N	−.273 ** .010 89	1.000 . 90	−.161 .130 90
CARDMINS	Pearson Correlation Sig. (2-tailed) N	−.109 .311 89	−.161 .130 90	1.000 . 90

** Correlation is significant at the 0.01 level (2-tailed).

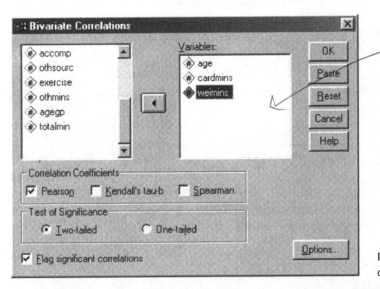

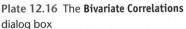

Plate 12.16 The **Bivariate Correlations** dialog box

Further operations in SPSS

Saving your data

You will need to save your data for future use. To do this, make sure that the **Data Editor** is the active window. Then,

→ **File** → **Save As** . . .

The **Save Data As** dialog box will then appear. You will need to provide a name for your data, which will be placed after **File name:**. We called the file 'gym study'. You also need to decide where you are going to save the data—for example, onto a floppy

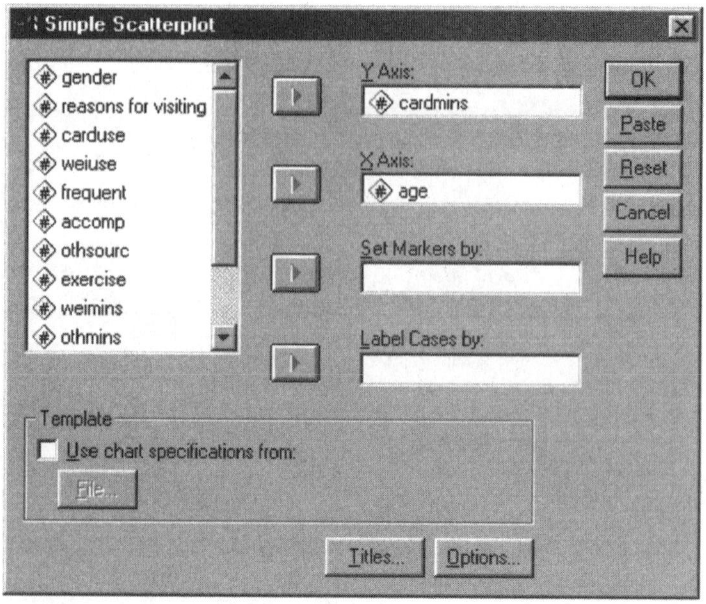

Plate 12.17 The **Simple Scatterplot** sub-dialog box

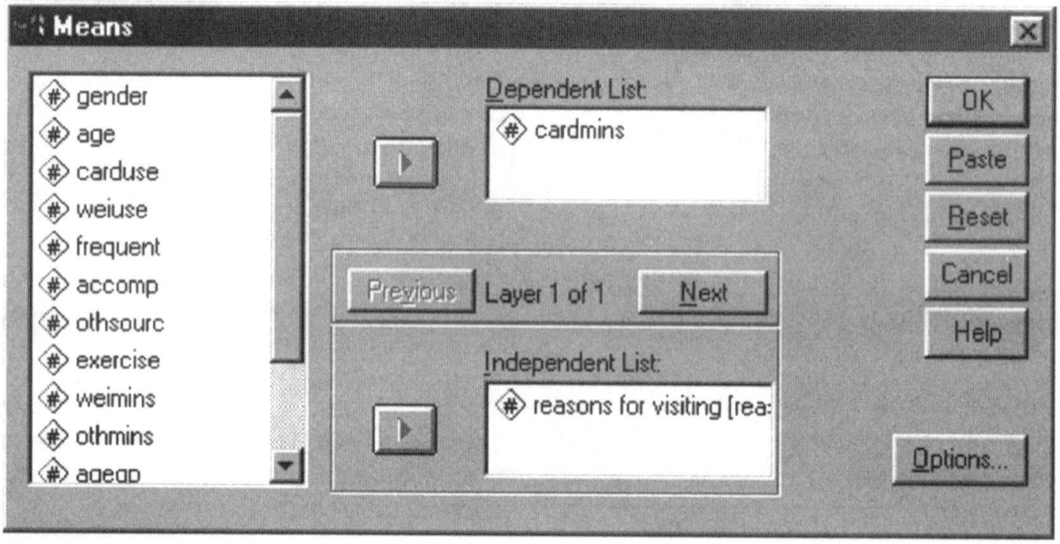

Plate 12.18 The **Means** dialog box

disk. To select the destination drive, → the downward pointing arrow to the right of the box by **Save in**. Then choose the drive to which you want to save your data. Then → **Save**.

Remember that this procedure saves your data *and* any other work you have done on your data—for example, value labels and recoded variables. If you subsequently use the data again and do more work on your data, such as creating a new variable, you will need to save the data again or the new work will be lost. SPSS will give you a choice of renaming your data, in which case you will have two files of data (one with the original data and one with any changes), or keeping the same name, in which case the file will be changed and the existing name retained.

Retrieving your data

When you want to retrieve the data file you have created, → **File** → **Open** . . . . The **Open File** dialog box will appear. You then need to go to the location in which you have deposited your data to retrieve the file containing your data and then → **Open**. A shortcut alternative to this procedure is to → the first button on the toolbar (it looks like an open file), which brings up the **Open File** dialog box.

Printing output

To print all the output in the **SPSS for Windows Output Viewer**, make sure that the **Viewer** is the active window and then → **File** → **Print** . . . . The **Print** dialog box will appear and then → **OK**. To print just some of your output, hold down the Ctrl button on your keyboard and click once on the parts you want to print. The easiest way to do this is to select all the elements you want in the output summary in the left-hand segment of the **Output Viewer** shown in Plate 12.10. Then bring up the **Print** dialog box. When the **Print** dialog box appears, make sure **Selection** under **Print Range** has been selected. The third button on the toolbar (which appears as a printer) provides a shortcut to the **Print** dialog box.

O OVERVIEW

The aim of this chapter has been to introduce the ways in which SPSS can be employed to implement the techniques learned in Chapter 11. Learning new software requires some perseverance and at times the work put in does not seem to be worth the learning process. But it is worth it. It would take you far longer to perform calculations on a sample of around 100 than to learn the software. If you find yourself moving into much more advanced techniques, the time saved is even more substantial, particularly with large samples. One final point is to remind you of the desirability of becoming familiar with SPSS *before* you begin designing your research instruments, because it is advisable to be aware of difficulties you might have in presenting your data in SPSS at an early stage.

Q REVISION QUESTIONS

Getting started in SPSS

- Outline the differences between: variable names, variable labels, and value labels.
- In what circumstances might you want to recode a variable?
- In what circumstances might you want to create a new variable?

Data analysis with SPSS

Using the gym survey data, create:

- a frequency table for *exercise*;
- a bar chart and pie chart for *exercise* and compare their usefulness;

- a histogram for *cardmins*;
- measures of central tendency and dispersion for *cardmins*;
- a contingency table and chi-square test for *exercise* and *gender*;
- Pearson's *r* for *age* and *cardmins*;
- Spearman's rho for *carduse* and *weiuse*;
- a scatter diagram for *age* and *cardmins*;
- a comparing means analysis for *totalmin* and reasons for visiting.

Part Three

Part Three of this book is concerned with qualitative research. Chapter 13 sets the scene by exploring the main features of this research strategy. Chapter 14 deals with ethnography and participant observation, which are among the main ways of collecting qualitative data. Chapter 15 is concerned with the kind of interviewing that is carried out in qualitative research. Chapter 16 addresses the focus group method, which is an increasingly popular technique that allows groups of people to be interviewed. Chapter 17 explores two approaches to the study of language in business research: conversation analysis and discourse analysis. Chapter 18 explores the types of documents with which qualitative researchers tend to be concerned and approaches to examining them. Chapter 19 examines different approaches to qualitative data analysis and offers advice on how it can be carried out. Chapter 20 shows you how to use computer software in the form of NVivo to conduct the kind of analysis discussed in Chapter 19.

These chapters will provide you with the essential tools for doing qualitative research. They will take you from the very general issues to do with the generic features of qualitative research to the very practical issues of conducting your own observational studies or interviews and analysing your own data.

13 The nature of qualitative research

CHAPTER GUIDE

Qualitative research is a research strategy that usually emphasizes words rather than quantification in the collection and analysis of data. As a research strategy it is inductivist, constructionist, and interpretivist, but qualitative researchers do not always subscribe to all three of these methods. This chapter is concerned with outlining the main features of qualitative research, which has become an increasingly popular approach to business research. The chapter explores:

- the main steps in qualitative research; delineating the sequence of stages in qualitative research is more controversial than with quantitative research, because it exhibits somewhat less codification of the research process;
- the relationship between theory and research;
- the nature of concepts in qualitative research and their differences from concepts in quantitative research;
- how far reliability and validity are appropriate criteria for qualitative researchers and whether alternative criteria

that are more tailored to the research strategy are necessary;

- the main preoccupations of qualitative researchers; five areas are identified in terms of an emphasis on: seeing through the eyes of research participants; description and context; process; flexibility and lack of structure; and concepts and theory as outcomes of the research process;
- some common criticisms of qualitative research;
- the main contrasts between qualitative and quantitative research;
- the stance of feminist researchers on qualitative research.

Introduction

We began Chapter 3 by noting that *quantitative* research had been outlined in Chapter 1 as a distinctive research strategy. Much the same kind of general point can be registered in relation to *qualitative* research. In Chapter 1 it was suggested that qualitative research differs from quantitative research in several ways. Most obviously, qualitative research tends to be concerned with words rather than numbers, but three further features were particularly noteworthy:

- an inductive view of the relationship between theory and research, whereby the former is generated out of the latter;
- an epistemological position described as interpretivist, meaning that, in contrast to the adoption of a natural scientific model in quantitative research, the stress is on the understanding of the social world through an examination of the interpretation of that world by its participants; and
- an ontological position described as constructionist, which implies that social properties are outcomes of the interactions between individuals, rather than phenomena 'out there' and separate from those involved in its construction.

As Bryman and Burgess (1999) observe, although there has been a proliferation of writings on qualitative

research since the 1970s, stipulating what it is and is not as a distinct research strategy is by no means straightforward. They propose three reasons for this state of affairs.

- As a term, 'qualitative research' is sometimes taken to imply an approach to business research in which quantitative data are not collected or generated. Many writers on qualitative research are critical of such a rendition of qualitative research, because (as we will see) the distinctiveness of qualitative research does not reside solely in the absence of numbers.
- Writers like Gubrium and Holstein (1997) have suggested that several different traditions in qualitative research can be identified (see Box 13.1).
- Sometimes, qualitative research is discussed in terms of the ways in which it differs from quantitative research. A potential problem with this tactic is that it means that qualitative research ends up being addressed in terms of what quantitative research is *not*.

Silverman (1993) has been particularly critical of accounts of qualitative research that do not acknowledge the variety of forms that the research strategy can assume. In other words, writers like Silverman

---

Box 13.1 Four traditions of qualitative research

Gubrium and Holstein (1997) suggest four traditions of qualitative research.

- *Naturalism*—seeks to understand social reality in its own terms; 'as it really is'; provides rich descriptions of people and interaction in natural settings.

- *Ethnomethodology*—seeks to understand how social order is created through talk and interaction; has a naturalistic orientation.

- *Emotionalism*—exhibits a concern with subjectivity and gaining access to 'inside' experience; concern with the inner reality of humans.

- *Postmodernism*—has an emphasis on 'method talk'; sensitive to the different ways social reality can be constructed.

We encountered the term *naturalism* in Box 2.4. The use of the term here is more or less the same as the second meaning referred to in Box 2.4. The naturalist tradition has probably been the most common one over the years. The second tradition will be encountered in Chapter 17, when we will be looking at an approach to the collection of qualitative data known as *conversation analysis*. The more recent postmodern standpoint will be addressed in Chapter 24. The third tradition—emotionalism—has not become the focus of a significant stream of research and will not be emphasized in this book. However, the mere presence of these four contrasting traditions points to the difficulty of creating a definitive account of what qualitative research is and is not.

---

are critical of attempts to specify the nature of qualitative research as a general approach. However, unless we can talk to a certain degree about the nature of qualitative research, it is difficult to see how it is possible to refer to qualitative research as a distinctive research strategy. In much the same way that in Chapter 3 it was recognized that quantitative researchers employ different research designs, in writing about the characteristics of qualitative research we will need to be sensitive to the different orientations of qualitative researchers. Without at least a sense of what is common to a set of many if not most studies that might be described as qualitative, the very notion of qualitative research would be rendered problematic. Yet it is clear that, for many social scientists, it is a helpful and meaningful category that can be seen in a variety of ways. Examples are: the arrival of specialist journals, such as *Qualitative Sociology* and *Qualitative Inquiry*; texts on qualitative research (e.g. Silverman 1993, 2000; Seale 1999); a huge *Handbook of Qualitative Research* (Denzin and Lincoln 2000); and a series of books on different facets of qualitative research (the Sage Qualitative Research Methods Series).

Several reasons might be proposed for the unease among some writers concerning the specification of the nature of qualitative research. Two reasons might be regarded as having particular importance. First, qualitative research subsumes several diverse research methods that differ from each other considerably. The following are the main research methods associated with qualitative research.

- *Ethnography/participant observation*. While some caution is advisable in treating ethnography and participant observation as synonyms, in many respects they refer to similar if not identical approaches to data collection in which the researcher is immersed in a social setting for some time in order to observe and listen with a view to gaining an appreciation of the culture of a social group. It has been employed in such business research classics as Dalton's (1959) study of managerial work in the USA and Lupton's (1963) exploration of shopfloor factory life and restriction of output in England.

- *Qualitative interviewing*. This is a very broad term to describe a wide range of interviewing styles (see Box 5.3 for an introduction). Moreover, qualitative researchers employing ethnography or participant observation typically engage in a substantial amount of qualitative interviewing.

- *Focus groups* (see Box 5.3).

- *Language-based approaches to the collection of qualitative data*, such as discourse and conversation analysis.

- *The collection and qualitative analysis of texts and documents*.

Each of these approaches to data collection will be examined in Part Three. The picture with regard to the very different methods and sources that comprise qualitative research is made somewhat more complex by the fact that a multi-strategy approach (see Chapter 22) is frequently employed. As noted above, researchers employing ethnography or participant observation frequently conduct qualitative interviews. However, they also often collect and analyze texts and documents as well. Thus, there is considerable variability in the collection of data among studies that are typically deemed to be qualitative. Of course, quantitative research also subsumes several different methods of data collection (these were covered in Part Two), but the inclusion of methods concerned with the analysis of language as a form of qualitative research implies somewhat greater variability.

A second reason why there is some resistance to a delineation of the nature of qualitative research is that the connection between theory and research is somewhat more ambiguous than in quantitative research. With the latter research strategy, theoretical issues drive the formulation of a research question, which in turn drives the collection and analysis of data. Findings then feed back into the relevant theory. This is rather a caricature, because what counts as 'theory' is sometimes little more than the research literature relating to a certain issue or area. In qualitative research, theory is supposed to be an outcome of an investigation rather than something that precedes it. However, some writers, like Silverman (1993: 24), have argued that such a depiction of qualitative research is 'out of tune with the greater sophistication of contemporary field research design, born out of accumulated knowledge of interaction and greater concern with issues of reliability and validity'. This is particularly the case with conversation analysis, an approach to the study of language that will be examined in Chapter 17. However, qualitative research is more usually regarded as denoting an approach in which theory and categorization emerge out of the collection and analysis of data. The more general point being made is that such a difference within qualitative research may account for the unease about depicting the research strategy in terms of a set of stages.

The main steps in qualitative research

The sequence outlined in Figure 13.1 provides a representation of how the qualitative research process can be visualized. In order to illustrate these steps, a study by Prasad (1993) of work computerization will be used.

- *Step 1. General research questions*. The starting point for Prasad's (1993) study of the computerization of work in a primary health-care organization was to focus on the symbolic processes involved in implementing information technology. Prasad chose to adopt a symbolic interactionist approach (see Chapter 1) to the study of technological change because this perspective emphasizes 'both process issues and the roles of meaning and symbols'

(1993: 1403). Informed by this theoretical perspective, she then sets out to explore the subjective meanings associated with computers that have hitherto, she suggests, been largely overlooked. This led her towards the development of research questions, including:

1. What are the multiple symbols associated with work computerization in the organization studied?

2. What are the local meanings of these symbolic representations?

3. What influences the process of sedimentation of symbols in the organization?

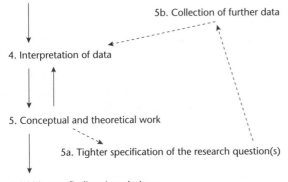

1. General research questions

2. Selecting relevant site(s) and subjects

3. Collection of relevant data

5b. Collection of further data

4. Interpretation of data

5. Conceptual and theoretical work

5a. Tighter specification of the research question(s)

6. Writing up findings/conclusions

Figure 13.1 An outline of the main steps of qualitative research

4. How do these symbolic realities influence the process of computerization and related organization-level action?

- *Step 2. Selecting relevant site(s) and subjects*. The organization studied was a medium-sized primary health-care provider (or health maintenance organization (HMO)) with 163 full-time staff, fictitiously named the 'Paragon Corporation'. Services offered included a medical centre, referrals, a pharmacy, and health education. The site was chosen on the basis that a recent decision had been made to computerize all administrative operations. It was expected that this would involve major changes in daily work practices and interactions between staff, as up until this point all administrative operations had been carried out manually.

- *Step 3. Collection of relevant data*. Prasad suggests that symbolic interaction 'rests on the assumption that every organizational situation is likely to be filled with multiple and frequently conflicting interpretations and meanings' (1993: 1404). This, she suggests, encourages the use of multiple research methods to capture complexity and contradictions in the data. In this way, Prasad neatly justifies her selection of multiple research methods in terms of the theoretical perspective she has already adopted in Step 1.

Prasad commenced her study of Paragon Corporation at the beginning of 1989 and concluded it more than a year and a half later. At the start of the study, the new technology had not yet arrived. This meant that Prasad was able to structure her data collection longitudinally, to cover the entire period of training and implementation and also to collect data after computerization was completed. During this period she visited the organization at least twice a week.

Prasad describes her methods as interview and observation. The latter involved regularly spending between two and five hours at a time observing work and interactions. She watched 'receptionists, physician assistants, nurses and records clerks at work and on several occasions even operated the appointment and billing system if a receptionist or clerk was particularly busy' (1993: 1407). After every fieldwork visit she wrote up 'extensive notes' documenting these observations.

The second strand to Prasad's data collection strategy involved 'in-depth interviews'. In total, she interviewed thirty-four employees, representing a diverse range of occupations and organizational positions. The interviews were carried out towards the end of the data collection period, after the computer system had been in use for more than five months. They focused on understanding organization members' meaningful experiences with computerized work. Most of the interviews were tape-recorded and transcribed later.

- *Step 4. Interpretation of data*. Prasad describes her approach to the analysis of the data as being based on techniques of grounded theory (Glaser and Strauss 1967). This provided guidelines for the classification and organization of the data, in particular through the creation and maintenance of 'concept cards' (see Chapter 19 and Box 19.5), through which Prasad grouped together incidents, events, or pieces of conversation related to a particular theme. As the analysis developed, new concepts were added and 'sometimes concept cards were reconstituted under different labels' (1993: 1411). Once patterns in the data had been identified, Prasad then started to place them in the context of relevant literature about technological change in organizations.

One of the key themes to emerge from the data is that employees associated the computerization of work with professionalism. Moreover, the symbolic meaning associated with professionalism held three distinct sets of meanings for different organizational members. First, it was linked to the notion that computers helped in the provision of good medical care. Secondly, it signalled the ability of the organization to move forward in keeping with technological advancement and progress. Thirdly, computerization was equated with professionalism because of its capacity to provide instant information and thereby transform employees into experts. These findings are linked to local circumstances that have shaped Paragon's history. Since its recent take-over by a large national health organization, there had been anxiety that Paragon did not 'measure up to the parent company's professional standards' (1993: 1417). 'Thus, the symbolic association of computerization with professionalism in part gained strength because it was seen as making the HMO a more professional member of the Paragon group of companies' (1993: 1417–18).

- *Step 5. Conceptual and theoretical work.* The primary contribution of Prasad's research stems from her application of a symbolic interactionist perspective, which helped to reveal some of the symbolic aspects of technological change. Her focus on meanings, local interpretations, and enactment revealed some of the hidden meanings of work computerization. This enabled the development of propositions about the nature of symbolic realities associated with technological change, which form the basis of the study's findings. Prasad concludes with a suggestion as to the broader generalizability

that may be associated with these findings: 'Understanding the nature of these broad symbolic realities may provide a way to understand resistance and adaptation to technological change in general' (1993: 1423).

- *Step 5a. Tighter specification of the research question(s),* and *Step 5b. Collection of further data.* There is some evidence from Prasad's account that she followed a process in which she collected further data and refined her research questions after several weeks of preliminary observations at the HMO. This approach corresponds with her grounded theory framework and emphasizes the interplay between interpretation and theorizing, on the one hand, and data collection, on the other. Such a strategy is frequently referred to as an *iterative* one. She does write at one point that data analysis was an iterative process, although the stages of data collection and analysis are presented as relatively sequential and discrete.

- *Step 6. Writing up findings/conclusions.* There is no real difference between the significance of writing up in quantitative research and qualitative research, so that exactly the same points made in relation to Step 11 in Figure 3.1 apply here. An audience has to be convinced about the credibility and significance of the interpretations offered. Researchers are not and cannot be simply conduits for the things they see and the words they hear. The salience of what researchers have seen and heard has to be impressed on the audience. Prasad does this by making clear to her audience that her methodology has implications for use in a variety of organizational situations that can benefit from the insights of symbolic interaction, including the phenomena of leadership transitions, mergers and acquisitions, new policy implementations, and organizational collaborations. She concludes that a symbolic interaction approach can provide insight into any situation that contains local meanings that influence organization-level action.

Two particularly distinctive aspects of the sequence of steps in qualitative research are the highly related issues of the links between theory and concepts with research data. It is to these issues that we now turn.

pre conceived

Theory and research

Most qualitative researchers when writing about their craft emphasize a preference for treating theory as something that emerges out of the collection and analysis of data. For example, Marshall (1984) describes her approach to the analysis of research data on women managers' career histories as 'immersion', clearly derived from an inductive approach (see Chapter 1). This involves trying to appreciate inherent patterns rather than to impose preconceived ideas on the data. For Marshall (1981) in the early stages of data analysis, impressions seem to dominate, but at this point, although there is a sense that something is coming out of the data, it is not clear what. At the same time Marshall explains 'there is a kind of fear that *nothing* is going to come out of the research and that I'm going to be left with a pile of tapes and nothing to say at the end' (1981: 396). Structuring the data involves picking certain things out and putting them under some headings, but again Marshall states: 'I'm a bit unsure about this, because this seems to *rob* the individual case of its wholeness. So I have to compensate for parcelling out little bits of a person and putting them under different categories and headings, and try to appreciate the wholeness of each person as well' (1981: 396). The final stage involves a lot of attention; it demands mental space in order to allow insights to emerge from an unconscious level so that connections can be made at lots of different levels. Towards the end of the analysis there comes a point that Marshall describes as feeling almost overloaded and things need to be brought together into a structure. At this point 'it's almost like having the *essence* of things that I can always fall back on now, so it does become more solid and understandable. That feeling gives me confidence

that I can put it together' (1981: 398). As will be seen in Chapter 19, practitioners of grounded theory—a frequently cited approach to the analysis of qualitative data—especially stress the importance of allowing theoretical ideas to emerge out of one's data. But some qualitative researchers argue that qualitative data can and should have an important role in relation to the *testing* of theories as well. Silverman (1993), in particular, has argued that in more recent times qualitative researchers have become increasingly interested in the testing of theories and that this is a reflection of the growing maturity of the strategy. Certainly, there is no reason why qualitative research cannot be employed in order to test theories that are specified in advance of data collection. In any case, much qualitative research entails the testing of theories in the course of the research process. So, in Figure 13.1, the loop back from Step 5*a* 'tighter specification of the research question(s)' to Step 5*b* 'collection of further data' implies that a theoretical position may emerge in the course of research and may spur the collection of further data to test that theory. This kind of oscillation between testing emerging theories and collecting data is a particularly prominent feature of grounded theory. It is presented as a dashed line in Figure 13.1, because it is not as necessary a feature of the process of qualitative research as the other steps.

One key point that is implied by Figure 13.1 is that the typical sequence of steps in qualitative research entails the generation of theories rather than the testing of theories that are specified at the outset. Silverman (1993) is undoubtedly correct that prespecified theories *can be* and sometimes *are* tested with qualitative data, but the generation of theory tends to be the preferred approach.

Concepts in qualitative research

A central feature of Chapter 3 was the discussion of concepts and their measurement. For most qualitative researchers, developing measures of concepts will

not be a significant consideration, but concepts are very much part of the landscape in qualitative research. However, the way in which concepts are developed and employed is often rather different from that implied in the quantitative research strategy. Blumer's (1954) distinction between 'definitive' and 'sensitizing' concepts captures aspects of the different ways in which concepts are thought about.

Blumer (1954) argued stridently against the use of definitive concepts in social research. The idea of definitive concepts is typified by the way in which, in quantitative research, a concept, once developed, becomes fixed through the elaboration of indicators. For Blumer, such an approach entailed the application of a straitjacket on the social world, because the concept in question comes to be seen exclusively in terms of the indicators that have been developed for it. Fine nuances in the form that the concept can assume or alternative ways of viewing the concept and its manifestations are sidelined. In other words, definitive concepts are excessively concerned with what is common to the phenomena that the concept is supposed to subsume rather than variety. Instead, Blumer recommended that social researchers should recognize that the concepts they use are sensitizing concepts in that they provide 'a general sense of reference and guidance in approaching empirical instances' (1954: 7). For Blumer, then, concepts should be employed in such a way that they give a very general sense of what to look for and act as a means for uncovering the variety of forms that the phenomena

to which they refer can assume. In providing a critique of definitive concepts, it is clear that Blumer had in mind the concept-indicator model described in Chapter 3. In other words, his views entailed in large part a critique of quantitative research and a programmatic statement that would form a springboard for an alternative approach that nowadays we would recognize as qualitative research.

Blumer's distinction is not without its problems. It is not at all clear how far a very general formulation of a concept can be regarded as a useful guide to empirical enquiry. If it is too general, it will simply fail to provide a useful starting point, because its guidelines are too broad; if too narrow, it is likely to repeat some of the difficulties Blumer identified in relation to definitive concepts. However, his general view of concepts has attracted some support, because his preference for not imposing preordained schemes on the social world chimes with that of many qualitative researchers. As the example in Box 13.2 suggests, the researcher frequently starts out with a broad outline of a concept, which is revised and narrowed during the course of data collection. For subsequent researchers, the concept may be taken up and revised as it is employed in connection with different social contexts or in relation to somewhat different research questions.

Reliability and validity in qualitative research

In Chapters 2 and 3 it was noted that reliability and validity are important criteria in establishing and assessing the quality of research for the quantitative researcher. However, there has been some discussion among qualitative researchers concerning their relevance for qualitative research. Moreover, even writers who do take the view that the criteria are relevant have considered the possibility that the meanings of the terms need to be altered. For example, the issue

of measurement validity almost by definition seems to carry connotations of measurement. Since measurement is not a major preoccupation among qualitative researchers, the issue of validity would seem to have little bearing on such studies. As foreshadowed briefly in Chapter 2, a number of different stances have been taken by qualitative researchers in relation to these issues.

Box 13.2 An example of the emergence of a concept in qualitative research: 'emotional labour'

Hochschild's (1983) idea of emotional labour—labour that 'requires one to induce or suppress feelings in order to sustain the outward countenance that produces the proper state of mind in others' (1983: 7)—has become a very influential concept in the sociology of work and in the developing area of the sociology of emotions. Somewhat ironically for a predominantly qualitative study, Hochschild's initial conceptualization appears to have emerged from a questionnaire she distributed to 261 university students. Within the questionnaire were two requests: 'Describe a real situation that was important to you in which you experienced a deep emotion' and 'Describe as fully and concretely as possible a real situation that was important to you in which you either changed the situation to fit your feelings or changed your feelings to fit the situation' (1983: 13). Thus, although a self-completion questionnaire was employed, the resulting data were qualitative. The data were analysed in terms of the idea of emotion *work*, which is the same as emotional labour but occurs in a private context. Emotional labour is essentially emotion work that is performed as part of one's paid employment. In order to develop the idea of emotional labour, Hochschild looked to the world of work. The main occupation she studied was the flight attendant. Several sources of data on emotional labour among flight attendants were employed. She gained access to Delta Airlines, a large American airline, and in the course of her investigations she:

- watched sessions for training attendants and had many conversations with both trainees and experienced attendants during the sessions;

- interviewed various personnel, such as managers in various sections, and advertising agents;

- examined Delta advertisements spanning thirty years;

- observed the flight attendant recruitment process at Pan American Airways, since she had not been allowed to do this at Delta;

- conducted 'open-ended interviews lasting three to five hours each with thirty flight attendants in the San Francisco Bay Area' (1983: 15).

As a contrasting occupational group that is nonetheless also involved in emotional labour, she also interviewed five debt-collectors. In her book, she explores such topics as the human costs of emotional labour and the issue of gender in relation to it. It is clear that Hochschild's concept of emotional labour began as a somewhat imprecise idea that emerged out of a concern with emotion work and that was gradually developed in order to address its wider significance.

The concept has been picked up by other qualitative researchers in management and organization studies. For example, Leidner (1993) has explored through ethnographic studies of a McDonald's restaurant and an insurance company the ways in which organizations seek to 'routinize' the display of emotional labour.

Adapting reliability and validity for qualitative research

One stance is to assimilate reliability and validity into qualitative research with little change of meaning other than playing down the salience of measurement issues. Mason, for example, in her book on qualitative research, argues that reliability, validity, and generalizability (which is the main component of external validity—see Chapter 2) 'are different kinds of measures of the quality, rigour and wider potential of research, which are achieved according to certain methodological and disciplinary conventions and principles' (1996: 21). She sticks very closely to the meaning that these criteria have in quantitative research, where they have been largely developed. Thus, validity refers to whether 'you are observing, identifying, or "measuring" what you say you are' (1996: 24). LeCompte and Goetz (1982) and Kirk and Miller (1986) also write about reliability and validity in relation to qualitative research but invest the terms with a somewhat different meaning from Mason. LeCompte and Goetz write about the following.

• *External reliability*, by which they mean the degree to which a study can be replicated. This is a difficult criterion to meet in qualitative research, since, as LeCompte and Goetz recognize, it is impossible to 'freeze' a social setting and the circumstances of an initial study to make it replicable in the sense in which the term is usually employed (see Chapter 3). However, they suggest several strategies that can be introduced in order to approach the requirements of external reliability. For example, they suggest that a qualitative researcher replicating ethnographic research needs to adopt a similar social role to that adopted by the original researcher. Otherwise what a researcher conducting a replication sees and hears will not be comparable to the original research.

• *Internal reliability*, by which they mean whether, when there is more than one observer, members of the research team agree about what they see and hear. This is a similar notion to *inter-observer consistency* (see Box 3.6).

• *Internal validity*, by which they mean whether there is a good match between researchers' observations and the theoretical ideas they develop. LeCompte and Goetz argue that internal validity tends to be a strength of qualitative research, particularly ethnographic research, because the prolonged participation in the social life of a group over a long period of time allows the researcher to ensure a high level of congruence between concepts and observations.

• *External validity*, which refers to the degree to which findings can be generalized across social settings. LeCompte and Goetz argue that, unlike internal validity, external validity represents a problem for qualitative researchers because of their tendency to employ case studies and small samples.

As this brief treatment suggests, qualitative researchers have tended to employ the terms reliability and validity in very similar ways to quantitative researchers when seeking to develop criteria for assessing research.

Alternative criteria for evaluating qualitative research

However, a second position in relation to reliability and validity in qualitative research can be discerned. Some writers have suggested that qualitative studies should be judged or evaluated according to quite different criteria from those used by quantitative researchers. Lincoln and Guba (1985) and Guba and Lincoln (1994) propose that it is necessary to specify terms and ways of establishing and assessing the quality of qualitative research that provide an alternative to reliability and validity. They propose two primary criteria for assessing a qualitative study: *trustworthiness* and *authenticity*.

Trustworthiness is made up of four criteria, each of which has an equivalent criterion in quantitative research:

• *credibility*, which parallels internal validity;
• *transferability*, which parallels external validity;
• *dependability*, which parallels reliability;
• *confirmability*, which parallels objectivity.

A major reason for Guba and Lincoln's unease about the simple application of reliability and validity standards to qualitative research is that the criteria presuppose that a single absolute account of social reality is feasible. In other words, they are critical of the view (described in Chapter 1 as *realist*) that there are absolute truths about the social world that it is the job of the social scientist to reveal. Instead, they argue that there can be more than one and possibly several accounts.

Credibility

The significance of this stress on multiple accounts of social reality is especially evident in the trustworthiness criterion of *credibility*. After all, if there can be several possible accounts of an aspect of social reality, it is the feasibility or credibility of the account that a researcher arrives at that is going to determine its acceptability to others. The establishment of the credibility of findings entails both ensuring that research is carried out according to the canons of good practice *and* submitting research findings to the members of the social world who were studied for confirmation that the investigator has correctly understood that social world. This latter technique is often referred to as *respondent validation* or *member validation* (see Box 13.3). Another technique they recommend is *triangulation* (see Box 13.4).

Transferability

Because qualitative research typically entails the intensive study of a small group, or of individuals sharing certain characteristics (that is, depth rather than the breadth that is a preoccupation in quantitative research), qualitative findings tend to be oriented to the contextual uniqueness and significance of the aspect of the social world being studied. As Guba and Lincoln put it, whether findings 'hold in some other context, or even in the same context at some other time, is an empirical issue' (Lincoln and Guba 1985: 316). Instead, qualitative researchers are encouraged to produce what Geertz (1973*a*) calls *thick description*— that is, rich accounts of the details of a culture. Guba and Lincoln argue that a thick description provides others with what they refer to as a database for making judgements about the possible transferability of findings to other milieux.

Dependability

As a parallel to reliability in quantitative research, Guba and Lincoln propose the idea of dependability and argue that, to establish the merit of research in terms of this criterion of trustworthiness, researchers should adopt an 'auditing' approach. This entails ensuring that complete records are kept of all phases of the research process—problem formulation, selection of research participants, fieldwork notes, interview transcripts, data analysis decisions, and so on—in an accessible manner. Peers would then act as auditors, possibly during the course of the research and certainly at the end to establish how far proper procedures are being and have been followed. This would include assessing the degree to which theoretical inferences can be justified. Auditing has not become a popular approach to enhancing the dependability of qualitative research within management and business, partly due to some of the problems that are associated with it. One is that it is very

demanding for the auditors, bearing in mind that qualitative research frequently generates extremely large data sets, and it may be that this is a major reason why it has not become a pervasive approach to validation.

Confirmability

Confirmability is concerned with ensuring that, while recognizing that complete objectivity is impossible in business research, the researcher can be shown to have acted in good faith; in other words, it should be apparent that he or she has not overtly allowed personal values or theoretical inclinations manifestly to sway the conduct of the research and findings deriving from it. Guba and Lincoln propose that establishing confirmability should be one of the objectives of auditors.

Authenticity

In addition to these four trustworthiness criteria, Guba and Lincoln suggest criteria of *authenticity*. These criteria raise a wider set of issues concerning the wider political impact of research. These are the criteria.

- *Fairness.* Does the research fairly represent different viewpoints among members of the social setting? For example, according to Starbuck (1981) one of the most serious deficiencies of the early (1963–72) Aston studies stems from the fact that the data about contexts and structures were collected primarily through interviews with senior managers. The first wave of interviews (1962–4) was conducted with chief executives and heads of departments, whereas the second set of interviews involved just one (senior) executive in the organization. Starbuck suggests that the data thus represent managerial perceptions and exclude the perceptions of other stakeholders, including first-line workers, customers, and suppliers.

- *Ontological authenticity.* Does the research help members to arrive at a better understanding of their social milieu?

- *Educative authenticity.* Does the research help members to appreciate better the perspectives of other members of their social setting?

Box 13.3 ⌐☼¬ *What is respondent validation?*

Respondent validation, which is also sometimes called *member validation*, is a process whereby a researcher provides the people on whom he or she has conducted research with an account of his or her findings. The aim of the exercise is to seek corroboration or otherwise of the account that the researcher has arrived at. Respondent validation has been particularly popular among qualitative researchers, because they frequently want to ensure that there is a good correspondence between their findings and the perspectives and experiences of their research participants. The form that respondent validation can assume varies. There are several different forms of respondent validation.

- The researcher provides each research participant with an account of what he or she has said to the researcher in an interview and conversations or of what the researcher observed by watching that person in the course of an observational study. For example, Marshall (1995) reports that she wanted to tell the stories of a small group of women managers who had left or are leaving senior organization positions from these women's points of view. To achieve this her proposed research approach involved a meeting with each woman manager, lasting between one and a half and two hours, in which she would tell her story—facilitated by Marshall if appropriate. Marshall stated that she would be happy to discuss her own views and experiences if relevant. She also stated a preference for the meeting to be tape-recorded. Marshall would then take responsibility for having the tape transcribed and writing an initial draft of the woman's story, to be read by the woman manager herself. It was intended that each story would eventually form one chapter of the book.

- The researcher feeds back to a group of people or an organization his or her impressions and findings in relation to that group or organization. In Marshall's (1995) research, after reading the case the respondent would then meet Marshall again, or exchange letters and phone calls, in order to develop the case to their mutual satisfaction. Most of the women were generally happy with the drafts but wanted minor amendments. Marshall revised the stories, taking research participants' comments into account. She states that, ultimately, the woman manager had the right of veto over what appeared in 'her' chapter.

  Later, all participants were invited to a one-day collaborative enquiry workshop, in which they would jointly review their experiences of employment and discuss issues of mutual interest.

In each case, the goal is to seek confirmation that the researcher's findings and impressions are congruent with the views of those on whom the research was conducted and to seek out areas in which there is a lack of correspondence and the reasons for it. However, the idea is not without practical difficulties.

- Respondent validation may occasion defensive reactions on the part of research participants and even censorship. Marshall was willing to accept this as a consequence of her collaborative approach. Hence one participant decided that her story made her too identifiable and vulnerable. Even though her reasons for this were highly relevant to the research, as they centred on the difficulties of establishing a positive, accepted identity as a lesbian manager, Marshall agreed only to write a brief account of 'Ruth's' experience, in a chapter amounting only to six pages.

- It is highly questionable whether research participants can validate a researcher's analysis, since this entails inferences being made for an audience of business and management academics. This means that, even though these methods of respondent validation may receive a corroborative response, the researcher still has to make a further leap, through the development of concepts and theories, in providing a framework for the resulting publications. Marshall was therefore careful to define the boundaries between data over which participants had a right of veto (the stories) and other material over which she wished to retain control, to put her own views and pursue her 'more academic concerns' (1995: 336), stressing from the outset that she would want to be able to use this in her publications.

To summarize, respondent validation can provide a means of confirming the validity of individual accounts. It can also help to redress the power imbalance between researcher and researched by providing the participants with a degree of authority in relation to the writing of the final research account. However, a distinction must be made between seeking validation from individuals and seeking validation from organizations, or—as is more likely—key groupings within organizations, such as senior managers. The latter option, by giving powerful groups within the organization control over the research, can introduce particular problems of censorship.

Box 13.4 💡 What is triangulation?

Triangulation entails using more than one method or source of data in the study of social phenomena. The triangulation metaphor is taken from navigation and military strategy, where it refers to the process whereby multiple reference points are used to locate an object's exact position. The term has been employed somewhat more broadly by Denzin (1970: 310) to refer to an approach that uses 'multiple observers, theoretical perspectives, sources of data, and methodologies', but the emphasis has tended to be on methods of investigation and sources of data. One of the reasons for the advocacy by Webb et al. (1966) of greater use of unobtrusive methods was their potential in relation to a strategy of triangulation (see Box 10.11). Triangulation can operate within and across research strategies. It was originally conceptualized by Webb et al. (1966) as an approach to the development of measures of concepts, whereby more than one method would be employed in the development of measures, resulting in greater confidence in findings. As such, triangulation was very much associated with a quantitative research strategy. However, triangulation can also take place within a qualitative research strategy. In fact, ethnographers often check out their observations with interview questions to determine whether they might have misunderstood what they had seen. Increasingly, triangulation is also being used to refer to a process of cross-checking findings deriving from both quantitative and qualitative research (Deacon, Bryman, and Fenton 1998). For example, Kanter draws attention to the *triangulation* of methods, which characterized her approach, stating 'I used each source of data, and each informant, as a check against the others' (1977: 337). She suggests that 'a combination of methods . . . emerges as the most valid and reliable way to develop understanding of such a complex social reality as the corporation' (1977: 337).

Another example of the way in which quantitative and qualitative methods can be combined in order to check the validity of findings is provided by Faules (1982), who conducted research in a local government agency in the USA to consider issues relating to performance appraisal.

Data were collected by survey questionnaire and semi-structured interviews. The questionnaire comprised fifty-one items concerned with contentious aspects of appraisal (such as goals, feedback, and judging its importance) and was administered to 250 employees in the agency, of whom 138 responded. The semi-structured interviews were conducted with sixty-two individuals and dealt with what people talk about in connection with appraisal and with 'stories' about performance appraisal in the agency. Faules concentrated on two areas: the functions of appraisal and the perceived quality of the system. Areas of convergence were found, for example, with both sets of data pointing to a questioning by employees of the relationship between performance ratings and job performance. Also, the questionnaire data provided evidence of differences in the responses of superiors and subordinates, which was supported by the analysis of stories. However, divergent findings emerged as well. The stories picked up a phenomenon referred to by Faules as a 'change in evaluation', which occurs when an initial appraisal by a person's superior is changed by someone else; this practice was seen as unfair by subordinates, but deemed acceptable by supervisors, who believed in the importance of comparing people's ratings and of ensuring that they were not excessively skewed. However, this element had not been included in the questionnaire and so was not addressed by this method. Although Faules believes that the results were broadly consistent, the nature of the information gleaned was often divergent— the questionnaire provided data on general attitudes, while the stories allowed access to issues of how people make sense of the appraisal process.

This example suggests that, in addition to allowing the cross-checking of data, the use of quantitative and qualitative research in conjunction may often allow access to different levels of reality. However, triangulation represents just one way in which it may be useful to think about the integration of these two research strategies; it is covered in Chapter 22.

• *Catalytic authenticity*. Has the research acted as an impetus to members to engage in action to change their circumstances?

• *Tactical authenticity*. Has the research empowered members to take the steps necessary for engaging in action?

The authenticity criteria are thought provoking but have not been influential, and their emphasis on the wider impact of research is controversial. However, the main point of discussing Guba and Lincoln's ideas is that they differ from writers like LeCompte and Goetz in seeking criteria for evaluating qualitative research that represent a departure from those employed by quantitative researchers. The authenticity criteria also have certain points of affinity with *action research*, which became popular as a research method within business and management during the 1980s and 1990s. The emphasis on practical outcomes differentiates action research from other forms of qualitative investigation. We will return to the subject of action research later in this chapter.

Between quantitative and qualitative research criteria

Hammersley (1992*a*) lies midway between the two positions outlined above. He proposes that validity is an important criterion but reformulates it somewhat. For Hammersley, validity means that an empirical account must be plausible and credible and should take into account the amount and kind of evidence used in relation to an account. In proposing this criterion, Hammersley shares with realism (see Box 1.9) the notion that there is an external social reality that can be accessed by the researcher. However, he simultaneously shares with the critics of the empirical realist position the rejection of the notion that such access is direct and in particular that the researcher can act as a mirror on the social world, reflecting its image back to an audience. Instead, the researcher is always engaged in representations or constructions of that world. The plausibility and credibility of a researcher's 'truth claims' then become the main considerations in evaluating qualitative research.

Hammersley also suggests *relevance* as an important criterion of qualitative research. Relevance is taken to be assessed from the vantage point of the importance of a topic within its substantive field or the contribution it makes to the literature on that field. Hammersley also discusses the question of whether the concerns of practitioners (that is, people who are part of the social setting being investigated and who are likely to have a vested interest in the research question and the implications of findings deriving from it) might be an aspect of considerations of relevance. In this way, his approach touches on the kinds of consideration that are addressed by Guba and Lincoln's authenticity criteria (Lincoln and Guba 1985; Guba and Lincoln 1994). However, he recognizes that the kinds of research questions and findings that might be of interest to practitioners and researchers are likely to be somewhat different. As Hammersley notes, practitioners are likely to be interested in research that helps them to understand or address problems with which they are confronted. These may not be (and perhaps are unlikely to be) at the forefront of a researcher's set of preoccupations. However, there may be occasions when researchers can combine the two and may even be able to use this capability as a means of securing access to organizations in which they wish to conduct research (see Chapter 14 for a further discussion of access issues).

Overview of the issue of criteria

There is a recognition—albeit to varying degrees—that a simple application of the quantitative researcher's criteria of reliability and validity to qualitative research is not desirable, but writers vary in the degree to which they propose a complete overhaul of those criteria. Nor do the three positions outlined above represent the full range of possible stances on this issue (Hammersley 1992*a*; Seale 1999). To a large extent, the differences between the three positions reflect divergences in the degree to which a realist position is broadly accepted or rejected. Writers on qualitative research who apply the ideas of reliability and validity with little if any adaptation broadly position themselves as realists— that is, as saying that social reality can be captured by qualitative researchers through their concepts and theories. Lincoln and Guba reject this view, arguing instead that qualitative researchers' concepts and theories are representations and that there may, therefore, be other equally credible representations of the same phenomena. Hammersley's position occupies a middle ground in terms of the axis, with realism at one end and anti-realism at the other, in that, while acknowledging the existence of social phenomena that are part of an external reality, he disavows any suggestion that it is possible to reproduce that reality for the audiences of social scientific endeavour. Most qualitative researchers nowadays probably operate around the midpoint on this realism axis, though without necessarily endorsing Hammersley's views. Typically, they treat their accounts as one of a number of possible representations rather than as definitive versions of social reality. They also bolster those accounts through some of the strategies advocated by Lincoln and Guba, such as thick descriptions, respondent validation exercises, and triangulation.

The main preoccupations of qualitative researchers

As was noted in Chapter 3, quantitative and qualitative research can be viewed as exhibiting a set of distinctive but contrasting preoccupations. These preoccupations reflect epistemologically grounded beliefs about what constitutes acceptable knowledge. In Chapter 1, it was suggested that at the level of epistemology, whereas quantitative research is profoundly influenced by a natural science approach of what should count as acceptable knowledge, qualitative researchers are more influenced by *interpretivism* (see Box 1.9). This position can itself be viewed as the product of the confluence of three related stances: Weber's notion of *Verstehen*; symbolic interactionism; and phenomenology. In this section, five distinctive preoccupations among qualitative researchers will be outlined and examined.

Seeing through the eyes of the people being studied

An underlying premise of many qualitative researchers is that the subject matter of the social sciences (that is, people and their social world) does differ from the subject matter of the natural sciences. A key difference is that the objects of analysis of the natural sciences (atoms, molecules, gases, chemicals, metals, and so on) cannot attribute meaning to events and to their environment. However, people *do*. This argument is especially evident in the work of Schutz (1962) and can particularly be seen in the passage quoted on page 17, where Schutz draws attention to the fact that, unlike the objects of the natural sciences, the objects of the social sciences—people—are capable of attributing meaning to their environment.

Consequently, many qualitative researchers have suggested that a methodology is required for studying people that reflects these differences between people and the objects of the natural sciences. As a result, many qualitative researchers express a commitment to viewing events and the social world through the eyes of the people that they study. The social world must be interpreted from the perspective of the people being studied, rather than as though those subjects were incapable of their own reflections on the social world. The epistemology underlying qualitative research has been expressed by the authors of one widely read text as involving two central tenets: '(1)...face-to-face interaction is the fullest condition of participating in the mind of another human being, and (2)...you must participate in the mind of another human being (in sociological terms, "take the role of the other") to acquire social knowledge' (Lofland and Lofland 1995: 16).

It is not surprising therefore that many researchers make claims in their reports of their investigations about having sought to take the views of the people they studied as the point of departure (see Box 13.5). This tendency reveals itself in frequent references to empathy and seeing through others' eyes. Here are some examples.

- Nichols and Beynon (1977) wanted to understand the working lives of workers, foremen and managers at 'ChemCo', a British-owned multinational chemical producer, from a Marxist perspective. Nichols and Beynon suggest that theory 'fails to connect with the lives that people lead, whereas most descriptive social surveys too often fail to grasp the structure of social relations and the sense

Box 13.5 Gaining an insider view of strategic change

In their study of strategic change in the context of a university, Gioia et al. (1994) describe themselves as adopting an interpretative approach to the research in attempting 'to represent the experience and interpretations of informants without giving precedence to prior theoretical views that might not be appropriate' (1994: 367). To this end, they give priority to the insider's perspective, in order to counterbalance the arrogant stance that they suggest organizational researchers tend to adopt towards their subjects of study. However, they also recognize the limitations of this reliance on informant views, which do not address the 'dimensions or structure of phenomena' (1994: 367). They therefore juxtapose this first-hand account with a grounded theoretical analysis of the case, to develop a triangulated approach.

Similarly, in another study of strategic change, Harfield and Hamilton (1997) suggest that the majority of research in strategic management has adopted a detached,

outsider approach, which is 'bound up in a straightjacket of "dated" organizational concepts and "multivariate statistical methodology" ' (1997: 61; citing Bettis 1991). As an alternative, they seek to accommodate managers' experiences by using the storytelling method, in the belief that this will have greater relevance to other managers in dealing with rapidly changing environments. They suggest that an interpretative methodology enables strategy to be presented as a continually unfolding experience, and not, as much of the traditional view of strategy explains it, as an end point or destination.

These examples illustrate the way that some researchers within the field of strategic management have suggested that qualitative approaches can provide an important complement to the explanations enabled by statistical methods that tend to be used within the strategic management literature.

---

which people make of them. It is almost as if another way of writing has to be developed; something which "tells it like it is", even though in any simple sense this is not possible' (1977: 2).

- Marshall (1984) describes herself as an 'interpretor' rather than a manipulator of data, 'concerned with capturing other people's meanings rather than testing hypotheses' (1984: 116).

- Jackall (1988), in his ethnographic study of bureaucracy and morality within large corporations, seeks to generate an understanding of 'how men and women in business actually experience their work' (1988: 5), in order to ascertain its moral salience for them;

- Casey (1995) acknowledges that her study interprets and analyses the speech of her interviewees, albeit highly selectively, and thereby does to some extent attempt to ' "give voice" to other voices' (1995: 203), even though the selection of data was based on her own interpretation as an academic researcher.

This predilection for seeing through the eyes of the people studied in the course of qualitative research is often accompanied by the closely related goal of

seeking to probe beneath surface appearances. After all, by taking the position of the people you are studying, the prospect is raised that they might view things differently from what an outsider with little direct contact might have expected. This stance reveals itself in:

- Dalton's (1959) research study of the informal organization, in which he found that the boundaries between unofficial reward obtained through expense accounting, and organizational theft, or pilfering, were defined quite differently by individual managers, depending on their position within the hierarchy;

- The work of Collinson (1992a), who found that shopfloor workers at 'Slavs' dealt with their occupational status partly by channelling their personal ambitions and energies outside the workplace into the alternative domains of family and home, investing in 'the self-sacrificing role of parental breadwinner' (1992: 185);

- Marshall's (1984) study of women in management, which showed that this issue could not be understood without taking into account the wider social context, including society's values about work, and the way of life in large organizations, in order to make sense of the kinds of job roles that women in employment adopt;

- Ram's (1994) study of management in small firms, which showed that workers were not just controlled through direct supervision and intensive working methods, as previous studies had suggested. Using ethnographic methods, Ram was able to pick up on a variety of largely informal negotiating processes, whereby employees negotiated a 'fair' rate for the job, taking into account considerations such as the time of the year, the type of work, caste, and culture.

The empathetic stance of seeking to see through the eyes of one's research participants is very much in tune with interpretivism and demonstrates well the epistemological links with phenomenology, symbolic interactionism, and *Verstehen*. However, it is not without practical problems. For example: the risk of 'going native' and losing sight of what you are studying (see Box 14.5); the problem of how far the researcher should go, such as the potential problem of participating in illegal or dangerous activities; and the possibility that the researcher will be able to see through the eyes of only some of the people who form part of a social scene but not others, such as only people of the same gender. These and other practical difficulties will be addressed in the chapters that follow.

Description and the emphasis on context

Qualitative researchers are much more inclined than quantitative researchers to provide a great deal of descriptive detail when reporting the fruits of their research. This is not to say that they are exclusively concerned with description. They *are* concerned with explanation, and indeed the extent to which qualitative researchers ask 'why?' questions is frequently understated. In addition, more critical or radical qualitative researchers are often concerned with understanding the political and economic interests that inform organizational actions, in order to

enhance the possibilities for changing them. For example, in her critical ethnography of a multinational corporation, Casey (1995) describes herself as concerned with understanding dominant social constructions about work, the self, and society, in the hope that this might increase the likelihood of societal transformation.

Many qualitative studies provide a detailed account of what goes on in the setting being investigated. Very often qualitative studies seem to be full of apparently trivial details. However, these details are frequently important for the qualitative researcher, because of their significance for their subjects and also because the details provide an account of the context within which people's behaviour takes place. It was with this point in mind that Geertz (1973a) recommended the provision of thick descriptions of social settings, events, and often individuals. As a result of this emphasis on description, qualitative studies are often full of detailed information about the social worlds being examined. On the surface, some of this detail may appear irrelevant, and, indeed, there is a risk of the researcher becoming too embroiled in descriptive detail. Lofland and Lofland (1995: 164–5), for example, warn against the sin of what they call 'descriptive excess' in qualitative research, whereby the amount of detail overwhelms or inhibits the analysis of data.

One of the main reasons why qualitative researchers are keen to provide considerable descriptive detail is that they typically emphasize the importance of the contextual understanding of social behaviour. This means that behaviour, values, or whatever must be understood in context. This recommendation means that we cannot understand the behaviour of members of a social group other than in terms of the specific environment in which they operate. In this way, behaviour that may appear odd or irrational can make perfect sense when we understand the particular context within which that behaviour takes place. The emphasis on context in qualitative research goes back to many of the classic studies in social anthropology, which often demonstrated how a particular practice, such as the magical ritual that may accompany the sowing of seeds, made little sense unless we understand the belief systems of that society. One of the chief reasons for the emphasis on descriptive detail is that it is often precisely this detail that provides the mapping of context in terms of which behaviour is understood. The propensity for description can also be interpreted as a manifestation of the naturalism that pervades much qualitative research (see Boxes 2.4 and 13.1), because it places a premium on detailed, rich descriptions of social settings.

Emphasis on process

Qualitative research tends to view social life in terms of processes. This tendency reveals itself in a number of different ways. One of the main ways is that there is often a concern to show how events and patterns unfold over time. As a result, qualitative evidence often conveys a strong sense of change and flux. As Pettigrew (1997: 338) usefully puts it, process is

'a sequence of individual and collective events, actions, and activities unfolding over time in context'. Qualitative research that is based in ethnographic methods is particularly associated with this emphasis on process. It is the element of participant observation that is a key feature of ethnography that is especially instrumental in generating this feature. Ethnographers are typically immersed in a social setting for a long time—sometimes years. Consequently, they are able to observe the ways in which events develop over time or the ways in which the different elements of a social system (values, beliefs, behaviour, and so on) interconnect. Such findings can inject a sense of process by seeing social life in terms of streams of interdependent events and elements (see Box 13.6 for an example).

This is not to say, however, that ethnographers are the only qualitative researchers who inject a sense of process into our understanding of social life. It can

---

Box 13.6 Process research in organizational settings

Process or processual research deals with the activities of individuals and organizations over time. It is concerned with understanding human conduct as a dynamic activity. The process analyst is therefore concerned with collecting data that illustrate the dynamic nature of organizational activity. This involves understanding how the past history of an organization shapes the present reality and how the 'interchange between agents and contexts occurs over time and is cumulative' (Pettigrew 1997: 339).

An example is provided by Isabella (1990), whose research focused on how managers construe organizational events at different stages. Her study was based on the selection of a sample of forty managers from a medium-sized financial-services institution. Each manager was asked to describe and discuss five events that had occurred in the organization over the past five years. This research strategy invited the managers to focus on events that they saw as critical. Isabella conducted two semi-structured interviews with each manager. The first interview focused on historical data, such as career history and the organizational culture. The second interview concentrated on five key organizational events, which had been identified as key on the basis of an earlier pilot study. Questions focused on encouraging managers to relate what had happened before, during, or after the event

occurred. The interviews were taped and transcribed and analysed following a grounded theory approach. Isabella found that managerial interpretation of key events evolves through a series of stages as they relate events to past experience and try to make sense of them in terms of their current frame of reference. Furthermore, the process whereby individuals move from one interpretative stage to another is informed by certain 'triggers' that cause the individual to rethink their current frame of reference, to assess what the change will mean to them, and how it will affect their job role.

We can see in this example the development of a sense of dynamic process through the analysis of events over a period of time. Key or critical events are assessed before, during, and after they happen, so that changing managerial interpretations can be brought out. However, processual research in business and management can also be developed through a strategy of data collection over a period of time. This method of time sampling is typical of longitudinal case study research and is recommended by Pettigrew (1997) as a means of connecting current organizational events with past beliefs and values using historical and other data. It is covered in more detail in Chapter 2 and in Chapter 22 (section on 'static and processual features').

also be achieved through semi-structured and unstructured interviewing, by asking participants to reflect on the processes leading up to or following on from an event. Broussine and Vince (1996), for example, were interested in the way that managers use metaphors in relation to the management of change. Research was undertaken in a public-sector organization at a time when the public services were experiencing a high level of uncertainty. Broussine and Vince chose a relatively unusual research method within management and organizational research, based on the analysis of managers' drawings. By drawing pictures, managers reflected on their experience of the change process. Analysis of the drawings involved 'listening to the drawing's story', its style, use made of colour, the way that space is represented, and the general atmosphere. A total of eighty-six managers produced drawings and individually and collectively they reflected on their emotional content. A picture of a ship swamped by a tidal wave was construed as reflecting the emotions of anxiety, fear, and dread, whereas drawings of piles of paperwork and queues of people reflected feelings of powerlessness and debility. The discussions were tape-recorded and comparisons were made between groups of senior and middle managers, to see if there were differences in the use of metaphor between colleagues at different hierarchical levels. Broussine and Vince suggest that on some occasions this process enabled managers to appreciate each other's perspectives; in other cases, it simply made apparent their differences.

The life history approach is another form of qualitative research, although one that is relatively little used in business and management research. This technique takes as research data accounts of individuals about their lives or specific areas of their social world. Accounts focus on the relationship between the individual and his or her social context. Jones (1983) suggests that the life history approach is useful as a means of researching organizational socialization and career development. This involves leading individuals through an account of their organizational careers and asking them to chart out significant events through which they came to an understanding of their social organizational context.

An example relating to experiences of work is provided by Terkel's (1974) anthology of working lives in the USA. Written as a series of first-person narratives detailing the everyday reality of working lives, the accounts link individuals' past and present experiences of employment with their hopes, fears, ambitions, home, and family lives. Although Terkel acknowledges that he used 'no one method or technique' in searching out the feelings of 'ordinary' people, this diverse set of narratives—which covers everyone from factory mechanics to washroom attendants—provides a colourful example of the life history approach.

Other qualitative studies begin with an ethnographic approach in order to gain access to organizational data and then proceed to analyse it using other methods. For example, in his study of a public inquiry concerning a fatal pipeline accident, Gephart (1993) employed what he calls a 'textual approach'. This involved systematically gathering together a set of documents concerning the event, which he subsequently analysed using a combination of theoretical sampling, computer-assisted qualitative data analysis, and expansion analysis. The documents, including official proceedings of the public inquiry, company documents, field notes, reports, and newspaper articles, enabled reconstruction of the events leading up to the pipeline disaster. Passages of text were selected to illustrate the unfolding sensemaking about key decisions relating to the disaster, highlighting issues such as risk, blame, and responsibility. These quite different approaches to data analysis and collection highlight the diverse nature of qualitative research within management and business.

Flexibility and limited structure

Many qualitative researchers are disdainful of approaches to research that entail the imposition of predetermined formats on the social world. This position is largely to do with the preference for seeing through the eyes of the people being studied. After all, if a structured method of data collection is employed, since this is bound to be the product of an investigator's ruminations about the object of enquiry, certain decisions must have been made about what he or she expects to find and about the nature of the social reality that is to be encountered. Therefore, the researcher is limited in the degree to which he or she can genuinely adopt the world view of the people being studied. Consequently, most qualitative researchers prefer a research orientation that entails as little prior contamination of the social world as possible. To do otherwise risks imposing an inappropriate frame of reference on people. Keeping structure to a minimum is supposed to enhance the opportunity of genuinely revealing the perspectives of the people you are studying. Also, in the process, aspects of people's social world that are particularly important to them, but that might not even have crossed the mind of a researcher unacquainted with it, are more likely to be forthcoming. As a result, qualitative research tends to be a strategy that tries not to delimit areas of enquiry too much and to ask fairly general rather than specific research questions (see Figure 13.1).

Because of the preference for a loosely structured approach to the collection of data, qualitative researchers adopt methods of research that do not require the investigator to develop highly specific research questions in advance and therefore to devise instruments specifically for those questions to be answered. Ethnography, with its emphasis on participant observation, is particularly well suited to this orientation. It allows researchers to submerge themselves in a social setting with a fairly general research focus in mind and gradually to formulate a narrower emphasis by making as many observations of that setting as possible. They can then formulate more specific research questions out of their collected data. Similarly, interviewing is an extremely prominent method in the qualitative researcher's armoury, but it is not of the kind we encountered in the course of

most of Chapter 5—namely, the structured interview. Instead, qualitative researchers prefer less structured approaches to interviewing, as we will see in Chapter 15. Blumer's (1954) argument for sensitizing rather than definitive concepts (that is, the kind employed by quantitative researchers) is symptomatic of the preference for a more open-ended, and hence less structured, approach.

An advantage of the unstructured nature of most qualitative enquiry (that is, in addition to the prospect of gaining access to people's world views) is that it offers the prospect of flexibility. The researcher can change direction in the course of his or her investigation much more easily than in quantitative research, which tends to have a built-in momentum once the data collection is under way: if you send out hundreds of postal questionnaires and realize after you have started to get some back that there is an issue that you would have liked to investigate, you are not going to find it easy to retrieve the situation. Structured interviewing and structured observation can involve some flexibility, but the requirement to make interviews as comparable as possible for survey investigations limits the extent to which this can happen. See Box 13.7 for an illustration of the ways in which the unstructured data collection style of qualitative research can be used to suggest alternative avenues of enquiry or ways of thinking about the phenomenon being investigated.

Concepts and theory grounded in data

This issue has already been addressed in much of the exposition of qualitative research above. For qualitative researchers, concepts and theories are usually inductively arrived at from the data that are collected (see Boxes 13.2 and 13.8).

The critique of qualitative research

In a similar way to the criticisms that have been levelled at quantitative research mainly by qualitative researchers, a parallel critique has been built up

of qualitative research. Some of the more common ones follow.

Box 13.7 An example of flexibility in action

Bryman and his colleagues carried out a multiple-case-study investigation of strategic responses to deregulation in nine British bus companies (Bryman, Gilingwater, and McGuinness 1996). The research was carried out largely through semi-structured interviews with senior managers and the examination of documents. The researchers were especially interested in the significance of organizational culture for types of strategic response. The bus companies were selected to reflect a range of post-deregulation experiences and ownership patterns. In spite of the diversity among the case-study companies, it became apparent after interviews at four of the companies that their responses to deregulation were remarkably similar, reflecting a concentration on survival at a time of declining passenger numbers. The rest of the findings reflected minor variations on this theme.

Having achieved theoretical saturation for their main concepts and interconnections, Bryman and his colleagues began to focus on the similarities between the companies and started to explore the possibility that organizational culture was far less significant to the nine companies than what the researchers had termed 'industry culture'. In their subsequent questioning this idea was explored further. This shift in focus was important because it helped the researchers to understand the firms and how they were coping with declining patronage, but it was also theoretically significant because of the attention that organizational culture had attracted among scholars in the 1980s and early 1990s. Although the research had been influenced by this stream of thinking, Bryman and his colleagues began to view organizational culture as less significant in this particular study.

Box 13.8 An example of emerging concepts

In the late 1980s and early 1990s, most UK universities were in the throes of introducing staff appraisal schemes for both academic and academic-related staff. Staff appraisal is employed to review the appraisee's performance and activities over a period of usually one or two years. Along with some colleagues, Bryman undertook an evaluation of staff appraisal schemes in four universities (Bryman, Haslam, and Webb 1994). The research entailed the collection of both quantitative and qualitative data within the framework of a comparative research design. The qualitative data were derived from large numbers of interviews with appraisers, appraisees, senior managers, and many others. In the course of conducting the interviews and analysing the subsequent data the researchers became increasingly aware of a cynicism among many of the people interviewed. This attitude revealed itself in several ways, such as: a view that appraisal had been introduced just to pacify the government; a belief that nothing happened of any significance in the aftermath of

an appraisal meeting; the view that it was not benefiting universities; and a suggestion that many participants to the appraisal process were just going through the motions. As one of the interviewees said in relation to this last feature: 'It's like going through the motions of it [appraisal]. It's just get it over with and signed and dated and filed and that's the end of it' (quoted in Bryman, Haslam, and Webb 1994: 180).

On the basis of these findings it was suggested that the attitudes towards appraisal and the behaviour of those involved in appraisal were characterized by *procedural compliance*, which was defined as 'a response to an organizational innovation in which the technical requirements of the innovation . . . are broadly adhered to, but where there are substantial reservations about its efficacy and only partial commitment to it, so that there is a tendency for the procedures associated with the innovation to be adhered to with less than a total commitment to its aims' (1994: 178).

Qualitative research is too subjective

Quantitative researchers sometimes criticize qualitative research as being too impressionistic and subjective. By these criticisms they usually mean that qualitative findings rely too much on the researcher's often unsystematic views about what is significant and important, and also upon the close personal relationships that the researcher frequently strikes up with the people studied. Precisely because qualitative research often begins in a relatively open-ended way and entails a gradual narrowing-down of research questions or problems, the consumer of the writings deriving from the research is given few clues as to why one area was the chosen area upon which attention was focused rather than another. By contrast, quantitative researchers point to the tendency for the problem formulation stage in their work to be more explicitly stated in terms of such matters as the existing literature on that topic and key theoretical ideas.

Difficult to replicate

Quantitative researchers also often argue that these tendencies are even more of a problem because of the difficulty of replicating a qualitative study, although replication in business and management research is by no means a straightforward matter regardless of this particular issue (see Chapter 3). Precisely because it is unstructured and often reliant upon the qualitative researcher's ingenuity, it is almost impossible to conduct a true replication, since there are hardly any standard procedures to be followed. In qualitative research, the investigator him- or herself is the main instrument of data collection, so that what is observed and heard and also what the researcher decides to concentrate upon is very much a product of his or her predilections. There are several possible components of this criticism: what qualitative researchers (especially perhaps in ethnography) choose to focus upon while in the field is a product of what strikes them as significant, whereas other researchers are likely to empathize with other issues; the responses of participants (people being observed or interviewed) to qualitative researchers is likely to be affected by the characteristics of the researcher (personality, age, gender, and so on); and, because of the unstructured nature of qualitative data, interpretation will be profoundly influenced by the subjective leanings of a researcher. Because of such factors it is difficult—not to say impossible—to replicate qualitative findings. The difficulties ethnographers experience when they revisit grounds previously trodden by another researcher (often referred to as a 'restudy')

do not inspire confidence in the replicability of qualitative research (Bryman 1994).

Problems of generalization

It is often suggested that the scope of the findings of qualitative investigations is restricted. When participant observation is used or when unstructured interviews are conducted with a small number of individuals in a certain organization or locality, they argue that it is impossible to know how the findings can be generalized to other settings. How can just one or two cases be representative of all cases? In other words, can we really treat Perlow's (1997; see Box 14.1) research on the time and the work–life balance of software engineers in a high-tech corporation in the USA as representative of all software engineers; or Prasad's (1993) research on computerization in a health management organization as representative of the symbolic effects of implementing new technology in other types of work organization? In the case of research based on interviews rather than participation, can we treat interviewees who have not been selected through a probability procedure or even quota sampling as representative? Are Watson's (1994a) managers typical of all managers working within the telecommunications industry, or are Ram's (1994; see Box 14.6) small firm case studies in the West Midlands typical of small firms elsewhere?

The answer in all these cases is, of course, emphatically 'no'. A case study is not a sample of one drawn from a known population. Similarly, the people who are interviewed in qualitative research are not meant to be representative of a population and indeed, in some cases, like managers, we may find it more or less impossible to enumerate the population in any precise manner. Instead, the findings of qualitative research are to generalize to theory rather than to populations. It is 'the cogency of the theoretical reasoning' (J. C. Mitchell 1983: 207), rather than statistical criteria, that is decisive in considering the generalizability of the findings of qualitative research. In other words, it is the quality of the theoretical inferences that are made out of qualitative data that is crucial to the assessment of generalization.

These three criticisms reflect many of the preoccupations of quantitative research that were discussed in Chapter 3. A further criticism that is often made of qualitative research, but that is perhaps less influenced by quantitative research criteria, is the suggestion that qualitative research frequently lacks transparency in how the research was conducted.

Lack of transparency

It is sometimes difficult to establish from qualitative research what the researcher actually *did* and how he or she arrived at the study's conclusions. For example, qualitative research reports are sometimes unclear about such matters as how people were chosen for observation or interview. This deficiency contrasts sharply with the sometimes laborious accounts of sampling procedures in reports of quantitative research. However, it does not seem plausible to suggest that outlining in some detail the ways in which research participants are selected constitutes the application of quantitative research criteria. Readers have a right to know how far research participants were selected to correspond to a wide range of people. Also, the process of qualitative data analysis is frequently unclear (Bryman and Burgess 1994a). It is often not obvious how the analysis was conducted—in other words, what the researcher was actually doing when the data were analysed and therefore how the study's conclusions were arrived at. To a large extent, these areas of a lack of transparency are increasingly being addressed by qualitative researchers.

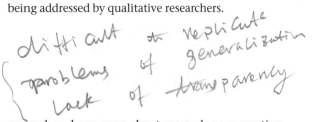

Is it always like this?

This was a heading that was employed in Chapter 3 in relation to quantitative research, but it is perhaps less easy to answer in relation to qualitative research. To a large extent, this is because qualitative research is less codified than quantitative research—that is, it is less influenced by strict guidelines and directions about how to go about data collection and analysis. For example, Dalton (1964; see Chapter 14) explains that no explicit hypotheses formed the basis for his participant-observational study of managerial work, for three reasons. First, he was not able to be sure what was relevant until he had gained 'some intimacy with the situation'; secondly, once uttered, a hypothesis becomes somewhat 'obligatory'; and, thirdly, there is a danger that the hypothesis carries a quasi-scientific status. Instead he worked on the basis of 'hunches', which guided him through the research.

As a result, and this may be noticed by readers of the chapters that follow this one, accounts of qualitative research are frequently less prescriptive in tone than those encountered in relation to quantitative research. Instead, they often exhibit more of a descriptive tenor, outlining the different ways qualitative researchers have gone about research or suggesting alternative ways of conducting research or analysis based on the writer's own experiences or those of others. To a large extent, this picture is changing, in that there is a growing number of books that seek to make clear-cut recommendations about how qualitative research should be carried out.

However, if we look at some of the preoccupations of qualitative research that were described above, we can see certain ways in which there are departures from the practices that are implied by these preoccupations. One of the main departures is that qualitative research is sometimes a lot more focused than is implied by the suggestion that the researcher begins with general research questions and narrows it down so that theory and concepts are arrived at during and after the data collection. There is no *necessary* reason why qualitative research cannot be employed to investigate a specific research problem. For example, Truss (2001; see Box 22.5) takes as her research problem the relationship between organizational performance and human resource management (HRM). However, instead of devising a list of 'best-practice' indicators from the literature and testing their impact on performance, this study looked at a firm that was successful—Hewlett-Packard—and asked what HR policies and practices were used and how they were being enacted. Using a variety of methods, including interviews and focus groups, Truss found that many of the company's human resource policies and practices were contradictory, particularly in relation to training and career management, where a large number of employees did not believe they received the training they needed. Yet, even though the company did not achieve a high level of 'fit' within its HR system, it still managed to achieve high levels of financial performance. Truss concludes that there is a disjuncture between formal policy and informal organization, which quantitative studies of

High Performance Work Systems fail to capture. A related way in which qualitative research differs from the standard model is in connection with the notion of a lack of structure in approaches to collecting and analysing data. As will be seen in Chapter 17, techniques like conversation analysis entail the application of a highly codified method for analysing talk. Moreover, the growing use of computer-assisted qualitative data analysis software (CAQDAS), which will be the subject of Chapter 20, is leading to greater transparency in the procedures used for analysing qualitative data. This greater transparency may lead to more codification in qualitative data analysis than has previously been the case.

Some contrasts between quantitative and qualitative research

Several writers have explored the contrasts between quantitative and qualitative research by devising tables that allow the differences to be brought out (e.g. Halfpenny 1979; Bryman 1988*a*; Hammersley 1992*b*). Table 13.1 attempts to draw out the chief contrasting features.

Table 13.1 Some common contrasts between quantitative and qualitative research

Quantitative	Qualitative
Numbers	Words
Point of view of researcher	Points of view of participants
Researcher distant	Researcher close
Theory testing	Theory emergent
Static	Process
Structured	Unstructured
Generalization	Contextual understanding
Hard, reliable data	Rich, deep data
Macro	Micro
Behaviour	Meaning
Artificial settings	Natural settings

- *Numbers vs. Words.* Quantitative researchers are often portrayed as preoccupied with applying measurement procedures to social life, while qualitative researchers are seen as using words in the presentation of analyses of society.

- *Point of view of researcher vs. Point of view of participants.* In quantitative research, the investigator is in the driving seat. The set of concerns that he or she brings to an investigation structures the investigation. In qualitative research, the perspective of those being studied—what they see as important and significant—provides the point of orientation.

- *Researcher is distant vs. Researcher is close.* In quantitative research, researchers are uninvolved with their subjects and in some cases, as in research based on postal questionnaires or on hired interviewers, may have no contact with them at all. Sometimes, this lack of a relationship with the subjects of an investigation is regarded as desirable by quantitative researchers, because they feel that their objectivity might be compromised if they become too involved with the people they study. The qualitative researcher seeks close involvement with the people being investigated, so that he or she can genuinely understand the world through their eyes.

- *Theory and concepts tested in research vs. Theory and concepts emergent from data.* Quantitative researchers typically bring a set of concepts to bear on the research instruments being employed, so that theoretical work precedes the collection of data, whereas in qualitative research concepts and theoretical elaboration emerge out of data collection.

- *Static vs. Process.* Quantitative research is frequently depicted as presenting a static image of social reality with its emphasis on relationships between variables. Change and connections between events over time tend not to surface, other than in a mechanistic fashion. Qualitative research is often depicted as attuned to the unfolding of events over time and to the interconnections between the actions of participants of social settings.

- *Structured vs. Unstructured.* Quantitative research is typically highly structured so that the investigator is able to examine the precise concepts and issues that are the focus of the study; in qualitative research the approach is invariably unstructured, so that the possibility of getting at actors' meanings and of concepts emerging out of data collection is enhanced.

- *Generalization vs. Contextual understanding.* Whereas quantitative researchers want their findings to be generalizable to the relevant population, the qualitative researcher seeks an understanding of behaviour, values, beliefs, and so on in terms of the context in which the research is conducted.

- *Hard, reliable data vs. Rich, deep data.* Quantitative data are often depicted as 'hard' in the sense of being robust and unambiguous, owing to the precision offered by measurement. Qualitative researchers claim, by contrast, that their contextual approach and their often prolonged involvement in a setting engender rich data.

- *Macro vs. Micro.* Quantitative researchers are often depicted as involved in uncovering large-scale social trends and connections between variables, whereas qualitative researchers are seen as concerned with small-scale aspects of social reality, such as interaction.

- *Behaviour vs. Meaning.* It is sometimes suggested that the quantitative researcher is concerned with people's behaviour and the qualitative researcher with the meaning of action.

- *Artificial settings vs. Natural settings.* Whereas quantitative researchers conduct research in a contrived context, qualitative researchers investigate people in natural environments.

However, as we will see in Chapter 21, while these contrasts depict reasonably well the differences between quantitative and qualitative research, they should not be viewed as constituting hard and fast distinctions. These issues will be returned to in the next three chapters.

Researcher–subject relationships

A further difference between quantitative and qualitative research arises in relation to the way that qualitative researchers relate to their research subjects. Specifically, qualitative researchers tend to take greater account of the power relations that exist between the researcher him- or herself and the people who are the main subject of study. This has led to the development of several qualitative approaches that enable research subjects to play a more active part in designing the research and influencing the outcomes of the process. Action research, feminism, collaborative and participative forms of enquiry all fall into this category. In the last section of this chapter we will consider the main features of each of these approaches and explore the implications that they have for researcher–subject relationships.

Action research

There is no single type of action research but broadly it can be defined as an approach in which the action researcher and a client collaborate in the diagnosis of

---

Box 13.9 An example of action research

Participatory action research can be seen as an emergent process; indeed it may not even begin as explicitly participatory. Based on their involvement with the US-based multinational Xerox corporation, Greenwood, Whyte, and Harkavy (1993) propose that the aim of participatory action research is to encourage continuous learning on the part of both the professional researchers and the members of the organization involved.

The case began as a 'fairly conventional consulting program' (1993: 181). However, in response to declining market share and profits, the company implemented a competitive benchmarking programme that threatened major job losses. This led to the emergence of a participatory action research project that focused on sociotechnical

change processes. The project involved management and union officials in the establishment of a team that worked together with researchers drawing on theories and ideas from a variety of fields. The team learnt how to address the internal cost accounting procedures that 'could lead management to make decisions adverse to the economic interests of both company and workers' (1993: 183).

Greenwood and his colleagues say little about how the shift from consulting programme to action research project was negotiated. However, they do say that a sense of organizational crisis was important in precipitating this shift. This in part depends on organizational leaders being willing to take risks and allow action researchers to engage in processes that senior management does not control.

---

a problem and in the development of a solution based on the diagnosis. A common theme amongst management and business researchers is that action research output results from 'involvement with members of an organization' over a matter of 'genuine concern to them' (Eden and Huxham 1996: 75). Many writers therefore stress the need for action research to be useful to the practitioner and suggest it should provide a means of empowering participants. For an example of action research see Box 13.9.

Action research is defined by Argyris, Putnam, and Smith (1985) as follows:

- Experiments are on real problems within an organization and are designed to assist in their solution.

- This involves an iterative process of problem identification, planning, action, and evaluation.

- Action research leads eventually to re-education, changing patterns of thinking and action. This depends on the participation of research subjects (who are often referred to in action research as clients) in identifying new courses of action.

- It is intended to contribute both to academic theory and practical action.

Eden and Huxham (1996) define the characteristics of action research in terms of outcomes and

processes. Good and effective action research should have the following outcomes.

- It should have implications that relate to situations other than the one that is studied.

- As well as being usable in everyday life, action research should also be concerned with theory.

- It leads to the generation of emergent or grounded theory, which emanates from the data in gradual incremental steps.

- Action researchers must recognize that their findings will have practical implications and they should be clear about what they expect participants to take away from the project.

In business and management, action research plays a particular role in bridging the gap between researchers and practitioners (by which it is usually meant managers). Gummesson (1999) stresses the need for business and management researchers to be involved in practice and he suggests that there is actually very little difference between the roles of the academic researcher and the management consultant (see Box 1.1). Action research seen as particularly useful in researching processual problems in organizations such as learning and change. Hence many action research projects are undertaken by part-time students who take their own work organization and problems within it to be their primary focus of study. These individuals are already immersed in the organizations as complete participants and have an understanding of it that is derived from being an actor in the processes being studied. They face three interrelated sets of issues that relate to:

- their preunderstanding of the setting;
- role duality;
- organizational politics (Coghlan 2001).

Preunderstanding refers to the knowledge, insight, and experience that researchers have about the lived experience of their own organization; for example they already know the history, key events, and jargon used within the organization and who to turn to for information. Their role duality sets them apart from other organizational members and can affect the data that are generated, particularly when they are engaged in research that may threaten existing organizational norms.

A further source of action research projects is related to organizational consultancy, which is conducted by some business school academics as a way of informing their own practice and as a source of additional income. However, this alternative source of research material can also cause problems. Even though consultancy settings provide access to data, a clear design must be formulated for the action research before the setting is encountered (Eden and Huxham 1996). In addition, the tendency to refer to research subjects as clients suggests that research participants are employing the services of the researcher. This can create conflicts of interest for the researcher and introduce bias towards those who are financially supporting the research. Action researchers must therefore possess a high degree of self-awareness in order to combine the roles of researcher and consultant and be prepared to defend their research in these terms.

The collection of data is likely to be involved in the formulation of the diagnosis of a problem and in the evaluation of a problem. Action research can involve the collection of both quantitative and qualitative data. Data collection methods can include keeping a diary of subjective impressions, a collection of documents relating to a situation, observation notes of meetings, questionnaire surveys, interviews, tape or video recordings of meetings, and written descriptions of meetings or interviews (which may be given to participants for them to validate or amend). In action research, the investigator becomes part of the field of study, and, as with participant observation, this has its own attendant problems. In their action research study of an outpatient health centre, Ramirez and Bartunek (1989) suggest that they were involved in dilemmas that related to conflicting organizational roles, which led to conflict over researcher loyalties. This affected how the action researcher (who was an internal consultant) was seen, as rumours were spread in order to discredit the action researcher by suggesting that she was using the project to set up a favourable position within the organization for herself.

A further claim of action research is that the research outputs are more readable, relevant, and interesting to practitioner as well as academic audiences. When the research is written up, the action research report is seen primarily as a discussion document, which presents a number of action strategies from which collaborators will jointly select a course to take. The narrative format is recommended as an appropriate way of expressing the sequence of practice and reflection that is entailed in the action research role (Winter 1989).

Action research is criticized, in a similar way to other qualitative methods, for its lack of repeatability and consequent lack of rigour and for concentrating too much on organizational action at the expense of research findings. In their defence, action researchers claim that involvement with practitioners concerning issues that are important to them provides a richness of insight that cannot be gained in other ways. It is also claimed that theory generated from action research is 'grounded in action' (Eden and Huxham 1996), thereby overcoming some of the difficulties of relying on talk as a source of data, instead of action or overt behaviour.

Action research should not be confused with *evaluation research* (Box 2.12), which usually denotes the study of the impact of an intervention, such as a new social policy or a new innovation in organizations. The research referred to in Box 13.8 was conducted broadly with an evaluation research frame of reference, in that it was concerned to evaluate the impact of the introduction of performance appraisal in British universities.

Cognitive mapping

Cognitive mapping is a predominantly qualitative method that has been used widely by business and management researchers in a variety of contexts (see Box 13.10 for an example), particularly in the field of strategy development. Cognitive mapping is seen as complementary to action research because the maps can be used as a problem-solving device by researchers, who work interactively with managers to address a particular organizational issue. Thus, in addition to its potential use as a research method, mapping is also commonly used as a management consulting technique.

Eden (1992) suggests that cognitive mapping is used to capture individual perspectives, because it is based on the assumption that people interpret data differently and they will therefore understand problems in different ways. The method draws on personal construct theory (Kelly 1955), which also informs the use of repertory grid technique (see Chapter 5), and is based on the assumption that people are actively engaged in constructing models, hypotheses, or representations that enable them to make sense of the world around them. Whilst cognitive maps can be seen as models of cognition, their primary function is as a tool for reflective thinking about a problem that enables steps to be taken towards its solution. Cause maps are a particular version of cognitive mapping that attempt to capture arguments and propositions in the form of a hierarchical structure that relates means to ends.

The mapping process involves participants identifying the factors that affect a particular decision-making 'goal'. Ideas or 'concepts' relating to the decision are generated on the basis of either individual or group interviews. The role of the interviewer in this context is to ask questions that explore *why* concepts are important to the individual and *how* they are related. This process, known as 'laddering' (Eden 1988), enables the researcher to understand an individual's construct system. It consists of

---

Box 13.10 An example of cognitive mapping

In their study of senior managerial decision making in a UK electrical retail company, Clarke and Mackaness (2001) began by conducting a collective group interview with all senior directors and managers who were involved in making new store investment decisions. The aim of this interview was to identify the problem-solving goal that would form the focus for cognitive mapping. This was defined as 'the opening of high performing superstores' (2001: 155). High-performing superstores were measured in terms of turnover per outlet and return on capital employed in investment. The group identified six 'prototype' stores that were seen as representative of high- and low-performing stores within the company.

The performance of these 'prototype' stores was then used as the focus for individual interviews with three senior managers who were jointly responsible for strategic decisions relating to investment in and construction of new superstores—the Managing Director, the Operations Manager, and the Estates Manager. All three interviewees knew about the 'prototype' stores and had been involved in the original investment decisions.

Illustrative materials were used to prompt discussion about each prototype store, including site maps and aerial photographs. Using these examples, they were asked to identify the most influential factors in producing high-performance superstores. These interviews were transcribed and used to generate a cognitive map for each manager, which was shown to each respondent for clarification and elaboration. Links between the concepts were also ascribed on three status levels: 'causal' links, in which one concept influences another directly; 'connotative' links, which imply indirect association; and 'temporal' links, which change over time and have either positive or negative dimensions.

Clarke and MacKaness conclude that senior managers tend to opt for simpler cognitive explanations of the decision-making process and rely on fewer constructs than their lower-level counterparts. They also tend to 'benchmark' their thoughts against previous decisions. This suggests that they are able to make use of past experience as well as factual information in a decision-making situation.

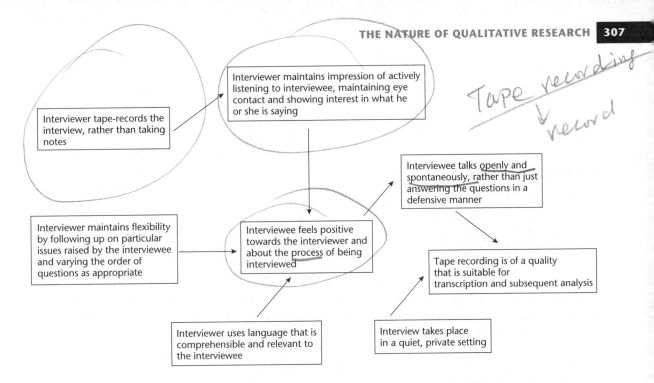

Figure 13.2 An example of a part of a cognitive map to show the process of qualitative interviewing
Source: adapted from Eden, Ackermann, and Cropper (1992).

'laddering up'—asking why a particular construct is important—and 'laddering down'—finding out how a particular construct is affected by the particular decision.

These data are then interpreted by the researcher and put into a diagram that reflects the relationship between the concepts. This process results in the construction of a maplike diagram that represents elements of understanding or thinking at a given time. A cognitive map is usually drawn as short pieces of text linked by arrows that show the direction of causality (see Figure 13.2 for a simplified example). This is intended to make it easy to see how concepts are related to each other and to show the overall structure of assertions, although some cognitive maps place less emphasis on the directional or causal nature of these relationships, focusing instead on the patterns or connections between them. In some cases, individuals are involved in validating their own maps; in others the interpretation of the data into a map is a task undertaken solely by the researcher.

The method is intended not only to enable understanding of an individual's construct system, but also to enable groups of individuals, usually managers, to understand the way that others in the group perceive a problem. The map can thus form the basis for discussion and provide a resource that can help them to form a coherent view in relation to an issue and decide on an appropriate course of action. Maps can therefore relate to the thinking processes of individuals, groups, organizations, or even industries, although there is a need for researchers to be clear about the level of analysis they are adopting. An underlying assumption of the approach is that the process of interaction between researcher and research subjects leads to the production of understanding.

There are several software packages on the market that have been developed to support the process of cognitive mapping. One of these is **Decision Explorer**, developed by Eden and other academics at the universities of Bath and Strathclyde. This enables the display and analysis of maps, and can be used interactively with research subjects or in problem-solving teams. The software, which is produced by a company called Banxia, has been used for a variety of academic and management consultancy projects. More information about the software and its potential applications can be found on their web site at:

www.banxia.com.

Feminism and qualitative research

A further dimension to add to this discussion is that, in the view of some writers, qualitative research is associated with a feminist sensitivity, and that, by implication, quantitative research is viewed by many feminists as incompatible with feminism. Moreover, feminist research could be seen as having a particularly important role to play in relation to business and management research, which has typically been pursued from a masculine perspective (see Box 13.11). Furthermore, the bias towards a masculine perspective in business and management research may be related to the dominance of quantitative methods, which are regarded as 'hard' or 'masculine', rather than qualitative methods, which are seen as 'soft' and lacking in concreteness (Gherardi and Turner 1987). However, the link between feminism and qualitative research is by no means a cut-and-dried issue, in that, although it

became something of an orthodoxy among some writers, it has not found favour with all feminists. Indeed, there are signs at the time of writing that views on this issue are changing.

The notion that there is an affinity between feminism and qualitative research has at least two main components to it: a view that quantitative research is inherently incompatible with feminism, and a view that qualitative research provides greater opportunity for a feminist sensitivity to come to the fore. Quantitative research is frequently viewed as incompatible with feminism for the following reasons.

- According to Mies (1993), quantitative research suppresses the voices of women either by ignoring them or by submerging them in a torrent of facts and statistics.

- The criteria of valid knowledge associated with quantitative research are ones that turn women, when they are the focus of research, into objects. This means that women are again subjected to exploitation, in that knowledge and experience are extracted from them with nothing in return, even when the research is conducted by women (Mies 1993).

Box 13.11 Is there a role for feminist research in business and management?

Organizational research has typically been pursued from a male-oriented perspective, which, according to Wilson (1995), regards men and women as alike and fails to consider gender as a significant variable within organizational processes. To illustrate this point, Wilson cites the example of the Hawthorne studies (see also Box 2.10), which involved the observational study of a group of female employees in the 'test room' and a group of male employees in the 'bank wiring room'. 'The men were observed under normal working conditions while the female group was pressured, by male supervisors, into an experimental situation. Despite the fact that output was increased by the women and restricted by the men, the overall findings were presented as an explanation of the behaviour of employees *per se*' (1995: 1–2).

Other studies have tended to treat women as entirely peripheral to organizational life; this bias is particularly evident in the study of management. As the majority of managers are men, studies of management have mainly focused on observation of male managers. Therefore, recommendations about what makes effective management often erroneously assume that better managers are more masculine, reinforcing this masculine gender stereotype. Despite the growth of feminist research in various disciplines, much of this has occurred outside the boundaries of business and management research. If, as Wilson suggests, we need to 'see reality differently' and reformulate the way in which work organizations are understood, feminist methods provide a means whereby the male-oriented values in business and management can be exposed and challenged.

- The emphasis on controlling variables further exacerbates this last problem, and indeed the very idea of control is viewed as a masculine approach.

- The use of predetermined categories in quantitative research results in an emphasis on what is already known and consequently in 'the silencing of women's own voices' (Maynard 1998: 128).

- The criteria of valid knowledge associated with quantitative research also mean that women are to be researched in a value-neutral way, when in fact the goals of feminist research should be to conduct research specifically *for* women.

By contrast, qualitative research was viewed by many feminists as either more compatible with feminism's central tenets or as more capable of being adapted to those tenets. Thus, in contrast to quantitative research, qualitative research allows:

- women's voices to be heard;

- exploitation to be reduced by giving as well as by receiving in the course of fieldwork;

- women *not* to be treated as objects to be controlled by the researcher's technical procedures; and

- the emancipatory goals of feminism to be realized.

How qualitative research achieves these goals will be addressed particularly in the next three chapters, since the issues and arguments vary somewhat from one method to the other. In fact, the issue of qualitative research as providing the opportunity for a feminist approach has somewhat different aspects when looking at ethnography, qualitative interviewing, and focus groups—the topics of the next three chapters. In business and management, feminist research is less well established than in the social science disciplines, but that is not to say that there are not important organizational issues that feminist research can address—for example, in the study of women entrepreneurs (see Box 13.12). However, it also ought to be recognized that there has been a softening of attitude among some feminist writers towards quantitative research in recent years. Examples of this softening are as follows.

- There is a recognition that many of the worst excesses of discrimination against women might

> **Box 13.12 Feminist research and the study of women entrepreneurs**
>
> Mirchandani (1999) suggests that much of the research on women's experiences of entrepreneurship focuses on identifying similarities and differences between female and male business-owners, and on providing explanations of these differences. Although this approach is useful in compensating for the exclusion of women in earlier studies, it does not explain why entrepreneurship is defined and understood only in terms of the behaviour of men. Mirchandani proposes that the construction of the category of 'the female entrepreneur' prioritizes gender over other important aspects of identity, such as social stratification, business ownership, organizational structure, and industry, that need to be explored in relation to female *and* male business-owners.

not have come to light so clearly were it not for the collection and analysis of statistics revealing discrimination (Maynard 1994; Oakley 1998). The very presence of factual evidence of this kind has allowed the case for equal opportunities legislation to be made much more sharply, although, needless to say, there is much more that still needs to be done in this field.

- As Jayaratne and Stewart (1991) and Maynard (1994, 1998) have pointed out, at the very least it is difficult to see why feminist research that combines quantitative and qualitative research would be incompatible with the feminist cause.

- There has also been a recognition of the fact that qualitative research is not *ipso facto* feminist in orientation. If, for example, ethnography, which is covered in the next chapter, provided for a feminist sensitivity, we would expect subjects like social anthropology, which have been virtually founded on the approach, to be almost inherently feminist, which is patently not the case (Reinharz 1992: 47–8). If this is so, the question of appropriate approaches to feminist research would seem to reside in the *application* of methods rather than something that is inherent in them. Consequently, some writers have preferred to write about *feminist research practice* rather than about *feminist methods* (Maynard 1998: 128).

Collaborative and cooperative enquiry

Like action research and some kinds of feminist research, collaborative forms of enquiry assume that the findings of research should relate to action. However, the distinguishing feature of collaborative methods of enquiry is their assumption that members of the organization being studied should actively participate in the research process in addition to being the subjects of it. Collaborative research can therefore be seen as an extended form of respondent validation (see Box 13.3), which attempts to break down the boundaries between researcher and researched. Also located under this umbrella is critical or emancipatory action research (Zuber-Skerritt 1996), which also casts itself as a form of collaborative enquiry by practitioners into a major problem or issue in their own practice.

An important milestone in the development of these research traditions was the publication of a book by Reason and Rowan (1981), which brought together writers from these traditions and argued for the legitimacy of a 'new paradigm' of research based on increased participation and collaboration with research subjects. (For an example of the kind of research that this book encouraged see Box 13.13). This set of perspectives broadly defined research as a two-way process whereby the researcher becomes involved in the participant's world and the practitioner gets involved in the generation of research outputs. At its most radical this leads to cooperative enquiry, where all those involved are both co-researchers and co-subjects (Reason 1999).

Collaborative methods of enquiry stem from a desire to challenge the conventional methods whereby knowledge is constructed in the social sciences. This involves challenging the monopoly, traditionally held by universities, over the processes and outcomes of research and offering a more democratic alternative whereby research participants are treated as active agents rather than as passive subjects. It is about doing research 'with people' rather than 'on people' (Heron and Reason 2000). It also seeks to acknowledge that the motivation to do research is related to our own personal needs for development, change, and learning (Reason and Marshall 1987) and that research often involves personal growth (see Box 13.14 for an illustration).

Box 13.13 An example of participative research

In the 1970s, Brown and Kaplan (1981) engaged in a five-year research and development project at Northern Chemical Works, a subsidiary of a large multinational corporation. The research focused on employee relations problems experienced by the firm. Interviews were held with managers and employees at the Textiles Plant and an 'empathic' questionnaire was devised using direct quotations from the interviews. Following analysis of this data, plant personnel met in small groups to discuss the findings and generate action steps to be taken.

Brown and Kaplan suggest that their research involvement illustrates five aspects of participative research.

1 It involved diverse parties, including management and union leaders, whose interactions could not be predicted or controlled.

2 The research involved ideological choices, in that the researchers were unable to remain neutral in their research as they were pressed to take sides with either union or management (eventually deciding to work exclusively with management—who had financially supported the research initially).

3 The diverse perspectives of different parties had somehow to be integrated, despite the high degree of misunderstanding and conflict that existed between them.

4 The research was organized in a way that enabled the use of resources to solve concrete problems as well as to generate abstract knowledge.

5 The outcomes of the research were complex and ambiguous, producing competing explanations that reflected multiple realities.

Box 13.14 An example of collaborative enquiry into workplace diversity

In order to consider the resources necessary to support an increasingly diverse workforce, Bond and Pyle (1998) used a social ecological perspective in order to suggest that the environment, and in particular the distribution of resources, exert a powerful influence on human behaviour. Their observations are based on an organizational case study called 'Chemical Products', where they used a collaborative enquiry process. They explain:

> We chose a collaborative inquiry process because of our ecologically-driven belief that organization members are not only in the best position to answer questions about their own setting, but they are also the most

knowledgeable about what questions to ask, how to ask the questions, and how to understand participants' responses. To facilitate such a participative process, we worked closely with the HR Manager and her staff. After getting approval for the project from the President, we reviewed goals with the Unit Managers Group. We then established a Steering Team to guide the Workplace Chemistry Project. We clarified project goals with other existing groups such as the cross-department People Team. These meetings were followed by 36 in-depth interviews, participant observation of meetings, and a series of feedback sessions.   (1998: 597)

K   KEY POINTS

- There is disagreement over what precisely qualitative research is.

- Qualitative research does not lend itself to the delineation of a clear set of linear steps.

- It tends to be a more open-ended research strategy than is typically the case with quantitative research.

- Theories and concepts are viewed as outcomes of the research process.

- There is considerable unease about the simple application of the reliability and validity criteria associated with quantitative research to qualitative research. Indeed, some writers prefer to use alternative criteria that have parallels with reliability and validity.

- Action research is an approach in which the researcher and a client collaborate in the diagnosis of a problem and in the development of a solution to the problem based on the diagnosis. It is connected with the method of cognitive mapping.

- Most qualitative researchers reveal a preference for seeing through the eyes of research participants.

- Several writers have depicted qualitative research as having a far greater affinity with a feminist standpoint than quantitative research can exhibit.

- Action research, feminism, and collaborative methods of enquiry have changed the relationship between the researcher and the research subject.

Q QUESTIONS FOR REVIEW

- What are some of the difficulties with providing a general account of the nature of qualitative research?

- Outline some of the traditions of qualitative research.

- What are some of the main research methods associated with qualitative research?

The main steps in qualitative research

- Does a research question in qualitative research have the same significance and characteristics as in quantitative research?

Theory and research

- Is the approach to theory in qualitative research inductive or deductive?

Concepts in qualitative research

- What is the difference between definitive and sensitizing concepts?

Reliability and validity in qualitative research

- How have some writers adapted the notions of reliability and validity to qualitative research?

- Why have some writers sought alternative criteria for the evaluation of qualitative research?

- Evaluate Lincoln and Guba's criteria.

- What is respondent validation?

- What is triangulation?

The main preoccupations of qualitative researchers

- Outline the main preoccupations of qualitative researchers.

- How do these preoccupations differ from those of quantitative researchers, which were considered in Chapter 3?

The critique of qualitative research

- What are some of the main criticisms that are frequently levelled at qualitative research?

- To what extent do these criticisms reflect the preoccupations of quantitative research?

Is it always like this?

- Can qualitative research be employed in relation to hypothesis testing?

Some contrasts between quantitative and qualitative research

- 'The difference between quantitative and qualitative research revolves entirely around the concern with numbers in the former and with words in the latter.' How far do you agree with this statement?

Researcher–subject relationships

- What is action research?

- How are cognitive maps used in problem solving?

- Is there a role for feminist research in the study of business and management?

- How have collaborative approaches to qualitative research changed the relationship between the researcher and the research subject?

Ethnography and participant observation

CHAPTER GUIDE

Ethnography and participant observation entail the extended involvement of the researcher in the social life of those he or she studies (see Box 13.1). However, the former term is also frequently taken to refer to the written output of that research. This chapter explores:

- the problems of gaining access to different settings and some suggestions about how they might be overcome;
- the issue of whether a covert role is practicable and acceptable;
- the role of key informants and gatekeepers for the ethnographer;

- the different kinds of roles that ethnographers can assume in the course of their fieldwork;
- sampling strategies in ethnography, in particular *theoretical sampling*, which is associated with the grounded theory approach to qualitative data analysis, which will be examined in Chapter 19;
- the role of field notes in ethnography and the varieties of forms they can assume;
- bringing ethnography to an end.

Introduction

Discussions about the merits and limitations of participant observation have been a fairly standard ingredient in textbooks on business research for many years. However, for some time, writers on research methods have increasingly preferred to write about ethnography rather than participant observation. It is difficult to date the point at which this change of terminology (though it is more than just this) occurred, but sometime in the 1970s ethnography began to become the preferred term. Prior to that, ethnography was primarily associated with social anthropological research, whereby the investigator visits a (usually) foreign land, gains access to a group (for example, a tribe or village), spends a considerable amount of time (often many years) with that group with the aim of uncovering its culture, watches and listens to what people say and do, engages people in conversations to probe specific issues of interest, takes copious field notes, and returns home to write up the fruits of his or her labours.

Ethnography could be viewed as a simple process of joining a group, watching what goes on, making some notes, and writing it all up. In fact, ethnography is nowhere nearly as straightforward as this implies. This chapter will outline some of the main decision areas that confront ethnographers, along with some of the many contingencies they face. However, it is not easy to generalize about the ethnographic research process in such a way as to provide definitive recommendations about research practice. As prefigured at the end of the previous chapter, the diversity of experiences that confront ethnographers and the variety of ways in which they deal with them does not readily permit clear-cut generalizations. The following comment in a book on ethnography makes this point well.

Every field situation *is* different and initial luck in meeting good informants, being in the right place at the right time and striking the right note in relationships may be just as important as skill in technique. Indeed, many successful episodes in the field do come about through good luck as much as through sophisticated planning, and many unsuccessful episodes are due as much to bad luck as to bad judgement. (Sarsby 1984: 96)

However, this statement should not be taken to imply that forethought and an awareness of alternative ways of doing things are irrelevant. It is with this kind of issue that the rest of this chapter will be concerned. However, issues to do with the conduct of interviews by ethnographers will be reserved for Chapter 15.

Organizational ethnography

Ethnography has also become a 'label of choice' for researchers working in professional and applied fields, who have discovered and adapted ethnographic methods to suit their own purposes. Among these are business researchers who have imported the methods and many of the conventions of ethnography into the study of organizational settings. Rosen (1991) understands organizational ethnography to be distinctive because it is concerned with social relations that are related to certain goal-directed activities. He suggests that the rules, strategies, and meanings within a structured work situation are different from those that affect other areas of social life. An ethnographic approach implies intense researcher involvement in the day-to-day running of an organization, in order for the researcher to be able to understand it from an insider's point of view. In order to become immersed in other people's realities, organizational ethnographers, like their anthropological predecessors, engage in fieldwork that tends to commit them to a period of time spent in the organization, or a long stay 'in the field'.

Indeed many of these early studies draw attention to the similarities between ethnography and participant observation (see Box 14.1 for an explanation of the relationship between these terms). Industrial sociologists working out of the Chicago School were followed by a group of writers who studied UK-based work organizations and relied heavily on the traditional ethnographic method of participant observation. These studies, which sometimes involved taking jobs in the research sites, included:

- Roy (1958), who spent two months working as a machine operator in the 'clicking room' of a factory in Chicago. The same factory was later used

as a research setting by Burawoy (1979), who also worked as a machine operator for ten months in the same plant.

- Lupton (1963), who became a participant-observer in Manchester factories in order to explore processes of work group influence on production levels. Lupton compared an engineering plant in which 'fiddles' were prevalent with a clothing factory where these practices were absent.

- Beynon (1975), who over a period of five years studied the Ford Motor Company's Halewood

Box 14.1 Ethnography and participant observation

Many definitions of ethnography and participant observation are very difficult to distinguish. Both draw attention to the fact that the participant observer/ethnographer immerses him- or herself in a group for an extended period of time, observing behaviour, listening to what is said in conversations both between others and with the fieldworker, and asking questions. It is possible that the term 'ethnography' is sometimes preferred because 'participant observation' seems to imply just observation, though in practice participant observers do more than simply observe. Typically, participant observers and ethnographers will gather further data through interviews and the collection of documents. It may be, therefore, that the apparent emphasis on observation in the term 'participant observation' has meant that an apparently more inclusive term would be preferable, even though in fact it is generally recognized that the method entails a wide range of methods of data collection and sources. Ethnography is also sometimes taken to refer to a study in which participant observation is the prevalent research method but that also has a specific focus on the culture of the group in which the ethnographer is immersed.

However, the term 'ethnography' has an additional meaning, in that it frequently simultaneously refers to both a method of research of the kind outlined above *and* the written product of that research. Indeed, 'ethnography' frequently denotes both a research process and the written outcome of the research. A typical account of the ethnographic research process is provided by Perlow (1997), in her study of work–life issues in post-industrial American corporations.

I spent much of each day wandering around, talking to people and observing their daily activities. I had an office in the same corridor, where I would type my field notes on a laptop computer. Even when typing notes, I left my office door open. I sat facing the door, looking up when people walked by, inviting conversation if an engineer or manager chose to enter.

In addition to being present and available to talk to the engineers, I conducted interviews and attended meetings . . . Later, I shadowed engineers . . . to get a sense of how they accomplished their work. Moreover, I sat for hours in each of the software labs observing and talking to the engineers at work and listening to the 'natural' interactions that occurred in the labs.   (1997: 143)

As part of this research was about the relationship between work and home domains, Perlow also wanted to understand the engineers' lives outside work. She therefore asked the married engineers to let her visit their homes and interview their spouses. Finally, Perlow describes how she participated in many social events during the fieldwork; she went to lunch with the engineers on a regular basis, joined them for 'happy hour' on Friday nights at one of the bars down-town, went with them on a three-day bus trip to New York city, and attended official celebrations organized by the company.

Perlow also describes how she adopted the role of confidante:

It was my job to listen, regardless of what I was doing or how I was feeling, I made myself available when the engineers wanted to tell me something. I found myself privy to many unsolicited conversations whether engineers had something specific they felt I should know or they were simply looking for a break in their work and wanted someone to chat with.   (1997: 146)

Practical tip 👉 micro-ethnography

If you are doing research for an undergraduate project or Master's dissertation, it is unlikely that you will be able to conduct a full-scale ethnography, because this will almost certainly involve you spending a considerable period of time in an organizational setting. Nevertheless, it may be possible for you to carry out a form of *micro-ethnography* (Wolcott 1995). This would involve focusing on a particular aspect of an organizational culture, such as the way the organization has implemented TQM, and showing how the culture is reflected through this managerial initiative. A shorter period of time (from a couple of weeks to a few months) could be spent in the organization—on either a full-time or a part-time basis—to achieve this more closely defined cultural understanding.

However, since the 1980s the popularity of organizational culture as a concept has meant that ethnographic methods have enjoyed something of a revival within business and management research. Ethnography, which denotes the practice of writing (*graphy*) about cultures (*ethno*), has provided researchers with an obvious method for understanding work organizations as cultural entities. Studies that focus on the construction of cultural norms, expressions of organizational values, and patterns of workplace behaviour include:

- Kunda's (1992) study of the fictitiously named high-technology company 'Lyndsville Tech' in Silicon Valley, USA.

- Watson's (1994*a*) account of managerial identity in a UK-based telecommunications firm.

- Casey's (1995) exploration of new-product development workers in an American-based multi-national corporation.

- Delbridge's (1998) study of the impact of new manufacturing techniques on worker experiences in a Japanese-owned consumer electronics plant, 'Nippon CTV', and a European-owned automotive components supplier, 'Valleyco'.

assembly plant in Liverpool to produce an account of factory life that described the process whereby people became shop stewards, the way they understood the job, and the kinds of pressures they experienced. This study also involved understanding the experience of people who worked on the assembly lines and the way they made sense of industrial politics.

Access

One of the key and yet most difficult steps in ethnography is gaining access to a social setting that is relevant to the research problem in which you are interested. The way in which access is approached differs according to whether the setting is a relatively open one or a relatively closed one (Bell 1969). The majority of organizational ethnography is done in predominantly closed or non-public settings of various kinds, such as factories or offices. The negotiation of access involves gaining permission to enter these privately managed spaces or situations. Gaining access to organizations can initially be a very formal process involving a lengthy sequence of letter writing and meetings, in order to deal with managerial concerns about your goals. However, the distinction between open and closed settings is not a hard-and-fast one. Organizations also have a highly public character, made visible through marketing and public relations activities.

Buchanan, Boddy, and McCalman (1988) suggest that researchers should adopt an opportunistic approach towards fieldwork in organizations, balancing what is desirable against what is possible. 'The research timetable must therefore take into account the possibility that access will not be automatic and instant, but may take weeks and months of meetings and correspondence to achieve' (1988: 56). As Van Maanen and Kolb (1985: 11) observe, 'gaining access to most organizations is not a matter to be taken lightly but one that involves some combination of strategic planning, hard work and dumb luck'. Sometimes, ethnographers will be able to have their paths smoothed by individuals who act as both sponsor and gatekeeper. Some of the most influential organizational research relationships are those made with senior management, who may act as 'gatekeepers' to the research setting. Gaining access is also sometimes seen as a process of exchange whereby the organizational ethnographer cannot expect to get something out, in the form of data, without giving something in return, often in the form of their physical, mental, or emotional labour.

In selecting a particular social setting to act as a case study in which to conduct an ethnographic investigation, the researcher may employ several criteria. These criteria should be determined by the general research area in which he or she is interested. Very often a number of potential cases (and sometimes very many) will be relevant to your research problem. Hence during his year of participant-observation at ZTC Ryland, Watson (1994a) used to joke with managers about the fact that he had chosen the company for the study because of its convenient location, just a twenty-minute walk from his house. The other reason he gave for choosing the company as a research site was because management had been involved in a succession of change initiatives associated with the development of a 'strong' corporate culture. These policies had been informed by the advice of consultants who were academics, providing Watson with potential insight into the processes whereby managerial ideas about culture building were transferred into practice.

You may also choose a certain case because of its 'fit' with your research questions, but there are no guarantees of success, as Van Maanen and Kolb's remark suggests. Sometimes, sheer perseverance pays off. Leidner (1993) was determined that one of the organizations in which she conducted ethnographic research on the routinization of service work should be McDonald's. She writes:

I knew from the beginning that I wanted one of the case studies to be of McDonald's. The company was a pioneer and exemplar of routinized interaction, and since it was locally based, it seemed like the perfect place to start. McDonald's had other ideas, however, and only after tenacious pestering and persuasion did I overcome corporate employees' polite demurrals, couched in terms of protecting proprietary information and the company's image. (Leidner 1993: 234–5)

This kind of determination is necessary for any instance in which you want to study a specific organization, where rejection is likely to require a complete rethink.

However, with many research questions, several potential cases are likely to meet your criteria. Organizational researchers have developed a range of tactics, many of which may seem rather unsystematic in tone, but they are worth drawing attention to.

- Use friends, contacts, colleagues, academics to help you gain access; provided the organization is relevant to your research question, the route should not matter.

- Try to get the support of someone within the organization who will act as your champion. This person may be prepared to vouch for you and the value of your research. Such people are placed in the role of 'sponsors'.

- Usually you will need to get access through top management/senior executives. Even though you may secure a certain level of agreement lower down the hierarchy, you will usually need clearance from them. Such senior people act as 'gatekeepers'.

- Offer something in return (e.g. a report). This helps to create a sense of being *trustworthy*. However, this strategy also carries risks, in that it may turn you into a cheap consultant and may invite restrictions on your activities, such as insistence on seeing what you write or restrictions on who is willing to talk to you. For example, Milkman (1997) in her study of General Motors (see Box 14.7) found that, although her research approach gained her legitimacy in the eyes of management, it stimulated scepticism and lack of trust among the workers.

- Provide a clear explanation of your aims and methods and be prepared to deal with concerns. Suggest a meeting at which you can deal with worries and provide an explanation of what you intend to do in terms that can readily be understood by others.

• Be prepared to negotiate—you will want complete access but it is unlikely you will be given a *carte blanche*. Milkman (1997) describes how, in negotiating access to the General Motors automobile assembly plant, the promise to produce 'hard', quantitative data to management, through survey research, was what eventually secured the researchers' access to the plant—even though she had no previous experience in designing or conducting surveys!

• Be reasonably honest about the amount of people's time you are likely to take up. This is a question you will almost certainly be asked if you are seeking access to commercial organizations and probably to many not-for-profit ones too.

'Hanging around' is another common access strategy. As a strategy, it typically entails either loitering in an area until you are noticed or gradually becoming incorporated into or asking to join a group. For example, as well as interviewing shop stewards who represented assembly-line workers and a selection of workers from each of the four main production departments, Beynon spent a day each week at the Ford plant, observing and listening to the shop stewards 'as they negotiated, argued and discussed issues amongst themselves and with their members' (1975: 13). He describes how he 'sat at tables in the canteens and at benches around the coffee-vending machines at break times' and 'talked with workers as they queued up for their dinner, for buses or to clock their cards at the beginning and the end of every day' (1975: 13). Similarly, Casey, in her study of a group of professional workers at the multinational 'Hephaestus' Corporation, tells how she 'spent a great deal of time lingering around individual people' (1995: 201). Similarly, Parker (2000: 236) describes how he spent time waiting 'outside managers' offices, often for long periods of time, and wandering around the factory or offices' just to collect small details or fragments of data.

Sometimes, as research relationships evolve, they come to a point where a degree of informal interaction becomes significant in developing insider status. For example, Heyes, whose research took place inside a chemical plant, lists the many social aspects

of organizational life in which he was eventually involved including 'general conversation, banter, smoke breaks' and rituals such as 'the take-away meals which were consumed on the weekend night-shift' (1997: 69).

As these anecdotes suggest, gaining access to social settings is a crucial first step in ethnographic research, in that, without access, your research plans will be halted in their tracks. As Ram (1994) illustrates in his study of employment relations in small firms (see Box 14.6), attention to cultural context and local norms and values can be very important considerations when seeking access to closed settings. Gender can also be an important dynamic when negotiating access to many male-dominated organizational settings (see Box 14.14). In sum, gaining access is often fraught with difficulties. Therefore this discussion of access strategies can be only a starting point in knowing what kinds of approach can be considered.

Overt versus covert?

One way to ease the access problem is to assume a *covert* role—in other words, not to disclose the fact that you are a researcher. This strategy obviates the need to negotiate access to organizations or to explain why you want to intrude into people's lives and make them objects of study. As we will see, seeking access is a highly fraught business and the adoption of a covert role removes some of these difficulties. An outline of the advantages and disadvantages of covert ethnography is given in Box 14.2.

Covert ethnography is relatively uncommon within studies of management and business. An exception is Dalton's (1959) classic study of managers, *Men Who Manage*, which focused on the gap between official and unofficial action. Dalton describes how, in setting up access, he made no formal approach to the top management of any of the four firms he studied in the heavily industrialized area of 'Mobile Acres' in the USA. He relied instead on his status as an employee in two of the firms he studied and relied primarily on the method of covert participant observation. Describing some of the difficulties associated with his covert research role, Dalton draws attention to the problem of 'knowing too much', describing

Box 14.2 The covert role in ethnography

Advantages

- *There is no problem of access.* Adopting a covert role largely gets around the access problem, because the researcher does not have to seek permission to gain entry to a social setting or organization.

- *Reactivity is not a problem.* Using a covert role also reduces reactivity (see Box 8.8), because participants do not know the person conducting the study is a researcher. Therefore, they are less likely to adjust their behaviour because of the researcher's presence.

Disadvantages

- *The problem of taking notes.* As Ditton (1977; see Box 14.3) discovered, it is difficult and probably in some circumstances impossible to take notes when people do not realize you are conducting research. As we will see below, notes are very important to an ethnographer, and it is too risky to rely exclusively on your memory.

- *The problem of not being able to use other methods.* Ethnography entails the use of several methods, but, if the researcher is in a covert role, it is difficult to steer conversations in a certain direction for fear of detection and it is essentially impossible to engage in interviewing.

- *Anxiety.* The ethnographer is under constant threat of having his or her cover blown. Ethnography is frequently a stressful research method and the worries about detection can add to those anxieties. Moreover, if the ethnographer *is* found out, the whole research project may be jeopardized.

- *Ethical problems.* Covert observation transgresses two important ethical tenets: it does not provide participants with the opportunity for 'informed consent' (whereby they can agree or disagree to participate on the basis of information supplied to them) and it entails deception. It can also be taken to be a violation of the principle of privacy. Also, many writers take the view that, in addition to being potentially damaging to research participants, it can also harm the practice of research, because of fears about social researchers being identified by the public as snoopers or voyeurs if they are found out. Ethical issues are considered in greater detail in Chapter 25.

However

- As the main text points out, in some circumstances the overt/covert distinction may be a matter of degree.

how his situation became more sensitive as he acquired more unofficial information about practices such as 'pilfering' (employee theft of materials).

Dalton describes his work role as giving him 'great freedom of movement and wide contacts' (1959: 278) within the firm. However, it is not clear from his accounts of the research process to what extent people in the firms actually knew what he was doing. Dalton draws attention to the importance of 'intimates', trusted individuals who gave information and aid to the research process. This circle of individuals had shown over a period of about three years that 'they could be counted on not to jeopardize the study' (Dalton 1964: 66) and did not pry too much into the information that he was getting from others. As far as these intimates were concerned, therefore, it is not clear to

what extent they encountered his research role as truly covert.

In another classic study, Donald Roy (1958) was similarly oblique with his co-workers about why he was working at the factory. Working under the pseudonym 'Danelly', he describes how workers knew that he had been attending 'college' but 'the specific course of study remained somewhat obscure' (1958: 164) to them. In answer to the question 'why are you working here?', Roy stressed the importance of working 'lots of overtime' and this, according to Roy, seemed to 'suffice' for the workers.

However, the overt versus covert distinction is not without problems. For example, while an ethnographer may seek access through an overt route, there may be many people with whom he or she comes into contact who will not be aware of the ethnographer's

---

Box 14.3 An example of the perils of covert observation: the case of field notes in the lavatory

Ditton's (1977) research on 'fiddling' in a bakery provides an interesting case of the practical difficulties of taking notes during covert observation as well as an illustration of an ethnographer who shifted his position from covert to overt observation at least in part because of those difficulties:

> Nevertheless, I *was* able to develop personal covert participant–observation skills. Right from the start, I found it impossible to keep everything that I wanted to remember in my head until the end of the working day . . . and so had to take rough notes as I was going along. But I was stuck 'on the line', and had nowhere to retire to privately to jot things down. Eventually, the wheeze of using innocently provided lavatory cubicles occurred to me.

> Looking back, all my notes for that third summer were on Bronco toilet paper! Apart from the awkward tendency for pencilled notes to be self-erasing from hard toilet paper . . . my frequent requests for 'time out' after interesting happenings or conversations in the bakehouse and the amount of time I was spending in the lavatory began to get noticed. I had to pacify some genuinely concerned work-mates, give up totally undercover operations, and 'come out' as an observer—albeit in a limited way. I eventually began to scribble notes more openly, but still not in front of people when they were talking. When questioned about this, as I was occasionally, I coyly said that I was writing things down that occurred to me about 'my studies'.   (1977: 5)

---

status as a researcher. Also, some ethnographers move between the two roles (see Box 14.3).

Another interesting case is provided by Glucksman (1994), who in the 1970s left her academic post to work on a factory assembly line to explore the reasons why feminism appeared not to be relevant to working-class women. In a sense, she was a covert observer, but her motives for the research were primarily political and she says that, at the time she was undertaking the research, she had no intention of writing the book that subsequently appeared and that was published under a pseudonym (Cavendish 1982). After the book's publication, it was treated as an example of ethnographic research. Was she an overt or a covert observer (or neither or both)? Whichever description applies, this is an interesting case of what might be termed *retrospective ethnography*.

Ethnographers are far more likely to be in an overt role than a covert one. Some of the reasons for this situation are extremely practical. For example, Freeman (2000) explains that being white and American made it impossible for her to adopt a covert role in her study of data entry workers in Barbados, and company production demands and limited space made it impossible for her to work on an unpaid temporary basis. However, as Box 14.2

reveals, the reasons for the preference of most ethnographers for an overt role are to do with ethical considerations. Because of the ethical problems that beset covert research (and indeed some of the practical difficulties), the bulk of the discussion of access issues that follows will focus upon ethnographers seeking to employ an overt role.

Ongoing access

But access does not finish when you have made contact and gained an entrée to the group. You still need access to *people*. Simply because you have gained access to an organization does not mean that you will have an easy passage through it. Securing access is in many ways an ongoing activity, which takes considerable effort and time. This is likely to prove a particular problem in closed contexts like organizations, as Delbridge (1998) so effectively illustrates when describing his attempts to become integrated as a worker on the shopfloor of a factory sited in a small Welsh valley community. At first, 'I stood out like a sore thumb, I was even noticed and looked at in the street'. However, 'my actual participation in the tasks which faced the workers helped to break down the barriers and several people approached me over the weeks and told me that when they actually saw me sitting there alongside them day after day they began to have some respect for what I was doing' (1998: 19).

Even so, there are various concerns that group members may have and these will affect the level of ongoing access that you are able to achieve.

- People will have suspicions about you, perhaps seeing you as an instrument of top management (it is very common for members of organizations to believe that researchers are placed there to check up on them or even to mistake them for other people). For example, Roethlisberger and Dickson (1939) describe how one of the interviewers in the Hawthorne studies was mistaken for a rate setter.

  There was a buzz of conversation and the men seemed to be working at great speed. Suddenly there was a sharp hissing sound. The conversation died away, and there was a noticeable slowing up in the work pace. The interviewer later discovered from an acquaintance in the department that he had been mistaken for a rate setter. One of the workmen, who acted as a lookout, had stepped on a valve releasing compressed air, a prearranged signal for slowing down. (1939: 386)

  Another example is provided by Freeman (2000), who found that her research access was halted because of fears that she was a corporate spy, sent by a competitor organization to poach members of the workforce.

- They will worry that what they say or do may get back to bosses or to colleagues. Van Maanen (1991a) notes from his research on the police that, when conducting ethnographic research among officers, you are likely to observe activities that may be deeply discrediting and even illegal. Your credibility among police officers will be determined by your reactions to situations and events that are known to be difficult for individuals.

- If they have these worries, they may go along with your research but in fact sabotage it, engaging in deceptions, misinformation, and not allowing access to 'back regions' (Goffman 1956).

There are four things you can do to smooth the path of ongoing access.

- Play up your credentials—past work and experience; your knowledge of the organization and/or its

sector; understanding of their problems—and be prepared for tests of either competence or credibility. An example of this is provided by Perlow (1997), who claims that a critical factor in gaining the support of engineers at the Ditto corporation was that she came from the Massachusetts Institute of Technology (MIT), as 'there is no institution that the engineers we studied hold in higher regard' (1997: 142).

- Pass tests—be non-judgemental when things are said to you about informal activities or about the organization; make sure information given to you does not get back to others, whether bosses or peers. Parker (2000) describes how, when at the end of his fieldwork he submitted his report to management, an uncomplimentary comment about the Managing Director was traced back to an insufficiently anonymized source. Parker subsequently came in for a humiliating grilling from three of the company directors. He claims that this event probably damaged the manager's reputation in the organization, and his trust in him.

- You may need a role—if your research involves quite a lot of participant observation, the role will be related to your position within the organization (see Box 14.7). Otherwise, you will need to construct a 'front', as Ditton (1977; see Box 14.3) did when referring to 'his studies'. This will involve thinking about your dress and your explanations about what you are doing there, and possibly helping out occasionally with work or offering advice. Make sure you have thought about ways in which people's suspicions can be allayed and be consistent and do not behave ambiguously or inconsistently.

- Be prepared for changes in circumstances that may affect your access, such as changes of senior management.

Key informants

One aspect of having sponsors or gatekeepers who smooth access for the ethnographer is that they may become *key informants* in the course of the subsequent fieldwork. The ethnographer relies a lot on informants, but certain informants may become particularly important to the research. They often develop an appreciation of the research and direct the ethnographer to situations, events, or people likely to be helpful to the progress of the investigation.

An interesting example is provided by Kanter (1977), who describes the relationships she developed with a small group of people with whom she worked closely at Indsco Corporation. 'These people were largely in functions where they were well placed to see a large number of people in a large number of levels . . . They could tell me about the history of the company and a variety of experiences in the organization as well as provide information about the issues in their own careers. I could also use them to check out stories I gathered elsewhere' (1977: 336). Similarly, Collinson (1992*b*) describes how being a man researching equal opportunities sometimes resulted in research respondents withholding cooperation. He describes how the identification of key women informants, who were prepared to assist the 'young lad from the university', was crucial in providing him with 'insider' information. One woman trade unionist in particular provided extensive help with the project. Working together, Collinson developed 'a much closer and mutually supportive working relationship than would usually be the case between researcher and respondents' (1992*b*: 115). This provided him with 'deeper insight into the difficulties faced by women in employment and within the trade union movement' (1992*b*: 115) and greater understanding of the problems of managing work and home.

In sum, key informants can clearly be of great help to the ethnographer and frequently provide a support that helps with the stress of fieldwork. However, it also needs to be borne in mind that they carry risks in that the ethnographer may develop an undue reliance on the key informant, and, rather than seeing social reality through the eyes of members of the social setting, the researcher is seeing social reality through the eyes of the key informant.

In addition, the ethnographer will encounter many other people who will also act as informants. Their accounts may be solicited or unsolicited (Hammersley and Atkinson 1995). Some researchers prefer the latter, because of its greater spontaneity and naturalism. Very often, research participants develop a sense of the kinds of events the ethnographer wants to see or encounters that it would be beneficial to be present at. Such unsolicited sources of information are highly attractive to the ethnographer because of their relative spontaneity, although, as Hammersley and Atkinson (1995: 130–1) observe, they may on occasions be staged for the ethnographer's benefit. Solicited accounts can occur in two ways: by interview (see Chapter 15) or by casual questioning during conversations (though in ethnographic research the boundary between an interview and a conversation is by no means clear-cut, as Burgess (1984) makes clear). When the ethnographer needs specific information concerning an issue that is not amenable to direct observation or that is not cropping up during 'natural' conversations, solicited accounts are likely to be the only way forward.

Roles for ethnographers

Related to the issue of ongoing access (or relationships in the field, as it is sometimes called) is the question of the kind of role the ethnographer adopts in relation to the social setting and its members. Several schemes have been devised by writers on research methods to describe the various roles that can be and have been adopted by ethnographers. One of the most widely cited schemes is Gold's (1958) classification of participant observer roles, which can be arrayed on a continuum of degrees of involvement with and detachment from members of the social setting (see Figure 14.1). There are four roles.

- *Complete participant.* According to Gold, the complete participant is a fully functioning member of the social setting and his or her true identity is not

Involvement ←——————→ Detachment

| Complete participant | Participant-as-observer | Observer-as-participant | Complete observer |

Figure 14.1 Gold's classification of participant observer roles

known to members. As such, the complete participant is a covert observer, like Roy (1958) and Dalton (1959).

- *Participant-as-observer*. This role is the same as the complete participant one, but members of the social setting are aware of the researcher's status as a researcher. The ethnographer is engaged in regular interaction with people and participates in their daily lives and is open about their research. In organizational ethnography this frequently involves taking up either paid or unpaid employment in the research setting, as did Delbridge (1998) in his study of contemporary manufacturing under TQM and Sharpe (1997) in her study of Japanese work practices in a UK-based car manufacturing plant.

- *Observer-as-participant*. In this role, the researcher is mainly an interviewer. There is some observation but very little of it involves any participation. Many of the studies covered in Chapter 15 are of this type. Prasad's (1993) study of the effects of computerization of work, described in Chapter 13, also fits into this category, as her research relied on structured periods of observation during which she would watch the staff at work and document these observations, only helping out occasionally on the reception desk when it was particularly busy. See also Box 14.4 for a further illustration.

- *Complete observer*. The researcher does not interact with people. According to Gold, people do not have to take the researcher into account. This kind of role relies on forms of observation that are unobtrusive in character. For example, in studies at the Western Electric Company's Hawthorne plant, investigators spent a total of six months observing the informal social relationships between operators in the Bank Wiring Observation Room. Investigations involved an observer, who maintained a role as 'disinterested spectator' with the aim of observing

> **Box 14.4 An example of observer-as-participant in the Magic Kingdom**
>
> An interesting illustration of research that comes very close to the observer-as-participant role is Raz's (1999) study of Tokyo Disneyland. His main sources of data were: many visits to the theme park, including being part of several official and unofficial tours; interviews with current and former employees; a textual analysis of company guidebooks; and an examination of the reception of the park by visitors through a focus group. Raz's goal was to explore the meeting place of the forces of globalization, in the form of the familiar themes associated with the Disney company, and forces of the 'local', in the form of the distinctive character of Japanese culture. He draws on ideas like 'globalization' in order to develop an understanding of the ways in which the combination of global and local forces is played out and on Hochschild's (1983) concept of 'emotional labour' (see Box 13.2) to develop an appreciation of the world of work for the Disney employee.

and describing what was going on. Observation involved certain general rules: the investigator should not give orders or answer any questions that necessitated the assumption of authority; he should not enter voluntarily into any argument and generally should remain as non-committal as possible; he should not force himself into any conversation or appear anxious to overhear; he should never violate confidences or give information to supervisors; and he should not by his manner of speech or behaviour 'set himself off from the group' (Roethlisberger and Dickson 1939: 388–9).

However, most writers would take the view that, since ethnography entails immersion in a social setting and fairly prolonged involvement, the complete observer role should not be considered as participant observation or ethnography at all, since participation is likely to be more or less entirely missing. Some writers might also question whether research based on the observer-as-participant role can genuinely be regarded as ethnography, but, since it is likely that certain situations are unlikely to be amenable to the

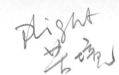

immersion that is a key ingredient of the method, it could be argued that to dismiss it totally as an approach to ethnography is rather restrictive. It is significant in this context that Gold referred to the four roles in relation to conducting 'fieldwork', which has the potential for a broader meaning than either participant observation or ethnography.

Each role carries its own advantages and risks. The issues concerning being a complete participant were covered in Box 14.2. According to Gold, the participant-as-observer role carries the risk of over-identification and hence of 'going native' (see Box 14.5), but offers the opportunity to get close to people. Gold argues that the observer-as-participant role carries the risk of not understanding the social setting and people in it sufficiently and therefore of making incorrect inferences. The complete observer role shares with complete participation the removal of the possible problem of reactivity, but it carries even further risks than the observer-as-participant role of failing to understand situations.

Gans (1968) has devised a classification of participant observer roles, but he views these as roles that will coexist in any project. In other words, the three roles he outlines will be employed at different times in the course of ethnographic research and for different purposes. The three roles are:

- *total participant*, in which the ethnographer is completely involved in a certain situation and has to

resume a researcher stance once the situation has unfolded and then write down notes;

- *researcher-participant*, whereby the ethnographer participates in a situation but is only semi-involved, so that he or she can function fully as a researcher in the course of the situation;

- *total researcher*, which entails observation without involvement in the situation, as in attendance at a public meeting or watching what is going on in a bar; when in this role, the researcher does not participate in the flow of events.

The advantage of Gans's classification is that, like Gold's, it reflects degrees of involvement and detachment, but has the advantage that it deals only with overt observation and recognizes that ethnographers do not typically adopt a single role throughout their dealings. For example, looking at the research process described by Ram (1994; see Box 14.6), it is clear that in one sense Ram was a total participant, running the firm, speaking Punjabi, and having first-hand experience of the clothing industry. However, in relation to the women shopfloor machinists, he was a total researcher, unable, because of the customary regulation of gender relationships in Asian society, to participate in the flow of events.

Table 14.1 outlines some of the working roles that organizational ethnographers take on in order to secure access to closed settings. However, it is evident from the table and the organizational ethnographies referred to in this chapter that more than one role may be involved in a particular setting. Holliday (1995), who took on the role of the apprentice, accounts for the value of her labour in exchange for access, which she estimates to have cost her approximately £2,500. Some more examples of working roles are given in Box 14.7.

Clearly these three organizational roles are overlapping and more than one may be adopted in a particular setting. They are also likely to change over time as the fieldwork progresses. It is arguably the case that, even if it were possible to adopt a single ethnographic role over the entire course of a project, it is likely that it would be undesirable, because there would be a lack of flexibility in handling situations and people, and risks of excessive involvement (and hence going native) or detachment would loom

---

Box 14.5 *What is 'going native'?*

'Going native' refers to a plight that is supposed sometimes to afflict ethnographers when they lose their sense of being a researcher and become wrapped up in the world view of the people they are studying. The prolonged immersion of ethnographers in the lives of the people they study, coupled with the commitment to seeing the social world through their eyes, lie behind the risk and actuality of going native. Going native is a potential problem for several reasons but especially because the ethnographer can lose sight of his or her position as a researcher and therefore find it difficult to develop a business angle on the collection and analysis of data.

Box 14.6 A complete participant?

One of the aims of Ram's (1994) ethnographic study of employment relations in small firms was to consider some of the ways in which employees and employers negotiated the labour process.

However, just getting into clothing companies in the West Midlands, which formed the focus of his study, was known to be 'notoriously difficult' (1994: 26). In order to gain access to the three clothing firms that formed the basis for his study, Ram relied on his family and community connections to establish the trust necessary for him to 'tap into the workplace culture' (1994: 23). Being able to speak fluent Punjabi was essential to understanding people in the workplace, but equally important for Ram in becoming an 'insider' was being able to understand how the shopfloor manufacturing industry culture worked. Crucial to this was his own first-hand experience of the clothing industry. Ram describes himself as having been involved in the clothing trade for most of his life.

> My two elder sisters and one younger sister are married into clothing families, where they work as sewing machinists and assist in the management of the in-laws'

firms. My elder brother runs a clothing manufacturing business with a cousin . . . My younger brother is in charge of the family-owned warehouse. (1994: 24)

Ram adopted an 'opportunistic' approach to the fieldwork, relying on his friends and relatives, and personal background as a member of a 'respected' family in the local Asian community. Ram's own father was in charge of 'Company A', which formed one of Ram's case studies. In addition, Ram himself had worked for this company either full- or part-time, 'since it came into being' (1994: 30). He had the power to 'sign cheques, purchase stock, make use of the firm's equipment and give instructions to the company's workers' (1994: 30) and during one period of the fieldwork his father went on holiday, leaving Ram and his younger brother to run the firm. However, despite his apparent role as a total participant, it was hard for Ram to talk to the shopfloor machinists, who were mostly women, because of the customary regulation of gender relationships within Asian society. He therefore used a chaperone, a senior female machinist, who accompanied him when he questioned individual female operatives.

Table 14.1 Three roles for organizational ethnographers

	Ethnographer's role		
	Consultant	Apprentice	Confidant
Characteristics	Competent, knowledgeable, professional A credible outsider who secures the trust of management Exchange of access for knowledge or information, often in the form of a written report or verbal presentation	Naïve, unthreatening, personable A younger person who can make him or herself useful within the organization Exchange of access for productive labour	Mature, attentive, trustworthy An impartial outsider who is able to listen to people's problems Exchange of access for psycho-social support or therapy
Examples	Ram (1994) Watson (1994*a*) Holliday (1995) Parker (2000)	Dalton (1959) Casey (1995) Perlow (1997) Freeman (2000) Parker (2000)	Collinson (1992) Crang (1994) Holliday (1995) Sharpe (1997) Delbridge (1998)

Active or Passive

Box 14.7 Finding a working role in the organization

Being an organizational ethnographer involves managing the impressions others have of you by developing a role that helps you to blend into a particular organizational setting. One way of doing this is by developing a working role, some examples of which can be found in Table 14.1. The first possibility involves the ethnographer casting him- or herself in the role of a management consultant. This involves being seen as a credible outsider, as someone who can be trusted and allowed to develop close relationships with management. Watson (1994a) illustrates how he used this role to gain access to and credibility within the organization. He agreed that his year-long access to the company would result in the development of a scheme identifying and expressing the competencies that the company could use in selecting and developing its future managers. However, there may be dangers in becoming too closely identified with managerial groupings, as this can cut off access to potentially valuable informants in other non-managerial roles within the organization. For example, Milkman (1997) describes how the very fact that she had legitimacy with both management and the union at General Motors rendered her untrustworthy in the eyes of workers whom she was most interested in studying. This was because, 'in the intensely political world of the factory, academic researchers were an entirely unknown quantity and could only be understood as servicing someone else's immediate interests' (1997: 192).

A second option involves becoming a confidant. Dalton (1959), for example, describes how a female secretary helped him to obtain confidential data about managerial salaries. In exchange, she asked Dalton, given his sociological training, to provide her with some relationship counselling to help her to work out the feelings she held towards a man she was seriously dating. Dalton obliged, in exchange for the data; the secretary married the man within a year. Similarly, Casey (1995: 203) describes how she was accorded the roles of witness, scribe, analyst, and therapist. She did not discourage the therapeutic role, as it gave her access to considerable data and insights and 'provided some catharsis for employees' who were trying to make sense of their organizational lives. Parker (2000) suggests the role of the confidant is the most productive one for revealing insights into the politics of the particular organization. He describes how his interviewees saw him as someone who would listen to their problems when others wouldn't.

A third potential role involves the researcher becoming an apprentice, adopting a more active work role in the setting. For example, Sharpe (1997) describes how she gained insider status by taking up employment as a shopfloor worker in a Japanese car manufacturing company on a six-month student job-placement contract. She explains: 'by immersing myself in the shopfloor life, I believed I would be able to offer a richer, reflexive understanding of social processes and dynamics than if I took a more conventional approach of research as an outsider or distant observer' (1997: 230).

large. This is a criticism that was levelled at Beynon (1975) in his ethnographic study of *Working for Ford* (see Box 14.8). The issue of the kind of role(s) the ethnographer adopts is therefore of considerable significance, because it has implications for field relationships in the various situations that are encountered.

Active or passive?

A further issue that is raised about any situation in which the ethnographer participates is the degree to which he or she should be or can be an active or a passive participant (Van Maanen 1978). Even when the ethnographer is in an observer-as-participant role, there may be contexts in which either participation is unavoidable or a compulsion to join in a limited way may be felt. For example, Fine's (1996) research on the work of chefs in restaurants was carried out largely by semi-structured interview. In spite of his limited participation, he found himself involved in washing up in the kitchens to help out during busy periods. Sometimes ethnographers may *feel* they have no choice but to get involved, because a failure to participate actively might indicate to members of the social setting a lack of commitment and lead to a loss of credibility. Another example is provided by Holliday (1995), who describes how in

Box 14.8 An example of going native

In the preface to the second edition of his classic study *Working for Ford* (1975: 11–12), Beynon describes how he was criticized by reviewers for 'going native' following publication of the first edition of the book. It was suggested that he had become a spokesperson for the Ford factory workers and his emotional involvement was seen as having gone a stage too far. He was accused of having a 'prolonged love affair' with 'foul mouthed shop stewards' and of having used the 'picturesque language of Billingsgate' in his 'confused, chatty, repetitive and ungrammatical' book, which was dismissed by one source as being of 'doubtful value as an objective sociological study'. The accuracy and validity of Beynon's account of working life at the Ford factory were thus called into question, and the study was dismissed by some as subjective, naive reportage.

Practical tip 👉 *being a participant observer in a familiar situation*

It is easy to gain the impression that, in order to become a participant observer, you need to gain access to an organization to which you do not belong as a member. However, it may be that you already have access to an organizational setting that could provide the basis for a more modest study using the method of participant observation. Several examples of this are provided by Spradley and McCurdy (1972), who encouraged their undergraduate students to engage in participant observation in organizations with which they were already familiar. This could include a place of work where you work either full- or part-time, or an organization where you are a volunteer or social member, such as a church group or the Territorial Army. The important thing to remember is that, if you are studying a cultural scene with which you are familiar, it is even more important to develop a high degree of self-awareness so that you don't take what you see for granted.

smaller organizations active work-role participation is more likely to be expected of the ethnographer than in larger companies where there is more space to 'hang around'. She describes how at FranTech she was given 'a variety of jobs, from typing and answering the telephone to "managerial" tasks such as auditing the production schedule and writing procedures for the BS5750' (Holliday 1995: 27). Similarly Ram (1994; see Box 14.6), in his study of family owned and managed firms in the West Midlands clothing industry, talks about helping with social security queries, housing issues, passport

problems, advising on higher education, and even tying turbans while in the field. However, the pressure to get involved raises ethical considerations, as the ethnographer may be asked to participate in an activity that involves a degree of deception or even illegal activity. We will consider ethical issues in greater detail in Chapter 25.

Sampling

The sampling of informants in ethnographic research is often a combination of convenience sampling and snowball sampling (see Chapter 4 for an explanation of these terms). Much of the time ethnographers are forced to gather information from whatever sources are available to them. Very often they face opposition or at least indifference to their research and are relieved to glean information or views from whoever is prepared to divulge such details. For example,

Dalton refers to the importance of 'conversational interviewing' as the basis for his data collection strategy. These are not interviews in the usual sense, but a series of broken and incomplete conversations that, when written up, may, according to Dalton, be 'tied together as one statement' (1959: 280). Conversational interviews are characterized by being precipitated by events. In some instances, these were prompted by Dalton, who asked managers at the end of an important meeting an open-ended question like 'how did things go?', but in others they were simply the result of overheard exchanges in shops or offices.

Ethnographers who take on a role that is closer to the observer-as-participant one rely somewhat more on formally asking for names of others who might be relevant and who could be contacted. For example, Marshall (1984) describes how, in order to identify her sample of thirty women managers, she would first make a contact within a particular company (sometimes a woman manager and sometimes a helpful member of the personnel department) and then ask him or her to suggest other potential interviewees.

In other instances, greater emphasis may be placed on how representative interviewees are of the overall population, using a *stratified sampling* approach. Casey (1995) describes how she interviewed sixty people during her research at the Hephaestus Corporation, in an effort to gain a wide sample of occupation, rank, tenure, and demographic features such as gender, race, ethnicity, and regional origin. She goes on to describe how interviewees came from a variety of occupational groupings, including engineers, computer professionals, scientists, technical analysts, financial analysts, administrators, managers, and manufacturing workers. Finally, some individuals were chosen on the basis of their strategic importance within the team or division, including the Vice-President, a union representative, a new entry employee, and a returned retiree.

Whichever of the two strategies is adopted, the question is raised as to the degree to which either can result in a representative sample of informants. Probability sampling is almost never used in ethnographic research and is even rarely employed in qualitative research based on interviews. In many cases, it is not feasible to conduct a probability sampling exercise because of the constraints of ongoing fieldwork and also because it can be difficult and often impossible to map 'the population' from which a random sample might be taken—that is, to create a sampling frame. Instead, ethnographers have to ensure that they gain access to as wide a range of individuals relevant to the research question as possible, so that many different perspectives and ranges of activity are the focus of attention.

Theoretical sampling

An alternative strategy is *theoretical sampling* (see Box 14.9), advocated by Glaser and Strauss (1967) and Strauss and Corbin (1998) in the context of an approach to qualitative data analysis they developed known as grounded theory. In Glaser and Strauss's view, because of its reliance on statistical rather than theoretical criteria, probability sampling is not appropriate to qualitative research. Theoretical sampling is meant to be an alternative strategy. As they put it: 'Theoretical sampling is done in order to discover categories and their properties and to suggest the interrelationships into a theory. Statistical

---

Box 14.9 ☼ *What is theoretical sampling?*

According to Glaser and Strauss (1967: 45), theoretical sampling 'is the process of data collection for generating theory whereby the analyst jointly collects, codes, and analyzes his data and decides what data to collect next and where to find them, in order to develop his theory as it emerges. The process of data collection is *controlled* by the emerging theory, whether substantive or formal.' This definition conveys a crucial characteristic of theoretical sampling—namely, that it is an ongoing process rather than a distinct and single stage, as it is, for example, in probability sampling. Moreover, it is important to realize

that it is not just people that are the 'objects' of sampling, as can be seen in a more recent definition: 'Data gathering driven by concepts derived from the evolving theory and based on the concept of "making comparisons", whose purpose is to go to places, people, or events that will maximize opportunities to discover variations among concepts and to densify categories in terms of their properties and dimensions' (Strauss and Corbin 1998: 201). For Charmaz (2000: 519), theoretical sampling is a 'defining property of grounded theory' and is concerned with the refinement of ideas, rather than boosting sample size.

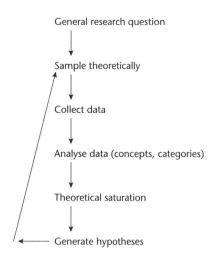

General research question

Sample theoretically

Collect data

Analyse data (concepts, categories)

Theoretical saturation

Generate hypotheses

Figure 14.2 The process of theoretical sampling

sampling is done to obtain accurate evidence on distributions of people among categories to be used in descriptions and verifications' (Glaser and Strauss 1967: 62).

Figure 14.2 outlines the main steps in theoretical sampling. The reference in Box 14.9 to 'places, people, or events' reminds us that, in ethnographic research, it is not just people who are being sampled but also events and contexts as well (see below).

In grounded theory, you carry on collecting data (observing, interviewing, collecting documents) until you have achieved *theoretical saturation* (see Box 14.10). This means that: successive interviews/observations have both formed the basis for the creation of a category and confirmed its importance; there is no need to continue with data collection in relation to that category or cluster of categories; instead, the researcher should move on and generate hypotheses out of the categories that are building up and then move on to collecting data in relation to these hypotheses. Proponents of grounded theory argue that there is a great deal of redundancy in statistical sampling. For example, committing yourself to interviewing *x* per cent of an organization's members may mean that you end up wasting time and resources because you could have confirmed the significance of a concept and/or its connections with other concepts by using a much smaller sample.

Instead, grounded theory advocates that you sample in terms of what is relevant to and meaningful for your theory. The key is to ensure you sample so as to test your emerging theoretical ideas.

The ideas of theoretical sampling and theoretical saturation will be encountered again when grounded theory is examined in greater detail in the context of qualitative data analysis in Chapter 19.

Not just people

As was pointed out in the last section, in ethnographic research sampling is not just about people but also about other things. Hammersley and Atkinson (1995) mention time and context as units that need to be considered in the context of sampling. Attending to *time* means that the ethnographer must make sure that people or events are observed at different times of the day and different days of the week. To do otherwise risks drawing inferences about certain people's behaviour or about events that are valid only for mornings or for weekdays rather than weekends. It is impossible to be an ethnographer all the time for several reasons: need to take time out to write up notes; other commitments (work or domestic); and body imperatives (eating, sleeping, and so on). When the group in question operates a different cycle from the ethnographer's normal regime (such as night shifts in a factory or hospital), the requirement to time sample may necessitate a considerable change of habit. Delbridge (1998), for example, describes how tired he felt after a day making windscreen wipers or circuit boards for televisions. In addition, he explains that 'there was real pressure and intensity during the fieldwork, particularly during the early stages when I was negotiating my informal access and acceptance into the group. I developed a nervous tic in my cheek during the first two weeks, something I have never experienced before or since' (1998: 19).

It can also be important to sample in terms of *context*. People's behaviour is influenced by contextual factors, so that it is important to ensure that such behaviour is observed in a variety of locations. For example, in his study of masculinity and workplace culture in a lorry-making factory in the north-west of England, Collinson (1992*a*) draws attention to the ways in which shopfloor workers resist managerial control, by spending time chatting and joking. By spending time with workers during lunch and unofficial breaks, in the toilet, the canteen, on the car park, on the works' bus, in the pub, and occasionally in people's homes, Collinson was able to explore these cultural practices in far more detail than if he had confined his study and himself to observing practices within formal workplace settings.

Field notes

Because of the frailties of human memory, ethnographers have to take notes based on their observations. These should be fairly detailed summaries of events and behaviour and the researcher's initial reflections on them. The notes need to specify key dimensions of whatever is observed or heard. There are some general principles.

- Write down notes, however brief, as quickly as possible after seeing or hearing something interesting.

- Write up full field notes at the very latest at the end of the day and include such details as location, who is involved, what prompted the exchange or whatever, date and time of the day, etc.

- Nowadays, people may prefer to use a tape recorder to record initial notes, but this may create a problem of needing to transcribe a lot of speech.

- Notes must be vivid and clear—you should not have to ask at a later date 'what did I mean by that?'

- You need to take copious notes, so, if in doubt, write it down. The notes may be of different types (see below).

Obviously, it can be very useful to take your notes down straight away—that is, as soon as something interesting happens. However, wandering around with a notebook and pencil in hand and scribbling notes down on a continuous basis runs the risk of making people self-conscious. It may be necessary, therefore, to develop strategies of taking small amounts of time out, though hopefully without generating the anxieties Ditton (1977) appears to have occasioned (see Box 14.3).

To some extent, strategies for taking field notes will be affected by the degree to which the ethnographer enters the field with clearly delineated research questions. As noted in Chapter 13, most qualitative research adopts a general approach of beginning with general research questions (as specifically implied by Figure 13.1), but there is considerable variation in the degree to which this is the case. Obviously, when there is some specificity to a research question, ethnographers have to orientate their observations to that research focus, but at the same time maintain a fairly open mind so that the element of flexibility that is such a strength of a qualitative research strategy is not eroded. Ditton (Box 14.3) provides an illustration of a very open-ended approach when he writes that his research 'was not set up to answer any empirical questions' (1977: 11).

Similarly, Kunda (1992) describes how he was swamped with information, partly because he did not seek to define his focus of study. His interest in any event that was occurring at the time led to the generation of a vast quantity of data. During his year in the field he 'generated thousands of pages of field-notes and interview transcripts, (produced each day from the fragmented notes hastily scribbled during and between events and interviews), collections of archival material, computer output, newsletters, papers, memos, brochures, posters, textbooks, and assorted leftovers' (1992: 237). This period of open-endedness usually cannot last long, because there is the temptation to try to record the details of absolutely everything, which can be very trying. Usually the ethnographer will begin to narrow down the focus of his or her research and to match observations to the emerging research focus. Hence, Parker (2000: 239) describes how, as each case study progressed, he began to focus down on certain key issues and ideas that began to guide his interviews and observation. This was partly a result of feeling the need to develop a framework that could enable him to cope with the 'huge quantity of ideas' and 'incoherent impressions' that he had generated. This approach is implied by the sequence suggested by Figure 13.1.

For most ethnographers, the main equipment with which they will need to supply themselves in the course of observation will be a note pad and pen (see e.g. Armstrong 1993: 28). A tape recorder can be another useful addition to one's hardware, but, as suggested above, it is likely to increase radically the amount of transcription and is possibly more obtrusive than writing notes. Most ethnographers report that after a period of time they become less obtrusive to participants in social settings, who become familiar with their presence (e.g. Atkinson 1981: 128). Speaking into a tape recorder may rekindle an awareness of the ethnographer's presence. Also, in shops, offices, and factories it may be difficult to use, without the availability of an interview room, because of the impact of extraneous noise.

Photography can be an additional source of data, which helps to stir the ethnographer's memory. Photographs, for example, can provide a graphic illustration of the organizational architecture, which is suggested to be influential in determining methods of organizational control and techniques of employee surveillance. Photography can also provide powerful illustration of organizational symbolism, enabling representation of logos, uniforms, and other visual artefacts, which can be interpreted as aspects of the organizational culture (Pondy et al. 1983). However, it is unlikely that photography will be suitable for all kinds of research; it may be less

---

Practical Tip 👉 *recording field notes*

Ethnographic field notes are traditionally handwritten and kept in a notebook or 'diary'. This medium for recording of data has a number of advantages, not least that it is flexible and discrete, the diary can be taken most places (including the toilet!), and it can be slipped out of the way into a pocket when not required. However, the main disadvantage with a handwritten diary is that at the end of the fieldwork you will be left with a huge quantity of notes (possibly not in very clear handwriting) and, if you want to analyse the data with the aid of CAQDAS (see Chapter 20) or even if you intend to quote extensively from your field notes in your dissertation, you will have to undertake the laborious and time-consuming task of typing them into word-processed form. An alternative is to consider using a palmtop computer—if you have access to one. In an organizational context, the presence of a palmtop is unlikely to make you stand out; in fact it may help you to blend into the setting and, by taking the palmtop with you into the field, you will be able to type your field notes straight into a word processor. On the down side, if you are a slow 'hunt-and-peck' typist it may be that this method of writing field notes proves too slow to be worthwhile. Also, palmtop machines are at risk of being stolen, so you will probably have either to carry the machine around with you or to find somewhere secure to keep it. In any case, the advantages and disadvantages of both methods for recording field notes should be considered carefully.

Scratch notes

appropriate for researching more abstract organizational issues, such as strategy or structure, which have fewer obvious physical manifestations.

Types of field notes

Some writers have found it useful to classify the types of field notes that are generated in the process of conducting an ethnography. The following classification is based on the similar categories suggested by Lofland and Lofland (1995) and Sanjek (1990).

- *Mental notes*—particularly useful when it is inappropriate to be seen taking notes.

- *Jotted notes* (also called *Scratch notes*)—very brief notes written down on pieces of paper or in small notebooks to jog one's memory about events that should be written up later. Lofland and Lofland (1995: 90) refer to these as being made up of 'little phrases, quotes, key words, and the like'. They need to be jotted down inconspicuously, preferably

out of sight, since detailed note taking in front of people may make them self-conscious. Crang (1994) refers to his use of scratch notes in his study of waiting staff in a restaurant (see Box 14.11).

- *Full field notes*—as soon as possible make detailed notes, which will be your main data source. They should be written at the end of the day or sooner if possible. Write as promptly and as fully as possible. Write down information about events, people, conversations, etc. Write down initial ideas about interpretation. Record impressions and feelings.

It is worth adding that field notes are often to do with the ethnographer as well as the social setting being observed. It is frequently in field notes that the ethnographer's presence is evident. For example, when Holliday (1995) describes the emotions associated with her fieldwork experience, she draws attention to her prevailing fear of incompetence, her concern about being liked, and her anxiety about whether or not to disagree with or challenge people. Precisely

---

Box 14.11 Writing field notes

Crang (1994) describes how whilst, working as a part-time waiter in a restaurant, Smoky Joe's, in the south-east of England, he decided to become a participant observer and started to take field notes about his workplace setting.

> Field notes were taken on my order pad when possible (this was not easy when very busy, so then I wrote single word 'scratch notes' and elaborated them in the break period at the end of the shift), and these were written from to produce shift-by-shift research diary entries (usually written through the morning after a shift, given that the evening rarely finished before 1.30 am). The latter included initial notes of 'factual detail' (that is, an expansion of field notes), followed by deliberately speculative reflections on these.   (1994: 676)

Crang's flexible strategy for taking field notes thus combines different types of notes that result in the eventual production of a research diary. Through them he describes the social relations with customers that helped to distinguish Smoky's from its competitors. Waiting staff were encouraged to 'put on a show'; and their uniform, a waistcoat and bowler hat, according to Crang, more closely resembled a costume. In his research diary Crang

relates the 'Tale of Dolly's socks', which illustrates the complex nature of the roles played by waiting staff.

> As I've often noted, socks are a big thing here. Wearing what are called 'jazzy' socks is pretty much compulsory and nearly all the competitions recently have had socks as their prizes! It's part of the 'fun atmosphere' don't you know. Dolly wears an extra pair of socks pinned to the back of her waistcoat, which she changes every night. Last night I finally asked her why. Oddly it felt silly to ask; it seems sensible in the context of Smoky's. Anyhow, she said she began when she won a pair, as bit of a piss-take about Mark [the manager] going on about socks. But . . . Dolly always talks and laughs about them with her tables, and the socks are a talking point; she gets great tips. But Mark thinks they are a great idea; he wants her to take the piss a bit. So laughing at his idea is actually part of the fun itself, and can't escape that. It becomes part of the atmosphere, the service, to laugh at that service. Dolly tells her customers what she told me, about Mark saying to wear jazzy socks but not saying where, and so distances herself from the idea, but she also sells Smoky's as a fun, lively place by 'rebelling' and I think she wants to . . .   (1994: 699)

because they record the quotidian as observed and experienced by ethnographers, it is here that they come to the surface. In the finished work—the ethnography in the sense of a written account of a group and its culture—the ethnographer is frequently written out of the picture (Van Maanen 1988). A major difference here is that field notes are invariably for personal consumption (Coffey 1999), whereas the written ethnography is for public consumption and has to be presented as a definitive account of the social setting and culture in question. To keep on allowing the ethnographer to surface in the text risks conveying a sense of the account as an artifice rather than an authoritative chronicle. This issue will be addressed in further detail in Chapter 24.

The end

Knowing when to stop is not an easy or straightforward matter in ethnography. Because of its unstructured nature and the absence of specific hypotheses to be tested (other than those that might emerge during data collection and analysis), there is a tendency for ethnographic research to lack a sense of an obvious end point. Traditions within anthropology have dictated that long-term continuous fieldwork should usually consist of a period of twelve months, so as to enable the study of a culture through a full seasonal cycle of activity (Davies 1999). These conventions apply to a lesser extent within organizational ethnography, where a 'long stay' in the field is still seen as crucial to securing 'insider' status (see Box 14.12 for a discussion of these issues). At some point, however, ethnographic research does come to an end! In organizational research it is likely that a deadline for data collection will be negotiated at the outset. Buchanan, Boddy, and McCalman (1988) recommend that leaving the research site, or 'getting out', is handled in such a way as to leave the door open to the possibility of future research or fieldwork visits. At this stage it is useful to confirm the conclusion of the research in writing, thanking staff for their cooperation. Sometimes, the rhythms of the ethnographer's occupational career or personal and

---

Box 14.12 Jet-plane ethnography

A note of caution is sounded by Bate (1997), who claims that there are more people writing about organizational ethnography these days but not very many people actually doing it. This means that 'thick description' turns out to be 'quick description' within many business and management research cases. As more and more researchers adopt the label of ethnography, it becomes more likely that the distinctive practices and cultural perspective associated with its practice may be lost and ethnography may come to mean 'observer-present' research (Wolcott 1995).

In what he refers to as 'jet-plane ethnography', Bate suggests that 'prolonged contact with the field' usually means a series of flying visits, rather than a long-term stay. This means, according to Bate, that organizational ethnographers rarely even take a toothbrush with them when they enter the field. The relative scarcity of organizational ethnography is partly because fieldwork is a time-consuming, personally tiresome, and stressful activity. This has led to increased interest in 'auto-ethnography' (Hayano 1979) as an alternative strategy within organizational research.

Auto-ethnography involves the ethnographic study of one's own work group. This implies that the researcher is already a complete participant in the organization under study. Indeed, Spradley and McCurdy (1972) suggest that the ethnographer's own place of work may even have special advantages as a research site, such as ease of access and already formed relationships with key informants. This may make the time needed to conduct the research shorter. However, this ethnographic approach is not without its own difficulties as, the more familiar you are with a social situation, the less you may be able to recognize the tacit cultural rules that are at work.

family life will necessitate withdrawal from the field or research funding commitments will bring fieldwork to a close. Such factors include: the end of a period of sabbatical leave; the need to write up and submit a doctoral thesis by a certain date; or funding for research drawing to a close.

Moreover, ethnographic research can be highly stressful for many reasons: the nature of the topic, which places the fieldworker in stressful situations; the marginality of the researcher in the social setting and the need constantly to manage a front; and the prolonged absence from one's normal life that is often necessary. The ethnographer may feel that he or she has simply had enough. A further possibility that may start to bring about moves to bring fieldwork to a close is that the ethnographer may begin to feel that the research questions on which he or she has decided to concentrate are answered, so that there are no new data worth generating. The ethnographer may even feel a strong sense of *déjà vu* towards the end of data collection. Altheide (1980: 310) has written that his decision to leave the various news organizations in which he had conducted ethnographic research was often motivated by 'the recurrence of familiar situations and the feeling that little worthwhile was being revealed'. In the language of grounded theory, all the researcher's categories are thoroughly *saturated*, although Glaser and Strauss's approach would invite you to be certain that there are no new questions to be asked of the area you are investigating, or no new comparisons to be made.

The reasons for bringing ethnographic research to a close can involve a wide range of factors from the personal to matters of research design. Whatever the reason, disengagement has to be *managed*. For one thing, this means that promises must be kept, so that, if you promised a report to an organization as a condition of entry, that promise should not be forgotten. It also means that ethnographers must provide good explanations for their departure. Members of a social setting always know that the researcher is a temporary fixture, but over a long period of time, and especially if there was genuine participation in activities within that setting, people may forget that the ethnographer's presence is finite. The farewells have to be managed and in an orderly fashion.

Also, the ethnographer's *ethical* commitments must not be forgotten, such as the need to ensure that persons and settings are anonymized. It is common practice within organizational ethnography to change the name of a company in order to protect the anonymity of the organization, as well as the names of individuals who participated in the study— even place names and locations may be changed. For example, Dalton (1959) protected the anonymity of his 'intimates' or informants by changing the place names and locations associated with the study. He also declined to disclose the nature of his formal work-roles at Milo and Fruhling, as he felt this would endanger the exposure of 'intimates' to their superiors. Whatever happens, it is wise to reach an agreement with senior members of the organization before disclosing the identity of an organization and it may be less threatening for senior managers and employers to offer anonymity as an explicit aspect of the access agreement.

Can there be a feminist ethnography?

In this final section we will review some of the central debates within feminist research within the social sciences and business research and relate them to the ethnographic tradition. However, it must be noted that it remains relatively unusual in business and management research for ethnography to be conducted in a way that involves applying a gender perspective with the aim of promoting the interests of women. Hence, in business and management research, there are several examples of ethnographies done by women and of women's work (e.g. Cavendish 1982; Westwood 1984; and Pollert 1981; see Box 14.13) but there are very few ethnographic studies that are informed by feminist tenets of the kind outlined in Chapter 13. However, it is our view that feminist research could inform innovative research in

---

Box 14.13 An ethnography of work from a woman's perspective

In her study of women employed in unskilled, manual jobs in Britain, Pollert (1981) set out to understand the lived experience of working under modern capitalism from a woman's perspective. The study is based on informal interviews and observation on the shopfloor of a Bristol tobacco factory in 1972. 'It is a glimpse into the everyday working lives of the young girls and older women who worked there: about how they got on with their jobs, their bosses and each other—and in a background sense, their boyfriends, their husbands and their families—and how all these strands wove together into their experience and consciousness' (1981: 6).

Pollert was not employed in the factory and was open about her status as a researcher. In this sense her role was one of observer-as-participant, according to Gold's classification scheme. Being a female researcher was, according to Pollert, vitally important to the study and an important factor in breaking down barriers with women workers. However, whilst she was a woman amongst women, she was also middle class, had a middle-class, accent, and was not there to earn money—factors that clearly set her apart from the women. To begin with she was 'naturally scrutinized with a mixture of hostility, suspicion

and curiosity' (1981: 7) and was called upon to answer more questions than she asked. In managing to break down some of these barriers, Pollert explains that she tried to be open with her opinions, in wanting to argue with and challenge attitudes as well as to learn, and not to set herself up as a 'reporter' who was interested in 'how the masses think'. Interestingly, unlike many male organizational ethnographers, Pollert kept a degree of social distance from her research subjects, having very little direct involvement with home, community, and social life. 'It was simply not on to suggest we meet for a drink in a pub, the normal "neutral" meeting-place for men.' Instead what she learned about home and social life was filtered through factory experience.

Pollert's research goes some of the way towards being what could be described as a feminist ethnography (she focuses on the working lives of women and seeks to understand the women from their own perspective and in their own context). However, as Pollert managed the power relations between herself and the women mainly as a one-way process, the study does not conform to the ideals of feminist ethnography in this respect.

---

this area by helping to expose the gendered nature of management and organizations (Collinson and Hearn 1996). This would help to counterbalance the tendency for organizational ethnographers to interpret male-dominated settings from their point of view as a male researcher, using their own gender to reinforce the authenticity of their account (see Box 14.14).

The title of this section is taken from a widely cited article by Judith Stacey (1988). It is a rebuttal of the view that there is and/or can be a distinctively feminist ethnography that combines the distinctive strengths of ethnography with a feminist position. Reinharz (1992) sees feminist ethnography as significant in terms of feminism, because:

• it documents women's lives and activities, which were previously largely seen as marginal and subsidiary to men's;

• it understands women from their perspective, so that the tendency that 'trivializes females' activities

and thoughts, or interprets them from the standpoint of men in the society or of the male researcher' (1992: 52) is militated against; and

• it understands women in context.

However, such commitments and practices go only part of the way. Of great significance to feminist researchers is the question of whether the research allows for a non-exploitative relationship between researcher and researched. One of the main elements of such a strategy is that the ethnographer does not treat the relationship as a one-way process of extracting information from others, but actually provides something in return. However, Stacey (1988) argues, on the basis of her fieldwork experience, that the various situations she encountered as a feminist ethnographer placed her,

in situations of inauthenticity, dissimilitude, and potential, perhaps inevitable betrayal, situations that I now believe are inherent in fieldwork method. For no matter how welcome,

Box 14.14 'Not one of the guys': ethnography in a male-dominated setting

In business and management research, gender and sexuality in the workplace constitute important subjects of study in their own right. However, these topics also raise particular methodological issues for the organizational ethnographer. The male-dominated nature of many typical business and management fieldwork settings, such as factory shopfloors or management boardrooms, means that gender and sexuality can often be an important and highly visible dynamic in the fieldwork encounter. Several organizational ethnographies, such as Dalton (1959), Collinson (1992*a*), and Watson (1994*a*), have explicitly focused on the masculine nature of these organizational settings: Collinson (1992*a*) writing about the collectivist, masculine practices of 'piss taking' and swearing on the shopfloor, and Watson drawing attention to the jokes and 'dirty talking' that reinforced his inclusion amongst managers at ZTC Ryland. This emphasis on jokes, humour, swearing, and 'becoming one of the lads' could be taken to suggest that the male ethnographer has privileged

'insider' status to a masculine subculture and is, as a result, able to produce an ethnography that is not only more entertaining but also more 'real'.

However, Emma Bell (1999) has argued that it is dangerous to assume that this necessarily enhances the authenticity of the research data. Even though female ethnographers may experience a work reality that differs from men in many ways, in terms of the experiences and opportunities that are available to them, it should not automatically be assumed that this necessarily generates worse or indeed better data. Instead, the gender of the researcher should be seen as a dynamic characteristic (Warren 1988), the significance of which changes as the research progresses. Bell concludes that it is necessary to dismantle some of the stereotypical gender myths that are applied to male and female ethnographers in order to appreciate the complexity of gendered fieldwork relationships.

---

even enjoyable the fieldworker's presence may appear to 'natives', fieldwork represents an intrusion and intervention into a system of relationships, a system of relationships that the researcher is far freer to leave.   (1988: 23)

Stacey also argues that, when the research is written up, it is the feminist ethnographer's interpretations and judgements that come through and have authority.

However, Reinharz (1992: 74–5) argues that, although ethnographic fieldwork relationships may sometimes *seem* manipulative, a clear undercurrent of reciprocity often lies beneath them. The researcher, in other words, may offer help or advice to her research participants, or she may be exhibiting reciprocity by

giving a public airing to normally marginalized voices (although the ethnographer is always the mouthpiece for such voices and may be imposing a particular 'spin' on them). Moreover, it seems extreme to abandon feminist ethnography on the grounds that the ethnographer cannot fulfil all possible obligations simultaneously. Indeed, this would be a recipe for the abandonment of all research, feminist or otherwise. What is also crucial is transparency—transparency in the feminist ethnographer's dealings with the women she studies and transparency in the account of the research process. Nonetheless, it is clear that the question of whether there is or can be a feminist ethnography is a matter of ongoing debate.

K **KEY POINTS**

- Ethnography is a term that refers to both a method and the written product of research based on that method.

- The ethnographer is typically a participant observer who also uses non-observational methods and sources such as interviewing and documents.

- The ethnographer may adopt an overt or a covert role, but the latter carries ethical difficulties.

- The negotiation of access to a social setting can be a lengthy process. It may depend on establishing an exchange relationship.

- Key informants frequently play an important role for the ethnographer, but care is needed to ensure that their impact on the direction of research is not excessive.

- There are several different ways of classifying the kinds of role that the ethnographer may assume. These are not necessarily mutually exclusive.

- Sampling considerations differ from those addressed in the context of quantitative research, in that issues of representativeness are emphasized less.

- Field notes are important for prompting the ethnographer's memory.

Q **QUESTIONS FOR REVIEW**

- Is it possible to distinguish ethnography and participant observation?

- How does participant observation differ from structured observation?

Organizational ethnography

- To what extent do participant observation and ethnography rely solely on observation?

- What distinguishes organizational ethnography from other forms of ethnography?

Access

- 'Covert ethnography obviates the need to gain access to inaccessible settings and therefore has much to recommend it.' Discuss.

- Examine some articles in business and management journals in which ethnography and participant observation figure strongly. Was the researcher in an overt or a covert role? How was access achieved?

- Does the problem of access finish once access to a chosen setting has been achieved?

- What might be the role of key informants in ethnographic research? Is there anything to be concerned about when using them?

Roles for ethnographers

- Compare Gold's and Gans's schemes for classifying participant observer roles.
- What is meant by 'going native'?
- Should ethnographers be active or passive in the settings in which they conduct research?

Sampling

- What is snowball sampling?
- What is theoretical sampling?
- How crucial is the idea of theoretical saturation to theoretical sampling?

Field notes

- Why are field notes important for ethnographers?
- Why is it useful to distinguish between different types of field notes?

The end

- How do you decide when to complete the data collection phase in ethnographic research?

Can there be a feminist ethnography?

- What are the main ingredients of feminist ethnography?

15 Interviewing in qualitative research

CHAPTER GUIDE

This chapter is concerned with the interview in qualitative research. The term *qualitative interview* is often used to capture the different types of interview that are used in qualitative research. Such interviews tend to be far less structured than the kind of interview associated with survey research, which was discussed in Chapter 5 in terms of structured interviewing. This chapter is concerned with individual interviews in qualitative research; the focus group method, which is a form of interview but with several people, is discussed in the next chapter. The two forms of qualitative interviewing discussed in this chapter

are unstructured and semi-structured interviewing. The chapter explores:

- the differences between structured interviewing and qualitative interviewing;

- the main characteristics of and differences between unstructured and semi-structured interviewing; this entails a recognition that the two terms refer to extremes and that in practice a wide range of interviews with differing degrees of structure lie between the extremes;

- how to devise and use an interview guide for semi-structured interviewing;

- the different kinds of question that can be asked in an interview guide;

- the importance of tape-recording and transcribing qualitative interviews;

- approaches to sampling in studies using qualitative interviews;

- the significance of qualitative interviewing in feminist research;

- the advantages and disadvantages of qualitative interviewing relative to participant observation.

Introduction

The interview is probably the most widely employed method in qualitative research. Of course, as we have seen in Chapter 14, ethnography usually involves a substantial amount of interviewing and this factor undoubtedly contributes to the widespread use of the interview by qualitative researchers. However, it is the flexibility of the interview that makes it so attractive. Since ethnography entails an extended period of participant observation, which is very disruptive for researchers because of the sustained absence(s) required from work and/or family life, research based more or less exclusively on interviews is a highly attractive alternative for the collection of qualitative data. Interviewing, the transcription of interviews, and the analysis of transcripts are all very time-consuming, but they can be more readily accommodated into researchers' personal lives.

In Box 5.3 several different types of interview were briefly outlined. The bulk of the types outlined there—other than the structured interview and the standardized interview—are ones associated with qualitative research. *Focus groups* and *group interviewing* will be examined in the next chapter and the remaining forms of interview associated with qualitative research will at various points be explored in this chapter. However, in spite of the apparent proliferation of terms describing types of interview in qualitative research, the two main types are the *unstructured interview* and the *semi-structured interview*. Researchers sometimes employ the term *qualitative interview* to encapsulate these two types of interview. There is clearly the potential for considerable confusion here, but the types and definitions offered in Box 5.3 are meant to inject a degree of consistency of terminology. One final point to note at the outset is that, in qualitative research, no single interview stands alone. 'It has meaning to the researcher only in terms of other interviews and observations' (Whyte 1953: 22).

Differences between the structured interview and qualitative research interviews

Qualitative interviewing is usually very different from interviewing in quantitative research in a number of ways.

- The approach tends to be much less structured in qualitative research. In quantitative research, the approach is structured to maximize the reliability and validity of measurement of key concepts. It is also more structured because the researcher has a clearly specified set of research questions that are to be investigated. The structured interview is designed to answer these questions. Instead, in qualitative research, there is an emphasis on greater generality in the formulation of initial research ideas and on interviewees' own perspectives.

- In qualitative interviewing, there is much greater interest in the interviewee's point of view; in quantitative research, the interview reflects the researcher's concerns. This contrast is a direct outcome of the previous one. For example, Ram (1994) describes his qualitative interviewing style as owing little to the 'textbook' approach, which 'exhorts the interviewer to remain aloof while seeking to extract information from the respondent' (1994: 32), as it would have been 'absurd and counter-productive' to assume this degree of social distance from family and friends whom he had known for years.

- In qualitative interviewing, 'rambling' or going off at tangents is often encouraged—it gives insight into what the interviewee sees as relevant and important; in quantitative research, it is usually regarded as a nuisance and discouraged.

- In qualitative interviewing, interviewers can depart significantly from any schedule or guide that is being used. They can ask new questions that follow up interviewees' replies and can vary the order of questions and even the wording of questions. In quantitative research, none of these things should be done, because they will compromise the standardization of the interview process and hence the reliability and validity of measurement.

- As a result, qualitative interviewing tends to be flexible (see Box 15.3 for an example), responding to the direction in which interviewees take the interview and perhaps adjusting the emphases in the research as a result of significant issues that

Box 15.1 Unstructured interviewing

Whyte (1953) presents an example of a 'non-directive', or unstructured, interview conducted during 1952 during a one-day visit to the Chicago plant of the Inland Steel Container Company. The aim of this interview was to catch up with developments in union–management relations that had taken place since his last visit to the plant and since Whyte's publication of a book on this subject. Whyte suggests that the book had been received favourably at the plant, as it showed management and union officials in a positive light. Publication was marked by a public meeting and every worker in the plant had been presented with a copy. This in Whyte's view helped to ensure positive rapport with the respondent on the day in question.

The interview was with Columbus Gary, vice-president of the union and chairman of its grievance committee. It was held in the management conference room of the plant. Whyte explains, 'Gary was neither a complete stranger to me nor a close acquaintance'. He goes on to suggest that he had no problem in establishing rapport with Gary, stating that Gary 'was willing to tell me anything I wanted to know' (1953: 16). Then follows a section of the verbatim interview with Gary, for which Whyte provides a commentary that involves analysing his own interviewing technique, including such 'mistakes' as presenting a leading question.

Although Whyte suggests that he was following the 'rules' of non-directive interviewing (by concentrating on listening, not interrupting or arguing with the informant, and periodically restating what had been said from time to time), he also suggests that in certain important respects he was not. In particular, Whyte attempted to direct Gary towards an account of the social process. Specifically, how did the problem come to the attention of the person concerned, and what were the steps involved in the action taken?

Right at the outset I sought to move him from a statement of sentiments to an account of interpersonal events. I was interested not only in what happened at a particular time, but in how that event related to others that took place before or afterwards. For all these events I wanted answers to the question: Who did what, with whom, and where? (1953: 21–2)

Whyte concludes that the interviewer must learn to recognize the difference between a statement of substance and an account of process in order to be able to guide an informant from one to the other. This enables the reconstruction of events by asking interviewees to consider how a sequence of events evolved. Therefore, we can see that, although Whyte describes his approach to organizational interviewing as non-directive, it is not as unstructured as it at first seems.

emerge in the course of interviews. By contrast, structured interviews are typically inflexible, because of the need to standardize the way in which each interviewee is dealt with.

- In qualitative interviewing, the researcher wants rich, detailed answers; in quantitative research the interview is supposed to generate answers that can be coded and processed quickly.

- In qualitative interviewing, the interviewee may be interviewed on more than one and sometimes even several occasions. In quantitative research, unless the research is longitudinal in character, the person will be interviewed on one occasion only.

Unstructured and semi-structured interviewing

However, qualitative interviewing varies a great deal in the approach taken by the interviewer. The two major types were mentioned at the beginning of the chapter.

- The almost totally *unstructured interview*. Here the researcher uses at most an *aide-mémoire* as a brief set of prompts to him- or herself to deal with a certain range of topics. There may be just a single question that the interviewer asks and the interviewee is then allowed to respond freely, with the interviewer simply responding to points that seem worthy of being followed up. Unstructured interviewing tends to be very similar in character to a conversation (Burgess 1984). See Box 15.1 for an illustration of an unstructured interview style.

- A *semi-structured interview*. The researcher has a list of questions on fairly specific topics to be covered, often referred to as an *interview guide*, but the interviewee has a great deal of leeway in how to reply. Questions may not follow on exactly in the way outlined on the schedule. Questions that are not included in the guide may be asked as the interviewer picks up on things said by interviewees. But, by and large, all the questions will be asked and a similar wording will be used from interviewee to interviewee. For example, Willman et al. (2002) carried out semi-structured interviews with traders in financial markets in London. The interviews covered a range of issues, including motivations, emotions, trading strategies, and questions about organizational culture. They also included questions about control incentives and management style. In this analysis, the researchers focused

on sections of the interview that dealt with the aversion and seeking of risk; this formed the basis for their conclusion that traders focus on avoiding losses rather than making gains. Boxes 15.2 and 15.3 provide further examples of these features.

In both cases, the interview process is *flexible*. Also, the emphasis must be on how the interviewee frames and understands issues and events—that is, what the interviewee views as important in explaining and understanding events, patterns, and forms of behaviour. Thus, Leidner (1993) describes the interviewing she carried out in a McDonald's restaurant as involving a degree of structure, but adds that the interviews also 'allowed room to pursue topics of particular interest to the workers' (1993: 238). Milkman (1997), in her study of auto workers at General Motors, describes how in the second stage of her research she interviewed a total of thirty buyout takers and workers, using a 'very general interview guide', trying to be as casual as she could, and never discouraging anyone from going off on tangents. Most interviews were with individuals. However, in a few cases workers invited their friends from the plant as well. Milkman claims that 'these turned out to be among the best interviews, since they developed a group dynamic in which my presence often became marginal' (1997: 198). In an interview study of secretarial work involving almost 500 office workers, Pringle (1988) followed an oral history format. She explains:

We did not restrict the subject matter to work. Initially people were asked to start by talking about a typical day . . . Over time, our interests shifted or became more focused on the relation

Box 15.2 Semi-structured interviewing

Spender (1989) carried out research investigating 'industry recipes'—the knowledge base that those socialized into an industry take to be professional common sense. His interviews were with managers in firms within three industries; they included iron founders, dairies, and fork-lift truck rental companies. After identifying a sample of firms using trade publications, buyers' guides, and the Yellow Pages, Spender set up all the interviews over the telephone.

There were three steps involved in this process. The first step in getting an interview involved asking for the senior manager by name, increasing the chance of being put straight through by the secretary. The second step was to stress the legitimacy of the research by drawing on the association with an academic institution, and the non-commercial, confidential nature of the research. The third

step was to make the research sound unthreatening and simple, by using questions such as 'I am looking into the problems of running firms in this industry and wonder if I could come and talk to you about it for half an hour?' (1989: 79) Having set up the interview, Spender's approach is 'focused' or semi-structured, as 'it combines unstructured interviews with a loose pattern of agreement with the interviewee about the context of enquiry' (1989: 79).

The interviews are focused in several ways before they start. First by introducing the interview as 'about the problems of running the firm'; secondly, by insisting on meeting senior managers with strategic responsibilites, and thirdly, by interviewing the managers at their workplaces, keeping them in the physical context of their organizational role.

Box 15.3 Flexibility in semi-structured interviewing

Between February and April 1990, Prasad (1993) interviewed thirty-four employees as part of her study of computerization at the Paragon Corporation. Interviews focused on understanding employees' experiences of computerized work. Each one lasted between forty-five minutes and one and a half hours and were 'semi-structured'. Prasad explains that in some cases the interviews corroborated her own assessment of the situation, whilst in others they offered a different interpretation that helped her to rethink her analysis. This meant that 'there was no one set of questions administered to all interviewees and no specific sequencing of the issues raised' (1993: 1408). She writes that the interviews were informed by the idea of 'grand tour' and 'mini tour' questions (Spradley and McCurdy 1972).

The somewhat broad and exploratory grand tour questions gave the interviews focus and were developed keeping my research interests in mind. For the most part, grand tour questions got interviewees talking about aspects of computerization and related organizational issues. If the interviewee touched on something that was closely connected with the symbolism of computers or seemed particularly concerned about certain aspects of computerization, I pursued those areas through the use of more specific and detailed mini tour questions. (Prasad 1993: 1409)

between different parts of their lives, on home and family, and their views on a range of political and social issues, and on their notions of a 'good boss' and 'good secretary'. (1988: 270)

Once again, we must remember that qualitative research is *not* quantitative research with the numbers missing. The kinds of interviewing carried out in qualitative research are typical also of *life history* and *oral history* interviewing (see Box 15.4).

The two different types of interview in qualitative research are extremes and there is quite a lot of variability between them, but most qualitative interviews are close to one type or the other. In neither case does the interviewer slavishly follow a schedule, as is done in quantitative research interviewing; but in semi-structured interviews the interviewer does follow a script to a certain extent. The choice of

Box 15.4 Life history and oral history interviews

Two special forms of the kind of interview associated with qualitative research are the *life history* and *oral history* interviews.

The *life history* interview is generally associated with the *life history method*, where it is often combined with various kinds of personal documents like diaries, photographs, and letters. This method is often referred to alternatively as the *biographical method*. A life history interview invites the subject to look back in detail across his or her entire life course. It has been depicted as documenting 'the inner experience of individuals, how they interpret, understand, and define the world around them' (Faraday and Plummer 1979: 776). However, the method is very much associated with the life history interview, which is a kind of unstructured interview covering the totality of an individual's life.

Life history methodology is suggested to be particularly useful in situations when the researcher is attempting to understand the complex processes whereby people make sense of their organizational reality. Musson (1998) suggests that it can help to provide answers to such research questions as: How does socialization take place in organizations? How are organizational careers created and maintained? How do certain managerial styles come to be accepted as natural? What influence do leaders and founders have on organizational culture?

However, despite the suggested relevance of life history interviews to organizational research, there has been only a trickle of empirical studies that have used this approach over the years. Bowen and Hisrich (1986) suggest that a very 'uneven picture' emerges of the female entrepreneur owing to a lack of published research. The few studies that exist tend to employ 'very small samples' and 'seldom attempt to be representative' (1986: 404). They suggest that longitudinal studies following the careers of entrepreneurs over time would enable development of a life cycle conception of the careers of female entrepreneurs and they recommend the use of a life history approach.

The life history method has tended to suffer because of an erroneous treatment of the life in question as a sample of one and hence of limited generalizability. However, it has certain clear strengths from the point of view of the qualitative researcher: its unambiguous emphasis on the point of view of the life in question and a clear commitment to the processual aspects of social life, showing how events unfold and interrelate in people's lives. The terms *life history* and *life story* are sometimes employed interchangeably, but Miller (2000: 19) suggests that the latter is an account someone gives about his or her life and that a life history dovetails a life story with other sources, such as diaries and letters (of the kind discussed in Chapter 18).

An example of the life history interview approach in organizational research is provided by Musson in the context of her doctoral research on how general medical practitioners in the UK experienced and understood the 1990 health-care reforms. As the research progressed, it became increasingly apparent to Musson that life histories of key actors were significant in the way that changes were understood and experienced.

> I directed the storytelling process to a large extent by asking individuals to tell me about when and how their understanding of the purpose of the organization shifted... These stories differed from focusing on the history of an individual's marital difficulties, to telling me a story about an individual patient and the way she was treated by the GPs in the practice... Likewise, I asked people to tell me about their lives in previous organizations and how they had experienced these; what they had found rewarding, constraining or difficult to make sense of, and how this differed in their current organization. Again, the open ended structure of the narratives allowed people to introduce subjects of major importance to them. (Musson 1998: 16).

Miller (2000) distinguishes between certain aspects of life history inteviews. One distinction has to do with age and life course effects. The former relates to the ageing process, in the sense of biological ageing and its effects and manifestations; life course effects are the patterned features associated with the stages of the life course. He also points to the need to distinguish cohort effects, which are the unique clusters of experiences associated with a specific generation.

Miller suggests there has been a resurgence of interest in recent years, and Chamberlayne, Bornat, and Wengraf (2000) argue that there has been a recent 'turn to biographical methods'. To a large extent, the revival of the approach derives from a growth of interest in the role and significance of agency in social life. The revival is largely associated with the growing use of life story interviews and especially those that are often referred to in association with *narrative analysis* (see Chapter 19). Moreover, the growing use of such interviews has come to be associated less and less with the study of a single life (or indeed just one or two lives) and increasingly with the study of several lives.

An *oral history* interview is usually somewhat more specific in tone in that the subject is asked to reflect upon specific events or periods in the past. It too is sometimes combined with other sources, such as documents. The chief problem with the oral history interview (which it shares with the life history interview) is the possibility of bias introduced by memory lapses and distortions (Grele 1998). On the other hand, oral history testimonies have allowed the voices to come through of groups that are typically marginalized in historical research (a point that also applies to life history interviews), either because of their lack of power or because they are typically regarded as unexceptional (Samuel 1976).

whether to veer towards one type rather than the other is likely to be affected by a variety of factors.

- Researchers who are concerned that the use of even the most rudimentary interview guide will not allow genuine access to the world views of members of a social setting or of people sharing common attributes are likely to favour an unstructured interview.

- If the researcher is beginning the investigation with a fairly clear focus, rather than a very general notion of wanting to do research on a topic, it is likely that the interviews will be semi-structured ones, so that the more specific issues can be addressed. More structure is also likely to be imposed when the researcher has a clear idea of how the data will be analysed. In the case of using interviews to generate data about critical incidents (see Box 15.5), a set of subject themes can be used to guide respondents who are asked to recall examples of specific events that illustrate each theme.

- If more than one person is to carry out the fieldwork, in order to ensure a modicum of comparability of interviewing style, it is likely that semi-structured interviewing will be preferred. See Boxes 15.2 and 15.3 for examples.

- If you are doing multiple-case-study research, you are likely to find that you will need some structure in order to ensure cross-case comparability. Certainly, all Bryman's qualitative research on different kinds of organization has entailed semi-structured interviewing and it is not a coincidence that this is because most of it has been multiple-case-study research (e.g. Bryman, Haslam, and Webb 1994—see Box 13.8; Bryman, Gillingwater, and McGuinness 1996).

In business and management research there are some additional considerations that relate to qualitative interviewing. Interviewing managers often raises specific issues; the status and power held, particularly at a senior level, mean that gaining access to this group of people can be extremely difficult, and arranging a mutually convenient time in which to conduct an interview, which may last several hours, even more so. Given the number of outside requests for information and assistance that most managers receive, it is particularly important to structure a request for interview in a way that is most likely to lead to a favourable response. A request for interview may be made either by letter or by telephone. Healey and Rawlinson (1993) recommend a dual approach: first make a telephone call, 'fishing' for a named person who is most likely to be appropriate for the interview, then follow this up with an introductory letter. In the letter, it may be appropriate to enclose a short outline of the nature and purpose of the project and an indication of how the findings might be useful to the respondent. If the research is supported by a high-profile sponsoring organization (e.g. a company or university business school) it may be worth enclosing a letter from a senior person within this organization endorsing the aims of the research. Finally, a telephone call made a few days after receipt of the letter can provide an opportunity for the researcher to deal with any queries the manager may have. The most important thing to remember, however, is that 'polite persistence' is often crucial (Healey and Rawlinson 1993).

Box 15.5 An example of the use of critical incident technique

Curran and Blackburn (1994) used a critical incident approach to examine the relationships between small and large businesses and their local economies. This involved focusing on particular events as a means of exploring how small business owner-managers related to their social and economic community. Forty-five owner-managers from a diverse range of businesses, including computer services, employment, secretarial and training agencies, and garages and vehicle repairers, were interviewed about a range of critical incidents that they had experienced over the past two years. Five themes were selected as a basis for exploring how owners articulate with their environments: customers and the market; investment and finance; co-directors and partners; family and kinship; and local authority connections and involvements. Respondents were sent the list of potential themes for discussion prior to the interview. This was a way of encouraging more detailed narratives than would have been possible if the subjects were first raised in the interview. Each theme was introduced by the interviewer, who gave a general preamble. For example, in the case of gaining or losing a major customer the interviewer would say:

> The success of any business greatly depends on its customers. Most businesses lose or gain a major customer from time to time and this can create problems—especially losing an important customer. We would like you to highlight any people who were involved, consulted or who helped you in this situation.   (1994: 107)

If the respondent had experienced an event like this in the previous two years, he or she was asked to talk through what happened, how he or she had coped, and with whom he or she had discussed it. Curran and Blackburn found that losing a major customer sometimes led owner-managers to seek outside help to resolve the problem; on other occasions they chose to deal with the problem themselves without any outside help. Critical incidents also revealed the conflicting pressures, particularly for female owner-managers, in managing business and family life. One explained how she had worked up to the last possible moment before she went into labour for the birth of one of her children:

> I was doing someone's wages when I went into labour and this poor man kept looking at me and saying 'Don't you think you'd better go now?' and I said 'No it's all right, I'll just finish the wages . . . Oh dear! Hang on a minute' [indicating a response to a pain contraction]. (Owner-manager, employment agency, Suffolk; 1994: 112)

The researchers suggest that critical incident analysis enables increased understanding of the reasons why owner-managers use links outside the business. They conclude that owner-managers tend to have relatively small networks and few external contacts such as accountants and bank managers. In addition, owner-managers rarely use non-economic contacts based on family, kinship, or social groupings for business information or advice. This example is illustrative of a more qualitative application of the critical incident technique than was used in the classic study of job satisfaction by Herzberg, Mausner, and Snyderman (1959) discussed in Chapter 5.

Interviewing within organizations also involves encroaching on an individual's work time and in some cases it may not be possible to take people away from their work during the hours of their employment. Managers may be unwilling to grant lower-level employees the time away from productive activity that is needed to conduct an interview, or there may simply be no one available to cover their duties. When employees are paid on an hourly basis, this becomes a particularly important issue. For example, in her research into work roles in restaurants, Elaine Hall (1993) wanted to interview a sample of the servers (waiters and waitresses) who worked in the five selected restaurants. To do this, she had to approach servers on duty to schedule individual interviews for off-duty times, usually before or after their work shift. This relied on servers' willingness to devote an hour of their unpaid time to this task.

However, sometimes managers demonstrate a willingness to enable the interview process despite the cost implications. For example, Freeman (2000) describes how one of the companies involved in the research provided release time for managers and workers so that she could interview them on

---

Practical Tip 👉 *where to conduct an interview?*

Finding a quiet, private space in which to conduct an interview uninterrupted can be one of the most difficult tasks for the qualitative researcher. Many organizations will struggle to find you a spare room that is not being used and is even remotely suitable. Think carefully before agreeing to interview someone in their own office; are there likely to be frequent telephone calls or interruptions that make the interview difficult? Also, traffic, aircraft, or machinery can contribute to background noise that can make the tape-recorded speech inaudible. It is a good idea to spend some time in the room prior to the interview; do a speech recording to test the acoustics of the room and

carefully position the furniture; if there is noise from outside the room, think about closing doors or windows. Similarly, you may wish to turn off a noisy heater. Position the microphone as near to your interviewees as possible and make sure that they are unlikely to knock it. You will, of course, need to balance these issues against the comfort and convenience of your interviewee (it would not be feasible to insist on having all the windows closed in a hot factory in the middle of summer!) But do not be afraid to explain what you need in order to conduct the interview, even though you may have to be prepared to compromise when it comes to actually getting it.

---

company premises. Similarly, Bell and colleagues (2001) were able to conduct a group interview with employees in one plant because the section manager and his team agreed to cease production for a period of time, in order to allow the interview to take place. However, this is not to suggest that it is only the interviewer who benefits from the interview process. Some interviewees, particularly senior managers, may welcome the opportunity to offload issues and concerns or think through a problem in a structured way, particularly if they are able to see a copy of the transcript afterwards. In these instances the interview is very much a two-way process, with both parties gaining something beneficial from it.

Preparing an interview guide

The idea of an interview guide is much less specific than the notion of a structured interview schedule. In fact, the term can be employed to refer to the brief list of memory prompts of areas to be covered that is often employed in unstructured interviewing or to the somewhat more structured list of issues to be addressed or questions to be asked in semi-structured interviewing. It is increasingly common in published accounts of research for researchers to offer to provide a copy of the interview guide or schedule to interested readers upon request. This can help to strengthen the dependability of the research

(see Chapter 13). What is crucial is that the questioning allows interviewers to glean the ways in which research participants view their social world and that there is flexibility in the conduct of the interviews. The latter is as much if not more to do with the conduct of the interview than with the nature of the interview guide as such.

In preparing for qualitative interviews, Lofland and Lofland (1995: 78) suggest asking yourself the question 'Just what about this thing is puzzling me?' This can be applied to each of the research questions you have generated or it may be a mechanism for generating some research questions. They suggest that your puzzlement can be stimulated by various activities: random thoughts in different contexts, which are then written down as quickly as possible; discussions with colleagues, friends, and relatives; and, of course, the existing literature on the topic. The formulation of the research question(s) should not be so specific that alternative avenues of enquiry that might arise during the collection of fieldwork data are closed off. Such premature closure of your research focus would be inconsistent with the process of qualitative research (Figure 13.1), with the emphasis on the world view of the people you will be interviewing, and with the approaches to qualitative data analysis like grounded theory that emphasize the importance of not starting out with too many preconceptions (see Chapter 19). Gradually, an order and structure will begin to emerge in your meanderings around your research question(s) and will form the basis for your interview guide.

You should also consider 'What do I need to know in order to answer each of the research questions I'm interested in?' This means trying to get an appreciation of what the interviewee sees as significant and important in relation to each of your topic areas. Thus, your questioning will need to cover the areas that you need but from the perspective of your interviewees. This means that, even though qualitative research is predominantly unstructured, it is rarely so unstructured that the researcher cannot at least specify a research focus.

Some basic elements in the preparation of your interview guide will be:

- create a certain amount of order on the topic areas, so that your questions about them flow reasonably well, but be prepared to alter the order of questions during the actual interview;

- formulate interview questions or topics in a way that will help you to answer your research questions (but try not to make them too specific);

- try to use a language that is comprehensible and relevant to the people you are interviewing;

- just as in interviewing in quantitative research, do not ask leading questions;

- remember to ensure that you ask or record 'facesheet' information of a general kind (name, age, gender, etc.) and a specific kind (position in company, number of years employed, number of years involved in a group, etc.), because such information is useful for contextualizing people's answers.

There are some practical details to attend to before the interview.

- Make sure you are familiar with the setting in which the interviewee works or lives or engages in the behaviour of interest to you. This will help you to understand what he or she is saying in the interviewee's own terms.

- Get hold of a good tape recorder and microphone. Qualitative researchers nearly always tape-record

and then transcribe their interviews. This procedure is important for detailed analysis required in qualitative research and to ensure that the interviewees' answers are captured in their own terms. If you are taking notes, it is easy to lose the phrases and language used. Also, because the interviewer is supposed not to be following a strictly formulated schedule of questions of the kind used in structured interviewing, he or she will need to be responsive to the interviewee's answers so that it is possible to follow them up. A good microphone is highly desirable, because many interviews are let down by poor recording.

- Make sure as far as possible that the interview takes place in a setting that is quiet (so there is no or little outside noise that might affect the quality of the tape recording) and private (so the interviewee does not have to worry about being overheard).

- Prepare yourself for the interview by cultivating as many of the criteria of a quality interviewer suggested by Kvale as possible (Box 15.6).

After the interview, make notes about:

- how the interview went (was interviewee talkative, cooperative, nervous, well-dressed/scruffy, etc.?);

- where the interview took place;

- any other feelings about the interview (did it open up new avenues of interest?);

- the setting (busy/quiet, many/few other people in the vicinity, new/old buildings, use of computers).

These various guidelines suggest the series of steps in formulating questions for an interview guide in qualitative research presented in Figure 15.1.

Kinds of question

The kinds of questions asked in qualitative interviews are highly variable. Kvale (1996) has suggested nine different kinds of question. Most interviews will contain virtually all of them, although interviews that rely on lists of topics are likely to follow a somewhat looser format. Kvale's nine types of question are as follows.

Box 15.6 Kvale's list of qualification criteria of an interviewer (plus two others)

Kvale (1996) has proposed a very useful list of ten criteria of a successful interviewer.

- *Knowledgeable*: is thoroughly familiar with the focus of the interview; pilot interviews of the kind used in survey interviewing can be useful here.

- *Structuring*: gives purpose for interview; rounds it off; asks whether interviewee has questions.

- *Clear*: asks simple, easy, short questions; no jargon.

- *Gentle*: lets people finish; gives them time to think; tolerates pauses.

- *Sensitive*: listens attentively to what is said and how it is said; is empathetic in dealing with the interviewee.

- *Open*: responds to what is important to interviewee and is flexible.

- *Steering*: knows what he or she wants to find out.

- *Critical*: is prepared to challenge what is said, for example, dealing with inconsistencies in interviewees' replies.

- *Remembering*: relates what is said to what has previously been said.

- *Interpreting*: clarifies and extends meanings of interviewees' statements, but without imposing meaning on them.

To Kvale's list we would add the following.

- *Balanced*: does not talk too much, which may make the interviewee passive, and does not talk too little, which may result in the interviewee feeling he or she is not talking along the right lines.

- *Ethically sensitive*: is sensitive to the ethical dimension of interviewing, ensuring the interviewee appreciates what the research is about, its purposes, and that his or her answers will be treated confidentially.

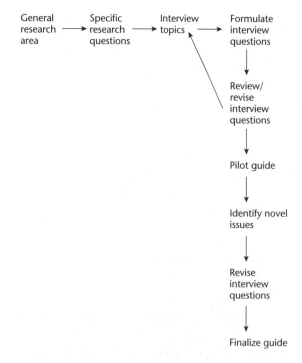

Figure 15.1 Formulating questions for an interview guide

Practical tip 👉 *interviewees and distance*

Sometimes you may need to contact interviewees who are a long way from you—perhaps even abroad. While interviewing in qualitative research is usually of the face-to-face kind, time and money restrictions may mean that you will need to interview such people in a less personal context. There are two possibilities. One is telephone interviewing. The cost of a telephone interview is much less than the cost involved in travelling long distances. Such interviewing is touched on in the context of the structured interview in Chapter 5. Another possibility is the online interview in which the interview is conducted by e-mail. This method is described in Chapter 23.

- *Introducing questions*: 'Please tell me about when your interest in X first began?'; 'Have you ever . . . ?'; 'Why did you go to . . . ?'
- *Follow-up questions*: getting the interviewee to elaborate his or her answer, such as 'Could you say some more about that?'; 'What do you mean by that . . . ?'; 'Can you give me an example . . . ?'; even 'Yeeees?'
- *Probing questions*: following up what has been said through direct questioning.
- *Specifying questions*: 'What did you do then?'; 'How did X react to what you said?'
- *Direct questions*: 'Do you find it easy to keep smiling when serving customers?'; 'Are you happy with the amount of on-the-job training you have received?' Such questions are perhaps best left until towards the end of the interview, in order not to influence the direction of the interview too much.
- *Indirect questions*: 'What do most people round here think of the ways that management treats its staff?', perhaps followed up by 'Is that the way you feel too?', in order to get at the individual's own view.
- *Structuring questions*: 'I would now like to move on to a different topic.'
- *Silence*: allow pauses to signal that you want to give the interviewee the opportunity to reflect and amplify an answer.
- *Interpreting questions*: 'Do you mean that your leadership role has had to change from one of encouraging others to a more directive one?'; 'Is it fair to say that you don't mind being friendly towards customers most of the time, but when they are unpleasant or demanding you find it more difficult?'

As this list suggests, one of the main ingredients of the interview is listening—being very attentive to what the interviewee is saying or even not saying. It means that the interviewer is active without being too intrusive—a difficult balance. But it also means that, just because the interview is being tape-recorded (the generally recommended practice whenever it is feasible), the interviewer cannot take things easy. In fact, an interviewer must be very attuned and responsive to what the interviewee is saying and doing. This is also important because something like body language may indicate that the interviewee is becoming uneasy or anxious about a line of questioning. An ethically sensitive interviewer will not want to place undue pressure on the person he or she is talking to and will need to be prepared to cut short that line of questioning if it is clearly a source of concern.

Remember as well that in interviews you are going to ask about different kinds of things, such as:

- values—of interviewee, of group, of organization;
- beliefs—of interviewee, of others, of group;
- behaviour—of interviewee, of others;
- formal and informal roles—of interviewee, of others;
- relationships—of interviewee, of others;
- places and locales;
- emotions—particularly of the interviewee, but also possibly of others;
- encounters;
- stories.

Try to vary the questioning in terms of types of question (as suggested by Kvale's nine types, which were outlined above) *and* the types of phenomena you ask about. Finally, you must think about how to end interviews satisfactorily, making sure that your interviewees have had a chance to comment fully on the topic concerned and giving them the opportunity to raise any issues that they think you have overlooked in your questions. The closing moments of an interview also provide an opportunity to include a final 'catch-all' question. Journalists sometimes refer to this as the 'doorknob question', since it is asked at the end, when rapport has been established and the interviewee has relaxed into the situation. This type of closing question tends to be directive—for example, 'If you were advising the organization on this subject, what are the main changes or improvements that you would recommend?' or 'From your experience in this area, what advice would you offer to other managers facing similar problems?' This encourages the interviewee to comment on specific issues and to put forward a personal opinion.

Using an interview guide: An example

Box 15.7 is taken from an interview from Bryman's (1999) study of visitors to Disney theme parks. The study was briefly mentioned in Chapter 4 as an

Box 15.7 Part of the transcript of a semi-structured interview

Interviewer	OK. What were your views or feelings about the presentation of different cultures, as shown in, for example, Jungle Cruise or It's a Small World at the Magic Kingdom or in World Showcase at Epcot?
Wife	Well, I thought the different countries at Epcot were wonderful, but I need to say more than that, don't I?
Husband	They were very good and some were better than others, but that was down to the host countries themselves really, as I suppose each of the countries represented would have been responsible for their own part, so that's nothing to do with Disney, I wouldn't have thought. I mean some of the landmarks were hard to recognize for what they were supposed to be, but some were very well done. Britain was OK, but there was only a pub and a Welsh shop there really, whereas some of the other pavilions, as I think they were called, were good ambassadors for the countries they represented. China, for example, had an excellent 360 degree film showing parts of China and I found that very interesting.
Interviewer	Did you think there was anything lacking about the content?

Husband Well I did notice that there weren't many black people at World Showcase, particularly the American Adventure. Now whether we were there on an unusual day in that respect I don't know, but we saw plenty of black Americans in the Magic Kingdom and other places, but very few if any in that World Showcase. And there was certainly little mention of black history in the American Adventure presentation, so maybe they felt alienated by that, I don't know, but they were noticeable by their absence.

Interviewer So did you think there were any special emphases?

Husband Well thinking about it now, because I hadn't really given this any consideration before you started asking about it, but thinking about it now, it was only really representative of the developed world, you know, Britain, America, Japan, world leaders many of them in technology, and there was nothing of the Third World there. Maybe that's their own fault, maybe they were asked to participate and didn't, but now that I think about it, that does come to me. What do you think, love?

Wife Well, like you, I hadn't thought of it like that before, but I agree with you.

example of a snowball sampling procedure. The interviews were concerned to elicit visitors' interpretations of the parks that had been visited. The interview is with a man who was in his sixties and his wife who was two years younger. They had visited Walt Disney World in Orlando, Florida, and were very enthusiastic about their visit.

The sequence begins with the interviewer asking what would be considered a 'direct question' in terms of the list of nine question types suggested by Kvale (1996) and outlined above. The replies are very bland and do little more than reflect the interviewees' positive feelings about their visit to Disney World. The wife acknowledges this when she says 'but I need to say more than that, don't I?' Interviewees frequently know that they are expected to be expansive in their answers. This sequence occurred around halfway

through the interview, so the interviewees were primed by then into realizing that more details were expected. There is almost a tinge of embarrassment that the answer has been so brief and unilluminating. The husband's answer is more expansive but not particularly enlightening.

There then follows the first of two important prompts by the interviewer. The husband's reponse is more interesting in that he now begins to answer in terms of the possibility that black people were under-represented in attractions like the American Adventure, which tells the story of America through tableaux and films via a debate between two audio-animatronic figures—Mark Twain and Benjamin Franklin. The second prompt yields further useful reflection, this time carrying the implication that Third World countries are under-represented in the

World Showcase in the Epcot Centre. The couple are clearly aware that it is the prompting that has made them provide these reflections when they say: 'Well thinking about it now, because I hadn't really given this any consideration before you started asking about it' and 'Well, like you, I hadn't thought of it like that before'. This is the whole point of prompting—to get the interviewee to think more about the topic and to provide the opportunity for a more detailed response. It is not a leading question, since the interviewees were not being asked 'Do you think that the Disney company fails to recognize the significance of Black history (or ignores the Third World) in its presentation of different cultures?' There is no doubt that it is the prompts that elicit the more interesting replies, but that is precisely their role.

Tape recording and transcription

The point has already been made on several occasions that, in qualitative research, the interview is usually tape-recorded and transcribed whenever possible (see Box 15.8). Qualitative researchers are frequently interested not just in *what* people say but also in the *way* that they say it. If this aspect is to be fully woven into an analysis, it is necessary for a complete account of the series of exchanges in an interview to be available. Also, because the interviewer is supposed to be highly alert to what is being said—following up interesting points made, prompting and probing where necessary, drawing attention to any inconsistencies in the interviewee's answers—it is best if he or she is not distracted by having to concentrate on getting down notes on what is said.

As with just about everything in conducting business research, there is a cost (other than the financial cost of tape recorders and tapes), in that the use of a tape recorder may disconcert respondents, who become self-conscious or alarmed at the prospect of their words being preserved. Most people accede to the request for the interview to be tape-recorded, though it is not uncommon for a small number to refuse (see Box 15.9). When faced with refusal, you should still go ahead with the interview, as it is highly likely that useful information will still be forthcoming. For example, Prasad (1993; see Chapter 13)

Box 15.8 Why should you record and transcribe interviews?

With approaches that entail detailed attention to language, such as conversation analysis and discourse analysis (see Chapter 17), the recording of conversations and interviews is to all intents and purposes mandatory. However, researchers who use qualitative interviews and focus groups (see Chapter 16) also tend to record and then transcribe interviews. Heritage (1984: 238) suggests that the procedure of recording and transcribing interviews has the following advantages.

- It helps to correct the natural limitations of our memories and of the intuitive glosses that we might place on what people say in interviews.

- It allows more thorough examination of what people say.

- It permits repeated examinations of the interviewees' answers.

- It opens up the data to public scrutiny by other researchers, who can evaluate the analysis that is carried out by the original researchers of the data (that is, a secondary analysis).

- It therefore helps to counter accusations that an analysis might have been influenced by a researcher's values or biases.

- It allows the data to be reused in other ways from those intended by the original researcher—for example, in the light of new theoretical ideas or analytic strategies.

However, it has to be recognized that the procedure is very time-consuming. It also requires good equipment, usually in the form of a good-quality tape recorder and microphone but also, if possible, a transcription machine. Transcription also very quickly results in a daunting pile of paper. Also, recording equipment may be offputting for interviewees.

Box 15.9 Getting it taped and transcribed: an illustration of two problems

Rafaeli et al. (1997) conducted semi-structured interviews with twenty female administrators in a university business school in order to study the significance of dress at the workplace. They write:

> Everyone we contacted agreed to participate. Interviews took place in participants' offices or in a school lounge and lasted between 45 minutes and three hours. We recorded and transcribed all but two interviews: 1 participant refused to be taped, and the tape recorder malfunctioned during another interview. For interviews

not taped, we recorded detailed notes. We assured all participants that their responses would remain confidential and anonymous and hired an outside contractor to transcribe the interviews.   (1997: 14)

Even though, overall this interview study was highly successful, generating eighteen interviews which were recorded and transcribed, it does show two kinds of problems qualitative interviewers can face—namely, hardware malfunctions and refusals to be recorded.

Practical tip 👉 *transcribing interviews*

If you are doing research for a project or dissertation, you may not have the resources to pay for professional transcription, and, unless you are an accurate touch typist, it may take you a lot longer than the suggested five to six hours per hour of speech. If you have access to a transcription machine with a foot-operated stop–start mechanism, this will make the task of transcription somewhat easier. However, the important thing to bear in mind is that you must allow sufficient time for transcription and be realistic about how many interviews you are going to be able to transcribe in the time available.

General Motors the length of the interviews ranged from between forty-five minutes and four hours. Similarly, Marshall's (1995; see Box 13.3) research into women managers involved interviews with women managers that lasted between one and a half and two hours. It should not be assumed that shorter interviews are necessarily inferior to longer ones, but very short ones that are a product of interviewee non-cooperation or anxiety about being tape-recorded are likely to be less useful. In the extreme, when an interview has produced very little of significance, it may not be worth the time and cost of transcription. Thankfully, such occasions are relatively unusual. If people do agree to be interviewed, they usually do so in a cooperative way and loosen up after initial anxiety about the microphone. As a result, even short interviews are often quite revealing.

recounts that, in the few instances where employees at Paragon indicated discomfort with being recorded, she took notes during the interview and wrote these up after the session. The summary notes were then shown to the interviewee, who evaluated their accuracy. This advice also applies to cases of tape-recorder malfunction (again see Box 15.9). Among those who do agree to be tape-recorded, there will be some who will not get over their alarm at being confronted with a microphone. As a result, some interviews may not be as interesting as you might have hoped. In qualitative research, there is often quite a large amount of variation in the amount of time that interviews take. For example, in Milkman's (1997) study of technological change at

The problem with transcribing interviews is that it is very time-consuming. Pettigrew (1985) notes that his interviews at Imperial Chemical Industries (ICI) produced around 500 hours of tape-recorded information for analysis, which were either completely transcribed or coded onto 8×5 inch cards according to predetermined and emergent categories. Similarly, in their study of traders and managers in four investment banks, Willman et al. (2002) interviewed 118 traders and trader-managers and ten senior managers. Interviews averaged one hour in duration and they were all taped and transcripts were produced. It is best to allow around five to six hours for transcription for every hour of speech. Also, transcription yields vast amounts of paper, which you will need to wade through when analysing the data. Prasad (1993) reports that her thirty-four interviews on computerization (see Chapter 13) generated nearly 800 pages of interview transcripts that needed to be analysed, in addition to over 1,800 pages of field notes from observations. It is clear, therefore, that, while transcription has the advantage of keeping intact the interviewee's (and interviewer's) words, it does so by piling up the amount of text to be analysed. It is no wonder that writers like Lofland and Lofland (1995) advise that the analysis of qualitative data is not left until all the interviews have been completed and transcribed. To procrastinate may give the researcher the impression that he or she faces a monumental task. Also, there are good grounds for making analysis an ongoing activity, because it allows the researcher to be more aware of emerging themes that he or she may want to ask about in a more direct way in later interviews. The preference for ongoing analysis is also very much recommended by proponents of approaches to qualitative data analysis like grounded theory (see Chapter 19).

It is easy to take the view that transcription is a relatively unproblematic translation of the spoken into the written word. However, given the reliance on transcripts in qualitative research based on

---

Practical tip ☞ transcribing sections of an interview

Some interviews or at least large portions of them are sometimes not very useful, perhaps because interviewees are reticent or not as relevant to your research topic as you had hoped. There seems little point in transcribing material that you know is unlikely to be fruitful. It may be that, for many of your interviews, it would be better to listen to them closely first, at least once or more usually twice, and then transcribe only those portions that you think are useful or relevant. However, this may mean that you miss certain things or that you have to go back to the tapes at a later stage in your analysis to try and find something that emerges as significant only later on.

---

interviews, the issue should not be taken lightly. The first question to consider is whether to do the transcription yourself, or use secretarial assistance. Transcribers need to be trained in much the same way that interviewers do. Moreover, even among experienced transcribers, errors can creep in. For example, Spender (1989) describes how, of the thirty-four interviews in his sample, twenty-five were transcribed. During the exploratory stages of the research this was done by assistants. However, this proved unsatisfactory, as 'there are important data in the respondent's intonations, hesitations, etc. which need to be available'. He concluded that 'the recording can help to recapture the actual data, which is neither the recording, nor the transcript, but the researcher's experience of the interview in its own context' (1989: 82). Poland (1995) has provided some fascinating examples of mistakes in transcription that can be the result of many different factors (mishearing, fatigue, carelessness). For example, one transcript contained the following passage:

I think unless we want to become like other countries, where people have, you know, democratic freedoms . . .

But the actual words on the audiotape were:

I think unless we want to become like other countries, where people have no democratic freedoms . . . (Poland 1995: 294)

Steps clearly need to be taken to check on the quality of transcription.

Flexibility in the interview

One further point to bear in mind is that you need to be generally flexible in your approach to interviewing in qualitative research. This advice is not just to do with needing to be responsive to what interviewees say to you and following up interesting points that they make. Such flexibility *is* important and is an important reminder that, with semi-structured interviewing, you should not turn the interview into a kind of structured interview but with open questions. Flexibility is important in such areas as varying the order of questions, following up leads, and clearing up inconsistencies in answers. Flexibility is important in other respects, such as coping with audio-recording equipment breakdown and refusals

---

Practical tip 👉 *translating interviews into English*

If you are interviewing people whose primary language is not English but another language in which you the interviewer are fluent, you may decide to interview respondents in their primary language, so that their ability to communicate effectively is not impaired by having to speak in a language with which they are less familiar. You should first transcribe the interviews in the language spoken during the interview and then translate the transcript into English so that you can analyse the data in the language that you will be using when you come to write up

your research. Differences in the meaning of words between the two languages may mean that the translation process leads to some distortion of the data. To overcome this, you may wish to back-translate the transcript into the primary language and then compare the back-translation with the original version, noting any discrepancies. However, it should be noted that this is bound to be a time-consuming process, so it needs to be borne in mind when deciding how many interviews to do.

---

by interviewees to allow a recording to take place (see Box 15.9). A further element is that interviewers often find that, as soon as they switch off their tape recorders, the interviewee continues to ruminate on the topic of interest and frequently will say more interesting things than in the interview. It is usually not feasible to switch the machine back on again, so try to take some notes, either while the person is talking or as soon as possible after the interview. Such 'unsolicited accounts' can often be the source of revealing information or views (Hammersley and Atkinson 1995). This is certainly what Parker (2000) found in connection with his research on three British organizations—a National Health Service District Health Authority, a building society, and a manufacturing company—which was based primarily on semi-structured interviews: 'Indeed, some of the most valuable parts of the interview took place

---

Practical tip 👉 *keeping the tape recorder going*

Since interviewees sometimes 'open up' at the end of the interview, perhaps just when the tape recorder has been switched off, there are good grounds for suggesting that you should keep it switched on for as long as possible. So, when you are winding the interview down, don't switch off the tape recorder immediately.

---

after the tape had been switched off, the closing intimacies of the conversation being prefixed with a silent or explicit "well, if you want to know what I really think...". Needless to say, a visit to the toilet to write up as much as I could remember followed almost immediately' (2000: 236).

Sampling

Many, if not most, of the issues raised in connection with sampling in ethnographic research apply more or less equally to sampling in qualitative interviewing. Very often, the lack of transparency that is sometimes a feature of qualitative research (referred to in Chapter 13) is particularly apparent in relation to sampling. It is sometimes more or less impossible to discern from researchers' accounts of their methods

either *how* their interviewees were selected or *how many* there were of them. Often, qualitative researchers are clear that their samples are convenience or opportunistic ones, and, on other occasions, the reader suspects that this is the case. This may be due to a belief that, because it aims to generate an in-depth analysis, issues of representativeness are less important in qualitative research than they are in quantitative research. For her study of women managers, Marshall (1984) made a number of decisions to limit certain potential influencing factors. First, to interview only in and around London, to reduce the significance of whether or not managers were geographically mobile; secondly, to impose an upper age limit of 45 years, to reduce the potential differences between generations. Thirdly, to contact several people in each company to provide a guide to the influence of the company; and, fourthly, to restrict the number of personnel managers in the sample, to avoid weighting her sample towards this 'traditional stronghold of female employment' (1984: 115). Sometimes, convenience samples may be the result of restrictions placed on the researcher—for example, when members of an organization select interviewees rather than give the researcher a free rein to do so.

Another example of opportunistic sampling is provided by Jackall (1988), who went into several large organizations in order to study how bureaucracy shapes moral consciousness. Analysis of the occupational ethics of corporate managers was based on core data of 143 intensive, semi-structured interviews with managers at every level of the organization. This formed the basis for selection of a smaller stratified group of twelve managers who were reinterviewed several times and asked to interpret materials that Jackall was collecting. However, as the study progressed Jackall realized that an investigation of organizational morality should also explore managerial dissenters, or 'whistleblowers', individuals who had taken stands against their organizations on grounds that they defined as moral. Between 1982 and 1988, Jackall conducted case studies of these dissenters, interviewing eighteen 'whistleblowers' and reviewing large amounts of documentary evidence. In order to explore managerial morality further, he then presented these cases to the stratified group of twelve managers, and asked them 'to assess the dissenters' actions and motives by their own standards' (1988: 206).

Snowball sampling is sometimes used to contact groups of people for whom there is no sampling frame. This approach was employed in Bryman's study of visitors to Disney theme parks and by Marshall (1984), who asked women managers to suggest other potential interviewees. Pettigrew and McNulty (1995) also describe their in-depth interview research into part-time board members of top UK firms as based on a 'snowball effect'. Pilot study interviews with twenty board members were used to get access to other prominent directors in the overall population. Pettigrew and McNulty's research approach is guided by the assumption that access to elites is best achieved through other elite members.

Sometimes, a probability sampling approach is employed. The research on organizational dress by Rafaeli et al. (1997; see Box 15.9) employed such an approach. The authors write: 'First, we identified a stratified random sample of 20 people from the population of full-time, permanent administrative employees in the organization' (1997: 13–14). The stratifying criteria were administrative section and hierarchical level. A similar kind of sampling strategy occurs when a sample of interviewees is taken (sometimes randomly, sometimes by ensuring a 'spread' in terms of stratifying criteria) from a much larger sample generated for social survey purposes. This approach allows the researcher to sample purposively (if not randomly) and so ensure a wide range of characteristics of interviewees. Pringle (1988) also used this approach in a study of power relations and secretarial work. This study involved interviews with secretarial students and with a range of workers, both secretarial and non-secretarial, in a variety of Australian workplaces. The first stage of this process involved groups of three secretarial students who were interviewed for 20–30 minutes about their course. A smaller sample ($n = 30$) were interviewed again near the end of their course and then followed into the workforce. Fifteen were interviewed a third time individually at home and asked to reflect on the value of their course. The second stage of interviews was carried out in a representative range of workplaces. 'Of 244 interviews 72 were with employees in the public sector, 32 with unions, 92 with large corporations and 44 with small companies, agencies and partnerships' (Pringle 1988: 268). A breakdown of interviewees by occupation is given in Table 15.1.

In addition, a theoretical sampling approach might be employed (see Box 14.9 and Figure 14.2).

This approach entails sampling interviewees until your categories achieve theoretical saturation (see Box 14.10) and selecting further interviewees on the basis of your emerging theoretical focus. The approach is supposed to be an iterative one—that is, one in which there is a movement backwards and forwards between sampling and theoretical reflection—but it may be that the researcher feels that his or her categories achieve theoretical saturation at a relatively early stage. For example, for their research on organization dress, which was referred to in Box 15.9, Rafaeli et al. (1997) initially employed a stratified random sampling approach (see above), but then evaluated their data 'after completing interviews with the 20 individuals selected and concluded that, because we had reached theoretical saturation (Glaser and Strauss 1967), no additional interviews were necessary' (1997: 14). A sampling approach that is more in tune with Glaser and Strauss's (1967) idea of theoretical sampling is provided by Gephart (1993) in his account of a study of disaster sensemaking (see Box 15.10).

The chief virtue of theoretical sampling is that the emphasis is upon using theoretical reflection on data as the guide to whether more data are needed. It therefore places a premium on theorizing rather than the statistical adequacy of a sample, which may be a limited guide to sample selection in many instances.

Table 15.1 A stratified interview sample

Interviewees by occupation	Number	Per cent
Top and middle management	54	22
Lower management	22	9
Administrative	18	7.5
Supervisory	9	3.5
Personal assistant	3	1.5
Secretary (1 boss)	67	27.5
Secretary (2+ bosses)	29	12
Word processor/typist	22	9
Clerical assistant	20	8
TOTAL	244	100

Source: adapted from Pringle (1988).

Box 15.10 Theoretical sampling

Gephart (1993) developed a theoretical sample in his study of disaster sensemaking, by deciding on analytic grounds which data to collect and analyse based on his emerging theory (see Box 18.6 for a more detailed account of this study). Sampling was determined by three main considerations.

- *Persons and documents*—Gephart chose to focus on the testimony and remarks of (1) the assistant district manager and district manager from the company; (2) a pipeline crew member; and (3) the government energy board members and its attorneys. This analytic choice was made because these three parties represented the main cultural groups involved in the enquiry.

- *Key issues*—ethnographic observation sensitized Gephart to the actors' concern with making sense of the disaster and determining who was responsible for the fire and related events. He then worked with the literature to review the theory of sensemaking and used this concept to further develop his analysis.

- *Limits*—sampling was also partly determined by Gephart's inability to gain access to publicly inaccessible settings. This meant that certain issues such as power and politics could not be addressed.

Feminist research and interviewing in qualitative research

Unstructured and semi-structured interviewing have become extremely prominent methods of data gathering within a feminist research framework. In part, this is a reflection of the preference for qualitative research among feminist researchers, but it also reflects a view that the kind of interview with which qualitative research is associated allows many of the goals of feminist research to be realized. Indeed, the view has been expressed that, 'Whilst several brave women in the 1980s defended quantitative methods, it is nonetheless still the case that not just qualitative methods, but the in-depth face-to-face interview has become the paradigmatic "feminist method"' (Kelly, Burton, and Regan 1994: 34). This comment is enlightening because it implies that it is not simply that qualitative research is seen by many writers and researchers as more consistent with a feminist position than quantitative research, but that specifically qualitative interviewing is seen as especially appropriate. The point that is being made here is not necessarily that such interviewing is somehow more in tune with feminist values than, say, ethnography (especially since it is often an ingredient of ethnographic research). Instead, it could be that the intensive and time-consuming nature of ethnography means that, although it has great potential as an approach to feminist research (see Chapter 14), qualitative interviewing is often preferred because it is usually less invasive in these respects.

However, it is specifically interviewing of the kind conducted in qualitative research that is seen as having potential for a feminist approach, not the structured interview with which survey research is associated. Why might one type of interview be consistent with a sensitivity to feminism and the other not? In a frequently cited article, Oakley outlines the following points about the standard survey interview.

- It is a one-way process—the interviewer extracts information or views from the interviewee.

- The interviewer offers nothing in return for the extraction of information. For example, interviewers using a structured interview do not offer information or their own views if asked. Indeed, they are typically advised not to do such things because of worries about contaminating their respondents' answers.

- The interviewer–interviewee relationship is a form of hierarchical or power relationship. Interviewers arrogate to themselves the right to ask questions, implicitly placing their interviewees in a position of subservience or inferiority.

- The element of power is also revealed by the fact that the structured interview seeks out information from the perspective of the researcher.

- Because of these points, the standard survey interview is inconsistent with feminism when women interview other women. This view arises because it is seen as indefensible for women to 'use' other women in these ways.

Instead of this framework for conducting interviews, feminist researchers advocate one that establishes:

- a high level of rapport between interviewer and interviewee;

- a high degree of reciprocity on the part of the interviewer;

- the perspective of the women being interviewed;

- a non-hierarchical relationship.

In connection with the reciprocity that she advocates, Oakley noted, for example, that, in her research on the transition to motherhood, she was frequently asked questions by her respondents. She argues that it was ethically indefensible for a feminist not to answer when confronted with questions of a certain kind. For Oakley, therefore, the qualitative interview was viewed as a means of resolving the dilemmas that she encountered as a feminist interviewing other women. However, as noted in previous chapters, while this broad adherence to a set of principles for interviewing in feminist research continues, it has been tempered by a greater recognition of the possible value of quantitative research.

An interesting dilemma that is perhaps not so easily resolved is the question of what feminist researchers should do when their own 'understandings and interpretations of women's accounts would either not be shared by some of them [i.e. the research participants], and/or represent a form of challenge or threat to their perceptions, choices and coping strategies' (Kelly, Burton, and Regan 1994: 37). It is the first type of situation that will be examined, at least in part, because, while it is of particular significance to feminist researchers, its implications are somewhat broader. It raises the tricky question of how far the commitment of seeing through the eyes of the people you study can and/or should be stretched. Two examples are relevant here. Reinharz (1992: 28–9) cites the case of an American study by Andersen (1981), who interviewed twenty 'corporate wives', who came across as happy with their lot and were supportive of feminism only in relation to employment discrimination. Andersen interpreted their responses to her questions as indicative of 'false consciousness'—in other words, she did not really believe her interviewees. When Andersen wrote an article on her findings, the women wrote a letter rejecting her account, affirming that women can be fulfilled as wives and mothers. A similar situation confronted Millen (1997) when she interviewed thirty-two British female scientists using 'semi-structured, in-depth individual interviewing' (1997: 4.6). As Millen puts it:

There was a tension between my interpretation of their reported experience as sex-based, and the meaning the participants themselves tended to attribute to their experience, since the majority of respondents did not analyse these experiences in terms of patriarchy or sex–gender systems, but considered them to be individualised, or as 'just something that had to be coped with'.... From my external, academically privileged vantage point, it is clear that sexism pervades these professions, and that men are assumed from the start by other scientists to be competent scientists of status whilst women have to prove themselves, overcome the barrier of their difference before they are accepted. These women, on the other hand, did not generally view their interactions in terms of gendered social systems. There is therefore a tension between their characterisation of their experience and my interpretation of it ...   (1997: 5.6, 5.9)

Three interesting issues are thrown up by these two accounts. First, how can such a situation arise? This is an issue that pervades qualitative research that makes claims to reveal social reality as viewed by members of the setting in question. If researchers are genuinely seeing through others' eyes, the 'tension' to which Millen refers should not arise. However, it clearly can and does, and this strongly suggests that qualitative researchers are more affected by their own perspectives and research questions when collecting and analysing data than might be expected from textbook accounts of the research process. Secondly, there is the question of how to handle such a 'tension'—that is, how do you reconcile the two accounts? Andersen's (1981) solution to the tension she encountered was to reinterpret her findings in terms of the conditions that engender the contentment she uncovered. Thirdly, given that feminist research is often concerned with wider political goals of emancipation, a tension between participants' world views and the researcher's position raises moral questions about the appropriateness of imposing an interpretation that is not shared by research participants themselves. Such an imposition could hardly be regarded as consistent with the principle of a non-hierarchical relationship in the interview situation.

Therefore, while qualitative interviewing has become a highly popular research method for feminist researchers because of its malleability into a form that can support the principles of feminism, interesting questions are raised in terms of the relationship between researchers' and participants' accounts. Such questions have a significance generally for the conduct of qualitative research.

Qualitative interviewing versus participant observation

The aim of this section is to compare the merits and limitations of interviewing in qualitative research with those of participant observation. These are probably the two most prominent methods of data collection in qualitative research, so there is some virtue in assessing their strengths, a debate that was first begun many years ago (Becker and Geer 1957*a,b*; Trow 1957). In this section, interviewing is being compared to participant observation rather than ethnography, because the latter invariably entails a significant amount of interviewing. So too does participant observation, but in this discussion we will be following the principle that we outlined in Box 14.1—namely, that the term will be employed to refer to the specifically observational activities in which the participant observer engages. As noted in Box 14.1, the term 'ethnography' is being reserved for the wide range of data collection activities in which ethnographers engage—one of which is participant observation—along with the written account that is a product of those activities.

Advantages of participant observation in comparison to qualitative interviewing

Seeing through others' eyes

As noted in Chapters 1 and 13, this is one of the main tenets of qualitative research, but, on the face of it, the participant observer would seem to be better placed for gaining a foothold on social reality in this way. The researcher's prolonged immersion in a social setting would seem to make him or her better equipped to see as others see. The participant observer is in much closer contact with people for a longer period of time; also, he or she participates in many of the same kinds of activity as the members of the social setting being studied. Research that relies on interviewing alone is likely to entail much more fleeting contacts,

though in qualitative research interviews can last many hours and reinterviewing is not unusual.

Learning the native language

Becker and Geer (1957*a*) argued that the participant observer is in the same position as a social anthropologist visiting a distant land, in that, in order to understand a culture, the language must be learned. However, it is not simply the formal language that must be understood in the case of the kinds of business research in which a participant observer in a complex organization engages. It is also very often the 'argot'—the special uses of words and slang that are important to penetrate that culture. Such an understanding is arrived at through the observation of language use.

The taken for granted

Although much important information can be obtained through interviews, some kinds of data cannot be captured through this particular research method. The interview relies primarily on verbal behaviour and as such matters that interviewees take for granted are less likely to surface than in participant observation, where implicit features in social life are more likely to be revealed as a result of the observer's continued presence and because of the ability to observe behaviour rather than just rely on what is said. For example, few interviewees will be able accurately to recollect the dynamics of a meeting involving several people—they may remember parts of what was said, and the nature of the problem under discussion, but are unlikely to recollect how decisions evolved as part of a social process (Whyte 1953), so for this researchers must continue to rely on observation.

Deviant and hidden activities

Much of what we know about patterns of resistance at work, industrial sabotage, and other criminal or deviant activity within organizations has been gleaned from participant observation. For example, Linstead's (1985) account of the practical jokes, general kidding, and games played by bakery workers was obtained through participant observation. Similarly, Collinson's (1988) analysis of humour in the context of a male-dominated workplace (see also Chapter 14) relied partly on non-participant observation to obtain data about the daily jibes, socialization rituals, and initiation ceremonies that characterized daily life on the shopfloor at Slavs. These are areas that insiders are likely to be reluctant to talk about in an interview context alone. Understanding is again likely to come through prolonged interaction. Ethnographers conducting participant observation are more likely to place themselves in situations in which their continued involvement allows them gradually to infiltrate such social worlds and to insinuate themselves into the lives of people who might be sensitive to outsiders.

Sensitivity to context

The participant observer's extensive contact with a social setting allows the context of people's behaviour to be mapped out fully. The participant observer interacts with people in a variety of different situations and possibly roles, so that the links between behaviour and context can be forged.

Encountering the unexpected and flexibility

It may be that, because of the unstructured nature of participant observation, it is more likely to uncover unexpected topics or issues. Except with the most unstructured forms of interview, the interview process is likely to entail some degree of closure as the interview guide is put together, which may blinker the researcher slightly. Also, participant observation may be more flexible because of the tendency for interviewers to instil an element of comparability (and hence a modicum of structure) in their questioning of different people. Ditton's (1977) decision at a very late stage in the data collection process to focus on pilferage in the bakery in which he was a participant observer is an example of this feature.

Naturalistic emphasis

Participant observation has the potential to come closer to a naturalistic emphasis, because the qualitative researcher confronts members of a social setting in their natural environments. Interviewing, because of its nature as a disruption of members' normal flow of events, even when it is at its most informal, is less amenable to this feature. It is unsurprising, therefore, that, when referring to naturalism as a tradition in qualitative research, Gubrium and Holstein (1997; see Box 13.1) largely refer to studies in which participant observation was a prominent component (e.g. Whyte 1955).

Advantages of qualitative interviewing in comparison to participant observation

Issues resistant to observation

It is likely that there is a wide range of issues that are simply not amenable to observation, so that asking people about them represents the only viable means of finding out about them within a qualitative research strategy. For example, in Bell's (2001) research on payment systems in the chemical industry it was not really possible to explore the systems and rules whereby payments were made by observing shopfloor practices, although the latter was very useful in gaining an understanding of the cultural context in which payment systems were located. For most workers, payment is an issue that surfaces through consideration of issues that relate to the 'effort-bargain' and this understanding was more readily accessed through interviews.

Reconstruction of events

Qualitative research frequently entails the reconstruction of events by asking interviewees to think back over how a certain series of events unfolded in relation to a current situation. An example is Isabella's research on how managers construe key organizational events at different stages (see Box 13.6). Another example is Pettigrew's (1985) research on Imperial Chemicals Industries (ICI), which entailed interviewing about contemporaneous events but also included 'retrospective interviewing', as Pettigrew defines it (see Box 2.17). This reconstruction of events is something that cannot be accomplished through participant observation alone.

Ethical considerations

There are certain areas that could be observed—albeit indirectly through hidden hardware like a microphone—but would raise ethical considerations. For example, Ditton (1977) never disclosed to his fellow workers in the bakery that he was interested in pilferage, although he did seek to protect their anonymity, by omitting names and changing other irrelevant facts in the published study. He goes on to claim that he could not have disclosed his interest in pilferage, partly because he did not decide to concentrate on this subject until some time after the conclusion of the study. However, in this case, participant observation does raise ethical issues relating to the observation of criminal activity and the extent to which the researcher actively participates in it.

Reactive effects

The question of reactive effects is by no means a straightforward matter. As with structured observation (see Chapter 8), it might be anticipated that the presence of a participant observer would result in reactive effects (see Box 8.8). People's knowledge of the fact that they are being observed may make them behave less naturally. However, participant observers, like researchers using structured observation, typically find that people become accustomed to their presence and begin to behave more naturally the longer they are around. Indeed, members of social settings sometimes express surprise when participant observers announce their imminent departure when they are on the verge of disengagement. Interviewers clearly do not suffer from the same kind of problem, but it could be argued that the unnatural character of the interview encounter can also be regarded as a context within which reactive effects may emerge. Participant observation also suffers from the related problem of observers disturbing the very situation being studied, because conversations and interactions will occur in conjunction with the observer that otherwise would not happen. This is by no means an easy issue to resolve and it seems likely that both participant observation and qualitative interviewing set in motion reactive effects but of different kinds.

Less intrusive in people's lives

Participant observation can be very intrusive in people's lives in that the observer is likely to take up a lot more of their time than in an interview. Interviews in qualitative research can sometimes be very long and reinterviewing is not uncommon, but the impact on people's time will probably be less than having to take observers into account on a regular basis, though it is likely that this feature will vary from situation to situation. Participant observation is likely to be especially intrusive in terms of the amount of people's time taken up when it is in organizational settings. In work organizations, there is a risk that the rhythms of work lives will be disrupted.

Longitudinal research easier

One of the advantages of participant observation is that it is inherently longitudinal in character because the observer is present in a social setting for a period of time. As a result, change and connections between events can be observed. However, there are limits to the amount of time that participant observers can devote to being away from their normal routines. Consequently, participant observation does not usually extend much beyond two to three years in duration. When participant observation is being conducted into an area of research that is episodic rather than requiring continued observation, a longer time period may be feasible. Pettigrew's (1985) research at ICI combined interviewing in late 1975, 1976, and early 1977, the latter parts of 1980 and early 1981, and again in 1982, with his interventions into the company as a consultant. During that period 134 people were interviewed from the ICI corporate headquarters and the four divisions under study. Several of these individuals were interviewed more than once and the total number of research interviews amounted to 175. Kanter (1977) employed a similar strategy combining consultant activity with research over a five-year period. In sum, interviewing can be carried out within a longitudinal research design somewhat more easily because repeat interviews may be easier to organize than repeat visits to participant observers' research settings, though the latter is not impossible. Following up interviewees on several occasions is likely to be easier than returning to research sites on a regular basis.

Greater breadth of coverage

In participant observation, the researcher is invariably constrained in his or her interactions and observations to a fairly restricted range of people, incidents, and localities. Participant observation in a large organization, for example, is likely to mean that knowledge of that organization beyond the confines of the department or section in which the observation is carried out is not likely to be very extensive. Interviewing can allow access to a wider variety of people and situations.

Specific focus

As noted in Chapter 13, qualitative research sometimes begins with a specific focus, and indeed Silverman (1993) has been critical of the notion that it should be regarded as an open-ended form of research. Qualitative interviewing would seem to be better suited to such a situation, since the interview can be directed at that focus and its associated research questions. Thus, the research by Bryman and his colleagues on the police had a very specific research focus in line with its Home Office funding—namely, conceptions of leadership among police officers (Bryman, Stephens, and Campo 1996). The bulk of the data gathering was in two police forces and entailed the interviewing of police officers at all levels using a semi-structured interview guide. Because it had such a clear focus, it was more appropriate to conduct the research by interview rather than participant observation, since issues to do with leadership notions may not crop up on a regular basis, which would make observation a very extravagant method of data collection.

Overview

When Becker and Geer (1957a: 28) proclaimed over forty years ago that the 'most complete form of the sociological datum . . . is the form in which the participant observer gathers it', Trow (1957: 33) reprimanded them for making such a universal claim and argued that 'the problem under investigation properly dictates the methods of investigation'. The latter view is very much the one taken in this book. Research methods are appropriate to researching some issues and areas but not others. The discussion of the merits and limitations of participant observation and qualitative interviews is meant simply to draw attention to some of the considerations that might be taken into account if there is a genuine opportunity to use one or the other in a study.

Equally, and to repeat an earlier point, the comparison is a somewhat artificial exercise, because participant observation is usually carried out as part of ethnographic research and as such it is usually accompanied by interviewing as well as other methods. In other words, participant observers frequently buttress their observations with methods of data collection that allow them access to important areas that are not amenable to observation. However, the aim of the comparison was to provide a kind of balance sheet in considering the strengths and limitations of a reliance on either participant observation or qualitative interview alone. Its aim is to draw attention to some of the factors that might be taken into account in deciding how to plan a study and even how to evaluate existing research.

Tandem [tændəm]

Checklist of issues to consider for your qualitative interview

✓ Have you devised a clear and comprehensive/informative way of introducing the research to interviewees?

✓ Does your interview guide clearly relate to your research questions?

✓ Have you piloted the guide with some appropriate respondents?

✓ Have you thought about what you will do if your interviewee does not turn up for the interview?

✓ Does the guide contain a good mixture of different kinds of questions, such as probing, specifying, and direct questions?

✓ Have you ensured that interviews will allow novel or unexpected themes and issues to arise?

✓ Is your language in the questions clear, comprehensible, and free of unnecessary jargon?

✓ Are your questions relevant to the people you are proposing to interview?

✓ Does your interview guide include requests for information about the interviewee, such as his or her age, work experience, position in the firm?

✓ Have your questions been designed to elicit reflective discussions so that they are not tempted to answer in 'yes' or 'no' terms?

✓ Do your questions offer a real prospect of seeing the world from your interviewees' point of view rather than imposing your own frame of reference on them?

✓ Are you familiar with the settings(s) in which the interviews will take place?

✓ Are you thoroughly familiar with and have you tested your recording equipment?

✓ Have you thought about how you will present yourself in the interview, such as how you will be dressed?

✓ Have you thought about how you will go about putting into operation the criteria of a good interviewer (Box 15.5)?

K KEY POINTS

• Interviewing in qualitative research is typically of the unstructured or semi-structured kind.

• In qualitative research, interviewing may be the sole method in an investigation or may be used as part of an ethnographic study, or indeed in tandem with another qualitative method.

• Qualitative interviewing is meant to be flexible and to seek out the world views of research participants.

• If an interview guide is employed, it should not be too structured in its application and should allow some flexibility in the asking of questions.

• The qualitative interview should be tape-recorded and then transcribed.

• As with ethnographic research, investigations using qualitative interviews tend not to employ random sampling to select participants.

- The qualitative interview has become an extremely popular method of data collection in feminist studies.

- Whether to use participant observation or qualitative interviews depends in large part on their relative suitability to the research questions being addressed. However, it must also be borne in mind that participant observers invariably conduct some interviews in the course of their investigations.

Q QUESTIONS FOR REVIEW

Differences between the structured interview and qualitative research interviews

- How does qualitative interviewing differ from structured interviewing?

Unstructured and semi-structured interviewing

- What are the differences between unstructured and semi-structured interviewing?
- Could semi-structured interviewing stand in the way of flexibility in qualitative research?
- What are the differences between life history and oral history interviews?
- What kinds of consideration need to be borne in mind when preparing an interview guide?
- What kinds of question might be asked in an interview guide?
- What kinds of skill does the interviewer need to develop in qualitative interviewing?
- Why is it important to tape-record and transcribe qualitative interviews?

Sampling

- Compare theoretical sampling and snowball sampling.

Feminist research and interviewing in qualitative research

- Why has the qualitative interview become such a prominent research method for feminist researchers?
- What dilemmas might be posed for feminist researchers using qualitative interviewing?

Qualitative interviewing versus participant observation

- Outline the relative advantages and disadvantages of qualitative interviewing and participant observation.
- Does one method seem more in tune with the preoccupations of qualitative researchers than the other?

CHAPTER GUIDE

The focus group method is an interview with several people on a specific topic or issue. This chapter explores:

- the possible reasons for preferring focus group interviews to individual interviews of the kind discussed in the previous chapter;

- the role of focus groups in market research;

- how focus groups should be conducted in terms of such features as the need for tape recording, the number and

size of groups, how participants can be selected, and how direct the questioning should be;

- the significance of interaction between participants in focus group discussions;

- the suggestion that the focus group method fits particularly well with a feminist research approach;

- some practical difficulties with focus group sessions, such as the possible loss of control over proceedings and the potential for unwanted group effects.

Introduction

We are used to thinking of the interview as something that involves an interviewer and one interviewee. Most textbooks reinforce this perception by concentrating on individual interviews. The focus group technique is a method of interviewing that involves more than one, usually at least four, interviewees. Essentially it is a group interview. Some authors draw a distinction between the focus group and the group interview techniques. Three reasons are sometimes put forward to suggest a distinction.

- Focus groups typically emphasize a specific theme or topic that is explored in depth, whereas group interviews often span very widely.

- Sometimes group interviews are carried out so that the researcher is able to save time and money by carrying out interviews with a number of individuals simultaneously. However, focus groups are not carried out for this reason.

- The focus group practitioner is invariably interested in the ways in which individuals discuss a certain issue *as members of a group*, rather than simply as individuals. In other words, with a focus group the researcher will be interested in such things as how people respond to each other's views and build up a view out of the interaction that takes place within the group.

However, the distinction between the focus group method and the group interview is by no means clear-cut and the two terms are frequently employed interchangeably. Nonetheless, the definition proposed in Box 16.1 provides a starting point.

Most focus group researchers undertake their work within the traditions of qualitative research. This means that they are explicitly concerned to reveal how the group participants view the issues with which they are confronted; therefore the researcher will aim to provide a fairly unstructured setting for the extraction of their views and perspectives. The person who runs the focus groups session is usually called the *moderator* or *facilitator* and he or she will be expected to guide each session but not to be too intrusive.

Another general point about the focus group method is that, although it has been used for many years in market research to test reactions to products and to advertising initiatives, it has more recently been developed for a wider variety of purposes. Hence focus groups are now used by politicians, not only quantitatively to predict the outcome of an election, but also qualitatively to shape their policies and images. Cowley (2000) reports that one politician used focus group research to determine that he should be filmed only from one side of his face, and he should be made to look older in order to increase voter support. Focus groups are used by film-makers to determine the end of a major film run, by art entrepreneurs to determine what paintings will sell, and by CEOs to test corporate communications. However, the popularization of the focus group method may have disadvantages for business and management researchers. For example, Blackburn and Stokes (2000) in their study of small businesses

---

Box 16.1 What is the focus group method?

The focus group method is a form of group interview in which: there are several participants (in addition to the moderator/facilitator); there is an emphasis in the questioning on a particular fairly tightly defined topic; and the accent is upon interaction within the group and the joint construction of meaning. As such, the focus group contains elements of two methods: the group interview, in which several people discuss a number of topics; and what has been called a *focused interview*, in which interviewees are selected because they 'are known to have been involved in a particular situation' (Merton et al. 1956: 3) and are asked about that involvement. The focused interview may be administered to individuals or to groups. Thus, the focus group method appends to the focused interview the element of interaction within groups as an area of interest and is more focused than the group interview.

suggest that it was more difficult to convince research audiences of the significance of their focus group research, partly because of the proliferation of the use of focus groups by political parties. Similarly Cowley (2000) suggests that, in order to distinguish research based on 'strategic qualitative market research focus groups' from research that is done by those who simply decide 'they can run' focus groups, despite their lack of experience, a professional code of conduct is needed. However, it must be remembered that, while the use of focus groups is gaining in popularity at the moment, it is by no means a new technique, as it has a long established use in various forms of social research.

Uses of focus groups

What are the uses of the focus group method? In many ways its uses are bound up with the uses of qualitative research in general, but, over and above these, the following points can be registered.

- The original idea for the focus group—the focused interview—was that people who were known to have had a certain experience could be interviewed in a relatively unstructured way about that experience. The bulk of the discussion by Merton et al. (1956) of the notion of the focused interview was in terms of individual interviews, but their book also considered the extension of the method into group interview contexts. Subsequently, the focus group has become a popular method for researchers examining the ways in which people in conjunction with one another construe the general topics in which the researcher is interested. In management and business, early use of the focus group technique was also seen as a way of helping individuals to define problems and work together to identify potential solutions (Hutt 1979). The dynamics of group discussion could lead individuals to define business problems in new and innovative ways and stimulate creative ideas for their solution.

- The technique allows the researcher to develop an understanding about *why* people feel the way they do. In a normal individual interview the interviewee is often asked about his or her reasons for holding a particular view, but the focus group approach offers the opportunity of allowing people to probe each other's reasons for holding a certain view. This can be more interesting than the sometimes predictable question-followed-by-answer approach of normal interviews. For one thing, an individual may answer in a certain way during a focus group, but, as he or she listens to others' answers, he or she may want to qualify or modify a view; or alternatively may want to voice agreement to something that he or she probably would not have thought of without the opportunity of hearing the views of others. These possibilities mean that focus groups may also be very helpful in the elicitation of a wide variety of different views in relation to a particular issue.

- In focus groups participants are able to bring to the fore issues in relation to a topic that they deem to be important and significant. This is clearly an aim of individual interviews too, but, because the moderator has to relinquish a certain amount of control to the participants, the issues that concern them can surface. This is clearly an important consideration in the context of qualitative research, since the viewpoints of the people being studied are an important point of departure.

- In conventional one-to-one interviewing, interviewees are rarely challenged; they might say things that are inconsistent with earlier replies or that patently could not be true, but we are often reluctant to point out such deficiencies. In the context of a focus group, individuals will often argue with each other and challenge each other's views. This process of arguing means that the researcher may stand a chance of ending up with more realistic accounts of what people think, because they are forced to think about and possibly revise their views.

- The focus group offers the researcher the opportunity to study the ways in which individuals collectively make sense of a phenomenon and construct meanings around it. It is a central tenet of theoretical positions like symbolic interactionism that the process of coming to terms with (that is, understanding) social phenomena is not undertaken by individuals in isolation from each other. Instead, it is something that occurs in interaction and discussion with others. In this sense, therefore, focus groups reflect the processes through which meaning is constructed in everyday life and to that extent can be regarded as more naturalistic (see Box 2.4 on the idea of naturalism) than individual interviews (Wilkinson 1998).

As we mentioned in the introduction, focus groups have been used extensively in market research for many years where the method is employed for such purposes as testing responses to new products and advertising initiatives (see Box 16.2 for an example). According to the UK Association of Qualitative Market Research Practitioners, focus groups represent the most commonly used research method in market research (see **www.aqrp.co.uk**). Focus groups typically involve groups of six–twelve consumers, who are brought together to discuss their reactions to new products, packaging, advertisements, or promotions. In fact there is a large literature within market research to do with the practices that are associated with focus group research and their implementation (e.g. Calder 1977).

However, the use of focus group methods in market research has attracted its fair share of controversy. Some researchers have suggested that it is a weaker method than say experiments or surveys (to name two research approaches that are common in market research). The most frequently mentioned problem is the perceived lack of generalizability—results are not always a reliable indicator of the reactions of the wider population. Criticism is also made of the unsystematic nature of the sample, which is not as rigorous as probability sampling (see Chapter 4). For example, Sudman and Blair (1999: 272) have suggested that, although the focus group method is an excellent tool for gaining insight about markets, 'it should be evident that a group of 10 or so people chosen haphazardly at a single location cannot be expected to reflect the total population of consumers'. A further difficulty stems from the lack of realism associated with focus groups. Participants may be given written or verbal descriptions of a product, or an artist's sketch, but this bears little relation to the real-life experience of choosing a product in

---

Box 16.2 The real and the unreal thing: focus groups in market research

On 23 April 1985 a product was launched that proved to be one of the greatest marketing blunders in business history. On that day, the Coca-Cola company not only launched what it called its New Coke but it removed from sale the old one, on which the massive corporation had been built. New Coke was a flop and the public clamoured for the return of its predecessor, in spite of assurances from the company that people would get used to the new formula and get to like it better. Yet close attention to data drawn from focus group research that the company had commissioned in the lead-up to the launch of New Coke might have prevented the disaster from happening. In 1982 and 1983, focus group research was conducted across the USA. At one point in each session, local consumers were presented with a scenario in which they were told that a new formula for a certain product had been introduced and that the response to it was very favourable. The participants were then asked how *they* would feel when it came to their town. The response to the prospect of new, improved Budweiser beer and of Hershey chocolate bars being replaced was met with a positive response. However, when the replacement of Coke was being considered, the consumers became vehemently antagonistic to the idea. Taste tests had shown that consumers liked New Coke but they had not been asked how they would feel if traditional Coke was taken off supermarket shelves. The focus groups made it clear how they would feel, but Coca-Cola's chief executive officer was determined to plough ahead and his assistant, who liaised with the firm conducting the focus groups, chose to follow his boss's lead.

Sources: Pendergrast (1993) and Greising (1998).

a competitive context. Criticisms also stem from problems of reliability. This relates to the role of the moderator and the suggestion that there can be variation in the interpretation of transcripts. Fern (2001) has provided a rebuttal of these criticisms by arguing that the generalizability of focus group findings, as with other research methods, depends on the scale of the sample—a two-group study may have limited generalizability but a thirty-two-group study is another matter. He also defends the reliability of focus groups, suggesting that representativeness can be achieved by stratifying the population and drawing random samples from each stratum. Fern suggests that greater reliability can be gained by using different moderators with different backgrounds (e.g. male and female) to conduct group discussions on a relevant topic (e.g. gender). The results from each group can then be compared for consistency of interpretation. Overall, however, what seems puzzling is that market researchers are attempting to defend their use of focus group methods in terms of quantitative rather than qualitative criteria; this is mainly because they are being criticized in terms of quantitative research criteria.

Conducting focus groups

There are a number of practical aspects of the conduct of focus group research that require some discussion.

Tape recording and transcription

As with interviewing for qualitative research, the focus group session will work best if it is tape-recorded and subsequently transcribed. The following reasons are often used to explain this preference.

- One reason is the simple difficulty of writing down not only exactly what people say but also who says it. In an individual interview you might be able to ask the respondent to hold on while you write something down, but to do this in the context of an interview involving several people would be extremely disruptive.

- The researcher will be interested in who expresses views within the group, such as whether certain individuals seem to act as opinion leaders or dominate the discussion. This also means that there is an interest in ranges of opinions within groups; for example, in a session, does most of the range of opinion derive from just one or two people or from most of the people in the group?

- A major reason for conducting focus group research is the fact that it is possible to study the processes whereby meaning is collectively constructed within each session (see above). It would be very difficult to do this by taking notes, because of the need to keep track of who says what (see also previous point). If this element is lost, the dynamics of the focus group session would also be lost, and a major rationale for doing focus group interviews rather than individual ones would be undermined.

- Like all qualitative researchers, the focus group practitioner will be interested in not just what people say but how they say it—for example, the particular language that they employ. There is every chance that the nuances of language will be lost if the researcher has to rely on notes.

It should be borne in mind that transcribing focus group sessions is more complicated and hence more time-consuming than transcribing traditional interview recordings. This is because you need to take account of who is talking in the session, as well as what is said. This is sometimes difficult, since people's voices are not always easy to distinguish. Also, people sometimes talk over each other, which can make transcription even more difficult. In addition, it is extremely important to ensure that you equip yourself with a very high-quality microphone, which is capable of picking up voices, some of which may be quite faint, from many directions. Focus group transcripts always seem to have more missing bits

Box 16.3 Virtual focus groups in market research

A recent development in marketing research involves the computerization of focus group interaction whereby group members interact with each other using specially designed software, rather than using a moderator (Kiely 1998).

Group members assemble in a room where there are networked computers. They type in their ideas about a given subject onto their own screen, where they see only the ideas that they type. A large screen at the front of the room then displays all the group members' comments simultaneously and anonymously. It is suggested that this process makes it easier for each group member to have an equal voice and more difficult for one person to dominate the discussion. The technology also makes it possible to reduce the time it takes to run a focus group, as all members of the group are able to express their ideas simultaneously rather than serially. As they see the ideas of others

on the main screen, individuals are able to build on the ideas already expressed.

However, focus group members do report feeling more anonymous within the encounter and therefore they find it less satisfactory. The technology implies that eventually focus groups may be held virtually—group members need not be in the same room with one another, or even in the same country.

Recent advances in computer graphics have also enabled innovation through virtual shopping, by simulating the atmosphere of an actual retail store on a computer screen (Burke 1996). Within this virtual environment focus group members are able to view shelves stocked with a range of products, examine the packaging, and decide whether or not to purchase it.

Practical tip *transcription of a focus group interview*

In Chapter 15, we provided the practical tip that it may be that it is not always desirable or feasible to transcribe the whole of the interview. The same applies to focus group research, which is often more difficult and time-consuming to transcribe than personal interview recordings because of the number of speakers who are involved. The suggestions we made in Chapter 15 in relation to transcribing sections of an interview therefore apply equally well to focus group recordings.

owing to lack of audibility than transcripts from conventional interviews. A recent development in market research has involved the introduction of virtual focus groups (see Box 16.3), who interact with each other via computer. This overcomes some of the problems associated with recording what goes on in focus groups, but it also raises difficulties.

How many groups?

How many groups do you need? Table 16.1 provides an example detailing the composition of a sequence of focus groups that was designed to reflect the impact of the local socio-economic context on small business owner-managers. This was a longitudinal focus group study, so the groups met on several occasions during an eighteen-month period (see Box 16.4). However, there is a good deal of variation in the numbers of focus groups that are used in any particular study, with the norm being somewhere between twelve and fifteen.

Clearly, it is unlikely that just one group will suffice the needs of the researcher, since there is always the possibility that the responses are particular to that one group. Obviously, time and resources will be a factor, but there are strong arguments for saying that too many groups will be a waste of time. Calder (1977) proposes that, when the moderator reaches the point that he or she is able to anticipate fairly accurately what the next group is going to say, then there are probably enough groups already. This notion is very similar to the *theoretical saturation* criterion that was briefly introduced in Box 14.10.

Table 16.1 Location and attendees from five focus groups

Location	Number of participants in each focus group			
	Sept. 1997	Mar. 1998	Nov. 1998	Mar. 1999
Reading	10	5	6	6
London	8	3	6	5
Kidderminster	7	7	3	6
Manchester	5	5	5	7
Glasgow/ Hartlepool	6	6	—	—
TOTAL	36	26	26	30

Source: adapted from Blackburn and Stokes (2000).

In other words, once your major analytic categories have been saturated, there seems little point in continuing, and so it would be appropriate to bring data collection to a halt. For their study of audience discussion programmes, Livingstone and Lunt (1994: 181) used this criterion: 'The number of focus groups was determined by continuing until comments and patterns began to repeat and little new material was generated.' When this point of theoretical saturation is reached, as an alternative to terminating data collection, there may be a case for moving on to an extension of the issues that have been raised in the focus group sessions that have been carried out.

One factor that may affect the number of groups is whether the researcher feels that the kinds and range of views are likely to be affected by socio-demographic factors such as age, gender, class, and so on. Many focus group researchers like to use stratifying criteria like these to ensure that groups with a wide range of features will be included. If so, a larger number of groups may be required to reflect the criteria. In connection with the research described in Box 16.4, Blackburn and Stokes (2000) explain that the composition of the groups was stratified according to business and personal criteria, including gender. A range of business sectors was represented within the focus groups, including manufacturing, construction, and services. Small businesses were defined quite

Practical tip 👉 *number of focus groups*

Focus groups take a long time to arrange and it takes a long time to transcribe the recordings that are made. It is likely that students will not be able to include as many focus group sessions for projects or dissertations as the studies cited in this chapter. You will, therefore, need to make do with a smaller number of groups in most instances. Make sure you are able to justify the number of groups you have chosen and why your data are still significant.

broadly in terms of certain turnover parameters—from a minimum of £50,000 to a maximum of £3,000,000. However, it may be that high levels of diversity are not anticipated in connection with some topics, in which case a large number of groups could represent an unnecessary expense.

One further point to bear in mind when considering the number of groups is that more groups will increase the complexity of your analysis. For example, Schlesinger et al. (1992: 29) report that the fourteen tape-recorded sessions they organized produced over 1,400 pages of transcription. This pile of paper was accumulated from discussions in each group of an average of one hour for each of the four screenings that session participants were shown. Although this means that the sessions were longer than is normally the case, it does demonstrate that the amount of data to analyse can be very large, even though a total of fourteen sessions may not sound a lot to someone unfamiliar with the workings of the method.

Size of groups

How large should groups be? Morgan (1998*a*) suggests that the typical group size is six to ten members, although in their study of small business owner-managers Blackburn and Stokes (2000) found that discussion in groups of more than eight was difficult to manage, so, as the research progressed, they scaled down the number of participants who were invited on each occasion. One major problem faced by focus group practitioners is people who agree to participate but who do not turn up on the day. It is almost impossible to control for 'no-shows' other than consciously over-recruiting, a strategy that is sometimes recommended (e.g. Wilkinson 1999*a*: 188).

In their research into small businesses, Blackburn and Stokes (2000) found that recruiting business-owners to attend a group discussion at a pre-set date and venue away from their business context proved to be a time-consuming process (see Box 16.4). The acceptance rate to invitations was as low as one to ten and the exercise of ensuring attendance involved a great number of telephone calls to ensure a broad spread of participants. However, after participants had attended one focus group and had got to know each other and exchanged business cards, they were more likely to attend a second time, as they were keen to hear how each other's businesses were developing. Overall the researchers found it very difficult to predict the 'no-show' rate. This meant that the size of their focus groups varied considerably, from three to ten (see Table 16.1). Blackburn and Stokes acknowledge that there was likely to be quite different dynamics in the different size groups; in particular, in the smaller groups greater demands were made on each participant to contribute more.

Almost the opposite problem was faced by Milkman (1997) in her study of auto factory workers

at the General Motors plant in New Jersey. Milkman and her colleague conducted three focus group discussions at the plant—two with production workers and one with skilled trades workers. Each discussion was held in a conference room inside the plant during regular working hours, lasted around two hours, and was tape-recorded and transcribed. Workers were selected randomly from the plant roster and they were paid their normal wage for the time spent in discussion. This, according to Milkman, 'ensured perfect attendance', but it also 'underscored the project's official status' (1997: 195). She suspects that this made some participants suspicious and less inclined to speak freely.

Morgan (1998*a*) recommends smaller groups when participants are likely to have a lot to say on the research topic. This is likely to occur when participants are very involved in or emotionally preoccupied with the topic. He also suggests smaller groups when topics are controversial or complex and when gleaning participants' personal accounts is a major goal. Morgan recommends larger groups when involvement with a topic is likely to be low or when the researcher wants 'to hear numerous brief suggestions' (1998*a*: 75). However, we are not convinced that larger groups are necessarily superior for topics in which participants have little involvement, since it may be more difficult to stimulate discussion in such a context. Larger groups may make it even more difficult if people are rather diffident about talking about a topic about which they know little or have little experience. This was a potential problem in Blackburn and Stokes's (2000) study, where external information, such as government proposals on late payment legislation, formed the basis for discussion. However, in these instances, the researchers found that participants relied more heavily on their own personal experiences and provided detailed accounts of payment practices in their industry.

Level of moderator involvement

How involved should the moderator/facilitator be? In qualitative research, the aim is to get at the perspectives of those being studied. Consequently, the approach should not be intrusive and structured.

Box 16.4 Using focus groups in small business research

Blackburn and Stokes (2000) used focus groups in their research into UK small firms across a range of sectors. Their decision was partly driven by a concern that much research into small firms has revealed little about the motivations, rationales, and experiences of business owner-managers. For this, more qualitative research is required and focus groups were seen as a means through which the culturally different world of the owner-manager can be encountered on a more equal basis.

One of the aims of the focus groups was to capture the immediate reactions of business owners to government statements and the launch of new initiatives. Focus groups were held on four occasions at six monthly intervals (see Table 16.1) in order to compare their initial reactions with later, more considered views.

Each focus group had three main objectives:

- to generate data on owner-managers' experiences of and reasons for running a business;
- to seek their views about the current business environment, including government policy;
- to explore how they see their world as business owner-managers and how they approach issues such as succession planning and finding new customers.

Focus groups were held in locations across the UK, based on the assumption that experiences would be different in particular local environments and socio-economic contexts. 'Whilst it is accepted that these focus groups can not aim to be truly *representative* of the small business population as a whole, it was important to ensure that the results could be *illustrative* of the possible regional and sectoral variations and therefore provide a limited level of generalizability for the results' (2000: 51). Potential participants were identified using local business

directories. The incentive they were offered was primarily social—participants would get the chance to meet other business owners and exchange experiences. The researchers also offered to pay for participants' expenses.

The meetings were held in the offices of a sponsor, a chartered accountancy practice. Blackburn and Stokes acknowledge that this location might have been a deterrent for business owners, presumably as it may be associated with taxation, but they argue that the impact of this possibility was minimized by informing business owners of the location only once they had agreed to participate!

Each moderator was accompanied by an assistant, who organized the layout of the room, took responsibility for audio-recording the event, and took notes to capture non-verbal signals and nuances. Room size constraints meant that the researchers decided against video recording.

Prior to the study, one of the concerns that the researchers had was about the extent to which business owners would be prepared to share the detail of their specific cases in a group setting. As the extract in Box 16.5 suggests, this proved not to be a problem: 'any reservations we had that business owners would be reluctant to open-up in front of their peers . . . were not borne out' (2000: 60).

The study also raised some ethical issues. In particular, although the researchers changed the names of participants in order to ensure their confidentiality, when the research was published, the research unit that had commissioned the research was approached by the media, seeking names and telephone numbers of the participants, to speak to them directly. Blackburn and Stokes contacted the focus group participants and asked them if were willing to talk to the press. Only if they were willing were their details passed on to the journalist.

Therefore, there is a tendency for researchers to use a fairly small number of very general questions to guide the focus group session. Moreover, there is a further tendency for moderators to allow quite a lot of latitude to participants, so that the discussion can range fairly widely. Box 16.5 provides an example of an extract from a focus group discussion where there is no moderator involvement. In this instance, three quite different opinions emerge in relation to the issue of succession planning without any moderator

prompting. Obviously, if the discussion goes off at a total tangent, it may be necessary to refocus the participants' attention, but even then it may be necessary to be careful, because what may appear to be digressions may in fact reveal something of interest to the group participants. The advantage of allowing a fairly free rein to the discussion is that the researcher stands a better chance of getting access to what individuals see as important or interesting. On the other hand, too much totally irrelevant discussion

---

Box 16.5 Extract from a focus group discussion showing no moderator involvement

Michael ...—talking about your family taking over the business—that's something I wouldn't do with my family because I don't think they've got the fire. I just don't think my daughters have got the same fire as I've got.

Mike You're forcing them down a particular channel—there are so many things they can do... I think that they may or may not have the right qualities to do that—they may wish to go out and do other things... plus you might think that in giving them a thriving business you're spoiling them so I just think this whole family business thing is an absolute can of worms.

Gary If they're in it already though it's a different situation.

Mike ...Well I accept that... my exit strategy is that at some point I've got to sell the business and I think the management team realise that. So they know when we're discussing share options there's only one point—you know we were discussing what's the point in owning shares in a private business—there is only one point when it is worth it and that's when the business is sold. So what it is, is when the business is sold they get a share of the benefit—so that's the sort of logic there. (Blackburn and Stokes 2000: 60)

Box 16.6 Extract from a focus group discussion showing some moderator involvement

Moderator Has anyone other than Gary taken advice on exit routes?

Lilian We took advice when we made our plan in the first place about moving ourselves away from the front end of the business. How we geared our pension schemes...

Mike I've taken advice and their advice was you need to be bigger... to make the amount of money you need to actually walk away from it... I'm in the process of doing that...

Marina We started this actually about two years ago and we have taken advice and put plans into place. I do believe it is very important to have those plans and the correct ones. They always advise you to get bigger and you have to be a certain size... (Blackburn and Stokes 2000: 59)

---

may prove too unproductive, especially in the commercial environment of market research. It is not surprising, therefore, that, as Wilkinson (1999*a*) observes, some writers on focus groups perceive the possibility that participants come to take over the running of a session from the moderator as a problem and offer advice on how to reassert control (e.g. Krueger 1988).

One way in which the moderator may need to be involved is in responding to specific points that are of potential interest to the research questions but that are not picked up by other participants. In the extract in Box 16.6 from the study of small business owner-managers (Blackburn and Stokes 2000), the moderator provides a prompt to guide the discussion of planned business succession to find out if any of the participants have taken advice on this issue. This encourages the group to share their experiences.

Clearly, the moderator has to straddle two positions: allowing the discussion to flow freely and intervening to bring out especially salient issues, particularly when group participants do not do so.

This is not an easy conundrum to resolve and each tactic—intervention and non-intervention—carries risks. The best advice is to err on the side of minimal intervention—other than to start the group on a fresh set of issues—but to intervene when the group is struggling in its discussions or when it has not alighted on something that is said in the course of the session that appears significant for the research topic.

Selecting participants

So who should participate in a focus group? This depends on who will find the topic relevant and who can represent specific occupational or organizational groupings that have an interest in the topic concerned. Usually, a wide range of organizational members or stakeholders from different organizations is required, but they are organized into separate groups in terms of stratifying criteria, such as age, gender, occupation, profession, hierarchical position within the organization, or length of service. Participants for each group can then be selected randomly or through some kind of snowball sampling method. The aim is to establish whether there is any systematic variation in the ways in which different groups discuss a matter.

A further issue in relation to the selection of group participants is whether to select people who are unknown to each other (for example, members of the same professional association or employees from different divisions within the same organization) or to use natural groupings (for example, co-workers or students on the same course). Some researchers prefer to exclude people who know each other on the grounds that pre-existing styles of interaction or status differences may contaminate the session. Not all writers accept this rule of thumb. Some prefer to select natural groups whenever possible. For example, in marketing research, companies like Procter and Gamble tend to go back repeatedly to the same pool from which they draw focus groups (Kiely 1998).

However, opting for a strategy of recruiting people entirely from natural groups is not always feasible, because of difficulties of securing participation. For example, it is not always feasible to remove a number of employees from work activity at the same time in

which case other strategies of selection may have to be used. Morgan (1998*a*) suggests that one problem with using natural groups is that people who know each other well are likely to operate with taken-for-granted assumptions that they feel do not need to be brought to the fore. He suggests that, if it is important for the researcher to bring out such assumptions, groups of strangers are likely to work better. On the other hand, if the focus group is intended to explore collective understandings or shared meanings held within a work group, this can be achieved more readily by using participants who are all members of the same group.

Asking questions

An issue that is close to the question of the degree of involvement on the part of the moderator is the matter of how far there should be a set of questions that must be addressed. This issue is very similar to the considerations about how unstructured an interview should be in qualitative interviewing (see Chapter 15). Some researchers prefer to use just one or two very general questions to stimulate discussion, with the moderator intervening as necessary along the lines outlined above. However, other researchers prefer to inject somewhat more structure into the organization of the focus group sessions. A clear example of this is the research on small business owner-managers in which moderators worked with a topic agenda with times allocated to the discussion of each topic (see Figure 16.1). Initial questions were designed to generate initial reactions in a relatively open-ended way, to put the owner-managers at ease and to get them talking as soon as possible in an informal manner. Then the moderator moved the discussion on to the substantive issues of trading climate, challenges in the business environment, government policies and business succession and exit strategies. Such a general approach to questioning, which is fairly common in focus group research, allows the researcher to navigate the channel between, on the one side, addressing the research questions and ensuring comparability between sessions, and, on the other side, allowing participants to raise issues they see as significant and in their own terms.

Topic Agenda

1. **Introduction (15 mins.)**
   Introduce the research team and roles
   Aim and format of the focus group
   Conventions (confidentiality, speak one at a time,
   recordings, everybody's views, open debate, report
   of proceedings)
   Personal introduction of participants and their businesses

2. **Discussion Topics**
   i)   *Current trading climate* (15 mins.)
        (e.g. comparative order levels)
   ii) *Main challenges in the business environment* (20 mins.)
        (e.g. exchange rates, recruitment, raising money)
   iii) *Government policies and small firms* (20 mins.)
        (e.g. the minimum wage, entry into the Euro)
   iv) *Topical issues* (20 mins.)
        (e.g. business succession and exit strategies)

3. **Summing Up**
   Thanks for participation and report back
   Invite back to next event in 6 months
   Reimburse expenses

4. **Lunch**
   Sandwiches and drinks
   Close

Figure 16.1 An example of a topic agenda for a small business owner-manager focus group

Clearly, there are different questioning strategies and approaches to moderating focus group sessions. Most seem to lie somewhere in between the rather open-ended approach employed by some business researchers and the somewhat more structured one used by Blackburn and Stokes (2000). There is probably no one best way and the style of questioning and moderating is likely to be affected by various factors, such as the nature of the research topic (for example, is it one that the researcher already knows a lot about, in which case a modicum of structure is feasible) and levels of interest and/or knowledge among participants in the research (for example, a low level of participant interest may require a somewhat more structured approach). Whichever strategy of questioning is employed, the focus group researcher should generally be prepared to allow at least some discussion that departs from the interview guide, since such debate may provide new and unexpected insights. A more structured approach to questioning might inhibit such spontaneity, but it is unlikely to remove it altogether.

Group interaction in focus group sessions

Kitzinger (1994) has observed that reports of focus group research frequently do not take into account interaction within the group. This is surprising, because it is precisely the operation of social interaction and its forms and impact that would seem to distinguish the focus group session from the individual interview. Yet, as Kitzinger observes, very few publications based on focus group research cite or draw inferences from patterns of interaction within the group. Wilkinson reviewed over 200 studies based on focus groups and published between 1946 and 1996. She concluded: 'Focus group data is most commonly presented as if it were one-to-one interview data, with interactions between group participants rarely reported, let alone analysed' (1998: 112).

Interactions between focus group participants may either be complementary or argumentative (Kitzinger 1994). The former brings out the elements of the social world that provide participants' own frameworks of understanding so that agreement emerges in people's minds. In the example provided by the data extract in Box 16.6, the first part of the discussion demonstrates broad agreement between Michael and Mike about the issues involved in handing over the business to a family member, with Mike building on the preceding remarks made by Michael. This complementary interaction is then interrupted by Gary, who suggests that this depends on whether or not the family member is actively involved in the day-to-day running of the business. This more argumentative interaction leads Mike to revert to an alternative exit strategy—one that relies ultimately on selling the business.

However, as Kitzinger suggests, arguments in focus groups can be equally revealing. She suggests that moderators can play an important role in identifying differences of opinion and exploring with participants the factors that may lie behind them. Disagreement can provide participants with the opportunity to revise their opinions or to think more about the reasons why they hold the view that they do. As Kitzinger argues, drawing attention to patterns of interaction within focus groups allows the researcher to determine how group participants view the issues with which they are confronted in their own terms. The posing of questions by, and agreement and disagreement among, participants help to bring out their own stances on these issues. The resolution of disagreements also helps to force participants to express the grounds on which they hold particular views.

The focus group as a feminist method

The use of focus groups by feminist researchers has grown considerably in recent years and Wilkinson (1998, 1999b) has argued that it has great potential in this regard. Three aspects of the method stand out in terms of their compatibility with the ethics and politics of feminism:

- Focus group research is less artificial than many other methods, because, in emphasizing group interaction, which is a normal part of social life, it does not suffer from the problem of gleaning information in an unnatural situation. Moreover, the tendency of many focus group researchers to recruit participants from naturally occurring groups underpins the lower level of artificiality of the method, since people are able to discuss in situations that are quite normal for them. As a result, there is greater opportunity to derive understandings that chime with the 'lived experience' of women. However, not all writers accept the contention that focus groups are more naturalistic than individual interviews. Even when natural groups are used, gathering people to discuss a certain topic (such as a television advertisement) is not inherently naturalistic, because the social setting is to a significant extent contrived (Morrison 1998: 154–5). Indeed, completing questionnaires or being interviewed may appear more natural, because such instruments are fairly commonplace, whereas being asked to discuss in a group an issue not necessarily of one's choosing is less so.

- Feminist researchers have expressed a preference for methods that avoid *decontextualization*—that is, that successfully study the individual within a social context. The tendency for most methods to treat the individual as a separate entity devoid of a social context is disliked by many feminist researchers, who prefer to analyse 'the self as relational or as socially constructed' (Wilkinson 1999b: 229–30). Because the individual is very much part of a group in the focus group method, this tendency towards decontextualization is avoided.

- As we have seen in previous chapters, feminist researchers are suspicious of research methods that are exploitative and create a power relationship between the female researcher and the female respondent. Wilkinson observes that the risk of this occurring is greatly reduced, because focus group participants are able to take over much of the direction of the session from the moderator. Indeed, they may even subvert the goals of the session in ways that could be of considerable interest to the moderator. As a result, participants' points of view are much more likely to be revealed than in a traditional interview.

Wilkinson does not argue that focus groups or indeed any method can be described as inherently feminist. Instead, she argues that, because of these three features and when employed with a sensitivity towards feminist concerns, the focus group method has considerable potential as a tool of feminist research.

The kinds of argument put forward regarding the fit between the focus group method and feminist research have been extended to suggest they may have a further role in allowing the voices of highly marginalized groups of women to surface. Madriz (2000: 843) argues that, for a group like lower-socio-economic-class women of colour, focus groups constitute a relatively rare opportunity for them to 'empower themselves by making sense of their experience of vulnerability and subjugation'.

Limitations of focus groups

Focus groups clearly have considerable potential for research questions in which the processes through which meaning is jointly constructed is likely to be of particular interest. Indeed, it may be that, even when this is not a prominent emphasis, the use of the focus group method may be appropriate and even advantageous, since it allows participants' perspectives—an important feature of much qualitative research (see Chapter 13)—to be revealed in ways that are different from individual interviews (for example, through discussion, participants' questions, arguments, and so on). It also offers considerable potential for feminist researchers. What, then, might be its chief limitations?

- The researcher probably has less control over proceedings than with the individual interview. As we have seen, by no means all writers on focus groups perceive this as a disadvantage and indeed feminist researchers often see it as an advantage. However, the question of control raises issues for researchers of how far they can allow a focus group to 'take over' the running of proceedings. There is clearly a delicate balance to be taken into account over how involved moderators should be and how far a set of prompts or questions should influence the conduct of a focus group, as some of the earlier discussions have suggested. What is not clear is the degree to which it is appropriate to surrender control of a focus group to its participants, especially when there is a reasonably explicit set of research questions to be answered, as is commonly the case, for example, in funded research.
- The data are difficult to analyse. A huge amount of data can be very quickly produced. Developing a strategy of analysis that incorporates both themes in what people say and patterns of interaction is not easy. Also, as previously pointed out, focus group recordings are particularly prone to inaudible elements, which affects transcription.

- They are difficult to organize. Not only do you have to secure the agreement of people to participate in your study; you also need to persuade them to turn up at a particular time. Small inducements, such as payment of expenses or provision of lunch, are sometimes made to induce participation, but nonetheless it is common for people not to turn up.

- The recordings are probably more time-consuming to transcribe than equivalent recordings of individual interviews, because of variations in voice pitch and the need to take account of who says what.

- There are possible problems of group effects. This includes the obvious problem of dealing with reticent speakers and with those who hog the stage! In this respect, they are a bit like tutorials. Krueger (1998) suggests in relation to the problem of overly prominent participants that the moderator should make clear to the speaker and other group participants that other people's views are definitely required; for example, he suggests saying something like 'That's one point of view. Does anyone have another point of view?' (1998: 59). As for those who do not speak very much, it is recommended that they are actively encouraged to say something. Also, as the well-known Asch experiments showed (see Box 16.7), an emerging group view may mean that a perfectly legitimate perspective held by just one individual may be suppressed. There is also evidence that, as a group comes to share a certain point of view, group members come to think uncritically about it and to develop almost irrational attachments to it (Janis 1982). It is not known how far such group effects have an adverse impact on focus group findings, but it is clear that they cannot be entirely ignored. In this context, it would be interesting to know how far agreement among focus group participants is more frequently encountered than disagreement (we have a hunch that it is), since the effects to which both Asch and Janis referred would lead us to expect more agreement than disagreement in focus group discussions.

- Madriz (2000) proposes that there are circumstances when focus groups may not be appropriate, because of their potential for causing discomfort among participants. When such discomfort might arise, individual interviews are likely to be preferable. Situations in which unease might be occasioned are: when intimate details of private lives need to be revealed; when participants may not be comfortable in each other's presence (for example, bringing together people in a hierarchical relationship to each other); and when participants are likely to disagree profoundly with each other.

Box 16.7 Group conformity and the focus group method

Asch's (1951) laboratory studies into individual conformity to group norms provide us with an indication of the risks that are associated with focus groups. One experiment involved seven men who were brought together as a group and seated at a table. The men were told that they were participating in a study on visual perception. However, only one of the men was a real participant, the rest were 'actors' paid by Asch to participate. The group was shown a series of lines and asked to judge which were equal in length.

However, the actor-participants had been instructed to lie about which of the lines was equal. Despite the obviousness of the task, in most of the trials that Asch conducted the individual subject conceded to the group judgement, rather than giving the response he or she judged to be correct. The research showed that it was difficult for individuals to express their opinions when they contradict the views of other group members.

These findings have obvious implications for the conduct of focus groups, particularly since Asch also found that conformity increased when group members had to continue working together in the future—a distinct possibility within organizational research. However, Asch also found that conformity decreased when subjects were not face to face, so there may be advantages in conducting virtual focus groups of the kind described in Box 16.3.

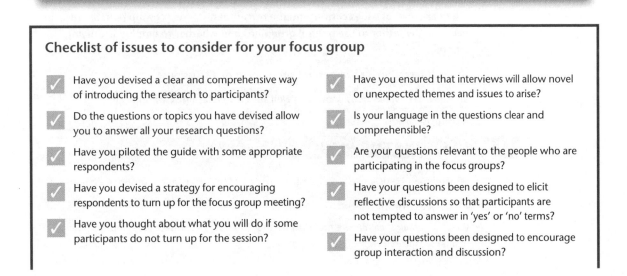

Checklist of issues to consider for your focus group

✓ Have you devised a clear and comprehensive way of introducing the research to participants?

✓ Do the questions or topics you have devised allow you to answer all your research questions?

✓ Have you piloted the guide with some appropriate respondents?

✓ Have you devised a strategy for encouraging respondents to turn up for the focus group meeting?

✓ Have you thought about what you will do if some participants do not turn up for the session?

✓ Have you ensured that interviews will allow novel or unexpected themes and issues to arise?

✓ Is your language in the questions clear and comprehensible?

✓ Are your questions relevant to the people who are participating in the focus groups?

✓ Have your questions been designed to elicit reflective discussions so that participants are not tempted to answer in 'yes' or 'no' terms?

✓ Have your questions been designed to encourage group interaction and discussion?

✓ Do your questions offer a real prospect of seeing the world from your interviewees' point of view rather than imposing your own frame of reference on them?

✓ Are you familiar with the setting(s) in which the interview will take place?

✓ Are you thoroughly familiar with and have you tested your recording or audio-visual equipment?

✓ Have you thought about how you will present yourself in the session, such as how you will be dressed?

✓ Have you devised a strategy for dealing with silences?

✓ Have you devised a strategy for dealing with participants who are reluctant to speak?

✓ Have you devised a strategy for dealing with participants who speak too much and hog the discussion?

✓ Do you have a strategy for how far you are going to intervene in the focus group discussion?

✓ Do you have a strategy for dealing with the focus group if the discussion goes off in a tangent?

✓ Have you tested out any aids that you are going to present to focus group participants (e.g. visual aids, segments of film, case studies)?

K KEY POINTS

- The focus group is a group interview that is concerned with exploring a certain topic.

- The moderator generally tries to provide a relatively free rein to the discussion. However, there may be contexts in which it is necessary to ask fairly specific questions, especially when cross-group comparability is an issue.

- There is concern with the joint production of meaning.

- Focus group discussions need to be tape-recorded and transcribed.

- There are several issues concerning the recruitment of focus group participants—in particular, whether to use natural groupings and whether to employ stratifying criteria.

- Group interaction is an important component of discussions.

- Some writers view focus groups as well suited to a feminist standpoint.

Q QUESTIONS FOR REVIEW

- Why might it be useful to distinguish between a focus group and a group interview?

Uses of focus groups

- What advantages might the focus group method offer in contrast to an individual qualitative interview?

Conducting focus groups

- How involved should the moderator be?
- Why is it necessary to tape-record and transcribe focus group sessions?
- Are there any circumstances in which it might be a good idea to select participants who know each other?
- What might be the advantages and disadvantages of using an interview guide in focus group sessions?

Group interaction in focus group sessions

- Why might it be important to treat group interaction as an important issue when analysing focus group data?

The focus group as a feminist method

- Evaluate the argument that the focus group can be viewed as a feminist method.
- To what extent are focus groups a naturalistic approach to data collection?

Limitations of focus groups

- Does the potential for the loss of control over proceedings and group effects damage the potential utility of the focus group as a method?
- How far do the greater problems of transcription and difficulty of analysis undermine the potential of focus groups?

17 Language in qualitative research

CHAPTER GUIDE

This chapter is concerned with two approaches to the examination of language: conversation analysis and discourse analysis. For the practitioners of both approaches, language is an object of interest in its own right and not simply a resource through which research participants communicate with researchers. The chapter explores:

- the roots of conversation analysis in ethnomethodology;

- some of its rules and principles;

- the assumptions of discourse analysis;

- some of its analytic strategies;

- points of difference between the two approaches.

Introduction

Language is bound to be of importance for business researchers. It is after all through language that we ask people questions in interviews and through which the questions are answered. Language is also central to the structuring of organizations, if only because people in work organizations rely so heavily on talk—in meetings, on the telephone, in the cafeteria—in order to accomplish their everyday business. It is through language that people in organizations exchange information, skills, services, and resources and make sense of their situation through interaction with each other. Furthermore, within managerial work a remarkably high emphasis is placed on verbal interaction, as findings from various research studies have suggested. For example, Mintzberg's (1973) study reports that verbal contacts, face to face and on the telephone, accounted for 75 per cent of senior managers' time and 67 per cent of their activities (see Chapter 8 for a more detailed explanation of Mintzberg's study). Other studies have shown that between 57 and 89 per cent of managerial time is spent in verbal interaction (Boden 1994). The role of the organizational researcher who focuses on language is to explore the nature of the relationship between language and action in these instances.

Understanding language categories has been an important component of research involving participant observation, because knowing how words are used and the meanings of specific terms in the local vernacular (often called 'argot') is frequently viewed as crucial to an appreciation of how the social world being studied is viewed by its members. In this chapter, however, two approaches will be examined that

treat language as their central focal points. They are called conversation analysis (CA) and discourse analysis (DA). What is crucial about these approaches is that, unlike traditional views of the role of language in business research, they treat language as a topic rather than as a resource (admittedly a clichéd phrase). This means that language is treated as significantly more than as a medium through which the business of research is conducted (such as asking questions in interviews). It becomes a focus of attention in its own right. This implies that language is not just seen as reflective of what goes on in an organization; instead language and organization become one and the same. This means, for example, that, as soon as managers in a public-sector organization start to talk of their client groups as 'customers', a whole new way of defining the organization's purpose and activities is introduced. While CA and DA do not exhaust the range of possibilities for studying language as a topic, they do represent two of the most prominent approaches. Each has evolved a technical vocabulary and set of techniques. This chapter will outline some of the basic elements of each of them and draw attention to some contrasting features.

Conversation analysis

The roots of CA lie in ethnomethodology, a sociological position developed in the USA under the general tutelage of Harold Garfinkel and Harvey Sacks, though it is the latter with whom CA is most associated. Ethnomethodology takes as its basic focus of attention 'practical, common-sense reasoning' in everyday life and as such is fundamentally concerned with the notion of social life as an accomplishment. Social order is not seen as a pre-existing force constraining individual action, but as something that is worked at and accomplished through interaction. Contrary to what its name implies, ethnomethodology is *not* a research methodology; it is the study of the methods employed in everyday life though which social order is accomplished.

Two ideas are particularly central to ethnomethodology and find clear expression in CA: indexicality and

reflexivity. The former means that the meaning of an act, which in CA essentially means spoken words or utterances including pauses and sounds, depends upon the context in which it is used. Reflexivity means that spoken words are constitutive of the social world in which they are located; in other words, the principle of reflexivity in ethnomethodology means that talk is not a 'mere' representation of the social world, so that it does much more than just stand for something else. In these ways, ethnomethodology fits fairly squarely with two aspects of qualitative research—the predilection for a contextual understanding of action (see Chapter 13) and an ontological position associated with constructionism (see Chapter 1).

In the years following its initial introduction into sociology, ethnomethodological research split into two camps. One entailed drawing on traditional social research methods, albeit in perhaps a somewhat altered form, and on ethnography in particular (e.g. Cicourel 1968). The other, which is mainly associated with Sacks and his co-workers (e.g. Sacks, Schegloff, and Jefferson 1974), sought to conduct fine-grained analyses of talk in naturally occurring situations. Moreover, it is not just talk in itself that is the object of interest but talk as it occurs in and through social interaction. CA concerns itself with the organization of such talk in the context of interaction (see Box 17.1). In order to conduct such investigations, a premium was placed on the recording of naturally occurring conversations and their transcription for the purpose of intensive analysis of the sequences of interaction revealed in the subsequent transcripts. As such, CA is a multifaceted approach—part theory, part method of data acquisition, part method of analysis. The predilection for the analysis of talk gleaned from naturally occurring situations suggests that CA chimes with another preoccupation among qualitative researchers—namely, a commitment to naturalism (see Boxes 2.4 and 13.1).

As the definition of CA in Box 17.1 and the preceding discussion suggest, CA takes from ethnomethodology a concern with the production of social order through and in the course of social interaction but takes conversation as the basic form through which that social order is achieved. The element of indexicality is also evident, in that practitioners of CA argue that the meaning of words is contextually grounded, whilst the commitment to reflexivity is revealed in the view that talk is constitutive of the social context in which it occurs.

Conversation analysts have developed a variety of procedures for the study of talk in interaction. Psathas (1995: 1) has described them as 'rigorous, systematic procedures' that can 'provide reproducible results'. Such a framework smacks of the commitment to the codification of procedures that generate valid, reliable, and replicable findings that are a feature of quantitative research. It is not surprising, therefore, that CA is sometimes described as having a positivist orientation. Thus, a cluster of features that are broadly in tune with qualitative research (contextual, naturalistic, studying the social world in its own terms and without prior theoretical commitments) are married to traits that are resonant of quantitative research. However, the emphasis on context in CA is somewhat at variance with the way in which contextual understanding is normally conceptualized in qualitative research. For CA practitioners, context refers to the specific here-and-now context of immediately preceding talk, whereas for most qualitative researchers it has a much wider set of resonances, which has to do with an appreciation of such things as the culture of the group within which action occurs. In other words, action is to be understood in terms of the values, beliefs, and typical modes of behaviour of that group. This is precisely the kind of attribution from which CA practitioners are keen to refrain. It is no wonder, therefore, that writers like Gubrium and Holstein (1997) treat it as a separate tradition within qualitative research (see Box 13.1), while Silverman (1993) finds it difficult to fit CA into broad descriptions of the nature of qualitative research.

Even though organizations are important contexts for talk and interaction, conversation analysis has rarely focused directly on the management of business and work organizations. A notable contribution is made by Boden (1994), who uses conversation analysis as a technique for the study of business firms and looks at the way that talk influences organizational structures. In her book, Boden highlights the importance of formal and informal meetings, which she sees as involving sequences of talk that enable people to transmit information, make decisions, and sort out misunderstandings. She suggests that conversation analysis can provide a means

---

Box 17.1 :💡: *What is conversation analysis?*

Conversation analysis (CA) is the fine-grained analysis of talk as it occurs in interaction in naturally occurring situations. The talk is recorded and transcribed so that the detailed analyses can be carried out. These analyses are concerned with uncovering the underlying structures of talk in interaction and as such with the achievement of order through interaction.

Box 17.2 Conversation analysis in action: the social organization of calculation in an entrepreneurial firm

In their study of entrepreneurial work, Anderson, Hughes, and Sharrock (1989) were concerned to understand the nature of the daily activities and business lives of senior personnel who worked in a UK-based fast food company, Leisure Time Catering (LTC). They approached the study from an ethnomethodological perspective, therefore, their primary concern was with how business practice at LTC was achieved.

The study involved the full-time attachment of one of the researchers to LTC for six months, followed by days and visits spent in and around the company catching up on recent developments. Data collection combined ethnographic methods, in particular the writing of field notes, with the use of a tape recorder to record the detail of meetings and conversations, the latter provided the focus for subsequent CA.

One of the aims of the study was to explore how transaction was arrived at, how prices were determined, and how supply and demand were coordinated within the firm. Hence, the researchers focused on the way that prices were negotiated, by looking in detail at the negotiation of a contract for the supply of beers and lagers to all LTC outlets.

They begin their analysis with an excerpt from field notes detailing an important meeting between the supplier and brewery manager—Graham—and the LTC purchasing manager—Giles. They point out that, although the parties had met before and engaged in previous negotiations, this meeting still involved a series of conversational moves—the results of which had not been fully worked out in advance. (An example of one of these sequences is provided in Box 17.5). Anderson and his colleagues suggest that negotiation involves, amongst other things, performing a role, being able to exploit an advantage, and arriving at a resolution or compromise between incompatible drives. They conclude that the determination of price at LTC is a socially organized process that cannot be understood only or even mainly in terms of economic forces.

---

of understanding these interactional contexts, by looking at the way that talk is organized in meetings. A further example of conversation analysis in work organizations is provided by Anderson, Hughes, and Sharrock (1989), who studied the social organization of calculation and entrepreneurship in a fast food business (see Box 17.2).

Assumptions of conversation analysis

Heritage (1984, 1987) has proposed that CA is governed by three basic assumptions.

- *Talk is structured.* Talk comprises invariant patterns—that is, it is structured. Participants are implicitly aware of the rules that underpin these patterns. As a result, conversation analysts eschew attempts to infer the motivations of speakers from what they say or to ascribe their talk to personal characteristics. Such information is unnecessary, since the

conversation analyst is oriented to the underlying structures of action, as revealed in talk.

- *Talk is forged contextually.* Action is revealed in talk and as such talk must be analysed in terms of its context. This means that we must seek to understand what someone says in terms of the talk that has preceded it and that therefore talk is viewed as exhibiting patterned sequences.

- *Analysis is grounded in data.* Conversation analysts shun prior theoretical schemes and instead argue that characteristics of talk and of the constitutive nature of social order in each empirical instance must be induced out of data. Heritage (1987: 258) has written: 'it is assumed that social actions work *in detail* and hence that the specific details of interaction cannot simply be ignored as insignificant without damaging the prospects for coherent and effective analyses.' This assumption represents a manifesto for the emphasis on fine-grained details (including length of pauses, prolongation of sounds, and so on) that is the hallmark of CA.

Transcription and attention to detail

As the third of the three assumptions associated with CA indicates, the approach requires the analyst to produce detailed transcripts of natural conversation. Consider the portion of transcript in Boxes 17.3 and 17.4 that contain some of the basic notational symbols employed in CA.

The transcript extract in Box 17.3 includes some basic symbols employed by conversation analysts:

(0.3)   A figure in parentheses indicates the length of a period of silence, usually measured in tenths of one second. Thus, (0.3) signals three-tenths of a second of silence.

?   Punctuation marks are used to capture characteristics of speech delivery rather than grammatical notation.

The transcript extract in Box 17.4 includes some further symbols employed by conversation analysts:

you, actually   Italics indicate emphasis in delivery.

-a   A hyphen represents a cut off of a prior word or syllable.

A number of other notational symbols are also used including:

Ye[s, two.]   Brackets indicate the point at which simultaneous speech overlaps.

We:ll   A colon indicates that the sound that occurs directly before the colon is prolonged. More than one colon means further prolongation (e.g. : : : :).

.hh   h's preceded by a dot indicate an intake of breath. If no dot is present, it means breathing out.

(.)   Indicates a very slight pause.

Box 17.3 A question and answer adjacency pair

Boden (1994) provides the following example from an exchange between two sales representatives, who have never met before, talking about a new sales manager they are about to work for.

Salesmen
1. **B:** The *reps* report to him?
2. **A:** Yeah.
3.   (0.3)
4. **A:** for *orders*.

5. **B:** Yeah, line stuff.
6. **A:** Yeah 'sright. All the time.   (1994: 67–8)

This is a typical series of adjacency pairs in conversation, even though only the first question, by Speaker B, is a typical grammatical unit. Speaker A's 'Yeah' provides the response to the first question. Boden also notes that, during the slight pause in line three, where Speaker B could have spoken, a gap is left for Speaker A, who continues.

Box 17.4 Two short adjacency pairs

The following two question and answer pairs from Boden (1994) illustrate the often brief nature of organizational talk. The first example is from a university and the second from an investment banking house.

University Prov
1. **Prov:** → *You* appoint the graduate advisers
2. don't you?

3.   (0.3)
4. **Dean:** No *actually* what happens is *you*
5. appoint them.

Investments-2
1. **A:** → Oh, th*at*'s the book you're talkin about?
2. **M:** Well, no this *isn't* a b*oo*k, this is just
3. a- a *research* report   (1994: 116).

The attention to detail in the sequence in Boxes 17.3 and 17.4 is very striking and represents a clear difference from the way in which talk is normally treated by social researchers—for example, in their transcription conventions when analysing qualitative interviews. It has sometimes been suggested that conversation analysis fails to capture body movements, but in recent times the use of video recordings has supplemented its tool kit of methods (e.g. Heath 1997). Attention to fine details is thus an essential ingredient of CA work. Pauses and emphases are not to be regarded as incidental or of little significance in terms of what the speaker is trying to achieve; instead, they are part of 'the specific details of interaction [that] cannot simply be ignored as insignificant', as Heritage (1987: 248) puts it.

Some basic tools of conversation analysis

The gradual accumulation of detailed analyses of talk in interaction has resulted in a recognition that there are recurring features of the ways in which that talk is organized. These features can be regarded as tools that can be applied to sequences of conversation. The following tools are presented merely to provide a flavour of the ways in which CA proceeds.

Turn-taking

One of the most basic ideas in CA is the notion that one of the ways in which order is achieved in everyday conversation is through turn-taking. This is a particularly important tool of conversation analysis, because it illustrates that talk depends on shared codes. If such

---

Practical tip 👉 *don't collect too much data*

If you are doing a project based on CA, do not be tempted to collect too much data. The real work of CA goes into the painstaking analysis that its underlying theoretical stance requires. It may be that just one or two portions of transcribed text will allow you to address your research questions using the technique.

---

codes did not exist, there would not be smooth transitions in conversation. In other words, there must be codes for indicating the ends of utterances.

Hutchby and Wooffitt (1998: 47) summarize this model as indicating that '(1) turn-taking occurs; (2) one speaker tends to talk at a time; and (3) turns are taken with as little gap or overlap between them as possible'. This is not to say that turn-taking 'errors' do not occur. They manifestly do, as the discussion of *repair mechanisms* below suggests. One of the ways in which turn-taking is revealed is through the examination of *adjacency pairs*, which are the focus of the next section.

Adjacency pairs

The idea of the *adjacency pair* draws attention to the well-attested tendency for some kinds of activity as revealed in talk to involve two linked phases: a question followed by an answer, as in Box 17.3; an invitation followed by a response (accept/decline); or a greeting followed by a returned greeting. The first phase invariably implies that the other part of the adjacency pair will be forthcoming—for example, that an invitation will be responded to. The second phase is of interest to the conversation analyst not just because it becomes a springboard for a response in its own right but because compliance with the putative normative structure of the pairing indicates an appreciation of how one is supposed to respond to the initial phase. In this way, 'intersubjective understandings' are continuously reinforced (Heritage 1987: 259–60). This is not to imply that the second phase will *always* follow the first; indeed, the response to a failure to comply with the expected response has itself been the focus of attention by conversation analysts.

Preference organization

While it is true to say that the second phase in an adjacency pair is always anticipated, some responses are clearly preferential to others. An example is that, when an invitation or a request is proffered, acceptance does not have to be justified, whereas a refusal does have to be justified. A further example is that, when an attempt to be self-deprecating is provided, it will be met with disagreement rather than agreement.

In each case, the former (acceptance, disagreement) is the *preferred response* and the latter (refusal, agreement) is the *dispreferred response*. Therefore, the preference structure is discovered by the conversation analyst through the response to an initial statement.

Speakers' awareness of the preference organization of such pairings has implications for the structure of a conversation. For example, a sequence may involve an offer being met with a straightforward preferred response of acceptance—'thank you' (Potter 1996: 59) or an invitation or request may be declined (the dispreferred response). In the case of a dispreferred response, several features contrast strikingly with the unequivocal 'thank you' that is associated with the case of acceptance. Potter argues that, in a typical acceptance rejection, which is, of course, a dispreferred response, the second speaker may delay the start of his or her response and fill it with 'hehh'. Also, the rejection is 'softened' and is accompanied by an explanation for failing to provide the preferred response.

For example, in their study of entrepreneurial activity, Anderson, Hughes, and Sharrock (1989; see Box 17.5) describe an instance of an adjacency pair involving a 'troubles telling sequence'; this is an opener that facilitates movement into the telling of troubles (Jefferson 1988). The initial opening by Graham, who works for a supplier of beers and lagers to the catering firm, might be seen as an attempt to gain the agreement of the second speaker, Giles (who manages LTC's purchasing) enabling Graham to talk about his problems. Indeed Graham's attempt at self-deprecation (utterance four) is met by a preferred response, in the form of Giles's protest and disagreement (utterance five). However, in this case,

Graham goes on, in utterance six, to make his response equivocal by filling it with 'Hhhehh huh'. This indicates that he is aware that, in the context of this business negotiation, despite his feigned interest, Giles cannot get involved in appreciating or sharing the problems that Graham faces. This leaves the way open for Giles to qualify his initial response (utterance seven) with a dispreferred response, thereby reasserting the depersonalized character of the conversation. This example is complex because it shows how an initial preferred response can actually be inverted as a conversation progresses.

However, Potter (1996) follows the admonition not to make inferences about speakers' motivations by observing that the notion of a preference structure is a feature of the talk and it does not necessarily reflect the motivations of the participants. After all, Giles may have wanted to listen to Graham's troubles but he was prevented from doing so by the nature of the business negotiation. The key point is that the participants recognize the preference structure of this kind of adjacency pairing and this affects the form of their response (that is, hesitancy, acknowledgement of the invitation, and providing an explanation) in the case of declining the offer or an unelaborated (or barely elaborated) response in the case of acceptance.

Accounts

The important feature to note about the treatment of accounts in CA is that they are analysed in context—that is, the form that they assume is handled as being occasioned by what precedes it (an invitation). A CA view of Graham's opening utterance in Box 17.5

Box 17.5 A preferred followed by a dispreferred response

Anderson, Hughes, and Sharrock (1989) provide the following example of a discussion involving a preferred followed by a dispreferred response.

1. Giles: So I would have thought eighty five lager and eighty five Fosters is er actually paying you a pound more on the differential between those two (6 secs)
2. Graham: Okay Giles we'll go along with that ( )
3. Giles: Okay
4. Graham: It does er well you don't want to know about our problems
5. Giles: I do I do
6. Graham: Hhhehh huh
7. Giles: But not to-day, hehhh right   (1989: 149).

involves recognition of the importance of the initial opening as one that invites a preferred response, even though this response cannot realistically be acted upon by Graham. The account thus establishes that both parties appreciate the problems faced by Graham, whilst it acknowledges that Giles is constrained by circumstances that don't allow him to dwell on the problems that his actions generate for his supplier. This allows the relationship between the two parties to be maintained. Moreover, in CA, accounts are not unusual phenomena to be deployed when things go wrong but are intrinsic to talk in a variety of situations. It is striking that many accounts are in essence simply a description or expression of a state of affairs. The sequence in Box 17.5 illustrates how, as corporate agents with different agendas (Giles being concerned to get the best deal and Graham to be sure that the discounts he has given are worth the business he has gained), both know that the other faces difficulties, yet they cannot share these difficulties (Anderson, Hughes, and Sharrock 1989). The factual nature of the account further allows the relationship between the two parties to be unharmed by Giles's final dispreferred response.

Repair mechanisms

Of course, things do go wrong in conversations, as occurs when turn-taking conventions are not followed so that there is overlapping of people talking. Silverman (1993: 132) notes several repair mechanisms, such as:

- when someone starts to speak before someone else has finished, the initial speaker stops talking before completing his or her turn;

- when a turn transfer does not occur at an appropriate point (for example, when someone does not respond to a question), the speaker may speak again, perhaps reinforcing the need for the other person to speak (for example, by reinforcing the question).

The crucial point to note about such repair mechanisms is that they allow the rules of turn-taking to be maintained in spite of the fact that they have been breached.

Overview

This review of CA can only scratch the surface of an approach that has developed a highly sophisticated way of studying talk in interaction. It is worth pointing out that the preoccupations of CA make it highly relevant to the study of business and management in several different ways—here we will mention two. The first relates to the study of formal institutional settings, and the distinction made by Sacks, Schegloff, and Jefferson (1974) between informal and formal talk, the latter being experienced as a breach from the normal, intersubjective model for managing talk in interaction, through such devices as turn-taking. Hence, although they have not tended to focus on work organizations *per se*, conversation analysts have studied talk in a number of other formal institutional settings, such as television news interviews, courtroom trials, and clinical interaction. There are thus potential parallels that could be drawn with, for example, recruitment, selection, and appraisal interviews, industrial tribunal hearings, and corporate boardroom meetings, as instances of formal, institutional talk in business and management settings. This would involve focusing on the devices and actions that people use when being questioned—to make a point, retain control of a topic, block interruptions, and so on. Button's (1998) study of job interviews provides one such illustration (see Box 17.6).

Another possible organizational application relates to the use of conversation analysis in relation to dispute resolution and conflict. Garcia (1991) suggests that institutional conflict resolution procedures are different from disputes in ordinary conversation, in terms of their interactional organization. Garcia analysed the hearings of a Californian mediation programme that provides an alternative to the small claims court in family, financial, and residential disputes. Nine hearings were video- and audio-taped and subsequently transcribed. Analysis focused on the way that speech was organized to promote agreement and minimize argument. Garcia found that, unlike in informal settings, the arguing techniques involved in these formal disputes tended to involve

Box 17.6 Conversation analysis in action: a study of the sequential practices used in job interviews

Button (1992) shows how job interviews are based on an 'orthodoxy' of sequential sequences that are quite different from those used in 'ordinary' conversation. The analysis was based on the interview of a comprehensive schoolteacher who was being considered for promotion to a more senior position as head of the arts faculty. The interview was video-taped but the interview panel would not allow any subsequent discussion to be recorded.

Button argues that the job interview is a form of speech exchange made up of a series of questions and answers that impart an order on the social setting as well as on the interactions that occur within it. Specifically, answers are used by hearers to monitor a speaker's apparent understanding of a question. Unlike in informal conversation, where turn-taking allows for misunderstandings to be corrected, in an interview speech exchange when the speaker is answering he or she is not usually interrupted. Button shows how, if a candidate 'misunderstands' an

interview question—in other words, if he or she fails to answer it in the way the hearers' do—the formality of the interaction makes this misunderstanding difficult to 'repair'. Moreover, Button shows how the pattern of interaction in an interview situation does not give the candidate the opportunity to return to his or her answer (to extend or modify it) later on in the exchange.

Interviewers assess candidates on their ability to understand what was being said, so misunderstanding is taken to imply that a candidate 'ducked the question'. Button suggests that, in the interview of the schoolteacher (who in the discussion following the interview was considered unsuitable for the position), the candidate was looked upon unfavourably partly because of this. However, Button argues that it is the very nature of the interview as a formal speech exchange, rather than some deficiency on the part of the candidate, that is to blame for the candidate's 'inability' to answer the question.

---

indirectly addressed exchanges; for example, accusations tended to be addressed to the person who was chairing the meeting. Garcia shows how mediation relies on eliminating adjacent exchanges between participants. Because the second participant's 'denial' in response to an accusation is delayed, 'a disputant may choose to bypass some accusations, focus on the more important accusations, or ignore accusations she or he cannot credibly deny. Thus, the speech exchange system in mediation facilitates the resolution of conflict by allowing for selective response to accusations' (1991: 830). These findings have relevance to the study of conflict at work, for example through the conversation analysis of wage negotiations and the decision-making processes that are associated with industrial action.

The insistence of conversation analysts that it is important to locate understanding in terms of sequences of talk, and therefore to avoid making extraneous inferences about the meanings of that talk, marks CA as representing a somewhat different approach from much qualitative research. As we have seen in previous chapters, qualitative researchers

often claim (perhaps erroneously from the perspective of CA) that they seek to achieve understanding from the perspective of those being studied. Conversation analysts claim to do this only in so far as that understanding can be revealed in the specific contexts of talk. To import elements that are not specifically grounded in the here and now of what has just been said during a conversation risks the implanting of understanding that is not grounded in participants' own terms (Schegloff 1997). Boden (1994), for example, points out that her concern is not automatically with 'typical' variables such as age, race, class, or gender, nor does she assume organizational structure or size as an important starting point for analysis. The status of the speaker is not assumed to dictate the talk; instead the point of interest for her as a conversation analyst is on how 'aspects of biography and social structure are made relevant in particular talk settings' (1994: 77).

Two points seem relevant here. First, this is a somewhat limiting stance, in that it means that the attribution of motives and meanings as a result of an in-depth understanding of a culture is illegitimate.

While an interpretative understanding of social action carries risks on misunderstanding, an approach that prohibits such speculation is potentially restrictive. Secondly, CA is contextual in that it locates understanding in the sequences of talk. However, for the participants of an exchange, much of their talk is informed by their mutual knowledge of contexts. The analyst is restricted from taking those additional components of the context into account if they are not specifically part of the organization of talk.

Again, this admonition seems to restrict the analyst more than is desirable in many circumstances and to consign CA to a range of research questions that are amenable solely to the location of meaning in talk alone. On the other hand, CA reduces the risk about making unwarranted speculations about what is happening in social interaction and has contributed much to our understanding of the accomplishment of social order, which is one of the classic concerns of social theory.

Discourse analysis

Unlike CA, DA is an approach to language that can be applied to forms of communication other than talk. As such, it can be and has been applied to forms like texts, such as company mission statements, and in this respect it is more flexible than CA. Moreover, in DA there is much less of an emphasis on naturally occurring talk, so that talk in research interviews can be a legitimate target for analysis. However, DA should not be treated totally in opposition or contradistinction to CA, since it incorporates insights from it.

Unlike CA, which by and large reveals a uniformity based on an orthodoxy associated with certain classic statements concerning its core practices (e.g. Sacks, Schegloff, and Jefferson 1974), there are several different approaches that are labelled as DA (Potter 1997). The version to be discussed here is one that is associated with such writers as Potter (1997); Potter and Wetherell (1987, 1994); Billig (1992); and Gilbert and Mulkay (1984). This version of DA (see Box 17.7) has been described as exhibiting two distinctive features at the level of epistemology and ontology (Potter 1997).

- It is *anti-realist*—in other words, it denies that there is an external reality awaiting a definitive portrayal by the researcher and it therefore disavows the notion that any researcher can arrive at a privileged account of the aspect of the social world being

---

Box 17.7 ⌖ *What is discourse analysis?*

There is no one version of discourse analysis (DA). The version described in the main body of this chapter is one that has been of particular interest to social scientists and that can be applied to both naturally occurring and contrived forms of talk and to texts. According to Potter, DA 'emphasizes the way versions of the world, of society, events and inner psychological worlds are produced in discourse' (1997: 146).

This definition of DA means that discourse is not just a mirror on the social world around us but in many ways plays a key role in producing that world. *How* we say

things—our phrases, our emphases, the things we leave out—is meant to accomplish certain effects in others. In so doing, we have an impact on others' perceptions and understandings and as such on their and our reality.

However, in business and management there has been a somewhat broader interpretation of this term, which is used to refer to a variety of analytical approaches that focus on the role of discourse, including the function of talk and the rhetorical devices whereby speech is constructed. This diversity is reflected in the examples used in this chapter.

investigated. Some discourse analysts, however, adopt a stance that is closer to a realist position, but most seem to be anti-realist in orientation.

• It is *constructionist*—in other words, the emphasis is placed on the versions of reality propounded by members of the social setting being investigated and on the fashioning of that reality through their renditions of it (see Box 1.14). More specifically, the constructionist emphasis entails a recognition that discourse entails a selection from many viable renditions and that in the process a particular depiction of reality is built up.

Thus, discourse is not simply a neutral device for imparting meaning. People seek to accomplish things when they talk or when they write; DA is concerned with the strategies they employ in trying to create different kinds of effect. In addition, DA shares with CA a preference for locating contextual understanding in terms of the situational specifics of talk. As Potter (1997: 158) puts it, discourse analysts prefer to avoid making reference in their analyses to what he refers to as 'ethnographic particulars' and argues that instead they prefer 'to see things as things that are worked up, attended to and made relevant in interaction rather than being external determinants'. However, DA practitioners are less wedded to this principle than conversation analysts, in that the former sometimes show a greater preparedness to make reference to 'ethnographic particulars'.

Discourse analysts resist the idea of a codification of their practices and indeed argue that such a

codification is probably impossible. Instead, they prefer to see their style of research as an 'analytic mentality' and as such as 'a craft skill, more like bike riding or chicken sexing than following the recipe for a mild chicken rogan josh' (Potter 1997: 147–8). One useful point of departure for DA research that has been suggested by Gill (1996), following Widdicombe (1993), is to treat the way that something is said as being 'a solution to a problem' (1993: 97, quoted in Gill 1996: 146). She also suggests adopting a posture of 'sceptical reading' (Gill 2000). This means searching for a purpose lurking behind the ways that something is said or presented.

The bulk of the exposition of DA that follows is based on four studies:

• research on the discourse of international business leaders (Hartog and Verburg 1997);

• the use of computer-based monitoring financial service organizations (Ball and Wilson 2000);

• the discourse used by bank managers to describe their customers (Graaf 2001);

• the framing of corporate mission statements (Swales and Rogers 1995).

The first study (Hartog and Verburg 1997; see Box 17.8) shows how charismatic leaders rely on the rhetorical construction of messages to overcome social and spatial distances between them and their followers; the second study (Ball and Wilson 2000 see Box 17.9) shows how interpretative repertoires can be used to analyse power and control in organizations; the third study (see Box 17.10) illustrates how discourse employed by bankers to describe their customers can reveal the nature of their ethical position; finally, the study of corporate mission statements (Swales and Rogers 1995; see Box 17.11) demonstrates that linguistic features are an important means of fostering organizational affiliation and identification. A further element to be sensitive to is that, as Gill (1996), following Billig (1991), suggests, what is said is always a way of *not* saying something else. In other words, either total silence on a topic, or formulating an argument in a conversation or article in one way rather than in another way, is a crucial component of seeing discourse as a solution to a

---

Practical tip 👉 *using existing material*

As some of the examples of DA show, you may well be able to employ the technique to illuminate issues of interest to you on materials that are in the public domain, such as speeches. In many cases, these will be available in electronic form. This means that you do not have to put a lot of effort into the collection of data, though it will still be necessary to seek out the materials. Instead, you can give greater emphasis to analysing the materials using the DA approach.

> **Box 17.8** Discourse analysis in action: the rhetorical construction of charismatic leadership
>
> Hartog and Verburg (1997) explore how the charismatic content of business leaders' speeches is constructed through the use of rhetorical devices, and consider what these speeches reveal about business leaders' attitudes towards internationalization. Using the method of DA, they focus on the speeches of three CEOs of international corporations:
>
> - Anita Roddick—the Body Shop;
> - Jan Timmer—former CEO of Philips;
> - Matthew Barrett—Bank of Montreal.
>
> They show how the literal meaning of the message is strengthened by presenting it in a specific form, using a range of rhetorical devices. They suggest that the use of different rhetorical devices reflects the orientation of speakers towards internationalization. Roddick has a universalistic approach towards global strategy formation, Barrett pays more attention to the differences between countries or regions in his speeches, and Timmer seeks simultaneously to acknowledge the differences between countries and subsidiaries whilst still retaining a strong sense of Philips identity. They conclude that the analysis of rhetoric can provide useful insight into the internationalization strategies of charismatic business leaders.

problem. As we will see, the way that Swales and Rogers (1995) were prevented from interviewing employees about their attitudes towards and uses of missions statements was important in revealing the distinction within the discourse between cultural insiders and outsiders.

Identifying rhetorical devices

In order to illustrate the importance of rhetorical devices in discourse analysis, a study of the message, style and delivery of charismatic business leaders' speeches will be employed. This research is outlined in some detail in Box 17.8. It highlights the importance of rhetorical devices in provoking identification and commitment amongst listeners. It suggests that how a leader's message is framed, through the use of metaphors, rhythm, contrasts, and lists, is as important as what the speech is about, in gaining commitment from followers. These 'tools for framing' define the form and construction of the message by providing vivid images for the audience. According to Hartog and Verburg (1997), they include the following.

- *Contrast*—where a subject is described in terms of its opposite in order to reinforce a point—for example, in Anita Roddick's speech she states:

3. Remember, corporations are invented. They are human institutions, not species found in nature. (Hartog and Verburg 1997: 367)

- *List*—this is usually composed of three parts—this being the minimum number to show that there is a group of items without adding too many elements that would make the list excessive. Here is an example, in the first sentence of a speech given by Jan Timmer:

6. That together we are strong, together we can make progress and that our destiny really is in our own hands. That we no longer say they ought to do something but that we continue to say after today we are going to do something. That will restore the Philips-image. That will make Philips again a very nice place to work in. That will make Philips a company we can all be proud of. (Hartog and Verburg 1997: 368)

This is analysed as:

1. Together we are strong;
2. Together we can make progress;
3. Our destiny really is in our own hands.

- *Headline–punchline/puzzle–solution*—in this instance the speaker creates the opportunity to present a punchline or solution by first presenting a headline or puzzle. This is illustrated using an excerpt from a speech given by Anita Roddick:

9. I came from an Italian immigrant family. At ten years of age, when my father died, my mother and us four kids worked in a large café. There were no family holidays, there were no family diversions, except for the weekly cinema, it was work! It was a livelihood. It was an extension of our home, our kitchen. Courtships flourished in that café, marriages formed, friendships connected, the eye was delighted, the music from the jukebox spoke personally to everyone and your heart was in the workplace. It taught me a huge lesson, you can bring your heart to work with you. It taught me business was not financial science, it is about trading, buying and selling. It is about creating a product or service so good that people will pay a higher price for that. (Hartog and Verburg 1997: 369)

According to Hartog and Verburg, the story of Roddick's youth provides the puzzle from which she constructs a solution: 'it taught me . . . you can bring your heart to work with you.'

- *Position taking*—the speaker begins by giving a fairly neutral description of a state of affairs and then he or she strongly agrees or disagrees with it. In a speech by Matthew Barrett he takes a position regarding the state of the Canadian economy stating:

10. As the weeks since October 30 have passed one by one, my optimism has slowly waned. What I hear are seductive voices calling us back to 'jobs and the economy'. Even the incoming premier of Quebec is saying as much. And the polls suggest the public agrees. I *don't* agree. (Hartog and Verburg 1997: 370)

- *Pursuit, repetition, alliteration*—the speaker may actively pursue audience reactions by repeating or otherwise stressing a point, for example by saying 'I repeat . . .'. For example, in the speech given by Jan Timmer he uses repetition in the delivery of his three part list:

1. *That will* restore the Philips-image.
2. *That will* make Philips again a very nice place to work in.
3. *That will* make Philips a company we can all be proud of. (Hartog and Verburg 1997: 370)

In the study of business and management, considerable emphasis has been placed on the persuasive acts and discursive strategies that help to engender identification and foster cooperation within a group. For example, industrial relations research has typically focused on how the behavioural compliance of workers is achieved, whereas studies of leadership, culture, and management have tended to concentrate on the ways that certain values can be inculcated. The rhetorical devices that we have described in this section provide an important means whereby organizational researchers are able to explore and systematically analyse this use of language.

Uncovering interpretative repertoires

Potter and Wetherell (1994) suggest that there are two tendencies within DA, although they acknowledge that the distinction is somewhat artificial. One is the identification of 'the general resources that are used to construct discourse and enable the performance of particular actions' (1994: 48–9), which is concerned with identifying *interpretative repertoires*. The other is concerned to identify 'the detailed procedures through which versions are constructed and made to look factual' (1994: 49). We will now explore these two strands of DA.

In order to illustrate the idea of an *interpretative repertoire*, a study of computer-based performance monitoring in two UK financial service organizations will be employed (Ball and Wilson 2000). This research is outlined in some detail in Box 17.9. Ball and Wilson found distinct differences between these two case-study organizations, in terms of the way that employees and managers made sense of the computer-based monitoring systems that were designed to monitor job performance. They identify four interpretative repertoires that reflect the ways that individuals make sense of power relations within their organizations.

- *The empowerment repertoire*—informants' talk that contains themes of 'self management', 'proactivity', 'choice', and 'freedom'. This is illustrated by

---

Box 17.9 Interpretative repertoires in computer-based performance monitoring

In a study of computer-based performance monitoring, Ball and Wilson (2000) collected observational and interview data in two departments, one in a building society (Case 1) and the other in a bank (Case 2). In Case 1, the open-plan physical layout of the offices meant that teams were highly visible to the department manager; performance statistics were fed back to individuals at the end of each week, detailing the financial value of the telephone calls to clients that had been made. In Case 2, there was a greater degree of separation between offices and the manager had little direct contact with his staff. Performance monitoring in this context focused on the relationship between work time and volume of work processed by each individual.

From their data analysis, Ball and Wilson suggest that, in Case 1, a repertoire of empowerment was dominant, whereas, in Case 2, a repertoire of legitimate authority prevailed. These were accompanied in each case by subordinate repertoires that enabled individuals to build alternative or resistant positions. They conclude that disciplinary power worked in quite different ways in the two organizations. In Case 1, individuals engage in subtle support of, or differentiation from the dominant repertoire; whereas, in Case 2, they developed outright opposition to them.

---

one manager who positions himself in these terms stating:

Extract 1: '. . . you empower people, people start throwing out ideas and actually manage themselves, and that's worked, we think, quite well in our area . . .'   (Ball and Wilson 2000: 551).

- *The 'life in work' repertoire*—this comprises a set of patterns that construe work as 'objective', 'neutral', and 'egalitarian' so that a manager may be seen, for example, as treating 'everybody as equal'.

- *The 'legitimate authority' repertoire*—typified by themes of 'discipline', 'rules', 'negative instruction', and 'inflexibility'. Ball and Wilson suggest that managers who claim a position based on legitimate authority repertoire tend to emphasize their access to, and control over, the computer-based performance monitoring statistics.

- *The 'power through experience' repertoire*—this is concerned with the knowledge and understanding that is needed to do the job; it can be mobilized as a form of resistance by showing how some managers do not have the experience to be able to manage. For example:

Extract 10: 'I was an inputter, and I've done grade two and now I'm a grade three [supervisor]. I know, from scratch, so it's easier for me so I can relate to the grade ones and the grade twos, because I've been there and I've done it, so I'm in a good position I would say.'   (Ball and Wilson 2000: 555)

Ball and Wilson locate these interpretative repertoires as mechanisms whereby disciplinary power is exercised over individuals. However, they also suggest that, through 'troubling' (Wetherell 1998), individuals are able to exercise resistance to the dominant discourse through their conversation. Resistance is thereby generated through *reciprocal positioning*; this is when individuals position themselves so that, even though they use the terms associated with the dominant discourse, they do so in a way that enables them to position themselves in opposition to it. Another form of resistance is generated by *alternative positioning*, whereby an individual positions him- or herself in terms of a discourse that represents an alternative to the dominant one.

The notion of the interpretative repertoire is interesting because it brings out the idea that belief and action take place within templates that guide and influence the writer or speaker. A further example is provided by Graaf (2001) in his study of Dutch bankers; Graaf identifies five overlapping discourses about customers, which he suggests will affect the way that bankers treat their customers (Box 17.10). Although Graaf does not use the analytical notion of interpretative repertoires, he *is* suggesting that discourses about customers will influence managerial action.

Finally, the four repertoires discussed by Ball and Wilson by no means exhaust the range of possibilities of analysis, as the advantages of the notion of

---

Box 17.10 How bankers conceptualize their customers

In a study of the three largest banks in Holland—ING, ABN-Amro, and Rabobank—Graaf (2001) explores the discourses that define how the bankers treat their customers. Following discourse theory, Graaf proposes that, 'if bank managers speak differently about their customers, they will treat them differently' (2001:303).

Analysing statements used internally by the banks about the different aspects of customers, Graaf focused on all sentences that used the word 'customer'. Ten interviews were also conducted with directors in local branches of the banks. From this data, Graaf formed a set of fifty-two statements about customers and dealing with customers.

The local bank directors were then asked to sort the statement set, according to how strongly they agreed or disagreed with each one. From this, Graaf identifies five overlapping discourses about customers:

- *Together for ourselves* (the relationship with customers must be mutually beneficial);

- *Using the bank to improve the region* (the direct interests of the customer are situated within a broader social and environmental context);
- *Customer as colleague and competitor in one* (the customer is someone with whom the bank has common and opposing interests—customers are out to make money and so is the bank);
- *Customer as buyer of profitable products* (providing a service to the customer is crucial to the bank's commercial success);
- *Customer as commercial relationship* (deliver the best products to the customer and they will bring their business to the bank).

The extent to which each bank identifies with each discourse gives a profile of its treatment of customers and provides a basis for evaluating its ethical position.

---

interpretative repertoires stem primarily from its flexibility in accounting for a diverse range of social practices. Hence, Potter and Wetherell (1987) suggest that repertoires are available to people with many different social group memberships. They also point out that there is no need to attempt to find consensus with regard to repertoires—because they are used to perform different sorts of accounting tasks, individuals are able to draw upon a variety of repertoires in different situations. Finally, they emphasize that 'the concept of repertoire is but one component in a systematic approach to the study of discourse' (Potter and Wetherell 1987: 157), one that in a few years time may be developed further or even discarded.

Producing facts

In discourse analytic research there is also an emphasis on the resources that are employed in conveying allegedly factual knowledge. In the study by Swales and Rogers (1995) of corporate mission statements (see Box 17.11), the researchers were especially interested in the way that mission statements were rhetorically designed to ensure maximum employee 'buy-in' and identification with the company. However, they note that mission statements operate at a general and ambiguous level and deal mainly with abstractions. From the mission statements they analyse, they observe that there is an almost total absence of 'support' (examples, quotations, or statistics)—or what Potter and Wetherell (1994) might describe as *quantification rhetoric*, by which is meant the ways in which numerical and non-numerical statements are made to support or refute arguments. Instead, the texts largely consist of general statements, claims, and conclusions. This is interesting given the importance of quantification in everyday life and in part in the tendency for many social scientists to make use of this strategy themselves (John 1992). Swales and Rogers (1995: 227) note that verb forms used within the mission statements are predominantly present, imperative (e.g. 'return to underwriting profit'), or purpose infinitive (e.g. 'to provide a caring environment...'; 'to be the safest carrier').

Box 17.11 The framing of corporate mission statements

Swales and Rogers (1995) use DA to explore how corporations project their philosophy through mission statements. From a collection of over 100 individual *texts*, they analyse a sample of thirty mission statements that reflect a diverse range of industries, organizational types, and countries of operation. They conclude that the content of these texts is 'pithy and up-beat', consisting of general statements with almost a total lack of 'support' such as examples, statistics, and so on. Mission statements 'tend to stress values, *positive* behaviour and guiding principles within the framework of the corporation's *announced* belief system and analysis' (1995: 227, emphasis in original).

Swales and Rogers show how mission statements use a number of linguistic features that are designed to foster affiliation and identification. Many use the rhetorical device of adopting the first-person-plural pronoun, 'we', to denote 'the employees of the corporation', rather than senior management or the corporation. In one instance they note that twenty-two of the sixty-six sentences in the document 'begin with the credo-like incantation "We believe..."' (1995: 234).

The second part of their research involved focusing on the mission statements of two well-known US companies—the Dana Corporation, a worldwide automotive parts supplier, and Honeywell, best known internationally for its temperature control systems.

In order to go beyond the surface of the text and explore the *framing content*, the researchers studied the companies' history, collected a wide range of documents, searched the business press, made site visits, and talked to key players. This enabled them to establish how mission statements get written and how they are perceived by their creators and users.

However, their original research plan also involved interviewing a stratified sample (see Chapter 4) of employees about their attitudes towards and uses of mission statements. This was not possible—'in both corporations, we were politely but firmly discouraged from such an ambition' (1995: 236)—apparently because they were perceived as cultural outsiders.

A number of further characteristics apply to DA. Some of the most important are presented in the list that follows.

- *Reading the detail*—discourse analysts incorporate the CA preference for attention to the details of discourse.

- *Looking for rhetorical detail*—attention to rhetorical detail entails a sensitivity to the ways in which arguments are constructed.

- *Looking for accountability*—discourse analysts draw on CA practitioners' interest in and approach to accounts. From the point of view of both CA and DA, discourse can, and should, be regarded as accounts. For DA practitioners, the search for accountability entails attending to the details through which these accounts are constructed.

- *Cross-referencing discourse studies*—Potter and Wetherell suggest that reading other discourse studies is itself an important activity. First, it helps to sharpen the analytic mentality at the heart of

DA. Secondly, other studies often provide insights that are suggestive for one's own data.

Overview

According to Oswick, Keenoy, and Grant (1997), discourse has rarely been a primary focus of management research. One of the reasons for this relates to the preference for action rather than talk: 'dialogue, discussion and debate are usually portrayed as being of secondary importance to action' (Grant, Keenoy, and Oswick 1998: 5). However, as these authors point out, the importance of discourse in understanding organizations is hard to underestimate; this is because discourse plays such a significant part in 'constructing, situating, facilitating and communicating the diverse cultural, institutional, political and socio-economic parameters of "organizational being"' (1998: 12). In other words, discourse does not just provide an account of what goes on in organizations; it is also a process whereby meaning is created.

As this discussion of DA has emphasized on several occasions, DA draws on insights from CA. Particularly when analysing strings of talk, DA draws on conversation analytic insights into the ways in which interaction is realized in and through talk in interaction. The CA injunction to focus on the talk itself and the ways in which intersubjective meaning is accomplished in sequences of talk are also incorporated into DA. This is not easy to accomplish, and, when one reads articles based on DA, it sometimes seems as though the practitioners come perilously close to invoking speculations that do not seem to be directly discernible in the sequences being analysed—that is, speculations about 'ethnographic particulars' and hence about motives.

Sometimes, there is a more explicit recognition of the potential contribution of an appreciation of the ethnographic context. For example, although Ball and Wilson (2000) do not present their work as ethnographic, their use of observational methods combined with interviewing, conducted within a DA framework, allowed them to relate the use of computer-based performance monitoring to the context or physical environment in which employees worked. This allowed them to draw on Bentham's Panopticon to suggest that the spatio-temporal location of individuals was significant in determining the interpretative repertoires that were adopted within each organization. Similarly, Heracleous and Barrett's (2001) longitudinal study of the implementation of an electronic risk-placing system in the London Insurance Market (Box 17.12) combined interview with documentary data that was collected over a five-year period. The key point is that it is clear that the periods of ethnographic observation at least in part informed the DA interpretation of the sequences of talk that had been recorded. Such research suggests that the proscription concerning the recourse to ethnographic particulars is honoured more by some discourse analysts than others. It is easy to see why: attention to ethnographic details may alert the analyst to nuances and understandings that are not directly entrenched in the flow of discourse.

DA is in certain respects a more flexible approach to language in business research than CA, because it is not solely concerned with the analysis of naturally occurring talk, since practitioners also use various kinds of documents and research interviews in their work. In business and management research, this often involves focusing on the rhetorical or linguistic features of the text, as a way of understanding the discourse. Also, it permits the intrusion of understandings of what is going on that are not specific to the immediacy of previous utterances. It is precisely this to which conversation analysts object, as when Schegloff (1997: 183) writes about DA: 'Discourse is too often made subservient to contexts not of its participants' making, but of its analysts' insistence.' For their part, discourse analysts object to the restriction that this injunction imposes, because it means that conversation analysts 'rarely raise their eyes from the next turn in the conversation, and, further, this is not an entire conversation or sizeable slice of social life but usually a tiny fragment' (Wetherell 1998: 402). Thus, for discourse analysts, phenomena like interpretative repertoires are very much part of the context within which talk occurs, whereas in CA they are inadmissible evidence. But it is here that we see the dilemma for the discourse analyst, for, in seeking to admit a broader sense of context (such as attention to interpretative repertoires in operation) while wanting to stick close to the conversation analysts' distaste for ethnographic particulars, they are faced with the uncertainty of just how far to go in allowing the inclusion of conversationally extraneous factors.

The anti-realist inclination of many DA practitioners has been a source of controversy, because the emphasis on representational practices through discourses sidelines any notion of a pre-existing material reality that can constrain individual agency. Reality becomes little more than that which is constituted in and through discourse. This lack of attention to a material reality that lies behind and underpins discourse has proved too abstracted for some social researchers and theorists. For example, writing from a critical-realist position (see Box 22.1), Reed (2000) has argued that discourses should be examined in relation to social structures, such as power relationships, that are responsible for the occasioning of those discourses. Attention would additionally be focused on the ways in which discourses then work through existing structures. Discourse is

Box 17.12 Discursive strategies used by individuals and groups to account for change

Coupland (2001) used a discursive approach to analyse the way that graduate trainees account for their changed identity when they join a company. She found that the newcomers used talk to emphasize simultaneously their similarity and their difference from the 'ideal' or typical 'Company A employee'. The graduates' talk also emphasized the need to adjust to the new 'environment' and to learn to behave 'appropriately' within the company. Failure to do so was seen as dangerous and talked about in terms of 'being bloodied'.

Another illustration of the way that discourse is used to account for change is provided by Heracleous and Barrett (2001), who examined the discourses used by different stakeholders involved in the implementation of an electronic 'risk-placing support system'. The electronic system was intended to support 'risk placing' in the London Insurance Market, the method by which brokers obtain insurance coverage for their client's risk by requesting the participation of underwriters.

The researchers chose to study three multinational brokers who were involved in the introduction of the electronic placing system. Within each of these firms, brokers and underwriters, information technology directors, and staff and senior managers were interviewed and multiple documentary sources were analysed. Three stakeholder groups were identified:

• market leaders—including senior managers who were proponents of the system;

• IT directors and staff—who were involved in implementation;

• brokers and underwriters.

Heracleous and Barrett's aim was to identify the rhetorical strategies that actors used in their arguments surrounding the introduction of the electronic placing system, by analysing the 'texts' (interview transcripts, strategy documents, media reports, and market publications) associated with this subject. They sought to elicit the meaning of different electronic trading systems to the different stakeholder groups and their expectations of the system. This approach enabled them to understand how the groups viewed each other and how they viewed the system, by exploring 'the deeper structures that guide agents' interpretation and actions' (2001: 775).

Although both of these studies involve discursive analysis of the way that people interpret change in organizational contexts, Coupland was more concerned with the way that *individuals* make sense of their changed identity through talk, whereas Heracleous and Barrett were interested in the way that particular *groups* use talk to guide interpretation and organizational action.

---

thereby conceived as a 'generative mechanism' rather than as a self-referential sphere in which nothing of significance exists outside it. Reed provides an interesting example of such an alternative view:

Discourses—such as the quantitatively based discourses of financial audit, quality control and risk management—are now seen as the generative mechanisms through which new regulatory regimes 'carried out' by rising expert groups—such as accountants, engineers and scientists—become established and legitimated in modern societies.

What they represent is less important than what they do in facilitating a radical re-ordering of pre-existing institutional structures in favour of social groups who benefit from the upward mobility which such innovative regulatory regimes facilitate . . . (2000: 529)

As this passage suggests, while many DA practitioners are anti-realist, an alternative, realist position in relation to discourse is feasible. Such an alternative position is perhaps closer to the classic concerns of the social sciences than an anti-realist stance.

K | KEY POINTS

- Both CA and DA approaches take the position that language is itself a focus of interest and not just a medium through which research participants communicate with researchers.

- CA is a systematic approach to conversation that locates action in talk.

- In CA, talk is deemed to be structured in the sense of following rules.

- Practitioners of CA seek to make inferences about talk that are not grounded in contextual details that are extraneous to talk.

- DA shares many features with CA but there are several different versions of it.

- DA can be applied to a wider variety of phenomena than CA, which is just concerned with naturally occurring talk.

- Discourse is conceived of as a means of conveying meaning.

- DA practitioners display a greater inclination to relate meaning in talk to contextual factors.

Q | QUESTIONS FOR REVIEW

- In what ways does the role of language in conversation and discourse analysis differ from that which is typical in most other research methods?

Conversation analysis

- In what ways is CA fundamentally about the production of social order in interaction?

- Why are tape recording and transcription crucial in CA?

- What is meant by each of the following: turn-taking; adjacency pair; preference organization; account; repair mechanism?

- How do the terms in the last question relate to the production of social order?

- Evaluate Schegloff's argument that CA obviates the need to make potentially unwarranted assumptions about participants' motives.

Discourse analysis

- What is the significance of saying that DA is anti-realist and constructionist?

- What is the purpose of rhetorical devices in DA?

- What is an interpretative repertoire?

- What techniques are available to the discourse analyst when trying to understand the ways in which facts are presented through discourse?

- What are the chief points of difference between CA and DA?

18 Documents as sources of data

CHAPTER GUIDE

The term 'documents' covers a very wide range of different kinds of sources. This chapter aims to reflect that variability by examining a wide range of different documentary sources that have been or can be used in qualitative business and management research. In addition, the chapter touches on approaches to the analysis of such sources. The chapter explores :

- personal documents in both written form—such as diaries and letters—and visual form—such as photographs;
- public documents deriving, for example, from an inquiry or legal investigation;

- official documents deriving from organizational sources— such as company annual reports, policy documents, and internal memoranda;
- mass media outputs—such as newspaper articles;
- virtual outputs—such as Internet resources;
- the criteria for evaluating each of the above sources;
- how far readers of documents are active or passive consumers of documents;
- three approaches to the analysis of documents: qualitative content analysis; semiotics; and hermeneutics.

Introduction

This chapter will be concerned with a fairly hetero-geneous set of sources of data, such as letters, memos, diaries, autobiographies, internal reports, newspa-pers, magazines, and photographs. The emphasis is placed on documents that have not been produced at the request of a business researcher—instead, the objects that are the focus of this chapter are simply 'out there' waiting to be assembled and analysed. However, this is not to suggest that the fact that docu-ments are available for the business and manage-ment researcher to work on renders them somehow less time-consuming or easier to deal with than need-ing to collect primary data. On the contrary, the search for documents relevant to your research can often be a frustrating and highly protracted process. Moreover, once they are collected, considerable in-terpretative skill is required to ascertain the meaning of the materials that have been uncovered.

In this chapter we will emphasize documents in the form of material that:

- can be read (though the term 'read' has to be under-stood in a somewhat looser fashion than is nor-mally the case when we come to visual materials, like photographs);

- has not been produced specifically for the purposes of research, although we will also refer to docu-ments that have been generated by researchers;

- is preserved so that it becomes available for analysis; and

- is relevant to the concerns of the business researcher.

Documents have already been encountered in this book, albeit in a variety of contexts or guises. For example, the kinds of source upon which content analysis is often carried out are documents, such as newspaper articles. However, the emphasis in this chapter will be upon the use of documents in quali-tative organizational research. A further way in which documents have previously surfaced was in the brief discussion in Box 10.11, which noted that archive materials are one form of unobtrusive meas-ure. Indeed, this points to an often-noted advantage of using documents of the kind discussed in this chapter—namely, they are non-reactive. This means that, because they have not been created specifically for the purposes of business research, the possibility of a reactive effect can be largely discounted as a lim-itation on the validity of data.

In discussing the different kinds of documents used in the social sciences, John Scott (1990) has use-fully distinguished between personal documents and official documents and has further classified the lat-ter in terms of private as opposed to state documents. These distinctions will be employed in much of the discussion that follows. A further set of important distinctions made by Scott relate to the criteria for assessing the quality of documents. He suggests (1990: 6) four criteria.

- *Authenticity*. Is the evidence genuine and of unquestionable origin?

- *Credibility*. Is the evidence free from error and distortion?

- *Representativeness*. Is the evidence typical of its kind, and, if not, is the extent of its untypicality known?

- *Meaning*. Is the evidence clear and comprehensible?

This is an extremely rigorous set of criteria against which documents might be gauged, and frequent reference to them will be made in the following discussion.

Personal documents

Diaries, letters, and autobiographies

Personal documents such as diaries and letters may be used as the primary source of data within a qualitative study or alternatively as adjuncts to other methods, such as interviews or participant observation. Diaries and letters kept for reasons other than research purposes tend to be used extensively by other groups of social researchers such as historians but less by business researchers. However, there is some scope for them to be used in the study of management, as Box 18.1 illustrates. In this example, Grey's (1996) analysis of managerialism is based upon the work of Simone Weil. In addition to his analysis of Weil's academic writings, Grey draws on Weil's published diaries, which document her experiences as a factory worker, arguing that these experiences were significant in informing her view of management as a form of oppression.

Personal documents can also be used to trace the history of an organization through the letters and diaries of its founders. For example, the company archives of the chocolate manufacturer Cadbury are held at the Birmingham factory. The archives include diaries and letters documenting more than 100 years of history of the family firm. Many of these documents are held in private collections, making access potentially difficult. However, it is likely that the use of personal diaries and letters in business and management research will be confined largely to retrospective, historical analysis. A classic example of the use of letters to build up a historical picture of working life is provided by E. P. Thompson (1968), in his comprehensive and enormously detailed account of the making of the English working classes. Research for the book draws upon numerous data sources such as legal records, autobiographies, notes, pamphlets, newspapers, minutes of committee meetings, and letters. This latter data source includes 'correspondence preserved by Sir Joseph Radcliffe, the exceedingly active Huddersfield magistrate who received his knighthood in recognition of his services in bringing leading Yorkshire Luddites to trial' (1968: 941). However, the emergence of alternative forms of communication has undoubtedly limited the use of letters as a source of data and it is likely that the emergence of e-mail will mean that the role of letters as a potential source of documentary data will continue to decline.

Another way that diaries can be used in qualitative research is as a method of data collection. In this instance, the diaries are produced specifically for the purpose of the research and the diarists are normally given some sort of topic guide to help them. They are different from quantitative diary studies (see Chapter 6), because a lesser degree of structure is imposed on the diarist. For example, in Bowey and Thorpe's (1986) study of incentive schemes (Box 18.2), although the coal miners were asked to keep diaries, they were given a large amount of scope in terms of what they wrote about in them. Hence, in addition to writing about the bonus incentive scheme, the diarists

---

Box 18.1 The diary of a French factory worker

The diaries and letters of Simone Weil (1909–43), a French philosopher and social-political writer, are used by Grey (1996) to gain insight into her conceptualization of management as a form of oppression. Grey suggests that Weil's views about management derive in part from her experiences as a factory worker. Quoting from her *Factory Journal* (Weil 1987), in which she records her experiences of working at the Alsthom electrical plant in Paris, a metal-working factory, and at Renault, Grey shows how these experiences shaped her view that mechanized work was degrading to the individual. He further argues that 'Weil's experience of factory work showed her that the condition of oppression was in part an outcome of the ways in which workers themselves were actors in the reproduction of their own servility' (1996: 604). In other words, it was her view that managerial oppression relies on employees being willing to submit themselves to managerial control and being active in maintaining and reinforcing this oppression.

Box 18.2 Using a diary study to investigate coal miners' attitudes to incentive schemes

In addition to the use of existing diaries as a source of data, qualitative researchers have used diary studies as a method of data collection in a way that bears some resemblance to the quantitative researchers' use of the diary methods (see Chapter 6).

For example, Bowey and Thorpe (1986) were interested in exploring coal miners' attitudes to incentive schemes as part of a larger, multi-method study. Over a three-month period the miners, who worked in the north-west of England, were asked to keep a daily written record of their feelings, observations and opinions about their life and work. The topics they were asked to consider included:

1 Relationships with other people, including supervisor, workmates etc.

2 Any particular difficulties encountered during the day, with machinery, raw materials or other people.

3 Details of how the incentive bonus scheme affected the individual's work. (Easterby-Smith, Thorpe, and Lowe 2001)

The diaries were returned to the researchers each week, so that they could keep track of their development and write back to the diarist asking for clarification of specific points. In addition to aiding the analysis, this process helped encourage the diarists, who felt an interest was being taken in what they were doing. A typical extract from one of the miner's diaries is given below.

Peter Gosnold, Wednesday, 19 April, 1980

> Back to work again after the Easter break also am now on afternoon shifts as face is now only producing on one shift and might as well follow this shift around. A bad turn up today, only 15 men, some of the team are taking their rest days making them a full week off so I can't see any improvement this week. We start off very well with machine but soon run into trouble. Floor lift over holidays has caused face conveyor to lift on face side. This causes the cutter to foul front legs on face supports, a common fault after any holiday period. This type of delay will not be paid for under incentive agreement, although we are cutting slow, we have not stopped. (Bowey and Thorpe 1986: 290)

This method was used as part of a *triangulated* research design that also involved a questionnaire survey of a much larger sample of firms ($n = 63$) in addition to semi-structured interviews with 438 respondents and three in-depth case studies. It therefore illustrates how diaries can be used to collect qualitative data as part of a multi-strategy research design (see Chapter 22).

---

were invited to write about workplace relationships and matters relating to production. The researchers were thus able to build up a picture of the operation of the incentive system that took into account the contextual features that framed its operation.

Whereas letters are a form of communication with other people, diarists invariably write for themselves. However, when they are written for wider consumption, diaries are difficult to distinguish from another kind of personal document—the autobiography. Like letters and diaries, autobiographies can be written at the behest of the researcher, particularly in connection with life history studies (see Box 15.4 for a full explanation of the life history method). However, commercially published autobiographical sources can also be used for research purposes. For example, in the research into organizational culture carried out by Martin and Siehl (1983; see Box 18.3), the authors relied extensively on a biography of the General Motors division manager, John DeLorean, written by Wright in 1979. Direct quotes and organizational stories from this source were analysed to build up a picture of the organizational counterculture that developed under DeLorean's influence.

However, the widespread distinction between biographies and autobiographies can sometimes break down. Walt Disney provides a case in point. As Bryman (1995) has shown, Disney provided, in short articles he authored and in articles written by others, many snippets about his life. The first biography of Disney, written by his daughter, Diane Disney Miller (1956), would almost certainly have been fed

---

Box 18.3 Using biographical accounts in the study of organizational culture

In an article about organizational counterculture at General Motors (GM), Martin and Siehl (1983) draw on data from two sources:

1 Ed Cray's *Chrome Colossus: General Motors and its Times* (1980)—a corporate history of GM.

2 J. P. Wright's *On a Clear Day You Can See General Motors* (1979)—an account of the activities of the influential manager John DeLorean at GM.

The former source was selected because it was the most current source at the time, it provides a detailed picture of the firm's dominant culture, and it includes some information that is critical of the firm. The second source was chosen because it is the most thorough published account of DeLorean's activities at GM. The two sources were supplemented by a number of interviews with present and former GM employees and by the use of other published books about the company.

An in-depth qualitative content analysis of the two books was conducted and this was used as the basis for the interpretations, using direct quotations and stories from the two accounts.

Martin and Siehl note a limitation of the two accounts is that they both focus primarily on the activities of 'relatively high ranking executives' without exploring 'how these activities were perceived by subordinates' (1983: 56).

They also note that, because Wright writes of DeLorean's experiences in the first person, the book is cited as representing DeLorean's point of view. However, they point out that DeLorean has disowned Wright's account and it is highly likely that their opinions differ on some issues. They acknowledge that 'in such cases the book is probably more representative of Wright's opinions than DeLorean's, in spite of the former's use of the first person' (1983: 64).

---

information by its subject. Moreover, several writers have noted the 'sameness' about subsequent biographies. This feature can be attributed to the tight control by the Disney Archive, which is itself controlled by the Walt Disney Corporation. It is from the primary materials of this archive (letters, notes of meetings, and so on) that biographies would be fashioned. As a result, while Walt Disney never wrote an autobiography in the conventional meaning of the term, his hand and subsequently that of the company can be seen in the biographies that have been written.

When we evaluate personal documents, the *authenticity* criterion is clearly of considerable importance. Is the purported author of the letter or diary the real author? In the case of autobiographies, this has become a growing problem in recent years as a result of the increasing use of 'ghost' writers by the famous. In Martin and Siehl's (1983) study of organizational counterculture (see Box 18.3) how can we be sure that interpretations of culture based on accounts of events and direct quotes from these biographical and historical sources are accurate? But the same is potentially true of other documents. Turning to the issue of *credibility*, John Scott (1990) observes that there are at least

two major concerns with respect to personal documents: the factual accuracy of reports and whether they do in fact report the true feelings of the writer. Scott recommends a strategy of healthy scepticism regarding the sincerity with which the writer reports his or her true feelings. Famous business people such as Richard Branson or Anita Roddick are likely to be fully aware that their letters or diaries will be of considerable interest to others and may, therefore, have one eye firmly fixed on the degree to which they really reveal themselves in their writings, or alternatively ensure that they convey a 'front' that they want to project. Authorized biographies and autobiographies have to be treated with similar caution, since they can frequently be exercises in reputation building.

Representativeness is an additional concern for these materials. Surviving historical documents are relatively few in number and they have been preserved only in relation to the most influential of companies, such as Cadbury, Unilever, or the Ford Foundation. Therefore, such historical documents are likely to be biased in terms of the organizations they represent. A further problem is the selective survival of documents like letters. Why do any survive at all and what proportion are damaged, lost, or thrown away? The question of *meaning* is often rendered problematic by such things as damage to letters and diaries and the use by authors of abbreviations or codes that are difficult to decipher.

Visual objects

There is a growing interest in the visual in business and management research. The photograph is the most obvious manifestation of this trend, in that, rather than being thought of as incidental to the research process, photographs are becoming objects of interest in their own right, as the example in Box 18.4 illustrates. Once again, there is a distinction between photographs and other visual objects that are produced as part of fieldwork and those that are naturally occurring. An interesting example of the use of both is provided by Schwartzman (1993), who neatly and somewhat poignantly juxtaposes three photographs of the General Electric Hawthorne works that was the focus of the famous Hawthorne studies (see Box 2.10): one contemporary image from the AT&T archives of one of the departments in which the studies were carried out (the Bank Wiring Observation Room, see Plate 2.1); a 1987 photograph from the *Chicago Sun-Times* of the demolished Hawthorne works buildings; and a photograph taken of the Hawthorne Works Shopping Centre that was built on the cleared land.

Box 18.4 Using photographs to capture organizational beliefs about customers

In seeking to develop a longitudinal and comparative research design for the study of organizational beliefs about customers, Dougherty and Kunda (1990) chose to focus on company annual reports because they were comparable across organizations and could be studied over time, thereby incorporating a longitudinal element into the study. They looked in particular at the photographs of customers found in the reports, which revealed 'aspects of an organization's theory of its customers in a nonverbalized yet substantive way' (1990: 187).

The study was limited to firms in the computer equipment manufacturing sector and annual reports from the five largest of these—IBM, Burroughs, Digital (DEC), Data General (DG), and Honeywell. Dougherty and Kunda analysed 425 photographs from the annual reports of these companies between 1975 and 1984. A major task for the researchers was to develop categories for the analysis of the data. After several weeks of scrutiny and discussion they decided on two broad descriptive dimensions. These related to the nature of:

1 *the customer organization*—how many people are shown in the photograph, what are they like e.g. sex, hierarchical position, what tasks are they undertaking?

2 *The relationship with customers*—where and how does the product fit into the customers' activities?

The photographs were categorized according to these dimensions to reveal the unique views of customers held across the firms. For example, in relation to the task theme, which conveys what the organization believes their customers do, the photographs illustrate how hospital, bank, and aircraft manufacturing customers are viewed differently by the five firms.

For example, in relation to the hospital customer, Dougherty and Kunda illustrate how DEC's photographs emphasize the importance of the task and its social contribution, combined with an emphasis on the high degree of technological sophistication that is involved. A typical image is therefore of a tense, dramatic moment in a hospital operating room. In contrast, both IBM and Burroughs use photographs to portray the more ordinary, repetitive aspects of hospital work; showing a relaxed, simple check-up, in the case of IBM, and featuring information processing in the image portrayed by Burroughs (see Plate 18.1). People are thus 'adjuncts to the task of information processing; data going into or coming out of the equipment dominate the scene' (1990: 193).

Moreover, Dougherty and Kunda show how many of these perceptions of customers remained consistent over the ten-year period, despite changes in users of computing products. They suggest that beliefs about customers are significant because they can affect an organization's ability to adapt to its environment. However, perhaps the more significant contribution made by this study lies in its methods; as the authors themselves acknowledge: 'We hope our findings at least suggest that much can be learned from the contrast of seemingly innocent photographs and the self conscious tales they tell'. (1990: 204)

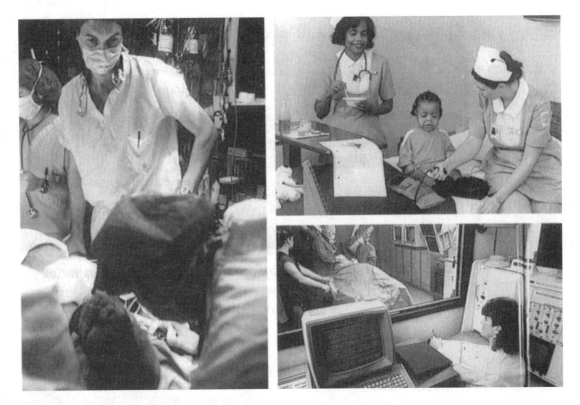

Plate 18.1 The Hospital customer: Left: Digital (DEC); top right: IBM; bottom right: Burroughs
Source: Dougherty and Kunda (1990: 191); reprinted with permission of Walter de Gruyter Publishing.

Sometimes the use of photographs and other visual records is not built into the researcher's plans at the outset. For example, Liff and Steward (2001) did not initially intend to use their case-study photographs as a data source, but as their research developed they found the photographs to have greater significance for their analysis than they had initially anticipated (see Box 18.5). By contrast, Buchanan (2001), in his study of the introduction of Business Process Re-engineering in Leicester General Hospital, included photography from the outset as part of the battery of data collection techniques he employed. As part of his focus on getting a sense of the 'patient trail', over 150 transparency slides were taken. Buchanan (2001: 151) argues that using photographs in conjunction with other methods of data collection helps the organizational researcher to:

- develop a richer understanding of organizational processes;

- capture data not disclosed in interview;

- reveal to staff aspects of work in other sections of the organization with which they have little or no regular contact;

- offer a novel channel for respondent validation of data; and

- involve staff in debate concerning the implications of research findings for organization process re-design and improvement.

The photograph provides a particularly important source of data in studies of organizational culture and symbolism (Gagliardi 1990). For example, in Berg and Kreiner's (1990) study of corporate buildings and architecture, they suggest physical structures are becoming an important part of building a successful organizational image. This is because managers are increasingly conscious of the way that physical layout can influence human behaviour, so

Lurking
effect

Box 18.5 Using photographs in the study of e-gateways

Plate 18.2 McNulty's Café, Newcastle: view from outside of tables and computers
Reprinted with the permission of Liff and Steward.

Plate 18.3 Project Cosmic, Devon: not likely to draw in those passing by
Reprinted with the permission of Liff and Steward.

E-gateways is the term used by Liff and Steward (2001) to refer to telecottages, cybercafés, and other similar organizations that provide public access to the Internet. Part of the research involved the study of a small number of UK e-gateways identified as illustrating different types of facility and location, which are successful in attracting users. In their research, Liff and Steward distinguish between:

- *shop front gateways*—which attract users through their prominent location and active promotion of facilities;

- *community e-gateways*—which draw on existing links into a neighbourhood to attract users.

Data collection involved observation, questionnaires to users and non-users, and interviews with staff and with those who had funding or other relationships with the centre. Photographs were also taken by the researchers—initially to be used as an *aide-mémoire* when writing up the cases.

Liff and Steward found the location and physical layout of the e-gateways to be significant in determining the way contrasting but successful facilities attracted users. For example, McNulty's Café, located in central Newcastle, has a corner location with large plate glass windows on both sides (Plate 18.2). Looking in, passers-by can see people eating, drinking, and using computers. Inside the computers and café tables are close together, making 'lurking' easy. The café has a relaxed atmosphere, and people use it for getting together with friends or for business or study meetings. These all reduce the barriers to entry and to the transition from a non-user to a user. Some users said that they had come into the café on several occasions before finally deciding to 'have a go' on the computers.

In contrast, Project Cosmic in rural Devon is based in a disused railway station, which is located on the edge of town and set back from the road (Plate 18.3). Liff and Steward explain that, even though the café is within comfortable walking distance of the shopping area, it is not in a very prominent location. Despite the sandwich board on the pavement, it would be hard to know what kind of place it was without going in.

When writing up the findings from their research and presenting it to sponsors and other research users, Liff and Steward have used the photographs from their case studies and other centres to illustrate the contrasts between shop front and community approaches and less successful approaches. In addition to reinforcing the *internal validity* of the research (see Chapter 13 for further discussion of validity in qualitative research), the photographs highlight a key finding of the research, which is that e-gateways can generate diverse forms of social inclusion.

comfortable chairs, for example, are suggested to produce less formal interaction. However, corporate architecture can also be used to reinforce a particular managerial philosophy; for example, a low, flat building design can be used to suggest the absence of a status hierarchy.

Marketing and advertising research also makes use of photographs as a source of data. Peñaloza (2000) looked at the way that the cultural meaning of the American West was produced through the activities of a cattle trade show. She suggests that the rich imagery of the American West, reflected by such examples as Marlboro cigarettes, Wrangler jeans, and Jeep Cherokees, is represented through the trade show where animals are bought and sold, but also where the culture of the American West is enacted and celebrated. In addition to participant observation and depth interviewing, her ethnographic study incorporated 550 photographs taken at the shows over a six-year period. These were mainly photographs of the events—including cattle sales, breed shows, and rodeos. As a visible record of people and activities, the photographs helped Peñaloza to build up a profile of the race/ethnicity and sex of attendees at particular events and of the type of activities that were involved in the show.

However, the photograph must not be taken at its face value when used as a research source; it is also necessary to have considerable additional knowledge of the social context to probe beneath the surface. Glossy photographs of happy, smiling employees in corporate brochures or newsletters, for example, might suggest that there is a gap between the photographic image of the company and the underlying reality as experienced at a day-to-day level. Scott sees the issue of *representativeness* as a particular problem for the analyst of photographs. As he suggests, the photographs that survive the passage of time—for example, in archives—are very unlikely to be representative. They are likely to have been subject to all sorts of hazards, such as damage and selective retention. A sensitivity to what is not photographed can reveal the 'mentality' of the person(s) behind the camera. What is clear is that the question of representativeness is much more fundamental than the issue of what survives, because it points to the way in which the selective survival of photographs may be constitutive of a reality that business owners and managers seek to fashion.

Public documents

The state is the source of a great deal of information of potential significance for business researchers. It produces a great deal of statistical information, some of which was touched on in Chapter 10. In addition to such quantitative data, the state is the source of a great deal of textual material of potential interest, such as Acts of Parliament and official reports.

An interesting use of official documents is Turner's (1994) employment of the reports of public inquiries into three disasters, one of which—the fire at the Summerland Leisure Centre, Douglas, Isle of Man, in 1973—is a particular emphasis in his discussion. The report was published in 1974. Turner was primarily interested in the preconditions of the fire—the factors that were deemed by the inquiry to have led to the fire itself and to the way in which the handling of the incident produced such disastrous consequences (fifty deaths). In his initial analysis, which was based on a grounded theory approach, Turner aimed to produce a theoretical account of the fire's preconditions. Turner describes the process for this and the other two public inquiry reports he examined as one of slowly going through the details of the report. He describes the process as follows:

I asked, for each paragraph, what names or 'labels for ideas' I needed in order to identify those elements, events or notions which were of interest to me in my broad and initially very unfocused concern to develop a theory of disaster preconditions. I then recorded each name or concept label on the top of a 5 inch by 8 inch card, together with a note of the source paragraph, and added further paragraph references to the card as I encountered additional instances of the concept identified.   (1994: 198)

He ended up with 182 of these cards, which provided the raw materials for building his theoretical model. Similar sources were employed by Weick (1990) in his study of the Tenerife plane crash in 1977, in that he used an official report of the Spanish Ministry of Transport and Communication and

a further report by the US-based Airline Pilots Association.

A further example of this kind of study is provided by Gephart (1993), who based his analysis on naturally occurring retrospective and archival qualitative data, including public inquiry transcripts and proceedings, newspaper reports, corporate and government documents (Box 18.6). This type of analysis, which uses publicly available data to

---

Box 18.6 Using public documents to analyse an organizational disaster

Gephart (1993) employed what he describes as a 'textual approach', using a variety of retrospective archival material in a way that treats researcher's observations and written documents as 'texts'. Two kinds of data were collected:

1 naturally occurring retrospective and archival qualitative data, including public inquiry transcripts and proceedings, newspaper reports, corporate and government documents;

2 self-generated texts including field notes describing inquiry events.

These texts were analysed in order to trace the life history of the focal event—a pipeline disaster—from the perspectives of a range of participants. The study sought to address the following research questions in the public inquiry context.

• What concepts and terms, or vocabularies are used by organizational members in sensemaking about disasters?

• How do people use risk and blame concepts in disaster sensemaking?

• How are sensemaking practices used in the interpretation of disasters?

• What role do collective and individual interpretative schemes play in disaster sensemaking?

The pipeline accident occurred in 1985 on the Western Pipe Lines system in Canada. A fireball erupted during attempts to control a leak of natural gas liquids and two employees of the company died of burns. There followed a public inquiry in which the federal government energy board took evidence about the causes and consequences of the disaster. The public inquiry provided Gephart with a

focus for his investigation through the series of texts that attempted to make sense of the disaster and tried publicly to attribute responsibility and blame.

Gephart attended the public inquiry throughout, informally interviewing managers, lawyers, and safety managers who were also attending the inquiry. This ethnographic aspect of his data collection resulted in 500 pages of field notes. These were combined with the other, naturally occurring, data used in the study, such as the official proceedings of the inquiry, and used to compile two electronically held data bases:

1 a word processor database containing all the information from the transcripts, company documents, field notes, newspaper articles and official report;

2 a textual database from the entire text of the inquiry proceedings.

Analysis, using a computer-based text retrieval programme, focused on creating 'textual exhibits' 'that tell the story of the disaster and the inquiry using actual segments of text'; this enabled Gephart in his analysis to 'remain close to the raw data' and to illustrate its richness (1993: 1483). A set of key words was then developed to reflect the way that participants saw concepts of risk, blame, and responsibility.

It was then possible to retrieve 'every occurrence of the key words in the data' using the textual analysis software and to show these frequencies speaker by speaker. Gephart claims that the textual approach offers a way of uncovering practices and processes that generate and sustain organizational interpretations of events. The use of archival materials enables the longitudinal study of events that are in this case complemented by the collection of primary, ethnographic data.

analyse critical events or disasters, has been referred to as 'organizational post mortem' research (Orton 1997) and there are an increasing number of research studies in business and management that use this approach. Other examples include Vaughan's (1990) analysis of the space shuttle *Challenger* tragedy in 1986 and Orton's (1997) study of three critical events in the history of the US intelligence community. In the former, Vaughan used documents gathered by the Presidential Commission and reports and transcripts that related to the disaster; he also interviewed journalists and people responsible for regulating safety at NASA. Orton instead relied on organizational and presidential libraries, in particular the Ford Library, which contained over fourteen million original documents from the Ford Administration. Familiarizing oneself with these kinds of research materials can be an extremely time-consuming activity, mainly because of the vastness and detail of documents associated with official events and inquiries, and this needs to be taken into account when planning to use such materials as a potential source of data.

In terms of John Scott's (1990) four criteria, such materials can certainly be seen as authentic and as having meaning (in the sense of being clear and comprehensible to the researcher), but the two other standards require somewhat greater consideration. The question of credibility raises the issue of whether the documentary source is biased. In other words, such documents can be interesting precisely because of the biases they reveal. Equally, this point suggests that caution is necessary in attempting to treat them as depictions of reality. The issue of representativeness is complicated in that materials like these are in a sense unique and it is precisely their official or quasi-official character that makes them interesting in their own right. There is also, of course, the question of whether the case itself is representative, but in the context of qualitative research this is not a meaningful question, because no case can be representative in a statistical sense. The issue is one of establishing a cogent theoretical account and possibly examining that account in other contexts. Turner (1994) in fact examined three disasters and noted many common factors that were associated with behaviour in crisis situations.

Organizational documents

This is a very heterogeneous group of sources that is of particular importance to the business and management researcher, not least because of the vast quantity of documentary information that is available within most organizations. Some of these documents are in the public domain, such as annual reports, mission statements, reports to shareholders, transcripts of chief executives' speeches, press releases, advertisements, and public relations material in printed form and on the World Wide Web. Other documents are not (or may not be) in the public domain, such as company newsletters, organizational charts, external consultancy reports, minutes of meetings, memos, internal and external correspondence, manuals for new recruits, policy statements, company regulations, and so on. Such materials can provide the researcher with valuable background information about the company; they are therefore often used by organizational ethnographers as part of their investigations. Similarly, in case-study research, documents can be used to build up a description of the organization and its history. Because documents can offer at least partial insights into past managerial decisions and actions, they can also be useful in building up a 'timeline', particularly in processual studies of organizational change (see Chapter 13 and Box 13.6).

However, the difficulty of gaining access to some organizations means that some researchers have to rely on public domain documents alone. Even if the researcher is an insider who has gained access to an organization, it may well be that certain documents that are not in the public domain will not be available to him or her. For his study of ICI, Pettigrew (see Box 2.17) was allowed access to company archives, so that, in addition to interviewing, he was allowed to

distortion

examine 'materials on company strategy and personnel policy, documents relating to the birth and development of various company OD (organizational development) groups, files documenting the natural history of key organizational changes, and information on the recruitment and training of internal OD consultants, and the use made of external OD consultants' (1985: 41). Such information can be very important for researchers conducting case studies of organizations using such methods as participant observation or (as in Pettigrew's case) qualitative interviews. Other writers have relied more or less exclusively on documents. For example, in Turner's (1994) study of large-scale disasters, his analysis relied entirely on the detailed accounts of action provided by the public inquiry records and these formed the basis for his own written notes, which constituted his data documents.

Such documents need to be evaluated using Scott's four criteria. As with the materials considered in the previous section, documents deriving from private sources like companies are likely to be authentic and meaningful, in the sense of being clear and comprehensible to the researcher, though this is not to suggest that the analyst of documents should be complacent. Issues of credibility and representativeness are likely to exercise the analyst of documents somewhat more. For instance, organizational documents that are in the public domain, such as company annual reports, may not be an accurate representation of how different organizational actors perceive the situations in which they are involved.

People who write organizational documents, such as managers, are likely to have a particular point of view that they want to get across. An interesting illustration of this simple observation is provided by a study of company documentation by Forster (1994). In the course of a study of career development issues in a major British retail company (referred to as TC), Forster carried out an extensive analysis of company documentation relating primarily to human resource management issues, as well as interviews and a questionnaire survey. Because he was able to interview many of the authors of the

documents about what they had written, 'both the accuracy of the documents and their authorship could be validated by the individuals who had produced them' (1994: 155). In other words, the authenticity of the documents was confirmed and it would seem that credibility was verified as well. However, Forster also tells us that the documents showed up divergent interpretations among different groupings of key events and processes:

One of the clearest themes to emerge was the apparently incompatible interpretations of the same events and processes amongst the three subgroups within the company—senior executives, HQ personnel staff and regional personnel managers.... These documents were not produced deliberately to distort or obscure events or processes being described, but their effect was to do precisely this.   (1994: 160)

In other words, members of the different groupings expressed through the documents certain perspectives that reflected their positions in the organization. Consequently, although authors of the documents could confirm the content of those documents, the latter could not be regarded as 'free from error and distortion', as John Scott puts it. Therefore, documents cannot be regarded as providing objective accounts of a state of affairs. They have to be interrogated and examined in the context of other sources of data. As Forster's case suggests, the different stances that are taken up by the authors of documents can be used as a platform for developing insights into the processes and factors that lie behind divergence. In this instance, the documents are interesting in bringing out the role and significance of subcultures within the organization.

Issues of representativeness are likely to loom large in most contexts of this kind. Did Forster have access to a totally comprehensive set of documents? It could be that some had been destroyed or that he was not allowed access to certain documents that were regarded as sensitive. Finally gaining access to confidential or potentially sensitive documents within an organization, such as personnel files, as Dalton (1959) did (see Chapter 14), raises particular ethical issues, which we will return to in Chapter 25.

Mass media outputs

Newspapers, magazines, television programmes, films, and other mass media are potential sources for business and management study. Of course, we have encountered these kinds of source before when exploring content analysis in Chapter 9. An example is given in Box 18.8 of a study that relied exclusively on articles about a well-known business leader published in the popular press. In addition to exploring mass media outputs using a quantitative form of data analysis like content analysis, such sources can also be examined so that their qualitative nature is preserved. Typically, such analysis entails searching for themes in the sources that are examined, but see the discussion on analysing documents below for a more detailed examination of this issue.

Authenticity issues are sometimes difficult to ascertain in the case of mass media outputs. While the outputs can usually be deemed to be genuine, the authorship of articles is often unclear (for example, editorials, some magazine articles), so that it is difficult to know whether the account can be relied upon as being written by someone in a position to provide an accurate version.

Credibility is also frequently an issue, but in fact it is often the uncovering of error or distortion that is the objective of the analysis. For example, Jackson and Carter (1998) have explored the constitution of management gurus through the analysis of a BBC management video featuring Frederick Herzberg giving a live lecture to an audience of UK managers on his Motivation-Hygiene theory. They compare this video with an earlier transmission of the lecture, which was shown on normal television in 1973, under the title 'Jumping for the Jelly Beans'. Comparison of the two versions reveals a number of differences between them; notably, in the video version a section subtitled 'KITA' (Herzberg's acronym for 'Kick in the Arse'), containing some offensive references including a joke about rape, has been edited out of the lecture. Jackson and Carter suggest that the reason for this careful editing relates to the need to maintain Herzberg's credibility as a management guru, ensuring that his image remains intact despite the fact that the editing distorts the presentation of his ideas.

Representativeness is rarely an issue for analyses of newspaper or magazine articles, since the corpus from which a sample has been drawn is usually ascertainable, especially when a wide range of newspapers is employed. Finally, the evidence is usually clear and comprehensible but may require considerable awareness of contextual factors relating to the organization or company, such as information about share prices, movements of key personnel, and merger speculation.

Virtual outputs

There is one final type of document that ought to be mentioned—the documents that appear on the Internet. The relative newness of the Internet means that this is an area that is fairly underused by business researchers. However, the vastness of the Internet and its growing accessibility make it a likely source of documents for both quantitative and qualitative data analysis.

There is clearly huge potential with the Internet as a source of documents, but John Scott's criteria need keeping in mind. First, authenticity: anyone could set up a web site, so that information and advice may be given by someone who is not an authority. Secondly, credibility: we need to be aware of possible distortions. For example, if we were studying advice about the purchase of shares, it is known that web sites have been set up encouraging people to buy or sell particular stocks held by the web-site authors, so that the prices of stocks can be manipulated. Thirdly, given the constant flux of the Internet, it is doubtful

whether we could ever know how representative web sites on a certain topic are. Finally, web sites are notorious for a kind of Webspeak, so that it may be difficult to comprehend what is being said without considerable insider knowledge. As the use of computers and in particular the Internet as a source of data is undoubtedly increasing, we will be returning to these issues and discussing them further in Chapter 23.

The world as text

There is one word that we have done our best to avoid using in the chapter so far—text. The word 'text' is frequently employed as a synonym for a term like 'written document'. We have clearly strayed from this association, in that photographs and films have been touched upon. But, in relatively recent times, the word 'text' has been applied to an increasingly wide range of phenomena, so that theme parks, landscapes, heritage attractions, technologies, and a wide range of other objects are treated as texts out of which a 'reading' can be fashioned (e.g. Grint and Woolgar 1997). Thus, in Barthes's (1972) influential collection of essays, objects as varied as wrestling matches, Citroën cars, and striptease acts are submitted to readings. In a sense, therefore, just about everything can be treated as a text and perhaps as a document. Box 18.6 provides an example of textual analysis in management and business. In this study Gephart (1993) treats both the written documents and his own ethnographic field notes as texts, analysing them both using the same methods. The aim using this approach is 'to account for how a given text is made meaningful to readers', seeking 'to uncover the general conventions, interests and cultural practices' (1993: 1468) that enable meaning to be created. This approach is based on two assumptions: first, that the texts have the interpretations of their creators embedded in them and, second, that a text acquires meaning through 'its embeddedness in a multiplicity of discourses and texts' (1993: 1469). Gephart thus seeks to interpret the meaning of texts in relation to events, both of which constitute aspects of culture.

Readers and audiences—active or passive?

A further important issue about texts and their nature is whether audiences/readers are active interpreters of what they see or hear. Do they passively derive the meanings that authors or designers infuse into their texts, or do they resist those meanings and arrive at resistant readings, or do they arrive at a middle point that incorporates both passive and active

---

Box 18.7 The difference between readers' and writers' intentions concerning managerial initiatives

In a study of the state-sponsored people management initiative, Investors in People, Bell, Taylor, and Thorpe (2002) explored the meaning of cultural artefacts (the badge, the plaque, and the flag) displayed in organizations that had achieved the Standard. On the basis of their case-study research in six organizations, the authors suggest there can be a significant gap between understanding of what the initiative ought to signify and what it comes to represent. For example, one story was told of an organization that had achieved the Standard. Whilst being formally recognized as an Investor in People, it was informally known by employees as a 'Divestor of People', partly as a result of a major, long-term redundancy programme. This finding confirms that readers, in this case employees, frequently come up with alternative readings to those that were intended by writers of the text, in this case managers and policy-makers working with the initiative.

elements? Much research on this issue suggests that audiences frequently come up with alternative readings to those that were intended by authors or designers, as the example given in Box 18.7 illustrates. Although the idea of the 'active audience' has not gone unchallenged (e.g. McGuigan 1992), the stream of research has been very influential and has placed a question mark over the readings of texts by social scientists. This means that we have to be cautious in concluding that the interpretations offered by social scientists of texts are going to be the same as those of another social scientist, or as those of the readers or audiences of these outputs. The business researcher is always providing his or her own 'spin' on the texts that are analysed. The same is true of all social science data: the conclusions you derive from your questionnaire or ethnographic data are always going to be a reflection of your own personal interpretation. However, the main point being made for the present is that caution is required when reading writers' renditions of texts of all kinds.

Interpreting documents

Although it means straying into areas that are relevant to the next chapter, this section will briefly consider the question of how to interpret documents qualitatively. Three possible approaches are outlined: qualitative content analysis; semiotics; and hermeneutics. In addition to these, discourse analysis, which was covered in Chapter 17, has been employed as an approach for the analysis of documents.

Qualitative content analysis

This is probably the most prevalent approach to the qualitative analysis of documents, although in business and management it remains less frequently used than quantitative content analysis (Insch et al. 1997). It comprises a searching-out of underlying themes in the materials being analysed and can be discerned in several of the studies referred to earlier, such as Dougherty and Kunda (1990) and Gephart (1993). A further example is provided in Chen and Meindl's (1991) study of the metaphors used to describe the entrepreneur and business leader Donald Burr (see Box 18.8). Unlike quantitative content analysis, the processes through which the themes are extracted is usually left implicit. The extracted themes are usually illustrated—for example, with brief quotations from a newspaper article or magazine. The procedures adopted by Turner (1994) in connection with his research on the Summerland disaster are an example of the search for themes in texts, although Turner provided greater detail about what he did than is often the case.

Altheide (1996) has outlined an approach that he calls *ethnographic content analysis* (which he contrasts with quantitative content analysis of the kind outlined in Chapter 9). Altheide's approach (referred to by him as ECA) represents a codification of certain procedures that might be viewed as typical of the kind of qualitative content analysis on which many of the studies referred to so far are based. He describes his approach as differing from traditional quantitative content analysis in that the researcher is constantly revising the themes or categories that are distilled from the examination of documents. As he puts it:

ECA follows a recursive and reflexive movement between concept development-sampling-data, collection-data, coding-data, and analysis-interpretation. The aim is to be systematic and analytic but not rigid. Categories and variables initially guide the study, but others are allowed and expected to emerge during the study, including an orientation to *constant discovery* and *constant comparison* of relevant situations, settings, styles, images, meanings, and nuances. (Altheide 1996: 16; emphases in original)

Thus, with ECA there is much more movement back and forth between conceptualization, data collection, analysis, and interpretation than is the case with the kind of content analysis described in

---

Box 18.8 Qualitative content analysis in leadership research

Chen and Meindl (1991) analysed articles in the popular press about Donald Burr, an entrepreneur who in 1980 started the low-cost US airline, People Express. Burr was widely revered as a charismatic leader because of the early success of his business and the high level of commitment exhibited by his staff. However, in 1984 the company began to founder and it was taken over by a rival in 1987.

The researchers carried out two analyses of magazine and newspaper articles about Burr. The first followed traditional content analysis methods (of the kind described in Chapter 9); it involved identifying themes and then recording the frequency of their occurrence in the text. However, the second analysis was more interpretative; it involved identification of the metaphors used to describe Burr over the course of the airline's history. The first analysis sought to analyse Burr's image from the perspective of the *reader* of the news article, whereas the second analysis concentrated on gaining an impression from the point of view of the *writer*.

Articles were presented to a sample of seventy-five undergraduate business students, who were asked to write a description of Burr based on the materials they had just read. Fourteen different themes were extracted from the image descriptions and these were subjected to traditional content analysis to establish a pattern of frequency. The analysis revealed that the themes used to describe Burr varied according to the time period in the company's history that the articles covered. For example, when the company was doing well, Burr was seen as ambitious, fair, and caring, but when it was doing badly he was seen as determined and instrumental.

In the qualitative content analysis, Chen and Meindl (1991) focused on the journalists' descriptions of Burr (i.e. the writers rather than readers of the text).

We screened, sentence by sentence, the same sampled journal articles that were presented to the respondents. Those words, phrases, or clauses that metaphorically described Burr's personality, his behaviours, or his impact were identified as metaphorical expressions. Altogether, 46 such expressions were identified. (1991: 539)

One of the commonest metaphors uncovered was that of Burr as an unorthodox preacher who was visionary, charismatic and dedicated to his mission, as these journalistic quotes illustrate:

Within the new structure . . . Burr will go on preaching his unorthodox management approach. (1991: 550)

Burr works hard when he talks. He paces, he sits; he stands; he throws out his arms; he condemns and praises, implores and jokes. (1991: 550)

The study found a high degree of correspondence between images constructed through metaphors and images constructed by the readers. This finding demonstrates the influence of the business press in constructing particular images of organizational leaders.

Chapter 9. Quantitative content analysis typically entails applying predefined categories to the sources; ECA employs some initial categorization, but there is greater potential for refinement of those categories and the generation of new ones.

Qualitative content analysis as a strategy for searching for themes in one's data lies at the heart of the coding approaches that are often employed in the analysis of qualitative data and as such will be encountered again in the next chapter.

Semiotics

Semiotics is invariably referred to as the 'science of signs'. It is an approach to the analysis of symbols in everyday life and as such can be employed in relation not only to documentary sources but also to all kinds of other data because of its commitment to treating phenomena as texts. The main terms employed in semiotics are:

- the *sign*—that is, something that stands for something else;

- the sign is made up of: a *signifier* and the *signified*;

- the *signifier* is the thing that points to an underlying meaning (the term *sign vehicle* is sometimes used instead of *signifier*);

- the *signified* is the meaning to which the signifier points;

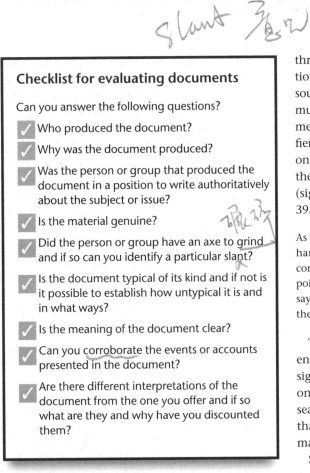

Checklist for evaluating documents

Can you answer the following questions?

☑ Who produced the document?

☑ Why was the document produced?

☑ Was the person or group that produced the document in a position to write authoritatively about the subject or issue?

☑ Is the material genuine?

☑ Did the person or group have an axe to grind and if so can you identify a particular slant?

☑ Is the document typical of its kind and if not is it possible to establish how untypical it is and in what ways?

☑ Is the meaning of the document clear?

☑ Can you corroborate the events or accounts presented in the document?

☑ Are there different interpretations of the document from the one you offer and if so what are they and why have you discounted them?

- a *denotative meaning* is the manifest or more obvious meaning of a signifier and as such indicates its function;

- a *sign-function* is an object that denotes a certain function;

- a *connotative meaning* is a meaning associated with a certain social context that is in addition to its denotative meaning;

- *polysemy* refers to a quality of signs—namely, that they are always capable of being interpreted in many ways;

- the *code* is the generalized meaning that interested parties may seek to instil in a sign; a code is sometimes also called a *sign system*.

Semiotic analysis focuses on the way that messages are communicated as systems of cultural meaning. It is based on semiotic theory, which suggests that the symbolic order of a culture is constructed and interpreted through a system of signs. A *sign* constitutes the relationship between the *signifier* (the recognizable word, sound, or picture that attracts our attention and communicates a particular message) and the *signified* (the message or concept itself). The link between the signifier and the signified is arbitrary; its meaning depends on the conventions held by groups of sign users about the mental concept (signified) that the material object (signifier) is intended to represent. Barley (1983: 395–6) provides the following example:

As you drive toward me in your speeding car, I hold up my hand, palm out, intending an expression signifying the content, 'Stop while I cross the street.' From your vantage point behind the wheel, you wonder why I am so brash as to say hello from the middle of the crosswalk and you step on the gas. Obviously our conventions differ.

This example places greater emphasis on the recipient of the message, who must actively interpret the signifier in order to establish its meaning by drawing on his or her cultural knowledge. The task of the researcher in semiotic analysis is to discover the rules that bind users of a sign together and enable them to make sense of their cultural world.

Signs contribute to systems of signification or *codes*, which provide a model for social action; these are composed of *denotative* and *connotative* elements. The denotative code represents meaning that is associated directly with the sign-vehicle itself, whereas the connotative code represents meaning that links the sign with its cultural context. An example from research into the UK state-sponsored people management initiative, Investors in People, by Bell et al. (2002), illustrates this distinction (see Box 18.7); the signifier of 'Investment in People' is a laurel wreath, a symbol that denotes victory, valour, or distinction. However, in certain organizational contexts, the connotative meaning of the sign can come to form part of a connotative code, conveying the message of 'divesting in people', which directly contradicts its intended denotative meaning.

Despite the potential for applying semiotic analysis in the study of organizational cultures, its use has instead been mainly confined to studies of marketing and advertising. In advertising, semiotic analysis encourages recognition of the way that individuals

Connotative
1 ⅞ ⅜ ⅛ ¼

interpret the same advertising message in slightly different ways. Combe and Crowther (2000) suggest, for example, that signs and symbols influence the positioning and repositioning of brands, such as Murphy's Irish stout, in recipients' minds. A further application of semiotic analysis in an organizational context is provided by Barley (1983), in his study of funeral work (see Box 18.9).

Semiotics is concerned to uncover the hidden meanings that reside in texts as broadly defined. Consider, by way of illustration, the curriculum vitae (CV) in academic life. The typical CV that an academic will produce contains such features as: personal details; education; previous and current posts; administrative responsibilities and experience; teaching experience; research experience; research grants acquired; and publications. We can treat the CV as a system of interlocking signifiers that signify at the level of denotative meaning a summary of the individual's experience (its sign function) and at the connotative level an indication of an individual's value, particularly in connection with his or her prospective employability. Each CV is capable of being interpreted in different ways, as anyone who has ever sat in on a short-listing meeting for a lectureship can testify, and is therefore polysemic, but there is a code whereby certain attributes of CVs are seen as especially desirable and that are therefore less contentious in terms of the attribution of meaning. Indeed, applicants for posts know this latter point and devise their CVs to amplify the desired qualities so that the CV becomes an autobiographical practice for the presentation of self, as Miller and Morgan (1993) have suggested.

Box 18.10 provides an illustration of a study from a semiotic perspective of Disneyland as a text. The chief strength of semiotics lies in its invitation to the

---

Box 18.9 Semiotic analysis of a funeral business

Over a three-month period, Barley (1983) engaged in observation and conducted interviews in a US funeral home, with the intention of uncovering the signs used by funeral directors to make sense of their work. After interviewing funeral directors about various aspects of their work, including the history of the business, the layout and decor of the home, and the tasks involved in preparing a body or making a removal, Barley began to develop maps of connotative codes through which he saw funeral directors as striving to achieve the quality of 'naturalness' in the funeral scene by making arrangements in a way that they believe is least likely to disturb mourners.

This might involve arranging the corpse in such a way as to convey the image of a restfully sleeping person or furnishing the funeral home in a way that simulates a comfortable living room, with coffee tables and comfortable chairs.

Barley concludes that the funeral director's role relies on a system of signs or codes that create a subtle illusion of everyday life, in order to obscure the strangeness of death and thereby to reassure mourners.

Box 18.10 A semiotic Disneyland

Gottdiener (1982; 1997: 108–15) has proposed that Disneyland in Los Angeles, California, can be fruitfully analysed through a semiotic analysis. In so doing, he was treating Disneyland as a text. One component of his analysis is that Disneyland's meaning 'is revealed by its oppositions with the quotidian—the alienated everyday life of residents of L.A.' (1982: 148). He identifies through this principle nine *sign systems* that entail a contrast between the park and its surrounding environment: transportation; food; clothing; shelter; entertainment; social control; economics; politics; and family. Thus, the first of these sign systems— transportation—reveals a contrast between the Disneyland visitor as pedestrian (walk in a group; efficient mass transportation, which is fun) and as passenger (car is necessary; poor mass transportation; danger on the congested freeways). A further component of his analysis entails an analysis of the connotations of the different 'lands' that make up the park. He suggests that each land is associated as a signifier with signifiers of capitalism, as follows:

- Frontierland—predatory capital
- Adventureland—colonialism/imperialism
- Tomorrowland—state capital
- New Orleans—venture capital
- Main Street—family capital.   (1982: 156)

analyst to try to see beyond and beneath the apparent ordinariness of everyday life and its manifestations. The main difficulty one often feels with the fruits of a semiotic analysis is that, although we are invariably given a compelling exposition of a facet of the quotidian, it is difficult to escape a sense of the arbitrariness of the analysis provided. However, in all probability this sensation is unfair to the approach, because the results of a semiotic analysis are probably no more arbitrary than any interpretation of documentary materials or any other data, such as a thematic, qualitative content analysis of the kind described in the previous section. Indeed, it would be surprising if we were not struck by a sense of arbitrariness in interpretation, in view of the principle of polysemy that lies at the heart of semiotics.

Hermeneutics

Hermeneutics refers to an approach that was originally devised in relation to the understanding or interpretation of texts and of theological texts in particular. It has been influential in the general formulation of interpretivism as an epistemology (see Chapter 1, where the idea of hermeneutics was briefly encountered) and is more or less synonymous with Weber's notion of *Verstehen*. The central idea behind hermeneutics is that the analyst of a text must seek to bring out the meanings of a text from the perspective of its author. This will entail attention to the social and historical context within which the text was produced. An approach to the analysis of texts like qualitative content analysis can be hermeneutic when it is sensitive to the context within which texts were produced. Hermeneutics is seen by its modern advocates as a strategy that has potential in relation both to texts as documents and to social actions and other non-documentary phenomena.

Phillips and Brown (1993) and Forster (1994) separately identify an approach to the interpretation of company documents that they describe as a *critical hermeneutic* approach. A hermeneutic approach, because of its emphasis on the location of interpretation within a specific social and historical context, would seem to represent an invitation to ensure that the analyst of texts is fully conversant with that

context. As such, the approach is likely to entail the collection and analysis of data that will allow an understanding in context to be forged. As noted previously, Forster's study of the company referred to as TC included interviews with senior managers and a questionnaire survey. For their study of the corporate image advertisements of a Canadian company that produces synthetic crude oil, Phillips and Brown also employed a large database of magazine and newspaper articles relating to the company, which also supplied the authors with additional documentary materials. Forster's critical hermeneutic analysis entailed the interrogation of the documents and the extraction of themes from them by reference to his knowledge of the organizational context within which the documents and the people and events within them were located.

Phillips and Brown's somewhat more formal approach entailed the examination of the advertisements in terms of three 'moments'.

- *The social–historical moment*, which involves 'an examination of the producer of the text, its intentional recipient, its referent in the world [i.e. what it refers to], and the context in which the text is produced, transmitted, and received' (1993: 1558).

- *The formal moment*, which involves 'a formal analysis of the structural and conventional aspects of the text' (1993: 1563). This means that the texts must be examined in terms of the constituent parts of each text and the writing conventions employed. This phase can involve the use of any of several techniques, such as semiotics or discourse analysis (see Chapter 17). Phillips and Brown used the former of these.

- *The interpretation–reinterpretation moment*, which 'involves the interpretation of the results of the first two moments' (1993: 1567); in other words, they are synthesized.

Through this strategy, Phillips and Brown show, for example, the ways in which the corporate image advertisements constitute an attempt to mobilize support for the company's activities from government (and from among the public, who were unlikely to be familiar with the company) at a time of intense competition for funding, and to ward off environmental legislation. The approach has points of affinity with the idea of the active audience (see above), in that there is an emphasis on the reception of texts and as such the notion that there may be a plurality of interpretations of them.

The critical hermeneutic approach thus can draw on practices associated with qualitative content analysis and can fuse them with ways of formally approaching texts, such as semiotics. What is crucial is the linkage that is made between understanding the text from the point of view of the author and the social and historical context of its production. Indeed, in many respects, for a hermeneutic approach, the latter is a precondition of the former. Its appeal to qualitative researchers is that it is an approach to the analysis of documents (and indeed other data) that explicitly draws on two central tenets of the qualitative research strategy: an emphasis on the point of view of the author of the text and a sensitivity to context.

K KEY POINTS

- Documents constitute a very heterogeneous set of sources of data, which include personal documents, official documents from both the state and private sources, and the mass media.

- Such materials can be the focus of both quantitative and qualitative enquiry, but the emphasis in this chapter has been upon the latter.

- Documents of the kinds considered may be in printed, visual, digital, or indeed any other retrievable format.

- For many writers, just about anything can be 'read' as a text.

- Criteria for evaluating the quality of documents are: authenticity; credibility; representativeness; and meaning. The relevance of these criteria varies somewhat according to the kind of document being assessed.

- There are several ways of analysing documents within qualitative research. In this chapter we have covered qualitative content analysis, semiotics, and hermeneutics.

Q QUESTIONS FOR REVIEW

- What is meant by a document?
- What are John Scott's four criteria for assessing documents?

Personal documents

- Outline the different kinds of personal documents.
- How do they fare in terms of John Scott's criteria?
- What might be the role of personal documents in relation to the life history or biographical method?
- What uses can photographs have in business research?

Public documents

- What do the studies by Gephart and Turner suggest in terms of the potential for business researchers to use official documents?

- How do such documents fare in terms of John Scott's criteria?

Organizational documents

- What kinds of documents might be obtained from organizational sources?

- How do such documents fare in terms of John Scott's criteria?

Mass media outputs

- What kinds of documents are mass media outputs?

- How do such documents fare in terms of John Scott's criteria?

Virtual outputs

- Do Internet documents and other virtual outputs raise special problems in terms of assessing them from the point of view of John Scott's criteria?

The world as text

- Can anything be treated as a text?

- What is the significance of audiences in connection with textual readings by academics?

Interpreting documents

- How does qualitative content analysis differ from the kind of content analysis discussed in Chapter 9?

- What is a sign? How central is it to semiotics?

- What is the difference between denotative meaning and connotative meaning?

- What is a hermeneutic approach to documents?

- What lessons can be learned from the studies by Phillips and Brown and by Forster concerning the potential uses of a hermeneutic approach?

19

Qualitative data analysis

CHAPTER GUIDE

Because qualitative data deriving from interviews or participant observation typically take the form of a large corpus of unstructured textual material, they are not straightforward to analyse. Moreover, unlike quantitative data analysis, clear-cut rules about how qualitative data analysis should be carried out have not been developed. In this chapter, some general approaches to qualitative data analysis will be examined, along with *coding*, which is the main feature of most of these approaches. The chapter explores:

- *analytic induction* as a general strategy of qualitative data analysis;

- *grounded theory* as a general strategy of qualitative data analysis; this is probably the most prominent of the general approaches to qualitative data analysis; the chapter

examines its main features, processes, and outcomes, along with some of the criticisms that are sometimes levelled at the approach;

- *coding* as a key process in grounded theory and in approaches to qualitative data analysis more generally; it is the focus of an extended discussion in terms of what it entails and some of the limitations of a reliance on coding;

- the criticism that is sometimes made of coding in relation to qualitative data—namely, that it tends to fragment data; the idea of *narrative analysis* is introduced as an approach to data analysis that is gaining a growing following and that does not result in data fragmentation;

- the possibility of conducting a secondary analysis of other researchers' qualitative data is examined.

Introduction

One of the main difficulties with qualitative research is that it very rapidly generates a large, cumbersome database because of its reliance on prose in the form of such media as field notes, interview transcripts, or documents. Miles (1979) has described qualitative data as an 'attractive nuisance', because of the attractiveness of its richness but the difficulty of finding analytic paths through that richness. The researcher must guard against being captivated by the richness of the data collected, so that there is a failure to give the data wider significance for the business and management community. In other words, it is crucial to guard against failing to carry out a true analysis. This means that you must protect yourself against the condition Lofland (1971: 18) once called 'analytic interruptus'.

Yet, finding a path through the thicket of prose that makes up your data is not an easy matter and is baffling to many researchers confronting such data for the first time. 'What do I do with it now?' is a common refrain. In large part, this is because, unlike the analysis of quantitative data, there are few well-established and widely accepted rules for the analysis of qualitative data. Although learning the techniques of quantitative data analysis may seem painful at the time, they do give you an unambiguous set of rules about how to handle your data. You still have to interpret your analyses, but at least there are relatively clear rules for getting to that point. Qualitative data analysis has not reached this degree of codification of analytic procedures and many writers would argue that this is not necessarily desirable anyway (see Bryman and Burgess 1994*b* on this point). What *can* be provided are broad guidelines (Okely 1994), and it is in the spirit of this suggestion that this chapter has been written.

This chapter has three main sections.

- *General strategies of qualitative data analysis*. In this section, we consider two approaches to data analysis—analytic induction and grounded theory.

- *Basic operations in qualitative data analysis*. This section builds on Chapter 18 and focuses on the steps, considerations, and problems that are associated with *coding*.

- *Narrative analysis*. This section explores an approach to qualitative data analysis that has become popular amongst some researchers in the field of management and business called narrative analysis.

In the next chapter, the use of computers in qualitative data analysis will be outlined.

General strategies of qualitative data analysis

This section considers two strategies of analysis—analytic induction and grounded theory. They are probably the most frequently cited approaches, though others do exist (e.g. Williams 1976; Hycner 1985). By a general strategy of qualitative data analysis, we simply mean a framework that is meant to guide the analysis of data. As we will see, one of the ways in which qualitative and quantitative data analysis sometimes differ is that, with the latter, analysis invariably occurs after your data have been collected. However, as noted in Chapter 13, general approaches like grounded theory (and analytic induction) are often described as *iterative*—that is, there is a repetitive interplay between the collection and analysis of data. This means that analysis starts after some of the data have been collected and the implications of that analysis then shape the next steps in the data collection process. Consequently, while grounded theory and analytic induction are described as strategies of analysis, they can also be viewed as strategies for the *collection* of data as well.

Analytic induction

The main steps in analytic induction are outlined in Figure 19.1. Analytic induction (see Box 19.1) begins with a rough definition of a research question, proceeds to a hypothetical explanation of that question, and then continues onto the collection of data (examination of cases). If a case that is inconsistent with the hypothesis is encountered, the analyst *either* redefines the hypothesis so as to exclude the deviant or negative case *or* reformulates the hypothesis and proceeds with further data collection. If the latter path is chosen, if a further deviant case is found, the analyst must choose again between reformulation or redefinition. An example of analytic induction used in a study of corporate ecological responsiveness is given in Box 19.2.

As this brief outline suggests, analytic induction is an extremely rigorous method of analysis, because encountering a single case that is inconsistent with a hypothesis is sufficient to necessitate further data collection or a reformulation of the hypothesis, and the selection of cases must be sufficiently diverse as to have adequately challenged the theory. This is reflected by Bansal and Roth's inclusion of Japanese companies in their sample, in order to test their model of corporate ecological responsiveness in a different cultural context. Nor should the alternative of reformulating the hypothetical explanation be regarded as a soft option. The rigours of analytic induction have not endeared the approach to qualitative researchers and most of the examples used in textbooks to illustrate analytic induction derive from the 1940s and early 1950s (Bryman and Burgess 1994*a*: 4); Bansal and Roth's (2000) work is unusual in being a relatively recent example.

Two further problems with analytic induction are worth noting. First, the final explanations that analytic induction arrives at specify the conditions that are *sufficient* for the phenomenon occurring but rarely specify the *necessary* conditions. This means that analytic induction may find out why companies with certain characteristics or in certain circumstances become ecologically responsive but it does not allow us to say why those particular companies became more responsive, rather than others in the same situation with the same characteristics. Secondly, it does not provide useful guidelines (unlike grounded theory) as to how many cases need to be investigated before the absence of negative cases and the validity of the hypothetical explanation (whether reformulated or not) can be confirmed.

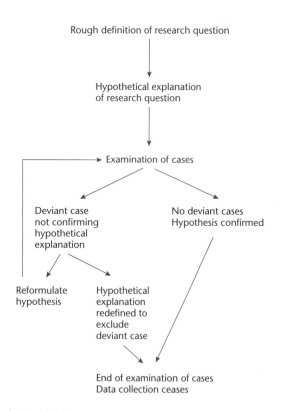

Figure 19.1 The process of analytic induction

Rough definition of research question

Hypothetical explanation of research question

Examination of cases

Deviant case not confirming hypothetical explanation

No deviant cases Hypothesis confirmed

Reformulate hypothesis

Hypothetical explanation redefined to exclude deviant case

End of examination of cases Data collection ceases

Box 19.1 *What is analytic induction?*

Analytic induction is an approach to the analysis of data in which the researcher seeks universal explanations of phenomena by pursuing the collection of data until no cases that are inconsistent with a hypothetical explanation (deviant or negative cases) of a phenomenon are found.

Box 19.2 An example of the use of analytic induction

The aim of Bansal and Roth's (2000) research was to develop a robust model of the motives for corporate ecological responsiveness, or 'greening'. They chose an analytic induction approach because it enabled them to accommodate existing theories of corporate greening. This allowed them to begin by reviewing the literature in order to develop a set of hypotheses and then to move back and forth between data collection and theory generation.

From the data they developed a preliminary model of corporate ecological responsiveness as driven by legislation, stakeholder pressures, economic opportunities, and ethical motives. To test this model, data were collected from fifty-three firms in the UK and Japan. Theoretical sampling was used to select the case studies from sectors that faced a wide range of ecological issues. These included:

- food retailers—chosen because they were facing issues relating to the location of sites, the distribution of products, packaging, labelling, and recycling;

- subsidiaries of the British-based multinational P&O—chosen to assess the importance of internal organizational structure and culture in motivating a corporate environmental policy;

- auto manufacturers—a sample of five firms based in the UK;

- oil companies—involved in the extraction or refining of oil in the UK;

- Japan-based companies—a sample of ten companies chosen in order to challenge the emerging theory in a different cultural context.

Data sources included:

- interviews—a selection of key informants within the firms, made based on their knowledge of the ecological initiatives of their firms;

- participant observation—of training seminars where environmental issues were discussed;

- public and private documents—including a newspaper search of the Reuters and Data Star databases, company accounts, annual reports, and corporate environmental reports.

Analysis involved an iterative process of collecting data from these sources, coding, developing, or refining emerging ideas, relating them to existing theory, and selecting further data for the next phase of analysis. Analysis focused on understanding why companies engaged in ecologically responsible initiatives. Three basic motives for ecological responsiveness were found:

1 competitiveness;

2 legitimation;

3 ecological responsibility.

Motives were also affected by three contextual dimensions, which influenced the dominant motivation of a firm. This led to the development of an advanced theoretical model that took the relationship between motives and context into account. By assessing the relationship between motives and context, Bansal and Roth suggest that it is possible to predict the kinds of ecological initiatives that firms will adopt.

The main weakness of the model, however, stems from the fact that Bansal and Roth were attempting to uncover a firm's motivations only after they had made the decision to act. This means that the research is subject to bias associated with retrospective accounts.

Grounded theory

Grounded theory (see Box 19.3) has become by far the most widely used framework for analysing qualitative data. The book that is the chief wellspring of the approach, *The Discovery of Grounded Theory: Strategies for Qualitative Research* by Barney G. Glaser and Anselm L. Strauss (published in 1967), must be one of the most widely cited books in the social sciences. However, providing a definitive account of the approach is by no means a straightforward matter, for the following reasons.

- Glaser and Strauss developed grounded theory along different paths after the publication of the above book. Glaser felt that the approach to

> **Box 19.3** 🔅 *What is grounded theory?*
>
> In its most recent incarnation, grounded theory has been defined as 'theory that was derived from data, systematically gathered and analyzed through the research process. In this method, data collection, analysis, and eventual theory stand in close relationship to one another' (Strauss and Corbin 1998: 12). Thus, two central features of grounded theory are that it is concerned with the development of theory out of data *and* the approach is *iterative*, or *recursive*, as it is sometimes called, meaning that data collection and analysis proceed in tandem, repeatedly referring back to each other.

grounded theory that Strauss was promoting (most notably in Strauss 1987, and Strauss and Corbin 1990) was too prescriptive and emphasized too much the development of concepts rather than of theories (Glaser 1992). However, because of the greater prominence of Strauss's writings, his version is largely the one followed in the exposition below. There is, however, considerable controversy about what grounded theory is and entails (Charmaz 2000).

- Straussian grounded theory has changed a great deal over the years. This is revealed in a constant addition to the tool chest of analytic devices that is revealed in his writings.

- Some writers have suggested that grounded theory is honoured more in the breach than in the observance, implying that claims are often made that grounded theory has been used but that evidence of this being the case is at best uncertain (Bryman 1988*a*: 85, 91; Locke 1996; Charmaz 2000). Sometimes the term is employed simply to imply that the analyst has grounded his or her theory in data. Grounded theory is more than this and refers to a set of procedures that are described below. Referencing academic publications is often part of a tactic of persuading readers of the legitimacy of one's work (Gilbert 1977) and this process can be discerned in the citation of grounded theory.

Alternatively, researchers sometimes appear to have used just one or two features of grounded theory but refer to their having used the approach without qualification (Locke 1996).

Against such a background, writing about the essential ingredients of grounded theory is not an easy matter.

It is not going to be possible to describe here grounded theory in all its facets; instead, its main features will be outlined. In order to organize the exposition, we find it helpful to distinguish between *tools* and *outcomes* in grounded theory.

Tools of grounded theory

Some of the tools of grounded theory have been referred to in previous chapters. Their location is indicated in the list that follows.

- *Theoretical sampling*—see Box 14.9.

- *Coding*—the key process in grounded theory, whereby data are broken down into component parts, which are given names. It begins soon after the collection of initial data. As Charmaz (2000: 515 puts it: 'We grounded theorists code our emerging data as we collect it.... Unlike quantitative research that requires data to fit into *pre-conceived* standardized codes, the researcher's interpretations of data shape his or her emergent codes in grounded theory' (emphasis in original). In grounded theory, different types or levels of coding are recognized (see Box 19.4).

- *Theoretical saturation*—see Box 14.10. Theoretical saturation is a process that relates to two phases in grounded theory: the coding of data (implying that you reach a point where there is no further point in reviewing your data to see how well they fit with your concepts or categories) and the collection of data (implying that, once a concept or category has been developed, you may wish to continue collecting data to determine its nature and operation but then reach a point where new data are no longer illuminating the concept).

- *Constant comparison*—an aspect of grounded theory that was prominent in Glaser and Strauss (1967) and that is often referred to as a significant phase by practitioners, but that seems to be an implicit, rather than an explicit, element in more recent writings. It refers to a process of maintaining a close connection between data and conceptualization, so that the correspondence between concepts and categories with their indicators is not lost. More specifically, attention to the procedure of constant comparison enjoins the researcher constantly to compare phenomena being coded under a certain category so that a theoretical elaboration of that category can begin to emerge. Glaser and Strauss advised writing a *memo* (see below) on the category after a few phenomena had been coded. It also entails being sensitive to contrasts between the categories that are emerging.

Outcomes of grounded theory

The following are the products of different phases of grounded theory.

- *Concept(s)*—refers to labels given to discrete phenomena; concepts are referred to as the 'building blocks of theory' (Strauss and Corbin 1998: 101). The value of concepts is determined by their usefulness or utility. One criterion for deciding if a concept is useful is that it will typically be found frequently and members of the organization under study will be able to recognize it and relate it to their experiences. Concepts are produced through *open coding* (see Box 19.4). Concepts can be recorded using concept cards (see Box 19.5), through which

---

Box 19.4 Coding in grounded theory

Coding is one of the most central processes in grounded theory. It entails reviewing transcripts and/or field notes and giving labels (names) to component parts that seem to be of potential theoretical significance and/or that appear to be particularly salient within the social worlds of those being studied. As Charmaz (1983: 186) puts it: 'Codes . . . serve as shorthand devices to *label, separate, compile,* and *organize* data' (emphases in original). Coding is a somewhat different process from coding in relation to quantitative data, such as survey data. With the latter, coding is more or less solely a way of managing data, whereas in grounded theory, and indeed in approaches to qualitative data analysis that do not subscribe to the approach, it is an important first step in the generation of theory. Coding in grounded theory is also somewhat more tentative than in relation to the generation of quantitative data, where there is a tendency to think in terms of data and codes as very fixed. Coding in qualitative data analysis tends to be in a constant state of potential revision and fluidity. The data are treated as potential indicators of concepts and the indicators are *constantly compared* (see under 'Tools of grounded theory') to see which concepts they best fit with. As Strauss (1987: 25) put it: 'Many indicators (behavioral actions/events) are examined comparatively by the analyst who then "codes" them, naming them as indicators of a class of events/behavioral actions.'

Strauss and Corbin (1990), drawing on their grounded theory approach, distinguish between three types of coding practice:

- *Open coding*—'the process of breaking down, examining, comparing, conceptualizing and categorizing data' (1990: 61); this process of coding yields concepts, which are later to be grouped and turned into categories.

- *Axial coding*—'a set of procedures whereby data are put back together in new ways after open coding, by making connections between categories' (1990: 96). This is done by linking codes to contexts, to consequences, to patterns of interaction, and to causes.

- *Selective coding*—'the procedure of selecting the core category, systematically relating it to other categories, validating those relationships, and filling in categories that need further refinement and development' (1990: 116). A *core category* is the central issue or focus around which all other categories are integrated. It is what Strauss and Corbin call the storyline that frames your account.

The three types of coding are really different levels of coding and each relates to a different point in the elaboration of categories in grounded theory.

incidents in the data can be recorded. An example of a concept card is provided in Figure 19.2.

- *Category, categories*—a concept that has been elaborated so that it is regarded as representing real-world phenomena. As noted in Box 14.10, a category may subsume two or more concepts. As such, categories are at a higher level of abstraction than concepts. A category may become a *core category* around which the other categories pivot (see Box 19.4). The number of core categories may, in fact, be relatively few. For example, Martin and Turner (1986) give an example of one study in which from a large data set and an initial 100 concepts, fewer than forty of these proved to be very useful and only ten provided the basis for the final analysis.

Box 19.5 Developing categories using concept cards

Prasad (1993) used techniques of grounded theory to analyse the vast quantity of field notes and interview transcripts that were generated by her study (see Chapter 13 for a detailed account of this research). Using *concept cards* to identify important *concepts* in the data, she accumulated incidents, events, or pieces of conversation—*elements*—that related to a particular theme and put them together under a meaningful *label* on a concept card, (see Fig. 19.2). The initial aim of labels was to find a level of abstraction that was high enough to avoid creating a separate card for every element observed but low enough to ensure that the concept accurately represented the phenomenon.

Maintaining the concept cards was an iterative process that began early in the research process. New concepts were generated and further elements were added to the cards as more data were collected. Prasad then scanned the concept cards for relationships among elements on the same and different cards. She states that this led to the development of 'a new set of second order cards that helped me make connections between certain symbolic representations of computerization and areas of organizational action' (1993: 1411).

Data source	Organization member	Incident, quotation, opinion, event
Field notes No. 7, p. 3	Project manager	Discussing possible resistance to computers: 'Yes . . . we have got to pull out all our weapons to fight this thing out. But until we win . . . It's going to mean confusion.'
Interview No. 8, p. 23	Receptionist	Describing the first two weeks of computerization: 'What I hated was the anger and well, the confusion. It was almost like my divorce all over again . . . blaming each other and mistakes every minute.'
Field notes No. 33, p. 24	Nurse supervisor	Official memo to trainers: 'We need to be well prepared for the next few weeks of chaos. Even the people you work with will not seem the same any more.'
Interview No. 24, pp. 8–9	Senior manager	'I finally know what army generals feel like . . . that's exactly what it was like. Fighting people all the time . . . the girls, the nurses, Joe, and the big brass at Paragon . . . and not knowing where the next attack would come from.'

Figure 19.2 An example of part of a concept card to show the symbolism of organizational turmoil related to work computerization

Source: adapted from Prasad (1993).

- *Properties*—attributes or aspects of a category.
- *Hypotheses*—initial hunches about relationships between concepts.
- *Theory*—according to Strauss and Corbin (1998: 22), 'a set of well-developed categories . . . that are systematically related through statements of relationship to form a theoretical framework that explains some relevant social . . . or other phenomenon'. Since the inception of grounded theory, writings have pointed to two types or levels of theory: *substantive theory* and *formal theory*. The former relates to theory in a certain empirical instance or substantive area, such as occupational socialization. A formal theory is at a higher level of abstraction and has a wider range of applicability to several substantive areas, such as socialization in a number of spheres, suggesting that higher-level processes are at work. The generation of formal theory requires data collection in contrasting settings.

The different elements are portrayed in Figure 19.3. As with all diagrams, this is a representation, and it is particularly so in the case of grounded theory, because the existence of different versions of the approach does not readily permit a more definitive rendition. Also, it is difficult to get across diagrammatically the iterative nature of grounded theory—in particular its commitment to the idea that data collection and analysis occur in parallel. This is partly achieved in the diagram through the presence of arrows pointing in both directions in relation to certain steps. The figure implies the following.

- The researcher begins with a general research question (step 1).
- Relevant people and/or incidents are theoretically sampled (step 2).
- Relevant data are collected (step 3).
- Data are coded (step 4), which may at the level of open coding generate concepts (step 4a).
- There is a constant movement backwards and forwards between the first four steps, so that early coding suggests the need for new data, which results in the need to sample theoretically, and so on.
- Through a constant comparison of indicators and concepts (step 5) categories are generated (step 5a).

The crucial issue is to ensure that there is a fit between indicators and concepts.

- Categories are saturated during the coding process (step 6).
- Relationships between categories are explored (step 7) in such a way that hypotheses about connections between categories emerge (step 7a).
- Further data are collected via theoretical sampling (steps 8 and 9).
- The collection of data is likely to be governed by the theoretical saturation principle (step 10) and by the testing of the emerging hypotheses (step 11),

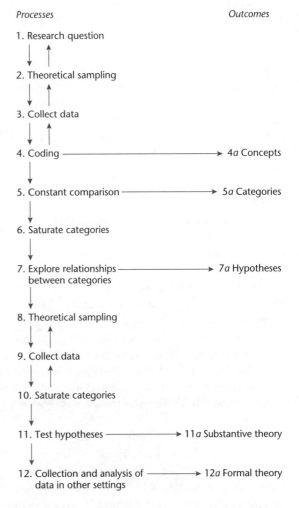

Processes   *Outcomes*

1. Research question

2. Theoretical sampling

3. Collect data

4. Coding   ⟶ 4a Concepts

5. Constant comparison   ⟶ 5a Categories

6. Saturate categories

7. Explore relationships   ⟶ 7a Hypotheses
   between categories

8. Theoretical sampling

9. Collect data

10. Saturate categories

11. Test hypotheses   ⟶ 11a Substantive theory

12. Collection and analysis of ⟶ 12a Formal theory
    data in other settings

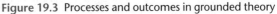

Figure 19.3 Processes and outcomes in grounded theory

which leads to the specification of substantive theory (step 11*a*).

• The substantive theory is explored using grounded theory processes in relation to different settings from that in which it was generated (step 12), so that formal theory may be generated (step 12*a*). A formal theory will relate to more abstract categories, which are not specifically related to the research area in question.

Step 12 is relatively unusual in grounded theory, because researchers typically concentrate on a certain setting. One way in which formal theory can be generated is through the use of existing theory and research in comparable settings.

Concepts and categories are perhaps the key elements in grounded theory. Indeed, it is sometimes suggested that, as a qualitative data analysis strategy, it works better for generating categories than theory. In part, this may be because studies purporting to use the approach often generate grounded *concepts* rather than grounded theory as such. Concepts and categories are nonetheless at the heart of the approach, and key processes such as coding, theoretical sampling, and theoretical saturation are designed to guide their generation.

Memos

One aid to the generation of concepts and categories is the *memo*. Memos in grounded theory are notes that researchers might write for themselves and for those with whom they work concerning such elements of grounded theory as coding or concepts. They serve as reminders about what is meant by the terms being used and provide the building blocks for a certain amount of reflection. Memos are potentially very helpful to researchers in helping them to crystallize ideas and not to lose track of their thinking on various topics. An illustration of a memo from research in which Bryman was involved is provided in Box 19.6.

Finding examples of grounded theory that reveal all its facets and stages is very difficult, and it is unsurprising that many expositions of grounded theory fall back on the original illustrations provided in Glaser and Strauss (1967). Many studies show some

of its ingredients but not others. For example, Prasad's (1994) study of technological change (see Chapter 13; Box 19.5 and Figure 19.2) certainly incorporates some of the features of a grounded theory approach, such as the use of concept cards to keep a record of coding, enabling a series of 'second-order' or core categories to be generated. However, other tools of grounded theory, such as memos, were not used as part of this study. Similarly, although Gersick (1994) claims to have used a grounded theory approach in her study of the effects of time on organizational adaptation, her coding was based partly on themes that she was interested in prior to data collection, in addition to those that emerged during the interviews. Gersick's approach thus relied on isolating and coding statements from the interview transcripts that related to time and identifying themes amongst them.

Criticisms of grounded theory

In spite of the frequency with which it is cited and the frequent lip-service paid to it, grounded theory is not without its limitations, of which the following can be briefly registered.

• Bulmer (1979) has questioned whether, as prescribed by the advocates of grounded theory, researchers can suspend their awareness of relevant theories or concepts until a quite late stage in the process of analysis. Business researchers are typically sensitive to the conceptual armoury of their disciplines and it seems unlikely that this awareness can be put aside. Indeed, nowadays it is rarely accepted that theory-neutral observation is feasible. In other words, it is generally agreed that what we 'see' when we conduct research is conditioned by many factors, one of which is what we already know about the social world being studied (in terms both of social scientific conceptualizations and as members of society). Also, many writers might take the view that it is desirable that researchers are sensitive to existing conceptualizations, so that their investigations are focused and can build upon the work of others.

• Related to this first point is that, in many circumstances, researchers are required to spell out the possible implications of their planned investigation. For example, a lecturer making a bid for

Box 19.6 A memo

In the course of research into the bus industry that Bryman carried out with colleagues in the early 1990s (Bryman, Gillingwater, and McGuinness 1996), the researchers noticed that the managers they interviewed frequently referred to the notion that their companies had inherited features that derived from the running of those companies before deregulation. They often referred to the idea of inheriting characteristics that held them back in trying to meet the competitive environment they faced in the 1990s. As such, inheritance is what Strauss (1987) calls an *in vivo code* (one that derives from the language of people in the social context being studied), rather than what he calls *sociologically constructed codes*, which are labels employing the analyst's own terminology. The following memo outlines the concept of inheritance, provides some illustrative quotations, and suggests some properties of the concept.

Memo for Inheritance

Inheritance: many of our interviewees suggest that they have inherited certain company traits and traditions from the period prior to deregulation (i.e. pre-1985). It is a term that many of them themselves employed to denote company attributes that are not of their choosing but have survived from the pre-deregulation period. The key point about inheritance is that the inherited elements are seen by our interviewees as hindering their ability to respond to the changing environment of the post-deregulation era. Inherited features include:

- expensive and often inappropriate fleets of vehicles and depots;
- the survival of attitudes and behaviour patterns, particularly among bus drivers, which are seen as inappropriate to the new environment (for example, lack of concern for customer service) and which hinder service innovation;
- high wage rates associated with the pre-deregulation era; means that new competitors can enter the market while paying drivers lower wages.

Sample comments:

We *inherited* a very high cost structure because of deregulation. 75% of our staff were paid in terms of conditions affected by [rates prior to deregulation]. (Commercial Director, Company B).

I suppose another major weakness is that we are very tied by conditions and practices we've *inherited*. (Commercial Director, Company G).

We have what we've *inherited* and we now have a massive surplus of double decks . . . We have to go on operating those. (Managing Director, Company B).

Managing Director of Company E said the company had inherited staff who were steeped in pre-deregulation attitudes, which meant that 'we don't have a staff where the message is "the customer is number one". We don't have a staff where that is emblazoned on the hearts and minds of everyone, far from it.'

Prepost-deregulation: interviewee makes a contrast between the periods before and after deregulation to show how they've changed. This shows in a sense the *absence* of inherited features and their possible impact; can refer to how the impact of possibly inherited features was negated or offset. For example, *X* referring to the recent end of the three-week strike: 'there was no way we were going to give in to this sort of thing, this sort of blackmail. We just refused to move and the trade unions had never experienced that. It was all part of the change in culture following deregulation . . .'.

Inheriting constraints: such as staff on high wage rates and with inappropriate attitudes.

Inheriting surplus capacity: such as too many buses or wrong size.

---

research funding or a student applying for funding for postgraduate research is usually required to demonstrate how his or her research will build upon what is already known or to demonstrate that he or she has a reasonably tightly defined research question, something which is also frequently disdained in grounded theory.

- There are practical difficulties with grounded theory. The time taken to transcribe tape recordings of interviews, for example, can make it difficult for researchers, especially when they have tight deadlines, to carry out a genuine grounded theory analysis with its constant interplay of data collection and conceptualization.

- It is somewhat doubtful whether grounded theory in many instances really results in *theory*. As previously suggested, it provides a rigorous approach to the generation of concepts, but it is often difficult to see what theory, in the sense of an explanation of something, is being put forward. Moreover, in spite of the frequent lip-service paid to the generation of formal theory, most grounded theories are substantive in character; in other words, they pertain to the specific social phenomenon being researched and not to a broader range of phenomena (though, of course, they *may* have such broader applicability).

- In spite of the large amount written on grounded theory, but perhaps because of the many subtle changes in its presentation, it is still vague on certain points, such as the difference between concepts and categories. For example, while Strauss and Corbin (1998: 73) refer to theoretical sampling as 'sampling on the basis of emerging *concepts*' (emphasis added), Charmaz (2000: 519) writes that it is used to 'develop our emerging *categories*' (emphasis added). The term 'categories' is increasingly being employed rather than concepts, but such inconsistent use of key terms is not helpful to people trying to understand the overall process.

- Grounded theory is very much associated with an approach to data analysis that invites researchers to fragment their data by coding the data into discrete chunks. However, in the eyes of some writers, this kind of activity results in a loss of a sense of context and of narrative flow (Coffey and Atkinson 1996), a point to which we will return below.

- The presence of competing accounts of the ingredients of grounded theory does not make it easy to characterize it or to establish how to use it. This situation has been made even more problematic by Charmaz's (2000) suggestion that most grounded theory is objectivist and that an alternative, constructionist (she calls it *constructivist*) approach is preferable. She argues that the grounded theory associated with Glaser, Strauss, and Corbin is objectivist in that it aims to uncover a reality that is external to social actors. She offers an alternative, constructionist version that 'assumes that people create and maintain meaningful worlds through dialectical processes of conferring meaning on their realities and acting within them... Thus, social reality does not exist independent of human action' (Charmaz 2000: 521). Such a position stands in contrast to earlier grounded theory texts that 'imply that categories and concepts inhere within the data, awaiting the researcher's discovery.... Instead, a constructivist approach recognizes that the categories, concepts, and theoretical level of an analysis emerge from the researcher's interaction within the field and questions about the data' (Charmaz 2000: 522). One difficulty here is that the two meanings of constructionism referred to in Box 1.14 seem to be conflated. The first quotation refers to constructionism as an ontological position in relating to social objects and categories; the second is a reference to constructionism in relation to the nature of knowledge of the social world. It is certainly fair to suggest that Glaser, Strauss, and Corbin in their various writings neglect the role of the researcher in the generation of knowledge, but it is not clear that they are indifferent to the notion that social reality exists independently of social actors. Strauss was, after all, the lead of the study referred to on page 20 concerning the hospital as a negotiated order, which was used as an illustration of constructionism (Strauss et al. 1973). However, there is little doubt that there is considerable confusion currently about the nature of grounded theory. According to Partington (2000), there is little evidence of the successful application of Strauss and Corbin's (1990) grounded theory within management and business research. This is partly because of the greater difficulty in following this more prescriptive, proceduralized approach, which contrasts sharply with Glaser and Strauss's (1967) earlier emphasis on the development of insight based on open-minded sensitivity.

Nonetheless, grounded theory probably represents the most influential general strategy for conducting qualitative data analysis, though how far the approach is followed varies from study to study. Locke (2001) argues that grounded theory is particularly well suited to organizational research. She suggests that it is particularly good at the following.

- *Capturing complexity*. Grounded theory is good at capturing the complexity of contexts as action unfolds.

- *Linking with practice*. It frequently facilitates an appreciation among organizational members of their situations. Such understanding can provide a helpful springboard for organizational action.

- *Facilitating theoretical work in substantive areas that have not been well researched by others*. As new forms of organizational or technological change emerge and become prominent in the business world, grounded theory is ideal for an open-ended research strategy that can then be employed for the generation of theory out of the resulting data.

- *Putting life into well-established fields*. Grounded theory can provide the basis for an alternative view of well-established fields, like group effectiveness and leadership, through its open-ended approach to data collection followed by a rigorous approach to theoretical work.

In addition, many of grounded theory's core processes, such as coding, memos, and the very idea of allowing theoretical ideas to emerge out of one's data, have been hugely influential. Indeed, it is striking that one of the main developments in qualitative data analysis in recent years—computer-assisted qualitative data analysis—has implicitly promoted many of these processes, because the software programs have often been written with grounded theory in mind (Richards and Richards 1994; Lonkila 1995).

More on coding

Coding is the starting point for most forms of qualitative data analysis, including ethnography (see Box 19.7 for an example). The principles involved have been well developed by writers on grounded theory and others. Some of the considerations in developing codes, some of which are derived from Lofland and Lofland (1995), are as follows.

- Of what general category is this item of data an instance?

- What does this item of data represent?

- What is this item of data about?

- Of what topic is this item of data an instance?

- What question about a topic does this item of data suggest?

- What sort of answer to a question about a topic does this item of data imply?

- What is happening here?

- What are people doing?

- What do people say they are doing?

- What kind of event is going on?

Steps and considerations in coding

The following steps and considerations need to be borne in mind in preparation for and during coding.

- *Code as soon as possible*. It is well worth coding as you go along, as grounded theory suggests. This may sharpen your understanding of your data and help with theoretical sampling. Also, it may help to alleviate the feeling of being swamped by your data, which may happen if you defer analysis entirely until the end of the data collection period. At the very least, you should ensure that, if your data collection involves recording interviews, you begin transcription at a relatively early stage.

- *Read through your initial set of transcripts, field notes, documents, etc.* without taking any notes or considering an interpretation; perhaps at the end jot down a few general notes about what struck you as especially interesting, important, or significant.

- *Do it again*. Read through your data again, but this time begin to make marginal notes about significant remarks or observations. Make as many as

Box 19.7 An example of ethnographic coding

Delbridge (1998) describes the process of analysing the hundreds of pages of handwritten field notes that described day-to-day events on the shopfloor of Valleyco and Nippon CTV as extremely challenging:

> Once the fieldnotes were completed, I read through the first set from Valleyco and began to pick out themes which emerged from these notes. At first this consisted of noting any type of event, interaction or comment which occurred more than once. After generating a very long list of such instances, I then grouped these around a set of tentative themes which had begun to emerge. In the first round of reviewing the data, I identified about 150 key events or notes from my first month at Valleyco and labelled these under one or more of the nine themes. I then grouped the second month's notes from Valleyco within these themes and added to or amended the themes to cope with additional instances. I repeated these iterative loops on a weekly basis for the Nippon CTV notes until I have centred on thirteen issues which came from the data.   (1998: 22).

The thirteen labels were:

QLTY   denoting systems of quality management;
SYS   the manufacturing system at the plants;
RELS   data regarding formal and informal relationships between actors;
UNTY   denoting issues of uncertainty and informality in the workplace;
CONT   issues of control and surveillance;
WORK   workers, their roles, and experiences;
COMM   communication issues and practices;
MGT   managers, their roles and perspectives;
ACCOMM issues of accommodation, indulgence, and resistance;
UNION   the role of unions in the workplace;
RES   issues pertaining to the research process;
COFACT factual data on the companies involved;
JAP   data relating specifically to Japan and the Japanese.

It is interesting to note that, in starting to identify themes based on events, interactions, or comments that occurred 'more than once', Delbridge was attempting to make an initial judgement about the significance of the data based on frequency. However, it is not that unusual for qualitative researchers to engage in some kind of quantitative assessment of qualitative data, as Chapter 22 illustrates.

possible. Initially, they will be very basic—perhaps key words used by your respondents, names that you give to themes in the data. When you do this you are *coding*—generating an index of terms that will help you to interpret and theorize in relation to your data.

- *Review your codes*. Begin to review your codes, possibly in relation to your transcripts. Are you using two or more words or phrases to describe the same phenomenon? If so, remove one of them. Do some of your codes relate to concepts and categories in the existing literature? If so, might it be sensible to use these instead? Can you see any connections between the codes? Is there some evidence that respondents believe that one thing tends to be associated with or caused by something else? If so, how do you characterize and therefore code these connections?

- *Consider more general theoretical ideas in relation to codes and data*. At this point, you should be beginning to generate some general theoretical ideas about your data. Try to outline connections between concepts and categories you are developing. Consider in more detail how they relate to the existing literature. Develop hypotheses about the linkages you are making and go back to your data to see if they can be confirmed.

- Remember that *any one item or slice of data can and often should be coded in more than one way*.

- *Do not worry about generating what seem to be too many codes*—at least in the early stages of your analysis; some will be fruitful and others will not—the important thing is to be as inventive and imaginative as possible; you can worry about tidying things up later.

- *Keep coding in perspective*. Do not equate coding with analysis. It is part of your analysis, albeit an important one. It is a mechanism for thinking about the meaning of your data *and* for reducing the vast amount of data that you are facing (Huberman and Miles 1994). Miles and Huberman (1984) have developed several techniques for the display of data that have been coded through content analysis as a way of overcoming the difficulty of representing the complexity of qualitative analysis. One of the most important of these is the matrix format, which identifies constructs along one axis and occurrences along the other. This technique introduces an element of quantification into the qualitative analysis by drawing attention to the frequency of occurrences in the data. Another data display mechanism described by Gersick (1994) in her study of a new business venture is the timeline; this is used to represent the company's history, including major events and decisions, the time period over which they were implemented, and the eventual outcome of the actions. Whatever data display techniques you use, you must still interpret your findings. This means attending to issues like the significance of your coded material for the lives of the people you are studying, forging interconnections between codes, and reflecting on the overall importance of your findings for the research questions and the research literature that have driven your data collection.

Turning data into fragments

The coding of such materials as interview transcripts has typically entailed writing marginal notes on them and gradually refining those notes into codes. In this way, portions of transcripts become seen as belonging to certain names or labels. In the past, this process was accompanied by cutting and pasting in the literal sense of using scissors and paste. It entailed cutting up one's transcripts into files of chunks of data, with each file representing a code. The process of cutting and pasting is useful for data retrieval, though it is always important to make sure that you have ways of identifying the origins of the chunk of text (for example, name, position, date). Word

processing programs allow this to be done in a way that does not rely on your DIY skills so much through the use of the 'find' function. Nowadays CAQDAS software is increasingly being used to perform these tasks (see Chapter 20).

There is no one correct approach to coding your data. As Box 19.4 suggests, grounded theory conceives of different types of code. Coffey and Atkinson (1996) point to different levels of coding. These levels can be related to the passage from an interview that was previously encountered in Chapter 15 about the study of visitors to Disney theme parks. Box 19.8 shows some coded text from the Disney project, illustrating three coding levels.

- First there is a very basic coding, which, in the passage in Box 19.8, could be in terms of liking or disliking the Disney theme parks. However, such a coding scheme is unlikely to get us very far from an analytical vantage point.

- A second level comprises much more awareness of the content of what is said. Themes reflect much more the language the interviewee uses. We see much more the kinds of issues with which the interviewee is concerned. Examples might be 'developed world', 'black people', and 'black history'.

- A third level moves slightly away from a close association with what the respondent says and towards a concern with broad analytic themes. This is the way that the passage in Box 19.8 has been coded. Here the passage has been coded in terms of such features as whether a response is uncritically enthusiastic ('uncritical enthusiasm') or is not critical of the Disney Corporation ('not critical of Disney'); reveals comments made about typical visitors ('visitors' ethnicity'); and makes critical comments ('aesthetic critique'; 'ethnicity critique'; 'nationality critique'). Interestingly, the passage also reveals the potential for a code employed by Coffey and Atkinson (1996: 43–5) in relation to one of their examples—namely, the use of a 'contrastive rhetoric'. This occurs when a person makes a point about something by comparing it to something else. This feature occurs when the husband makes a point about the representation of British culture, which in fact he regards as poor, by comparing it to that of

---

Box 19.8 Coded text from the Disney project

Interviewer	OK. What were your views or feelings about the presentation of different cultures, as shown in, for example, Jungle Cruise or It's a Small World at the Magic Kingdom or in World Showcase at Epcot?	
Wife	Well, I thought the different countries at Epcot were wonderful, but I need to say more than that, don't I?	uncritical enthusiasm
Husband	They were very good and some were better than others, but that was down to the host countries themselves really, as I suppose each of the countries represented would have been responsible for their own part, so that's nothing to do with Disney, I wouldn't have thought.	not critical of Disney — aesthetic critique
	I mean some of the landmarks were hard to recognise for what they were supposed to be, but some were very well done. Britain was OK, but there was only a pub and a Welsh shop there really, whereas some of the other pavilions, as I think they were called, were good ambassadors for the countries they represented. China, for example, had an excellent 360 degree film showing parts of China and I found that very interesting.	content critique
Interviewer	Did you think there was anything lacking about the content?	
Husband	Well I did notice that there weren't many black people at World Showcase, particularly the American Adventure. Now whether we were there on an unusual day in that respect I don't know, but we saw plenty of black Americans in the Magic Kingdom and other places, but very few if any in that World Showcase. And there was certainly little mention of black history in the American Adventure presentation, so maybe they felt alienated by that, I don't know, but	visitors' ethnicity — ethnicity critique
	they were noticeable by their absence.	visitors' ethnicity
Interviewer	So did you think there were any special emphases?	
Husband	Well thinking about it now, because I hadn't really given this any consideration before you started asking about it, but thinking about it now, it was only really representative of the developed world, you know, Britain, America, Japan, world leaders many of them in technology, and there was nothing of the Third World there. Maybe that's their own fault, maybe they were asked to participate and didn't, but now that I think about it, that does come to me. What do you think, love?	nationality critique
Wife	Well, like you, I hadn't thought of it like that before, but I agree with you.	

China, which he regards as good. The poor showing of Britain is brought out by comparing it in a negative light to China. However, this coding category was not employed in relation to this research.

As Coffey and Atkinson (1996) observe, following Strauss and Corbin's account (1990) of grounded theory, codes should not be thought of purely as mechanisms for the fragmentation and retrieval of text. In other words, they can do more than simply manage the data you have gathered. For example, if we ask about the properties and interconnections between codes, we may begin to see that some of them may be dimensions of a broader phenomenon. For example, as shown in the next chapter (see especially Figure 20.1), 'ethnicity critique' came to be seen as a dimension of 'ideology critique', along with 'class critique' and 'gender critique'. In this way, we can begin to map the more general or formal properties of concepts that are being developed.

Problems with coding

One of the most commonly mentioned criticisms of the coding approach to qualitative data analysis is the possible problem of losing the context of what is said. By plucking chunks of text out of the context within which they appeared, such as a particular interview transcript, the social setting can be lost.

A second criticism of coding is that it results in a fragmentation of data, so that the narrative flow of what people say is lost (Coffey and Atkinson 1996). Sensitivity to this issue has been heightened by a growing interest in narrative analysis since the late 1980s (see below). Riessman became concerned about the fragmentation of data that occurs when coding themes when she came to analyse data she had collected through structured interviews on divorce and gender. She writes:

Some [interviewees] developed long accounts of what had happened in their marriages to justify their divorces. I did not realize these were narratives until I struggled to code them. Applying traditional qualitative methods, I searched the texts for common thematic elements. But some individuals knotted together several themes into long accounts that had coherence and sequence, defying easy categorization. I found myself not wanting to fragment the long accounts into distinct thematic categories. There seemed to be a common structure beneath talk about a variety of topics. While I coded one interview, a respondent provided language for my trouble. As I have thought about it since, it was a 'click moment' in my biography as a narrative researcher... (Riessman 1993: p. vi).

Riessman's account is interesting because it suggests several possibilities: that the coding method of qualitative data analysis fragments data; that some forms of data may be unsuitable for the coding method; and that researchers can turn narrative analysis on themselves, since what she provides in this passage is precisely a narrative. Interest in narrative analysis certainly shows signs of growing and in large part this trend parallels the revival of interest in the life history approach (see Box 15.4). Nonetheless, the coding method is unlikely to become less prominent, because of several factors: its widespread acceptance in the research community; not all analysts are interested in research questions that lend themselves to the elicitation of narratives; the influence of grounded theory and its associated techniques; and the growing use and acceptance of computer software for qualitative data analysis, which frequently invites a coding approach.

Regardless of which analytical strategy you employ, what you must not do is simply say—'this is what my subjects said and did—isn't that incredibly interesting'. It may be reasonably interesting, but your work can acquire significance only when you theorize in relation to it. Many researchers are wary of this—they worry that, in the process of interpretation and theorizing, they may fail to do justice to what they have seen and heard; that they may contaminate their subjects' words and behaviour. This is a risk, but it has to be balanced against the fact that your findings acquire significance in our intellectual community only when you have reflected on, interpreted, and theorized your data. You are not there as a mere mouthpiece.

Secondary analysis of qualitative data

One final point to bear in mind is that this discussion of qualitative data analysis may have been presumed to be solely concerned with the analysis of data in which the analyst has played a part in collecting. However, in recent years, secondary analysis of qualitative data has become a growing focus of discussion and interest. While the secondary analysis of quantitative data has been on the research agenda for many years (see Chapter 10), similar use of qualitative data has only recently come to the fore. The general idea of secondary analysis was addressed in Box 10.1.

There is no obvious reason why qualitative data cannot be the focus of secondary analysis, though it is undoubtedly the case that such data do present certain problems that are not fully shared by quantitative data. The possible grounds for conducting a secondary analysis are more or less the same as those associated with quantitative data (see Chapter 10). With such considerations in mind, Qualidata, an archival resource centre, was created in the UK in 1994. The centre is not a repository for qualitative data (unlike the Data Archive, which does house quantitative data); instead, it is concerned with 'locating, assessing and documenting qualitative data and arranging their deposit in suitable public archive repositories' (Corti et al. 1995). It has a very useful web site:

www.qualidata.essex.ac.uk

and its online catalogue—Qualicat—can be searched at the following address:

www.qualidata.essex.ac.uk/search/qualicat.asp

Qualidata acknowledges certain difficulties with the reuse of qualitative data, such as the difficulty of making settings and people anonymous and the ethical problems involved in such reuse associated with promises of confidentiality. Also, Hammersley (1997)

has suggested that reuse of qualitative data may be hindered by the secondary analyst's lack of an insider's understanding of the social context within which the data were produced. This possible difficulty may hinder the interpretation of data but would seem to be more of a problem with ethnographic field notes than with interview transcripts. Such problems even seem to afflict researchers revisiting their own data many years after the original research had been carried out (Mauthner, Parry, and Backett-Milburn 1998: 742). There are also distinctive ethical issues deriving from the fact that the original researcher(s) may not have obtained the consent of research participants for the analysis of data by others. This is a particular problem with qualitative data in view of the fact that it invariably contains detailed accounts of contexts and people that can make it difficult to conceal the identities of institutions and individuals in the presentation of raw data (as opposed to publications in which such concealment is usually feasible). Nonetheless, in spite of certain practical difficulties, secondary analysis offers rich opportunities not least because the tendency for qualitative researchers to generate large and unwieldy sets of data means that much of the material remains under-explored.

Narrative analysis

Narrative analysis is an approach to the elicitation and analysis of data that is sensitive to the sense of temporal sequence that people, as tellers of stories about their lives or events around them, detect in their lives and surrounding episodes and inject into their accounts. Proponents of narrative analysis argue that most approaches to the collection and analysis of data neglect the fact that people perceive their lives in terms of continuity and process and that attempts to understand social life that are not attuned to this feature neglect the perspective of those being studied. Life history research (Box 15.4) is an obvious location for the application of a narrative analysis, but its use can be much broader than this. Mishler (1986: 77), for example, has argued for

greater interest in 'elicited personal narratives'. In his view, and that of many others, the answers that people provide, in particular in qualitative interviews, can be viewed as stories that are potential fodder for a narrative analysis. In other words, narrative analysis relates not just to the life span but also to accounts relating to episodes and to the interconnections between them. Some researchers apply narrative analysis to interview accounts (e.g. Riessman 1993), while others deliberately ask people to recount stories (e.g. Miller 2000). A further type of qualitative analysis that is related to narrative analysis involves dramatism (see Box 19.9).

Coffey and Atkinson (1996) argue that a narrative should be viewed in terms of the functions that the

Box 19.9 Drama and executive action

Dramaturgy is a method for analysing social action and people's explanations of social action. It builds on Goffman's (1969) work and in particular on the notion of impression management. Analysis focuses on understanding the roles, scenes, scripts, and performances that people engage in as they interact with each other in a given setting.

Mangham's (1986) study of the executive function is based on the activities of a small group of managers as they think, talk, feel, and act on one afternoon during a boardroom discussion. Using a dramaturgical perspective, Mangham treats the processes whereby the executives interact with each other as 'performances', through which each member of the group asserts his power or status.

The study is interesting from a methodological point of view, partly because it focuses on just one short sequence of social activity, from which Mangham generates a series of 'readings' or interpretations of events. He states:

I have spent more hours of my life with these executives than I care to remember and recorded in one form or another thousands of lines of text. Out of this mass of material I have selected less than fifteen minutes and from these confused and confusing minutes I have shaped my presentation. A verbatim transcript of what was actually said—the entire repertoire of false starts, incomplete sentences, talkings over and the like—together with a detailed description of their non-verbal behaviour—the scratching, the fidgeting, the movement of feet, the twitching of brows, the coughs, stomach rumbles and so on—would fill several volumes and still be but a poor record of the actual scenes and exchanges. (1986: 153).

Mangham's analysis draws attention to the way that social actors construct their own power and status. This involves great skill in working with scripted roles such as 'the boss' combined with appropriate displays of emotion.

---

narrative serves for the teller. The aim of narrative interviews is to elicit interviewees' reconstructed accounts of connections between events and between events and contexts. A narrative analysis will then entail a seeking-out of the forms and functions of narrative. Miller (2000) proposes that narrative interviews in life story or biographical research are far more concerned with eliciting the interviewee's perspective as revealed in the telling of the story of his or her life or family than with the facts of that life. There is a concern with how that perspective changes in relation to different contexts. The interviewer is very much a part of the process in that he or she is fully implicated in the construction of the story for the interviewee.

Narrative analysis has made inroads into management research in recent years (Czarniawska 1998; Boje 2001). For the management researcher, narrative analysis can prove extremely helpful in providing a springboard for understanding what Weick (1995) has termed 'organizational sensemaking'. In one of the best-known studies using a narrative approach, Boje (1991) analyses the types and uses of stories in an office supply firm based upon his participant observation in the organization and interviews with key actors. Stories became a common focus of attention when researchers became interested in organizational culture in the 1980s and this interest in organizational stories has continued, but they have tended to form just one of a number of aspects of culture in which researchers have been interested (for example, rituals and mission statements). Thus, Boje (1991) provides an example of a strategic planning session in which during a fairly brief interlude a number of stories are recounted that serve the function of conveying to participants that printing was a different enterprise at the time of the stories in question from the current situation (see also Boje 2001: 118–21). For the CEO, the story helps participants to make sense of their current situation and conveys a sense of things being better now than they were in the past at the time that the less than desirable features relating to printing orders pertained. In the process, the CEO is able to gain a certain amount of political advantage by portraying the current context in a more favourable light.

The significance of narrative for understanding the internal politics of organizations is further indicated by the study referred to in Box 19.10. As Brown notes in relation to this study, one of the advantages of narrative analysis in a context such as this is that it conveys a clear sense of an organization as an arena in which a variety of perspectives and viewpoints coexist, rather than a monolithic entity with a single voice.

However, as Brown notes, his rendition of the three narratives of the implementation is itself a narrative. As such, it is either a compelling one or one that fails to convince us. This point presages the kind of issue that will receive more treatment in Chapter 24. In this sense, all research when it is written up entails a narrative analysis because the researcher/author always has a story to tell about his or her data.

Box 19.10 An example of storytelling in a hospital

Brown (1998) has examined the competing narratives involved in the aftermath of the introduction of a hospital information support system (HISS) at a British hospital trust referred to as 'The City'. The IT implementation was largely seen as unsuccessful because of the absence of clear clinical benefits and cost over-runs. Drawing on his interviews with key actors regarding the IT implementation and its aftermath, Brown presents three contrasting narratives: the ward narrative; the laboratory narrative; and the implementation team's narrative, thereby presenting the perspectives of the main groups of participants in the implementation.

The three contrasting narratives provide a very clear sense of the organization as a political arena in which groups and individuals contest the legitimacy of others' interpretations of events. Thus, 'the representations of each group's narrative are described as vehicles for establishing its altruistic motives for embarking on the project, and for attributing responsibility for what had come to be defined as a failing project to others' (Brown 1998: 49).

Thus, while the three groups had similar motivations for participating in the initiative, largely in terms of the espousal of an ethic of patient care, they had rather different latent motivations and interpretations of what went wrong. In terms of the former, whereas the ward narrative implied a latent motivation to save doctors' and nurses' time, the laboratory team emphasized the importance of retaining the existing IT systems, and the implementation team placed the accent on the possible advantages for their own careers, in large part by the increased level of dependence on their skills. In terms of the contrasting narratives of what went wrong, the ward narrative was to do with the failure of the implementation team to coordinate the initiative and meet deadlines, and the laboratory team emphasized the tendency for the implementation team not to listen or communicate. As for the implementation team, their diagnosis was to do with the ward staff failing to communicate their needs, lack of cooperation from the laboratory staff, and poorly written software.

K **KEY POINTS**

- The collection of qualitative data frequently results in the accumulation of a large volume of information.

- Qualitative data analysis is not governed by codified rules in the same way as quantitative data analysis.

- There are different approaches to qualitative data analysis, of which grounded theory is probably the most prominent.

- Coding is a key process in most qualitative data analysis strategies, but it is sometimes accused of fragmenting and decontextualizing text.

- Secondary analysis of qualitative data is becoming a more prominent activity than in the past.

Q QUESTIONS FOR REVIEW

- What is meant by suggesting that qualitative data are an 'attractive nuisance'?

General strategies of qualitative data analysis

- What are the main ingredients of analytic induction?

- What makes it a rigorous method?

- What are the main ingredients of grounded theory?

- What is the role of coding in grounded theory and what are the different types of coding?

- What is the role of memos in grounded theory?

- Charmaz has written that theoretical sampling 'represents a defining property of grounded theory' (2000: 519). Why do you think she feels this to be the case?

- What are some of the main criticisms of grounded theory?

More on coding

- Is coding associated solely with grounded theory?

- What are the main steps in coding?

- To what extent does coding result in excessive fragmentation of data?

- To what extent does narrative analysis provide an alternative to data fragmentation?

Secondary analysis of qualitative data

- How feasible is it for researchers to analyse qualitative data collected by another researcher?

Narrative analysis

- What might be the main purpose in seeking to uncover organizational stories?

20

Computer-assisted qualitative data analysis: using NVivo

CHAPTER GUIDE

One of the most significant developments in qualitative research in the last twenty years is the emergence of computer software that can assist in the use of qualitative data analysis. This software is often referred to as computer-assisted (or computer-aided) qualitative data analysis software (CAQDAS). CAQDAS removes many if not most of the clerical tasks associated with the manual coding and retrieving of data. There is no industry leader among the different programs (in the sense that SPSS holds this position among quantitative data analysis software). This chapter introduces a relatively new entrant that is having a big impact—NVivo. It was developed out of an earlier program—NUD*IST—which is still available. This chapter explores:

- some of the debates about the desirability of CAQDAS;
- how to set up your research materials for analysis with NVivo;
- how to code using NVivo;
- how to retrieve coded text;
- how to create memos;
- basic computer operations in NVivo.

Introduction

One of the most notable developments in qualitative research in recent years has been the arrival of computer software that facilitates the analysis of qualitative data. Computer-assisted qualitative data analysis software, or CAQDAS as it is conventionally abbreviated, has been a growth area in terms of both the proliferation of programs that perform such analysis and the numbers of people using them. The term and its abbreviation were coined by Lee and Fielding (1991).

Most of the best-known programs are variations on the code-and-retrieve theme. This means that they allow the analyst to code text while working at the computer and to retrieve the coded text. Thus, if we code a large number of interviews, we can retrieve all those sequences of text to which a code (or combination of codes) was attached. This means that the computer takes over manual tasks associated with the coding process referred to in the previous chapter. Typically, the analyst would:

- go through a set of data marking sequences of text in terms of codes (coding); and

- for each code, collect together all sequences of text coded in a particular way (retrieving).

The computer takes over the physical task of writing marginal codes, making photocopies of transcripts or field notes, cutting out all chunks of text relating to a code, and pasting them together. CAQDAS does not automatically do these things: the analyst must still interpret his or her data, code, and then retrieve the data, but the computer takes over the manual labour involved (wielding scissors and pasting small pieces of paper together, for example).

Is CAQDAS like quantitative data analysis software?

One of the comments often made about CAQDAS is that it does not and cannot help with decisions about the coding of textual materials or about the interpretation of findings (Sprokkereef et al. 1995; Weitzman and Miles 1995). However, this situation is little different (if at all) from quantitative data analysis software. In quantitative research, the investigator sets out the crucial concepts and ideas in advance rather than generating them out of his or her data. Also, it would be wrong to represent the use of quantitative data analysis software like SPSS as purely mechanical: once the analyses have been performed, it is still necessary to interpret them. Indeed, the choice of variables to be analysed and the techniques of analysis to be employed are themselves areas in which a considerable amount of interpretive expertise is required. Creativity is required by both forms of software.

CAQDAS differs from the use of quantitative data analysis software largely in terms of the environment within which it operates.

No industry leader

With quantitative data analysis, SPSS is both widely known and used. It is not the only statistical software used by social researchers, but it is certainly dominant. It has competitors, such as Minitab, but SPSS is close to being the industry leader. No parallel situation exists with regard to CAQDAS. Up until the early 1990s, The Ethnograph was probably the best known and most widely used CAQDAS. Lee and Fielding (1991: 11) report that, between March 1988 and January 1990, 1,600 copies of the software were sold. However, at that time more and more programs were coming onto the market: ten other programs were referred to in an appendix to the book in which Lee and Fielding's (1991) article appeared, and since then further programs have appeared. Seven years later, the situation had changed. The same authors observed that, in the UK, The Ethnograph 'seems . . . to have lost ground to both NUD*IST and Atlas/ti over the last few years. NUD*IST is now probably the package that most people at least know by name' (Fielding and Lee 1998: 15).

NUD*IST (Non-numerical Unstructured Data Indexing Searching and Theorizing) became very popular in the 1990s and has been built upon more recently with the emergence of QSR NUD*IST Vivo, known as NVivo. This software is the one featured in this chapter. It draws upon many features in NUD*IST, so that, if you have access to NUD*IST, most of what you read in this chapter will be applicable to you. If you are unsure about which software is likely to meet your needs, demonstration copies of many of the main packages (The Ethnograph, NUD*IST, NVivo, winMax, and ATLAS/ti) can be downloaded from either of the distributor's Internet sites:

www.scolari.co.uk
www.scolari.com.

These demonstration copies are full working programs but you cannot save changes to the project work you carry out using them.

Lack of universal agreement about the utility of CAQDAS

Unlike quantitative data analysis, in which the use of computer software is both widely accepted and to all intents and purposes a necessity, among qualitative data analysts its use is by no means universally embraced. There are several concerns.

- Some writers are concerned that the ease with which coded text can be quantified, either within qualitative data analysis packages or by importing coded information into quantitative data analysis packages like SPSS, will mean that the temptation to quantify findings will prove irresistible to many researchers. As a result, there is a concern that qualitative research will then be colonized by the reliability and validity criteria of quantitative research (Hesse-Biber 1995).

- It has been suggested that CAQDAS reinforces and even exaggerates the tendency for the code-and-retrieve process that underpins most approaches to qualitative data analysis to result in a fragmentation of the textual materials on which researchers

work (Weaver and Atkinson 1994). As a result, the narrative flow of interview transcripts and events recorded in field notes may be lost.

- It has also been suggested that the fragmentation process of coding text into chunks that are then retrieved and put together into groups of related fragments risks decontextualizing data (Buston 1997; Fielding and Lee 1998: 74). Having an awareness of context is crucial to many qualitative researchers and the prospect of this element being sidelined is not an attractive prospect.

- Catterall and Maclaran (1997) have argued on the basis of their experience that CAQDAS is not very suitable for focus group data because the code and retrieve function tends to result in a loss of the communication process that goes on when this method is used. Many writers view the interaction that occurs in focus groups as an important feature of the method (Kitzinger 1994).

- Stanley and Temple (1995) have suggested that most of the coding and retrieval features that someone is likely to need in the course of conducting qualitative data analysis are achievable through powerful word-processing software. They show how this can be accomplished using Word for Windows. The key point here is that the advantage of using such software is that it does not require a lengthy period of getting acquainted with the mechanics of its operations. Also, of course, if someone already has the necessary word-processing software, the possible cost of a CAQDAS program is rendered unnecessary.

- Researchers working in teams may experience difficulties in coordinating the coding of text when different people are involved in this activity (Sprokkereef et al. 1995).

- Coffey, Halbrook, and Atkinson (1996) have argued that the style of qualitative data analysis enshrined in most CAQDAS software (particularly the more prominent ones such as The Ethnograph, NUD*IST, and NVivo) is resulting in the emergence of a new orthodoxy. This arises because these programs presume and are predicated on a certain style of analysis—one based on coding and retrieving text—that owes a great deal to grounded theory.

Coffey et al. argue that the emergence of a new orthodoxy is inconsistent with the growing flirtation with a variety of representational modes in qualitative research, partly as a result of the influence of postmodernism (see Chapter 24 for a discussion of these considerations).

On the other hand, several writers have sought to extol the virtues of such packages on a variety of grounds:

- Most obviously, CAQDAS can make the coding and retrieval process faster and more efficient.

- It has been suggested that new opportunities are offered. For example, Mangabeira (1995) has argued on the basis of her experience with The Ethnograph that her ability to relate her coded text to what are often referred to as 'face-sheet variables' (socio-demographic and personal information, such as age, title of job, number of years in school education) offered new opportunities in the process of analysing her data. Thus, CAQDAS may be helpful in the development of explanations.

- It is sometimes suggested that CAQDAS enhances the transparency of the process of conducting qualitative data analysis. It is often noted that the ways in which qualitative data are analysed are unclear in reports of findings (Bryman and Burgess 1994b). CAQDAS may force researchers to be more explicit and reflective about the process of analysis.

- CAQDAS, like NVivo, invites the analyst to think about codes that are developed in terms of 'trees' of inter-related ideas. This can be a useful feature,

in that it urges the analyst to consider possible connections between codes.

- Writers like Silverman (1985) have commented on the tendency towards anecdotalism in much qualitative research—that is, the tendency to use quotations from interview transcripts or field notes but with little sense of the prevalence of the phenomenon they are supposed to exemplify. CAQDAS invariably offers the opportunity to count such things as the frequency with which a form of behaviour occurred or a viewpoint was expressed in interviews. However, as previously noted, some qualitative researchers perceive risks in the opportunity offered for quantification of findings.

To use or not to use CAQDAS? If you have a very small data set, it is probably not worth the time and trouble navigating your way around new software. On the other hand, if you think you may use it on a future occasion, taking the time and trouble may be worth it. If you do not have easy access to CAQDAS, it is likely to be too expensive for your personal purchase, though the afore-mentioned Scolari Internet sites do outline student and educational discounts. It is also worth bearing in mind that learning new software does provide you with useful skills that may be transferable on a future occasion. By and large, we feel it is worthwhile, but you need to bear in mind some of the factors mentioned above in deciding whether to use it. The rest of this chapter provides an introduction to NVivo. It is based on Bryman's study of visitors to Disney theme parks, where he used NVivo as a tool to assist him in the process of qualitative data analysis.

Learning NVivo

This exposition of NVivo and its functions addresses just its most basic features. There may be features not covered here that you would find useful in your own work, so try to explore it. There is a very good help facility and tutorials have been included to assist learners. In the following account, as in Chapter 12, → signifies 'click once with the left-hand button of your mouse'—that is, select.

On opening NVivo, you will be presented with a welcome screen (known as the **Launch Pad**), offering four options: create a project; open a project; open tutorial project; and exit NVivo. If you are starting a new project, as we will be in the example that follows, select the first of these. You will then be offered the option of opening either a 'typical' or a 'custom' project. First-time users are strongly advised to select the former and this selection was made for this example. You are then presented with a screen offering you an opportunity to give your project a name. I have chosen 'Disney project'. Then, → **Next** >. The details of your Project will then be presented to you, and, if you are happy with them, → **Finish**.

You will then be faced with a window, known as the **Project Pad** (see Plate 20.1), offering several options. My aim is to import into NVivo documents I have created using a standard word processor (Word). This is probably the most common route to creating documents for processing by NVivo. The

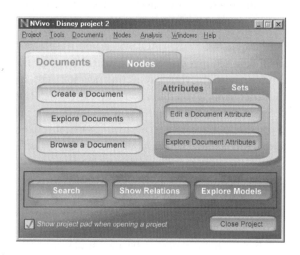

Plate 20.1 The **Project Pad**

Project Pad can be hidden so that only the menu bar is visible (→ **Windows** and then **Project Pad**). You can access all the functions on the **Project Pad** from the menu bar that is left behind, but when learning NVivo you may find it reassuring to have the **Project Pad** visible.

In order to import word-processed documents, you need to save your project documents as either .txt files (plain text files) or .rtf files (rich text files, which contain the text with some formatting features retained). I chose the latter. To do this if you are working in Word, → **Save As . . . .** Then in the box at the bottom of the dialog box, which is called **Save as type**, → the downward pointing arrow and select **Rich Text Format**. Doing this will not over-write your existing document as an .rtf document. Instead, two documents will exist: the original Word one and the .rtf one. You may want to give them clearly different names. Then:

1. From the **Project Pad** (Plate 20.1) → **Create a document** [the **New Document Wizard: Creation** dialog box opens].

2. → **Locate and import readable external text file[s]** → **Next** > [the **Select file to read** dialog box in Plate 20.2 opens].

3. Select the file or files you want to use in your project; more than one can be selected by holding down the Ctrl key and selecting the files.

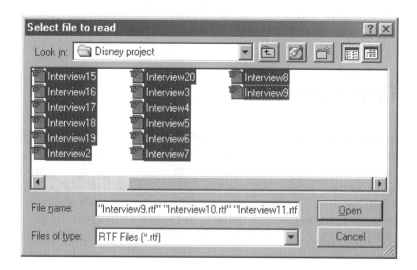

Plate 20.2 The **Select file to read** dialog box

4. → **Open** [the **New Document Wizard: Obtain Name** dialog box opens].

5. → **Use the source file name as the document name.**

6. → **Finish**.

The selected files will then be copied into your NVivo project and you will be taken back to the **Project Pad** (Plate 20.1). At this point, you can elect to edit any of the documents you have entered into your project by selecting **Browse a Document.** The **Choose Document** dialog box will open. Select the document you want and then → **Open**. This opens the **Document Browser** (Plate 20.3). From the **Document Browser**, you can edit the document as if you were using a word processor.

Coding

Coding your data is obviously one of the key phases in the whole process of qualitative data analysis. For NVivo, coding is accomplished through nodes (see Box 20.1).

There are several ways of going about the coding process in NVivo. The approach I took in relation to the coding of the Disney Project was to follow these steps:

1. I read through the interviews both in printed form and in the **Document Browser** (Plate 20.3).

2. I worked out some codes that seemed relevant to the documents.

3. I went back into the documents and coded them using the **Node Browser** (see below).

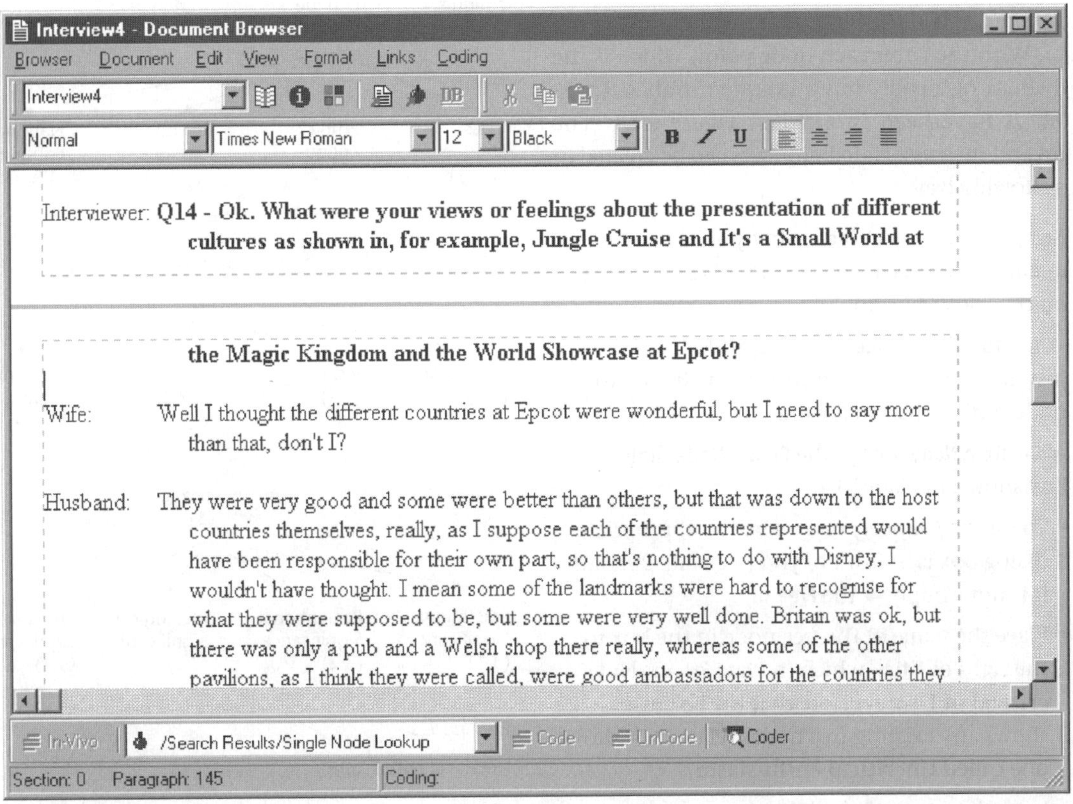

Plate 20.3 The **Document Browser**

Box 20.1 🔆 *What is a node?*

NVivo's help system defines coding as 'the process of marking passages of text in a project's documents with *nodes*' (emphasis added). Nodes are, therefore, the route by which coding is undertaken. In turn, nodes are 'items that you create to represent anything at all in or about your project, and to hold information about it, code text about it, etc. A node belongs to a particular project and is kept inside its database.' When a document has been coded, the node will incorporate references to those portions of documents in which the code appears. Once established, nodes can be changed or deleted. Nodes can be held in any of three ways, but only two are covered in this chapter. First, there are *tree nodes*, whereby nodes are held in a treelike structure, implying connections between them. In this way, you can have groups (trees) of related nodes. The other type covered here are *free nodes*, which are independent of any tree.

An alternative strategy is to code while browsing the documents.

Creating nodes

The nodes that I used that were relevant to the passage in Box 19.7 are presented in Figure 20.1. Notice that there are two *free nodes* and three groups of *tree nodes*. With the latter each node point, which is the equivalent of a code, has a unique number. These numbers have been inserted in Figure 20.1. The nodes and their associated numbers can be created in the following way.

1. Bring up the **Project Pad** again by exiting the document browser. You can do this by clicking on the 'close' button.

2. ➔ the tab titled **Nodes**. The **Project Pad** looks just like the one in Plate 20.1, but will refer to nodes rather than to documents.

3. ➔ **Create a Node** [opens the **Create Node** dialog box shown in Plate 20.4].

4. • To form a *free node*, make sure the appropriate dialog box is in front of you (see Plate 20.4). If it is not, simply ➔ the **Free** tab.

   • Place the name of the free node in the box to the right of **Title:**, which in Plate 20.4 is **Not critical of Disney**. Note that the box also shows any existing free nodes (Plate 20.4 shows one called **Uncritical enthusiasm**).

   • In the box under **Description:** you can place a brief summary of what the node is about. This is

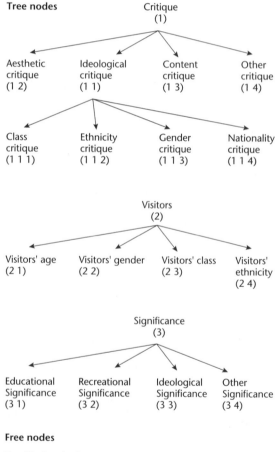

Figure 20.1 Nodes used in the Disney project

not essential but can be useful as a reminder and may form a useful aid to creating memos (see below on the procedure for creating memos).

- **→ Create**.

5. • To form a *tree node*, make sure the appropriate dialog box is on your screen (see Plate 20.5). To activate it, simply → the **Tree** tab.

- Make sure you have a good idea of what your Tree Node should look like. Place the starting point of the tree in the box by **Title** (in this case it was **Critique**) and then → **Create**. This Node will then move into the large box under **Tree Nodes:**.

- As with free nodes, in the box under **Description:** you can place a brief summary of what the node

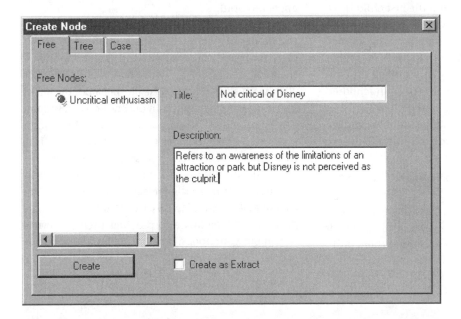

Plate 20.4 The **Create Node** dialog box (free nodes)

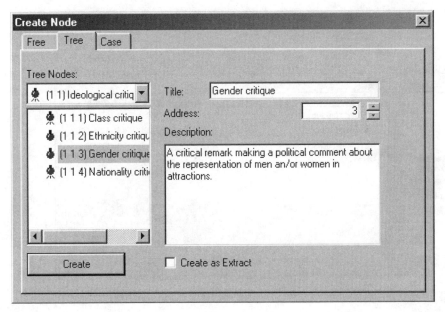

Plate 20.5 The **Create Node** dialog box (tree nodes)

is about. This is not essential but can be useful as a reminder and may form a useful aid to creating memos.

- Then double-click on the new tree node so that it appears in the small box under **Tree Nodes:**. You can then place in the box by **Title:** the name of the first 'child' (as it is known in NVivo language) of the 'parent'. In this case, the parent is *Critique* and the first child is **Ideological Critique**. Make sure that it is in the box by **Address:** the number is that of the parent (in this case **1**) and the child (**1**, so that it is **1 1**). Carry on doing this until all the children have been dealt with. For 'grandchildren', as we have with the four children of **Ideological Critique**, simply double-click on **Ideological Critique** and follow the same procedure as for the children.

- When each child has been created, remember to → **Create**.

6. When you have finished, close the dialog box. Remember that you can always create new nodes using this procedure or you can add them during coding.

Editing and browsing

At any time, you can browse and edit your nodes. To browse your nodes, from the **Project Pad → Explore Nodes**. The **Node Explorer** dialog box will appear (see Plate 20.6). Selecting any nodes will allow you to see their children or parents and any descriptions you might have provided. Nodes that have already been used at some point in coding documents will appear in **bold**.

From the **Node Explorer** you can delete or change the names of nodes. To delete a node, simply click once on it and then → **Tools** and → **Cut**. To change the name of a Node, click once on the node and then click again after a short pause (i.e. *not* a double-click). The node will then appear in outline and a new name can be provided. When you have carried out some coding, the **Node Explorer** will reveal such details as the number of occurrences (**Passages**) of that Node.

A child or sibling of a Node can be created by → **Browse a Node** on the **Project Pad** (Plate 20.1). The **Choose Node** sub-dialog box (see Plate 20.7) will appear. This dialog box also provides useful information about your nodes, but clicking on the ✳ button

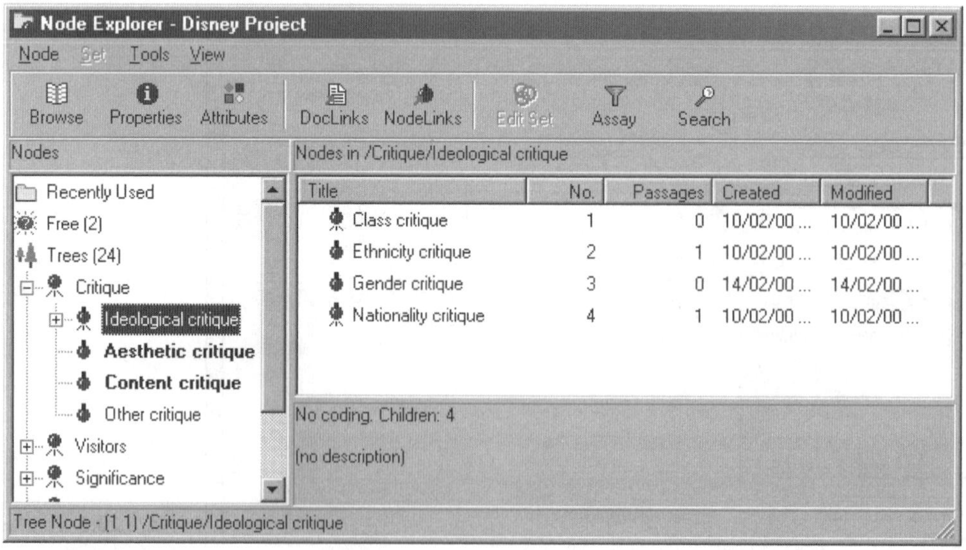

Plate 20.6 The **Node Explorer**

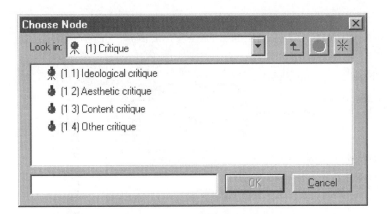

Look in: (1) Critique

- (1 1) Ideological critique
- (1 2) Aesthetic critique
- (1 3) Content critique
- (1 4) Other critique

OK   Cancel

Plate 20.7 The **Choose Node** sub-dialog box

will give you the option of whether to create a child or sibling node for the node that you have selected.

Applying nodes in the coding process

Coding is carried out by applying nodes to segments of text. Once you have set up some nodes (and do remember you can add and alter at any time), follow this procedure:

1. → the **Documents** tab on the **Project Pad** (Plate 20.1).
2. → **Browse a Document** [opens the **Choose Document** dialog box].
3. Select the document you want to code, which in this case is **Interview4**, since it contains the passage in Table 19.7 (p. 438) that will be the focus of attention in this account of NVivo's operations, and then → **OK**.
4. When you find a passage that you want to code using one of your nodes, highlight that passage.
5. Then → **Coding** and then → **Coder** . . . *or* simply → **Coder** on the bar at the bottom of the screen [opens the **Coder** dialog box—see Plate 20.8, which shows the **Document Browser** and the **Coder** dialog box].
6. Select the node you want to apply to the selected (i.e. highlighted) text and then → **Code**.

To *uncode* at any point, simply highlight the passage to be uncoded, and from the **Coder** dialog box → **UnCode** or simply choose **Uncode** from the toolbar at the bottom of the screen.

These instructions apply to the application of both free nodes and tree nodes.

Coding stripes

It is very helpful to be able to see the areas of text that have been coded and the nodes applied to them. NVivo has a very useful aid to this called *coding stripes*. Selecting this facility allows you to see multi-coloured stripes that represent portions of coded text and the nodes that have been used. Overlapping codes do not represent a problem at all.

To activate this facility, → **View** and then → **Coding Stripes**. The screen then splits and the right-hand section contains the coding stripes. Plate 20.9 shows these stripes. We can see that there is a segment that has been coded with two nodes—**visitors ethnicity** and **ethnicity critique**. All the nodes that have been used are clearly displayed and are visible even when the **Coder** dialog box is open.

Speed coding

At the bottom of the **Document Browser** is the *speed coding* bar (see Plate 20.9). If you are coding a passage or series of passages using recurring nodes, you may find it easier to use this facility. If you click on the downward pointing arrow to the immediate right of the box by it, the most recently used nodes will be displayed. You can then select the appropriate node and then → **Code** to the right of the selected node to code a highlighted section of text.

Another useful facility on this bar is the opportunity to generate *in vivo codes* (see Box 19.6 for an example of such a code). This is a code that is derived

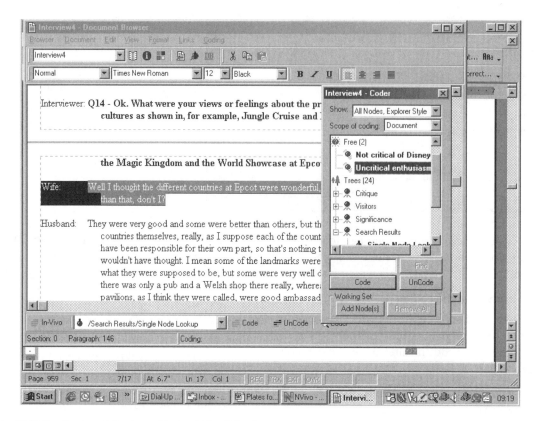

Plate 20.8 The **Document Browser** with the **Coder** dialog box

from the language of research participants and that is found in the interview transcripts or field notes. To create an in vivo code, highlight the word or short passage that strikes you as significant and from which you want to create a node. An example might be 'black history', which can be seen in the unhighlighted passage in Plate 20.9. Once you have highlighted the word or passage, → the **InVivo** button. This action will create a new node entitled **black history**. This will be a free node and NVivo will adjust your list of free nodes accordingly. You then need to highlight the area that you want to code in terms of this new free node and then code it, using either the speed coding bar or the **Coder** dialog box.

Searching text

Once you have coded your data, however preliminary that may be, you will want to conduct searches of your data at some point. To conduct a search, → **Search** on the **Project Pad**. This will bring up the **Search Tool** dialog box (see Plate 20.10). The **Search Tool** facilitates a variety of different types of search, but just three simple types will be presented below.

To search for occurrences of a single node

These steps describe how to conduct a search for sequences of text that have been coded in terms of the node **ethnicity critique**.

1. While in the **Search Tool** dialog box, → **Node ...** to the right of **Single Item:** [opens the **Single Node Lookup** dialog box shown in Plate 20.11].

2. If you know the name of the node you want to search for, enter it in the window beneath **Search for text coded by this node:** and then → **OK**.

3. If you do *not* know the name of the node, → **Choose** [opens the **Choose Node** sub-dialog

Coder
dialog box

Coding
stripes

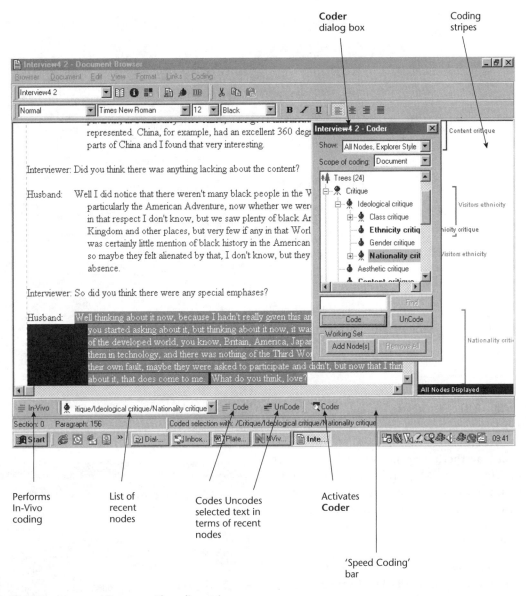

Performs
In-Vivo
coding

List of
recent
nodes

Codes Uncodes
selected text in
terms of recent
nodes

Activates
Coder

'Speed Coding'
bar

Plate 20.9 The **Document Browser** with coding stripes

box—see Plate 20.12] and then ➔ the downward
pointing arrowhead to the right of the window
by **Look in:**. Find the node that you want to
use. The node will be listed as either a free or
a tree node. If the latter, simply keep clicking
on the appropriate branches until you find the
node you need. When you have found the node
➔ **OK**.

4. You then need to define the scope of your search.
The default in NVivo is **All Documents**.

5. ➔ **Run Search**.

**To search for the intersection of two or
more nodes**

These steps describe how to conduct a search for
sequences of text that have been coded in terms of

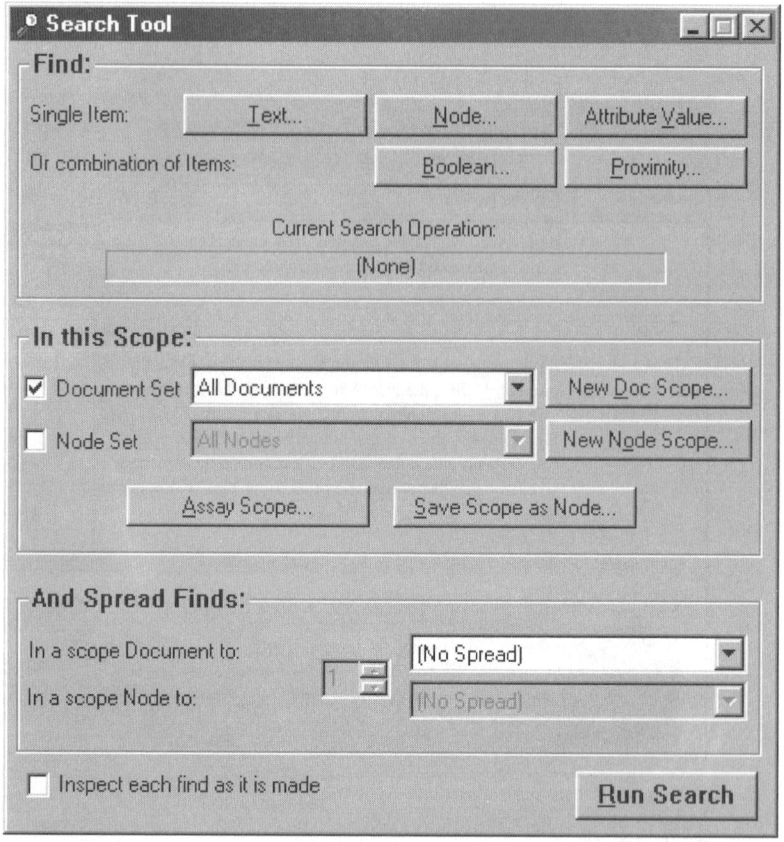

Plate 20.10 The **Search Tool** dialog box

two nodes: **aesthetic critique** and **not critical of Disney**. This type of search is known as a 'Boolean search'. It will locate not text coded in terms of each of the two nodes, but text coded in terms of the two nodes together (that is, where they intersect). The following steps need to be followed:

1. In the **Search Tool** dialog box (Plate 20.10)
   → **Boolean** ... [opens the **Boolean Search** dialog box shown in Plate 20.13].

2. → **Choose Nodes** ... [opens the **Choose Nodes** dialog box shown in Plate 20.14].

3. Select a node and → the **Node** button underneath **Add:**. Do this for the second node and any other nodes.

4. → **OK**, which takes you back to the **Boolean Search** dialog box (Plate 20.13).

5. → **OK**, which takes you back to the **Search Tool** dialog box (Plate 20.10).

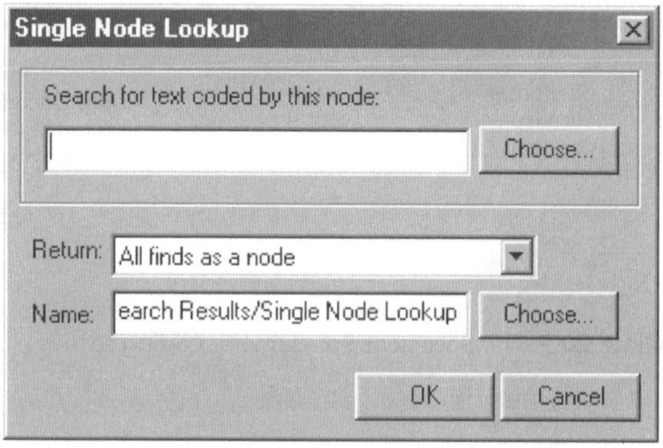

Plate 20.11 The **Single Node Lookup** dialog box

6. → **OK**.

To search for specific text

NVivo can also perform searches for specific words or phrases, often referred to as 'strings' in computer

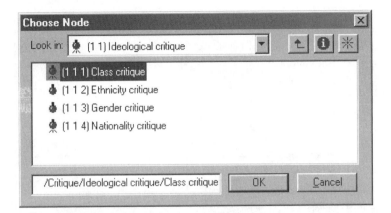

Plate 20.12 The **Choose Node** dialog box

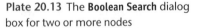

Plate 20.13 The **Boolean Search** dialog box for two or more nodes

jargon. For example, to search for **Magic Kingdom**, the following steps would need to be taken:

1. In the **Search Tool** dialog box (Plate 20.10) → **Text** [opens the **Text Search** dialog box shown in Plate 20.15].
2. After **Search for this Text:**, type in the text you want to search for (e.g. **Magic Kingdom**).
3. → **OK**, which takes you back to the **Search Tool** dialog box (see Plate 20.10).
4. → **OK**.

Text searching can be useful for the identification of possible in vivo codes. You would then need to go back to the documents to conduct in vivo coding.

Output

The default is that, for each search you carry out, a node will be created into which the results of your search will be printed. These results can then be inspected using the **Node Browser** and printed. Plate 20.16 shows the results of a search for the node **ethnicity critique** in **Interview4**.

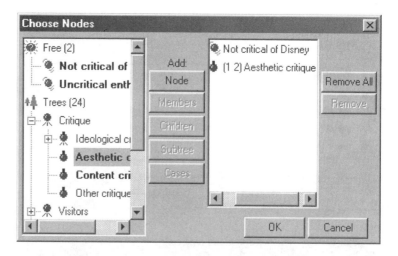

Plate 20.14 The **Choose Nodes** dialog box for two or more nodes

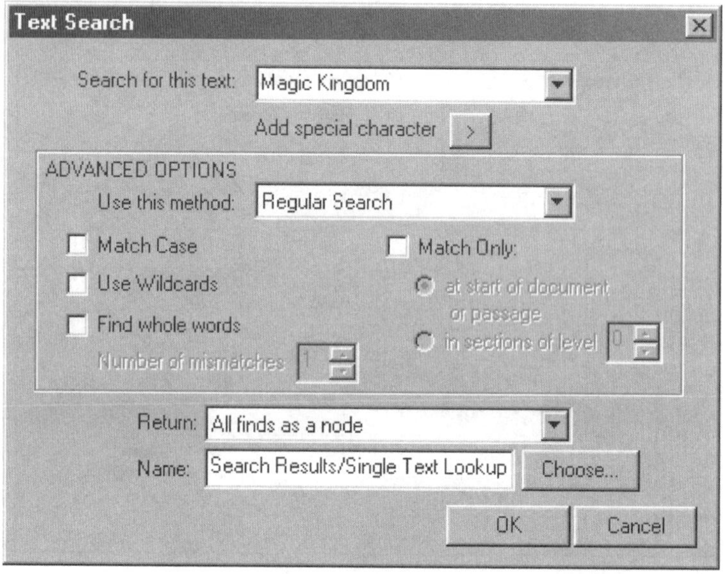

Plate 20.15 The **Text Search** dialog box

Memos

In Chapter 19, it was noted that one feature of the grounded theory approach to qualitative data analysis is the use of memos in which ideas and illustrations might be stored. Memos can be easily created in NVivo, but it is important to realize that the software makes no distinction between memos and other kinds of document. In other words, when you create a memo, so far as NVivo is concerned, it is indistinguishable from your data (for example, your interview transcripts or field notes) and as such becomes part of your data set. Memos can be created in the **Document Browser** (see Plate 20.16 for an example). The following steps should be followed:

1. On the **Project Pad**, → **Create a Document** [opens the **New Document Wizard:Creation** dialog box].

2. → **Make a new blank document** and → **Create document as a memo**.

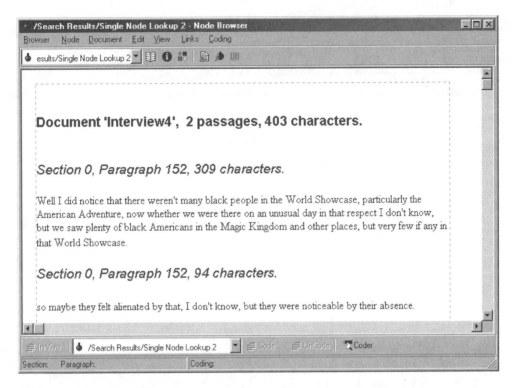

Plate 20.16 The **Node Browser** with the results of a node search

3. → **Next**> [opens the **New Document Wizard:Name** dialog box].

4. After **Name:**, type in a name for the document (e.g. **gender critique memo**). You can also provide a brief description of the document in the window under **Description**.

5. → **Finish**.

6. On the **Project Pad**, → **Browse a Document** [opens the **Choose Document** dialog box].

7. → the name of the document you have just created (e.g. **gender critique memo**) and provide the kind of description you feel you need to clarify the code or concepts you are developing (see Plate 20.17).

8. → **Browser**

9. → **Close**

You may find that a brief description is all you require, in which case Steps 1–5 will be sufficient for your needs.

Saving an NVivo project

When you have finished working on your data, you will need to save it for future use. To do this, on the **Project Pad** → **Close Project**. You will then be prompted to save changes to your project. You should → **Yes**. You will then be given the opportunity to exit NVivo or to create or open a project.

Opening an existing NVivo project

To retrieve a project you have created, at the welcome screen, → **Open a Project**. This opens the **Open Project—NVivo** dialog box. Select the project you want to work on. If you only have one, this will come up as the default as in Plate 20.18. Then → **OK**. The **Project Pad** will then appear (see Plate 20.1).

To import a NUD*IST project, from the **Project Pad** → **Tools** and then → **Import NUD*IST Project.…** You will then be faced with a dialog box requesting that

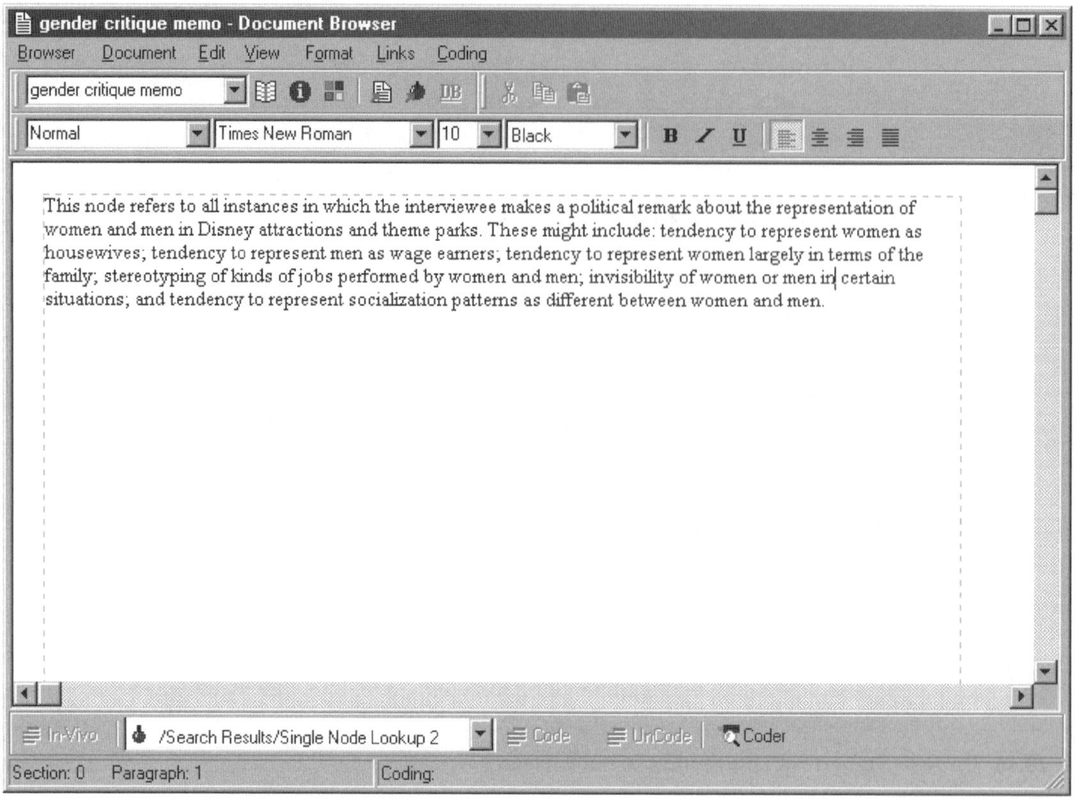

Plate 20.17 The **Document Browser** with a memo

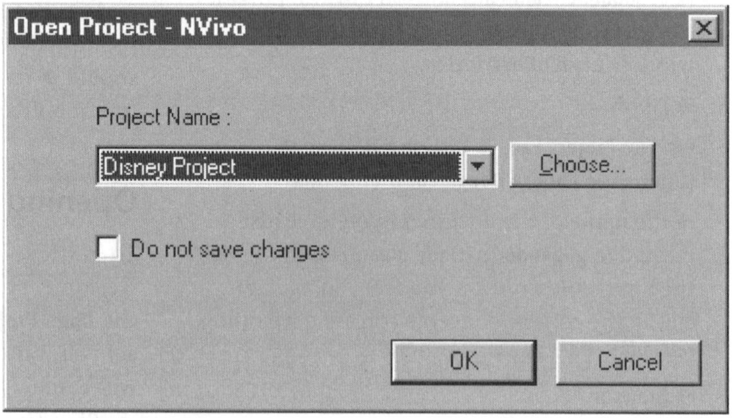

Plate 20.18 The **Open Project** dialog box

you identify the project you wish to open. When you have located it, → **Open**.

Final thoughts

As with the chapter on SPSS (Chapter 12), a short chapter like this can provide help only with the most basic features of the software. In so doing, we hope that it will have given students who may be uncertain about whether CAQDAS is for them an impression of what the software is like. Doubtless, some readers will decide it is not for them and that the tried-and-tested scissors and paste will do the trick. On the other hand, the software warrants serious consideration because of its power and flexibility.

R REVISION QUESTIONS

Is CAQDAS like quantitative data analysis software?

- What are the main points of difference between CAQDAS and quantitative data analysis software like SPSS?

- Why is CAQDAS controversial?

- To what extent does CAQDAS help with qualitative data analysis?

Learning NVivo

- What is a node?

- What is the difference between a free node and a tree node?

- What is in vivo coding?

- Do nodes have to be set up in advance?

- What is speed coding?

- In NVivo, what is the difference between a document and a memo?

- How do you go about searching for a single node and the intersection of two nodes?

- Why might it be useful to display coding stripes?

- How do you search for specific text?

Part Four

In Part Four, we will explore areas that transcend the quantitative/qualitative distinction. Chapter 21 invites readers to consider how useful the distinction is. This may seem a contrary thing to do, since the book has been organized around the quantitative/qualitative divide. However, the aim is to show that the distinction is not a hard-and-fast one. Chapter 22 considers the different ways in which quantitative and qualitative research can be combined. Such combinations are referred to as *multi-strategy research*. Chapter 23 considers the growing possibilities for e-research and focuses on the use of the Internet both as a source of data and as a research method. Chapter 24 examines issues relating to the writing-up of business research and explores some features of good writing in both quantitative and qualitative research. Chapter 25 is concerned with some of the ethical principles that arise in business research and the difficulties of applying them in practice. Chapter 26 has been written to offer advice to students faced with the often daunting prospect of having to produce a dissertation. It will also be helpful to those who have to do mini-projects as part of the coursework requirement associated with modules.

These chapters draw together certain issues from previous parts but also address others that have been raised already but this time in much greater depth. In addition, they offer advice for those students who are confronted with the need to produce a lengthy piece of work, which is an increasingly common requirement.

21

Breaking down the quantitative/qualitative divide

CHAPTER GUIDE

This chapter is concerned with the degree to which the quantitative/qualitative divide should be regarded as a hard-and-fast one. It shows that, while there are many differences between the two research strategies, there are also many examples of research that transcend the distinction. One way in which this occurs is through research that combines quantitative and qualitative research, which is the focus of the next chapter. The present chapter is concerned with points of overlap between them. This chapter explores:

- aspects of qualitative research that can contain elements of the natural science model;

- aspects of quantitative research that can contain elements of interpretivism;

- the idea that research methods are more independent of epistemological and ontological assumptions than is sometimes supposed;
- ways in which aspects of the quantitative/qualitative contrast sometimes break down;

- studies in which quantitative and qualitative research are employed in relation to each other, so that qualitative research is used to analyse quantitative research and vice versa;
- the use of quantification in qualitative research.

Introduction

With this book structured so far around the distinction between quantitative and qualitative research, it might appear perverse to raise at this stage the prospect that the distinction might be overblown. The distinction has been employed so far for two main reasons.

- There *are* differences between quantitative and qualitative research in terms of research strategy, and many researchers and writers on research methodology perceive this to be the case.
- It is a useful means of organizing research methods and approaches to data analysis.

However, while epistemological and ontological commitments may be associated with certain research methods—such as the often-cited links between a natural science epistemology (in particular, positivism) and survey research, or between an interpretivist epistemology (for example, phenomenology) and qualitative interviewing—the connections are not deterministic. In other words, while qualitative interviews may often reveal a predisposition towards or a reflection of an interpretivist and constructionist position, this is not always the case, as an early example suggested (see the discussion of the study by Hochschild (1983) in Chapter 1). This means that the connections that were posited in Chapter 1 between epistemology and ontology, on the one hand, and research method, on the other, are best thought of as tendencies rather than as definitive connections. Such connections were implied by

the suggestion that within each of the two research strategies—quantitative and qualitative—there is a distinctive mix of epistemology, ontology, and research methods (see Table 1.1). However, we cannot say that the use of a structured interview or self-completion questionnaire *necessarily* implies a commitment to a natural scientific model or that ethnographic research *must* mean an interpretivist epistemology. We should not be surprised at this: after all, quantitative research teaches us that it is rarely the case that we find perfect associations between variables. We should not be surprised, therefore, that the practice of business research similarly lacks absolute determinism.

Research methods are much more free-floating than is sometimes supposed. A method of data collection like participant observation can be employed in such a way that it is in tune with the tenets of constructionism, but equally it can be used in a manner that reveals an objectivist orientation. Also, it is easy to underemphasize the significance of practical considerations in the way in which business research is conducted (though look again at Figure 1.2). Conducting a study of humour and resistance on the shopfloor by postal questionnaire may not be totally impossible, but it is unlikely to succeed in terms of yielding valid answers to questions.

In the rest of this chapter, we will examine a variety of ways in which the contrast between quantitative and qualitative research should not be overdrawn.

The natural science model and qualitative research

One of the chief difficulties with the links that are frequently forged between issues of epistemology and matters of research method or technique is that they often entail a characterization of the natural sciences as necessarily or inherently positivist in orientation. There are three notable difficulties here.

- There is no agreement on the epistemological basis of the natural sciences. As noted in Chapter 1, writers like Harré (1972) and Keat and Urry (1975) have argued that positivism is but one version of the nature of the natural sciences, *realism* being one alternative account (Bhaskar 1975).

- If we assume that the practices of natural scientists are those that are revealed in their written accounts of what they do (and most of the discussions of the nature of the natural sciences do assume this), we run into a problem because studies by social researchers of scientists' practices suggest that there is often a disparity between their work behaviour and their writings. Research by Gilbert and Mulkay (1984) suggested that the ways in which scientists talked about their work frequently revealed a different set of practices from those inscribed in their articles.

- As Platt (1981) has argued, a term like 'positivist' has to be treated in a circumspect way, because, while it does refer to a distinctive characterization of scientific enquiry (see Box 1.7), it is also frequently employed in a polemical way. When employed in this manner, it is rarely helpful, because the term is usually a characterization (a negative one) of the work of others rather than of one's own work.

Quite aside from the difficulty of addressing the natural science model and positivism, there are problems with associating them solely with quantitative research. Further, qualitative research frequently exhibits features that one would associate with a natural science model. This tendency is revealed in several ways:

- *Empiricist overtones.* Although empiricism (see Box 1.4) is typically associated with quantitative research, many writers on qualitative research display an equal emphasis on the importance of direct contact with social reality as the springboard for any investigation. Thus, writers on qualitative research frequently stress the importance of direct experience of social settings and fashioning an understanding of social worlds via that contact. The very idea that theory is to be grounded in data (see Chapter 19) seems to constitute a manifesto for empiricism, and it is unsurprising, therefore, that some writers claim to detect 'covert positivism' in qualitative research. Another way in which empiricist overtones are revealed is in the suggestion that social reality must be studied from the vantage point of research participants but that the only way to gain access to their interpretations is through extended contact with them, implying that meaning is accessible to the senses of researchers. The empiricism of qualitative research is perhaps most notable in conversation analysis, which was examined in Chapter 17. This is an approach that takes precise transcriptions of talk as its starting point and applies rules of analysis to such data. The analyst is actively discouraged from engaging in speculations about intention or context that might derive from an appreciation of the ethnographic particulars of the social setting.

- *A specific problem focus.* As noted in Chapter 13, qualitative research can be employed to investigate quite specific, tightly defined research questions of the kind normally associated with a natural science model of the research process.

- *Hypothesis- and theory-testing.* Following on from the last point, qualitative researchers typically discuss hypothesis- and theory-testing in connection with hypotheses or theories generated in the course of conducting research, as in analytic induction or grounded theory. However, there is no obvious reason why this cannot occur in relation to previously specified hypotheses or theories. Scott's (1994) ethnographic study of British workers under human resource management, for example, was designed to test the theory that British management was operating according to a 'new' model of industrial relations, based on a unitaristic view of organizational life, where workers and managers are seen to have a similar interest in the success of the firm. Scott wanted to test whether workers and managers in his case-study firms actually shared similar interests or if they still adhered to ideas based on an 'old' industrial relations model founded on adversarial relationships. In the event, the research showed a complex picture, concluding that 'any cultural transformation of British management has only been partial, and the embrace of the "new IR" piecemeal' (Scott 1994: 131).

• *Realism.* Realism (Box 1.9) is one way in which the epistemological basis of the natural sciences has been construed. It has entered into the social sciences in a number of ways, but one of the most significant of these is Bhaskar's (1989) notion of *critical realism*. This approach accepts neither a constructionist nor an objectivist ontology and instead takes the view that the 'social world is reproduced and transformed in daily life' (1989: 4). Social phenomena are produced by mechanisms that are real, but that are not directly accessible to observation and are discernible only through their effects. For critical realism the task of business research is to construct hypotheses about such mechanisms and to seek out their effects. However, the application of critical realism in business research is relatively rare and empirical examples are not common. Despite this, there is increasing interest in this approach, which is, according to Reed (1997), undergoing something of an intellectual revitalization. Whittington's (1989) analysis of the strategic choices made by companies during periods of recession and recovery provides an exception (Box 1.2). Whittington suggests that the capitalist structures, in which his case-study

organizations are located, exist independently of the discursive construction of individual managers who are involved in strategic action. However, he also argues that 'the plural and contradictory nature of the social structures embodied within the firm precludes unambiguous determination and allows sufficient autonomy for individual actors to choose which powers to use and how' (Whittington 1989: 77). In other words, the relationship between structure and agency is a fluid one, with social structures providing the resources that enable autonomy and social actors exercising genuine choice between the alternatives that are presented to them. This implies, according to Whittington, that different companies will respond to similar structural conditions of recession in quite different ways, resulting in differing outcomes in terms of the effectiveness of firm recovery. In this way, Whittington discerns the influence of capitalist structures through analysis of the effects of recession. Porter's (1993) critical realist ethnography is also interesting in this connection (see Box 21.1), because it demonstrates the use of ethnography in connection with an epistemological position that derives from the natural sciences. It also relates to the previous point in providing an illustration of hypothesis-testing qualitative research.

In addition, writers on qualitative research sometimes distinguish stances on qualitative research that contain elements of both quantitative and qualitative research. Miller (2000), in connection with an examination of life history interviews (see Box 15.4), distinguishes three approaches to such research. One of these, which he calls 'neo-positivist', uses 'pre-existing networks of concepts . . . to make theoretically based predictions concerning people's experienced lives' (2000: 12). Therefore, one approach to the life history method, which is associated with qualitative rather than quantitative research, would seem to entail a theory-testing approach to the collection and analysis of qualitative data. A further illustration is Charmaz's (2000) suggestion that two approaches to grounded theory can be distinguished: objectivist

---

Box 21.1 A critical realist ethnography

A critical realist stance was employed by Porter (1993) in connection with an ethnographic study in a large Irish hospital in which the author was employed for three months as a staff nurse. Porter's interest was in the possible role of racism in this setting. He suggests that racism and professionalism were in operation such that the latter tempered the effects of the former in the context of interactions between doctors and nurses. Thus, racism and professionalism were conceptualized as generative structures—that is, mechanisms—that could be productive of certain kinds of effect. Two hypotheses were proposed: that racism would play some part in the relationships between white staff and those from 'racialized minorities' and that the 'occupational situation would affect the way in which racism was expressed' (1993: 599). Porter found that racism was not a significant factor in relationships between members of racialized minorities and the other staff but did manifest itself behind the backs of the former in the form of racist remarks. Racism did not intrude into work relationships, because of the operation of the greater weight given to people's achievements and performance (such as qualifications and medical skills) rather than their ascriptive qualities (that is, 'race') when judging members of professions. The emphasis on values associated with professionalism counteracted the potential role of those associated with racism. Thus, 'racism can be seen as a tendency that is realised in certain circumstances, but exercised unrealised in others' (1993: 607). In terms of critical realism, one possible structural mechanism (racism) was countered by the operation of another structural mechanism (professional ideology).

---

and constructionist (she uses the term 'constructivist'). She argues that, in spite of the differences that developed between Glaser (1992) and Strauss (e.g. Strauss and Corbin 1998), both held to the view of an objective, external reality. In other words, in the eyes of both the major writers on grounded theory, there is a social world beyond the researcher, whose job it is to reveal its nature and functioning.

Quantitative research and interpretivism

Qualitative research would seem to have a monopoly of the ability to study meaning. Its proponents essentially claim that it is only through qualitative research that the world can be studied through the eyes of the people who are studied. As Platt (1981: 87) observes, this contention seems rather at odds with the widespread study of attitudes in surveys based on interviews and questionnaires. In fact, it would seem that quantitative researchers frequently address meanings. An example is the well-known concept of 'orientation to work' associated with the *Affluent Worker* research in the 1960s, which sought to uncover the nature and significance of the meanings that industrial workers bring with them to the workplace (Goldthorpe et al. 1968).

The widespread inclusion of questions about attitudes in surveys suggests that quantitative researchers are interested in matters of meaning. It might be objected that survey questions do not really tap issues of meaning because they are based on categories devised by the designers of the interview schedule or questionnaire. Two points are relevant here. First, in the absence of respondent validation exercises, the notion that qualitative research is more adept at gaining access to the point of view of those being studied than quantitative research is invariably assumed rather than demonstrated. Qualitative researchers frequently claim to have tapped into participants' world views because of, for example, their extensive participation in the daily round of those they study, the length of time they spent in the setting being studied, or the lengthy and intensive interviews conducted. However, the explicit demonstration that interpretative understanding has been accomplished—for example, through respondent validation (see Box 13.3)—is rarely undertaken. Secondly, if the design of attitude questions is based on prior questioning that seeks to bring out the range of possible attitudinal positions on an issue, as in the research discussed in Box 7.4, attitudinal questions may be better able to gain access to meaning.

Also, as Marsh (1982) has pointed out, the practice in much survey research of asking respondents the reasons for their actions also implies that quantitative researchers are frequently concerned to uncover issues of meaning. For example, Stewart's (1967) diary study of how managers use their time (see Box 6.5) focused on recording how much time was spent by each individual on different kinds of activity. However, Stewart followed up the diary study by sending each manager a summary of how he or she had spent his or her time, together with comparative figures for managers in similar jobs. Managers were then asked to comment on any unusual features in their figures and to explain individual and contextual reasons for these differences. Examples such as these further point to the possibility that the gulf between quantitative and qualitative research is not as wide as is sometimes supposed.

Quantitative research and constructionism

It was noted in Chapter 1 that one keynote of constructionism is a concern with issues of representation, as these play an important role in the construction of the social world. Qualitative content analysis has played an important role in developing just such an understanding, just as discourse analysis has in relation to the social construction of events and meanings in business leaders' speeches and mission statements. However, it is easy to forget that conventional quantitative content analysis can also be useful in this way.

Chen and Meindl's (1991) research into the entrepreneurial leadership of the founder of the low-cost US airline People Express, Donald Burr, which was referred to in Box 18.8, provides an example of the combined use of quantitative and qualitative content analysis. Much of their understanding of Burr's leadership style was derived from qualitative content analysis, but they also employed a quantitative content analysis, 'identifying leader-charismatic themes, recording frequency, and analyzing trends' (1991: 530) using data from magazine and newspaper articles that focused on the company. However, rather than simply content analysing the articles themselves, the researchers involved seventy-two undergraduate business students, who were asked to read the new articles and write a description of Burr, as a person and as a CEO, based on the materials they had read. Content analysis was then conducted on the students' descriptions. This showed that the language used by the students to describe Burr changed as the performance of the company varied. Chen and Meindl conclude that images portrayed of Burr in the past interacted with indications of current performance to determine the reconstruction of the leader's image. In other words, instead of being rejected, old themes were modified and injected with new meaning. The second stage of the content analysis was more qualitative in nature. It involved qualitative content analysis of the actual newspaper articles in order to identify the metaphors used to describe Burr. The results of this analysis were broadly consistent with the first, thereby reinforcing the validity of the overall findings. More generally, this example shows how quantitative research can play a significant role in relation to a constructionist stance.

Epistemological and ontological considerations

If we review the argument so far, it is being suggested:

- there are differences between quantitative and qualitative research in terms of their epistemological and ontological commitments; *but*

- the connection between research strategy, on the one hand, and epistemological and ontological commitments, on the other, is not deterministic. In other words, there is a *tendency* for quantitative and qualitative research to be associated with the epistemological and ontological positions outlined in Chapter 1 (for example, in Table 1.1), but the connections are not perfect.

However, some writers have suggested that research methods carry with them a cluster of epistemological and ontological commitments such that to elect to use a self-completion questionnaire is more or less simultaneously and inevitably to select a natural science model and an objectivist world view. Similarly, the use of participant observation is often taken to imply a commitment to interpretivism and constructionism. Such a view implies that research methods are imbued with specific clusters of epistemological and ontological commitments and can be seen in comments of the following kind: 'the choice and adequacy of a method embodies a variety of assumptions regarding the nature of knowledge and the methods through which that knowledge can be obtained, as well as a set of root assumptions about the nature of the phenomena to be investigated'

(Morgan and Smircich 1980: 491). The difficulty with such a view is that, if we accept that there is no perfect correspondence between research strategy and matters of epistemology and ontology, the notion that a method is inherently or necessarily indicative of certain wider assumptions about knowledge and the nature of social reality begins to founder.

In business and management research, if Burrell and Morgan's (1979) influential 'four-paradigm' framework were consistently applied, one would expect to see a clear correspondence between the paradigm adopted (see Chapter 1) and the research methods used, in a manner similar to that illustrated by Hassard (see Box 1.17): the functionalist paradigm community using, for example, questionnaire surveys, and the interpretative paradigm community using, for example, ethnographic methods. In fact, research methods are much more 'free-floating' in terms of epistemology and ontology than this proposition suggests and it is often not possible to uncover an unambiguous pattern linking the grounding of an article in one of the four paradigms with the research methods used. Furthermore, because of the dominance of multi-strategy case-study research in the business and management field, it is common for several methods to be used within the same research study. In sum, although there is undoubtedly a general tendency for specific paradigm communities to favour certain research methods, the reality is more complex than this picture at first suggests.

Problems with the quantitative/ qualitative contrast

The contrasts between quantitative and qualitative research that were drawn in Chapter 13 suggest a somewhat hard-and-fast set of distinctions and differences (see, in particular, Table 13.1). However, there is a risk that this kind of representation tends to exaggerate the differences between them. A few of the distinctions will be examined to demonstrate this point.

Behaviour versus meaning

The distinction is sometimes drawn between a focus on behaviour and a focus on meanings. However, quantitative research frequently involves the study of meanings in the form of attitude scales (such as the Likert scaling technique) and other techniques. Qualitative researchers may feel that the tendency for attitude scales to be preformulated and imposed on research participants means that they do not really gain access to meanings (see above). The key point being made here is that at the very least quantitative researchers frequently *try* to address meanings. Also, somewhat ironically, many of the techniques with which quantitative research is associated, most notably survey research based on questionnaires and interviews, have been shown to relate poorly to people's actual behaviour. Moreover, looking at the other side of the divide, qualitative research frequently, if not invariably, entails the examination of behaviour in context. Qualitative researchers often want to interpret people's behaviour in terms of the norms, values, and culture of the group or organization in question. In other words, quantitative and qualitative researchers are typically interested in both what people do and what they think, but go about the investigation of these areas in different ways. Therefore, the degree to which the behaviour versus meaning contrast coincides with quantitative and qualitative research should not be overstated.

Theory tested in research versus emergent from data

A further related point is that the suggestion that theory and concepts are developed prior to undertaking a study in quantitative research is something of a caricature that is true only up to a point. It reflects a tendency to characterize quantitative research as driven by a theory-testing approach. However, while experimental investigations probably fit this model well, survey-based studies are often more exploratory than this view implies. Although concepts have to be measured, the nature of their interconnections is frequently not specified in advance. Quantitative research is far less driven by a hypothesis-testing strategy than is frequently supposed. As a result, the analysis of quantitative data from social surveys is often more exploratory than is generally appreciated and consequently offers opportunities for the generation of theories and concepts. As one American survey researcher has commented in relation to a large-scale survey he conducted in the 1950s, but which has much relevance today: 'There are so many questions which might be asked, so many correlations which can be run, so many ways in which the findings can be organized, and so few rules or precedents for making these choices that a thousand different studies could come out of the same data' (Davis 1964: 232).

The common depiction of quantitative research as solely an exercise in testing preformulated ideas fails to appreciate the degree to which findings frequently suggest new departures and theoretical contributions. Therefore, the suggestion that, unlike an interpretivist stance, quantitative research is concerned solely with the testing of ideas that have previously been formulated (such as hypotheses) fails to recognize the creative work that goes into the analysis of quantitative data and into the interpretation of findings. Equally, as noted above, qualitative research can be used in relation to the testing of theories (see Box 21.1 for an example).

Numbers versus words

Even perhaps this most basic element in the distinction between quantitative and qualitative research is not without problems. Qualitative researchers sometimes undertake a limited amount of quantification of their data. Silverman (1984, 1985) has argued that some quantification of findings from qualitative research can often help to uncover the generality of the phenomena being described. However, he warns that such quantification should reflect research participants' own ways of understanding their social world. Similarly, Miles and Huberman (1994), whose approach is commonly used in business and management research, recommend the use of a contact summary sheet as a means of recording themes that arise during a qualitative interview. Using the interview

Interviewee responses:	Frequency
'The role of the board of directors is to . . .'	
be involved in strategy	32
take responsibility for monitoring the health of the firm	20
hire, appraise, and fire executives	7
converse with shareholders/stakeholders	6
ensure corporate renewal	5
develop the corporate vision	5
take responsibility for developing an ethical framework	4
ensure corporate survival	3
determine risk position	3
lead strategic change	2
review social responsibilities	2
act as ambassadors for the firm	2
understand current and forthcoming legislation	1
TOTAL	92

Figure 21.1 A contact summary sheet to show interviewee interpretations of the role of boards of directors

Source: adapted from Stiles (2001).

transcript, the researcher categorizes interview responses by theme, eventually generating a single page summary of the interview. Not only does the contact summary sheet highlight the main concepts, themes, and issues, it also provides a record of their frequency of occurrence. Figure 21.1 illustrates an example of the contact summary sheet used by Stiles (2001) (this study is discussed in Chapter 22). This technique illustrates how qualitative interview data can be analysed in a way that involves a degree of quantification. In any case, it has often been noted that qualitative researchers engage in 'quasi-quantification' through the use of terms like 'many', 'often', and 'some' (see below). All that is happening is that the researcher is injecting greater precision into such estimates of frequency.

Artificial versus natural

The artificial/natural contrast referred to in Table 13.1 can similarly be criticized. It is often assumed that, because much quantitative research employs research instruments that are applied to the people being studied (questionnaires, structured interview schedules, structured observation schedules, and so on), it provides an artificial account of how the social world operates. Qualitative research is often viewed as more naturalistic (see Box 2.4 on naturalism). Ethnographic research in particular would seem to exhibit this quality, because the participant observer studies people in their normal social worlds and contexts—in other words, as they go about normal activities. However, when qualitative research is based on interviews (such as semi- and unstructured interviewing and focus groups), the depiction 'natural' is possibly less applicable. Interviews still have to be arranged and interviewees have to be taken away from activities that they would otherwise be engaged in, even when the interviewing style is of the more conversational kind. We know very little about interviewees' reactions to and feelings about being interviewed. Parker (2000), in describing his ethnographic role as a confidant (see Table 14.1), recounts a comment made by one of his interviewees: 'it's nice to have somebody to talk to and moan to you know. I try to talk to my wife like this but she doesn't listen' (2000: 237). While this interviewee clearly enjoyed being interviewed, it is likely that he was very conscious of the fact that he had been engaged in an interview rather than a conversation. The interview was clearly valuable in allowing this individual to express his concerns, but the point being made here is that the view that the methods associated with qualitative research are naturalistic is to exaggerate the contrast with the supposed artificiality of the research methods associated with quantitative research. Atkinson and Silverman (1997) have further suggested that qualitative researchers' obsession with the semi-structured interview as a naturalistic form of enquiry reflects a media-led societal trend towards confessional interviewing as a source of truth and meaning. They suggest that descriptive research of this nature is little different from chat shows or human interest journalism.

As noted in Chapter 16, focus group research is often described as more natural than qualitative interviewing because it emulates the way people discuss issues in real life. Natural groupings are often used to emphasize this element. However, whether this is how group participants view the nature of their participation is unclear. In particular, when it is borne in mind that people are sometimes strangers, have to travel to a site where the session takes place, are paid for their trouble, and frequently discuss topics they rarely if ever talk about, it is not hard to take the view that the naturalism of focus groups is assumed rather than demonstrated.

In participant observation, the researcher can be a source of interference that renders the research situation less natural than it might superficially appear to be. Whenever the ethnographer is in an overt role, a certain amount of reactivity is possible—even inevitable. It is difficult to estimate the degree to which the ethnographer represents an intrusive element that has an impact on what is found, but once again the naturalism of such research is often assumed rather than demonstrated, although it is admittedly likely that it will be less artificial than the methods associated with quantitative research. However, when the ethnographer also engages in interviewing (as opposed to casual conversations), the naturalistic quality is likely to be less pronounced.

These observations suggest that there are areas and examples of studies that lead us to question the degree to which the quantitative/qualitative contrast is a rigid one. Once again, this is not to suggest that the contrast is unhelpful, but that we should be wary of assuming that in writing and talking about quantitative and qualitative research we are referring to two absolutely divergent and inconsistent research strategies.

Reciprocal analysis

One further way in which the barriers between quantitative and qualitative research might be undermined is by virtue of developments in which each is used as an approach to analyse the other.

Qualitative analysis of quantitative data

There has been a growing interest in the examination of the writings of quantitative researchers using some of the methods associated with qualitative research. In part, this trend can be seen as an extension of the growth of interest among qualitative researchers in the writing of ethnography, which can be seen in such work as Van Maanen (1988) and Atkinson (1990). The attention to quantitative research is very much part of this trend because it reveals a concern in both cases with the notion that, not only does the written account of research constitute the presentation of findings but it is also an attempt to persuade the reader of the credibility of those findings. This is true of the natural sciences too; for example, in relation to the research by Gilbert and Mulkay (1984) mentioned earlier in this chapter, it was shown that scientists employed an empiricist repertoire when writing up their findings. This writing strategy was used to show how proper procedures were followed in a systematic and linear way. However, Gilbert and Mulkay demonstrated that, when the scientists discussed in interviews how they did their research, it is clear that the process was suffused with the influence of factors to do with their personal biographies.

One way in which a qualitative research approach to quantitative research is manifested is through what Gephart (1988: 9) has called *ethnostatistics*, by which is meant 'the study of the construction, interpretation, and display of statistics in quantitative social research'. Gephart shows that there are a number of ways in which the idea of ethnostatistics can be realized, but it is with just one of these—approaching statistics as rhetoric—that we will be concerned here. Directing attention to the idea of statistics as rhetoric means becoming sensitive to the ways in which statistical arguments are deployed to bestow credibility on research for target audiences. More specifically, this means examining the language used in persuading audiences about the validity of research. Indeed, the very use of statistics themselves can be regarded as a rhetorical device because the use of quantification means that business research can bestow upon itself the appearance of a natural science and thereby achieve greater legitimacy and credibility by virtue of that association (McCartney 1970; John 1992). Some of the rhetorical strategies identified by analysts are presented in Box 24.3. However, the chief point being made here is that the nature of quantitative research can be illuminated by being approached from the vantage point of qualitative research.

Quantitative analysis of qualitative data

In Chapter 9, the research by Hodson (1996), which was based on the content analysis of workplace ethnographies, was given quite a lot of attention (see Box 9.5). Essentially, Hodson's approach was to apply a quantitative research approach—in the form of content analysis—to qualitative research. This is a form of research that may have potential in other areas of business research in which ethnography has been a popular method and as a result a good deal of ethnographic evidence has been built up. Hodson (1999) suggests that the study of social movements may be one such field; managerial fads and fashions may be yet another. Hodson's research is treated as a solution to the problem of making comparisons between ethnographic studies in a given area. One approach to synthesizing related qualitative studies is *meta-ethnography*, which is a qualitative research approach to such aggregation (Noblit and Hare 1988). However, whereas the practice of meta-ethnography is meant to be broadly in line with the goals of qualitative research, such as a commitment to interpretivism and a sensitivity to the social context, Hodson's approach is one that largely ignores contextual factors in order to explore relationships between variables that have been abstracted out of the ethnographies.

Certain key issues need to be resolved when conducting analyses of the kind carried out by Hodson. One relates to the issue of conducting an exhaustive literature search for suitable studies for possible inclusion. Hodson chose to analyse just books, rather than articles, because of the limited amount of information that can usually be included in the latter. Even then, criteria for the inclusion of a book needed to be stipulated. Hodson employed three: 'The criteria for inclusion were (*a*) the book had to be based on ethnographic methods of observation over a period of at least 6 months, (*b*) the observations had to be in a single organization, and (*c*) the book had to focus on at least one clearly identified group of workers...' (Hodson 1999: 22). The application of these criteria resulted in the exclusion of 279 out of 365 books uncovered. A second crucial area relates to the coding of the studies, which was briefly covered in Box 9.5. Hodson stresses the importance of having considerable knowledge of the subject area, adopting clear coding rules, and pilot testing the coding schedule. In addition, he recommends checking the *reliability* of coding by having 10 per cent of the documents coded by two people. The process of coding was time-consuming, in that Hodson calculates that each book-length ethnography took forty or more hours to code.

The approach has many attractions, not the least of which is the impossibility of a quantitative researcher being able to conduct investigations in such a varied set of organizations. Also, it means that more data of much greater depth can be used than can typically be gathered by quantitative researchers. It also allows hypotheses deriving from established theories to be tested, such as the 'technological implications' approach, which sees technologies as having impacts on the experience of work (Hodson 1996). However, the loss of a sense of social context is likely to be unattractive to many qualitative researchers.

However, of particular significance for this discussion is the remark that 'the fundamental contribution of the systematic analysis of documentary accounts is that it creates an analytic link between the in-depth accounts of professional observers and the statistical methods of quantitative researchers' (Hodson 1999: 68). In other words, the application of quantitative methods to qualitative research may provide a meeting ground for the two research strategies.

Quantification in qualitative research

As noted in Chapter 13, the numbers versus words contrast is perhaps the most basic in many people's minds when they think about the differences between quantitative and qualitative research. After all, it seems to relate in a most fundamental way to the very terms used to denote the two approaches that seem to imply the presence and absence of numbers. However, it is simply not the case that there is a complete absence of quantification in qualitative research. As we will see in the next chapter, when qualitative researchers incorporate research methods associated with quantitative research into their investigations, a certain amount of quantification is injected into the research.

Quite aside from the issue of combining quantitative and qualitative research, three observations are worth making about quantification in the analysis and writing-up of qualitative data.

Thematic analysis

In Chapter 19, it was observed that one of the commonest approaches to qualitative data analysis is undertaking a search for themes in transcripts or field notes. However, as Bryman and Burgess (1994b: 224) point out, the criteria employed in the identification of themes are often unclear. One possible factor that these authors suggest may be in operation is the frequency of the occurrence of certain incidents, words, phrases, and so on that denote a theme. In other words, a theme is more likely to be identified the more times the phenomenon it denotes occurs in the course of coding. This process may also account for the prominence given to some themes over others when writing up the fruits of qualitative data analysis. In other words, a kind of implicit quantification may be in operation that influences the identification of themes and the elevation of some themes over others.

Quasi-quantification in qualitative research

It has often been noted that qualitative researchers engage in 'quasi-quantification' through the use of terms such as 'many', 'frequently', 'rarely', 'often', and 'some'. In order to be able to make such allusions to quantity, the qualitative researcher should have some idea of the relative frequency of the phenomena being referred to. However, as expressions of quantities, they are imprecise, and it is often difficult to discern why they are being used at all. The alternative would seem to be to engage in a limited amount of quantification when it is appropriate, such as when an expression of quantity can bolster an argument. This point leads directly on to the next section.

Combating anecdotalism through limited quantification

One of the criticisms that is often levelled against qualitative research is that the publications on which it is based are often anecdotal, giving the reader little guidance as to the prevalence of the issue to which the anecdote refers. The widespread use of brief sequences of conversation, snippets from interview transcripts, and accounts of encounters between people provides little sense of the prevalence of whatever such items of evidence are supposed to indicate. There is the related risk that a particularly striking statement by someone or an unexpected activity may have more significance attached to it than might be warranted in terms of its frequency.

Perhaps at least partly in response to these problems, qualitative researchers sometimes undertake a limited amount of quantification of their data. Numbers can be used to give a fairly straightforward indication of the scale of the research project. Casey (1995), for example, explains that she interviewed sixty people during the course of her ethnographic study. However, numbers can also be used to interpret the significance of qualitative data. For example, in their research on concepts of leadership employed by British police officers, Bryman, Stephens, and Campo (1996) counted the frequency with which certain leadership styles were cited in interview transcripts. This exercise allowed them to demonstrate that the kind of leadership preferred by police officers was different from what was in vogue among theorists of leadership at the time. Similarly, Gabriel (1998) describes how he studied organizational culture in a variety of organizations by collecting during interviews stories about the organizations in question. Computers and information technology were a particular focus of the stories elicited. Altogether 377 stories were collected in the course of 126 interviews in five organizations. Gabriel shows that the stories were of different types, such as: comic stories (which were usually a mechanism for disparagement of others); epic stories (survival against the odds); tragic stories (undeserved misfortune); gripes (personal injustices); and so on. He counted the number of each type: comic stories were the most numerous at 108; then epic stories (82); tragic stories (53); gripe stories (40); and so on. Themes in the stories were also counted, such as whether they involved a leader, a personal trauma, an accident, and so forth. In all these cases, the types of stories and the themes could have been treated in an anecdotal way, but the use of such simple counting conveys a clear sense of their relative prevalence.

Exercises like these can be used to counter the suggestion that is sometimes made that the approach to presenting qualitative data can be too anecdotal, so that readers are given too little sense of the *extent* to which certain beliefs are held or a certain form of behaviour occurs. All that is happening in such cases

is that the researcher is injecting greater precision into estimates of frequency than can be derived from quasi-quantification terms. Moreover, it is not inconceivable that there might be greater use of limited amounts of quantification in qualitative research in the future as a result of the use of Computer-Assisted Qualitative Data Analysis Software (CAQDAS). Most of the major software programs include a facility that allows the analyst to produce simple counts of such things as the frequency with which a word or a coded theme occurs. In many cases, they can also produce simple cross-tabulations—for example, relating the occurrence of a coded theme to gender. Writing when CAQDAS was used far less than it is today, Ragin and Becker (1989) concluded their review of the impact of microcomputers on sociologists' 'analytic habits' with the following remark: 'Thus, the microcomputer provides important technical means for new kinds of dialogues between ideas and evidence and, at the same time, provides a common technical ground for the meeting of qualitative and quantitative researchers' (1989: 54). Weaver and Atkinson (1994) further suggest that the introduction of CAQDAS may be bound up with attempts to make qualitative research more respectable within the scientific community and more acceptable to 'gatekeepers' of research—that is, funding bodies. The greater use of quantification by qualitative researchers may turn out to be one of the more significant areas for this 'meeting'.

K KEY POINTS

- There are differences between quantitative and qualitative research but it is important not to exaggerate them.

- The connections between epistemology and ontology, on the one hand, and research methods, on the other, are not deterministic.

- Qualitative research sometimes exhibits features normally associated with a natural science model.

- Quantitative research aims on occasions to engage with an interpretivist stance.

- Research methods are more autonomous in relation to epistemological commitments than is often appreciated.

- The artificial/natural contrast that is often an element in drawing a distinction between quantitative and qualitative research is frequently exaggerated.

- A quantitative research approach can be employed for the analysis of qualitative studies and a qualitative research approach can be employed to examine the rhetoric of quantitative researchers.

- Some qualitative researchers employ quantification in their work.

Q | QUESTIONS FOR REVIEW

The natural science model and qualitative research

- Are the natural sciences positivistic?

- To what extent can some qualitative research be deemed to exhibit the characteristics of a natural science model?

Quantitative research and interpretivism

- To what extent can some quantitative research be deemed to exhibit the characteristics of interpretivism?

Quantitative research and constructionism

- To what extent can some quantitative research be deemed to exhibit the characteristics of constructionism?

Epistemological and ontological considerations

- How far do research methods necessarily carry epistemological and ontological implications?

Problems with the quantitative/qualitative contrast

- Outline some of the ways in which the quantitative/qualitative contrast may not be as hard and fast as is often supposed.

Reciprocal analysis

- How have statistics been used to bestow credibility upon management and business research?

- How might Hodson's approach to the analysis of qualitative data be applied in business and management research?

Quantification in qualitative research

- How far is quantification a feature of qualitative research?

22

Combining quantitative and qualitative research

CHAPTER GUIDE

This chapter is concerned with multi-strategy research—that is, research that combines quantitative and qualitative research. While this may seem a straightforward way of resolving and breaking down the divide between the two research strategies, it is not without controversy. Moreover, there may be practical difficulties associated with multi-strategy research. This chapter explores:

- arguments against the combination of quantitative and qualitative research; two kinds of argument are distinguished and are referred to as the embedded methods and paradigm arguments;

- the suggestion that there are two versions of the debate about the possibility of combining quantitative and qualitative research: one that concentrates on methods of research and another that is concerned with epistemological issues;

- the different ways in which multi-strategy research has been carried out;

- the need to recognize that multi-strategy research is not inherently superior to research that employs a single research strategy.

Introduction

So far throughout the book an emphasis has been placed upon the strengths and weaknesses of the research methods associated with quantitative and qualitative research. One possible response to this kind of recognition is to propose combining them. After all, such a strategy would seem to allow the various strengths to be capitalized upon and the weaknesses offset somewhat. However, not all writers on research methods agree that such integration is either desirable or feasible. On the other hand, it is probably the case that the amount of combined research has been increasing since the early 1980s and in business and management research combined research is particularly popular. Therefore, in discussing the combination of quantitative and qualitative research, this chapter will be concerned with three main issues:

1. an examination of the arguments against integrating quantitative and qualitative research;

2. the different ways in which quantitative and qualitative research have been combined;

3. an assessment of combined research, which asks whether it is necessarily superior to investigations relying on just one research strategy and whether there are any additional problems deriving from it.

In this chapter, we will use the term *multi-strategy research*, which is borrowed from Layder (1993), as a simple shorthand to stand for research that integrates quantitative and qualitative research within a single project. Of course, there is research that, for example, combines structured interviewing with structured observation or ethnography with semi-structured interviewing. However, these instances of the combination of research methods are associated with just one research strategy. By multi-strategy research we are referring to research that combines research methods that cross the two research strategies.

The argument against multi-strategy research

The argument against multi-strategy research tends to be based on either and sometimes both of two kinds of argument:

- the idea that research methods carry epistemological commitments; and

- the idea that quantitative and qualitative research are separate *paradigms*.

These two arguments will now be briefly reviewed.

The embedded methods argument

This first position, which was outlined in Chapter 21, implies that research methods are ineluctably rooted in epistemological and ontological commitments. Such a view of research methods can be discerned in statements like the following:

every research tool or procedure is inextricably embedded in commitments to particular versions of the world and to knowing that world. To use a questionnaire, to use an attitude scale, to take the role of participant observer, to select a random sample, to measure rates of population growth, and so on, is to be involved in conceptions of the world which allow these instruments to be used for the purposes conceived.   (Hughes 1990: 11)

According to such a position, the decision to employ, for example, participant observation is not simply about how to go about data collection but a commitment to an epistemological position that is inimical to positivism and that is consistent with interpretivism.

This kind of view of research methods has led some writers to argue that multi-strategy research is not feasible or even desirable. An ethnographer may collect questionnaire data to gain information about a slice of social life that is not amenable to participant observation, but this does not represent an integration of quantitative and qualitative research, because the epistemological positions in which the two methods are grounded constitute irreconcilable views about how social reality should be studied. Smith (1983: 12, 13), for example, argues that each of the two research strategies 'sponsors different procedures and has different epistemological implications' and therefore counsels researchers not to 'accept the unfounded assumption that the methods are complementary'. Smith and Heshusius (1986) criticize the integration of research strategies, because it ignores the assumptions underlying research methods and transforms 'qualitative inquiry into a procedural variation of quantitative inquiry' (1986: 8).

The chief difficulty with the argument that writers like Smith present is that, as was noted in Chapter 21, the idea that research methods carry with them fixed epistemological and ontological implications is very difficult to sustain. They are capable of being put to a wide variety of tasks.

The paradigm argument

The paradigm argument was introduced in Chapter 1 in order to categorize some of the ontological and epistemological assumptions that are made in business research. It conceives of quantitative and qualitative research as *paradigms* (see Box 1.16) in which epistemological assumptions, values, and methods are inextricably intertwined and are incompatible between paradigms (e.g. Guba 1985; Morgan 1998*b*). Therefore, when researchers combine participant observation with a questionnaire, they are not really combining quantitative and qualitative research, since paradigms are incommensurable—that is, they are incompatible: the integration is only at a superficial level and within a single paradigm.

The problem with the paradigm argument is that it rests, as with the embedded methods argument, on contentions about the interconnectedness of method, and epistemology in particular, that cannot—in the case of business research—be demonstrated. Moreover, while Kuhn (1970) certainly argued that paradigms are incommensurable, it is by no means clear that quantitative and qualitative research are in fact paradigms. As suggested in Chapters 1 and 21, there are areas of overlap and commonality between them.

Two versions of the debate about quantitative and qualitative research

There would seem to be two different versions about the nature of quantitative and qualitative research, and these two different versions have implications in writers' minds about whether the two can be combined.

- An *epistemological version*, as in the embedded methods argument and the paradigm argument, sees quantitative and qualitative research as grounded in incompatible epistemological principles (and ontological ones too, but these tend not to be given as much attention). According to this version of their nature, multi-strategy research is not possible.

- A *technical version*, which is the position taken by most researchers whose work is mentioned in the

next section, gives greater prominence to the strengths of the data collection and data analysis techniques with which quantitative and qualitative research are each associated and sees these as capable of being fused. There is a recognition that quantitative and qualitative research are each connected with distinctive epistemological and ontological assumptions, but the connections are not viewed as fixed and ineluctable. Research methods are perceived, unlike in the epistemological version, as autonomous. A research method from one research strategy is viewed as capable of being pressed into the service of another. Indeed, in some instances, as will be seen in the next section, the notion that there is a 'leading' research strategy in a multi-strategy investigation may not even apply in some cases.

The technical version about the nature of quantitative and qualitative research essentially views the two research strategies as compatible. As a result, multi-strategy research becomes both feasible and desirable. It is in that spirit that we now turn to a discussion of the ways in which quantitative and qualitative research can be combined.

Approaches to multi-strategy research

This section will be structured in terms of a classification Bryman developed many years ago of the different ways in which multi-strategy research has been undertaken (Bryman 1988*a*, 1992). The classification has been changed slightly from the one presented in his earlier publications. Several other ways of classifying such investigations have been proposed by other authors, and two of these are presented in Boxes 22.1 and 22.2.

The logic of triangulation

The idea of triangulation has been previously encountered in Boxes 10.11 and 13.4. When applied to the present context, it implies that the results of an investigation employing a method associated with one research strategy are cross-checked against the results of using a method associated with the other research strategy. It is an adaptation of the argument by writers like Webb et al. (1966) that confidence in the findings deriving from a study using a quantitative research strategy can be enhanced by using more than one way of measuring a concept. For example, in their longitudinal study of culture in a governmental organization in the USA, Zamanou and Glaser (1994) collected different types of data in order to examine different aspects of organizational reality. By using survey, interview, and observational data, they were able to combine 'the specificity and accuracy of quantitative data with the ability to interpret idiosyncracies and complex perceptions, provided by qualitative analysis' (1994: 478). Ratings on the 190 questionnaires were combined with data from the interviews, 76 of which were conducted before and 94 after the introduction of a communication intervention program, which was designed to change the organizational culture. One of the researchers also became a participant observer in the organization for a period of two months. Zamanou and Glaser suggest that this triangulated approach enabled the collection of different types of data that related to different cultural elements, from values to material artefacts—something that other cultural researchers have found difficult to achieve.

As mentioned in Box 13.4, triangulation can also be associated with a quantitative strategy, as an approach to the development of multiple measures in order to improve confidence in findings (Webb et al. 1966); some writers have suggested that this kind of triangulation is declining in use. This can be

---

Box 22.1 Hammersley's classification of approaches to multi-strategy research

Hammersley (1996) has proposed three approaches to multi-strategy research.

- *Triangulation*. This refers to the use of quantitative research to corroborate qualitative research findings or vice versa.

- *Facilitation*. This approach arises when one research strategy is employed in order to aid research using the other research strategy.

- *Complementarity*. This approach occurs when the two research strategies are employed in order that different aspects of an investigation can be dovetailed.

Box 22.2   Morgan's classification of approaches to multi-strategy research

Morgan (1998*b*) has proposed four approaches to multi-strategy research. His classification is based on two criteria.

- *The priority decision.* How far is a qualitative or a quantitative method the principal data-gathering tool?

- *The sequence decision.* Which method precedes which? In other words, does the qualitative method precede the quantitative one or vice versa?

These criteria yield four possible types.

   This is an interesting approach to take, but the chief difficulty with this scheme is that it relies upon being able to identify both (*a*) that either quantitative or qualitative research had priority in research and (*b*) that one was

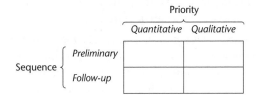

preliminary to the other. This is not necessarily possible in all cases. Boxes 22.4 and 22.6 provide examples of research projects that combined quantitative and qualitative research strategies through the use of several methods. However, no single method or research strategy was dominant.

---

demonstrated by reference to an article that has reviewed the methods used within business and management research. Scandura and Williams (2000) analysed all articles published in three top-ranking American journals, *Academy of Management Journal*, *Administrative Science Quarterly*, and the *Journal of Management* over two time periods, 1995–7 and 1985–7. They were particularly interested in tracing changing practice in triangulation of methods and use of different measures of validity. A total of 614 articles was coded for the primary research methodologies they employed. The research showed that, 'to publish in these three top-tier general management journals, researchers are increasingly employing research strategies and methodological approaches that compromise triangulation' (2000: 1259). A further finding indicated that internal, external, and construct validity had also declined during the period. They conclude that 'management research may be moving even further away from rigour', limiting the applicability of findings by failing to triangulate, using various designs in a programme of research in order to help counterbalance the strengths and weaknesses of each.

   Another illustration of a study that uses a triangulation approach is an investigation by Stiles (2001)

into the impact of boards of directors on corporate strategy. Stiles used a multi-method research design, which involved the following methods.

- *In-depth semi-structured interviews with fifty-one main board directors of UK public companies.* This was Stiles's primary means of collecting data. In order to develop a grounded understanding of board activities, he sought to allow directors 'to reveal their perceptions' (2001: 632). Pilot interviews, using a schedule based on analysis of existing literature, were carried out with five directors, and these were used to develop the final set of topics. Stiles also carried out a number of supplementary interviews with other stakeholders, these included a city journalist, a representative from the Consumers' Association, and a number of leading academics.

- *A questionnaire survey of 121 company secretaries.* Stiles's quantitative element in his research design relied on a questionnaire, which was sent to 900 members of the Institute of Company Secretaries and Administrators. This generated a response rate of 14 per cent. Had this been the main research method upon which the study relied, the low response rate would have called into question the external validity of the findings. However,

Stiles points out that questionnaire results are used 'to support the main findings, which emerged from the qualitative data and . . . are meant to be illustrative rather than definitive' (Stiles 2001: 633).

- *Four case studies of UK plcs, where several board members were interviewed, and secondary, archival data were collected.* Stiles chose four large UK businesses in which to test findings that emerged from data collected using his two preliminary research methods. The cases were chosen because they had strong reputations but had experienced periods of turbulence and change. Stiles claims that 'this buttressing of the original findings through testing in four different research sites affords a further element of triangulation into the study, with the new data from the case testing the validity and generality of the initial findings' (2001: 634). Validity was also improved through respondent validation (see Box 13.3), involving a draft of the findings being sent to the case companies on which individuals were invited to comment.

Stiles's main finding, that multiple perspectives are required in order to understand fully the nature of board activity, owes something to his research approach, which enabled exploration of the strategy-making role of the board and its multifunctional nature. In this research, the use of a triangulation strategy seems to have been planned by the researcher and the two sets of results were broadly consistent. However, researchers may carry out multi-strategy research for other purposes, but in the course of doing so discover that they have generated quantitative and qualitative findings on related issues, so that they can treat such overlapping findings as a triangulation exercise. Liff and Steward (2001) provide an example of unplanned triangulation, in that they gathered data about e-gateways through several quantitative and qualitative research methods (see Box 18.5), but they had not intended the photographs that were taken to be deployed as part of a triangulation exercise. However, their analysis of their data found location and physical layout of the gateways to be significant in reducing barriers to entry and in attracting Internet-users. The

photographs therefore provided an additional source of data through which the researchers were able to corroborate these findings.

Whether planned or unplanned, when a triangulation exercise is undertaken, the possibility of a failure to corroborate findings always exists. This raises the issue of what approach should be taken towards inconsistent results. One approach is to treat one set of results as definitive. However, simply and often arbitrarily favouring one set of findings over another is not an ideal approach to reconciling conflicting findings deriving from a triangulation exercise.

Qualitative research facilitates quantitative research

There are several ways in which qualitative research can be used to guide quantitative research.

- *Providing hypotheses.* Because of its tendency towards an unstructured, open-ended approach to data collection, qualitative research is often very helpful as a source of hypotheses or hunches that can be subsequently tested using a quantitative research strategy. An example is Prasad's study of computerization in a health-care organization (see Chapter 13). On the basis of her qualitative investigation, which relied on the methods of participant observation and in-depth semi-structured interviewing, Prasad suggests a number of hypotheses, or propositions, that can be drawn in relation to the impact of technological symbolism on organizational-level action. Although Prasad does not say that these should be tested using a quantitative research strategy, it is clear that some of them could form the basis for a quantitative, deductive research project.

- *Aiding measurement.* The in-depth knowledge of social contexts acquired through qualitative research can be used to inform the design of survey questions for structured interviewing and self-completion questionnaires. In their study of work relationships in telephone call centres, Deery, Iversen, and Walsch (2002) analysed data from a questionnaire survey of 480 telephone service operators in five call centre locations in Melbourne and Sydney, Australia. The questionnaire was constructed following 'site visits and extensive discussions with focus groups of employees and meetings with shop stewards, team leaders and call centre managers' (2002: 481), and this helped the researchers to develop their understanding of the possible negative effects of this kind of work on the psychological well-being of employees. This preliminary, qualitative stage of the research, and the fact that the survey was endorsed both by the company and the union, may have contributed towards the high overall survey response rate of 88 per cent, a further benefit gained from the multi-strategy research approach.

Quantitative research facilitates qualitative research

One of the chief ways in which quantitative research can prepare the ground for qualitative research is through the selection of people to be interviewed, or

companies to be selected as case studies. For example, Scase and Goffee (1989) used the results of their questionnaire survey of 374 UK managers (see Box 2.16) to generate a smaller, representative sample of eighty managers for in-depth interviews. Similarly, in the research by Storey et al. (2002) on flexible employment (see Box 22.3), the postal questionnaire survey of 2,700 companies provided a basis for selection of eight case-study firms where the survey data had suggested there was an association between innovation and flexible employment. The case studies were then explored using a qualitative research strategy based on in-depth semi-structured interviewing in order to investigate internal sources of knowledge and expertise within the organization.

Filling in the gaps

This approach to multi-strategy research occurs when the researcher cannot rely on either a quantitative

---

Box 22.3 Using quantitative research to facilitate qualitative research

In a study that examined the relationship between increasing use of 'flexible employment contracts' and the incidence of product and process innovations, Storey et al. (2002) describe their use of two complementary research methods: (*a*) a postal survey and (*b*) eight case studies.

In the postal survey of 2,700 companies, random sampling methods were used to select a representative cross-section of UK private-sector companies. Data collection in the case studies was used to help unpack some of the main findings from the survey. This second part of the research design relied on *theoretical sampling*; from the survey data the researchers identified instances of organizations where there was an association between high performance in innovation and various forms of flexible employment and outsourcing. They then approached these firms on the basis of their emerging theoretical focus and requested case-study access, in order to explore some of the processes and rationales surrounding innovation and flexible employment in greater detail.

The case-study part of the research then used in-depth semi-structured interviews, which were tape-recorded

and transcribed. Interviewees were selected on the basis of snowball sampling, by moving from initial contacts to colleagues who were identified as 'important to the research'. In several cases, the researchers also carried out interviews in supplier and customer organizations in order to investigate external sources of knowledge and expertise. In total, fifty-seven interviews were conducted. However Storey et al. do not explain how the decision to stop sampling was reached—that is, whether or not this was when theoretical saturation was achieved.

Findings from the large-scale survey suggest that in most firms the rhetoric of the strategic importance of innovation is not reflected by the proportion of resources devoted to it. Findings from both the survey and the case studies show that employers rarely use flexible working as a lever to achieve innovation; instead the two phenomena are relatively decoupled at an organizational level. They conclude that an increase in the use of flexible labour has occurred in parallel with the greater emphasis on innovation but that the pursuit of innovation has occurred independently of increased use of flexible employment contracts.

or a qualitative method alone and must buttress his or her findings with a method drawn from the other research strategy. Its most typical form is when ethnographers employ structured interviewing or possibly a self-completion questionnaire, because not everything they need to know about is accessible through participant observation. This kind of need can arise for several reasons, such as the need for information that is not accessible to observation or to qualitative interviewing (for example, systematic information about social backgrounds of people in a particular setting), or the difficulty of gaining access to certain groups of people. Equally, qualitative methods may be used to provide important contextual information that supplements the findings from a larger quantitative study. For example, Zamanou and Glaser (1994) used semi-structured interviews and participant observation in order to help interpret and place in context the results of statistical analyses of the Organizational Culture Scale (OCS), which formed the basis for their questionnaire survey of culture change in a government organization. They state:

the results of the OCS provided a quantitative description of the culture of the organization, but the study still lacked an exploration of the deeper, more subjective, and less observable layers of culture. Thus qualitative measures (i.e. interviews, observations) were combined with the questionnaire results to illustrate the quantitative findings and to provide an examination of the depth of the culture.   (1994: 479)

Static and processual features

One of the contrasts suggested by Table 13.1 is that, whereas quantitative research tends to bring out a static picture of social life, qualitative research is more processual. The term 'static' can easily be viewed in a rather negative light. In fact, it is very valuable on many occasions to uncover regularities, and it is often the identification of such regularities that allows a processual analysis to proceed. A multi-strategy research approach offers the prospect of being able to combine both elements.

For example, Zamanou and Glaser (1994) wanted to explore the impact of a communication intervention programme designed to change the culture of

a governmental organization from hierarchical and authoritarian to participative and involved. They argue that the study of organizational culture lends itself to a multi-strategy research approach because different methods can be used to capture different cultural elements and processes. In addition, as we mentioned in Chapter 13, a longitudinal research design can enable understanding of events over time and is therefore often used in the study of organizational change (see Box 13.6 for an example). The questionnaire survey used by Zamanou and Glaser provided a static picture of the organizational culture prior to the intervention (Time 1) and again after it had ended (Time 2). It was hypothesized that ratings on scales such as teamwork, morale, and involvement would be significantly higher after the intervention than before it. Interviews were then used to explore employees' perceptions of culture in more detail, asking them to describe cultural incidents, events, and stories that had helped to form their perceptions. However, it is not only qualitative research that can incorporate processual analysis. Quantitative diary study research by Stewart (1967) analysed the way in which 160 managers spent their time during a four-week period in order to discover similarities and differences in their use of time and the reasons for them (see Box 6.5). In focusing on managerial activity over a period of time this study provided a dynamic, rather than a static analysis of what managers actually do.

Research issues and participants' perspectives

Sometimes, researchers want to gather two kinds of data: qualitative data that will allow them to gain access to the perspectives of the people they are studying; and quantitative data that will allow them to explore specific issues in which they are interested. When this occurs, they are seeking to explore an area in both ways, so that they can both adopt an unstructured approach to data collection in which participants' meanings are the focus of attention and investigate a specific set of issues through the more structured approach of quantitative research. An example of this is Milkman's (1997) study of a General Motors car manufacturing plant in the USA, referred to in Chapter 14.

Milkman was interested in the nature of the labour process in the late twentieth century and whether new factory conditions were markedly different for car workers from the negative portrayals of such work in the 1950s and early 1960s (e.g. Blauner 1964). As such, she was interested in the meaning of industrial work. She employed semi-structured interviews and focus groups with car production workers to elicit data relevant to this aspect of her work. However, in addition she had some specific interests in a 'buyout' plan that the company's management introduced in the mid-1980s after it had initiated a variety of changes to work practices. The plan gave workers the opportunity to give up their jobs for a substantial cash payment. In 1988, Milkman carried out a questionnaire survey of workers who had taken up the company's buyout offer. These workers were surveyed again the following year and in 1991. The reason for the surveys was that Milkman had some very specific interests in the buyout scheme, such as reasons for taking the buyout, how they had fared since leaving General Motors, how they felt about their current employment, and differences between social groups (in particular, different ethnic groups) in current earnings relative to those at General Motors.

The problem of generality

As noted in Chapter 21, a problem that is often referred to by critics of qualitative research is that the tendency for findings to be presented in an anecdotal fashion is frequently frustrating, since we are given little sense of the relative importance of the themes identified. Silverman (1984, 1985) has argued that some quantification of findings from qualitative research can often help to uncover the generality of the phenomena being described.

In addition, the combined use of qualitative and quantitative research methods represents a common pattern in case-study research in business and management, used by researchers in order to enhance the generality of their findings. An illustration of this tendency is given in Box 22.4, where Kanter (1977) describes the diverse range of methods that she used

in her case study of a single organization, Indsco Supply Corporation. Even though the fieldwork was undertaken in just one company and the case constituted a focus of interest in its own right, Kanter claims that its findings are typical of other large corporations. However, it is more than coincidental that she makes this claim only after having accounted in some detail for the complex set of methods that were involved in her multi-strategy research design.

Other studies have attempted to counter the criticism of anecdotalism, which is levelled at qualitative research by introducing a quantitative aspect into their analysis. These include Bryman, Stephens, and A Campo's (1996) study of leadership in the British police force and Gabriel's study of organizational culture (Chapter 21), both of which calculate the frequency of themes in order to provide a sense of their relative importance. However, Silverman warns that such quantification should reflect research participants' own ways of understanding their social world. If this occurs, the quantification is more consistent with the goals of qualitative research.

Qualitative research may facilitate the interpretation of the relationship between variables

One of the problems that frequently confront quantitative researchers is how to explain relationships between variables. One strategy is to look for what is called an intervening variable, which is influenced by the independent variable but which in turn has an effect on the dependent variable. Thus, if we find a relationship between gender and small business ownership, we might propose that entrepreneurial attitude is one factor behind the relationship implying:

gender → entrepreneurial attitude → small business ownership.

This sequence implies that the variable gender has an impact on how an individual feels about taking on an entrepreneurial role and becoming committed to the ideals associated with it (for example, belief in economic self advancement, individualism, self-reliance, and a strong work ethic), which in turn has

---

Box 22.4 A multi-strategy case study

Kanter (1977) describes her research at Indsco as a 'case study of a single organization'. Kanter describes how, over a five-year period, she spent time as a consultant, participant-observer, and researcher at Indsco Supply Corporation. Her sources of data included:

- a postal questionnaire survey, taking 2–3 hours to complete, of 205 sales workers and managers out of a population of 350;

- semi-structured interviews with the first twenty women to enter the sales force;

- access to a survey of employees on attitudes towards promotion;

- content analysis of 100 performance appraisal forms;

- group discussions with employees—from managers to secretaries, recorded verbatim;

- participation in meetings;

- participant observation in training programmes;

- internal reports, memoranda, and public documents relating to personnel policies;

- conversations in offices, at social gatherings, or in people's homes.

Overall, Kanter suggests that she spent over 120 personal contact days on-site and the number of people with whom she held conversations at well over 120. A further 500 people participated in written surveys—the primary source of quantitative data used in the study. Kanter draws attention to the potential for *generalizability* from a single case, by suggesting that 'the case provided material out of which to generate the concepts and flesh for giving meaning to the abstract propositions I was developing' (1977: 332).

Although Kanter does not claim statistical generalizability for her data, she does draw attention to the way that she used the data from the case to generate concepts that could be transferred to other organizational contexts. Hence she states that, after having formulated her initial impressions about Indsco, she had conversations with informants in three other large corporations 'in order to satisfy myself that Indsco . . . was not particularly unique in the relationships I observed. I learned that Indsco, indeed, was typical, and its story could be that of many large corporations' (1977: 332).

---

implications for the kinds of choices they make within the labour market. However, an alternative approach might be to seek to explore the relationship between the variables further by conducting a qualitative investigation of the ways in which entrepreneurial work is situated within gendered processes that are embedded within society (Mirchandani 1999). This would involve challenging the sequence of these variables, drawing attention to the gendered nature of entrepreneurial values.

Truss (2001) argues that more qualitative research is needed in order to increase our understanding of the link between HRM and organizational performance (see Box 22.5). She suggests many existing studies rely on a single informant in each organization and focus on financial performance, rather than on a broader range of outcome variables. In contrast, adopting a multi-strategy longitudinal research design, Truss was able to explain how Hewlett-Packard's

people management philosophy, known as 'The HP Way', was translated into policies by the HR function.

The questionnaire data enabled comparison with other companies, showing, for example, that employees were significantly more positive regarding the effectiveness of recruitment at HP. Overall, employees received more training and development than in the other high-performance companies and appraisals were regularly conducted. However, once the researchers attempted to probe beneath the surface, it emerged that, 'The HP Way' was open to quite different interpretations. For example, during the first wave of data collection it was found that, prior to the redundancies in the 1980s, employees had believed that 'The HP Way' meant they would have 'jobs for life'. It was also found that the move towards flexible working was having an adverse effect on staff loyalty. In terms of recruitment and selection, the strength of corporate values expressed in

Box 22.5 A multi-strategy approach to the study of HRM and performance

In her research on the relationship between human resource management and performance at Hewlett-Packard, Truss (2001) used a triangulated approach in order to overcome the limitations of research on this topic, which has tended to rely heavily on quantitative methods. She also incorporated a longitudinal element into the research design, by collecting data at two points in time, once in 1994 and again in 1996. Four principal research methods were used on each occasion:

- questionnaires—400 distributed to a random sample of employees at middle-manager level and below, generating a response rate of 56 per cent in 1994 and 52 per cent in 1996; in order to provide an indicative point of comparison with the questionnaire data, Truss also makes reference to data that were collected from six other high-performance organizations at the same

time and using the same questionnaire instrument, as part of a larger study with which she was involved;

- focus groups—with senior members of the HR department;
- semi-structured interviews—with employees from all levels of the firm;
- secondary data—from documents on topics such as recruitment and selection, training, career management, appraisal and reward from within the organization.

This approach results in the generation of an extremely in-depth case study from which it is possible to explore 'not only the "rhetoric" of what the HR group was trying to achieve, but also the reality experienced by employees' (Truss 2001: 1128).

'The HP Way' had given rise to a rather narrow view of the HP employee and individuals who did not fit this profile were unlikely to survive within the company. These findings suggest that changes in the company's environment, which was becoming increasingly competitive and hostile, were having a negative effect on HRM. In conclusion, the research provides only limited support for the view that effective HRM is the key to achieving sustained competitive advantage, instead suggesting that environmental events and conditions play a significant part. Finally, Truss concludes that these findings are the direct result of the qualitative aspect of the study:

Had we relied on questionnaire data obtained from a single informant (the HR director, as in other studies) and carried out a quantitative analysis linking performance with human resource processes, we would have concluded that this organization was an example of an organization employing 'High Performance Work Practices' to good effect. However, employing a contextualized, case-study method has enabled us to see below the surface and tap into the reality experienced by employees, which often contrasts sharply with the company rhetoric.   (Truss 2001: 1145)

The quantitative research results could thus be seen as somewhat misleading, in that they reflect the

organization's rhetorical position, rather than the reality experienced by employees. Truss is suggesting that the latter would not have been exposed without the addition of qualitative methods of investigation.

Studying different aspects of a phenomenon

This category of multi-strategy research incorporates two forms Bryman has referred to in earlier work as 'the relationship between "macro" and "micro" levels' and 'stages in the research process', but provides a more general formulation (Bryman 1988a: 147–51). The former draws attention to the tendency to think of quantitative research as most suited to the investigation of 'macro' phenomena (such as social mobility) and qualitative research as better suited to 'micro' ones (such as small group interaction).

In the example shown in Box 22.6, Wajcman and Martin (2002) used quantitative methods in the form of a questionnaire survey to explore the career patterns of male and female managers. However, they also carried out qualitative, semi-structured interviews to explore the way that managers made sense

---

Box 22.6 Combining survey research and qualitative interviewing in a study of managers

Wajcman and Martin (2002) conducted survey research using a questionnaire on male and female managers (470 in total) in six Australian companies. The authors were interested in career orientations and attitudes. They also conducted semi-structured interviews with 136 managers in each company. The survey evidence showed that male and female managers were generally more similar than different in terms of most variables. Thus, contrary to what many people might have anticipated, women's career experiences and orientations were *not* distinctive. They then examined the qualitative interviews in terms of narratives of identity. Wajcman and Martin found that both male and female managers depicted their careers in 'market' terms

(as needing to respond to the requirements of the managerial labour market to develop their skills, experience, and hence career). *But*, whereas, for men, narratives of career meshed seamlessly with narratives of domestic life, for women there was a disjuncture. Female managers found it much harder to reconcile managerial identities with domestic ones. They needed to opt for one. Thus, choices about career and family are still gendered. This research shows how a multi-strategy research approach was able to reveal much more than could have been gleaned through one approach alone by collecting evidence on both career patterns and expectations and identities using research methods suited to each issue area.

---

of their career patterns in terms of their identity; their choice of methods was therefore determined by the particular aspect of career orientation they were interested in.

Table 13.1 also illustrates this distinction. The category 'stages in the research process' draws attention to the possibility that quantitative and qualitative research may be suited to different phases in a study. However, it now seems to us that these are simply aspects of a more general tendency for quantitative and qualitative researchers to examine different aspects of their area of interest.

A further illustration of the use of multi-strategy research to explore different aspects of a phenomenon can be found in a study of how people use their time at work conducted by Perlow (1997, 1999), which was previously encountered in Chapter 13 and Box 14.1. Although this study mainly comprised ethnographic methods, which included participant observation and semi-structured interviewing, Perlow also used a time-use diary (see Chapter 6) similar to the one used by Stewart (1967; see Box 6.5), to record and measure quantitatively the time that software engineers spent on various activities each day. She explains:

On randomly chosen days, I asked three or four of the twelve software engineers to track their activities from when they woke up until they went to bed. I asked them to

wear a digital watch that beeped on the hour and, at each beep, to write down everything that they had done during the previous hour. I encouraged them to write down interactions as they occurred and to use the beeps as an extra reminder to keep track of their activities.   (Perlow 1999: 61)

The ethnographic methods were intended to capture the cultural norms and values held by the software engineers, while the time-use diary was specifically directed towards measurement of their time use. Using this combined approach, Perlow was able to build up a picture of *how* the engineers use their work time (using a quantitative strategy) and an understanding of *why* they use their work time in this way (using qualitative methods). In this study, multi-strategy research was geared to addressing different kinds of research question. After each tracking log had been completed, Perlow conducted a debriefing interview with each engineer, who explained the patterns of interaction recorded on the log sheets. From this Perlow was able to calculate the total time the engineer spent at work and the proportion of that time spent on interactive versus individual activities. Perlow found that, although 60 per cent of the engineers' time was spent on individual activities, and just over 30 per cent was spent on interactive activities, the time spent alone did not occur in one consecutive block.

Rather, examination of the sequences of individual and interactive activities revealed that a large proportion of the time spent uninterrupted on individual activities was spent in very short blocks of time, sandwiched between interactive activities. Seventy-five percent of the blocks of time spent uninterrupted on individual activities were one hour or less in length, and, of those blocks of time, 60 percent were half an hour or less in length.   (1999: 64)

This finding forms the basis for the theoretical conclusions that Perlow is able to draw, in relation to the crisis mentality induced by the engineers, work patterns and the heroic acts that this culture encourages and rewards. In her analysis she is able to illustrate these themes through presentation of the ethnographic research data. However, it is the *quantitative* analysis of time use that provides the initial impetus for the theoretical conclusions that Perlow is able to draw.

This form of multi-strategy research entails making decisions about which kinds of research question are best answered using a quantitative research method and which by a qualitative research method and about how best to interweave the different elements, especially since, as suggested in the context of the discussion about triangulation, the outcomes of mixtures of methods are not always predictable.

Solving a puzzle

The outcomes of research are, as suggested by the last sentence, not always easy to anticipate. Although people sometimes cynically suggest that social scientists find what they want to find or that social scientists just convey the obvious, the capacity of the obvious to provide us with puzzling surprises should never be underestimated. When this occurs, employing a research method associated with the research strategy not initially used can be helpful. One context in which this might occur is when qualitative research is used as a salvage operation, when an anticipated set of results from a quantitative investigation fails to materialize (Weinholtz, Kacer, and Rocklin 1995). Box 22.7 provides an interesting illustration of this use of multi-strategy research. Another situation arises when questionnaire response rates are too low to be used as the sole data source upon which to base findings. Stiles (2001; see Chapter 21), for example, generated only a 14 per cent response rate from the 900 questionnaires that were sent to members of the Institute of Company Secretaries and Administrators. Interview and case-study data provided him with alternative data sources upon which to focus.

Like unplanned triangulation, this category of multi-strategy research is more or less impossible to plan for. It essentially provides the quantitative researcher with an alternative either to reconstructing a hypothesis or to filing the results away (and probably never looking at them again) when findings are inconsistent with a hypothesis. It is probably not an option in all cases in which a hypothesis is not confirmed. There may also be instances in which a quantitative study could shed light on puzzling findings drawn from a qualitative investigation.

Reflections on multi-strategy research

There can be little doubt that multi-strategy research is becoming far more common than when one of us first started writing about it (Bryman 1988a). Two particularly significant factors in prompting this development are:

1. a growing preparedness to think of research methods as techniques of data collection or analysis that are not as encumbered by epistemological and ontological baggage as is sometimes supposed; and

2. a softening in the attitude towards quantitative research among feminist researchers, who had previously been highly resistant to its use (see Chapter 13 for a discussion of this point).

Other factors are doubtlessly relevant, but these two developments do seem especially significant. Yet lingering unease among some practitioners of qualitative research, particularly regarding issues to do with reliability and generalizability of findings, has led to

Box 22.7 Using multi-strategy research to solve a puzzle: the case of displayed emotions in convenience stores

An example of combining quantitative and qualitative research to solve a puzzle is Sutton and Rafaeli's (1988) study of the display of emotions in organizations. Following a traditional quantitative research strategy, based on their examination of studies like Hochschild (1983), Sutton and Rafaeli formulated a hypothesis suggesting a positive relationship between the display of positive emotions to retail shoppers (smiling, friendly greeting, eye contact) and the level of retail sales. In other words, we would expect that, when retail staff are friendly and give time to shoppers, sales will be better than when they fail to do so. Sutton and Rafaeli had access to data that allowed this hypothesis to be tested. The data derived from a study of 576 convenience stores in a national retail chain in the USA.

Structured observation of retail workers provided the data on the display of positive emotions, and sales data provided information for the other variable. The hypothesis implied that there would be a positive relationship—that is, that stores in which there was a more pronounced display of positive emotions would report superior sales. When the data were analysed, a relationship was confirmed, but it was found to be negative; that is, stores in which retail workers were *less* inclined to smile, be friendly, and so on tended to have better sales than those in which such emotions were in evidence. This was the reverse of what the authors had anticipated they would uncover. Sutton and Rafaeli (1992: 124) considered restating their hypothesis to make it seem that they had found what they had expected, but fortunately resisted the temptation!

Instead, they conducted a qualitative investigation of four case-study stores to help understand what was happening. This involved a number of methods: unstructured observation of interactions between staff and customers; semi-structured interviews with store managers; brief periods of participant observation; casual conversations with store managers, supervisors, executives, and others; and data gathered through posing as a customer in stores. The stores were chosen in terms of two criteria: high or low sales and whether staff typically displayed positive emotions. The qualitative investigation suggested that the relationship between the display of positive emotions and sales *was* negative, but that sales were likely to be a cause rather than a consequence of the display of emotions. This pattern occurred because, in stores with high levels of sales, staff were under greater pressure and encountered longer queues at checkouts. Staff therefore had less time and inclination for the pleasantries associated with the display of positive emotions. The quantitative data were then reanalysed with this alternative interpretation in mind and it was supported.

Thus, instead of the causal sequence being

display of positive emotions $\rightarrow$ retail sales

it was

retail sales $\rightarrow$ display of positive emotions.

This exercise also highlights the main difficulty associated with inferring causal direction from a cross-sectional research design (see Box 2.13 and Figure 2.2).

some calls for a consideration of the possible use of quantitative research in tandem with qualitative methods (e.g. Schrøder 1999). However, it is important to realize that multi-strategy research is not intrinsically superior to mono-method or mono-strategy research. It is tempting to think that multi-strategy research is more or less inevitably superior to research that relies on a single method on the grounds that more and more varied findings are inevitably 'a good thing'. However, four points must be borne in mind.

1. Multi-strategy research, like mono-method research, must be competently designed and conducted. Poorly conducted research will yield suspect findings no matter how many methods are employed.

2. Just like mono-method or mono-strategy research, multi-strategy research must be appropriate to the research questions or research area with which you are concerned. There is no point collecting more data simply on the basis that 'more is better'. Multi-strategy research has to be

dovetailed to research questions, just as all research methods must be. It is, after all, likely to consume considerably more time and financial resources than research relying on just one method.

3. Any research project has limited resources. Employing multi-strategy research may dilute the research effort in any area, since resources would need to be spread.

4. By no means all researchers have the skills and training to carry out both quantitative and qualitative research, so that their 'trained incapacities' may act as a barrier to integration (Reiss 1968: 351). However, there is a growing recognition of the potential of multi-strategy research, so that this point probably carries less weight than it did when Reiss was writing.

In other words, multi-strategy research should not be considered as an approach that is universally applicable or as a panacea. It may provide a better understanding of a phenomenon than if just one method had been used. It may also frequently enhance our confidence in our own or others' findings—for example, when a triangulation exercise has been conducted. It may even improve our chances of access to settings to which we might otherwise be excluded; Milkman (1997: 192), for example, has suggested in the context of her research on a General Motors factory that the promise that she 'would produce "hard", quantitative data through survey research was what secured [her] access', even though she had no experience in this method. But the general point remains, that multi-strategy research, while offering great potential in many instances, is subject to similar constraints and considerations as research relying on a single method or research strategy.

K KEY POINTS

- While there has been a growth in the amount of multi-strategy research, not all writers support its use.

- Objections to multi-strategy research tend to be the result of a view that there are epistemological and ontological impediments to the combination of quantitative and qualitative research.

- There are several different ways of combining quantitative and qualitative research and of representing multi-strategy research.

- The outcomes of combining quantitative and qualitative research can be planned or unplanned.

Q QUESTIONS FOR REVIEW

- What is multi-strategy research?

The argument against multi-strategy research

- What are the main elements of the embedded methods and paradigm arguments in terms of their implications for the possibility of multi-strategy research?

Two versions of the debate about quantitative and qualitative research

• What are the main elements of the technical and epistemological versions of the debate about quantitative and qualitative research? What are the implications of these two versions of the debate for multi-strategy research?

Approaches to multi-strategy research

• What are the main differences between Hammersley's and Morgan's classifications of multi-strategy research?

• What are the chief ways in which quantitative and qualitative research have been combined?

• What is the logic of triangulation?

• Traditionally, qualitative research has been depicted as having a preparatory role in relation to quantitative research. To what extent do the different forms of multi-strategy research reflect this view?

Reflections on multi-strategy research

• Why has multi-strategy research become more prominent?

• Is multi-strategy research necessarily superior to single strategy research?

23 Using the Internet as object and method of data collection

CHAPTER GUIDE

This chapter is concerned with the ways in which the Internet can be used in research. Most readers will be familiar with using the Internet as a means of searching for material on companies or on topics for essays and various other uses. It can be very valuable for such purposes, but this kind of activity is not the focus of this chapter. Instead, we are concerned with the ways in which Internet web sites can be used as objects of analysis in their own right and with the ways that the Internet can be used as a means of collecting data, much like the post and the telephone.

Introduction

There can be little doubting that the Internet and on-line communication have proliferated since the early 1990s and it would be surprising if this boom did not have implications for business research methods. In May 2001 *The Times* reported that the number of households using the Internet had increased to ten million from six million in the previous year. Use of the Internet is particularly high among university students, many of whom have been brought up with technology and for whom it is a very natural medium. A survey of Internet use among American college students found particularly high rates of use in comparison with the population at large, with 86 per cent of students being compared with 59 per cent of the population (Jones 2002). Nearly 80 per cent of university students felt that the Internet had had a positive impact on their college experience. The situation in the UK is likely to be similar to that found in the USA.

Given this background, it is plausible that many students will be drawn to the Internet as an environment within which to conduct business research. The Internet offers several opportunities in this regard and in this chapter we will focus upon:

• World Wide Web sites or pages as objects of analysis;

• ethnographic study of the Internet;

• qualitative research using online focus groups;

• qualitative research using online personal interviews;

• online social surveys.

The ongoing and burgeoning nature of the Internet and online communication makes it difficult to characterize this field and its impact on business research and its conduct in any straightforward

and simple way. In this chapter, we will be concerned with the following areas of e-research:

1. World Wide Web sites or pages as objects of analysis;

2. using the World Wide Web or online communications as a means of collecting data from individuals and organizations.

In addition, we will address some of the broader implications and ramifications of the Internet for conducting business research.

While the choice of these two areas of online research and their classification is rather arbitrary and tend to shade into each other somewhat, they provide the basis for a reasonably comprehensive overview in the face of a highly fluid field. This chapter does not consider the use of the Internet as an information resource or as a means of finding references. Some suggestions about the latter can be found in Chapter 26. The Internet is a vast information resource and has too many possible forms to be covered in a single chapter. Moreover, we advise caution about the use of such materials; while the Internet is a cornucopia of data and advice, it also contains a great deal of misleading and downright incorrect information. Healthy scepticism should guide your searches.

World Wide Web sites or pages as objects of analysis

Web sites and web pages are potential sources of data in their own right and can be regarded as potential fodder for both quantitative and qualitative content analysis of the kind discussed in Chapters 9 and 18. Indeed, in the latter chapter, there is a section on 'virtual outputs' that draws attention to web sites as a form of document. Aldridge (1998), for example, examined both written consumer guides to personal finance published in the UK and several Internet web sites. Through an analysis of such documents Aldridge extracted a number of themes that he saw as part of the 'promotional culture' in which we live. Examples of such themes are:

1. the necessity for members of the public to assume responsibility for their personal finances,

particularly in the light of the reductions in welfare provision; and

2. the depiction of the professional–client relationship as unthreatening and relatedly as one in which the client might legitimately ask informed questions.

However, there are clearly difficulties with using web sites as sources of data in this way. Four issues were mentioned in Chapter 18. In addition to the issues raised there, the following additional observations are worth considering:

• You will need to find the web sites relating to your research questions. This is likely to mean trawling the Web using a search engine of the kind used by Ho et al. (see Box 23.1). As these authors point out,

Box 23.1 Conducting an analysis of web sites

Ho, Baber, and Khondker (2002) were interested in 'alternative web sites' in Singapore against the backcloth of a country whose government has been concerned to facilitate the spread of online access as a means of building a knowledge-based economy capable of participating fully in a global economic order. The Singapore government is depicted as concerned to create a knowledge-based workforce with the skills and mindset capable of responding to and capitalizing upon the diffusion of new technologies. Alternative web sites are in a sense a paradox, because they have been facilitated by the spread of Internet access but at the same time challenge the status quo. Ho et al. chose to emphasize web sites concerned with politics, religion, and alternative sexuality. The research was conducted over a four-month period and employed five search engines (Yahoo, Alta Vista, Google, Infoseek, and Webcrawler) to trawl for suitable sites. The team of researchers used for each web site a two-page report sheet to record information about:

(a) web-content in the form of 'alternative culture', via recourse to complaints, criticisms, promotion of alternative values, practices and lifestyles; (b) the target audience: whether the site targets its own community or 'outsiders'; and (c) website characteristics which included guest book entries, links, sponsors, interactive functions, and evidence of Web-rings (clusters of inter-linked sites representing a general theme).   (2002: 135)

On the basis of their analyses, the authors proceeded to classify the different types of alternative web site. For example, some were concerned with civil rights and used the Singapore constitution or general civil-rights issues as the basis for advancing their position. Another type was made up of web sites that sought to reduce or even purge censorship. Thus, while the Internet is often associated with technologies of surveillance and control, it also contains spaces in which surveillance and control can be resisted.

---

any search engine provides access to only a portion of the Web and there is evidence, which they cite, that even the combined use of several search engines will allow access to only just under a half of the total population of web sites. While this means that the use of several search engines is highly desirable when seeking out appropriate web sites, it has to be recognized that not only will they allow access to a just a portion of the available web sites but also they may be a biased sample.

• Related to this point, seeking out web sites on a topic can only be as good as the keywords that are employed in the search process. The researcher has to be very patient to try as many relevant keywords as possible (and combinations of them—known as Boolean searches) and may be advised to ask other people (librarians, supervisors, etc.) to advise on whether the most appropriate ones are being used.

• New web sites are continually appearing and others disappearing. Researchers basing their investigations on web sites need to recognize that their analyses may be based on web sites that no longer

Practical tip: ☞ referring to web sites

There is a growing practice in academic work that, when referring to web sites, you should include the date you consulted them. This convention is very much associated with the fact that web sites often disappear and frequently change, so that, if subsequent researchers want to follow up your findings, or even to check on them, they may find that they are no longer there or that they have changed. Citing the date you consulted the web site may help to relieve any anxieties about someone not finding a web site you have referred to or finding it has changed. This does mean, however, that you will have to keep a running record of the dates you consulted the web sites to which you refer.

exist and that new ones may have appeared since data collection was terminated.

- Web sites are also continually changing, so that an analysis may be based upon at least some web sites that have been quite considerably updated.

Most researchers who use documents as the basis for their work have to confront the issue that it is difficult to determine the universe or population from which they are sampling. Therefore, the problems identified here and in Chapter 18 are not entirely unique to web sites. However, the rapid growth and speed of change in the Web accentuate these kinds of problems for business researchers, who are likely to feel that the experience is like trying to hit a target that not only continually moves but is in a constant state of metamorphosis. The crucial issue is to be sensitive to the limitations of the use of web sites as material that can be content analysed, as well as to the opportunities they offer. Employing both printed and web-site materials, as Aldridge (1998) did, has the potential to bring out interesting contrasts in such sources and can also provide the basis for cross-validating sources.

In addition, it is important to bear in mind the four quality criteria recommended by John Scott (1990) in connection with documents (see Chapter 18). Scott's suggestions invite us to consider quite why a web site is constructed. Why is it there at all? Is it there for commercial reasons? Does it have an axe to grind? In other words, we should be no less sceptical about web sites than about any other kind of document.

Using web sites to collect data from individuals

In this section, we examine research methods that entail the use of either the Web or online communications, such as e-mail, as a platform for collecting data from individuals. At the time of writing, the bulk of the discussion concerned with this issue has emphasized four main areas:

1. ethnography of the Internet;
2. qualitative research using online focus groups;
3. qualitative research using online personal interviews;
4. online social surveys.

These types of Internet-based research method do not exhaust the full range of possibilities but they do represent recurring emphases in the emerging literature on this subject. All of them offer certain advantages over their traditional counterparts because:

- they are usually more economical in terms of time and money;
- they can reach large numbers of people very easily;
- distance is no problem, since the research participant need only be accessible by computer—it does not matter whether he or she is in the same building or across the world;
- data can be collected and collated very quickly.

The chief general disadvantages tend to revolve around the following issues:

- Access to the Internet is still nowhere near universal, so that certain people are likely to be inaccessible.
- Invitations to take part in research may be viewed as just another nuisance e-mail.
- There is loss of the personal touch owing to lack of rapport between interviewer and interviewee, inability to pick up visual or auditory cues.
- There are concerns among research participants about confidentiality of replies at a time of widespread anxiety about fraud and hackers.

More specific balance sheets of advantages and disadvantages relating to some of the individual e-research methods will be covered below.

There are two crucial distinctions that should be borne in mind when examining Internet-based research methods.

1. There is a distinction between *web-based* and *communication-based* methods. The former is a research method whereby data are collected through the Web—for example, a questionnaire that forms a web page and that the respondent then completes. A communication-based research method is one where e-mail or a similar communication medium is the platform from which the data collection instrument is launched.

2. There is a distinction between *synchronous* and *asynchronous* methods of data collection. The former occur in real time. An example would be an interview in which an online interviewer asks a question and the respondent, who is also online, replies immediately, as in a chat room. An asynchronous method is not in real time so that there is no immediate response from the respondent, who is unlikely to be on online at the same time as the interviewer (or, if the respondent is on online, he or she is extremely unlikely to be in a position to reply immediately). An example would be an interview question posed by the interviewer in an e-mail that is opened and answered by the respondent some time later, perhaps days or weeks later.

With these distinctions in mind we can now move on to examine the four main forms of online research methods previously identified.

An ethnography of the Internet?

Ethnography may not seem to be an obvious method for collecting data on Internet use. The image of the ethnographer is that of someone who visits places or locations, and particularly in the context of business research—organizations. The Internet seems to go against the grain of ethnography, in that it seems a decidedly placeless space. In fact, as Hine (2000) has observed, conceiving of the Internet as a place—a cyberspace—has been one strategy for an ethnographic study of the Internet and from this it is just a short journey to the examination of communities in the form of online communities or virtual communities. In this way, our concepts of place and space that are constitutive of the way in which we operate in the real world are grafted onto the Internet and its use. A further issue is that, as noted in Chapter 14, ethnography entails participant observation, but in cyberspace what is the ethnographer observing and in what is he or she participating?

Markham's (1998) approach to an ethnography of life on the Net involved interviews. The interviews followed a period of 'lurking' (reading but not participating) in computer-mediated communication forums like chat rooms and multi-user domains (MUDS). The interviews allowed synchronous questioning and answering; in other words, the asking and answering of questions were in real time, rather than the kind of questioning and answering that might occur via e-mail, where a question might be answered several hours or days later. She used an interview guide and the interviews lasted between one hour and over four hours. Such interviews are a very real challenge for both interviewer and interviewee, because neither party can pick up on visual cues (for example, puzzlement, anxiety) or auditory cues (sighs, groans).

One of Markham's interests lay in the reality or otherwise of online experiences. This can be seen in the following brief online interview sequence (Markham is Annette):

ANNETTE: 'How real are your experiences in the Internet?'

SHERIE: 'How real are experiences off the internet?' (Markham 1998: 115)

In fact, Markham notes how her notion of 'real' was different from that of her interviewees. For Markham 'real' or 'in real life' carried a connotation of genuiness or authenticity, but for her interviewees it was more to do with distinguishing experiences that occur offline. Indeed, Markham increasingly felt that her interviewees were questioning the validity of the dichotomous distinction between the real and the non-real, so far as online interaction was concerned. However, it is likely that these distinctions between life online and life offline will become less significant as younger people who are growing up with the Internet conduct large portions of their lives online. This development would have considerable implications for business researchers, since for many research participants the online world may become very naturalistic.

An interesting question about this research is—in what sense is it an ethnography? At one level, Markham was simply an interviewer who used a semi-structured interview guide to elicit information and the worldview of her correspondents. At another level, she was indeed a participant in and observer of life online, although the life that she was participating in and observing was very much a product of her promptings, no matter how open the questions she asked and no matter how willing she was to allow her interviewees leeway in what they wanted to discuss. In much the same way that her interviewees were questioning the nature of reality, Markham's investigation invites us to question the nature of ethnography so far as research on the Internet is concerned.

Kendall (1999) was probably closer to the traditional concept of the ethnographer in that she describes her research as comprising three years of online participant observation in a MUD, as well as face-to-face interviews and attendance at face-to-face gatherings. Such research is probably closer to the conventional

notion of ethnographic research in its use of several methods of data collection and a sense of participation in the lives of those being studied, as well as interviewing them.

A further example of the use of ethnography in relation to the study of online worlds can be found in Box 23.2, which shows how the study of online discussion groups can be revealing about enthusiasms in our era of consumerism and brands.

Miller and Slater's (2000) ethnography of Internet use takes an approach that is rather more redolent of traditional ethnography than Markham's (see Box 23.3). Its location in a particular place (Trinidad), its use of several methods of gathering data, and its commitment to observation (for example, in cyber-cafés) are probably for many people closer to the traditional meanings of ethnography. As the authors put it: 'For us an ethnography does include participating, which may mean going on a chat line for the eight hours that informants will remain online, or participating in a room full of people playing networked Quake . . .' (Miller and Slater 2000: 22).

One of Miller and Slater's chief interests lay in the state of e-commerce in Trinidad. They found a situation in which there was considerable uncertainty at the time about how far to get into this business medium. There was recognition that the Internet

---

Box 23.2 Netnography

Kozinets (2002) has coined the term 'netnography' to refer to a marketing research method that investigates computer-mediated communications in connection with market-related topics. As the author points out: 'Online communities are contexts in which consumers often partake in discussions whose goals include attempts to inform and influence fellow consumers about products and brands' (2002: 61). Kozinets illustrates his approach with reference to a study of the meanings surrounding coffee and its consumption. As with most specialized online discussion forums, groups that engage in computer-mediated communications about a certain topic are likely to be knowledgeable enthusiasts. Therefore, they are well placed to provide interesting market-related information about trends and meanings in relation to a consumer topic like coffee. Kozinets began with a search for

newsgroups that contained the word 'coffee' and homed in on one—<alt.coffe>—that contained a large amount of traffic. He read hundreds of posted messages but narrowed these down to 179. He followed through particular threads (for example, those to do with Starbucks) in terms of their connection with his research questions. For example, the netnography suggests that, among many of these enthusiasts, Starbucks is seen as having commodified coffee and as a result its 'baristas' lack passion in their craft. There is a sense that the discussion participants felt that this lack of passion was transmitted to the quality of the coffee. Kozinets suggests that his analysis shows that 'coffee marketers have barely begun to plumb the depths of taste, status, and snob appeal that are waiting to be explored by discriminating coffee consumers' (2002: 70).

Box 23.3 An ethnography of Internet use in Trinidad

Miller and Slater (2000) conducted ethnographic research on the use of the Internet in Trinidad. The first author had previously conducted research on the unfolding of modernity in Trinidad and drew on his prior research to help appreciate the context of the reception of the Internet in the country; Slater had previously conducted research on computer-mediated communication in the UK. This preamble is significant because it forms part of the authors' justification for describing their investigation as ethnographic. For Miller and Slater, an important component of ethnography is that it entails protracted involvement with the people one studies. In fact, the authors spent just five weeks in Trinidad for this study, so their prior experiences are invoked as a way of legitimizing the label 'ethnography'. Further, the authors consulted Internet web sites on their return and interviewed Trinidadians in London and New York. They also maintained contact with informants after their return through e-mail and 'chat'. Overall, the following were the main methods:

1 interviews 'largely devoted to the study of the political economy of the Internet, including businesses, the ISPs [Internet service providers] and government officers' (2000: 22);

2 hanging around 'in cybercafes watching people go online and chatting with them. We also interviewed them more formally' (2000: 22);

3 an exploration with friends of how the Internet had become intertwined with their lives;

4 a house-to-house survey in the same four areas in which Miller had previously conducted a similar investigation to ascertain levels of Internet usage;

5 in-depth interviews with some of those contacted through the survey.

Like Markham, Miller and Slater found that the worlds of the Internet and of everyday life beyond the Internet are highly intertwined.

---

should provide more than a means of advertising wares but little agreement beyond that. Thus, the clothing firms they studied recognized that the Internet could provide more than just a catalogue on a monitor screen, but the nature of any kind of alternative or additional interface represented an area of some uncertainty. Generally, however, consumers did little of their purchasing of goods on the Net. Indeed, a Trinidadian cultural trait of seeking out things that are free would seem to militate against the use of the Net for online purchasing.

A feature that is striking about all these studies from the point of view of anyone familiar with organizational behaviour research on technology is the way in which it treats the Internet as a technology as a 'given'. Recent thinking on technology and work has preferred to view technologies as texts that have 'interpretive flexibility' (Grint and Woolgar 1997). This notion means that the researcher needs to approach any technology through an examination of both the principles inscribed into it and how it is interpreted by users. Such a position is very much associated with the notion, previously encountered in Chapter 18, which suggests that the audiences of texts need to be the focus of attention as much as the texts themselves. Taking this position, Hine (2000: 9) locates the Internet 'as a product of culture: a technology that was produced by particular people with contextually situated goals and priorities. It is also a technology which is shaped by the ways in which it is marketed, taught and used.'

Hine describes her approach as one of 'virtual ethnography' (see Box 23.4), which intendedly has a dual meaning: it is at once an ethnography of being online—that is, of the virtual—but it is also a virtual ethnography—that is, not quite an ethnography in any of the term's conventional settings. In particular, a virtual ethnography requires getting away from the idea that an ethnography is of or in a place in any traditional sense. It is also an ethnography of a domain that infiltrates other spaces and times of its participants, so that its boundedness is problematic to participants and analysts alike. As regards the issue of the interpretative flexibility of the Internet, Hine

---

Box 23.4   Virtually an ethnography

Hine's (2000) research was concerned with the trial in 1997 in Boston of a British nanny (Louise Woodward) for the murder of the child in her charge, as well as the aftermath of the trial. While not an area relevant in any direct way to business and management research, Hine's research is relevant as an approach that could be adapted to such a substantive focus. Hine's data collection strategy included: searching out web sites concerned with the case, which attracted a great deal of Internet interest; contacting web authors by e-mail and asking a series of questions about their intentions, familiarity with the Web, experiences, and so on; examining communication in newsgroups in which ten or more postings about the case had been made and posting a message in those groups; and contact with the official site that campaigned for Louise Woodward. In contacting web developers and newsgroup participants, Hine writes:

> I introduced myself as a researcher in communications who was looking at the specific case of Louise Woodward

on the Internet. I explained that I was concerned with how people got interested in the case, where they got their information from, and what they thought of the quality of information on newsgroups and web pages. . . . I offered people a promise of confidentiality and the chance to check my own credentials through my web site.   (2000: 78)

Hine did not receive a very good response to the newsgroup postings, which may reflect a tendency noticed by other researchers for newsgroup, MUD, listserv, and other participants to be sceptical about the use of their cyberdomains for research and suspicious about researchers who contact them. In her examination of newsgroup communication, Hine employed an approach that was heavily influenced by discourse analysis (see Chapter 17)—for example, by showing the discursive moves through which participants sought to construe the authenticity or factual nature of their information.

---

shows that there was some general agreement about its purposes as a technology. However, these purposes were not inscribed in the technology in the way that a technological determinist position might imply, but they had arisen in the course of the use of the Internet. Moreover, Hine argues that the nature and capacities of the Internet have not become totally stabilized in the minds of participants and that gradual increments of change are likely in response to particular needs and purposes of participants.

Studies like these are clearly inviting us to consider the nature of the Internet as a domain for investigation, but they also invite us to consider the nature and the adaptiveness of our research methods. In the examples discussed in this section, the question of what is and is not ethnography is given a layer of complexity that adds to the considerations about this issue that were referred to in Chapter 14. But these studies are also cases of using Internet-based research methods to investigate Internet use. Future online ethnographic investigations of issues unrelated to the Internet will give a clearer indication of the possibilities that the method offers.

Qualitative research using online focus groups

There is a crucial distinction between synchronous and asynchronous online focus groups. With the former, the focus group is in real time, so that contributions are made more or less immediately after previous contributions (whether from the moderator or other participants) among a group of participants all of whom are simultaneously online. Contributions can be responded to as soon as they are typed (and with some forms of software, the contributions can be seen as they are being typed). As Mann and

---

Box 23.5 An asynchronous focus group study

Adriaenssens and Cadman (1999) report their experiences of conducting a market research exercise to explore the launch of an online share-trading platform in the UK. Participants were in two groups: one group of active shareholders (twenty participants) and a second group of passive shareholders (ten participants). They were identified through the MORI Financial Services database as 'up-market shareholders who were also Internet users' (1999: 418–19). The participants who were identified were very geographically spread, so online focus groups were ideal. Questions were e-mailed to participants in five phases with a deadline for returning replies, which were then copied anonymously to the rest of the participants. The questions were sent in the body of the e-mail, rather than as attachments, to solve problems of software incompatibility. After each phase, a summary document was produced and circulated to participants for comment, thus injecting a form of respondent validation into the project. The researchers found it difficult to ensure that participants kept to the deadlines, which in fact were rather tight, although it was felt that having a schedule of deadlines that was kept to as far as possible was helpful in preventing drop-outs. The researchers felt that the group of active shareholders was too large to manage and suggest groups of no more than ten participants.

Stewart (2000) observe, because several participants can type in a response to a contribution at the same time, the conventions of normal turn-taking in conversations are largely sidelined. If participants are in considerably different time zones, the organization of such groups can be slightly more difficult.

With asynchronous groups, focus group exchanges are not in real time. E-mail is one form of asynchronous communication that is sometimes used (see Box 23.5 for an example). For example, the moderator might ask a question and then send the e-mail containing it to focus group participants. The latter will be able to reply to the moderator and to other group members at some time in the future. Such groups get around the time zone problem and are probably easier than synchronous groups for participants who are not skilled at using the keyboard.

Conferencing software is used for synchronous groups and is often used for asynchronous groups as well. This may mean that focus group participants will require access to the software, which can be undesirable if the software needs to be loaded onto their computers. Participants may not feel confident about loading the software and there may be compatibility problems with particular machines and operating systems.

Selecting participants for online focus groups is potentially difficult, not least because they must normally have access to the necessary hardware and software. One possibility is to use questionnaires as a springboard for identifying possible participants. For their study of virtual communities concerned with consumption issues Evans et al. (2001) used a combination of questionnaires (both paper and online) and focus groups made up of respondents to the questionnaires who had indicated a willingness to take further part in the research. The British focus groups were of the face-to-face kind, but, in addition, international respondents to the questionnaire who were prepared to be further involved in the research participated in an online focus group. Other sources of participants for online focus groups might involve postings on appropriate special interest web sites or on such outlets as special interest bulletin boards or chat rooms.

The requisite number of participants is affected by the question of whether the online focus group is being conducted synchronously or asynchronously. Mann and Stewart (2000) advocate that, with the former type, the group should not be too large, because it can make it difficult for some people to participate, possibly because of limited keyboard skills, and they recommend groups of between six and eight participants. Also, moderating the session can be more difficult with a large number. In asynchronous mode, such problems do not exist and very large groups can be accommodated—certainly much larger ones than could be envisaged in a face-to-face context, although Adriaenssens and Cadman (1999) suggest that large groups can present research management problems.

Before starting the focus group, moderators are advised to send out a welcome message introducing the research and laying out some of the ground rules for the ongoing discussion. There is evidence that participants respond more positively if the researchers reveal something about themselves (Curasi 2001). This can be done in the opening message or by creating links to personal web sites.

One problem with the asynchronous focus group is that moderators cannot be available online twenty-four hours a day, although it is not inconceivable that moderators could have a shift system to deal with this limitation. This lack of continuous availability means that e-mails or postings may be sent and responded to without any ability of the moderator to intervene or participate. This feature may not be a problem, but could become so if offensive messages were being sent or if it meant that the

discussion was going off at a complete tangent from which it would be difficult to redeem the situation. Further, because focus group sessions in asynchronous mode may go on for a long time, perhaps several days or even weeks, there is a greater likelihood of participants dropping out of the study.

Online focus groups are unlikely to replace their face-to-face counterparts. Instead, they are likely to be employed in connection with certain kinds of research topic and/or sample. As regards the latter, dispersed or inaccessible people are especially relevant to online focus group research. As Sweet (2001) points out, relevant topics are likely to be ones like those involving sensitive issues and ones concerned with Internet use—for example, the study discussed in Box 23.5 and studies like O'Connor and Madge (2001).

Box 23.6 summarizes the chief advantages and disadvantages of online relative to face-to-face focus groups. The discussion is combined with online personal interviews, which are the subject of the next section, since most of the elements in the balance sheet of advantages and disadvantages are the same.

Box 23.6 Advantages and disadvantages of online focus group and personal interviews compared to face-to-face interviews in qualitative research

This box summarizes the main advantages and disadvantages of online focus groups and personal interviews compared to their face-to-face counterparts. The two methods are combined because the tally of advantages and disadvantages applies more or less equally well to both of them.

Advantages

- Online interviews and focus groups are extremely cheap to conduct compared to comparable face-to-face equivalents. They are likely to take longer, however, especially when conducted asynchronously.

- Interviewees or focus group participants who would otherwise normally be inaccessible (for example, because they are located in another country) or hard to involve in research (for example, very senior executives, people with almost no time for participation) can more easily be involved.

- Interviewees and focus group participants are able to reread what they (and, in the case of focus groups, others) have previously written in their replies.

- People participating in the research may be better able to fit the interviews into their own time.

- People participating in the research do not have to make additional allowances for the time spent travelling to a focus group session.

- The interviews do not have to be audio-recorded, thus eliminating interviewee apprehension about speaking and being recorded.

- There is no need for transcription. This represents an enormous advantage because of time and cost involved in getting recorded interview sessions transcribed.

- Because of the previous point, the interview transcripts can be more or less immediately entered into a Computer-assisted qualitative data analysis software (CAQDAS) program of the kind introduced in Chapter 20.

- The transcripts of the interviews are more likely to be accurate, because the problems that may arise from mishearing or not hearing at all what is said do not arise. This is a particular advantage with focus group discussions, because it can be difficult to establish who is speaking and impossible to distinguish what is said when participants speak at the same time.

- Focus group participants can employ pseudonyms so that their identity can be more easily concealed from others in the group. This can make it easier for participants to discuss potentially embarrassing issues or to divulge potentially unpopular views. The ability to discuss sensitive issues generally may be greater in electronic than face-to-face focus groups.

- In focus groups, shy or quiet participants may find it easier to come to the fore.

- Equally, in focus groups overbearing participants are less likely to predominate, but in synchronous groups variations in keyboard skills may militate slightly against equal participation.

- Participants are less likely to be influenced by characteristics like the age, ethnicity, or appearance (and possibly even gender if pseudonyms are used) of other participants in a focus group.

- Similarly, interviewees and focus group participants are much less likely to be affected by characteristics of interviewers or moderators respectively, so that interviewer bias is less likely.

- When interviewees and participants are online at home, they are essentially being provided with an 'anonymous, safe and non-threatening environment' (O'Connor and Madge 2002: 11.2), which may be especially helpful to vulnerable groups.

- Similarly, researchers are not confronted with the potentially discomfiting experience of having to invade other people's homes or workplaces, which can themselves sometimes be unsafe environments.

Disadvantages

- Only people with access to online facilities and/or who find them relatively straightforward are likely to be in a position to participate.

- It can be more difficult for the interviewer to establish rapport and to engage with interviewees. However, when the topic is of interest to participants, this may not be a great problem.

- It can be difficult in asynchronous interviews to retain over a longer term any rapport that has been built up.

- Probing is more difficult though not impossible. Curasi (2001) reports some success in eliciting further

information from respondents, but it is easier for interviewees to ignore or forget about the requests for further information or for expansion on answers given.

- Asynchronous interviews may take a very long time to complete, depending on cooperativeness.

- With asynchronous interviews, there may be a greater tendency for interviewees to discontinue their participation than is likely to be the case with face-to-face interviews.

- There is less spontaneity of response, since interviewees can reflect on their answers to a much greater extent than is possible in a face-to-face situation. However, this can be construed as an advantage in some respects, since interviewees are likely to give more considered replies (though some commentators see the ability to provide more considered replies an advantage—see Adriaenssens and Cadman 1999).

- There may be a tendency for non-response to be higher in online personal interviews.

- The researcher cannot be certain that the people who are interviewed are who they say they are (though this issue may apply on occasion to face-to-face interviews as well).

- In synchronous focus groups, variations in keyboard skills may make equal levels of participation difficult.

- Online interviews and focus groups from home require considerable commitment from interviewees and participants if they have to install software onto their computers and remain online for extended periods of time, thereby incurring expense (though it is possible to offer remuneration for such costs) and blocking their telephone lines.

- The interviewer/moderator may not be aware that the interviewee/participant is distracted by something and in such circumstances will continue to ask questions as if he or she had the person's full attention.

- Online connections may be lost, so research participants need to know what to do in case of such an eventuality.

- Interviewers cannot capitalize upon body language that might suggest puzzlement or in the case of focus groups a thwarted desire to contribute to the discussion.

Sources: Clapper and Massey (1996); Adriaenssens and Cadman (1999); Tse (1999); Mann and Stewart (2000); Curasi (2001); O'Connor and Madge (2001); Sweet (2001).

Qualitative research using online personal interviews

The issues involved in conducting online personal interviews for qualitative research are essentially the same as those to do with conducting online focus groups. In particular, the researcher must decide whether the interviews should take place in synchronous or asynchronous mode. The factors involved in deciding which to use are also largely the same, although issues to do with variable typing speed or computer-related knowledge among focus group participants will not apply.

Although online interviews run the risk relative to face-to-face interviews that the respondent is somewhat more likely to drop out of the exchange (especially in asynchronous mode, since the interviews can sometimes be very protracted), Mann and Stewart (2000: 138–9) suggest that in fact a relationship of mutual trust can be built up. This kind of relationship can make it easier for a longer-term commitment to the interview to be maintained, but also makes it easier for the researcher to go back to his or her interviewees for further information or reflections, something that is difficult to do with the face-to-face personal interview. The authors also suggest that it is important for interviewers to keep sending messages to respondents to reassure them that their written utterances are helpful and significant, especially since interviewing through the Internet is still an unfamiliar experience for most people.

A further issue for the online personal interviewer to consider is whether to send all the questions at once or to interview on a question followed by reply basis. The problem with the former tactic is that respondents may read all the questions and then reply only to those that they feel interested in or to which they feel they can make a genuine contribution, so that it is likely that asking one question at a time is likely to be more reliable.

There is evidence that prospective interviewees are more likely to agree to participate if their agreement is solicited prior to sending them questions and if the researcher uses some form of self-disclosure, such as directing the person being contacted to the researcher's web site, which contains personal information, particularly information that might be relevant to the research issue (Curasi 2001; O'Connor and Madge 2001). The argument for obtaining prior agreement from interviewees before sending them questions to be answered is that unsolicited e-mails, often referred to as 'spamming', are regarded as a nuisance among online users and receiving them can result in an immediate refusal to take the message seriously.

Curasi (2001) conducted a comparison in which twenty-four online interviews carried out through e-mail correspondence (and therefore asynchronous) were contrasted with twenty-four parallel face-to-face interviews. The interviews were concerned with shopping on the Internet. She found the following.

- Face-to-face interviewers are better able than online interviewers to maintain rapport with respondents.

- Greater commitment and motivation are required for completing an online interview, but, because of this, replies are often more detailed and considered than with face-to-face interviews.

- Online interviewers are less able to have an impact on whether the interview is successful or not because they are more remote.

- Online interviewees' answers tend to be more considered and grammatically correct because they have more time to ponder their answers and because they can tidy them up before sending them. Whether this is a positive feature is debateable: there is the obvious advantage of a 'clean' transcript, but there may be some loss of spontaneity.

- Follow-up probes can be carried out in online interviews, as well as in face-to-face ones.

On the other hand, Curasi also found that the worst interviews in terms of the amount of detail forthcoming were from online interviews. It may be that this and the other differences are to do with the fact that, whereas a qualitative face-to-face interview is *spoken*, the parallel online interview is *typed*. The full significance of this difference in the nature of the respondent's mode of answering has not been fully appreciated.

Thus far, most of the discussion of online personal interviewing assumes that the exchange is conducted entirely in a textual context (particularly by e-mail). However, the webcam may offer further possibilities for synchronous online personal interviews should the technology become widespread. Such a development would make the online interview similar to a telephone interview, in that it is mediated by a technology, but also similar to an in-person interview, since those involved in the exchange would be able to see each other. However, one of the main advantages of the online interview would be lost, in that the respondent's answers would need to be transcribed, as in traditional qualitative interviewing.

The possibilities associated with conducting online focus groups has probably attracted greater attention than online personal interviews, perhaps because the potential advantages are greater with the former. For example, with focus groups, a great deal of time and administration can be saved by online focus groups, whereas there is less comparable saving with online personal interviews unless a great deal of travel is involved.

Online social surveys

There has been a considerable growth in the number of surveys being administered online. It is questionable whether the research instruments should be regarded as structured interviews (see Chapter 5) or as self-completion questionnaires (see Chapter 6)—in a sense they are both. So far as online social surveys are concerned, there is a crucial distinction between surveys administered by e-mail (e-mail surveys) and surveys administered via the Web (Web surveys). In the case of the former, the questionnaire is sent via e-mail to a respondent, whereas, with a Web survey, the respondent is directed to a web site in order to answer a questionnaire. Sheehan and Hoy (1999) suggest that there has been a tendency for e-mail surveys to be employed in relation to 'smaller, more homogeneous on-line user groups', whereas Web surveys have been used to study 'large groups of on-line users'.

E-mail surveys

With e-mail surveys it is important to distinguish between embedded and attached questionnaires sent by e-mail. In the case of the embedded questionnaire, the questions are to be found in the body of the e-mail. There may be an introduction to the questionnaire followed by some marking that partitions the introduction from the questionnaire itself. Respondents have to indicate their replies using simple notations, such as an 'x', or they may be asked to delete alternatives that do not apply. If questions are open, they are asked to type in their answers. They then simply need to select the reply button to return their completed questionnaires to the researcher. With an attached questionnaire, the questionnaire arrives as an attachment to an e-mail that introduces it. As with the embedded questionnaire, respondents must select and/or type their answers. To return the questionnaire, it must be attached to a reply e-mail, although respondents may also be given the opportunity to fax or send the completed questionnaire by postal mail to the researcher (Sheehan and Hoy 1999).

The chief advantage of the embedded questionnaire is that it is easier for the respondent to return to the researcher and requires less computer expertise. Knowing how to read and then return an attachment requires a certain facility with handling online communication that is still not universally applicable. Also, the recipients' operating systems or software may present problems with reading attachments, while many respondents may refuse to open the attachment because of concerns about a virus. On the other hand, the limited formatting that is possible with most e-mail software, such as using bold, variations in font size, indenting, and other features, makes the appearance of embedded questionnaires rather dull and featureless, although this limitation is rapidly changing. Furthermore, it is slightly easier for the respondent to type material into an attachment that uses well-known software like Microsoft Word, since, if the questionnaire is embedded in an e-mail, the alignment of questions and answers may be lost.

Dommeyer and Moriarty (2000) compared the two forms of e-mail survey in connection with an attitude study. The attached questionnaire was given a much wider range of embellishments in terms of appearance than was possible with the embedded one. Before conducting the survey, undergraduate students were asked about the relative appearance of the two formats. The attached questionnaire was deemed to be better looking, easier to complete, clearer in appearance, and better organized. The two formats were then administered to two random samples of students, all of whom were active e-mail users. The researchers found a much higher response rate with the embedded than with the attached questionnaire (37 per cent versus 8 per cent), but there was little difference in terms of speed of response or whether questions were more likely to be omitted with one format rather than the other. Although Dommeyer and Moriarty (2000: 48) conclude that 'the attached e-mail survey presents too many obstacles to the potential respondent', it is important to appreciate that this study was conducted during what were still early days in the life of online surveys. It may be that, as prospective respondents become more adept at using online communication methods and as viruses become less of a threat (for example, as virus-checking software improves in terms of accessibility and cost), the concerns that led to the lower response rate for the attached questionnaire will be less pronounced. Also, the researchers do not appear to have established a prior contact with the students before sending out the questionnaires; it may be that the reaction to such an approach, which is frowned upon in the online community, may have been more negative in the case of the attached questionnaire format.

Web surveys

Web surveys operate by inviting prospective respondents to visit a web site at which the questionnaire can be found and completed online. The web survey has an important advantage over the e-mail survey in that it can use a much wider variety of embellishments in terms of appearance. Plate 23.1 presents part of the questionnaire from the gym survey from Chapter 11 in a Web survey format and answered in the same way as in Box 11.2. Common features include 'radio buttons' (whereby the respondent makes a choice between closed question answers by clicking on a circle in which a dot appears—see question 8 in Plate 23.1) and pull-down menus of possible answers (see Plate 23.2). There are also greater possibilities in terms of the use of colour. With open questions, the respondent is invited to type directly into a boxed area (for example, question 2 in Plate 23.1).

However, the advantages of the Web survey are not just to do with appearance. The questionnaire can be designed so that, when there is a filter question (for example, 'if yes, go to question 12, if no go to question 14'), it skips automatically to the next appropriate question. The questionnaire can also be programmed so that only one question ever appears on the screen or so that the respondent can scroll

---

Box 23.7 Combining a paper survey with a Web survey

As part of their research into virtual communities concerned with consumption issues, Evans et al. (2001) carried out a survey using two methods of administration; first, a paper-based questionnaire, which was distributed at various locations at the University of Bristol and the University of West of England, Bristol, and at three cybercafés; secondly, a Web survey, hosted by the Bristol Business School, which was linked via BBC Bristol Online and a cybercafé. The authors write: 'Invitations to respond to the on-line questionnaire were posted on several electronic lists within the two Bristol universities, and several international discussion lists' (2001: 152). As a result of these two strategies, over 300 questionnaires were returned.

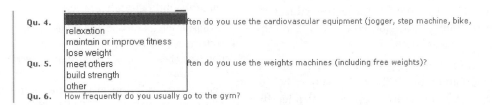

Qu. 1. Are you male or female?

Male

Qu. 2. How old are you?

21

Qu. 3. Which of the following best describes your main reason for going to the gym?

maintain or improve fitness

Qu. 4. When you go to the gym, how often do you use the cardiovascular equipment (jogger, step machine, bike, rower)?

always

Qu. 5. When you go to the gym, how often do you use the weights machines (including free weights)?

always

Qu. 6. How frequently do you usually go to the gym?

2 or 3 days a week

Qu. 7. Are you usually accompanied when you to to the gym or do you usually go on your own?

on my own

Qu. 8. Do you have sources of regular exercise other than the gym?

Yes No

Plate 23.1 Gym survey in web survey format

Qu. 4. relaxation | ften do you use the cardiovascular equipment (jogger, step machine, bike,
maintain or improve fitness
lose weight
Qu. 5. meet others | ften do you use the weights machines (including free weights)?
build strength
other
Qu. 6. How frequently do you usually go to the gym?

Plate 23.2 A pull-down menu

down and look at all questions in advance. Finally, respondents' answers can be automatically programmed to download into a database, thus eliminating the daunting coding of a large number of questionnaires. One of the chief problems with the Web survey is that, in order to produce the attractive text and all the other features, the researcher will either have to be highly sophisticated in the use of HTML or will need to use one of a growing number of software packages that are designed to produce questionnaires with all the features that have been described.

Potential respondents need to be directed to the Web site containing the questionnaire. Box 23.7 provides an example of the kind of approach that might be used. Where there are possible problems to do with restricting who may answer the questionnaire, it may

be necessary to set up a password system to filter out people for whom the questionnaire is not appropriate.

Sampling issues

Anyone who has read Chapter 4 must be wondering how the sampling principles described there might apply to online surveys. A major issue and limitation is that not everyone in any nation is online and has the technical ability to handle questionnaires online in either e-mail or Web formats. Certain other features of online communications make the issue more problematic.

- Many people have more than one e-mail address.

- Many people use more than one Internet Service Provider (ISP).

Practical tip: 👉 *using Internet surveys to supplement traditional postal questionnaire surveys*

There is a growing tendency for researchers who conduct postal questionnaire surveys to offer their respondents the opportunity to complete their questionnaires online (Couper 2000). This can be done by indicating in the covering letter that goes out with the postal questionnaire that they can have the questionnaire e-mailed to them, or, if the questionnaire is accessible via the Web, they can be directed to the Web address. The advantage of doing this is that some of the samples of respondents may feel more comfortable completing the questionnaire on-line because of the long periods of time they spend online and it removes the need to return the questionnaire by post. There is the question of whether the mode of administration (postal as against online) influences the kinds of response received. This is an issue that is likely to attract research in the future.

- A household may have one computer but several users.

- Internet-users are a biased sample of the population, in that they tend to be better educated, wealthier, younger, and not representative in ethnic terms (Couper 2000).

- Few sampling frames exist of the general online population and most of these are likely to be expensive to acquire, since they are controlled by ISPs or may be confidential.

Such issues make the possibilities of conducting online surveys using probability sampling principles difficult to envisage. This is not to say that online surveys should not be considered. Indeed, for researchers in the field of business and management, there may be more opportunities than for researchers in other areas. For example, in many organizations, most if not all non-manual workers are likely to be online and to be familiar with the details of using e-mail and the Internet. Thus surveys of samples of online populations can be conducted using essentially the same probability sampling procedures. Similarly, surveys of members of commercially relevant online groups can be conducted using these principles. Smith (1997) conducted a survey of Web presence providers (people or organizations that are involved in creating and maintaining Web content). She acquired her sample from a directory of providers, which acted as her sampling frame.

A further example of the use of a directory to generate a probability sample can be found in Box 23.8.

As Couper (2000) notes of surveys of populations using probability sampling procedures:

Intra-organizational surveys and those directed at users of the Internet were among the first to adopt this new survey technology. These restricted populations typically have no coverage problems . . . or very high rates of coverage. Student surveys are a particular example of this approach that are growing in popularity. (2000: 485)

The chief problem with sampling strategies of the kind employed by Evans et al. (Box 23.7) is that we have no idea about the representativeness of those who answered the web survey questionnaire (though the same applies to the respondents to their paper-based questionnaire too). On the other hand, given that we have so little knowledge and understanding of online behaviour and attitudes relating to online issues, it could reasonably be argued that some information about these areas is a lot better than none at all, provided the limitations of the findings in terms of their generalizability is appreciated.

A further issue in relation to sampling and sampling-related error is the matter of *non-response* (see Box 4.5). There is growing evidence that online surveys typically generate lower response rates than postal questionnaire surveys (Tse 1998; Sheehan 2001). In the early years, in the late 1980s, response rates for e-mail surveys were quite encouraging (Sheehan and Hoy 1999), but since the mid-1990s

---

Box 23.8 Sampling for an online survey

Cobanoglu, Ward, and Moreo (2001) report the results of a study in which three different modes of survey administration were used: post, fax, and online. The questionnaires were administered to 300 hospitality professors in the USA, who had been randomly sampled from the online directory of the Council on Hotel, Restaurant, and Institutional Education. The sampling was carried out only from those who had an e-mail address. The 300 professors were randomly assigned to one of the three modes of survey administration. The authors write:

> For the web-based survey, an email message was sent to the professors along with a cover letter and the website

address. The respondents were informed that they could request a paper copy of the survey should they have problems accessing the survey online. A unique website address was created for each respondent . . . (2001: 447)

Compared with the postal administration of the questionnaire, the online administration achieved a higher response rate (26 per cent versus 44 per cent) and a faster response speed, and was cheaper.

---

they have been declining and are at lower levels than those for most postal questionnaires (Sheehan 2001), though there are clear exceptions to this tendency (for example, see Box 23.8). Two factors may account for this decline: the novelty of e-mail surveys in the early years and a growing antipathy towards unsolicited e-mails among online communities. However, response rates can be boosted by following two simple strategies.

1. Contact prospective respondents before sending them a questionnaire. This is regarded as basic 'netiquette'.
2. As with postal questionnaire surveys, follow up non-respondents at least once.

The case for the first of these two strategies in boosting response rates is not entirely clear (Sheehan 2001), but seems to be generally advisable.

Box 23.9 summarizes the main factors to take into account when comparing online surveys with postal questionnaire surveys.

Overview

Online surveys are clearly in their infancy, but they have considerable potential. There is evidence that

having a web survey or even an e-mail option can boost response rates to postal questionnaires (Yun and Trumbo 2000). Several problems have been identified with Web and e-mail surveys, but it is too early to dismiss them because methodologists are only beginning to get to grips with this approach to survey research and may gradually develop ways of overcoming the limitations that are being identified. Moreover, as we have pointed out, for certain kinds of populations and as more and more people and organizations go online, some of the sampling-related problems will diminish. As Yun and Trumbo (2000) observe: 'the electronic-only survey is advisable when resources are limited and the target population suits an electronic survey.'

It is also worth making the obvious point that, when conducting an online survey, you should bear in mind the principles about sampling, interview design, and question construction that were posed in Chapters 4 through 7 in particular. While online surveys are distinctive in certain ways, they require the same rigorous considerations that go into the design of conventional surveys that are conducted by postal questionnaire or by personal or telephone interview.

Box 23.9 Advantages and disadvantages of online surveys compared to postal questionnaire surveys

This box summarizes the main advantages and disadvantages of online surveys compared to postal questionnaire surveys. The tally of advantages and disadvantages in connection with online surveys relates to both e-mail and Web surveys. It should also be made clear that by and large online surveys and postal questionnaires suffer from one disadvantage relative to personal and telephone interviews—namely, that the researcher can never be certain that the person answering questions is who the researcher believes him or her to be.

Advantages

1 *Low cost.* Even though postal questionnaire surveys are cheap to administer, there is evidence that e-mail surveys in particular are cheaper. This is in part due to the cost of postage, paper, envelopes, and the time taken to stuff covering letters and questionnaires into envelopes with postal questionnaire surveys. However, with Web surveys there may be start-up costs associated with the software needed to produce the questionnaire.

2 *Faster response.* Online surveys tend to be returned considerably faster than postal questionnaires.

3 *Attractive formats.* With web surveys, there is the opportunity to use a wide variety of stylistic formats for presenting questionnaires and closed question answers. Also, automatic skipping when using filter questions and the possibility of immediate downloading of questionnaire replies into a database make this kind of survey quite attractive for researchers.

4 *Mixed administration.* They can be combined with postal questionnaire surveys so that respondents have the option of replying by post or online. Moreover, the mode of reply does not seem to make a significant difference to the kinds of replies generated (Box 23.8).

5 *Unrestricted compass.* There are no constraints in terms of geographical coverage. The same might be said of postal questionnaire surveys, but the problems of sending respondents stamped addressed envelopes that can be used in their own countries is overcome.

6 *Fewer unanswered questions.* There is evidence that online questionnaires are completed with fewer unanswered questions than postal questionnaires, resulting in less missing data. However, there is also evidence of little difference between the two modes of administering surveys.

7 *Better response to open questions.* To the extent that open questions are used, they tend to be more likely to be answered online and to result in more detailed replies.

Disadvantages

1 *Low response rate.* Typically, response rates to online surveys are lower than those for comparable postal questionnaire surveys.

2 *Restricted to online populations.* Only people who are available online can reasonably be expected to participate in an online survey. This restriction may gradually ease over time, but, since the online population differs in significant ways from the non-online population, it is likely to remain a difficulty. On the other hand, if online populations are the focus of interest, this disadvantage is unlikely to prove an obstacle.

3 *Requires motivation.* Because online survey respondents must be online to answer the questionnaire, if they are having to pay for the connection and perhaps are tying up their telephone lines, they may need a higher level of motivation than postal questionnaire respondents. This suggests that the solicitation to participate must be especially persuasive.

4 *Confidentiality and anonymity issues.* It is normal for survey researchers to indicate that respondents' replies will be confidential and that they will be anonymous. The same suggestions can and should be made with respect to online surveys. However, with e-mail surveys, since the recipient must return the questionnaire either embedded within the message or as an attachment, respondents may find it difficult to believe that their replies really are confidential and will be treated anonymously. In this respect, Web surveys may have an advantage over e-mail surveys.

5 *Multiple replies.* With Web surveys, there is a risk that some people may mischievously complete the questionnaire more than once. There is much less risk of this with e-mail surveys.

Sources: Schaeffer and Dillman (1998); Tse (1998); Kent and Lee (1999); Sheehan and Hoy (1999); Cobanoglu, Ward, and Moreo (2001).

Table 23.1 The strengths of e-mail and web-based surveys in relation to face-to-face interview, telephone interview, and postal questionnaire surveys

Issues to consider	Mode of survey administration				
	Face-to-face interview	Telephone interview	Postal questionnaire	E-mail	Web
Resource issues Is the cost of the mode of admistration relatively low?	✓	✓✓	✓✓✓	✓✓✓	✓ (unless access to low-cost software)
Is the speed of the mode of administration relatively fast?	✓	✓✓✓	✓✓✓	✓✓✓	✓✓✓
Is the cost of handling a dispersed sample relatively low?	✓ (✓✓ if clustered)	✓✓✓	✓✓✓	✓✓✓	✓✓✓
Does the researcher require little technical expertise for devising a questionnaire?	✓✓✓	✓✓✓	✓✓✓	✓✓	✓
Sampling-related issues Does the mode of administration tend to produce a good response rate?	✓✓✓	✓✓	✓	✓	✓
Is the researcher able to control who responds (i.e. the person at whom it is targeted is the person who answers)?	✓✓✓	✓✓✓	✓✓	✓✓	✓✓
Is the mode of administration accessible to all sample members?	✓✓✓	✓✓	✓✓✓	✓ (because of need for respondents to be accessible online)	✓ (because of need for respondents to be accessible online)
Questionnaire issues Is the mode of administration suitable for long questionnaires?	✓✓✓	✓✓	✓✓	✓✓	✓✓
Is the mode of administration suitable for complex questions?	✓✓✓	✓	✓✓	✓✓	✓✓
Is the mode of administration suitable for open questions?	✓✓✓	✓✓	✓	✓✓	✓✓
Is the mode of administration suitable for filter questions?	✓✓✓ (especially if CAPI used)	✓✓✓ (especially if CATI used)	✓	✓	✓✓✓ if allows jumping
Does the mode of administration allow control over order questions are answered?	✓✓✓	✓✓✓	✓	✓	✓
Is the mode of administration suitable for sensitive questions?	✓	✓✓	✓✓✓	✓✓✓	✓✓✓

Issues to consider	Mode of survey administration				
	Face-to-face interview	**Telephone interview**	**Postal questionnaire**	**E-mail**	**Web**
Is the mode of administration less likely to result in non-reponse to some questions?	✓✓✓	✓✓✓	✓✓	✓✓	✓✓
Does the mode of administration allow the use of visual aids?	✓✓✓	✓	✓✓✓	✓✓	✓✓✓
Answering context issues					
Does the mode of administration give respondents the opportunity to consult others for information?	✓✓	✓	✓✓✓	✓✓✓	✓✓✓
Does the mode of administration minimize the impact of interviewers' characteristics (gender, class, ethnicity)?	✓	✓✓	✓✓✓	✓✓✓	✓✓✓
Does the mode of administration minimize the impact of the social desirability effect?	✓	✓✓	✓✓✓	✓✓✓	✓✓✓
Does the mode of administration allow control over the intrusion of others in answering questions?	✓✓✓	✓✓	✓	✓	✓
Does the mode of administration minimize need for respondents to have certain skills to answer questions?	✓✓✓	✓✓✓	✓✓	✓ (because of need to have online skills)	✓ (because of need to have online skills)
Does the mode of administration enable respondents to be probed?	✓✓✓	✓✓✓	✓	✓✓	✓

Notes: Number of ticks indicates the strength of the mode of administration of a questionnaire in relation to each issue. More ticks correspond to more advantages in relation to each issue. A single tick implies that the mode of administering a questionnaire does not fare well in terms of the issue in question. Three ticks imply that it does very well, but two ticks imply that it is acceptable. This table has been influenced by the authors' own experience and by Dillman (1978) and Czaja and Blair (1996). CAPI is computer-assisted personal interviewing; CATI is computer-assisted telephone interviewing.

K KEY POINTS

- The growth in the use of the Internet offers significant opportunities for business researchers in allowing them access to a large and growing body of people.

- Many research methods covered elsewhere in this book can be adapted to online investigations.

- There is a distinction between research that uses Web sites as objects of analysis and research that uses the Internet to collect data from others.

- Online surveys may be of either of two major types: Web surveys and e-mail surveys.

- Most of the same considerations that go into designing research that is not online apply to e-research.

- Both quantitative and qualitative research can be adapted to e-research.

Q QUESTIONS FOR REVIEW

World Wide Web sites or pages as objects of analysis

- In what ways might the analysis of Web sites pose particular difficulties that are less likely to be encountered in the analysis of non-electronic documents?

Using web sites to collect data from individuals

- What are the chief ways of collecting data from individuals using the World Wide Web and online communications?

- What advantages do they have over traditional research methods for collecting such data?

- What disadvantages do they have in comparison to traditional research methods for collecting such data?

- What is the difference between Web-based and communication-based research methods?

An ethnography of the Internet?

- How does ethnography need to be adapted in order to collect data on the use of the Internet?

- Does the study of the impact of the Internet necessarily mean that we end up as technological determinists?

- Are ethnographies of the Internet really ethnographic?

Qualitative research using online focus groups

- What is the significance of the distinction between synchronous and asynchronous focus groups?

- How different is the role of the moderator in online, as against face-to-face, focus groups?

Qualitative research using online personal interviews

- Can online personal interviews really be personal interviews?

- To what extent does the absence of direct contact mean that the online interview cannot be a true interview?

Online social surveys

- What is the significance of the distinction between e-mail and Web surveys?

- Are there any special circumstances in which embedded e-mail questionnaires will be more likely to be effective than attached questionnaires?

- Do sampling problems render online social surveys too problematic to warrant serious consideration?

- Are response rates in online surveys worse or better than in traditional surveys?

24

Writing up business research

CHAPTER GUIDE

It is easy to forget that one of the main stages in any research project, regardless of its size, is that it has to be written up. Not only is this how you will convey your findings, but being aware of the significance of writing is crucial, because your audience must be persuaded about the credibility and importance of your research. This chapter presents some of the characteristics of the writing-up of business research. The chapter explores:

- why writing, and especially good writing, is important to business research;

- how quantitative and qualitative research are composed, using examples;

- the influence and implications of postmodernism for writing;

- key issues raised by discussions about the writing of ethnography, an area in which discussions about writing have been especially prominent.

Introduction

The aim of this chapter is to examine some of the strategies that are employed in writing up business research. Initially, we will explore the question of whether quantitative and qualitative research reveal divergent approaches. As we will see, the similarities are frequently more striking and apparent than the differences. However, the main point of this chapter is to extract some principles of good practice that can be developed and incorporated into your own writing. This is an important issue, since many people find writing up research more difficult than carrying it out. On the other hand, many people treat the writing-up stage as relatively unproblematic. But no matter how well research is conducted, others (that is, your readers) have to be convinced about the credibility of the knowledge claims you are making. Good writing is, therefore, very much to do with developing your style so that it is *persuasive* and *convincing*. Flat, lifeless, uncertain writing does not have the power to persuade and convince. In exploring these issues, we will touch on rhetorical strategies in the writing of business research (see Box 24.1). As Atkinson (1990: 2) has observed in relation to social research, 'the conventions of text and rhetoric are among the ways in which reality is *constructed*'.

This chapter will review some of the ways in which business research is written up in a way that will provide some basic ideas about structuring your own

written work if you have to produce something like a dissertation. There will be more advice on writing up for a dissertation in Chapter 26.

Two research-based articles that have been published in journals are examined to detect some helpful features. One is based on quantitative research and the other on qualitative research. This raises the question of whether practitioners of the two research strategies employ different writing approaches. It is sometimes suggested that they do, though, when Bryman compared two articles based on research in the sociology of work, he found that the differences were less pronounced than he had anticipated on the basis of reading the literature on the topic (Bryman 1998). One difference that we have noticed is that, in journals, quantitative researchers often give more detailed accounts of their research design, research methods, and approaches to analysis than qualitative researchers. This is surprising, because, in books reporting their research, qualitative researchers provide detailed accounts of these areas. Indeed, the chapters in Part Three of the book rely heavily on these accounts. Wolcott (1990: 27) has also noticed this tendency: 'Our [qualitative researchers'] failure to render full and complete disclosure about our data-gathering procedures give our methodologically oriented colleagues fits. And rightly so, especially for those among them willing to accept our contributions if we would only provide more careful data about our data.' Being informed that a study was based on a year's participant observation or a number of semi-structured interviews is not enough to gain an acceptance of the claims to credibility that a writer might be wishing to convey.

However, this point aside, in the discussion that follows, although one article based on quantitative research and one based on qualitative research will be examined, we should not be too surprised if they turn out to be more similar than might have been expected. In other words, although we might have expected clear differences between the two in terms of their approaches to writing, the similarities are more noticeable than the differences.

Box 24.1 ⌇(ᵕ)⌇ *What is rhetoric?*

The study of rhetoric is fundamentally concerned with the ways in which attempts to convince or persuade an audience are formulated. We often encounter the term in a negative context, such as 'mere rhetoric' or the opposition of 'rhetoric and reality'. However, rhetoric is an essential ingredient of writing, because when we write our aim is to convince others about the credibility of our knowledge claims. To suggest that rhetoric should somehow be suppressed makes little sense, since it is in fact a basic feature of writing. The examination of rhetorical strategies in written texts based on business research is concerned with the identification of the techniques in those texts that are designed to convince and persuade.

Writing quantitative research: an example

To illustrate some of the characteristics of the way quantitative research is written up for academic journals, we will take an article by Coyle-Shapiro and Kessler (2000). We are not suggesting that this article is somehow exemplary or representative, but rather that it exhibits some features that are often regarded as desirable qualities in terms of presentation and structure. The article is a secondary analysis of data from two surveys conducted in a large local-authority government organization and it was accepted for publication in one of the most prestigious European journals in business and management—the *Journal of Management Studies*. The vast majority of published articles in academic journals entail the blind refereeing of articles submitted. This means that an article will be read by two or three peers, who comment on the article and give the editors a judgement about its merits and hence whether it is worthy of publication. Most articles submitted are rejected. With highly prestigious journals, it is common for in excess of 90 per cent of articles to be rejected. It is unusual for an article to be accepted on its first submission. Usually, the referees

will suggest areas that need revising and the author (or authors) is expected to respond to that feedback. Revised versions of articles are usually sent back to the referees for further comment and this process may result in the author having to revise the draft yet again. It may even result in rejection. Therefore, an article like Coyle-Shapiro and Kessler's is not just the culmination of a research process, but is also the outcome of a feedback and review process. The fact that it has been accepted for publication, when many others have been rejected, testifies to its merits as having met the standards of the journal. That is not to say it is perfect, but the refereeing process is an indication that it does possess certain crucial qualities.

The article has the following components, aside from the abstract:

1. introduction;
2. theory and hypotheses;
3. methods;
4. results;
5. discussion.

Introduction

Right at the beginning of the introduction, the opening sentences attempt to grab our attention, to give a clear indication of where the article's focus lies, and to provide an indication of the significance and importance of the subject of study for practitioners, policy-makers, and academics. This is what the authors write:

The implications of globalization, organizational restructuring and downsizing on employment relations have renewed interest in the concept of the psychological contract. It has captured the attention of policy-makers in their efforts to 'change the deal' in response to increasing pressures to adapt to changing circumstances. For academics, the psychological contract presents another opportunity to re-examine the fundamental aspect of organizational life, the employee–employer relationship. (Coyle-Shapiro and Kessler 2000: 903)

This is an impressive start, because, in just over sixty words, the authors set out what the article is about and persuade us of its significance. Let us look at what each sentence achieves.

- The first sentence locates the article's focus as addressing an important aspect of business and management research that is currently the focus of renewed interest.

- The second sentence notes that the concept of the psychological contract has been used by policy-makers in response to pressure to adapt to changing circumstances.

- The third sentence goes on to suggest that this subject has also been of longstanding interest to academics. This sentence also widens the focus of the article by suggesting that the psychological contract is just one way of looking at the employee–employer relationship.

The rest of the paragraph then hints towards current challenges faced in managing the employment relationship, citing two further sources on this subject and hinting that the psychological contract has been proposed as a potential framework for understanding changes in the employee–employer exchange relationship. So, by the end of this paragraph, the contribution that the article is claiming to make to our understanding of the psychological contract has been outlined and situated within an established literature on the topic. This is quite a powerful start to the article, because the reader knows what the article is about and the particular case the authors are making for their contribution to the literature on the subject.

The authors go on to draw attention to the specific organizational context of their study, highlighting changes in the public sector that have led to increased financial and managerial accountability. Then they set out in much more precise terms exactly what this article will achieve, providing a summary of exactly where the researchers claim their contribution to this subject lies:

In this study, we set out to examine the content and state of the psychological contract from the employer and employee perspective. The inclusion of the employer's perspective goes some way towards countering the exclusive emphasis on the employee perspective adopted in the majority of empirical studies undertaken to date. (2000: 904)

Notice how the second sentence aims to persuade us that this really is an important contribution to our understanding of this research area. The authors draw attention to a deficiency in existing knowledge (the tendency towards an 'exclusive emphasis on the employee perspective') and tell us that they are going to correct this situation.

This aim is then broken down into three distinct stages:

1. First, 'we explore employees' and managers' perceptions of employer obligations and how well the employer has fulfilled its obligations to its employees (i.e. contract behaviour)';

2. 'Subsequently, we investigate the consequences of perceived employer contract behaviour on employees' perceived organizational support, organizational commitment and organizational citizenship behaviour [OCB]';

3. This then enables examination of 'whether the psychological contract contributes to our understanding of the employee–employer exchange relationship . . .' (2000: 904).

Two important concepts—'contract behaviour' and 'organizational citizenship behaviour [OCB]'— are thereby introduced; the latter is defined as a 'readiness to contribute beyond literal contractual obligations' (Organ 1988: 22, cited in Coyle-Shapiro and Kessler 2000: 910). The authors then go on to review the literature on the psychological contract, from early contributions to recent developments.

Theory and hypotheses

Although this is not presented as a separate section of the paper—in fact it forms an extension of the intro-duction—it is where existing ideas and research on the topic of the psychological contract are presented; it is thus where the theory that the study builds on is introduced. The authors point to a tendency within the literature to downplay the mutuality in the exchange relationship and the 'near exclusive emphasis on the employee perspective' (2000: 905). They treat managers as agents of the organization and suggest 'their interpretation of the psychological con-tract may provide one way of capturing the em-ployer's perspective' (2000: 907). The authors suggest that capturing the employer's perspective may add to understanding of employer violation or breach of the psychological contract and go on to cite empirical studies that suggest employer violations of the psy-chological contract are increasing in frequency. Importantly, they point out that 'none of the empir-ical studies have examined the relationship between employer contract behaviour and perceived organi-zational support' (2000: 909). Coyle-Shapiro and Kessler's ruminations on this issue lead them to pro-pose the first of three hypotheses.

- *Hypothesis 1*. 'Fulfilment of the psychological con-tract by the employer will have a positive effect on employees' perceived organizational support' (2000: 909).

This hypothesis stipulates that fulfilment of the psy-chological contract by the employer has an impact on employee perception concerning the extent to which the organization values their contributions and cares for their well-being. This leads them to suggest two further related hypotheses.

- *Hypothesis 2*. 'Fulfilment of the psychological contract by the employer will have a positive effect on employees' commitment to the organization' (2000: 910).

- *Hypothesis 2b*. 'An employee's perception of who their employer is will moderate the relationship between psychological contract fulfilment and organizational commitment' (2000: 910).

Finally, the authors suggest a third hypothesis:

- *Hypothesis 3*. 'Fulfilment of the psychological contract by the employer will have a positive effect on employees' OCB behaviour' (2000: 911).

These three hypotheses suggest a relationship between fulfilment of the psychological contract by the employer—the dependent variable—and employees' perceived organizational support, com-mitment to the organization, and OCB behaviour, which constitute the independent variables in this study. We thus end up with very clear research ques-tions, which have been arrived at by reflecting on existing ideas and research in this area.

Methods

In this section, the authors outline the methods that were used in conducting the research and provide details about the data that they draw on. They begin by describing the case-study organization in which the data for the study were collected. The section then gives a general outline of the data sets and provides details of the sample sizes and response rates for the two questionnaire surveys that were conducted, one of managers and the other of employees. Information about the sample is given, including mean organiza-tional and job tenure, mean age, gender proportions, and average earnings. The section also outlines the different ways in which the relationships between the variables might be conceptualized and discusses the control variables included in the study. The con-trol variables are additional variables that may have an influence on the nature of the relationships be-tween the main variables in the study. They then go on to explain how the main variables in their research were measured using a series of psychological scales.

Results

In this section, the authors provide a general description of their findings, which are based on factor analysis (see Chapter 3), and then consider whether their hypotheses are supported. In fact, it turns out that hypotheses 1 and 2 are supported, but hypothesis 3, which predicted that contract fulfilment would have a positive effect on OCB, is not supported. In fact, the effect of transactional fulfilment on OCB is found to be negative. They then offer a potential explanation that may account for this contrary finding related to the difficulties in conceptualizing OCB, arguing that what is measured in the study as citizenship behaviour and thus discretionary 'may actually be considered in-role behaviours from the employees' viewpoint' (2000: 920). They thus highlight differences in interpretation that OCB is prone to.

Discussion

In this final section, Coyle-Shapiro and Kessler return to the issues that have been driving their investigation. These are the issues they presented in the introduction and theory sections. They begin this section with a strong statement of their findings:

Our findings suggest that the majority of employees are experiencing contract breach. Furthermore, managers responding as representatives of the employer broadly support this. The extent of perceived employer contract fulfilment has a significant effect on employees' perceived organizational support, organizational commitment and organizational citizenship behaviour. (2000: 922)

They go on to claim that their results are consistent with other empirical studies that suggest violation of the psychological contract, adding that 'our inclusion of the employer's perspective adds significant weight to the findings' (2000: 922).

In the last few paragraphs of the paper, Coyle-Shapiro and Kessler reflect upon the implications of their findings for our understanding of the consequences of employer contract behaviour and the nature of the psychological contract, concluding that 'overall, this study highlights the importance of employer's contract behaviour regarding the fulfilment of specific obligations in affecting

employees' attitudes and behaviour' (2000: 923). After drawing attention to some of the limitations of the study, they then outline possibilities for further research. Finally, they outline some practical implications of the study, suggesting that 'employers need to take steps to understand employees' perceptions of the content of the psychological contract and from this alter the terms of the contract where circumstances permit' (2000: 925). Many articles have a section called 'conclusion' in which the kinds of discussion that appear in these last few paragraphs are presented. Regardless of whether there is a separate conclusion, a presentation of the main conclusions will invariably be provided.

Lessons

What lessons can be learned from Coyle-Shapiro and Kessler's article? To some extent, these have been alluded to in the course of the above exposition, but they are worth spelling out.

- There is a clear attempt to grab the reader's attention with strong opening statements, which also act as signposts to what the article is about.

- The authors spell out clearly the rationale of their research. This entails pointing to the significance of the psychological contract as a framework for analysis of the employment relationship highlighting reasons for renewed interest in this concept, along with the neglect of the employer's perspective in most research.

- The research questions are spelled out in a very specific way. In fact, the authors present hypotheses that are a highly specific form of research question. As noted in Chapter 3, by no means all quantitative research is driven by hypotheses, even though outlines of the nature of quantitative research often imply that it is. Nonetheless, Coyle-Shapiro and Kessler chose to frame their research questions in this form.

- The research methods employed, the nature of the data, the measurement of concepts, the sampling, and the approaches to the analysis of the data are clearly and explicitly summarized.

- The presentation of the findings is oriented very specifically to the questions that drive the research.

- The discussion returns to the research questions and spells out the implications of the findings for them and for the theories examined earlier on in the paper. This is an important element. It is easy to forget that you should think of the research process as closing a circle in which you must return unambiguously to your research questions. There is no point inserting extraneous findings if they do not illuminate your research questions. Digressions of this kind can be confusing to readers, who might be inclined to wonder about the significance of the extraneous findings. In this section there is an attempt to consider the limitations of the study, in addition to its strengths, and to identify possibilities for further research. In addition, because business and management are an applied field of research, it is also common at this stage to draw attention to practical implications that arise from the study.

We also see that there is a clear sequential process moving from the formulation of the research questions through the exposition of the nature of the data and the presentation of the findings to the conclusions. Each stage is linked to and follows on from its predecessor (but see Box 24.2). The structure used by Coyle-Shapiro and Kessler is based on a common one employed in the writing-up of quantitative research for academic journals in business and management. Sometimes, there is a separate Theory section that appears between the Introduction and the Data sections. Another variation is that issues of measurement and analysis appear in separate sections from the one dealing with research methods. Finally, the structure employed by Coyle-Shapiro and Kessler involved just one final section entitled Discussion, in which the authors drew their conclusions, but in other articles these may be treated as separate sections.

Box 24.2 An empiricist repertoire?

At this point, it is worth recalling the discussion in Chapter 21 of Gilbert and Mulkay's (1984) research on scientists. The authors drew a distinction between an *empiricist repertoire* and a *contingent repertoire*. The former derived from 'the observation that the texts of experimental papers display certain recurrent stylistic, grammatical and lexical features which appear to be coherently related' (1984: 55–6). We should bear in mind that the same is true of papers written for social science journals. These too display certain features that suggest a degree of inevitability to the outcome of the research. In other words, the reader is given a sense that, in following the rigorous procedures outlined in the article, the researchers logically arrived at their conclusions. The contingent repertoire, with its recognition of the role of the researcher in the production of findings, is far less apparent in scientists' published work. Thus, we have to recognize the possibility that the impression of a series of linked stages leading to an inescapable culmination is to a large extent a reconstruction of events designed to persuade referees (who, of course, use the same tactics themselves) of the credibility and importance of one's findings. This

means that the conventions about writing up a quantitative research project, some of which are outlined in this chapter, are in many ways an invitation to reconstruct an investigation in a particular way. The whole issue of the ways in which the writing-up of research represents a means of persuading others of the credibility of one's knowledge claims has been a particular preoccupation among qualitative researchers (see below) and has been greatly influenced by the surge of interest in postmodernism. However, in Box 24.3, some of the rhetorical strategies involved in writing up quantitative research are outlined. Three points are worth making about these strategies in the present context. First, they are characteristic of the empiricist repertoire. Secondly, while the writing of qualitative research has been a particular focus in recent times (see below), some attention has also been paid to quantitative research. Thirdly, when Bryman (1998) compared the writing of quantitative and qualitative research articles, he found they were not as dissimilar in terms of rhetorical strategies as is sometimes proposed. However, he did find greater evidence of a management metaphor (see Box 24.3).

Box 24.3 Rhetorical strategies in writing up quantitative research

The rhetorical strategies used by quantitative researchers include the following.

- There is a tendency to remove the researcher from the text as an active ingredient of the research process in order to convey an impression of the objective nature of the findings—that is, as part of an external reality that is independent of the researcher (Gusfield 1976). Woolgar (1988) refers to this as an externalizing device.

- The researcher surfaces in the text only to demonstrate his or her ingenuity in overcoming obstacles (Bazerman 1987; Bryman 1998).

- Key figures in the field are routinely cited to bestow credibility on the research (McCloskey 1985).

- The research process is presented as a linear one to convey an air of inevitability about the findings arrived at (Gusfield 1976).

- Relatively strict rules are followed about what should be reported in published research and how it should be reported (Bazerman 1987).

- The use of a *management* metaphor is common in the presentation of findings in which the researcher is depicted as ingeniously ' "designing" research, "controlling" variables, "managing" data, and "generating" tables' (Bryman 1998: 146). See Shapiro (1985–6) and Richardson (1990) on this point.

Note that the first two are somewhat inconsistent. There is some evidence that disciplines within the social sciences differ in respect of their use of an impersonal style of writing. But it may well also be that it sometimes depends on what the writer is trying to do; for example, sometimes getting across a sense of one's cunning in overcoming practical difficulties can be just as useful as giving a sense of the external nature of the findings. Therefore, sometimes the style of presentation may vary somewhat.

Writing qualitative research: an example

Now we will look at an example of a journal article based on qualitative research. Again, we are not suggesting that the article is exemplary or representative, but that it exhibits some features that are often regarded as desirable qualities in terms of presentation and structure. The article is one that has been referred to in Chapters 13 and 22 and Box 14.1: a study of time use at work by Perlow (1999). The study is based predominantly on ethnographic methods and was published in *Administrative Science Quarterly*, a leading American journal.

The structure runs as follows:

1. introduction;
2. review of the literature;
3. methods;
4. presentation of main themes;
5. discussion;
6. implications.

What is immediately striking about the structure is that it is not dissimilar to Coyle-Shapiro and Kessler's (2000). Nor should this be all that surprising. After all, a structure that runs

Introduction ➔ Literature review ➔ Research design/ methods ➔ Results ➔ Discussion ➔ Conclusions

is not obviously associated with one research strategy rather than the other. One difference from quantitative research articles is that the presentation of the results and the discussion of them are frequently rather more interwoven in qualitative research articles. We will see this in the case of Perlow's article. As with Coyle-Shapiro and Kessler's article, we will examine the writing in terms of the article's structure.

Introduction

The first two paragraphs give us an immediate sense of what the article is about and where its focus lies. Like Coyle-Shapiro and Kessler, Perlow uses the introduction to locate the article in relation to a subject of wide interest to business and management researchers, referring to the tendency for many workers routinely to work extremely long hours and to suffer as a result. She explains: 'The purpose of this paper is to explore what I refer to as their time famine—their feeling of having too much to do and not enough time to do it—and to question whether this famine must exist' (Perlow 1999: 57).

In the second paragraph, Perlow begins simply by stating what type of workers she intends to focus on: 'I chose to study a group of software engineers in a high-tech corporation' (Perlow 1999: 57).

She then goes on to outline precisely the position that will be taken in the article:

Several recent books have described with awe the fast-paced, high-pressure, crisis-filled environment in which software engineers work (Kidder 1981; Moody 1990; Zachary 1994). These authors portray the engineers as heroes for their willingness to work extremely long hours and celebrate the engineers' intensity and total devotion to work. I, in contrast, explore the engineers' actual use of time at work and the impact their use of time has on other individuals and the groups to which individuals belong, which reveals the problematic nature of the current way of using time. Ultimately, I therefore challenge the assumption that the current way of using time, which is so destructive to individuals' lives outside of work, is in the corporation's best interests (Perlow 1995, 1997).   (Perlow 1999: 57)

Like Coyle-Shapiro and Kessler's, this is a strong introduction. Although it must be noted that for the purpose of this analysis we have been selective in our direct quotation from these two paragraphs, it is useful to look again at what each of these sentences achieves.

- The first sentence introduces a primary theme, the idea of 'time famine', which is the main subject of this article.

- The second sentence provides a specific research focus—the study of software engineers.

- In the four sentences of the final block of text, however, our attention is jolted by the assertions that the author makes in relation to the existing literature. Like Coyle-Shapiro and Kessler, Perlow begins by pointing to a line of research interest in this subject, but interestingly, unlike them, she cites the work of these authors critically, using it to draw the reader's attention to what she is *not* going to do in *this* article. In addition, by highlighting the limitations of the existing literature, Perlow is preparing the reader for delivery of her alternative viewpoint.

- In the second to last sentence, Perlow claims that, unlike previous studies, this article explores 'engineers' actual use of time', thereby implying her preference for qualitative, ethnographic research.

- The final sentence allows Perlow to elaborate on the argument that she is making, in which she directly contradicts some of the claims made by other writers.

Thus, after around 100 words, the reader has a clear idea of the focus of the research and has been led to anticipate that some of the findings presented within the article are likely to be unsupportive or indeed indirectly critical of existing studies of how people use their time at work. Unlike the previous article by Coyle-Shapiro and Kessler, Perlow is more forthright in presenting an argument that is sometimes almost polemical in its criticism of other writers for their tendency to glamorize high-pressure work.

Review of the literature

This short section reviews existing theory and research on time use at work. Perlow proposes that the theory and research 'on time use contributes to a partial understanding of both how and why individuals do and should spend their time at work' (1999: 57). This point is important because it enables Perlow to acknowledge, yet also to distance her study, from existing literature in order to be able to develop an alternative theoretical position throughout the remainder of the article. Interestingly, even though this section is relatively short, approximately 600 words, it contains twenty-eight references. Many of these are string references—this means that they are grouped together to indicate a theoretical association. In contrast, there are only two references in the whole of the two subsequent sections.

Methods

This section covers a number of important issues relating to the methods and the analytical processes used within the study. The author outlines:

- what the organization that the software engineers worked for is like and why it was chosen as the research site for the study;
- how respondents were selected and access negotiated;
- the data sources used, which included participant observation, semi-structured interviews, shadowing and tracking logs (see Box 14.1 and Chapter 22) and how the data were collected;
- the approach to analysing the data; this involved an iterative process of generating inferences that were related to emerging themes.

Presentation of main themes

The chief findings are outlined under separate headings: interdependent work patterns, enactment of work patterns, and effectiveness of work patterns. The presentation of the results is carried out so that there is some discussion of their meaning or significance in such a way as to lead onto the next section, which provides more detailed discussion of them. For example, in the first paragraph of the second main theme, which deals with enactment of work patterns, Perlow writes:

Two components of the social context help explain why engineers perpetuated this disruptive pattern of interacting. I found that engineers experience both constant pressure to respond to crises and a reward system based on individual heroics. These two components, together, resulted in engineers doing whatever it took to solve the crisis of the moment. When individuals attempted to solve crises at the expense of all else, they frequently interrupted each other,

thereby further perpetuating crises and the perceived need for individuals to do whatever it took to solve crises. I refer to this dynamic as the vicious work–time cycle. (1999: 65)

In this way, the presentation of the results is pointing forward to some themes that are taken up in the following sections and this demonstrates the significance of certain findings in relation to some of the previously discussed literature.

Discussion

This section discusses the findings in the light of the study's research questions about how people use time at work. The results are also related to many of the ideas introduced in the previous sections of the article, in particular to the notions of the 'vicious work–time cycle', which the author suggests is reinforced by 'individual heroics'. However, in this section the author takes these ideas in a more ambitious direction, suggesting that the emerging 'framework' lays the 'foundation' for development of 'a sociology of work time' that 'integrates components from several existing streams of research' (1999: 77). To support this claim she draws on the work of a number of highly regarded sociologists of work time (including Zerubavel 1981 and Roy 1958) and calls for a structuration approach (Giddens 1979) to writing work ethnographies (see Box 1.2 for a summary of structuration theory). 'Researchers would consider simultaneously the role that these interdependent patterns play in the work process and both the social and temporal contexts that perpetuate and are perpetuated by these patterns' (Perlow 1999: 77–8).

Implications

In this section, the author spells out the implications of the research, which are claimed to be practical as well as theoretical in nature. To this end, Perlow suggests that the 'vicious circle' may be changed into a 'virtuous circle' through the actions of managers. She states: 'instead of interruptions perpetuating crises, reactive behaviour, and long work hours, synchronizing individual and interactive activities may minimize crises, perpetuate proactive behaviour, and even reduce the demand for such long work hours' (1999: 79). Thus, similarly to Coyle-Shapiro and Kessler, Perlow rounds off the article by drawing attention to the relevance of the findings for those who manage. The final sentence returns to the primary theme of 'time famine' and reiterates the main findings of the study in order to drive home this point: to mitigate the time famine experienced by employees whose

work involves both individual and interactive activities a new type of collective time management is needed—one that takes into account individuals' interdependent work patterns, the macro context in which they work, and the interconnections between this context and their work patterns.   (1999: 80)

Lessons

As with Coyle-Shapiro and Kessler's article, it is useful to review some of the lessons learned from this examination of Perlow's article.

- Just like the illustration of quantitative research writing, there are strong opening sentences, which attract our attention and give a clear indication of the nature and content of the article.

- The rationale of the research is clearly identified. To a large extent, this revolves around noting the limitations of existing literature that celebrates heroic attitudes towards time-use at work and challenging the assumption that this is in either the individual's or the organization's interests.

- Research questions are specified but they are somewhat more open-ended than in Coyle-Shapiro and Kessler's article, which is in keeping with the general orientation of qualitative researchers. The

research questions revolve around the engineers' use of time at work and the impact that this has on other individuals and groups to which the engineers belong.

- The research methods are outlined and an indication is given of the approach to analysis. The section in which these issues are discussed demonstrates greater transparency than is sometimes the case with articles reporting qualitative research.

- The presentation of main themes is geared to the broad research questions that motivated the researcher's interest in time-use at work. However, this section also represents a major opportunity for the idea of the vicious work–time cycle and its dimensions to be articulated. The inductive nature of qualitative research means that the concepts and theories that are generated from an investigation must be clearly identified and discussed, as in this case.

- The discussion section allows concepts and theories to be developed into a more general framework, which is used to characterize the present study in the context of other qualitative studies of work time.

- The implications elucidate in a more specific way the significance of these results for managers, thereby addressing a requirement that is specifically made of business and management researchers to highlight the practical relevance of research findings.

In Chapter 26, the implications of the writing practices revealed in this review of the articles by Coyle-Shapiro and Kessler and Perlow will be returned to in the context of exploring some possible implications for a dissertation or report that you might need to produce.

Postmodernism and its implications for writing

Postmodernism (see Box 13.1) is an extremely difficult idea to pin down. In one sense, it can be seen as a form of sensitivity—a way of seeing and understanding that results in a questioning of the taken-for-granted. It questions the very notion of the dispassionate social

scientist seeking to uncover a pre-given external reality. Instead, postmodernists view the social scientist's account as only one among many ways of rendering social reality to audiences. The social world itself is viewed as a context out of which many accounts can be hewn. As a result, 'knowledge' of the social world is relative; any account is just one of many possible ways of rendering social reality. As Rosenau (1992: 8) puts it, postmodernists 'offer "readings" not "observations," "interpretations" not "findings"...'.

One of the effects of the impact of postmodernism since the 1980s has been a growing interest in the writing of social science. For postmodernists, reporting findings in a journal article provides merely one version of the social reality that was investigated. Postmodernists mistrust the knowledge claims that are frequently boldly made when findings are reported and instead they adopt an attitude of investigating the bases and forms of those knowledge claims. While the writing of all types of social science is potentially in the postmodernist's firing line, it has been the kinds of text produced by ethnographers that have been a particular focus of attention. This focus has led to a particular interest in the claims to ethnographic authority that are inscribed into ethnographic texts (Clifford 1983). The ethnographic text 'presumes a world out there (the real) that can be captured by a "knowing" author through the careful transcription and analysis of field materials (interviews, notes, etc.)' (Denzin 1994: 296). Postmodernism problematizes such accounts and their authority to represent a reality because there 'can never be a final, accurate representation of what was meant or said, only different textual representations of different experiences' (Denzin 1994: 296).

However, it would be wrong to depict the growing attention being focused on ethnographic writing as exclusively a product of postmodernism. Atkinson and Coffey (1995) have argued that there are other intellectual trends in the social sciences that have stimulated this interest. Writers in the area of theory and research known as the social studies of science have been concerned with the limitations of accepted distinctions between rhetoric and logic and between the observer and the observed (e.g. Gilbert and Mulkay 1984). The problematizing of these distinctions, along with doubts about the possibility of a neutral language through which the natural and social worlds can be revealed, opened the door for an evaluation of scientific and social scientific writing. Some illustrations of these analyses can be discerned

in Boxes 24.2 and 24.3. Atkinson and Coffey also point to the antipathy within feminism towards the image of the neutral 'observer-author' who assumes a privileged stance in relation to members of the social setting being studied. This stance is regarded as revealing a position of domination of the observer-author over the observed that is inconsistent with the goals of feminism (see Chapter 13 for an elaboration of this general point). This concern has led to an interest in the ways in which privilege is conveyed in ethnographic texts and how voices, particularly of marginal groups, are suppressed.

The concerns within these and other traditions (including postmodernism) have led to experiments in writing ethnography (Richardson 1994). An example is the use of a 'dialogic' form of writing that seeks to raise the profile of the multiplicity of voices that can be heard in the course of fieldwork. As Lincoln and Denzin (1994: 584) put it: 'Slowly it dawns on us that there may...be...not one "voice", but polyvocality; not one story, but many tales, dramas, pieces of fiction, fables, memories, histories, autobiographies, poems, and other texts to inform our sense of lifeways, to extend our understandings of the Other...'. This postmodern preference for seeking out multiple voices and for turning the ethnographer into a 'bit player' reflects the mistrust among postmodernists of 'meta-narratives'—that is, positions or grand accounts that implicitly make claims about absolute truths and that therefore rule out the possibility of alternative versions of reality. On the other hand, 'mini-narratives, micro-narratives, local narratives are just stories that make no truth claims and are therefore more acceptable to postmodernists' (Rosenau 1992: p. xiii).

Postmodernism has also encouraged a growing reflexivity in considerations about the conduct of business research, and the growing interest in the writing of ethnography is very much a manifestation of this trend (see Box 24.4). This reflexivity can be discerned in the way in which many ethnographers have turned inwards to examine the truth claims inscribed in their own classic texts, which is the focus of the next section.

In the end, what postmodernism leaves us with is an acute sense of uncertainty. It raises the issue of

Box 24.4 *What is reflexivity?*

Reflexivity has several meanings in the social sciences. The term is employed by ethnomethodologists to refer to the way in which speech and action are constitutive of the social world in which they are located; in other words, they do more than merely act as indicators of deeper phenomena (see Chapter 17). The other meaning of the term carries the connotation that business researchers should be reflective about the implications of their methods, values, biases, and decisions for the knowledge of the social world they generate. It assumes that all researchers enter the field carrying cultural 'baggage', personal idiosyncracies and implicit assumptions about the nature of reality. Reflexivity involves a willingness to probe beyond the level of straightforward interpretation (Woolgar 1988) and to explore how these biases and characteristics affect the research process. This is described as resembling having an ongoing conversation with oneself about an experience whilst simultaneously living in the moment.

There has been evidence of a growing reflexivity in organizational research in the form of an industry of books that collect together inside stories of the research process that detail the nuts and bolts of research as distinct from the often sanitized portrayal in research articles. An early volume on the sociological research process edited by Hammond (1964) paved the way for a large number of imitators (e.g. Bell and Newby 1977; Bell and Roberts 1984; Bryman 1988*b*; Shaffir and Stebbins 1991) and the confessional tales referred to in Box 24.6 are invariably manifestations of this development. Therefore, the rise of reflexivity largely predates the growing awareness of postmodern thinking since the late 1980s. What distinguishes the reflexivity that has followed in the wake of postmodernism is a greater awareness and acknowledgement of the role of the researcher as part and parcel of the construction of knowledge. In other words, the reflexive attitude within postmodernism is highly critical of the notion that the researcher is someone who extracts knowledge from observations and conversations with others and then transmits knowledge to an audience. The researcher is viewed as implicated in the construction of knowledge through the stance that he or she assumes in relation to the observed and through the ways in which an account is transmitted in the form of a text. This understanding entails an acknowledgement of the implications and significance of the researcher's choices as both observer and writer.

Box 24.5 Identity and ethnographic writing

In her study of everyday life on the shopfloor of a Japanese factory, Kondo (1990) provides an example of ethnographic writing in which the self is central to the account. Kondo describes how, as a Japanese–American academic studying Japanese factory life, she had to learn how to act and behave as a Japanese woman: 'My first nine months of fieldwork were characterised by an attempt to reduce the distance between expectation and inadequate reality, as my informants and I conspired to rewrite my identity as Japanese' (1990: 25). Her sense of self and identity was thereby mediated 'by the experiences, relations and interactions of her fieldwork' (Coffey 1999: 24).

Writing partly in the first person, Kondo seeks to reveal her identity through the text in order to emphasize the point that the ethnographic text is constructed through the stance assumed in relation to the observed. For example she states: 'what I write is no mere academic exercise; for me it matters, and matters deeply' (1990: 302).

Kondo is also critical of conventional ethnographic writing, which 'sandwiches the "data" into the body of the book, leaving "theory" for beginning and the end' (1990: 304). Instead she 'scatters' theoretical discussion 'in different parts of the text, and the "ethnographic" vignettes and anecdotes are marshaled analytically' (1990: 304).

Kondo's work thus provides an example of a contemporary organizational ethnography that seeks to achieve a postmodern reflexivity, partly through exploration of experimental writing strategies.

how we can ever know or capture the social reality that belongs to others and in so doing it points to an unresolvable tension that will not go away and that is further revealed in the issues raised in the next section, because, to quote Lincoln and Denzin (1994: 582) again: 'On the one hand there is the concern for validity, or certainty in the text as a form of isomorphism and authenticity. On the other hand there is the sure and certain knowledge that all texts are socially, historically, politically, and culturally located. We, like the texts we write, can never be transcendent.' At the same time, of course, such a view renders problematic the very idea of what knowledge is or comprises.

Writing ethnography

The term 'ethnography', as noted in Chapter 14, is interesting, because it refers to both a method of business research and the finished product of ethnographic research. In other words, it is both something that is carried out in doing research and something one reads. Thus, writing seems to be at the heart of the ethnographic enterprise. In recent years, the production of ethnographic texts has become a focus of interest in its own right. This means that there has been a growth of interest not just in how ethnography is carried out in the field but also in the rhetorical conventions employed in the production of ethnographic texts.

Ethnographic texts are designed to convince readers of the *reality* of the events and situations described, and the plausibility of the analyst's explanations. The ethnographic text must not simply present a set of findings: it must provide an 'authoritative' account of the group or culture in question. In other words, the ethnographer must convince us that he or she has arrived at an account of social reality that has strong claims to truth.

The ethnographic text is permeated by stylistic and rhetorical devices whereby the reader is persuaded to enter into a shared framework of facts and interpretations, observations and reflections. Just like the scientific paper and the kind of approach to writing found in reporting quantitative business research, the ethnographer typically works within a writing strategy that is imbued with *realism*. This simply means that the researcher presents an authoritative, dispassionate account that represents an external, objective reality. In this respect, there is very little difference between the writing styles of quantitative and qualitative

researchers. Van Maanen (1988) calls ethnography texts that conform to these characteristics *realist tales*. These are the most common type of ethnographic writing, though he distinguishes other types (see Box 24.6). However, the *form* that this realism takes differs. Van Maanen distinguishes four characteristics of realist tales: experiential authority; typical forms; the native's point of view; and interpretative omnipotence. Realist tales are particularly prevalent in business and management research writing (see Box 24.7).

Experiential authority

Just as in much quantitative research writing, the author disappears from view. We are told what members of a group say and do, and they are the only people directly visible in the text. The author provides a narrative in which he or she is no longer to be seen. As a result, an impression is conveyed that the findings presented are what any reasonable, similarly placed researcher would have found. As readers, we have to accept that this is what the ethnographer saw and heard while working as a participant observer or whatever. The personal subjectivity of the author/ ethnographer is essentially played down by this strategy. The possibility that the fieldworker may have his or her own biases or may have become too involved with the people being studied is suppressed. To this end, when writing up the results of their ethnographic work, authors play up their academic credentials and qualifications, their previous experience, and so on. All this enhances the degree to which the author's account can be relied upon.

Box 24.6 Three forms of ethnographic writing

Van Maanen (1988) has distinguished three major types of ethnographic writing.

- *Realist tales*—apparently definitive, confident, and dispassionate third person accounts of a culture and of the behaviour of members of that culture. This is the most prevalent form of ethnographic writing.

- *Confessional tales*—personalized accounts in which the ethnographer is fully implicated in the data-gathering and writing-up processes. These are warts-and-all accounts of the trials and tribulations of doing ethnography. They have become more prominent since the 1970s and reflect a growing emphasis on reflexivity in qualitative research in particular. In the edited volume *Doing Research in Organizations* (Bryman 1988*b*) several of the contributors provide inside accounts of doing qualitative research in industrial enterprises. Beynon (1988), for example, describes how his account published in *Working for Ford* (1975) of how a dead man was left lying on the factory floor for ten minutes while the line continued to run provoked a response from the Ford Motor Company, which sought to discredit his research. As this example illustrates, confessional tales are more concerned with detailing how research was carried out than with presenting findings. Very often the confessional tale is told in a particular context (such as an invited chapter in a book of similar tales), but the main findings are written up in realist tale form.

- *Impressionist tales*—accounts that place a heavy emphasis on 'words, metaphors, phrasings, and . . . the expansive recall of fieldwork experience' (Van Maanen 1988: 102). There is a heavy emphasis on stories of dramatic events that provide 'a representational means of cracking open the culture and the fieldworker's way of knowing it' (1988: 102). However, as Van Maanen notes, impressionist tales 'are typically enclosed within realist, or perhaps more frequently, confessional tales' (1988: 106).

Box 24.7 Realism in organizational ethnography

Many organizational ethnographies tend to be written as realist tales (see Box 24.6) and narrated dispassionately in order to reinforce the authenticity of the account. Typically, the author is absent from the text, or is a minor character in the story, and methods are revealed only at the end, in the form of a 'confessional' chapter or appendix, where the ethnographer 'reveals his hand' (Watson 1994*a*) by disclosing personal details about the fieldwork experience. However, this is not to say that organizational ethnographers are unaware of the representational difficulties caused by such an approach to writing. Consider, for example, the first few sentences of the methodological appendix that is provided by Kunda (1992) in the book *Engineering Culture: Control and Commitment in a High-Tech Corporation*.

This study belongs to the genre of ethnographic realism described in Box 24.6. Although this identification says much about presentational style, it gives away little about the research process. The descriptive style presents an author functioning more or less as a fly on the wall in the course of his sojourn in the field, as an objective, unseen observer following well-defined procedures for data collection and verification. It requires no great insight to recognize that this is a distortion of convenience. Fieldwork, as those who have engaged in it will testify, is an intensely personal and subjective process and there are probably at least as many methods as there are fieldworkers.

Kunda (1992) questions the extent to which the ethnographer is an objective observer, suggesting instead that he or she experiences organizational life from a situated position as an insider. He implies that it is therefore impossible for ethnographers to distance themselves from the fieldwork experience. However, despite this recognition of the need for greater 'reflexivity' within organizational ethnography, only a few organizational ethnographies are actually written in the first person, with the researcher as a main character who is telling the story. Even in cases when this does occur, the main character narrative tends to be located peripherally, in the appendixes or footnotes of an article or book (Hatch 1996), such as Kunda himself has done.

The author/ethnographer can then appear as a reliable witness.

A further element of experiential authority is that, when describing their methods, ethnographers invariably make a great deal of the intensiveness of the research that they carried out—they spent so many months in the field, had conversations and interviews with countless individuals, worked hard to establish rapport, and so on. These features are also added to by drawing the reader's attention to such hardships as the inconvenience of the fieldwork—the danger, the poor food, the disruptive effect on normal life, the feelings of isolation and loneliness, and so on.

Also worth mentioning are the extensive quotations from conversations and interviews that invariably form part of the ethnographic report. These are also obviously important ingredients of the author's use of *evidence* to support points. However, they are a mechanism for establishing the credibility of the report in that they demonstrate the author's ability to encourage people to talk and so demonstrate that he or she achieved rapport with them. The copious descriptive details—of places, patterns of behaviour, contexts, and so on—can also be viewed as a means of piling on the sense of the author being an ideally placed witness for all the findings that have been uncovered.

Typical forms

The author often writes about typical forms of institutions or of patterns of behaviour. What is happening here is that the author is generalizing about a number of recurring features of the group in question to create a typical form that that feature takes. He or she may use examples based on particular incidents or people, but basically the emphasis is upon the general. For example, in Watson's (1994*a*) conclusion to his ethnographic study of managers in a UK telecommunications company, which was cited several times in Chapter 14, we encounter the following statement:

The image which has taken shape is one of management as essentially and inherently a social and moral activity; one

whose greatest successes in efficiently and effectively producing goods and services is likely to come through building organisational patterns, cultures and understandings based on relationships of mutual trust and shared obligation among people involved with the organisation. (1994*a*: 223)

The study is thus meant to portray managers in general and individuals are important only in so far as they represent such general tendencies.

The native's point of view

The point has been made several times that one of the distinguishing features of much qualitative research is the commitment to seeing through the eyes of the people being studied. This is an important feature for qualitative researchers, because it is part of a strategy of getting at the meaning of social reality from the perspective of those being studied. However, it also represents an important element in creating a sense of authoritativeness on the part of the ethnographer. After all, claiming that he or she takes the native's point of view and sees through their eyes means that he or she is in an excellent position to speak authoritatively about the group in question. The very fact that the ethnographer has taken the native's point of view testifies to the fact that he or she is well placed to write definitively about the group in question. Realist tales frequently include numerous references to the steps taken by the ethnographer to get close to the people studied and his or her success in this regard. Thus, in her study of Afro-Carribean women working in high-tech informatics (see Chapter 14), Freeman (2000) writes about the small group of six women at Multitext, who became the focus of more intense, long-term data collection:

After many Sunday lunches, picnics, church services, birthday celebrations, and family outings, I got to know these few women better, seeing them not only as workers but also as members of families, as partners in complex relationships, as mothers, as daughters, as co-workers, and as friends. We spent time together in my rented flat, and in their wood and 'wall house' homes, cooking and eating meals together, sometimes watching videos as we talked. I persuaded them, on rare occasions, to picnic at the beach, and they took me to their churches and fetes and on special outings—to the circus, to the calypso contests, and to national sites enjoyed by tourists and locals alike. Sometimes we went shopping, and sometimes we bought ice cream after work.   (2000: 17)

Interpretative omnipotence

When writing up an ethnography, the author rarely presents possible alternative interpretations of an event or pattern of behaviour. Instead, the phenomenon in question is presented as having a single meaning or significance, which the fieldworker alone has cracked. Indeed, the evidence provided is carefully marshalled to support the singular interpretation that is placed on the event or pattern of behaviour. We are presented with an inevitability. It seems obvious or inevitable that someone would draw the inferences that the author has drawn when faced with such clear-cut evidence.

These four characteristics of realist tales imply that what the researcher did qua researcher is only one part of creating a sense of having figured out the nature of a culture. It is also very much to do with how the researcher represents what he or she did through writing about ethnography. For the postmodernist position, any realist tale is merely one 'spin'—that is one version, which can be or has been formulated in relation to the culture in question.

K KEY POINTS

- Good writing is probably just as important as good research practice. Indeed, it is probably better thought of as a part of good research practice.

- Clear structure and statement of your research questions are important components of writing up research.

- Be sensitive to the ways in which writers seek to persuade us of their points of view.

- The study of rhetoric and writing strategies generally teaches us that the writings of scientists and social scientists do more than simply report findings. They are designed to convince and to persuade.

- The emphasis on rhetoric is not meant to imply that there is no external social reality; it merely suggests that our understanding of that reality is profoundly influenced by the ways it is represented by writers.

- While postmodernism has exerted a particular influence on this last point, writers working within other traditions have also contributed to it.

- The basic structure of and the rhetorical strategies employed in most quantitative and qualitative research articles are broadly similar.

- We need to get away from the idea that rhetoric and the desire to persuade others of the validity of our work are somehow bad things. They are not. We all want to get our points across and to persuade our readers that we have got things right. The question is—do we do it well? Do we make the best possible case? We all have to persuade others that we have got the right angle on things; the trick is to do it well. So when you write an essay or dissertation, do bear in mind the significance of your writing strategy.

Q **QUESTIONS FOR REVIEW**

- Why is it important to consider the ways in which business research is written up?

Writing quantitative research: an example

- Read an article based on quantitative research in an American business and management journal (e.g. *Academy of Management Journal* or *Administrative Science Quarterly*). How far does it exhibit the same characteristics as Coyle-Shapiro and Kessler's article?

- What is meant by rhetorical strategy? Why might rhetorical strategies be important in relation to the writing-up of business research?

- Do Coyle-Shapiro and Kessler employ an empiricist repertoire?

Writing qualitative research: an example

- Read an article based on quantitative research in a European business and management journal (e.g. *Organization Studies, Journal of Management Studies*, or *Organization*). How far does it exhibit the same characteristics as Perlow's article?

- How far is the structure of Perlow's article different from Coyle-Shapiro and Kessler's?

Postmodernism and its implications for writing

- Why has postmodernism produced a growth of interest in writing business research?

- What is reflexivity?

Writing ethnography

- How far is it true to say that ethnographic writing is typically imbued with realism?

- What forms of ethnographic writing other than realist tales can be found?

- What are the main characteristics of realist tales?

25 Ethics in business research

CHAPTER GUIDE

Ethical issues arise at a variety of stages in business and management research. This chapter is concerned with the concerns about ethics that might arise in the course of conducting research. The professional bodies concerned with the social sciences have been keen to spell out the ethical issues that can arise, and some of their statements will be reviewed in this chapter. Ethical issues cannot be ignored, in that they relate directly to the integrity of a piece of research and of the disciplines that are involved. This chapter explores:

- some famous, even infamous, cases in which transgressions of ethical principles have occurred, though it is important not to take the view that ethical concerns arise only in relation to these extreme cases;

- different stances that can be and have been taken on ethics in business research;

- the significance and operation of four areas in which ethical concerns particularly arise: whether harm comes to participants; informed consent; invasion of privacy; and deception;

- some of the difficulties associated with ethical decision making.

Introduction

Discussions about the ethics of business and management research bring us into a realm in which the role of values in the research process becomes a topic of concern. They revolve around such issues as the following.

- How should we treat the people on whom we conduct research?

- Are there activities in which we should or should not engage in our relations with them?

Questions about ethics in business and management research also bring in the role of professional associations, such as the American Academy of Management (AoM) and the Market Research Society (MRS), which have formulated codes of ethics on behalf of their members. Statements of professional principles are frequently accessible from the Internet. Some useful codes of ethics for business and management researchers can be found at the following Internet addresses.

Academy of Management (AoM), *Code of Ethical Conduct*: **www.aomonline.org/aom.asp?ID=185**

Market Research Society (MRS), *Code of Conduct and Guidelines*: **www.mrs.org.uk/standards/guidelines** (also includes specific MRS guidelines on qualitative and quantitative research, doing Internet and employee research).

However, it is also useful to look at the way that researchers within the social sciences more generally have dealt with ethical research issues—for example, the Social Research Association (SRA) and the British Sociological Association (BSA). In this chapter, the codes of these professional associations will also be referred to on several occasions.

Social Research Association (SRA), *Ethical Guidelines* **www.the-sra.org.uk/ethicals.htm**

British Sociological Association (BSA), *Statement of Ethical Practice* **www.britsoc.org.uk/about/ethic.htm**

American Sociological Association (ASA), *Code of Ethics* **www.asanet.org/members/ecoderev.html**

Writings about ethics in social research are frequently frustrating for four reasons.

1. Writers often differ quite widely from each other over ethical issues and questions. In other words, they differ over what is and is not ethically acceptable.

2. The main elements in the debates do not seem to move forward a great deal. The same kinds of points that were made in the 1960s were being rehashed in the late 1990s and at the start of the present century.

3. Debates about ethics have often accompanied well-known cases of alleged ethical transgression. Some of them, such as Dalton's (1959) covert ethnography of unofficial managerial activity, have already been encountered earlier on in this book (Chapter 14 and Box 14.7). One of the central issues that Dalton addresses in his study is the unofficial use of company resources, including pilfering or corporate theft (see Box 25.1). There is considerable debate as to whether it was ethical to obtain such data through the method of covert observation. There are also several well-known psychological studies (e.g. Milgram 1963; Haney, Banks, and Zimbardo 1973) that continue to be widely cited in the field of organizational behaviour, despite the fact that they were based on research designs that would now be widely considered extremely unethical (see Box 25.3). However, the problem with this emphasis on notoriety is that it can be taken to imply that ethical concerns reside only in such extreme cases, when in fact the potential for ethical transgression is much more general than this.

4. Related to this last point is that these extreme and notorious cases of ethical violation tend to be associated with particular research methods—notably disguised observation and the use of deception in experiments. Again, the problem with this association of ethics with certain studies (and methods) is that it implies that ethical concerns only or even primarily reside in some methods but not others. As a result, the impression can be gleaned that other methods, such as questionnaires or overt ethnography, are immune from ethical problems.

In this chapter, we will introduce the main ethical issues and debates about ethics. We are not going to try to resolve them, because they are not readily capable of resolution. This is why the ethical debate has scarcely moved on since the 1960s. What *is* crucial is to be aware of the ethical principles involved and of the nature of the concerns about ethics in business research. It is only if researchers are aware of the issues involved that they can make informed

Box 25.1 A covert study of unofficial rewards

One of Dalton's (1959) central themes in his study of American managers and unofficial action revolves around the use of company materials and services as supplementary rewards for the variable contributions of individuals. He presents several cases, including the Milo carpenter, Ted Berger, who was rewarded for his loyalty by not being required to operate machines, instead making such things as baby beds, tables, and rocking horses—custom built-objects for various managers, in exchange for which he was given 'gifts'. Another case concerns staff who routinely filled their car fuel tank from the company garage and with this obtained free washing and waxing. Similarly, there is the case of Jim Speier, a factory foreman, who made use of machinery and materials to have constructed a rose arch, storm windows, and a set of wooden lawn sprinklers cut in the form of dancing girls and brightly painted!

Dalton's main strategy for preventing harm to his participants is to protect their anonymity, but the reader is left in no doubt as to the seriousness of consequences for individuals concerned if their identities were to have been discovered. As Dalton explains, these individuals 'gave information and aid that, if generally known, would have jeopardized their careers' (1959: 275). One of the key ethical issues in this study concerns the lack of informed consent, as participants were in no position to be able to judge whether or not to become involved in the research, as they were only vaguely aware of the nature of Dalton's interest. Furthermore, they were almost certainly unaware of the risk of harm that could result from the study in relation to their employment prospects. In his defence, Dalton adopts a situational stance (see Box 25.2), arguing that it is impossible to study unofficial action, other than using covert methods that enable the researcher to get sufficiently close to the subject. As there has been very little study of this subject, it is very difficult to see how we could compare Dalton's findings with those produced using overt methods and therefore we have little choice but to take his word for this.

Practical tip ☞ *ethics committees*

In addition to needing to be familiar with the codes of practice produced by several professional associations like the Academy of Management, the Market Research Society, and the Social Research Association, you should be acquainted with the ethical guidelines of your university or college. Most higher education organizations have ethics committees that issue guidelines about ethical practice. These guidelines are often based on or influenced by the codes developed by professional associations. Universities' and colleges' guidelines will provide indications of what are considered ethically unacceptable practices. Sometimes, you will need to submit your proposed research to an ethics committee of your university or college. This is likely to occur if there is some uncertainty about whether your proposed research is likely to be in breach of the guidelines or if you want to go ahead with research that you know is ethically dubious but you wish to obtain permission to do it anyway. The ethical guidelines and the ethics committee are there to protect research participants, but they are also involved in protecting institutions, so that researchers will be deterred from behaving in ethically unacceptable ways that might rebound on institutions. Such behaviour could cause problems for institutions if ethically inappropriate behaviour gave rise to legal action against them or to adverse publicity. However, ethics committees and their guidelines are there to help and protect researchers too, so that they are less likely to conduct research that could damage their reputations.

decisions about the implications of certain choices. If nothing else, you should be aware of the possible opprobrium that will be coming your way if you make certain kinds of choice. Our chief concern lies with the ethical issues that arise in relations between researchers and research participants in the course of an investigation. This focus by no means exhausts the range of ethical issues and dilemmas that arise,

---

Box 25.2 Stances on ethics

Authors on social research ethics can be characterized in terms of the stances they take on the issue. The following stances can be distinguished.

- *Universalism.* A universalist stance takes the view that ethical precepts should never be broken. Infractions of ethical principles are wrong in a moral sense and are damaging to social research. This kind of stance can be seen in the writings of Erikson (1967), Dingwall (1980), and Bulmer (1982). Bulmer does, however, point to some forms of what appears to be disguised observation that may be acceptable. One is retrospective covert observation, which occurs when a researcher writes up his or her experiences in social settings in which he or she participated but not as a researcher. An example would be Van Maanen (1991b), who wrote up his experiences as a ride operator in Disneyland many years after he had been employed there in vacation jobs. Even a universalist like Erikson (1967: 372) recognizes that it 'would be absurd . . . to insist as a point of ethics that sociologists should always introduce themselves as investigators everywhere they go and should inform every person who figures in their thinking exactly what their research is all about.'

- *Situation ethics.* Goode (1996) has argued for deception to be considered on a case-by-case basis. In other words, he argues for what Fletcher (1966: 31) has called a 'situation ethics', or more specifically 'principled relativism', which can be contrasted with the universalist ethics of some writers. This argument has two ways of being represented:

  1 *The end justifies the means.* Some writers argue that, unless there is some breaking of ethical rules, we would never know about certain social phenomena. Dalton (1959) essentially argues for this position in relation to his study of managers and the differences between official and unofficial action. Without some kind of disguised observation, this important aspect of organizational life would not have been studied. This is usually linked to the second form

of a situationist argument in relation to social research ethics.

  2 *No choice.* It is often suggested that we have no choice but to engage in dissimulation on occasions if we want to investigate the issues in which we are interested.

- *Ethical transgression is pervasive.* It is often observed that virtually all research involves elements that are at least ethically questionable. This occurs whenever participants are not given absolutely all the details on a piece of research, or when there is variation in the amount of knowledge about research. Punch (1994: 91), for example, observes that 'some dissimulation is intrinsic to social life and, therefore, to fieldwork'. He quotes Gans (1962: 44) in support of this point: 'If the researcher is completely honest with people about his activities, they will try to hide actions and attitudes they consider undesirable, and so will be dishonest. Consequently, the researcher must be dishonest to get honest data.'

- *Anything goes (more or less).* The writers associated with arguments relating to situation ethics and a recognition of the pervasiveness of ethical transgressions are not arguing for an 'anything-goes' mentality, but for a certain amount of flexibility in ethical decision making. However, Douglas (1976) has argued that the kinds of deception in which social researchers engage are trivial compared to those perpetrated by powerful institutions in modern society (such as the mass media, the police, and industry). His book is an inventory of tactics for deceiving people so that their trust is gained and they reveal themselves to the researcher. Very few researchers subscribe to this stance. Denzin (1968) comes close to an anything-goes stance when he suggests that social researchers are entitled to study anyone in any setting provided the work has a 'scientific' purpose, does not harm participants, and does not deliberately damage the discipline. The harm-to-participants criterion can also be seen in the cases reported in Box 25.3.

---

such as those that might arise in relation to the funding of business research or how findings are used by non-researchers. However, the ethical issues that arise in the course of doing research are the ones that are most likely to impinge on students.

Writers on research ethics adopt different stances concerning the ethical issues that arise in connection with relationships between researchers and research participants. Box 25.2 outlines some of these stances.

Ethical principles

Discussions about ethical principles in business research, and perhaps more specifically transgressions of them, tend to revolve around certain issues that recur in different guises but that have been usefully broken down by Diener and Crandall (1978) into four main areas:

- whether there is *harm to participants*;
- whether there is a *lack of informed consent*;
- whether there is an *invasion of privacy*;
- whether *deception* is involved.

We will look at each of these in turn, but it should be appreciated that these four principles overlap somewhat. For example, it is difficult to imagine how the principle of informed consent could be built into an investigation in which research participants were deceived. However, there is no doubt that these four areas form a useful classification of ethical principles in and for business research.

Harm to participants

Research that is likely to harm participants is regarded by most people as unacceptable. But what is harm? Harm can entail a number of facets: physical harm; harm to participants' development or self-esteem; stress; harm to career prospects or future employment; and 'inducing subjects to perform reprehensible acts', as Diener and Crandall (1978: 19) put it. In several studies that we have encountered in this book, there has been real or potential harm to participants.

- In Dalton's (1959) study his 'counselling' relationship with the female secretary in exchange for access to valuable personnel files (Box 14.7) was potentially harmful to her, both in terms of the personal relationship and in jeopardizing the security of her employment.
- In Haney, Banks, and Zimbardo's (1973) prison experiments (Box 25.3), several participants experienced severe emotional reactions, including mental breakdown.

- Many of the participants in the Milgram experiment (1963) on obedience to authority (Box 25.3) experienced high levels of stress and anxiety as a consequence of being incited to administer electric shocks. It could also be argued that Milgram's observers were 'inducing subjects to perform reprehensible acts'. Indeed, yet another series of studies in which Milgram was involved placed participants in positions where they were being influenced to steal (Milgram and Shotland 1973).

The AoM *Code of Ethical Conduct* states that it is the responsibility of the researcher to assess carefully the possibility of harm to research participants, and, to the extent that is possible, the possibility of harm should be minimized. Similar sentiments are expressed by the MRS's *Code of Conduct*, which advocates that 'the researcher must take all reasonable precautions to ensure that respondents are in no way directly harmed or adversely affected as a result of their participation in a marketing research project'.

The issue of harm to participants is further addressed in ethical codes by advocating care over maintaining the confidentiality of records and anonymity of accounts. This means that the identities and records of individuals and organizations should be maintained as confidential. For example, the AoM *Code of Ethical Conduct* recommends that issues relating to confidentiality and anonymity should be negotiated and agreed with potential research participants, and, 'if confidentiality or anonymity is requested, this must be honored'. This injunction also means that care needs to be taken when findings are being published to ensure that individuals and organizations are not identified or identifiable, unless permission has been given for data to be passed on in a form that allows them to be identified. The MRS *Code of Conduct* states that, as a general rule, anonymity must be preserved. If a respondent's identity is to be revealed, '(*a*) the respondent must first have been told to whom the information would be supplied and the purposes for which it will be used, and also (*b*) the researcher must

Box 25.3 Two infamous studies of obedience to authority

Milgram's (1963) electric shock experiments and Haney, Banks, and Zimbardo's (1973) prison studies have come to be seen as infamous because of the ethical issues they raise. Both studies were concerned to measure the effects of group norms on the behaviour of the individual and they have been widely applied in the field of organizational behaviour. Milgram was concerned with the processes whereby a person can be induced to cause extreme harm to another by virtue of being ordered to do so. To investigate this issue further he devised a laboratory experiment. Volunteers were recruited to act out the role of teachers who punished learners (who were accomplices of the experimenter) by submitting them to electric shocks when they gave incorrect answers to questions.

The shocks were not, of course, real, but the teachers/volunteers were not aware of this. The level of electric shock was gradually increased with successive incorrect answers until the teacher/volunteer refused to administer more shocks. Learners had been trained to respond to the rising level of electric shock with simulated but appropriate howls of pain. In the room was a further accomplice of Milgram's, who cajoled the teacher/volunteer to continue to administer shocks, suggesting that it was part of the study's requirements to continue and that they were not causing permanent harm, in spite of the increasingly shrill cries of pain. However, in a later adaptation of the experiment, the teacher/volunteer was accompanied by a colleague who acted out the part of someone who refused to administer the shocks beyond a certain level. In this situation, the real subject continued to administer the shocks for a shorter period and then declined as the first teacher/volunteer had done. Milgram's study demonstrates the extent to which individuals display obedience to authority even if this involves causing considerable pain

to others. It also shows how peer rebellion can be a powerful means of resisting the experimenter's authority.

Experiments conducted by Zimbardo and his graduate students from the Department of Psychology at Stanford University, California, involved creating a mock prison, in order to examine the roles played by prisoners and guards. Twenty-one male participants were selected from a group of seventy-five who responded to an advertisement in a local newspaper. Individuals were selected on the basis that they were mature, emotionally stable, middle class, well educated, and had no criminal record. Each was paid $15 per day to participate in the study. A coin was flipped in order to decide if the participant was to play the role of prisoner or guard. There were ten prisoners and eleven guards. However, only a few days into the planned fourteen-day study, the experiment took an unexpected turn. The relationship between prisoners and guards deteriorated to such an extent that guards began to subject prisoners to psychological cruelty. Within the first few days several of the prisoners had been released, suffering from severe depression and mental breakdown. Only six days into the study the experiment was abandoned owing to the extreme symptoms experienced by the prisoners. Haney, Banks, and Zimbardo's study shows that individual behaviour is determined by social and environmental conditions to a far greater extent than is commonly assumed.

Both studies raise complex ethical issues, particularly in relation to the potential harm incurred by participants as a result of the experiments. It is worth noting that both studies were conducted over thirty years ago and it is extremely unlikely that either would be considered acceptable by a university human subjects committee or indeed by most social researchers today.

---

ensure that the information will not be used for any non-research purpose and that the recipient of the information has agreed to conform to the requirements of the Code.'

In quantitative research, it is often easier to anonymize records and to report findings in a way that does not allow individuals to be identified. However, even in quantitative studies there are sometimes instances where it is virtually impossible to make a company anonymous. The use of pseudonyms

is a common recourse, but it may not eliminate entirely the possibility of identification. For example, in the case of Hofstede's (1984) research, although a company pseudonym was used throughout the published study, it was virtually impossible to conceal the company's identity without completely distorting the original data, partly because IBM is such a large and well-known organization. Similarly, although Scott et al. (1956) did not actually name their case-study organization, the details they provided in their

---

Practical tip 👉 confidentiality agreements

As part of the process of negotiating access, it is becoming increasingly common for companies to ask their legal departments to prepare a confidentiality agreement, which you may be asked to sign on your own behalf, or someone from your university may be asked to sign it on behalf of the institution. The main purpose of this is to define what type of information you can have access to and to establish what information you are and are not able to disclose about the company. This usually involves agreeing that you will not pass on information to a third party, particularly that which pertains to commercially sensitive or valuable issues, such as new-product development. In addition, there may be a clause that specifies that the company must have sight of the research once it has been written up, so that it can comment on the findings, particularly if they are going to be published. This legally binding agreement can thus grant a considerable amount of power to the company and it has the potential to cause considerable difficulties if your research throws up issues that the company would rather were kept out of the public domain. If you are asked to sign a confidentiality agreement, before signing it, take it to your supervisor to ask for advice and get it checked by someone who deals with legal issues on behalf of the university. It may be that there is some room for negotiation in relation to the exact wording of the agreement and the company may be reassured if there is an undertaking that the research will guarantee its anonymity.

---

analysis about the firm's size, location, history, and activities made it clear to Bacon and Blyton (2001; see Box 2.18), and to other researchers, exactly which large steel works in North Wales they had focused on.

The issues of confidentiality and anonymity raise particular difficulties for many forms of qualitative research, where particular care has to be taken with regard to the possible identification of persons, organizations, and places. The consequences of failing to protect individual anonymity are illustrated by Parker (2000: 238; see Chapter 14), who describes how a quote in his report about the managing director was traced to an 'insufficiently anonymized source', whose reputation was damaged as a result of the incident. As the MRS guidelines on employee research note:

Sample sizes in specialised areas may be very small to the point where employees themselves could be identified. If there is a reasonable risk of an employee being identified, due to the sample size of the population or sub-population being covered, the employee *must* be informed of this risk at the beginning of the interview and given the opportunity to withdraw.

They therefore recommend that researchers examine the results of subgroups only in situations where there are ten or more respondents involved.

The issues of confidentiality and anonymity involve legal as well as ethical considerations. For example, in Cavendish's (1982) study of women factory workers on an assembly line, great care was taken by the researcher to invent names for all the women so that they could not be identified, to protect them from possible victimization by the company. However, Cavendish deliberately left the name of the firm unchanged in order to preserve the realism of the study and to provide 'concrete facts about the factory' (1982: p. vi). However, as Cavendish explains, this proved very naive: 'if the firm was named, here was a risk both to me and to the publisher that the firm might bring a libel action against us' (1982: p. vi). For this reason, after consultation with lawyers, she decided to rewrite the account prior to publication in order to make the firm unidentifiable. This involved changing not only the name of the firm, but also its location, the details of the components manufactured, and the name of the trade union representing the women. In contrast, there are other instances where organizations do consent to be named in publication, for example in Pettigrew's (1985) study of changing culture at Imperial Chemical Industries.

The issues of confidentiality and anonymity also raise particular problems with regard to the secondary analysis of qualitative data (see Chapter 19), since it is very difficult, though by no means impossible, to present field notes and interview transcripts in a way that will prevent people and places from being identified. As Alderson (1998) has suggested, the difficulty is one of being able to ensure that the same safeguards concerning confidentiality can be guaranteed when secondary analysts examine such records as those provided by the original primary researcher.

One of the problems with the harm-to-participants principle is that it is not possible to identify in all circumstances whether harm is likely, though that fact should not be taken to mean that there is no point in seeking to protect them. For example, in the prison experiments conducted by Honey, Banks, and Zimbardo (Box 25.3) the extreme reactions of participants surprised the researchers. Arguably they did not anticipate this level of harm to be incurred when they planned the study. This is partly why the AoM *Code of Ethical Conduct* recommends third-party review as a means of protecting the interests of research participants, stating that: 'research plans involving human participants should be reviewed by an appropriate third party such as a university human subjects committee or a focus group of potential participants.' In addition, the ASA *Code of Ethics* suggests that, if there is any prospect of harm to participants, informed consent, the focus of the next section, is essential: 'Informed consent must be obtained when the risks of research are greater than the risks of everyday life. Where modest risk or harm is anticipated, informed consent must be obtained.'

Lack of informed consent

The issue of informed consent is in many respects the area within business research ethics that is most hotly debated. The bulk of the discussion tends to focus on what is variously called disguised or covert observation. Such observation can involve covert participant observation (Box 14.2), or simple or contrived observation (see, for example, Boxes 8.9 and 8.10), in which the researcher's true identity is unknown. The principle means that prospective research participants should be given as much information as might be needed to make an informed decision about whether or not they wish to participate in a study. Covert observation transgresses that principle, because participants are not given the opportunity to refuse to cooperate. They are involved whether they like it or not.

Lack of informed consent is a feature of the research in Boxes 25.1 and 25.3. For example, in Dalton's research informed consent is almost entirely absent. Dalton went to great lengths in order to keep the purpose of his research from participants, presumably to maximize his chances of obtaining specific information about such things as unofficial use of resources or pilfering. Even those who became key informants, or 'intimates', knew only of Dalton's general interest in 'personnel problems', and great care was taken not to arouse suspicion. Dalton describes his undercover role as similar in indirect actions to that of an espionage agent or spy, although he stresses that his interest was in scientific rather than criminal evidence. The principle of informed consent also entails the implication that, even when people know they are being asked to participate in research, they should be fully informed about the research process. As the AoM *Code of Ethical Conduct* suggests:

It is the duty of Academy members to preserve and protect the privacy, dignity, well being, and freedom of research participants. This duty requires both careful research design and informed consent from all participants . . . Informed consent means explaining to potential participants the purposes and nature of the research so they can freely choose whether or not to become involved. Such explanations include warning of possible harm and providing explicit opportunities to refuse to participate and to terminate participation at any time. Because students and employees are particularly subject to possible coercion, even when unintended, special care must be taken in obtaining their informed consent.

Similarly, the MRS *Code of Conduct* states that informed consent means that respondents should be told, normally at the beginning of the interview, if observation techniques or recording equipment are to be used. Thus, while Milgram's and Honey, Banks, and Zimbardo's experimental subjects (see Box 25.3) were volunteers and therefore knew they were going to participate in research, there is a lack of informed consent, because they were not given full information about the nature of the research and its possible implications for them.

However, as Homan (1991: 73) has observed, implementing the principle of informed consent 'is easier said than done'. At least two major points stand out here.

- It is extremely difficult to present prospective participants with absolutely all the information that might be required to make an informed decision about their involvement. In fact, relatively minor transgressions probably pervade most business research, such as deliberately underestimating the amount of time that an interview is likely to take so that people are not put off being interviewed and not giving absolutely all the details about one's research for fear of contaminating people's answers to questions.

- In ethnographic research, the researcher is likely to come into contact with a wide spectrum of people, and ensuring that absolutely everyone has the opportunity for informed consent is not practicable, because it would be extremely disruptive in everyday contexts. Also, even when all research participants in a certain setting are aware that the ethnographer is a researcher, it is doubtful whether they are all similarly (let alone identically) informed about the nature of the research. For example, in Lee's (1998) study of women factory workers in Hong Kong and China, she found it difficult to convey her 'version' of what she was doing to her co-workers. This was partly because the academic term 'thesis' did not make sense to them, so the women developed an alternative explanation, which involved the idea that Lee was writing a novel based on her experiences as a worker 'toiling side by side with "real" workers'. Lee explains: 'I had to settle for that definition too ...' (1998: 173). This example aptly illustrates how it is not always possible for the researcher fully to explain the purposes and nature of the research and so sometimes a compromise understanding is reached.

In spite of the widespread condemnation of violations of informed consent and the view that covert observation is especially vulnerable to accusations of unethical practice in this regard, studies such as Dalton's (1959) are still regarded as important in providing insight into subversive or illegitimate organizational behaviour. The defence is usually of the 'end-justifies-the-means' kind, which is further discussed below. What is interesting in the context of this discussion is that some ethical codes essentially leave the door ajar for covert observation. The BSA *Statement of Ethical Practice* does suggest that researchers should 'as far as possible' seek to achieve informed consent, but it then goes even further in relation to covert research:

There are serious ethical dangers in the use of covert research but covert methods may avoid certain problems. For instance, difficulties arise when research participants change their behaviour because they know they are being studied. Researchers may also face problems when access to spheres of social life is closed to social scientists by powerful or secretive interests. However, covert methods violate the principles of informed consent and may invade the privacy of those being studied. Participant or non-participant observation in non-public spaces or experimental manipulation of research participants without their knowledge should be resorted to only where it is impossible to use other methods to obtain essential data. In such studies it is important to safeguard the anonymity of research participants. Ideally, where informed consent has not been obtained prior to the research it should be obtained post-hoc.

While this statement hardly condones the absence of informed consent associated with covert research, it is not unequivocally censorious either. It recognizes that covert research 'may avoid certain problems' and refers, without using the term, to the possibility of reactivity associated with overt observational methods. It also recognizes that covert methods can help to get over the difficulty of gaining access to certain kinds of setting. The passage entails an acknowledgement that informed consent is jeopardized, along with the privacy principle (see below), but implies that covert research can be used 'where it is impossible to use other methods to obtain essential data'. The difficulty here clearly is how a researcher is to decide whether it is in fact impossible to obtain data other than by covert work. We suspect that, by and large, covert observers typically make their judgements in this connection on the basis of the *anticipated* difficulty of gaining access to a setting or of encountering reactivity problems, rather than as a response to difficulties they have actually experienced. For example, Dalton (1959) has written that it is impossible to get sufficiently close to unofficial managerial activities to access the meanings assigned to them by participants, other than through covert observation. The issue of the circumstances in which violations of ethical principles, like informed consent, are deemed acceptable will reappear in the discussion below.

The principle of informed consent is also bound up to some extent with the issue of harm to participants. Erikson (1967) has suggested that, if the principle is not followed and if participants are harmed as a result of the research, the investigator is more culpable than if they did not know. For example, he writes: 'If we happen to harm people who have agreed to act as subjects, we can at least argue that they knew something of the risks involved...' (1967: 369). While this might seem like a recipe for seeking a salve for the researcher's conscience, it does point to an important issue— namely, that the business researcher is more likely to be vilified if participants are adversely affected when they were not willing accomplices, than when they were. However, it is debatable whether that means that the researcher is any less culpable for that harm. Erikson implies researchers are less culpable, but this is a potential area for disagreement.

Invasion of privacy

This third area of ethical concern relates to the issue of the degree to which invasions of privacy can be condoned. The right to privacy is a tenet that many of us hold dear, and transgressions of that right in the name of research are not regarded as acceptable. The MRS guidance is clear: 'the objectives of any study do not give researchers a special right to intrude on a respondent's privacy nor to abandon normal respect for an individual's values.' Privacy is very much linked to the notion of informed consent, because, to the degree that informed consent is given on the basis of a detailed understanding of what the research participant's involvement is likely to entail, he or she in a sense acknowledges that the right to privacy has been surrendered for that limited domain. Of course, the research participant does not abrogate the right to privacy entirely by providing informed consent. As we have seen, when people agree to be interviewed, they will frequently refuse to answer certain questions on whatever grounds they feel are justified. Often, these refusals will be based

on a feeling that certain questions delve into private realms or cover topic areas that they find sensitive and they do not wish to make these public, regardless of the fact that the interview is conducted in private. However the MRS acknowledges that, although there are some topics that can be judged sensitive to everyone, because of the nature of the subject, it is impossible for the researcher to know beforehand which topics may be sensitive to a particular individual. It therefore recommends that the researcher 'treat each case sensitively and individually, giving respondents a genuine opportunity to withdraw'.

Covert methods are usually deemed to be violations of the privacy principle on the grounds that participants are not being given the opportunity to refuse invasions of their privacy. Such methods also mean that they might reveal confidences or information that they would not have revealed if they had known about the status of the confidant as researcher. The issue of privacy is invariably linked to issues of anonymity and confidentiality in the research process, an area that has already been touched on in the context of the question of whether harm comes to participants. The BSA *Statement* forges this kind of connection: 'The anonymity and privacy of those who participate in the research process should be respected. Personal information concerning research participants should be kept confidential. In some cases it may be necessary to decide whether it is proper or appropriate to record certain kinds of sensitive information.'

Raising issues about ensuring anonymity and confidentiality in relation to the recording of information and the maintenance of records relates to all methods of business research. In other words, while covert research may pose certain kinds of problem regarding the invasion of privacy, other methods of business research are implicated in possible difficulties in connection with anonymity and confidentiality.

Data Protection Legislation

Issues of privacy must also be handled in the light of relevant data protection legislation. In the UK this is encompassed by the 1998 Data Protection Act. The principles of data protection enshrined in the Act relate specifically to personal data, which are data that relate to a living individual who can be identi-fied either from the data or from other information in the possession of the data-holder. It includes expressions of opinion as well as factual information. The Act is intended to restrict the processing of this data. Processing includes obtaining, recording, or holding the data or carrying out analytical opera-tions on it. The definition of processing is thus quite broad. In addition to the use of data, processing also refers to disclosure of data, data blocking, and data destruction. The 1998 Act states that personal data must:

1. be processed fairly and lawfully;

2. be obtained only for one or more specified and lawful purposes and not further processed in any manner incompatible with that purpose or those purposes;

3. be adequate, relevant, and not excessive in rela-tion to the purpose or purposes for which they are processed;

4. be accurate and, where necessary, kept up to date;

5. not be kept longer than necessary.

In addition, the Act states:

• appropriate technical and organizational measures must be taken to protect against unauthorized or unlawful processing of personal data and against accidental loss or destruction of, or damage to, personal data;

• personal data shall not be transferred to a country or territory outside the European Economic Area, unless that country or territory ensures an ad-equate level of protection for the rights and free-doms of data subjects in relation to the processing of personal data.

There is a further category in the Act that relates to sensitive personal data, such as information about a data subject's political or religious beliefs or ethnic origin. This type of data is more rigorously protected and there is greater onus on the researcher to obtain explicit, usually written, consent from data subjects for the processing of this type of personal data. However, the Act does provide for certain exemptions

in the case of personal data that are collected for research purposes—namely, that where personal data are processed for research that is not likely to cause damage or distress to any of the data subjects concerned, it may be kept and further processed at a later stage for other purposes. Additionally, as long as the results of the research are not published in any form that identifies any particular data subject, re-spondents do not have right of access to the data. Data protection legislation thus provides another reason for researchers to take steps to adequately protect the anonymity of individual respondents unless there is a sound reason for not doing so.

Deception

Deception occurs when researchers represent their research as something other than what it is. The obedience to authority study by Milgram referred to in Box 25.3 involves deception because participants are led to believe they are administering real electric shocks. Another less extreme example is provided by Holliday (1995) in her ethnographic study of small firms (Box 25.4), in pretending to be a student inter-ested in small firms in order to get information about a competitor's product, Holliday was clearly engaged in an element of deception. The AoM *Code of Ethical Conduct* states:

Deception should be minimized, and, when necessary, the degree and effects must be mitigated as much as pos-sible. Researchers should carefully weigh the gains achieved against the cost in human dignity. To the extent that con-cealment or deception is necessary, the researcher must provide a full and accurate explanation to participants at the conclusion of the study, including counselling, if appropriate.

Deception in various degrees is probably quite widespread in much research, because researchers often want to limit participants' understanding of what the research is about so that they respond more naturally to the experimental treatment. Indeed, some ethical codes appear to condone the strictly bounded use of deception, in order to preserve the naturalness of the data. For example, in the section on Informed Consent it was mentioned that the

---

Box 25.4 An example of an ethical fieldwork dilemma

Holliday (1995: 17–18) describes an ethical dilemma that she faced during her fieldwork.

> I arranged to visit a small electronics company owned by a friend of a colleague. The night before I was due to visit the company my temperature soared to 103 degrees and I went down with 'flu. However, I felt that I could not break the arrangement at such short notice, so I decided to go the factory anyway...I got to the factory at 10 am. Eventually Raj, the owner-manager, arrived. We had spent 10 minutes touring the factory when he asked me if I could drive. I said that I could, so he asked me if I would drive him to another factory about fifteen miles south... Business and lunch over we walked back to the car (to my great relief—at last I could go home). This time I drove. As we pulled out of the car park, Raj turned to me and said, 'I'd just like to pop down to an exhibition in Birmingham—is that okay?' My heart sank, but I didn't have the strength to protest, so off to Birmingham we went.
>
> During the journey down, Raj told me about a crisis which had occurred very recently within his company.

> Another small firm had ordered a very substantial piece of equipment from him, which had required a huge amount of development work. Once the item was supplied the company which placed the order promptly declared itself bankrupt and refused to pay...By the time we reached Birmingham my sense of injustice was well and truly inflamed... 'So', Raj continued, 'this company has a display of *our product* here today and I want to get their brochure on it. The trouble is they'll know me, so you'll have to get it. We'll split up at the door and I'll meet you in an hour. Tell them you're a customer or something...' I couldn't believe it. I was being asked to commit industrial espionage in my first few hours of fieldwork...

> I got the brochure pretending to be a student—from Southampton, interested in researching small firms. I even got an invitation to the factory to come and research them. Then I passed the intelligence to Raj and began the long drive back. I arrived home at 8.30 pm exhausted and feverish, and with a very guilty conscience.

MSR *Code of Conduct* states that respondents should be told at the *beginning* of an interview if observation techniques or recording equipment are to be used. However, if it is felt that this knowledge might bias the respondent's subsequent behaviour, the respondent may be told about the recording at the *end* of the interview. They should then be given the opportunity to see or hear the relevant section of the record, and, if they so wish, 'the record or relevant section of it must be destroyed or deleted'.

The ethical objection to deception seems to turn on two points. First, it is not a nice thing to do. While the SRA *Guidelines* recognizes that deception is widespread in social interaction, it is hardly desirable. Secondly, there is the question of professional self-interest. If business researchers became known as snoopers who deceived people as a matter of professional course, the image of our work would be adversely affected and we might experience difficulty in gaining financial support and the cooperation of future prospective research participants. As the SRA *Guidelines* puts it:

It remains the duty of social researchers and their collaborators, however, not to pursue methods of inquiry that are likely to infringe human values and sensibilities. To do so, whatever the methodological advantages, would be to endanger the reputation of social research and the mutual trust between social researchers and society which is a prerequisite for much research.

One of the chief problems with the discussion of this aspect of ethics is that deception is, as some writers observe, widespread in business research (see the stance *Ethical transgression is pervasive*, in Box 25.2). As the example from Lee's (1998) research illustrates, it is rarely feasible or desirable to provide participants with a totally complete account of what your research is about. Bulmer (1982), whose stance is predominantly that of a universalist in ethics terms (see Box 25.2), nonetheless recognizes that there are bound to be instances such as this and deems them justifiable. However, it is very difficult to know where the line should be drawn here.

The difficulties of ethical decision making

The difficulty of drawing the line between ethical and unethical practices can be revealed in several ways. The issue of some members of social settings being aware of the researcher's status and the nature of his or her investigation has been mentioned on several occasions. Manuals about interviewing are full of advice about how to entice interviewees to open up about themselves. Researchers using Likert scales reword items to identify yeasayers and naysayers. Interviewers frequently err on the low side when asked how long an interview will take. Women may use their identity as women to influence female interviewees in in-depth interviews to probe into their lives and reveal inner thoughts and feelings, albeit with a commitment to feminist research (Oakley 1981; Finch 1984; Freeman 2000). Qualitative research is frequently very open-ended, and, as a result, research questions are either loose or not specified, so that it is doubtful whether ethnographers in particular are able to inform others

accurately about the nature of their research. Perhaps, too, some interviewees find the questions we ask unsettling or find the cut and thrust of a focus group discussion stressful, especially if they inadvertently reveal more than they might have intended.

There are, in other words, many ways in which there is the potential for deception and, relatedly, lack of informed consent in business research. These instances are, of course, a far cry from the deceptions perpetrated in the research summarized in Boxes 25.1 and 25.3, but they point to the difficulty of arriving at ethically informed decisions. Ethical codes give advice on patently inappropriate practices, though sometimes leaving some room for manœuvre, as we have seen, but less guidance on marginal areas of ethical decision making. Indeed, guidelines may even be used by research participants *against* the researcher when they seek to limit the boundaries of a fieldworker's investigation (Punch 1994).

Checklist of issues to consider in connection with ethical issues

- ☑ Have you read and incorporated into your research the principles associated with at least one of the major professional associations mentioned in this book?

- ☑ Have you read and incorporated the requirements for doing ethical research in your institution?

- ☑ Have you found out whether all proposed research needs to be submitted to the body in your institution that is responsible for the oversight of ethical issues?

- ☑ If only certain types of research need to be submitted, have you checked to see whether your proposed research is likely to require clearance?

- ☑ Have you checked to ensure that there is no prospect of any harm coming to participants?

- ☑ Does your research conform to the principle of informed consent, so that research participants

understand:

- ☑ what the research is about?

- ☑ the purposes of the research?

- ☑ who is sponsoring it?

- ☑ the nature of their involvement in the research?

- ☑ how long their participation is going to take?

- ☑ that their participation is voluntary?

- ☑ that they can withdraw from participation in the research at any time?

- ☑ what is going to happen to the data (e.g. how it is going to be kept)?

- ☑ Are you confident that the privacy of the people involved in your research will not be violated?

✓ Do you appreciate that you should not divulge information or views to your research participants that other research participants have given you?

✓ Have you taken steps to ensure that your research participants will not be deceived about the research and its purposes?

✓ Have you taken steps to ensure that the confidentiality of data relating to your research participants will be maintained?

✓ Once the data have been collected, have you taken steps to ensure that the names of your research

participants and the location of your research (such as the name of the organization(s) in which it took place) are not identifiable?

✓ Does your strategy for keeping your data in electronic form comply with data protection legislation?

✓ Once your research has been completed, have you met obligations that were a requirement of doing the research (e.g. submitting a report to an organization that allowed you access)?

K KEY POINTS

- This chapter has been concerned with a limited range of issues concerning ethics in business research, in that it has concentrated on ethical concerns that might arise in the context of collecting and analysing data. Our concern has mainly been with relations between researchers and research participants. Other ethical issues can arise in the course of business research.

- While the codes and guidelines of professional associations provide some guidance, their potency is ambiguous and they often leave the door open for some autonomy with regard to ethical issues.

- The main areas of ethical concern relate to: harm to participants; lack of informed consent; invasion of privacy; and deception.

- Covert observation and certain notorious studies have been particular focuses of concern.

- The boundaries between ethical and unethical practices are not clear-cut.

- Writers on social research ethics have adopted several different stances in relation to the issue.

- While the rights of research participants are the chief focus of ethical principles, concerns about professional self-interest are also of concern.

Q QUESTIONS FOR REVIEW

- Why are ethical issues important in relation to the conduct of business research?

- Outline the different stances on ethics in social research.

Ethical principles

- Does 'harm to participants' refer to physical harm alone?

- What are some difficulties with following this ethical principle?

- Why is the issue of informed consent so hotly debated?

- What are some of the difficulties of following this ethical principle?

- Why is the privacy principle important?

- What principles concerning the use of personal data are expressed in the 1998 Data Protection Act?

- Why does deception matter?

- How helpful are studies like Milgram's, Honey, Banks, and Zimbardo's, and Dalton's in terms of understanding the operation of ethical principles in business research?

The difficulties of ethical decision making

- How easy is it to conduct ethical research?

- Read one of the ethical guidelines referred to in this chapter. How effective is it in guarding against ethical transgressions?

- Were the actions taken by Holliday (1995) and described in Box 25.4 ethical? (Justify your viewpoint in terms of the framework provided in this chapter.) Would you have behaved differently in these circumstances? If so, how?

26 Doing a research project

22/03 오

CHAPTER GUIDE

The goal of this chapter is to provide advice to students on some of the issues that they need to consider if they have to prepare a dissertation based upon a relatively small-scale project. Increasingly, business and management students are required to produce such a dissertation as part of the requirements for their degrees. In addition to needing help with the conduct of research, which it is hoped has been provided by the bulk of this book up to this point, more specific advice on tactics in doing and writing up research for a dissertation can be useful. It is against this background that this chapter has been written. The chapter explores a wide variety of issues such as:

- advice on timing;

- advice on generating research questions;

- dealing with the existing literature on the subject;

- advice on writing to help you produce compelling findings.

외 나 칠입이

정정 제시이

Introduction

This chapter has been written to provide some advice for readers who might be carrying out a small-scale project of their own. Hopefully, the previous twenty-five chapters will have provided helpful information about the choices available to you and how to implement them. But, beyond this, how might you go about conducting a small project of your own? We have in mind here the kind of situation that is increasingly common among business and management degree programmes—the requirement to write a dissertation of around 10,000 to 15,000 words. In particular, we have in mind the needs of undergraduate students, as well as students on postgraduate degree programmes, who will also find some of the observations we make helpful. Also, the advice is really concerned with students conducting projects with a component of empirical research in which they collect new data or perhaps conduct a secondary analysis of existing data.

Get to know what is expected of you by your institution

Your institution or department will have specific requirements concerning a wide variety of different features that your dissertation should comprise and a range of other matters relating to it. These include such things as: the form of binding; how it is to be presented; whether an abstract is required; how big the page margins should be; the format for referencing; number of words; perhaps the structure of the dissertation; how much advice you can get from your supervisor; plagiarism; deadlines; how much (if any) financial assistance you can expect; and so on.

The advice here is simple: *follow the requirements, instructions, and information you are given*. If anything in this book conflicts with your institution's guidelines and requirements, ignore this book! We very much hope this is not something that will occur very much, but if it does, keep to the guidelines your institution gives you.

Start thinking about your research area early on

The chances are that you will be asked to start thinking about what you want to do research on well before you are due to start work on your dissertation. It is worth giving yourself a good deal of time. As you are doing your various modules, begin to think about whether there are any topics that might interest you and that might provide you with a researchable area. This may at times feel like a rather unproductive process in which a number of false starts or changes of direction are made. However, taking the time to explore different avenues at the point of problem identification can prevent difficulties at a much later stage.

Identifying research questions

Many students want to conduct research into areas that are of personal interest to them. This is not a bad thing at all and, as we noted in Chapter 1, many business researchers start from this point as well (see also Lofland and Lofland 1995: 11–14). However, you must move on to develop research questions. This recommendation applies to qualitative research as well as quantitative research. We realize that we said in Chapter 13 that qualitative research is more open-ended than quantitative research, and that in Chapter 14 we mentioned some notable studies that appear not to have been driven by specific research questions. However, very open-ended research is risky and can lead to the collection of too much data and, when it comes to writing up, to confusion about your focus. So, unless your supervisor advises you to the contrary, we would definitely advise that you formulate some research questions, even if they turn out to be somewhat less specific than the kinds we often find in quantitative research. In other words, what is it about your area of interest that you want to know?

Research questions are, therefore, important. In Chapter 2 we provided some advice on the role that research questions play in the research process and about possible sources of research questions. In addition, Box 2.5 provides some suggestions about some features that your research questions should exhibit. Figure 2.1 tries to bring out the main steps in developing research questions. It is worth returning to these discussions for some insights into the process of formulating research questions. Watson (1994a, b) has also provided a useful account of the process of 'crafting research', as he puts it. Before embarking on the task of research design and choice of research methods, it is a good idea to ask yourself a series of questions about your research and the findings that you hope to produce. Crafting a research design relies on addressing a series of what, why and how questions (see Figure 26.1), which eventually result in the production of a set of 'findings' or conclusions. Watson (1994b) sees management research as an intellectual craft that relies on the acquisition of a set of skills, which, when combined imaginatively, result in the production of an artefact.

Watson's figure illustrates how central research questions are to the overall research process and the way in which they are embedded in the many decisions that have to be made during it. In the case of his own research, Watson found that his research

What?	Why?
What puzzles/intrigues me! What do I want to know more about/understand better? What are my key research questions?	Why will this be of enough interest to others to be published as a thesis, book, paper, guide to practitioners or policy-makers? Can the research be justified as a 'contribution to knowledge'?
How—conceptually? What models, concepts, and theories can I draw on/develop to answer my research questions? How can these be brought together into a basic conceptual framework to guide my investigation?	How—practically? What investigative styles and techniques shall I use to apply my conceptual framework (both to gather material and analyse it)? How shall I gain and maintain access to information sources?

Figure 26.1 A 'what, why, and how' framework for crafting research

Source: Watson (1994b: S80). Reprinted with permission of Wiley Publishing.

> **Box 26.1** Marx's sources of research questions
>
> Marx (1997) suggests the following as possible sources of research questions.
>
> - Intellectual puzzles and contradictions.
> - The existing literature.
> - Replication.
> - Structures and functions. For example, if you point to a structure such as a type of organization, you can ask questions about the reasons why there are different types and the implications of the differences.
> - Opposition. Marx identifies the sensation of feeling that a certain theoretical perspective or notable piece of work is misguided and exploring the reasons for your opposition.
> - A social problem. But remember that this is just a source of a research question; you still have to identify business and management research issues in relation to a social problem: 'Gaps between official versions of reality and the facts on the ground'
>
> (Marx 1997: 113). An example here is something like Delbridge's (1998) fascinating ethnographic account of company rhetoric about Japanized work practices and how they operate in practice.
> - The counter-intuitive. For example, when common sense seems to fly in the face of social scientific truths.
> - 'Empirical examples that trigger amazement' (Marx 1997: 114). Marx gives, as examples, deviant cases and atypical events.
> - New methods and theories. How might they be applied in new settings?
> - 'New social and technical developments and social trends' (Marx 1997: 114).
> - Personal experience.
> - Sponsors and teachers. But do not expect your teachers to provide you with detailed research questions.

questions were pushing him in the direction of needing to appreciate 'issues of language and meaning'. He goes on to say:

This implies investigative techniques which take one close to individuals, which allow close attention to the way people use language and which enable the researcher to relate closely the individual to the context in which they work. The basic research design shaped to meet these criteria was one of participant observation within the management team of a single organization combined with detailed interviews with a cross-section of that group of managers. (Watson 1994b: S82)

In other words, the way in which Watson's research questions were framed profoundly influenced

both his research design (a case study) and his research methods (participant observation and semi-structured interviewing). Decisions about research questions are therefore crucial to how research is designed and how data are collected.

If you are still stuck about how to formulate research questions (or indeed about other phases of your research), it is always a good idea to look at journal articles or research monographs to see how other researchers have formulated them. Also, look at past dissertations for ideas as well. Marx (1997) has suggested a wide range of sources of research questions (see Box 26.1).

Using your supervisor

Most institutions that require a dissertation or similar component allocate students to supervisors. Institutions vary quite a lot in what can be expected of supervisors; in other words, they vary in terms of what kinds of and how much assistance supervisors

will give to students allocated to them. Equally, students vary a great deal in how frequently they see their supervisors and in their use of them. Our advice here is simple: use your supervisor to the fullest extent that you are allowed and follow the pointers you are given by him or her. Your supervisor will almost certainly be someone who is well versed in the research process and who will be able to provide you with help and feedback at all stages of your research, subject to your institution's strictures in this regard. If your supervisor is critical of your research questions, your interview schedule, drafts of your dissertation, or whatever, try to respond positively. Follow the suggestions that he or she provides, since the criticisms will invariably be accompanied by reasons for the criticisms and suggestions for revision. It is not a personal attack. Supervisors regularly have to go through the same process themselves when they submit an article to a peer-refereed journal or apply for a research grant or give a conference paper. So respond to criticisms and suggestions positively and be glad that you are being given the opportunity to address deficiencies in your work before it is formally examined.

A further point is that students who get stuck at the start of their dissertations or who get behind with their work sometimes respond to the situation by avoiding their supervisors. They then get caught up in a vicious circle that results in their work being neglected and perhaps rushed at the end. Try to avoid this situation by confronting the fact that you are experiencing difficulties in getting going or are getting behind and seek out your supervisor for advice.

Managing time and resources

All research is constrained by time and resources. There is no point in working on research questions and plans that cannot be seen through because of time pressure or because of the costs involved. Two points are relevant here.

1. Work out a timetable—preferably in conjunction with your supervisor—detailing the different stages of your research (including the review of the literature and writing-up). The timetable should specify the different stages and the calendar points at which you should start and finish them. Some stages are likely to be ongoing—for example, searching the literature for new references (see below)—but that should not prove an obstacle to developing a timetable.

2. Find out what, if any, resources can be put at your disposal for carrying out your research. For example, will you receive help from your institution with such things as travel costs, photocopying, secretarial assistance, postage, stationery, and so on? Will the institution be able to loan you hardware such as tape recorders and transcription machines if you need to record and transcribe your interviews? Has it got the software you need, such as SPSS or a qualitative data analysis package like NVivo? This kind of information will help you to establish how far your research design and methods are financially feasible and practical. The imaginary gym survey that was used in Chapter 11 is an example of an investigation that would be feasible within the kind of time frame usually allocated to undergraduate and postgraduate dissertations. However, it would require such facilities as: typing up the questionnaire, which nowadays students can usually do for themselves with the help of word-processing programs; photocopying covering letters and questionnaires; postage for sending the questionnaires out and for any follow-up letters to non-respondents; return postage for the questionnaires; and the availability of a quantitative data analysis package like SPSS.

Searching the existing literature and looking for business information

Usually, students know a few initial references when they begin on a project. The bibliographies in these references will usually provide you with a raft of further relevant references. Nowadays, online bibliographical databases that are accessible on the Internet are an invaluable source of journal references. An increasing number of these will also provide access to the full text of an article in electronic format—these are usually referred to as e-journals. However, you will need to find out whether your institution can give you a user name and password to gain access to these databases. Here are three that we would recommend.

1. ABI/INFORM Global provides business information from a wide range of periodicals and reports, coverage is international and it is possible to search by keyword or use <u>BROWSE LISTS</u> or <u>TOPIC FINDER</u> to search for relevant articles by subject. ABI/INFORM can be accessed at the following address:

   http://proquest.umi.com/pqdweb.

2. Business Source Premier is a less widely used business periodical database than ABI/INFORM. However, it is becoming increasingly popular owing to its provision of extremely comprehensive full text access to certain key business and management journals including *Harvard Business Review* and *Academy of Management Review*. In addition, it provides indexing and abstracts for over 3,000 business journals. It can be accessed via EBSCO Publishing at:

   http://search.epnet.com.

3. However, we also recommend use of the Social Sciences Citation Index (SSCI), which fully indexes over 1,700 major social science journals covering all social science disciplines dating back to 1981. It can be accessed from the Web

of Science (WoS) home page at the following address:

   http://wos.mimas.ac.uk.

Unlike the first two databases, SSCI does not provide full text access to journals. However, it does provide references and abstracts for articles from some 120 of the most important business and management journals published worldwide. The database also covers related fields such as accountancy and finance, economics and public administration. It is therefore very useful as an initial source in your literature search because, if you search the database effectively, you can be relatively confident that you have covered the majority of recent academic journals that may have published articles on your topic of interest. You can then obtain the full text of the most relevant either in electronic or hard copy form. Here are some introductory guidelines for searching SSCI:

> Just click on the WoS button in the centre of the Screen and after logging in you will be asked to choose between Full Search and Easy Search. Unless you are very unfamiliar with using the Internet, the former is likely to be preferable. Once you have done this, → Social Sciences Citation Index. At this point, you can also narrow down your search to specific years. If you do not elect to do this, your search will cover all years from 1981. To activate your search, → GENERAL SEARCH. The General Search window will then open. If you are searching for references on a particular topic, insert the key word(s) in *TOPIC* and then → SEARCH.

A feature of SSCI is its complete coverage of journal contents, so in addition to research and scholarly articles it also contains book reviews and editorial material, which invariably can be identified through keyword searches. You will need to experiment with the use of keywords, because this is usually the way in which databases like these are searched, though author searches are also possible.

To search for books, good places to start are the databases of online bookshops. Useful Internet addresses for these are:

www.amazon.com
www.amazon.co.uk
www.bookshop.co.uk.

The catalogue of your own institution is an obvious route to finding books, but so too are the catalogues of other universities. COPAC contains the holdings of twenty-two of the largest university research libraries plus the British Library. It can be found at:

www.copac.ac.uk/copac.

You may also need to find out background information about the markets or companies in which you are interested. There are numerous database sources that can provide you with this kind of company and market research data, including the **General Market Information Database** (GMID), which contains marketing profiles, consumer market sizing for fifty-two countries, consumer lifestyle reports, data for over 200 countries, market forecasts to 2012, and information about 100,000 brands and 12,000 companies. **Mintel** provides comprehensive market research reports on the UK retail and leisure sectors and conducts its own market research, and **Reuters Business Insight** provides access to hundreds of market research reports focused on: energy, consumer goods, finance, health care, and technology. Again, you will need to check with your library to find out which of these is available to you.

For all of these online databases, you will need to work out some good keywords that can be entered into the search engines and that will allow you to identify suitable references. There are a number of business dictionaries that can help you to define your area of research and to identify changes in the language used to describe the subject. For example, the term 'personnel management' has now been largely superseded by 'HRM' and 'payment systems' are now more widely referred to under the umbrella of 'reward management'. You will also need to think of synonyms and try to match your language to that

of the source you are searching. For example, performance management may be more usually referred to in practitioner publications as 'employee evaluation' or 'appraisal'. Two dictionaries that are widely available for this purpose are:

Collins Dictionary of Business, 2nd edition (1995)
The IEBM Dictionary of Business and Management (1999).

You should explore the existing literature to identify the following issues.

- What is already known about this area?
- What concepts and theories are relevant to this area?
- What research methods and research strategies have been employed in studying this area?
- Are there any significant controversies?
- Are there any inconsistencies in findings relating to this area?
- Are there any unanswered research questions in this area?

This last issue points to the possibility that you will be able to revise and refine your research questions in the process of reviewing the literature.

Why do you need to review the existing literature? The most obvious reason is that you want to know what is already known about your area of interest so that you do not simply 'reinvent the wheel'. Beyond this, using the existing literature on a topic is a means of developing an argument about the significance of your research and where it leads. The simile of a *story* is sometimes used in this context (see below). A competent review of the literature is also at least in part a means of affirming your credibility as someone who is knowledgeable in your chosen area.

When you are reading the existing literature try to do the following.

- Take good notes, including the details of the material you read. It is infuriating to find that you forgot to record the volume number of an article you read and that needs to be included in your Bibliography. This may necessitate a trip to the library on occasions when you are already hard pressed for time.

Practical tip 👉 *reasons for writing a literature review*

The following is a list of reasons for writing a literature review:

1 You need to know what is already known in connection with your research area because you do not want to be accused of reinventing the wheel.

2 You can learn from other researchers' mistakes and avoid making the same ones.

3 You can learn about different theoretical and methodological approaches to your research area.

4 It may help you to develop an analytic framework.

5 It may lead you to consider the inclusion of variables in your research that you might not otherwise have thought about.

6 It may suggest further research questions for you.

7 It will help with the interpretation of your findings.

8 It gives you some pegs on which to hang your findings.

9 It is expected!

• Develop critical reading skills. Your review of the literature will need to be critical rather than merely descriptive, so it is worth developing these skills and recording relevant critical points in the course of taking notes. Developing a critical approach is not necessarily one of simply criticizing the work of others. It entails moving beyond mere description and asking questions about the significance of the work. It entails attending to such issues as: How does the item relate to others you have read? Are there any apparent strengths and deficiencies—perhaps in terms of methodology or in terms of the credibility of the conclusions drawn? What theoretical ideas have influenced the item?

In some areas of research, there are very many references. Try to identify the major ones and work outwards from there. Move on to the next stage of your research at the point that you identified in your timetable (see above) so that you can dig yourself out of the library. This is not to say that your search for the literature will cease, but that you need to force yourself to move on. Seek out your supervisor's advice on whether you need to search the literature much more.

Preparing for your research

Do not begin your data collection until you have identified your research questions reasonably clearly. Develop your data collection instruments with these research questions at the forefront of your thinking. If you do not do this, there is the risk that your results will not allow you to illuminate the research questions. If at all possible, conduct a small pilot study to determine how well your research instruments work.

You will also need to think about access and sampling issues. If your research requires you to gain access to or the cooperation of one or more closed settings like an organization, you need to confirm at the earliest opportunity that you have the necessary permission to conduct your work. You also need to consider how you will go about gaining access to people. These issues lead you into sampling considerations, such as the following.

• Who do you need to study in order to investigate your research questions?

• How easily can you gain access to a sampling frame?

• What kind of sampling strategy will you employ (e.g. probability sampling, quota sampling, theoretical sampling, convenience sampling)?

• Can you justify your choice of sampling method?

Also, at this stage, if you are using a case-study design, you will almost certainly need to find out more about the organization that you intend to investigate. What is its financial position? Has it been in the news recently? Where are its premises? What market conditions does it face? There are a wide variety of sources available on the Web that can provide this kind of background information to inform your research. Company accounts are available through Companies House and some free company information is available from this site:

www.companies-house.co.uk

In addition, the largest multinational corporations often make their annual report and accounts available through their homepages. Although this is for them primarily a marketing exercise, you can often obtain the full text, as it appears in hard copy free of charge. The best way to find these pages is using a search engine and entering the full company name as a phrase.

Newspapers such as the *Financial Times* are also accessible on the Web, although there are some limitations on the amount of information that you can obtain free of charge. Newslink is a collection of links to countries and then to newspapers all over the world. It can be found at:

www.newslink.org

Also, while preparing for your data collection you should consider whether there are any possible ethical problems associated with your research methods or your approach to contacting people.

Doing your research and analysing your results

This is what the bulk of this book has been about, so it seems (superfluous) to go over this ground again. Here are some useful reminders of practicalities.

- Keep good records of what you do. A research diary can be helpful here, but there are several other things to bear in mind. For example, if you are doing a survey by postal questionnaire, keep good records of who has replied, so that you know who should be sent reminders. If participant observation is a component of your research, remember to keep good field notes and not to rely on your memory.

- Make sure that you are thoroughly familiar with any hardware you are using in collecting your data, such as tape recorders for interviewing, and make sure it is in good working order (for example, that the batteries are not flat or close to being flat).

- Do not wait until all your data have been collected to begin coding. This recommendation applies to both quantitative and qualitative research. If you are conducting a questionnaire survey, begin coding your data and entering them into SPSS or whatever package you are using after you have put together a reasonably sized batch of completed questionnaires. In the case of qualitative data, such as interview transcripts, the same point applies, and, indeed, it is a specific recommendation of the proponents of grounded theory that data collection and analysis should be intertwined.

- Remember that the transcription of tapes with recorded interviews takes a long time. Allow at least six hours' transcription for every one hour of recorded interview talk, at least in the early stages of transcription.

- Become familiar with any data analysis packages as soon as possible. This familiarity will help you to establish whether you definitely need them and will ensure that you do not need to learn everything about them at the very time you need to use them for your analysis.

The deadly habit of procrastination
拖拖拉拉事性是个害人坏习惯.

Writing up your research

It is easy to neglect the writing stage of your work because of the difficulties that you often encounter in getting your research underway. But—obvious though this point is—your dissertation has to be written. Your findings must be conveyed to an audience, something that all of us who carry out research have to face. The first bit of advice is . . .

Start early

It is easy to take the view that the writing-up of your research findings is something that you can think about after you have collected and analysed your data. There is, of course, a (grain) of truth in this view, in that you could hardly write up your findings until you know what they are, which is something that you can know only once you have gathered and analysed your data. However, there are good reasons for beginning writing early on, since you might want to start thinking about such issues as how best to present and justify the research questions that are driving your research or how to structure the theoretical and research literature that will have been used to frame your research questions. A further reason why it is advisable to begin writing earlier rather than later is an entirely practical one: many people find it difficult to get started and employ (probably unwittingly) (procrastination) strategies to put off the inevitable. This tendency can result in the writing being left until the last minute and consequently rushed. Writing under this kind of pressure is not ideal. How you represent your findings and conclusions is a crucial stage in the research process. If you do not provide a convincing account of your research, you will not do justice to it.

Be persuasive

This point is crucial. Writing up your research is not simply a matter of reporting your findings and drawing some conclusions. Writing up your research will contain many other features, such as referring to the literature on which you drew, explaining how you did your research, and outlining how you conducted your analysis. But above all, you must be *persuasive.* This means that you must convince your readers of the credibility of your conclusions. Simply saying 'this is what I found; isn't it interesting' is not enough. You must persuade your readers that your findings and conclusion are significant and that they are plausible.

Get feedback

Try to get as much feedback on your writing as possible and respond positively to the points anyone makes about what they read. Your supervisor is likely to be the main source of feedback, but institutions vary in what supervisors are allowed to comment on. Provide your supervisor with drafts of your work to the fullest extent that regulations will allow. Give him or her plenty of time to provide feedback. There will be others like you who will want your supervisor to comment on their work, and, if he or she feels rushed, the comments may be less helpful. Also, you could ask others on the same degree programme to read your drafts and comment on them. They may ask you to do the same. Their comments may be very useful, but, by and large, your supervisor's comments are the main ones you should seek out.

Avoid sexist, racist, and disablist language

Remember that your writing should be free of sexist, racist, and disablist language. The British Sociological Association provides very good general and specific advice about this issue, which can be found at:

www.britsoc.org.uk/about/antisex.htm
www.britsoc.org.uk/about/antirace.htm
www.britsoc.org.uk/about/ablist.htm.

Practical tip 🖝 non-sexist writing

One of the biggest problems (but by no means the only one) when trying to write in a non-sexist way is avoiding complex his/her formulations. The easiest way of dealing with this is to write in the plural in such circumstances. For example: 'I wanted to give each respondent the opportunity to complete the questionnaire in his or her own time and in a location that was convenient for him or her.' This is a rather tortuous sentence and, although grammatically correct, it could be phrased more helpfully as: 'I wanted to give respondents the opportunity to complete their questionnaires in their own time and in a location that was convenient for them.'

Structure your writing

What lessons might be gleaned from the examination in Chapter 24 of the journal articles by Coyle-Shapiro and Kessler (2000) and Perlow (1999) for your own research project? It may be that you have to write a dissertation of around 10,000 to 15,000 words for your degree. How might it be structured? The following is typical of the structure of a dissertation.

Title page

You should examine your institution's rules about what should be entered here.

Acknowledgements

You might want to acknowledge the help of various people, such as gatekeepers who gave you access to an organization, people who have read your drafts and provided you with feedback, or your supervisor for his or her advice.

List of contents

Your institution may have recommendations or prescriptions about the form this should take.

An abstract

A brief summary of your dissertation. Not all institutions require this component, so check on whether it is required. Journal articles usually have abstracts, so you can draw on these for guidance on how to approach this task.

Introduction

- You should explain what you are writing about and why it is important. Saying simply that it interests you because of a long-standing personal interest is not enough.

- You might indicate in general terms the theoretical approach or perspective you will be using and why.

- You should also at this point outline your research questions. In the case of dissertations based on qualitative research, it is likely that your research questions will be rather more open-ended than is the case with quantitative research. But do try to identify some research questions. A totally open-ended research focus is risky and can lead to the collection of too much data, and, when it comes to writing up, it can result in a lack of focus.

- The opening sentence or sentences are often the most difficult of all. Becker (1986) advises strongly against opening sentences that he describes as 'vacuous' and 'evasive'. He gives the example of 'This study deals with the problem of careers', and adds that this kind of sentence employs 'a typically evasive manœuvre, pointing to something without saying anything, or anything much, about it. *What about careers?*' (Becker 1986: 51). He suggests that such evasiveness often occurs because of concerns about giving away the plot. In fact, he argues, it is much better to give readers a quick and clear indication of what is going to be meted out to them and where it is going. Coyle-Shapiro and Kessler's (2000) opening sentences do rather well in this regard, whereas Perlow (1999) is slightly more elusive.

Literature review

This chapter will review the main ideas and research relating to your area of interest. However, you should do more than simply summarize the relevant literature.

- You should, whenever appropriate, be critical in your approach.

- You should use your review of the literature as a means of showing why your research questions are important. For example, if one of your arguments in arriving at your research questions is that, although a lot of research has been done on X (a general topic or area, such as the psychological contract, female entrepreneurship, or employee absenteeism), little or no research has been done on X_1 (an aspect of X), the literature review is the point where you can justify this assertion. Alternatively, it might be that there are two competing positions with regard to X_1 and you are going to investigate which one provides a better understanding. In the literature review, you should outline the nature of the differences between the competing positions. The literature review, then, allows you to locate your own research within a tradition of research in an area. Indeed, reading the literature is itself often an important source of research questions.

- Bear in mind that you will want to return to much of the literature that you examine in the discussion of your findings and conclusion.

- Do not try to get everything you read into a literature review. Trying to force everything you have read into your review (because of all the hard work involved in uncovering and reading the material) is not going to help you. The literature review must assist you in developing an argument, and bringing in material of dubious relevance may undermine your ability to get your argument across.

- Bear in mind that reading the literature is not something that you should stop doing once you begin designing your research. You should continue your search for and reading of relevant literature more or less throughout your research. This means that, if you have written a literature review before beginning your data collection, you will need to regard it as provisional. Indeed, you may want to make quite substantial revisions of your review towards the end of writing up your work.

- Further useful thoughts about how to develop the literature can be found in Box 26.2. The different ways of construing the literature that are presented in this box are derived from a review of qualitative studies of organizations, but the approaches identified have a much broader applicability, including to quantitative research.

Research methods

The term 'research methods' is meant here as a kind of catch-all for several issues that need to be outlined: your research design; your sampling approach; how access was achieved if relevant; the procedures you used (such as, if you sent out a postal questionnaire, did you follow up non-respondents); the nature of your questionnaire, interview schedule, participant observation role, observation schedule, coding frame, or whatever (these will usually appear in an appendix, but you should comment on such things as your style of questioning or observation and why you asked the things you did); problems of non-response; note taking; issues of ongoing access and cooperation; coding matters; and how you proceeded with your analysis. When discussing each of these issues, you should describe and defend the choices that you made, such as why you used a postal questionnaire rather than a structured interview approach, or why you focused upon that particular population for sampling purposes.

Results

In this chapter you present the bulk of your findings. If you intend to have a separate Discussion chapter, it is likely that the results will be presented with little commentary in terms of the literature or the implications of your findings. If there will be no Discussion chapter, you will need to provide some reflections on the significance of your findings for your research questions and for the literature. Bear these points in mind.

- Whichever approach you take, remember not to include *all* your results. You should present and discuss only those findings that relate to your research questions. This requirement may mean a rather painful process of leaving out many findings, but it is necessary, so that the thread of your argument is not lost.

- Your writing should point to particularly salient aspects of the tables, graphs, or other forms of analysis you present. Do not just summarize what a table shows; you should direct the reader to the component or components of it that are especially striking from the point of view of your research

Box 26.2 Presenting the literature in articles based on qualitative research on organizations

Further useful advice on relating your own work to the literature can be gleaned from an examination of the ways in which articles based on qualitative research on organizations are composed. In their examination of such articles, Golden-Biddle and Locke (1993, 1997) argue that good articles in this area develop a story—that is, a clear and compelling framework around which the writing is structured. This idea is very much in tune with Wolcott's (1990: 18) recommendation to 'determine the basic story you are going to tell'. Golden-Biddle and Locke's research suggests that the way the author's position in relation to the literature is presented is an important component of storytelling. They distinguish two processes in the ways that the literature is conveyed.

- **Constructing intertextual coherence**—refers to the way in which existing knowledge is represented and organized; the author shows how contributions to the literature relate to each other and the research reported. The techniques used are:

  - *Synthesized coherence*—puts together work that is generally considered unrelated; theory and research previously regarded as unconnected are pieced together. There are two prominent forms:

    1 the organization of very incompatible references (bits and pieces);

    2 connections forged between established theories or research programmes.

  - *Progressive coherence*—portrays the building up of an area of knowledge around which there is considerable consensus.
  - *Non-coherence*—recognition that there have been many contributions to a certain research programme, but there is considerable disagreement among practitioners.

Each of these strategies is designed to leave room for a contribution to be made.

- **Problematizing the situation**—the literature is then subverted by locating a problem. The following techniques were identified:

  - *Incomplete*—the existing literature is not fully complete; there is a gap.
  - *Inadequate*—the existing literature on the phenomenon of interest has overlooked ways of looking at it that can greatly improve our understanding of it; alternative perspectives or frameworks can then be introduced.
  - *Incommensurate*—argues for an alternative perspective that is superior to the literature as it stands; differs from 'inadequate problematization' because it portrays the existing literature as 'wrong, misguided, or incorrect' (Golden-Biddle and Locke 1997: 43).

The key point about Golden-Biddle and Locke's account of the way the literature is construed in this field is that it is used by writers to achieve a number of things.

- They can demonstrate their competence by referring to prominent writings in the field (Gilbert 1977).
- They develop their version of the literature in such a way to show and to lead up to the contribution they will be making in the article.
- The gap or problem in the literature that is identified corresponds to the research questions.

The idea of writing up one's research as storytelling acts as a useful reminder that reviewing the literature, which is part of the story, should link seamlessly with the rest of the article and not be considered a separate element.

questions. Try to ask yourself what story you want the table to convey and try to relay that story to your readers.

- Another sin to be avoided is simply presenting a graph or table or a section of the transcript of a semi-structured interview or focus group session

without any comment whatsoever, because the reader is left wondering why you think the finding is important.

- When reporting quantitative findings, it is quite a good idea to vary wherever possible the method of presenting results—for example, provide a mixture of diagrams and tables. However, you must remember the lessons of Chapter 11 concerning the methods of analysis that are appropriate to different types of variable.

- A particular problem that can arise with qualitative research is that students find it difficult to leave out large parts of their data. As one experienced qualitative researcher has put it: 'The major problem we face in qualitative inquiry is not to get data, but to get rid of it!' (Wolcott 1990: 18). He goes on to say that the 'critical task in qualitative research is not to accumulate all the data you can, but to "can" (i.e., get rid of) most of the data you accumulate' (Wolcott 1990: 35). You simply have to recognize that much of the rich data you accumulate will have to be jettisoned. If you do not do this, any sense of an argument in your work is likely to be lost. There is also the risk that your account of your findings will appear too descriptive and lack an analytical edge. This is why it is important to use research questions as a focus and to orient the presentation of your findings to them.

- If you are writing a thesis, for example for an M.Phil. or Ph.D. degree, it is likely that you will have more than one and possibly several chapters in which you present your results. Cryer (1996) recommends showing at the beginning of each chapter the particular issues that are being examined in the chapter. You should indicate which research question or questions are being addressed in the chapter and provide some signposts about what will be included in the chapter. In the conclusion of the chapter, you should make clear what your results have shown and draw out any links that might be made with the next results chapter.

Discussion

In the Discussion, you reflect on the implications of your findings for the research questions that have driven your research. In other words, how do your results illuminate your research questions? If you have specified hypotheses, as Coyle-Shapiro and Kessler (2000) did, the discussion will revolve around whether the hypotheses have been confirmed or not, and, if not, you might speculate about some possible reasons for and the implications of their refutation. In the case of Perlow's (1999) article, section 6 acts as a discussion section, and it is here that the author brings out the main theoretical contribution of her research—the idea of the 'vicious work–time cycle'—and explores its implications.

Conclusion

The main points here are as follows.

- A Conclusion is not the same as a summary. However, it is frequently useful to bring out in the opening paragraph of the Conclusion your argument thus far. This will mean relating your findings and your discussion of them to your research questions. Thus, your brief summary should be a means of hammering home to your readers the significance of what you have done. However, the Conclusion should do more than merely summarize.

- You should make clear the implications of your findings for your research questions.

- You might suggest some ways in which your findings have implications for theories relating to your area of interest.

- You might also suggest some ways in which your findings have implications for practice in the field of business and management.

- You might draw attention to any limitations of your research with the benefit of hindsight, but it is probably best not to overdo this element and provide examiners with too much ammunition that might be used against you!

- It is often valuable to propose areas of further research that are suggested by your findings.

- Two things to avoid are engaging in speculations that take you too far away from your data, or that cannot be substantiated by the data, and introducing issues or ideas that have not previously been brought up.

Appendices

In your appendices you might want to include such things as your questionnaire, coding frame, or observation schedule, letters sent to sample members, and letters sent to and received from gatekeepers where the cooperation of an organization was required.

References

Include here all references cited in the text. For the format of the References section you should follow whichever one is prescribed by your department. Nowadays, the format is usually a variation of the Harvard method, such as the one employed for this book.

Finally

Remember to fulfil any obligations you entered into, such as supplying a copy of your dissertation, if, for example, your access to an organization was predicated on providing one, and maintaining the confidentiality of information supplied and the anonymity of your informants and other research participants.

Checklist of issues to consider for writing up a piece of research

✓ Have you clearly specified your research questions?

✓ Have you clearly indicated how the literature you have read relates to your research questions?

✓ Is your discussion of the literature critical and organized so that it is not just a summary of what you have read?

✓ Have you clearly outlined your research design and your research methods, including:

 ✓ why you chose a particular research design?

 ✓ why you chose a particular research method?

 ✓ how you selected your research participants?

 ✓ whether there were any issues to do with cooperation (e.g. response rates)?

 ✓ why you implemented your research in a particular way (e.g. how the interview questions relate to your research questions, why you observed participants in particular situations, why your focus group guide asked the questions in a particular way and order)?

 ✓ if your research required access to an organization, how and on what basis was agreement for access forthcoming?

 ✓ steps you took to ensure that your research was ethically responsible?

✓ how you analysed your data?

✓ any difficulties you encountered in the implementation of your research approach?

✓ Have you presented your data in a manner that relates to your research questions?

✓ Does your discussion of your findings show how they relate to your research questions?

✓ Does your discussion of your findings show how they shed light on the literature that you presented?

✓ Are the interpretations of your data that you offer fully supported with tables, figures, or segments from transcripts?

✓ If you have presented tables and/or figures, are they properly labelled with a title and number?

✓ If you have presented tables and/or figures, are they commented upon in your discussion?

✓ Do your conclusions clearly allow the reader to establish what your research contributes to the literature?

✓ Have you explained the limitations of your study?

✓ Do your conclusions consist solely of a summary of your findings? If they do, rewrite them!

✓ Do your conclusions make clear the answers to your research questions?

✓ Does your presentation of the findings and the discussion allow a clear argument and narrative to be presented to the reader?

✓ Have you broken up the text in each chapter with appropriate subheadings?

✓ Does your writing avoid sexist, racist, and disablist language?

✓ Have you included all appendices that you might need to provide (e.g. interview schedule, letters requesting access, communications with research participants)?

✓ Have you checked that your list of references includes *all* the items referred to in your text?

✓ Have you checked that your list of references follows precisely the style that your institution requires?

✓ Have you followed your supervisor's suggestions when he or she has commented on your draft chapters?

✓ Have you got people other than your supervisor to read your draft chapters for you?

✓ Have you checked to ensure that there is not excessive use of jargon?

✓ Do you provide clear signposts in the course of writing, so that readers are clear about what to expect next and why it is there?

✓ Have you ensured that your institution's requirements for submitting projects are fully met in terms of such issues as word length (so that it is neither too long nor too short) and whether an abstract and table of contents are required?

✓ Have you ensured that you do not quote excessively when presenting the literature?

✓ Have you fully acknowledged the work of others so that you cannot be accused of plagiarism?

✓ Is there a good correspondence between the title of your project and its contents?

✓ Have you acknowledged the help of others where this is appropriate (e.g. your supervisor, people who may have helped with interviews, people who read your drafts)?

Glossary

Terms appearing elsewhere in the Glossary are in **bold**.

Action research An approach in which the action researcher and a client collaborate in the diagnosis of a problem and in the development of a solution based on the diagnosis.

***Ad libitum* sampling** A sampling approach in **structured observation** whereby whatever is happening at the moment that observation is due to occur is recorded.

Adjacency pair The tendency for certain kinds of activity in talk to be characterized by linked phases.

Analytic induction An approach to the analysis of qualitative data in which the researcher seeks universal explanations of phenomena by pursuing the collection of data until no cases that are inconsistent with a hypothetical explanation (deviant or negative cases) of a phenomenon are found.

Arithmetic mean Also known simply as the **mean**, this is the everyday average—namely, the total of a distribution of values divided by the number of values.

Asynchronous online interview or focus group Online interviews may be asynchronous or **synchronous**. In the case of the former, the transactions between participants are not in real time, so that there may be long spaces of time between interviewers' questions and participants' replies, and in the case of focus groups, between participants' contributions to the discussion.

Attached e-mail survey A survey in which respondents are sent a questionnaire, which is received as an e-mail attachment. Compare with **embedded e-mail survey**.

Behaviour sampling A sampling approach in **structured observation** whereby an entire group is watched and the observer records who was involved in a particular kind of behaviour.

Biographical method See **life history method**.

Bivariate analysis The examination of the relationship between two variables, as in **contingency tables** or **correlation**.

CAQDAS An abbreviation of **c**omputer-**a**ssisted (or -aided) **q**ualitative **d**ata **a**nalysis **s**oftware.

Case study A **research design** that entails the detailed and intensive analysis of a single case. The term is sometimes extended to include the study of just two or three cases for comparative purposes.

Causality A concern with establishing causal connections between variables, rather than mere **relationships** between them.

Cell The point in a table, such as a **contingency table**, where the rows and columns intersect.

Census The enumeration of an entire **population**. Unlike a **sample**, which comprises a count of *some* units in a population, a census relates to *all* units in a population. Thus, if a **postal questionnaire** is mailed to every person in a town or to all members of a profession, the research should be characterized as a census.

Chi-square test Chi-square (χ^2) is a test of **statistical significance**, which is typically employed to establish how confident we can be that the findings displayed in a **contingency table** can be generalized from a **probability sample** to a **population**.

Closed question A question employed in an **interview schedule** or **self-completion questionnaire** that presents the respondent with a set of possible answers to choose from. Also called **fixed-choice question** and **pre-coded question**.

Cluster sample A sampling procedure in which at an initial stage the researcher samples areas (i.e. clusters) and then samples units from these clusters, usually using a **probability sampling** method.

Code, coding In **quantitative research**, codes act as tags that are placed on data about people or other units of analysis. The aim is to assign the data relating to each **variable** to groups, each of which is considered to be a category of the variable in question. Numbers are then assigned to each category to allow the information to be processed by the computer. In **qualitative research**, coding is the process whereby data are broken down into component parts, which are given names.

Coding frame A listing of the codes used in relation to the analysis of data. In relation to answers to a structured interview schedule or questionnaire, the coding frame will delineate the categories used in connection with each question. It is particularly crucial in relation to the coding of **open questions**. With **closed questions**, the coding frame is essentially incorporated into the pre-given answers, hence the frequent use of the term **pre-coded question** to describe such questions.

Coding manual In **content analysis**, this is the statement of instructions to coders that outlines all the possible categories for each dimension being coded.

Coding schedule In **content analysis**, this is the form onto which all the data relating to an item being coded will be entered.

Cognitive mapping A method used to map the thought processes and decision-making sequences used by an individual or a group to solve a problem.

Collaborative enquiry A tradition founded on the assumption that the people who are the focus of study should be fully involved in the research process at all stages, from the identification of aims to the writing-up of findings. The tradition stems from a desire to challenge the conventional methods whereby knowledge is constructed in the social sciences and to dismantle the assumed authority of the researcher and for this reason it is sometimes referred to as 'new paradigm' research or cooperative enquiry.

Comparative design A **research design** that entails the comparison of two or more cases in order to illuminate existing theory or generate theoretical insights as a result of contrasting findings uncovered through the comparison.

Concept A name given to a category that organizes observations and ideas by virtue of their possessing common features.

Concurrent validity One of the main approaches to establishing **measurement validity**. It entails relating a measure to a criterion on which cases (e.g. people) are known to differ and that is relevant to the **concept** in question.

Connotation A term used in **semiotics** to refer to the principal and most manifest meaning of a **sign**. Compare with **denotation**.

Constant An attribute in terms of which cases do not differ. Compare with **variable**.

Constructionism, constructionist An **ontological** position (often also referred to as **constructivism**) that asserts that social phenomena and their meanings are continually being accomplished by social actors. It is antithetical to **objectivism** and **essentialism**.

Constructivism See **constructionism**.

Content analysis An approach to the analysis of documents and texts that seeks to quantify content in terms of predetermined categories and in a systematic and replicable manner. The term is sometimes used in connection with qualitative research as well—see **qualitative content analysis**.

Contingency table A table, comprising rows and columns, that shows the **relationship** between two **variables**. Usually, at least one of the variables is a **nominal variable**. Each cell in the table shows the frequency of occurrence of that intersection of categories of each of the two variables and usually a percentage.

Continuous recording A procedure in **structured observation**, whereby observation occurs for extended periods, so that the frequency and duration of certain types of behaviour can be carefully recorded.

Convenience sample A sample that is selected because of its availability to the researcher. It is a form of **non-probability sample**.

Conversation analysis The fine-grained analysis of talk as it occurs in interaction in naturally occurring situations. The talk is recorded and **transcribed** so that the detailed analyses can be carried out. The analysis is concerned with uncovering the underlying structures of talk in interaction and as such with the achievement of order through interaction. Conversation analysis is grounded in **ethnomethodology**.

Correlation An approach to the analysis of relationships between **interval/ratio variables** and/or **ordinal variables** that seeks to assess the strength and direction of the relationship between the variables concerned. **Pearson's r** and **Spearman's rho** are both methods for assessing the level of correlation between variables.

Covert research A term frequently used in connection with **ethnographic** research in which the researcher does not reveal his or her true identity. Such research violates the ethical principle of **informed consent**.

Cramér's V A method for assessing the strength of the relationship between two variables, at least one of which must have more than two categories.

Critical incident method A technique that usually relies on **structured interviewing** to elicit from respondents an account of key events or specific kinds of behaviour (critical incidents) and their consequences. Analysis involves interpretation of critical incidents so as to identify common patterns of behaviour.

Critical realism A **realist** epistemology that asserts that the study of the social world should be concerned with the identification of the structures that generate that world. Critical realism is critical because its practitioners aim to identify structures in order to change them, so that inequalities and injustices may be counteracted. Unlike a **positivist** epistemology, critical realism accepts that the structures that are identified may not be amenable to the senses. Thus, whereas **positivism** is **empiricist**, critical realism is not.

Cross-sectional design A **research design** that entails the collection of data on more than one case (usually quite a lot more than one) and at a single point in time in order to collect a body of quantitative or quantifiable data in connection with two or more variables (usually many more than two), which are then examined to detect patterns of association.

Deductive An approach to the relationship between theory and research in which the latter is conducted with reference to hypotheses and ideas inferred from the former. Compare with **inductive**.

Denotation A term used in **semiotics** to refer to the meanings of a **sign** associated with the social context within which it operates that are supplementary to and less immediately apparent than its **connotation**.

Diary A term that in the context of social research methods can mean different things. Three types of diary can be distinguished: diaries written or completed at the behest of a researcher; personal diaries that can be analysed as a **personal document**, but that were produced spontaneously; and diaries written by social researchers as a log of their activities and reflections.

Dependent variable A **variable** that is causally influenced by another variable (i.e. an **independent variable**).

Dichotomous variable A variable with just two categories.

Dimension Refers to an aspect of a **concept**.

Discourse analysis An approach to the analysis of talk and other forms of discourse that emphasizes the ways in which versions of reality are accomplished through language.

Distribution of values A term used to refer to the entire data relating to a **variable**. Thus, the ages of members of a **sample** represent the distribution of values for that variable for that sample.

Ecological fallacy The error of assuming that inferences about individuals can be made from findings relating to aggregate data.

Ecological validity A concern with the question of whether social scientific findings are applicable to people's everyday, natural social settings.

Embedded e-mail survey A **social survey** in which respondents are sent an e-mail that contains a **questionnaire**. Compare with **attached e-mail survey**.

Empiricism An approach to the study of reality that suggests that only knowledge gained through experience and the senses is acceptable.

Epistemology, epistemological A theory of knowledge. It is particularly employed in this book to refer to a stance on what should pass as acceptable knowledge. See **positivism**, **realism**, and **interpretivism**.

Essentialism A position that has close affinities with naive **realism**. Essentialism suggests that objects have essences that denote their authentic nature. Compare with **constructionism**.

Eta A test of the strength of the **relationship** between two **variables**. The **independent variable** must be a **nominal variable** and the **dependent variable** must be an **interval variable** or **ratio variable**. The resulting level of correlation will always be positive.

Ethnographic content analysis See **qualitative content analysis**.

Ethnography, ethnographer Like **participant observation**, a research method in which the researcher immerses him- or herself in a social setting for an extended period of time, observing behaviour, listening to what is said in conversations both between others and with the fieldworker, and asking questions. However, the term has a more inclusive sense than participant observation, which seems to emphasize the observational component. Also, the term 'an ethnography' is frequently used to refer to the written output of ethnographic research.

Ethnomethodology A sociological perspective concerned with the way in which social order is accomplished through talk and interaction. It provides the intellectual foundations of **conversation analysis**.

Evaluation research Research that is concerned with the evaluation of real-life interventions in the social world.

Experiment A **research design** that rules out alternative explanations of findings deriving from it (i.e. possesses **internal validity**) by having at least (*a*) an experimental group, which is exposed to a treatment, and a control group, which is not, and (*b*) **random assignment** to the two groups.

External validity A concern with the question of whether the results of a study can be generalized beyond the specific research context in which it was conducted.

Face validity A concern with whether an **indicator** appears to reflect the content of the **concept** in question.

Facilitator See **moderator**.

Factor analysis A statistical technique used for large numbers of **variables** to establish whether there is a tendency for groups of them to be inter-related. It is often used with **multiple-indicator measures** to see if the **indicators** tend to bunch to form one or more groups of indicators. These groups of indicators are called factors and must then be given a name.

Field stimulation A study in which the researcher directly intervenes in and/or manipulates a natural setting in order to observe what happens as a consequence of that intervention.

Field notes A detailed chronicle by an **ethnographer** of events, conversations, and behaviour, and the researcher's initial reflections on them.

Frequency table A table that displays the number and/or percentage of units (e.g. people) in different categories of a variable.

Focal sampling A sampling approach in **structured observation** whereby a sampled individual is observed for a set period of time. The observer records all examples of whatever forms of behaviour are of interest.

Focus group A form of group interview in which: there are several participants (in addition to the **moderator/facilitator**); there is an emphasis in the questioning on a particular fairly tightly defined topic; and the emphasis is upon interaction within the group and the joint construction of meaning.

Generalization, generalizability A concern with the **external validity** of research findings.

Grounded theory An approach to the analysis of qualitative data that aims to generate theory out of research data by achieving a close fit between the two.

Hawthorne effect See **reactivity, reactive effect**.

Hermeneutics A term drawn from theology, which, when imported into the social sciences, is concerned with the theory and method of the interpretation of human action. It emphasizes the need to understand from the perspective of the social actor.

Hypothesis An informed speculation, which is set up to be tested, about the possible relationship between two or more variables.

Independent variable A **variable** that has a causal impact on another variable (i.e. a **dependent variable**).

Index See **scale**.

Indicator A measure that is employed to refer to a **concept** when no direct measure is available.

Inductive An approach to the relationship between theory and research in which the former is generated out of the latter. Compare with **deductive**.

Informed consent A key principle in social research ethics. It implies that prospective research participants should be given as much information as might be needed to make an informed decision about whether or not they wish to participate in a study.

Inter-coder reliability The degree to which two or more individuals agree about the **coding** of an item. Inter-coder reliability is likely to be an issue in **content analysis, structured observation**, and when **coding** answers to **open questions** in research based on **questionnaires** or **structured interviews**.

Internal reliability The degree to which the indicators that make up a **scale** are consistent.

Internal validity A concern with the question of whether a finding that incorporates a causal relationship between two or more variables is sound.

Internet survey A very general term used to include any survey conducted online. As such, it includes the **Web Survey** and the **attached e-mail survey** and the **embedded e-mail survey**.

Interpretative repertoire A collection of linguistic resources that are drawn upon in order to characterize and assess actions and events.

Interpretivism An **epistemological** position that requires the social scientist to grasp the subjective meaning of social action.

Interval variable A **variable** where the distances between the categories are identical across its range of categories.

Intervening variable A **variable** that is affected by another variable and that in turn has a causal impact on another variable. Taking an intervening variable into account often facilitates the understanding of the relationship between two variables.

Interview guide A rather vague term that is used to refer to the brief list of memory prompts of areas to be covered that is often employed in **unstructured interviewing** or to the somewhat more structured list of issues to be addressed or questions to be asked in **semi-structured interviewing**.

Interview schedule A collection of questions designed to be asked by an interviewer. An interview schedule is always used in a **structured interview**.

Intra-coder reliability The degree to which an individual differs over time in the **coding** of an item. Intra-coder reliability is likely to be an issue in **content analysis, structured observation**, and when **coding** answers to **open questions** in research based on **questionnaires** or **structured interviews**.

Key informant Someone who offers the researcher, usually in the context of conducting an **ethnography**, perceptive information about the social setting, important events, and individuals.

Life history interview Similar to the **oral history interview**, but the aim of this type of **unstructured interview** is to glean information on the entire biography of each respondent.

Life history method Also often referred to as the **biographical method**, this method emphasizes the inner experience of individuals and its connections with changing events and phases throughout the life course. The method usually entails **life history interviews** and the use of **personal documents** as data.

Likert scale A widely used format developed by Rensis Likert for asking attitude questions. Respondents are typically asked their degree of agreement with a series of statements that together form a **multiple-indicator** or **-item** measure. The scale is deemed then to measure the intensity with which respondents feel about an issue.

Longitudinal research A **research design** in which data are collected on a **sample** (of people, documents, etc.) on at least two occasions.

Mail questionnaire Traditionally, this term has been synonymous with the **postal questionnaire**, but, with the arrival of e-mail-based questionnaires (see **embedded e-mail survey** and **attached e-mail survey**), many writers prefer to refer to postal rather than mail questionnaires.

Mean See **arithmetic mean**.

Measure of central tendency A statistic, like the **arithmetic mean**, **median**, or **mode**, that summarizes a **distribution of values**.

Measure of dispersion A statistic, like the **range** or **standard deviation**, that summarizes the amount of variation in a **distribution of values**.

Measurement validity The degree to which a measure of a concept truly reflects that concept. See also **face validity** and **concurrent validity**.

Median The mid-point in a **distribution of values**.

Meta-analysis A method for determining the overall effect of the relationship between variables by drawing together the findings from more than one, and often many more research studies. This is typically achieved through quantitative measurement and the use of statistical procedures.

Missing data Data relating to a case that are not available, for example, when a respondent in **survey** research does not answer a question. These are referred to as 'missing values' in **SPSS**.

Mode The value that occurs most frequently in a **distribution of values**.

Moderated relationship A **relationship** between two **variables** is said to be moderated when it holds for one category of a third variable but not for another category or other categories.

Moderator The person who guides the questioning of a **focus group**. Also called a **facilitator**.

Multiple-indicator measure A measure that employs more than one **indicator** to measure a **concept**.

Multi-strategy research A term used to describe research that combines **quantitative** and **qualitative research**.

Multivariate analysis The examination of relationships between three or more **variables**.

Narrative analysis An approach to the elicitation and analysis of data that is sensitive to the sense of temporal sequence that people, as tellers of stories about their lives or events around them, detect in their lives and surrounding episodes and inject into their accounts. However, the approach is not exclusive to a focus on life histories.

Naturalism A confusing term that has at least three distinct meanings: a commitment to adopting the principles of natural scientific method; being true to the nature of the phenomenon being investigated; and a style of research that seeks to minimize the intrusion of artificial methods of data collection.

Negative relationship A **relationship** between two **variables**, whereby as one increases the other decreases.

Nominal variable Also known as a **categorical variable**, this is a variable that comprises categories that cannot be rank ordered.

Non-manipulable variable A **variable** that cannot readily be manipulated either for practical or for ethical reasons and that therefore cannot be employed in an **experiment**.

Non-probability sample A sample that has not been selected using a random sampling method. Essentially, this implies that some units in the population are more likely to be selected than others.

Non-response A source of **non-sampling error** that occurs whenever some members of a sample refuse to cooperate, cannot be contacted, or for some reason cannot supply the required data.

Non-sampling error Differences between the **population** and the **sample** that arise either from deficiencies in the sampling approach, such as an inadequate **sampling frame** or **non-response**, or from such problems as poor question wording, poor interviewing, or flawed processing of data.

Null hypothesis A hypothesis of no relationship between two variables.

Objectivism An **ontological** position that asserts that social phenomena and their meanings have an existence that is independent of social actors. Compare with **constructionism**.

Observation schedule A device used in **structured observation** that specifies the categories of behaviour that are to be observed and how behaviour should be allocated to those categories.

Official statistics Statistics compiled by or on behalf of state agencies in the course of conducting their business.

Ontology, ontological A theory of the nature of social entities. See **objectivism** and **inductivism**.

Open question A question employed in an **interview schedule** or **self-completion questionnaire** that does not present the respondent with a set of possible answers to choose from. Compare with **closed question**.

Operational definition The definition of a **concept** in terms of the operations to be carried out when measuring it.

Operationism, operationalism A doctrine, mainly associated with a version of physics, that emphasizes the search for **operational definitions** of **concepts**.

Oral history interview A largely **unstructured interview** in which the respondent is asked to recall events from his or her past and to reflect on them.

Ordinal variable A variable whose categories can be rank ordered (as in the case of **interval** and **ratio variables**), but the distances between the categories are not equal across the range.

Outlier An extreme value in a distribution of values. If a **variable** has an extreme value—either very high or very low—the **arithmetic mean** or the **range** will be distorted by it.

Paradigm A term deriving from the history of science, where it was used to describe a cluster of beliefs and dictates that for scientists in a particular discipline influence what should be studied, how research should be done, and how results should be interpreted.

Participant observation Research in which the researcher immerses him- or herself in a social setting for an extended period of time, observing behaviour, listening to what is said in conversations both between others and with the fieldworker, and asking questions. Participant observation usually includes interviewing key informants and studying documents and as such is difficult to distinguish from **ethnography**. In this book, participant observation is employed to refer to the specifically observational aspect of ethnography.

Pearson's r A measure of the strength and direction of the **relationship** between two **interval/ratio variables**.

Personal documents Documents such as **diaries**, letters, and autobiographies that are not written for an official purpose. They provide first-person accounts of the writer's life and events within it.

Phenomenology A philosophy that is concerned with the question of how individuals make sense of the world around them and how in particular the philosopher should bracket out preconceptions concerning his or her grasp of that world.

Phi A method for assessing the strength and direction of the **relationship** between two **dichotomous variables**.

Population The universe of units from which a **sample** is to be selected.

Positive relationship A **relationship** between two **variables**, whereby as one increases the other increases as well.

Positivism An **epistemological** position that advocates the application of the methods of the natural sciences to the study of social reality and beyond.

Postal questionnaire A form of **self-completion questionnaire** that is sent to respondents and usually returned by them by non-electronic mail.

Postmodernism A position that displays a distaste for master-narratives and for a **realist** orientation. In the context of research methodology, postmodernists display a preference for qualitative methods and a concern with the modes of representation of research findings.

Pre-coded question Another name for a **closed question**. The term is often preferred, because such a question removes the need for the application of a **coding frame** to the question after it has been answered. This is because the range of answers has been predetermined and a numerical **code** will have been pre-assigned to each possible answer. The term is particularly appropriate when the codes appear on the **questionnaire** or **interview schedule**.

Probability sample A sample that has been selected using **random sampling** and in which each unit in the population has a known probability of being selected.

Projective techniques A method involving the presentation of ambiguous stimuli to individuals, which are interpreted by the researcher to reveal the underlying characteristics of the individual.

QSR NVivo A **CAQDAS** package that derives from but goes beyond NUD*IST (Non-numerical Unstructured Data Indexing Searching and Theorizing).

Qualitative content analysis An approach to documents that emphasizes the role of the investigator in the construction of the meaning of and in texts. There is an emphasis on allowing categories to emerge out of data and on recognizing the significance for understanding the meaning of the context in which an item being analysed (and the categories derived from it) appeared.

Qualitative research Qualitative research usually emphasizes words rather than quantification in the collection and analysis of data. As a **research strategy** it is **inductivist, constructivist**, and **interpretivist**, but qualitative researchers do not always subscribe to all three of these features. Compare with **quantitative research**.

Quantitative research Quantitative research usually emphasizes quantification in the collection and analysis of data. As a **research strategy** it is **deductivist** and **objectivist** and incorporates a natural science model of the research process (in particular, one influenced by **positivism**), but quantitative researchers do not always subscribe to all three of these features. Compare with **qualitative research**.

Quasi-experiment A **research design** that is close to being an **experiment** but that does not meet the requirements fully and therefore does not exhibit complete **internal validity**.

Questionnaire A collection of questions administered to respondents. When used on its own, the term usually denotes a **self-completion questionnaire**.

Quota sample A **sample** that non-randomly samples a **population** in terms of the relative proportions of people in different categories. It is a type of **non-probability sample**.

Random assignment A term used in connection with **experiments** to refer to the random allocation of research participants to the experimental group and the control group.

Random sampling Sampling whereby the inclusion of a unit of a **population** occurs entirely by chance.

Range The difference between the maximum and the minimum value in a **distribution of values** associated with an **interval** or **ratio variable**.

Ratio variable An **interval variable** with a true zero point.

Reactivity, reactive effect A term used to describe the response of research participants to the fact that they know they are being studied, also sometimes referred to as the Hawthorne effect. Reactivity is deemed to result in untypical behaviour.

Realism An epistemological position that acknowledges a reality independent of the senses that is accessible to the researcher's tools and theoretical speculations. It implies that the categories created by scientists refer to real objects in the natural or social worlds. See also **critical realism**.

Reflexivity A term used in research methodology to refer to a reflectiveness among social researchers about the implica-

tions for the knowledge of the social world they generate of their methods, values, biases, decisions, and mere presence in the very situations they investigate.

Relationship An association between two variables whereby the variation in one variable coincides with variation in another variable.

Reliability The degree to which a measure of a concept is stable.

Repertory grid technique A method for mapping the relationship between constructs used by an individual or a group of individuals to construct meaning. The method results in the production of a diagrammatic matrix representing the various constructs and elements involved in analysing this relationship, i.e. the repertory grid.

Replication, replicability The degree to which the results of a study can be reproduced. See also **internal reliability**.

Representative sample A **sample** that reflects the population accurately, so that it is a microcosm of the **population**.

Research design This term is employed in this book to refer to a framework for the collection and analysis of data. A choice of research design reflects decisions about the priority being given to a range of dimensions of the research process (such as **causality** and **generalization**).

Research strategy A term used in this book to refer to a general orientation to the conduct of social research (see **quantitative research** and **qualitative research**).

Respondent validation Sometimes called *member validation*, this is a process whereby a researcher provides the people on whom he or she has conducted research with an account of his or her findings and requests feedback on that account.

Response set The tendency among some respondents to **multiple-indicator measures** to reply in the same way to each constituent item.

Rhetoric A concern with the ways in which appeals to convince or persuade are devised.

Sample The segment of the population that is selected for research. It is a subset of the **population**. The method of selection may be based on **probability sampling** or **non-probability sampling**.

Sampling error Differences between a **random sample** and the **population** from which it is selected.

Sampling frame The listing of all units in the **population** from which a **sample** is selected.

Scale A term that is usually used interchangeably with **index** to refer to a **multiple-indicator measure** in which the score a person gives for each component **indicator** is used to provide a composite score for that person.

Scan sampling A sampling approach in **structured observation** whereby an entire group of individuals is scanned at regular intervals and the behaviour of all of them is recorded at each occasion.

Secondary analysis The analysis of data by researchers who will probably not have been involved in the collection of those data for purposes that may not have been envisaged by those responsible for the data collection. Secondary analysis may entail the analysis of either quantitative data or qualitative data.

Self-administered questionnaire See **self-completion questionnaire**.

Self-completion questionnaire A **questionnaire** that the respondent answers without the aid of an interviewer. Sometimes called a **self-administered questionnaire**.

Semiotics The study/science of **signs**. An approach to the analysis of documents and other phenomena that emphasizes the importance of seeking out the deeper meaning of those phenomena. A semiotic approach is concerned to uncover the processes of meaning production and how signs are designed to have an effect upon actual and prospective consumers of those signs.

Semi-structured interview A term that covers a wide range of types. It typically refers to a context in which the interviewer has a series of questions that are in the general form of an **interview guide** but is able to vary the sequence of questions. The questions are frequently somewhat more general in their frame of reference from that typically found in a **structured interview** schedule. Also, the interviewer usually has some latitude to ask further questions in response to what are seen as significant replies.

Sensitizing concept A term devised by Blumer to refer to a preference for treating a **concept** as a guide in an investigation, so that it points in a general way to what is relevant or important. This position contrasts with the idea of an **operational definition**, in which the meaning of a concept is fixed in advance of carrying out an investigation.

Sign A term employed in **semiotics**. A sign is made up of a signifier (the manifestation of a sign) and the signified (that idea or deeper meaning to which the signifier refers).

Simple observation The passive and unobtrusive observation of behaviour.

Simple random sample A **sample** in which each unit has been selected entirely by chance. Each unit of the **population** has a known and equal probability of inclusion in the sample.

Snowball sample A **non-probability sample** in which the researcher makes initial contact with a small group of people who are relevant to the research topic and then uses these to establish contacts with others.

Social survey See survey research.

Social desirability bias A distortion of data that is caused by respondents' attempts to construct an account that conforms to a socially acceptable model of belief or behaviour.

Spearman's rho (ρ) A measure of the strength and direction of the **relationship** between two **ordinal variables**.

SPSS Originally short for Statistical Package for the Social Sciences, SPSS is a widely used computer program that allows quantitative data to be managed and analysed.

Spurious relationship A **relationship** between two **variables** is said to be spurious if it is being produced by the impact of a third variable on each of the two variables that form the spurious relationship. When the third variable is controlled, the relationship disappears.

Standard deviation A measure of dispersion around the **mean**.

Standard error of the mean An estimate of the amount that a sample mean is likely to differ from the population mean.

Statistical inference See **statistical significance (test of)**.

Statistical significance (test of) Allows the analyst to estimate how confident he or she can be that the results deriving from a study based on a randomly selected **sample** are generalizable to the **population** from which the sample was drawn. Such a test does not allow the researcher to infer that the findings are of substantive importance. The **chi-square test** is an example of this kind of test. The process of using a test of statistical significance to generalize from a sample to a population is known as **statistical inference**.

Stratified random sample A **sample** in which units are randomly sampled from a **population** that has been divided into categories (strata).

Structured interview A research interview in which all respondents are asked exactly the same questions in the same order with the aid of a formal **interview schedule**.

Structured observation Often also called **systematic observation**, structured observation is a technique in which the researcher employs explicitly formulated rules for the observation and recording of behaviour. The rules inform observers about what they should look for and how they should record behaviour.

Survey research A **cross-sectional design** in relation to which data are collected predominantly by **self-completion questionnaire** or by **structured interview** on more than one case (usually quite a lot more than one) and at *a single point in time* in order to collect a body of quantitative or quantifiable data in connection with two or more **variables** (usually many more than two) which are then examined to detect patterns of **relationship**.

Symbolic interactionism A theoretical perspective in sociology and social psychology that views social interaction as taking place in terms of the meanings actors attach to action and things.

Synchronous online interview or **focus group** Online interviews may be **asynchronous** or synchronous. In the case of the latter, the transactions between participants are in real time, so that there will be only brief time lapes between interviewers' questions and participants' replies, and, in the case of focus groups, between participants' contributions to the discussion.

Systematic observation See **structured observation**.

Systematic sample A **probability sampling** method in which units are selected from a **sampling frame** according to fixed intervals, such as every fifth unit.

Text A term that is used either in the conventional sense of a written work or in more recent years to refer to a wide range of phenomena. For example, in arriving at a **thick description**, Geertz refers to treating culture as a text.

Theoretical sampling A term used mainly in relation to **grounded theory** to refer to sampling carried out so that emerging theoretical considerations guide the selection of cases and/or research participants. Theoretical sampling is supposed to continue until a point of **theoretical saturation** is reached.

Theoretical saturation In **grounded theory**, the point when emerging **concepts** have been fully explored and no new insights are being generated. See also **theoretical sampling**.

Thick description A term devised by Geertz to refer to detailed accounts of a social setting that can form the basis for the creation of general statements about a culture and its significance in people's social lives.

Time sampling A sampling method in **structured observation**, which entails using a criterion for deciding when observation will occur.

Transcription, transcript The written translation of a tape-recorded **interview** or **focus group** session.

Triangulation The use of more than one method or source of data in the study of a social phenomenon so that findings may be cross-checked.

Trustworthiness A set of criteria advocated by some writers for assessing the quality of **qualitative research**.

Turn-taking The notion from **conversation analysis** that order in everyday conversation is achieved through orderly taking of turns in conversations.

Univariate analysis The analysis of a single **variable** at a time.

Unobtrusive methods Methods that do not entail the awareness among research participants that they are being studied and that are therefore not subject to **reactivity**.

Unstructured interview An interview in which the interviewer typically only has a list of topics or issues, often called an **interview guide**, that are typically covered. The style of questioning is usually very informal. The phrasing and sequencing of questions will vary from interview to interview.

Validity A concern with the integrity of the conclusions that are generated from a piece of research. There are different aspects of validity. See, in particular, **measurement validity**, **internal validity**, **external validity**, and **ecological validity**. When used on its own, **validity** is usually taken to refer to **measurement validity**.

Variable An attribute in terms of which cases vary. See also **dependent variable** and **independent variable**. Compare with **constant**.

Verbal protocol approach A method that involves asking respondents to think aloud while they are performing a task in order to capture their thought processes while they are making a decision or judgement or solving a problem.

Web survey A **social survey** conducted so that respondents complete a **questionnaire** via a web site.

References

Addison, J. T., and Belfield, C. R. (2000), 'The Impact of Financial Participation and Employee Involvement on Financial Performance: A Reiteration Using the 1998 WERS', *Scottish Journal of Political Economy*, 47(5): 571–83.

Adler, N. (1983), 'A Typology of Management Studies Involving Culture', *Journal of International Business Studies*, Fall: 29–47.

Adriaenssens, C., and Cadman, L. (1999), 'An Adaptation of Moderated E-Mail Focus Groups to Assess the Potential of a New Online (Internet) Financial Services Offer in the UK', *Journal of the Market Research Society*, 41: 417–24.

Altheide, D. L. (1980), 'Leaving the Newsroom', in W. Shaffir, R. A. Stebbins, and A. Turowetz (eds), *Fieldwork Experience: Qualitative Approaches to Social Research* (New York: St Martin's Press).

——(1996), *Qualitative Media Analysis* (Thousand Oaks, Calif.: Sage).

Aitken, I. (1998), 'The Documentary Film Movement: The Post Office Touches All Branches of Life', in J. Hassard and R. Holliday (eds), *Organization-Representation: Work and Organization in Popular Culture* (London: Sage).

Alderson, P. (1998), 'Confidentiality and Consent in Qualitative Research', *Network: Newsletter of the British Sociological Association*, 69: 6–7.

Aldrich, H. E. (1972), 'Technology and Organizational Structure: A Re-Examination of the Findings of the Aston Group', *Administrative Science Quarterly*, 17(1): 26–43.

Aldridge, A. (1998), 'Reproducing the Value of Professional Expertise in Post-Traditional Culture: Financial Advice and the Creation of the Client', *Cultural Values*, 2: 445–62.

Altschuld, J. W., and Lower, M. A. (1984), 'Improving Mailed Questionnaires: Analysis of a 96 Percent Return Rate', in D. C. Lockhart (ed.), *Making Effective Use of Mailed Questionnaires* (San Francisco, Calif.: Jossey-Bass).

Andersen, M. (1981), 'Corporate Wives: Longing for Liberation or Satisfied with the Status Quo?', *Urban Life*, 10: 311–27.

Anderson, N. (1990), 'Repertory Grid Technique in Employee Selection', *Personnel Review*, 19(3): 9–15.

Anderson, R. J., Hughes, J. A., and Sharrock, W. W. (1989), *Working for Profit: The Social Organization of Calculation in an Entrepreneurial Firm* (Aldershot: Avebury).

Argyris, C., Putnam, R., and Smith, M. (1985), *Action Science: Concepts, Methods and Skills for Research and Intervention* (San Francisco, Calif.: Jossey-Bass).

Armstrong, G. (1993), 'Like that Desmond Morris?', in D. Hobbs and T. May (eds), *Interpreting the Field: Accounts of Ethnography* (Oxford: Clarendon Press).

Arnold, H. J., and Feldman, D. C. (1981), 'Social Desirability Response Bias in Self-Report Choice Situations', *Academy of Management Journal*, 24: 377–85.

Aronson, E., and Carlsmith, J. M. (1968), 'Experimentation in Social Psychology', in G. Lindzey and E. Aronson (eds), *The Handbook of Social Psychology* (Reading, Mass.: Addison-Wesley).

Arthur, J. (1994), 'Effects of Human Resource Systems on Manufacturing, Performance and Turnover', *Academy of Management Journal*, 37(3): 670–87.

Asch, S. E. (1951), 'Effect of Group Pressure upon the Modification and Distortion of Judgments', in H. Guetzkow (ed.), *Groups, Leadership and Men* (Pittsburgh: Carnegie Press).

Atkinson, P. (1981), *The Clinical Experience* (Farnborough: Gower).

——(1990), *The Ethnographic Imagination: Textual Constructions of Society* (London: Routledge).

——and Coffey, A. (1995), 'Realism and its Discontents: On the Crisis of Cultural Representation in Ethnographic Texts', in B. Adam and S. Allan (eds), *Theorizing Culture: An Interdisciplinary Critique after Postmodernism* (London: UCL Press).

——and Silverman, D. (1997), 'Kundera's Immortality: The Interview Society and the Invention of Self', *Qualitative Inquiry*, 3(3): 324–45.

Bacon, N., and Blyton, P. (2001), 'Management Practices and Employee Attitudes: A Longitudinal Study Spanning Fifty Years', *Sociological Review*, 49(2): 254–74.

Ball, K., and Wilson, D. C. (2000), 'Power, Control and Computer-Based Performance Monitoring: Repertoires, Resistance and Subjectivities', *Organization Studies*, 21(3): 539–65.

Bansal, P., and Roth, K. (2000), 'Why Companies Go Green: A Model of Ecological Responsiveness', *Academy of Management Journal*, 43(4): 717–36.

Barley, S. (1983), 'Semiotics and the Study of Occupational and Organizational Cultures', *Administrative Science Quarterly*, 28: 393–413.

Barley, S., Meyer, G., and Gash, D. (1988), 'Cultures of Culture: Academics, Practitioners and the Pragmatics of Normative Control', *Administrative Science Quarterly*, 33: 24–60.

Barthes, R. (1972), *Mythologies* (London: Jonathan Cape).

Bartunek, J. M., Bobko, P., and Venkatraman, N. (1993). 'Toward Innovation and Diversity in Management Research Methods', *Academy of Management Journal*, 36(6): 1362–73.

Bate, S. (1997), 'Whatever Happened to Organizational Ethnography? A Review of the Field of Organizational Ethnography and Anthropological Studies', *Human Relations*, 50(9): 1147–75.

Bauman, Z. (1978), *Hermeneutics and Social Science: Approaches to Understanding* (London: Hutchison).

Baumgartner, R. M., and Heberlein, T. A. (1984), 'Applying Attitude Theories to the Return of Mailed Questionnaires', in D. C. Lockhart (ed.), *Making Effective Use of Mailed Questionnaires* (San Francisco: Jossey-Bass).

Bazerman, C. (1987), 'Codifying the Social Scientific Style: The APA *Publication Manual* as a Behaviorist Rhetoric', in J. S. Nelson, A. Megill, and D. N. McClosky (eds), *The Rhetoric of the Human Sciences* (Madison: University of Wisconsin Press).

——(1988), *Shaping Written Knowledge: The Genre and Activity of the Experimental Article in Science* (Madison: University of Wisconsin Press).

Beardsworth, A. (1980), 'Analysing Press Content: Some Technical and Methodological Issues', in H. Christian (ed.), *Sociology of Journalism and the Press* (Keele: Keele University Press).

Bechhofer, F., Elliott, B., and McCrone, D. (1984), 'Safety in Numbers: On the Use of Multiple Interviewers', *Sociology*, 18: 97–100.

Becker, H. S. (1958), 'Problems of Inference and Proof in Participant Observation', *American Sociological Review*, 23: 652–60.

——(1982), 'Culture: A Sociological View', *Yale Review*, 71: 513–27.

——(1986), *Writing for Social Scientists: How to Start and Finish your Thesis, Book, or Article* (Chicago: University of Chicago Press).

——and Geer, B. (1957a), 'Participant Observation and Interviewing: A Comparison', *Human Organization*, 16: 28–32.

————(1957b), ' "Participant Observation and Interviewing": A Rejoinder', *Human Organization*, 16: 39–40.

Belk, R. W., Ger, G., and Askegaard, S. (1997), 'Consumer Desire in Three Cultures: Results from Projective Research', *Advances in Consumer Research*, 24: 24–8.

Bell, C. (1969), 'A Note on Participant Observation', *Sociology*, 3: 417–18.

——and Newby, H. (1977), *Doing Sociological Research* (London: George Allen & Unwin).

——and Roberts, H. (1984), *Social Researching: Politics, Problems, Practice* (London: Routledge & Kegan Paul).

Bell, E. (1999), 'The Negotiation of a Working Role in Organizational Ethnography', *International Journal of Social Research Methodology*, 2(1): 17–37.

——(2001), 'The Social Time of Organizational Payment Systems', *Time & Society*, 10(1): 45–62.

——and Bryman, A. (2003), 'Ethical Issues in Critical Management Research', Critical Management Studies Conference, Lancaster, 7–9 July.

——Taylor, S., and Thorpe, R. (2001), 'Investors in People and the Standardization of Professional Knowledge in Personnel Management', *Management Learning*, 32(2): 201–19.

————(2002), 'Organizational Differentiation through Badging: Investors in People and the Value of the Sign', *Journal of Management Studies*, 39(8): 1071–85.

Belson, W. A. (1981), *The Design and Understanding of Survey Questions* (Aldershot: Gower).

Berelson, B. (1952), *Content Analysis in Communication Research* (New York: Free Press).

Berg, P. O., and Kreiner, K. (1990), 'Corporate Architecture: Turning Physical Settings into Symbolic Resources', in P. Gagliardi (ed.), *Symbols and Artifacts: Views of the Corporate Landscape* (Berlin: DeGruyter).

Bettis, R. (1991), 'Strategic Management and the Straightjacket: An Editorial Essay', *Organization Science*, 2(3): 315–19.

Bettman, J., and Weitz, B. (1983), 'Attributions in the Board Room: Causal Reasoning in Corporate Annual Reports', *Administrative Science Quarterly*, 28: 165–83.

Beynon, H. (1975), *Working for Ford*, 2nd edn. (Harmondsworth: Penguin).

——(1988), 'Regulating Research: Politics and Decision Making in Industrial Organizations', in A. Bryman (ed.), *Doing Research in Organizations* (London: Routledge).

Bhaskar, R. (1975), *A Realist Theory of Science* (Leeds: Leeds Books).

——(1989), *Reclaiming Reality: A Critical Introduction to Contemporary Philosophy* (London: Verso).

Billig, M. (1991), *Ideology and Opinions: Studies in Rhetorical Psychology* (Cambridge: Cambridge University Press).

——(1992), *Talking of the Royal Family* (London: Routledge).

——Condor, S., Edwards, D., Gane, M., Middleton, D., and Radley, A. (1988), *Ideological Dilemmas: A Social Psychology of Everyday Thinking* (London: Sage).

Blackburn, R., and Stokes, D. (2000), 'Breaking Down the Barriers: Using Focus Groups to Research Small and Medium-Sized Enterprises', *International Small Business Journal*, 19(1): 44–67.

Blauner, R. (1964), *Alienation and Freedom* (Chicago: University of Chicago Press).

Bloomfield, B. P., and Vurdubakis, T. (1994), 'Re-Presenting Technology: IT Consultancy Reports as Textual Reality Constructions', *Sociology*, 28: 455–77.

Bloor, M. (1978), 'On the Analysis of Observational Data: A Discussion of the Worth and Uses of Inductive Techniques and Respondent Validation', *Sociology*, 12: 545–52.

Blumer, H. (1954), 'What is Wrong with Social Theory?', *American Sociological Review*, 19: 3–10.

—— (1956), 'Sociological Analysis and the "Variable"', *American Sociological Review*, 21: 683–90.

—— (1962), 'Society as Symbolic Interaction', in A. M. Rose (ed.), *Human Behavior and Social Processes* (London: Routledge & Kegan Paul).

Blyton, P., Bacon, N., and Morris, J. (1996), 'Working in Steel: Steelworkers' Attitudes to Change Forty Years On', *Industrial Relations Journal*, 27(2): 155–65.

Boden, D. (1994), *The Business of Talk: Organizations in Action* (Cambridge: Polity).

Bogdan, R., and Taylor, S. J. (1975), *Introduction to Qualitative Research Methods: A Phenomenological Approach to the Social Sciences* (New York: Wiley).

Boje, D. (1991), 'The Storytelling Organization: A Study of Performance in an Office Supply Firm', *Administrative Science Quarterly*, 36: 106–26.

—— (2001), *Narrative Methods for Organizational and Communication Research* (London: Sage).

Bond, M., and Pyle, J. (1998), 'The Ecology of Diversity in Organizational Settings: Lessons from a Case Study', *Human Relations*, 51(5): 589–623.

Bottomore, T. B., and Rubel, M. (1963), *Karl Marx: Selected Writings in Sociology and Social Philosophy* (Harmondsworth: Penguin).

Bowen, D. D., and Hisrich, R. D. (1986), 'The Female Entrepreneur: A Career Development Perspective', *Academy of Management Review*, 11: 393–407.

Bowey, A., and Thorpe, R. (1986), *Payment Systems and Productivity* (Basingstoke: Macmillan).

Bradburn, N. A., and Sudman, S. (1979), *Improving Interview Method and Questionnaire Design* (San Francisco: Jossey-Bass).

Braverman, H. (1974), *Labor and Monopoly Capital: The Degradation of Work in the Twentieth Century* (London: Monthly Review Press).

Brayfield, A., and Rothe, H. (1951), 'An Index of Job Satisfaction', *Journal of Applied Psychology*, 35: 307–11.

Brewster, C., and Hegewisch, A. (1994), *Policy and Practice in European Human Resource Management: The Price Waterhouse Cranfield Study* (London: Routledge).

Bridgman, P. W. (1927), *The Logic of Modern Physics* (New York: Macmillan).

Briggs, C. L. (1986), *Learning How to Ask: A Sociolinguistic Appraisal of the Role of the Interview in Social Science Research* (Cambridge: Cambridge University Press).

Broussine, M., and Vince, R. (1996), 'Working with Metaphor Towards Organizational Change', in C. Oswick and D. Grant (eds), *Organization Development: Metaphorical Explanations* (London: Pitman Publishing).

Brown, A. D. (1998), 'Narrative, Politics and Legitimacy in an IT Implementation', *Journal of Management Studies*, 35: 35–58.

Brown, L. D., and Kaplan, R. E. (1981), 'Participative Research in a Factory', in P. Reason and J. Rowan (eds), *Human Inquiry* (London: Wiley).

Bryman, A. (1974), 'Sociology of Religion and Sociology of Elites', *Archives de sciences sociales des religions*, 38: 109–21.

—— (1988a), *Quantity and Quality in Social Research* (London: Routledge).

—— (1988b), *Doing Research in Organizations* (London: Routledge).

—— (1989a), *Research Methods and Organization Studies* (London: Routledge).

—— (1989b), 'The Value of Re-Studies in Sociology: The Case of Clergy and Ministers, 1971 to 1985', *Sociology*, 23: 31–54.

—— (1992), 'Quantitative and Qualitative Research: Further Reflections on their Integration', in J. Brannen (ed.), *Mixing Methods: Qualitative and Quantitative Research* (Aldershot: Avebury).

—— (1994), 'The Mead/Freeman Controversy: Some Implications for Qualitative Researchers', in R. G. Burgess (ed.), *Studies in Qualitative Methodology*, Vol. 4 (Greenwich, Conn.: JAI Press).

—— (1995), *Disney and his Worlds* (London: Routledge).

—— (1997), 'Animating the Pioneer versus Late Entrant Debate: An Historical Case Study', *Journal of Management Studies*, 34: 415–38.

—— (1998), 'Quantitative and Qualitative Research Strategies in Knowing the Social World', in T. May and M. Williams (eds), *Knowing the Social World* (Buckingham: Open University Press).

—— (1999), 'Global Disney', in P. Taylor and D. Slater (eds), *The American Century* (Oxford: Blackwell).

—— (2000), 'Telling Technological Tales', *Organization*, 7: 455–75.

—— and Burgess, R. G. (1994a), 'Developments in Qualitative Data Analysis: An Introduction', in A. Bryman and R. G. Burgess (eds), *Analyzing Qualitative Data* (London: Routledge).

———— (1994b), 'Reflections on Qualitative Data Analysis', in A. Bryman and R. G. Burgess (eds), *Analyzing Qualitative Data* (London: Routledge).

———— (1999), 'Introduction: Qualitative Research Methodology—A Review', in A. Bryman and R. G. Burgess (eds), *Qualitative Research* (London: Sage).

Bryman, A., and Cramer, D. (2001), *Quantitative Data Analysis with SPSS Release 10 for Windows: A Guide for Social Scientists* (London: Routledge).

—— Gillingwater, D., and McGuinness, I. (1996), 'Industry Culture and Strategic Response: The Case of the British Bus Industry', *Studies in Cultures, Organizations and Societies*, 2: 191–208.

Bryman, A., Haslam, C., and Webb, A. (1994), 'Performance Appraisal in UK Universities: A Case of Procedural Compliance?', *Assessment and Evaluation in Higher Education*, 19: 175–88.

——Stephens, M., and A Campo, C. (1996), 'The Importance of Context: Qualitative Research and the Study of Leadership', *Leadership Quarterly*, 7: 353–70.

Buchanan, D. R. (1992), 'An Uneasy Alliance: Combining Qualitative and Quantitative Research Methods', *Health Education Quarterly*, 19: 117–35.

Buchanan, D. A. (2001), 'The Role of Photography in Organization Research: A Reengineering Case Illustration', *Journal of Management Inquiry*, 10: 151–64.

——Boddy, D., and McCalman, J. (1988), 'Getting In, Getting Out and Getting Back', in A. Bryman (ed.), *Doing Research in Organizations* (London: Routledge).

Bulmer, M. (1979), 'Concepts in the Analysis of Qualitative Data', *Sociological Review*, 27: 651–77.

——(1980), 'Why Don't Sociologists Make More Use of Official Statistics?', *Sociology*, 14: 505–23.

——(1982), 'The Merits and Demerits of Covert Participant Observation', in M. Bulmer (ed.), *Social Research Ethics* (London: Macmillan).

——(1984), 'Facts, Concepts, Theories and Problems', in M. Bulmer (ed.), *Social Research Methods* (London: Macmillan).

Bunce, D., and West, M. (1996), 'Stress Management and Innovation Interventions at Work', *Human Relations*, 49(2): 209–32.

Burawoy, M. (1979), *Manufacturing Consent* (Chicago: University of Chicago Press).

Burgess, R. G. (1984), *In the Field* (London: Allen & Unwin).

Burke, R. R. (1996), 'Virtual Shopping: Breakthrough in Marketing Research', *Harvard Business Review*, 74(2): 120–31.

Burrell, G. (1997), *Pandemonium: Towards a Retro-Organization Theory* (London: Sage).

——and Morgan, G. (1979), *Sociological Paradigms and Organisational Analysis* (Aldershot: Gower).

Business Week (1973), 'The Public Clams up on Survey Takers', 15 Sept.: 216–20.

Buston, K. (1997), 'NUD*IST in Action: Its Use and its Usefulness in a Study of Chronic Illness in Young People', *Sociological Research Online*, 2, **www.socresonline.org.uk/socresonline/2/3/6.html**.

Butcher, B. (1994), 'Sampling Methods—an Overview and Review', *Survey Methods Centre Newsletter*, 15: 4–8.

Butterfield, K., Treviño, L., and Weaver, G. (2000), 'Moral Awareness in Business Organizations: Influences of Issue-Related and Social Context Factors', *Human Relations*, 53(7): 981–1018.

Button, G. (1992), 'Answers as Interactional Products: Two Sequential Practices Used in Job Interviews', in P. Drew and J. Heritage (eds), *Talk at Work: Interaction in Institutional Settings* (Cambridge: Cambridge University Press).

——(1998), 'Answers as Interactional Products: Two Sequential Practices Used in Job Interviews', in P. Drew and J. Heritage (eds), *Talk at Work: Interaction in Institutional Settings* (Cambridge: Cambridge University Press).

Cable, D., and Graham, M. (2000), 'The Determinants of Job Seekers' Reputation Perceptions', *Journal of Organizational Behavior*, 21: 929–47.

Calder, B. J. (1977), 'Focus Groups and the Nature of Qualitative Marketing Research', *Journal of Marketing Research*, 14: 353–64.

Cameron, J. (2001), 'Negative Effects of Reward on Intrinsic Motivation: A Limited Phenomenon: Comment on Deci, Koestner, and Ryan (2001)', *Review of Educational Research*, 71(1): 29–42.

——and Pierce, W. (1994), 'Reinforcement, Reward and Intrinsic Motivation: A Meta-Analysis', *Review of Educational Research*, 64: 363–423.

Campbell, D. T. (1957), 'Factors Relevant to the Validity of Experiments in Social Settings', *Psychological Bulletin*, 54: 297–312.

Caplan, R., Cobb, S., French, J., Harrison, R., and Pinneau, S. (1975), *Job Demands and Worker Health* (Washington: US Department of Health, Education and Welfare).

Casey, C. (1995), *Work, Self and Society: After Industrialism* (London: Routledge).

Catterall, M., and Maclaran, P. (1997), 'Focus Group Data and Qualitative Analysis Programs: Coding the Moving Picture as well as Snapshots', *Sociological Research Online*, 2, **www.socresonline.org.uk/socresonline/2/1/6.html**.

Cavendish, R. (1982), *Women on the Line* (London: Routledge & Kegan Paul).

Chamberlayne, P., Bornat, J., and Wengraf, T. (2000), 'Introduction: The Biographical Turn', in P. Chamberlayne, J. Bornat, and T. Wengraf (eds), *The Turn to Biographical Methods in Social Science: Comparative Issues and Examples* (London: Routledge).

Champoux, J. (1991), 'A Multivariate Analysis of Curvilinear Relationships among Job Scope, Work Context Satisfactions and Affective Outcomes', *Human Relations*, 45: 87–111.

Charmaz, K. (1983), 'The Grounded Theory Method: An Explication and Interpretation', in R. M. Emerson (ed.), *Contemporary Field Research: A Collection of Readings* (Boston: Little, Brown).

——(2000), 'Grounded Theory: Objectivist and Constructivist Methods', in N. K. Denzin and Y. S. Lincoln (eds), *Handbook of Qualitative Research*, 2nd edn. (Thousand Oaks, Calif.: Sage).

Chen, C. C., and Meindl, J. R. (1991), 'The Construction of Leadership Images in the Popular Press: The Case of Donald Burr and People Express', *Administrative Science Quarterly*, 36: 521–51.

Child, J. (1972), 'Organization Structure and Strategies of Control: A Replication of the Aston Study', *Administrative Science Quarterly*, 17: 163–77.

Cicourel, A. V. (1964), *Method and Measurement in Sociology* (New York: Free Press).

——(1968), *The Social Organization of Juvenile Justice* (New York: Wiley).

——(1982), 'Interviews, Surveys, and the Problem of Ecological Validity', *American Sociologist*, 17: 11–20.

Clapper, D. L., and Massey, A. P. (1996), 'Electronic Focus Groups: A Framework for Exploration', *Information and Management*, 30: 43–50.

Clarke, I., and Mackaness, W. (2001), 'Management Intuition: An Interpretative Account of Structure and Content Using Cognitive Maps', *Journal of Management Studies*, 38(2): 147–72.

Clegg, S. (2002), ' "Lives in the Balance": A Comment on Hinings and Greenwood's "Disconnects and Consequences in Organization Theory?" ', *Administrative Science Quarterly*, 47: 428–41.

Cleveland, C. E. (1986), 'Semiotics: Determining what the Advertising Message Means to the Audience', in J. Olson and K. Sentis (eds), *Advertising and Consumer Psychology*, 3: 227–41.

Clifford, J. (1983), 'On Ethnographic Authority', *Representations*, 1: 118–46.

——and Marcus, G. E. (1986), *Writing Culture: The Poetics and Politics of Ethnography* (Berkeley and Los Angeles: University of California Press).

Cobanoglu, C., Ward, B., and Moreo, P. J. (2001), 'A Comparison of Mail, Fax and Web-Based Survey Methods', *International Journal of Market Research*, 43: 441–52.

Coffey, A. (1999), *The Ethnographic Self: Fieldwork and the Representation of Reality* (London: Sage).

——and Atkinson, P. (1996), *Making Sense of Qualitative Data: Complementary Research Strategies* (Thousand Oaks, Calif.: Sage).

——Holbrook, B., and Atkinson, P. (1996), 'Qualitative Data Analysis: Technologies and Representations', *Sociological Research Online*, 2, **www.socresonline. org.uk/socresonline/ 1/1/4.html.**

Coghlan, D. (2001), 'Insider Action Research Projects: Implications for Practising Managers', *Management Learning*, 32(1): 49–60.

Coleman, C., and Moynihan, J. (1996), *Understanding Crime Data: Haunted by the Dark Figure* (Buckingham: Open University Press).

Coleman, J. S. (1958), 'Relational Analysis: The Study of Social Organization with Survey Methods', *Human Organization*, 16: 28–36.

Collins, M. (1997), 'Interviewer Variability: A Review of the Problem', *Journal of the Market Research Society*, 39: 67–84.

Collins, R. (1994), *Four Sociological Traditions*, rev. edn. (New York: Oxford University Press).

Collinson, D. L. (1988), 'Engineering Humour: Masculinity, Joking and Conflict in Shop Floor Relations', *Organisation Studies*, 9(2): 181–99.

——(1992a), *Managing the Shopfloor: Subjectivity, Masculinity and Workplace Culture* (Berlin: DeGruyter).

——(1992b), 'Researching Recruitment: Qualitative Methods and Sex Discrimination', in R. Burgess (ed.), *Studies in Qualitative Methodology*, Vol 3 (London: JAI Press).

——and Hearn, J. (1996), *Men as Managers, Managers as Men* (London: Sage).

Combe, I. A., and Crowther, D. E. (2000), 'The Semiology of an Advertising Campaign: Brand Repositioning', University of North London, Social Marketing Working Paper Series, 1–32.

Conger, J. A., and Kanungo, R. N. (1998), *Charismatic Leadership in Organizations* (Thousand Oaks, Calif.: Sage).

Conway, N., and Briner, R. (2002), 'A Daily Diary Study of Affective Responses to Psychological Contract Breach and Exceeded Promises', *Journal of Organizational Behaviour*, 23: 287–302.

Cook, T. D., and Campbell, D. T. (1979), *Quasi-Experimentation: Design and Analysis for Field Settings* (Boston, Mass.: Houghton Mifflin).

Corti, L. (1993), 'Using Diaries in Social Research', *Social Research Update*, 2.

——Foster, J., and Thompson, P. (1995), 'Archiving Qualitative Research Data', *Social Research Update*, 10.

Cotterill, P. (1992), 'Interviewing Women: Issues of Friendship, Vulnerability, and Power', *Women's Studies International Forum*, 15(5–6): 593–606.

Couper, M. P. (2000), 'Web Surveys: A Review of Issues and Approaches', *Public Opinion Quarterly*, 64: 464–94.

Coupland, C. (2001), 'Accounting for Change: A Discourse Analysis of Graduate Trainees' Talk of Adjustment', *Journal of Management Studies*, 38(8): 1103–19.

Coutrot, T. (1998), 'How Do Institutional Frameworks Affect Industrial Relations Outcomes? A Micro-Statistical Comparison of France and Britain', *European Journal of Industrial Relations*, 4(2): 177–205.

Cowley, J. C. P. (2000), 'Strategic Qualitative Focus Group Research: Define and Articulate our Skills or We Will Be Replaced by Others', *International Journal of Market Research*, 42(1): 17–38.

Coyle-Shapiro, J., and Kessler, I. (2000), 'Consequences of the Psychological Contract for the Employment Relationship: A Large Scale Survey', *Journal of Management Studies*, 37(7): 903–30.

Cramer, D. (1998), *Fundamental Statistics for Social Research* (London: Routledge).

Crang, P. (1994) 'It's Showtime: On the Workplace Geographies of Display in a Restaurant in South East England', *Environment and Planning D: Society and Space*, 12: 675–704.

Crapanzano, V. (1986), 'Hermes' Dilemma: The Masking of Subversion in Ethnographic Description', in J. Clifford and G. E. Marcus (eds), *Writing Culture: The Poetics and Politics of Ethnography* (Berkeley and Los Angeles: University of California Press).

Cring, A., Smith, D., and Neale, J. (1994). 'Individual Differences in Dispositional Expressiveness: Development and Validation of the Emotional Expressivity Scale', *Journal of Personality and Social Psychology*, 66: 935–49.

Croll, P. (1986), *Systematic Classroom Observation* (London: Falmer Press).

Cryer, P. (1996), *The Research Student's Guide to Success* (Buckingham: Open University Press).

Cullen, D. (1997) 'Maslow, Monkeys and Motivation Theory', *Organization*, 4(3): 355–73.

Cully, M., Woodland, S., O'Reilly, A., and Dix, G. (1999), *Britain at Work: As Depicted by the 1998 Workplace Employee Relations Survey* (London: Routledge).

Culler, J. (1981), *The Pursuit of Signs: Semiotics, Literature and Deconstruction* (Ithaca, NY: Cornell University Press).

Cunha, R. C., and Cooper, C. L. (2002), 'Does Privatization Affect Corporate Culture and Employee Wellbeing?' *Journal of Managerial Psychology*, 17(1): 21–49.

Curasi, C. F. (2001), 'A Critical Exploration of Face-to-Face Interviewing vs. Computer-Mediated Interviewing', *International Journal of Market Research*, 43: 361–75.

Curran, J., and Blackburn, R. (1994), *Small Firms and Local Economic Networks: The Death of the Local Economy?* (London: Paul Chapman).

Czaja, R., and Blair, J. (1996), *Designing Surveys: A Guide to Decisions and Procedures* (Thousand Oaks, Calif.: Sage).

Czarniawska, B. (1998), *A Narrative Approach to Organization Studies* (Thousand Oaks, Calif.: Sage).

Dale, A., Arber, S., and Proctor, M. (1988), *Doing Secondary Analysis* (London: Unwin Hyman).

Dalton, M. (1959), *Men who Manage: Fusion of Feeling and Theory in Administration* (New York: Wiley).

——(1964), 'Perceptions and Methods in Men who Manage', in P. Hammond (ed.), *Sociologists at Work* (New York: Basic Books).

Daniel, W. W. (1968), *Racial Discrimination in Britain* (Harmondsworth: Penguin).

Davies, C. A. (1999), *Reflexive Ethnography: A Guide to Researching Selves and Others* (London: Routledge).

Davies, J. (2001), 'International Comparisons of Labour Disputes in 1999', *Labour Market Trends*, April: 195–201.

Davis, J. A. (1964), 'Great Books and Small Groups: An Informal History of a National Survey', in P. Hammond (ed.), *Sociologists at Work* (New York: Basic Books).

Deacon, D., Bryman, A., and Fenton, N. (1998), 'Collision or Collusion? A Discussion of the Unplanned Triangulation of Quantitative and Qualitative Research Methods', *International Journal of Social Research Methodology*, 1: 47–63.

Deci, E. L., Koestner, R., and Ryan, R. (2001), 'Extrinsic Rewards and Intrinsic Motivation in Education: Reconsidered Once Again', *Review of Educational Research*, 71(1): 1–27.

Deery, S., Iverson, R., and Walsch, J. (2002), 'Work Relationships in Telephone Call Centres: Understanding Emotional Exhaustion and Employee Withdrawal', *Journal of Management Studies*, 39(4): 471–96.

Delamont, S., and Hamilton, D. (1984), 'Revisiting Classroom Research: A Continuing Cautionary Tale', in S. Delamont (ed.), *Readings on Interaction in the Classroom* (London: Methuen).

Delbridge, R. (1998), *Life on the Line: The Workplace Experience of Lean Production and the 'Japanese' Model* (Oxford: Oxford University Press).

Denzin, N. K. (1968), 'On the Ethics of Disguised Observation', *Social Problems*, 15: 502–4.

——(1970), *The Research Act in Sociology* (Chicago: Aldine).

——(1994), 'Evaluating Qualitative Research in the Poststructural Moment: The Lessons James Joyce Teaches us', *International Journal of Qualitative Studies in Education*, 7: 295–308.

——and Lincoln, Y. S. (2000), *Handbook of Qualitative Research*, 2nd edn. (Thousand Oaks, Calif.: Sage).

Diener, E., and Crandall, R. (1978), *Ethics in Social and Behavioral Research* (Chicago: University of Chicago Press).

Dillman, D. A. (1978), *Mail and Telephone Surveys: The Total Design Method* (New York: Wiley).

——(1983), 'Mail and Other Self-Administered Questionnaires', in P. H. Rossi, J. D. Wright, and A. B. Anderson (eds), *Handbook of Survey Research* (Orlando, Fl.: Academic Press).

Dingwall, R. (1980), 'Ethics and Ethnography', *Sociological Review*, 28: 871–91.

Ditton, J. (1977), *Part-Time Crime: An Ethnography of Fiddling and Pilferage* (London: Macmillan).

Dommeyer, C. J., and Moriarty, E. (2000), 'Comparison of Two Forms of an E-Mail Survey: Embedded vs. Attached', *International Journal of Market Research*, 42: 39–50.

Dougherty, D., and Kunda, G. (1990), 'Photograph Analysis: A Method to Capture Organizational Belief Systems', in P. Gagliardi (ed.), *Symbols and Artefacts: Views of the Corporate Landscape* (Berlin: DeGruyter).

Douglas, J. D. (1976), *Investigative Social Research: Individual and Team Field Research* (Beverly Hills, Calif.: Sage).

Durkheim, E. (1938), *The Rules of Sociological Method*, trans. S. A. Solavay and J. H. Mueller (New York: Free Press).

Dyer, W. G., and Wilkins, A. L. (1991), 'Better Stories, not Better Constructs, to Generate Better Theory: A Rejoinder to Eisenhardt', *Academy of Management Review*, 16: 613–19.

Easterby-Smith, M., and Malina, D. (1999), 'Cross Cultural Collaborative Research', *Academy of Management Journal*, 42(1): 76–86.

——Thorpe, R., and Holman, D. (1996), 'Using Repertory Grids in Management', *Journal of European Industrial Training*, 20(3): 3–30.

————and Lowe, A. (2001), *Management Research*, 2nd edn. (London: Sage).

Eden, C. (1988), 'Cognitive Mapping: A Review', *European Journal of Operational Research*, 36: 1–13.

——(1992), 'On the Status of Cognitive Maps', *Journal of Management Studies*, 29(3): 261–5.

——and Huxham, C. (1996), 'Action Research for Management Research', *British Journal of Management*, 7(1): 75–86.

——Ackermann, F., and Cropper, S. (1992), 'The Analysis of Cause Maps', *Journal of Management Studies*, 29(3): 309–24.

——Jones, S., and Sims, D. (1983), *Messing About in Problems* (Oxford: Pergamon).

Edwards, P. (1995), 'Human Resource Management, Union Voice and the Use of Discipline: An Analysis of WIRS 3', *Industrial Relations Journal*, 26(3): 204–20.

Edwards, R. (1979), *Contested Terrain* (New York: Basic Books).

Eisenhardt, K. M. (1989), 'Building Theories from Case Study Research', *Academy of Management Review*, 14: 532–50.

Elliott, H. (1997), 'The Use of Diaries in Sociological Research on Health Experience', *Sociological Research Online*, 2, **www.socresonline.org.uk/socresonline/2/2/7.html**.

Erikson, K. T. (1967), 'A Comment on Disguised Observation in Sociology', *Social Problems*, 14: 366–73.

Evans, M., Wedande, G., Ralston, L., and van't Hul, S. (2001), 'Consumer Interaction in the Virtual Era: Some Qualitative Insights', *Qualitative Market Research*, 4: 150–9.

Faraday, A., and Plummer, K. (1979), 'Doing Life Histories', *Sociological Review*, 27: 773–98.

Faules, D. (1982), 'The Use of Multi-Methods in the Organizational Setting', *Western Journal of Speech Communication*, 46: 150–61.

Felstead, A., Gallie, D., and Green, F. (2002), *Work Skills in Britain* (Nottingham: DfES Publications).

——Jewson, N., Phizacklea, A., and Walters, S. (2001), 'Working at Home: Statistical Evidence for Seven Key Hypotheses', *Work, Employment and Society*, 15(2): 215–31.

Fenton, N., Bryman, A., and Deacon, D. (1998), *Mediating Social Science* (London: Sage).

Fern, E. F. (2001), *Advanced Focus Group Research* (Thousand Oaks, Calif.: Sage).

Fiedler, E. E. (1967), *A Theory of Leadership Effectiveness* (New York: McGraw Hill).

Fielding, N., and Lee, R. M. (1998), *Computer Analysis and Qualitative Research* (London: Sage).

Filmer, P., Phillipson, M., Silverman, D., and Walsh, D. (1972), *New Directions in Sociological Theory* (London: Collier-Macmillan).

Finch, J. (1984), ' "It's great to have someone to talk to": The Ethics and Politics of Interviewing Women', in C. Bell and H. Roberts (eds), *Social Researching: Politics, Problems, Practice* (London: Routledge & Kegan Paul).

——(1987), 'The Vignette Technique in Survey Research', *Sociology*, 21: 105–14.

——and Mason, J. (1990), 'Decision Taking in the Fieldwork Process: Theoretical Sampling and Collaborative Working', in R. G. Burgess (ed.), *Studies in Qualitative Methodology*, 2: 25–50.

Fine, G. A. (1996), 'Justifying Work: Occupational Rhetorics as Resources in Kitchen Restaurants', *Administrative Science Quarterly*, 41: 90–115.

Flanagan, J. C. (1954), 'The Critical Incident Technique', *Psychological Bulletin*, 1: 327–58.

Fletcher, J. (1966), *Situation Ethics* (London: SCM Press).

Foddy, W. (1993), *Constructing Questions for Interviews and Questionnaires: Theory and Practice in Social Research* (Cambridge: Cambridge University Press).

Forster, N. (1994), 'The Analysis of Company Documentation', in C. Cassell and G. Symon (eds), *Qualitative Methods in Organizational Research* (London: Sage).

Fowler, F. J. (1993), *Survey Research Methods*, 2nd edn. (Newbury Park, Calif.: Sage).

——and Mangione, T. W. (1990), *Standardized Survey Interviewing: Minimizing Interviewer-Related Error* (Beverly Hills, Calif.: Sage).

Frankwick, G., Ward, J., Hutt, M., and Reingen, P. (1994), 'Evolving Patterns of Organizational Beliefs in the Formation of Strategy', *Journal of Marketing*, 58: 96–110.

Freeman, C. (2000), *High Tech and High Heels in the Global Economy: Women, Work and Pink-Collar Identities in the Carribean* (Durham, NC: Duke University Press).

Frey, J. H., and Oishi, S. M. (1995), *How to Conduct Interviews by Telephone and in Person* (Thousand Oaks, Calif.: Sage).

Fritzsche, D. J. (1988), 'An Examination of Marketing Ethics: Role of the Decision Maker, Consequences of the Decision, Management Position, and Sex of the Respondent', *Journal of Macromarketing*, 8: 29–39.

Gabriel, Y. (1998), 'The Use of Stories', in G. Symon and C. Cassell (eds), *Qualitative Methods and Analysis in Organizational Research* (London: Sage).

Gagliardi, P. (1990), *Symbols and Artifacts: Views of the Corporate Landscape* (Berlin: DeGruyter).

Gallup, G. (1947), 'The Quintamensional Plan of Question Design', *Public Opinion Quarterly*, 11: 385–93.

Gallupe, R. B., Dennis, A. R., Cooper, W. H., Valacich, J. S., Bastianutti, L. M., and Nunamaker, J. F. (1992), 'Electronic Brainstorming and Group Size', *Academy of Management Journal*, 35: 350–69.

Galton, M., Simon, B., and Croll, P. (1980), *Inside the Primary Classroom* (London: Routledge & Kegan Paul).

Gans, H. J. (1962), *The Urban Villagers* (New York: Free Press).

—— (1968), 'The Participant-Observer as Human Being: Observations on the Personal Aspects of Field Work', in H. S. Becker (ed.), *Institutions and the Person: Papers Presented to Everett C. Hughes* (Chicago: Aldine).

Ganster, D. (1980), 'Individual Differences and Task Design', *Organizational Behaviour and Human Performance*, 26(1): 131–48.

Garcia, A. (1991), 'Dispute Resolution without Disputing: How the Interactional Organization of Mediation Hearings Minimizes Argument', *American Sociological Review*, 56: 818–35.

Garfinkel, H. (1967), *Studies in Ethnomethodology* (Englewood Cliffs, NJ: Prentice-Hall).

Geertz, C. (1973*a*), 'Thick Description: Toward an Interpretive Theory of Culture', in C. Geertz, *The Interpretation of Cultures* (New York: Basic Books).

—— (1973*b*), 'Deep Play: Notes on the Balinese Cockfight', in C. Geertz, *The Interpretation of Cultures* (New York: Basic Books).

Gephart, R. P. (1988), *Ethnostatistics: Qualitative Foundations for Quantitative Research* (Newbury Park, Calif.: Sage).

—— (1993), 'The Textual Approach: Risk and Blame in Disaster Sensemaking', *Academy of Management Journal*, 36(6): 1465–514.

Gersick, C. J. G. (1994), 'Pacing Strategic Change: The Case of a New Venture', *Academy of Management Journal*, 37(1): 9–45.

Gherardi, S., and Turner, B. (1987), 'Real Men Don't Collect Soft Data', *Quaderno 13* (Department of Social Policy, University of Trento).

Ghobadian, A., and Gallear, D. (1997), 'TQM and Organization Size', *International Journal of Operations and Production Management*, 17(2): 121–63.

Gibbons, M., Limoges, C., Nowotny, H., Schwartzman, S., Scott, P., and Trow, M. (1994), *The New Production of Knowledge* (London: Sage).

Giddens, A. (1979), *Central Problems in Social Theory* (Berkeley, Calif.: University of California Press).

—— (1984), *The Constitution of Society* (Cambridge: Polity).

Gilbert, G. N. (1977), 'Referencing as Persuasion', *Social Studies of Science*, 7: 113–22.

—— and Mulkay, M. (1984), *Opening Pandora's Box: A Sociological Analysis of Scientists' Discourse* (Cambridge: Cambridge University Press).

Gill, R. (1996), 'Discourse Analysis: Practical Implementation', in J. T. E. Richardson (ed.), *Handbook of Qualitative Research*

Methods for Psychology and the Social Sciences (Leicester: BPS Books).

—— (2000), 'Discourse Analysis', in M. W. Bauer and G. Gaskell (eds), *Qualitative Researching with Text, Image and Sound* (London: Sage).

Gioia, D., Thomas, J., Clark, S., and Chittipeddi, K. (1994), 'Symbolism and Strategic Change in Academia: The Dynamics of Sensemaking and Influence', *Organization Science*, 5(3): 363–83.

Glaser, B. G. (1992), *Basics of Grounded Theory Analysis* (Mill Valley, Calif.: Sociology Press).

—— and Strauss, A. L. (1967), *The Discovery of Grounded Theory: Strategies for Qualitative Research* (Chicago: Aldine).

Glock, C. Y. (1988), 'Reflections on Doing Survey Research', in H. J. O'Gorman (ed.), *Surveying Social Life* (Middletown, Conn.: Wesleyan University Press).

Glucksmann, M. (1994), 'The Work of Knowledge and the Knowledge of Women's Work', in M. Maynard and J. Purvis (eds), *Researching Women's Lives from a Feminist Perspective* (London: Taylor & Francis).

Goffman, E. (1956), *The Presentation of Self in Everyday Life* (New York: Doubleday).

—— (1963), *Stigma: Notes on the Management of Spoiled Identity* (Harmondsworth: Penguin).

Gold, R. L. (1958), 'Roles in Sociological Fieldwork', *Social Forces*, 36: 217–23.

Golden-Biddle, K., and Locke, K. D. (1993), 'Appealing Work: An Investigation of how Ethnographic Texts Convince', *Organization Science*, 4: 595–616.

—— —— (1997), *Composing Qualitative Research* (Thousand Oaks, Calif.: Sage).

Goldthorpe, J. H., Lockwood, D., Bechhofer, F., and Platt, J. (1968), *The Affluent Worker: Industrial Attitudes and Behaviour* (Cambridge: Cambridge University Press).

Goode, E. (1996), 'The Ethics of Deception in Social Research: A Case Study', *Qualitative Sociology*, 19: 11–33.

Goode, W. J., and Hatt, P. K. (1952), *Methods of Social Research* (New York: McGraw Hill).

Gottdiener, M. (1982), 'Disneyland: A Utopian Urban Space', *Urban Life*, 11: 139–62.

—— (1997), *The Theming of America: Dreams, Visions and Commercial Spaces* (Boulder, Colo.: Westview Press).

Graaf, G. (2001), 'Discourse Theory and Business Ethics: The Case of Bankers' Conceptualizations of Customers', *Journal of Business Ethics*, 31: 299–319.

Grant, D., Keenoy, T., and Oswick, C. (1998), *Discourse + Organization* (London: Sage).

Greene, J. C. (1994), 'Qualitative Program Evaluation: Practice and Promise', in N. K. Denzin and Y. S. Lincoln (eds), *Handbook of Qualitative Research* (Thousand Oaks, Calif.: Sage).

——(2000), 'Understanding Social Programs through Evaluation', in N. K. Denzin and Y. S. Lincoln (eds), *Handbook of Qualitative Research*, 2nd edn. (Thousand Oaks, Calif.: Sage).

Greenwood, D., Whyte, W., and Harkavy, I. (1993), 'Participatory Action Research as a Process and as a Goal', *Human Relations*, 46(2): 175–91.

Greising, D. (1998), *I'd Like the World to Buy a Coke: The Life and Leadership of Robert Goizueta* (New York: Wiley).

Grele, R. J. (1998), 'Movement without Aim: Methodological and Theoretical Problems in Oral History', in R. Perks and A. Thomson (eds), *The History Reader* (London: Routledge).

Grey, C. (1996) 'Towards a Critique of Managerialism: The Construction of Simone Weil', *Journal of Management Studies*, 33(5): 591–611.

Grint, K. (2000) *The Arts of Leadership* (Oxford: Oxford University Press).

——and Woolgar, S. (1997), *The Machine at Work: Technology, Work and Organization* (Cambridge: Polity).

Grinyer, P., and Yasai-Ardekani, M. (1980), 'Dimensions of Organizational Structure: A Critical Replication', *Academy of Management Journal*, 23: 405–21.

Grunig, L. A. (1990), 'Using Focus Group Research in Public Relations', *Public Relations Review*, 16(2): 36–49.

Guba, E. G. (1985), 'The Context of Emergent Paradigm Research', in Y. S. Lincoln (ed.), *Organization Theory and Inquiry: The Paradigm Revolution* (Beverly Hills, Calif.: Sage).

——and Lincoln, Y. S. (1994), 'Competing Paradigms in Qualitative Research', in N. K. Denzin and Y. S. Lincoln (eds), *Handbook of Qualitative Research* (Thousand Oaks, Calif.: Sage).

Gubrium, J. F., and Holstein, J. A. (1997), *The New Language of Qualitative Method* (New York: Oxford University Press).

Guest, D. E., and Dewe, P. (1991), 'Company or Trade Union? Which Wins Worker's Allegiance? A Study of Commitment in the UK Electronics Industry', *British Journal of Industrial Relations*, 29(1): 73–96.

Gully, S., Incalaterra, K., Joshi, A., and Beaubien, J. (2002), 'A Meta-analysis of Team-Efficacy, Potency, and Performance: Interdependence and Level of Analysis as Moderators of Observed Relationships', *Journal of Applied Psychology*, 87(5): 819–32.

Gummesson, E. (2000), *Qualitative Methods in Management Research* (London: Sage).

Gusfield, J. (1976), 'The Literary Rhetoric of Science: Comedy and Pathos in Drinking Driving Research', *American Sociological Review*, 41: 16–34.

Hackman, J., and Oldham, G. (1976), 'Motivation through the Design of Work: Test of a Theory', *Organizational Behavior and Human Performance*, 16(2): 250–79.

——————(1980), *Work Redesign* (Reading, Mass.: Addison-Wesley).

Halfpenny, P. (1979), 'The Analysis of Qualitative Data', *Sociological Review*, 27: 799–825.

Hall, E. (1993), 'Smiling, Deferring and Flirting: Doing Gender by Giving "Good Service" ', *Work and Occupations*, 20(4): 452–71.

Hall, R., Workman, J., and Marchioro, C. (1998), 'Sex, Task, and Behavioral Flexibility Effects on Leadership Perceptions', *Organizational Behavior and Human Decision Processes*, 74(1): 1–32.

Hall, W. S., and Guthrie, L. F. (1981), 'Cultural and Situational Variation in Language Function and Use—Methods and Procedures for Research', in J. L. Green and C. Wallatt (eds), *Ethnography and Language in Educational Settings* (Norwood, NJ: Ablex).

Hammersley, M. (1989), *The Dilemma of Qualitative Method: Herbert Blumer and the Chicago Tradition* (London: Routledge).

——(1992a), 'By what Criteria should Ethnographic Research be Judged?', in M. Hammersley, *What's Wrong with Ethnography* (London: Routledge).

——(1992b), 'Deconstructing the Qualitative–Quantitative Divide', in M. Hammersley, (ed.) *What's Wrong with Ethnography* (London: Routledge).

——(1996), 'The Relationship between Qualitative and Quantitative Research: Paradigm Loyalty versus Methodological Eclecticism', in J. T. E. Richardson (ed.), *Handbook of Research Methods for Psychology and the Social Sciences* (Leicester: BPS Books).

——(1997), 'Qualitative Data Archiving: Some Reflections on its Prospects and Problems', *Sociology*, 31: 131–42.

——and Atkinson, P. (1995), *Ethnography: Principles in Practice*, 2nd edn. (London: Routledge).

Hammond, P. (1964), *Sociologists at Work* (New York: Basic Books).

Haney, C., Banks, C., and Zimbardo, P. (1973), 'Interpersonal Dynamics in a Simulated Prison', *International Journal of Criminology and Penology*, 1: 69–97.

Hantrais, L. (1996), 'Comparative Research Methods', *Social Research Update*, 13.

Harfield, T., and Hamilton, R. (1997), 'Journeys in a Declining Industry: Stories of Footwear Manufacturing', *Journal of Organizational Change Management*, 10(1): 61–70.

Harré, R. (1972), *The Philosophies of Science* (Oxford: Oxford University Press).

Harris, H. (2001), 'Content Analysis of Secondary Data: A Study of Courage in Managerial Decision Making', *Journal of Business Ethics*, 34(3–4): 191–208.

Hartog, D. N., and Verburg, R. M. (1997), 'Charisma and Rhetoric: Communicative Techniques of International Business Leaders', *Leadership Quarterly*, 8(4): 355–91.

Haslam, C., and Bryman, A. (1994), 'The Research Dissemination Minefield', in C. Haslam and A. Bryman (eds), *Social Scientists Meet the Media* (London: Routledge).

Hassard, J. (1990), 'Ethnomethodology and Organizational Research: An Introduction', in J. Hassard and D. Pym (eds), *The Theory and Philosophy of Organizations* (London: Routledge).

—— (1991), 'Multiple Paradigms and Organizational Analysis: A Case Study', *Organization Studies*, 12(2): 275–99.

Hatch, M. J. (1996), 'The Role of the Researcher: An Analysis of Narrative Position in Organization Theory', *Journal of Management Inquiry*, 5(4): 359–74.

Hawkes, N. (2003), 'Close Shaves Beat Death by a Whisker', *The Times*, 6 February, 1.

Hayano, D. (1979), 'Auto-Ethnography: Paradigms, Problems and Prospects', *Human Organization*, 38(1): 99–104.

Healey, M. J., and Rawlinson, M. B. (1993), 'Interviewing Business Owners and Managers: A Review of Methods and Techniques', *Geoforum*, 24(3): 339–55.

Heap, J. L., and Roth, P. A. (1973), 'On Phenomenological Sociology', *American Sociological Review*, 38: 354–67.

Heath, C. (1997), 'The Analysis of Activities in Face to Face Interaction Using Video', in D. Silverman (ed.), *Qualitative Research: Theory, Method and Practice* (London: Sage).

Heracleous, L., and Barrett, M. (2001), 'Organizational Change as Discourse: Communicative Actions and Deep Structures in the Context of Information Technology Implementation', *Academy of Management Journal*, 44(4): 755–78.

Heritage, J. (1984), *Garfinkel and Ethnomethodology* (Cambridge: Polity).

—— (1987), 'Ethnomethodology', in A. Giddens and J. H. Turner (eds), *Social Theory Today* (Cambridge: Polity).

Heron, J., and Reason, P. (2000), 'The Practice of Co-operative Inquiry', in P. Reason and H. Bradbury (eds), *Handbook of Action Research* (London: Sage).

Herzberg, F., Mausner, B., and Snyderman, B. B. (1959), *The Motivation to Work*, 2nd edn. (New York: Wiley).

Hesse-Biber, S. (1995), 'Unleashing Frankenstein's Monster? The Use of Computers in Qualitative Research', *Studies in Qualitative Methodology*, 5: 25–41.

Heyes, J. (1997), 'Annualised Hours and the Knock: The Organisation of Working Time in a Chemicals Plant', *Work, Employment and Society*, 11(1): 65–81.

Hilton, G. (1972), 'Causal Inference Analysis: A Seductive Process', *Administrative Science Quarterly*, 17(1): 44–54.

Hine, V. (2000), *Virtual Ethnography* (London: Sage).

Hinings, C. R., and Bryman, A. (1974), 'Size and the Administrative Component in Churches', *Human Relations*, 27: 457–75.

—— and Greenwood, R. (2002), 'ASQ Forum: Disconnects and Consequences in Organization Theory?', *Administrative Science Quarterly*, 47: 411–21.

—— Ranson, S., and Bryman, A. (1976), 'Churches as Organizations', in D. S. Pugh and C. R. Hinings (eds), *Organization Structure: Extensions and Replications, The Aston Programme II* (Saxon House, 1976).

Ho, K. C., Baber, Z., and Khondker, H. (2002), ' "Sites of Resistance": Alternative Websites and State-Society Relations', *British Journal of Sociology*, 53: 127–48.

Hobbs, D. (1993), 'Peers, Careers, and Academic Fears: Writing as Fieldwork', in D. Hobbs and T. May (eds), *Interpreting the Field: Accounts of Ethnography* (Oxford: Clarendon Press).

—— and May, T. (1993), *Interpreting the Field: Accounts of Ethnography* (Oxford: Clarendon Press).

Hochschild, A. R. (1983), *The Managed Heart* (Berkeley and Los Angeles: University of California Press).

Hodges, L. (1998), 'The Making of a National Portrait', *The Times Higher*, 20 Feb.: 22–3.

Hodson, R. (1996), 'Dignity in the Workplace under Participative Management', *American Sociological Review*, 61: 719–38.

—— (1999), *Analyzing Documentary Accounts* (Thousand Oaks, Calif.: Sage).

Hofstede, G. (1984), *Culture's Consequences: International Differences in Work Related Values* (Beverly Hills, Calif.: Sage).

Holdaway, E. A., Newberry, J. F., Hickson, D. J., and Heron, R. P. (1975), 'Dimensions of Structure in Complex Societies: The Educational Sector', *Administrative Science Quarterly*, 20: 37–58.

Holliday, R. (1995), *Investigating Small Firms: Nice Work?* (London: Routledge).

Holsti, O. R. (1969), *Content Analysis for the Social Sciences and Humanities* (Reading, Mass.: Addison-Wesley).

Homan, R. (1991), *The Ethics of Social Research* (London: Longman).

—— and Bulmer, M. (1982), 'On the Merits of Covert Methods: A Dialogue', in M. Bulmer (ed.), *Social Research Ethics* (London: Macmillan).

Hoque, K. (2003), 'All in All, It's Just Another Plaque on the Wall: The Incidence and Impact of the Investors in People Standard', *Journal of Management Studies*, 40(2): 543–71.

House, J. (1981), *Work Stress and Social Support* (Reading, Mass.: Addison-Wesley).

Howell, J. M., and Frost, P. J. (1989), 'A Laboratory Study of Charismatic Leadership', *Organizational Behavior and Human Decision Processes*, 43: 243–69.

Huberman, A. M., and Miles, M. B. (1994), 'Data Management and Analysis Methods', in N. K. Denzin and Y. S. Lincoln (eds), *Handbook of Qualitative Research* (Thousand Oaks, Calif.: Sage).

Hudson, S, Snaith, T., Miller, G., and Hudson, P. (2001), 'Distribution Channels in the Travel Industry: Using Mystery Shoppers to Understand the Influence of Travel Agency Recommendations', *Journal of Travel Research*, 40: 148–54.

Hughes, J. A. (1990), *The Philosophy of Social Research*, 2nd edn. (Harlow: Longman).

Huselid, M. (1995), 'The Impact of Human Resource Management Practices on Turnover, Productivity and Corporate Financial Performance', *Academy of Management Journal*, 38(3): 635–72.

Hutchby, I., and Wooffitt, R. (1998), *Conversation Analysis* (Cambridge: Polity).

Hutt, R. W. (1979), 'The Focus Group Interview: A Technique for Counseling Small Business Clients', *Journal of Small Business Management*, 17(1): 15–20.

Hycner, R. H. (1985), 'Some Guidelines for the Phenomenological Analysis of Interview Data', *Human Studies*, 8: 279–303.

Insch, G., Moore, J., and Murphy, L. (1997), 'Content Analysis in Leadership Research: Examples, Procedures and Suggestions for Future Use', *Leadership Quarterly*, 8(1): 1–25.

Isabella, L. A. (1990), 'Evolving Interpretations as a Change Unfolds: How Managers Construe Key Organizational Events', *Academy of Management Journal*, 33(1): 1–41.

Jackall, R. (1988), *Moral Mazes: The World of the Corporate Manager* (Oxford: Oxford University Press).

Jackson, N., and Carter, P. (1991), 'In Defence of Paradigm Incommensurability', *Organization Studies*, 12(1): 109–27.

——— (1998), 'Management Gurus: What are we to Make of Them?', in J. Hassard and R. Holliday (eds), *Organization-Representation: Work and Organization in Popular Culture* (London: Sage).

Jackson, T. (2001), 'Cultural Values and Management Ethics: A Ten Nation Study', *Human Relations*, 54(10): 1267–302.

Janis, I. L. (1982), *Groupthink: Psychological Studies of Policy Decisions and Fiascos*, 2nd edn. (Boston: Houghton-Mifflin).

Jayaratne, T. E., and Stewart, A. J. (1991), 'Quantitative and Qualitative Methods in the Social Sciences: Current Feminist Issues and Practical Strategies', in M. M. Fonow and J. A. Cook (eds), *Beyond Methodology: Feminist Scholarship as Lived Research* (Bloomington, Ind.: Indiana University Press).

Jefferson, G. (1988), 'On the Sequential Organization of Troubles: Talk in Ordinary Conversation', *Social Problems*, 35(4): 418–41.

Jenkins, G. D., Nader, D. A., Lawler, E. E., and Cammann, C. (1975), 'Standardized Observations: An Approach to Measuring the Nature of Jobs', *Journal of Applied Psychology*, 60: 171–81.

John, I. D. (1992), 'Statistics as Rhetoric in Psychology', *Australian Psychologist*, 27: 144–9.

Johns, G., Xie, J., and Fang, Y. (1992), 'Mediating and Moderating Effects in Job Design', *Journal of Management*, 18(4): 657–76.

Johnson, P. (1998), 'Analytic Induction', in G. Symon and C. Cassell (eds), *Qualitative Methods and Analysis in Organizational Research* (London: Sage).

——and Duberley, J. (2000), *Understanding Management Research* (London: Sage).

Jones, G. (1983), 'Life History Methodology', in G. Morgan (ed.), *Beyond Method: Strategies for Social Research* (London: Sage).

——(2002), *The Internet Goes to College* (Washington: Pew Internet & American Life Project).

Kabanoff, B., Waldersee, R., and Cohen, M. (1995), 'Espoused Values and Organizational Change Themes', *Academy of Management Journal*, 38(4): 1075–104.

Kanter, R. M. (1977), *Men and Women of the Corporation* (New York: Basic Books).

Keat, R., and Urry, J. (1975), *Social Theory as Science* (London: Routledge & Kegan Paul).

Kelly, A. (1985), 'Action Research: What Is It and What Can It Do?', in R. G. Burgess (ed.), *Issues in Educational Research: Qualitative Methods* (London: Falmer Press).

Kelly, G. A. (1955), *The Psychology of Personal Constructs* (New York: Norton).

Kelly, L., Burton, S., and Regan, L. (1994), 'Researching Women's Lives or Studying Women's Oppression? Reflections on what Constitutes Feminist Research', in M. Maynard and J. Purvis (eds), *Researching Women's Lives from a Feminist Perspective* (London: Taylor & Francis).

Kendall, L. (1999), 'Recontextualizing "Cyberspace": Methodological Considerations for On-Line Research', in S. Jones (ed.), *Doing Internet Research: Critical Issues and Methods for Examining the Net* (Thousand Oaks, Calif.: Sage).

Kent, R., and Lee, M. (1999), 'Using the Internet for Market Research: A Study of Private Trading on the Internet', *Journal of the Market Research Society*, 41: 377–85.

Kidder, T. (1981), *The Soul of a New Machine* (New York: Avon).

Kiely, T. (1998), 'Wired Focus Groups', *Harvard Business Review*, Jan.–Feb.: 12–16.

Kimmel, A. J. (1988), *Ethics and Values in Applied Social Research* (Newbury Park, Calif.: Sage).

King, N. (1994), 'The Qualitative Research Interview', in C. Cassell and G. Symon (eds), *Qualitative Methods in Organizational Research* (London: Sage).

Kirk, J., and Miller, M. L. (1986), *Reliability and Validity in Qualitative Research* (Newbury Park, Calif.: Sage).

Kitsuse, J. I., and Cicourel, A. V. (1963), 'A Note on the Use of Official Statistics', *Social Problems*, 11: 131–9.

Kitzinger, J. (1994), 'The Methodology of Focus Groups: The Importance of Interaction between Research Participants', *Sociology of Health and Illness*, 16: 103–21.

Knight, K., and Latreille, P. (2000), 'Discipline, Dismissals and Complaints to Employment Tribunals', *British Journal of Industrial Relations*, 38(4): 533–55.

Knights, D., and Collinson, D. (1985), *Job Redesign: Critical Perspectives on the Labour Process* (Aldershot: Gower).

Knights, D., and McCabe, D. (1997), ' "How Would You Measure Something Like That?": Quality in a Retail Bank', *Journal of Management Studies*, 34(3): 371–88.

——and Willmott, H. (1990), *Labour Process Theory* (London: Macmillan).

Kondo, D. K. (1990), *Crafting Selves: Power, Gender and Discourses of Identity in a Japanese Workplace* (Chicago: University of Chicago Press).

Kozinets, R. V. (2002), 'The Field behind the Screen: Using Netnography for Marketing Research in Online Communities', *Journal of Marketing Research*, 39: 61–72.

Kristof-Brown, A. (2000), 'Perceived Applicant Fit: Distinguishing between Recruiters' Perceptions of Person–Job and Person–Organization Fit', *Personnel Psychology*, 53: 643–71.

Krueger, R. A. (1988), *Focus Groups: A Practical Guide for Applied Research* (Newbury Park, Calif.: Sage).

——(1998), *Moderating Focus Groups* (Thousand Oaks, Calif.: Sage).

Kuhn, T. S. (1970), *The Structure of Scientific Revolutions*, 2nd edn. (Chicago: University of Chicago Press).

Kunda, G. (1992), *Engineering Culture: Control and Commitment in a High-Tech Corporation* (Philadelphia: Temple University Press).

Kvale, S. (1996), *InterViews: An Introduction to Qualitative Research Interviewing* (Thousand Oaks, Calif.: Sage).

LaPiere, R. T. (1934), 'Attitudes vs. Actions', *Social Forces*, 13: 230–7.

Lawrence, P. R., and Lorsch, J. W. (1967), *Organization and Environment* (Boston: Addison Wesley).

Layder, D. (1993), *New Strategies in Social Research* (Cambridge: Polity).

Lazarsfeld, P. (1958), 'Evidence and Inference in Social Research', *Daedalus*, 87: 99–130.

LeCompte, M. D., and Goetz, J. P. (1982), 'Problems of Reliability and Validity in Ethnographic Research', *Review of Educational Research*, 52: 31–60.

Lee, C. K. (1998), *Gender and the South China Miracle: Two Worlds of Factory Women* (Berkeley and Los Angeles: University of California Press).

Lee, R. M. (2000), *Unobtrusive Methods in Social Research* (Buckingham: Open University Press).

——and Fielding, N. G. (1991), 'Computing for Qualitative Research: Options, Problems and Potential', in N. G. Fielding and R. M. Lee (eds), *Using Computers in Qualitative Research* (London: Sage).

Leidner, R. (1993), *Fast Food, Fast Talk: Service Work and the Routinization of Everyday Life* (Berkeley and Los Angeles: University of California Press).

Levitas, R., and Guy, W. (1996), 'Introduction', in R. Levitas and W. Guy (eds), *Interpreting Official Statistics* (London: Routledge).

Liff, S., and Steward, F. (2001), 'Community E-Gateways: Locating Networks and Learning for Social Inclusion', *Information, Communication and Society*, 4(3): 317–40.

Lincoln, Y. S., and Guba, E. (1985), *Naturalistic Inquiry* (Beverly Hills, Calif.: Sage).

——and Denzin, N. K. (1994), 'The Fifth Moment', in N. K. Denzin and Y. S. Lincoln (eds), *Handbook of Qualitative Research* (Thousand Oaks, Calif.: Sage).

Linstead, S. (1985), 'Jokers Wild: The Importance of Humour and the Maintenance of Organizational Culture', *Sociological Review*, 33(4): 741–67.

Livingstone, S., and Lunt, P. (1994), *Talk on Television: Audience Participation and Public Debate* (London: Routledge).

Locke, K. (1996), 'Rewriting *The Discovery of Grounded Theory* after 25 Years?', *Journal of Management Inquiry*, 5: 239–45.

——(2001), *Grounded Theory in Management Research* (London: Sage).

Lofland, J. (1971), *Analyzing Social Settings: A Guide to Qualitative Observation and Analysis* (Belmont, Calif.: Wadsworth).

——and Lofland, L. (1995), *Analyzing Social Settings: A Guide to Qualitative Observation and Analysis*, 3rd edn. (Belmont, Calif.: Wadsworth).

Lonkila, M. (1995), 'Grounded Theory as an Emergent Paradigm for Computer-Assisted Qualitative Data Analysis', in U. Kelle (ed.), *Computer-Aided Qualitative Data Analysis* (London: Sage).

Lucas, R. (1997), 'Youth, Gender and Part-Time Work: Students in the Labour Process', *Work, Employment and Society*, 11: 595–614.

Lund, D. (2000), 'An Empirical Examination of Marketing Professionals' Ethical Behaviour in Differing Situations', *Journal of Business Ethics*, 24: 331–42.

Lupton, T. (1963), *On the Shopfloor* (Oxford: Pergamon Press).

McCall, M. J. (1984), 'Structured Field Observation', *Annual Review of Sociology*, 10: 263–82.

——and Lombardo, M. (1982), 'Using Simulation for Leadership and Management Research: Through the Looking Glass', *Management Science*, 28(5): 533–49.

McCartney, J. L. (1970), 'On Being Scientific: Changing Styles of Presentation of Sociological Research', *American Sociologist*, 5: 30–5.

McClelland, D.C. (1961), *The Achieving Society* (Princeton: Van Nostrand).

McCloskey, D. N. (1985), *The Rhetoric of Economics* (Brighton: Wheatsheaf).

McDonald, G. (2000), 'Cross-Cultural Methodological Issues in Ethical Research', *Journal of Business Ethics*, 27: 89–104.

McEnery, J., and Blanchard, P. (1999), 'Validity of Multiple Ratings of Business Student Performance in a Management Simulation', *Human Resource Development Quarterly*, 10(2): 155–172.

McGuigan, J. (1992), *Cultural Populism* (London: Routledge).

McPhail, C., and Rexroat, C. (1979), 'Mead vs. Blumer: The Divergent Methodological Perspectives of Social Behaviorism and Symbolic Interactionism', *American Sociological Review*, 44: 449–67.

Madriz, M. (2000), 'Focus Groups in Feminist Research', in N. K. Denzin and Y. S. Lincoln (eds), *Handbook of Qualitative Research*, 2nd edn. (Thousand Oaks, Calif.: Sage).

Malinowski, B. (1967), *A Diary in the Strict Sense of the Term* (London: Routledge & Kegan Paul).

Mangabeira, W. (1995), 'Qualitative Analysis and Microcomputer Software: Some Reflections on a New Trend in Sociological Research', *Studies in Qualitative Methodology*, 5: 43–61.

Mangham, I. (1986), *Power and Performance in Organizations: An Exploration of Executive Process*. Oxford: Blackwell.

——and Overington, M. A. (1983), 'Dramatism and the Theatrical Metaphor', in G. Morgan (ed.). *Beyond Method* (Beverly Hills, Calif.: Sage).

Mangione, T. W. (1995), *Mail Surveys: Improving the Quality* (Thousand Oaks, Calif.: Sage).

Mann, C., and Stewart, F. (2000), *Internet Communication and Qualitative Research: A Handbook for Researching Online* (London: Sage).

Manning, P. K. (1995), 'The Challenge of Postmodernism', in J. Van Maanen (ed.), *Representation in Ethnography* (Thousand Oaks, Calif.: Sage).

Marginson, P. (1998), 'The Survey Tradition in British Industrial Relations Research: An Assessment of the Contribution of Large-Scale Workplace and Enterprise Surveys', *British Journal of Industrial Relations*, 36(3): 361–88.

Markham, A. (1998), *Life Online: Researching the Real Experience in Virtual Space* (London and Walnut Creek, Calif.: AltaMira Press).

Marsh, C. (1982), *The Survey Method: The Contribution of Surveys to Sociological Explanation* (London: Allen & Unwin).

——and Scarbrough, E. (1990), 'Testing Nine Hypotheses about Quota Sampling', *Journal of the Market Research Society*, 32: 485–506.

Marshall, J. (1981), 'Making Sense as a Personal Process' in P. Reason and J. Rowan (eds), *Human Inquiry* (Chichester: John Wiley).

——(1984), *Women Managers: Travellers in a Male World* (Chichester: Wiley).

——(1995), *Women Managers Moving On: Exploring Career and Life Choices* (London: Routledge).

Martin, J. (1992), *Cultures in Organizations: Three Perspectives* (Oxford: Oxford University Press).

——and Siehl, C. (1983), 'Organizational Culture and Counterculture: An Uneasy Symbiosis', *Organizational Dynamics*, Autumn: 52–64.

Martin, P., and Bateson, P. (1986), *Measuring Behaviour: An Introductory Guide* (Cambridge: Cambridge University Press).

Martin, P. Y., and Turner, B. A. (1986), 'Grounded Theory and Organizational Research', *Journal of Applied Behavioral Science*, 22(2): 141–57.

Martinko, M. J., and Gardner, W. L. (1990), 'Structured Observation of Managerial Work: A Replication and Synthesis', *Journal of Management Studies*, 27(3): 329–57.

Marx, G. T. (1997), 'Of Methods and Manners for Aspiring Sociologists: 37 Moral Imperatives', *American Sociologist*, 102–25.

Maslach, C., and Jackson, S. (1981), 'The Measurement of Experienced Burnout', *Journal of Occupational Behavior*, 2: 99–113.

Maslow, A. (1943), 'A Theory of Human Motivation', *Pschological Review*, 50: 370–96.

Mason, J. (1994), 'Linking Qualitative and Quantitative Data Analysis', in A. Bryman and R. G. Burgess (eds), *Analyzing Qualitative Data* (London: Routledge).

——(1996), *Qualitative Researching* (London: Sage).

Masterman, M. (1970), 'The Nature of a Paradigm', in I. Lakatos and A. Musgrave (eds), *Criticism and the Growth of Knowledge* (Cambridge: Cambridge University Press).

Matza, D. (1969), *Becoming Deviant* (Englewood Cliffs, NJ: Prentice-Hall).

Mauthner, N. S., Parry, O., and Backett-Milburn, K. (1998), 'The Data are Out There, or Are They? Implications for Archiving and Revisiting Qualitative Data', *Sociology*, 32: 733–45.

Maynard, M. (1994), 'Methods, Practice and Epistemology: The Debate about Feminism and Research', in M. Maynard and J. Purvis (eds), *Researching Women's Lives from a Feminist Perspective* (London: Taylor & Francis).

——(1998), 'Feminists' Knowledge and the Knowledge of Feminisms: Epistemology, Theory, Methodology and Method', in T. May and M. Williams (eds), *Knowing the Social World* (Buckingham: Open University Press).

Meltzer, B. N., Petras, J. W., and Reynolds, L. T. (1975), *Symbolic Interactionism: Genesis, Varieties and Criticism* (London: Routledge & Kegan Paul).

Menard, S. (1991), *Longitudinal Research* (Newbury Park, Calif.: Sage).

Merton, R. K. (1967), *On Theoretical Sociology* (New York: Free Press).

——Fiske, M., and Kendall, P. L. (1956), *The Focused Interview: A Manual of Problems and Procedures* (New York: Free Press).

Meyer, J., and Rowan, B. (1977), 'Institutionalized Organizations: Formal Structure as Myth and Ceremony', *American Journal of Sociology*, 83: 340–63.

Mies, M. (1993), 'Towards a Methodology for Feminist Research', in M. Hammersley (ed.), *Social Research: Philosophy, Politics and Practice* (London: Sage).

Miles, M. B. (1979), 'Qualitative Data as an Attractive Nuisance', *Administrative Science Quarterly*, 24: 590–601.

Miles, N. B., and Huberman, A. M. (1984), *Qualitative Data Analysis: A Sourcebook of New Methods* (London: Sage).

——— (1994), *Qualitative Data Analysis: An Expanded Sourcebook* (London: Sage).

Milgram, S. (1963), 'A Behavioral Study of Obedience', *Journal of Abnormal and Social Psychology*, 67: 371–8.

—— (1974), *Obedience to Authority* (London: Tavistock).

—— and Shotland, L. (1973), *Television and Antisocial Behavior: Field Experiments* (New York: Academic Press).

Milkman, R. (1997), *Farewell to the Factory: Auto Workers in the Late Twentieth Century* (Berkeley and Los Angeles: University of California Press).

Millen, D. (1997), 'Some Methodological and Epistemological Issues Raised by Doing Feminist Research on Non-Feminist Women', *Sociological Research Online*, 2, www.socresonline.org.uk/socresonline/2/3/3.html.

Miller, D., and Slater, D. (2000), *The Internet: An Ethnographic Approach* (Oxford: Berg).

Miller, D. Disney (1956), *The Story of Walt Disney* (New York: Dell).

Miller, N., and Morgan, D. (1993), 'Called to Account: The CV as an Autobiographical Practice', *Sociology*, 27: 133–43.

Miller, R. L. (2000), *Researching Life Stories and Family Histories* (London: Sage).

Millward, N., Bryson, A., and Forth, J. (2000), *All Change at Work? British Employment Relations 1980–1998, as Portrayed by the Workplace Industrial Relations Survey Series* (London: Routledge).

Mintzberg, H. (1973), *The Nature of Managerial Work* (New York: Harper & Row).

Mirchandani, K. (1999), 'Feminist Insight on Gendered Work: New Directions in Research on Women and Entrepreneurship', *Gender, Work and Organization*, 6(4): 224–35.

Mishler, E. G. (1986), *Research Interviewing: Context and Narrative* (Cambridge, Mass.: Harvard University Press).

Mitchell, J. C. (1983), 'Case and Situation Analysis', *Sociological Review*, 31: 186–211.

Mitchell, T. (1985), 'An Evaluation of the Validity of Correlational Research Conducted in Organizations', *Academy of Management Review*, 10(2): 192–205.

Moody, F. (1990), *I Sing the Body Electronic: A Year with Microsoft on the Multimedia Frontier* (New York: Viking).

Morgan, D. L. (1998a), *Planning Focus Groups* (Thousand Oaks, Calif.: Sage).

—— (1998b), 'Practical Strategies for Combining Qualitative and Quantitative Methods: Applications for Health Research', *Qualitative Health Research*, 8: 362–76.

Morgan, G., and Smircich, L. (1980), 'The Case for Qualitative Research', *Academy of Management Review*, 5: 491–500.

Morrison, D. E. (1998), *The Search for a Method: Focus Groups and the Development of Mass Communication Research* (Luton: University of Luton Press).

Moser, C. A., and Kalton, G. (1971), *Survey Methods in Social Investigation* (London: Heinemann).

Musson, G. (1998), 'Life Histories', in G. Symon and C. Cassell (eds), *Qualitative Methods and Analysis in Organizational Research* (London: Sage).

Newell, A., and Simon, H. A. (1972), *Human Problem Solving* (Englewood Cliffs, NJ: Prentice Hall).

Nichols, T., and Beynon, H. (1977), *Living with Capitalism: Class Relations and the Modern Factory* (London: Routledge).

Noblit, G. W., and Hare, R. D. (1988), *Meta-Ethnography: Synthesizing Qualitative Studies* (Newbury Park, Calif.: Sage).

Noordengraaf, M., and Stewart, R. (2000), 'Managerial Behaviour Research in Private and Public Sectors: Distinctiveness, Disputes and Directions', *Journal of Management Studies*, 37(3): 427–43.

Oakley, A. (1981), 'Interviewing Women: A Contradiction in Terms', in H. Roberts (ed.), *Doing Feminist Research* (London: Routledge & Kegan Paul).

—— (1998), 'Gender, Methodology and People's Ways of Knowing: Some Problems with Feminism and the Paradigm Debate in Social Science', *Sociology*, 32: 707–31.

O'Connor, H., and Madge, C. (2001), 'Cyber-Mothers: Online Synchronous Interviewing using Conferencing Software', *Sociological Research Online*, 2, www.socresonline.org.uk/5/4/o'connor.html.

Okely, J. (1994), 'Thinking through Fieldwork', in A. Bryman and R. G. Burgess (eds), *Analyzing Qualitative Data* (London: Routledge).

Oppenheim, A. N. (1966), *Questionnaire Design and Attitude Measurement* (London: Heinemann).

—— (1992), *Questionnaire Design, Interviewing and Attitude Measurement* (London: Pinter).

Organ, D. W. (1988), *Organizational Citizenship Behaviour: The Good Soldier Syndrome* (Lexington, Mass.: Lexington Books).

Orpen, C. (1979), 'The Effects of Job Enrichment on Employee Satisfaction, Motivation, Involvement, and Performance: A Field Experiment', *Human Relations*, 32(3): 189–217.

Orton, J. D.(1997), 'From Inductive to Interative Grounded Theory: Zipping the Gap between Process Theory and Process Data', *Scandinavian Journal of Management*, 13(4): 419–38.

Oswick, C., Keenoy, T., and Grant, D. (1997), 'Managerial Discourses: Words Speak Louder than Actions?', *Journal of Applied Management Studies*, 6(1): 5–12.

Park, S. H. (1996), 'Relationships between Involvement and Attitudinal Loyalty Constructs in Adult Fitness Programmes', *Journal of Leisure Research*, 28(4): 233–50.

Parker, M. (2000), *Organizational Culture and Identity* (London: Sage).

Partington, D. (2000), 'Building Grounded Theories of Management Action', *British Journal of Management*, 11: 91–102.

Pawson, R., and Tilley, N. (1997), *Realistic Evaluation* (London: Sage).

Peñaloza, L. (2000), 'The Commodification of the American West: Marketers' Production of Cultural Meanings at the Trade Show', *Journal of Marketing*, 64: 82–109.

Pendergrast, M. (1993), *For God, Country and Coca-Cola: The Unauthorized History of the World's Most Popular Soft Drink* (London: Weidenfeld & Nicolson).

Penn, R., Rose, M., and Rubery, J. (1994), *Skill and Occupational Change* (Oxford: Oxford University Press).

Peräkylä, A. (1997), 'Reliability and Validity in Research Based on Transcripts', in D. Silverman (ed.), *Qualitative Research: Theory, Method and Practice* (London: Sage).

Perlow, L. A. (1995), 'The Time Famine: The Unintended Consequences of the Way Time is Used at Work', unpublished Ph.D. thesis, MIT.

——(1997), *Finding Time: How Corporations, Individuals and Families can Benefit from New Work Practices* (Ithaca, NY: ILR Press).

——(1999), 'Time Famine: Toward a Sociology of Work Time', *Administrative Science Quarterly*, 44: 57–81.

Pettigrew, A. (1985), *The Awakening Giant: Continuity and Change in Imperial Chemical Industries* (Oxford: Blackwell).

——(1990), 'Longitudinal Field Research on Change: Theory and Practice', *Organization Science*, 1(3): 267–92.

——(1997), 'What is a Processual Analysis?', *Scandinavian Journal of Management*, 13: 337–48.

——and McNulty, T. (1995), 'Power and Influence in and around the Boardroom', *Human Relations*, 48(8): 845–73.

——and Whipp, R. (1991), *Managing Change for Competitive Success* (Oxford: Blackwell).

Pfeffer, J. (1997), 'Pitfalls on the Road to Measurement: The Dangerous Liaison of Human Resource Management with the Ideas of Accounting and Finance', *Human Resource Management*, 36(3): 357–65.

Phillips, D. L. (1973), *Abandoning Method* (San Francisco: Jossey-Bass).

Phillips, N., and Brown, J. L. (1993), 'Analyzing Communications in and around Organizations: A Critical Hermeneutic Approach', *Academy of Management Journal*, 36: 1547–76.

Piercy, N. F., Harris, L. C., and Lane, N. (2002), 'Market Orientation and Retail Operatives' Expectations', *Journal of Business Research*, 55: 261–73.

Platt, J. (1981), 'The Social Construction of "Positivism" and its Significance in British Sociology, 1950–80', in P. Abrams, R. Deem, J. Finch, and P. Rock (eds), *Practice and Progress: British Sociology 1950–1980* (London: George Allen & Unwin).

——(1983), 'The Development of the "Participant Observation" Method in Sociology: Origin Myth and History', *Journal of the History of the Behavioral Sciences*, 19: 379–93.

Podsakoff, P. M., and Dalton, D. R. (1987), 'Research Methodology in Organizational Studies', *Journal of Management*, 13: 419–44.

Poland, B. D. (1995), 'Transcription Quality as an Aspect of Rigor in Qualitative Research', *Qualitative Inquiry*, 1: 290–310.

Pollert, A. (1981), *Girls, Wives, Factory Lives* (London: Macmillan).

Pondy, L. Frost, P., Morgan, G., and Dandridge, T. (1983), *Organizational Symbolism* (London: JAI Press).

Porter, S. (1993), 'Critical Realist Ethnography: The Case of Racism and Professionalism in a Medical Setting', *Sociology*, 27: 591–609.

Potter, J. (1996), *Representing Reality: Discourse, Rhetoric and Social Construction* (London: Sage).

——(1997), 'Discourse Analysis as a Way of Analysing Naturally Occurring Talk', in D. Silverman (ed.), *Qualitative Research: Theory, Method and Practice* (London: Sage).

——and Wetherell, M. (1987), *Discourse and Social Psychology: Beyond Attitudes and Behaviour* (London: Sage).

————(1994), 'Analyzing Discourse', in A. Bryman and R. G. Burgess (eds), *Analyzing Qualitative Data* (London: Routledge).

Powell, G. N., and Butterfield, D. A. (1997), 'Effect of Race on Promotions to Top Management in a Federal Department', *Academy of Management Journal*, 40: 112–28.

Powell, T. C. (1995), 'Total Quality Management as Competitive Advantage: A Review and Empirical Study', *Strategic Management Journal*, 16: 15–37.

Prasad, P. (1993), 'Symbolic Processes in the Implementation of Technological Change: A Symbolic Interactionist Study of Work Computerization', *Academy of Management Journal*, 36(6): 1400–29.

Pringle, R. (1988), *Secretaries Talk: Sexuality, Power and Work* (London: Verso).

Psathas, G. (1995), *Conversation Analysis: The Study of Talk-in-Interaction* (Thousand Oaks, Calif.: Sage).

Pugh, D. S. (1983), 'Studying Organizational Structure and Process', in G. Morgan (ed.), *Beyond Method*. Newbury Park, Calif.: Sage.

——(1988), 'The Aston Research Programme', in A. Bryman (ed.) *Doing Research in Organizations* (London: Routledge).

——(1998) 'Introduction', in D. S. Pugh (ed.), *The Aston Programme, I. The Aston Study and its Developments* (Dartmouth: Ashgate).

——Hickson, D. J., Hinings, C. R., and Turner, C. (1968), 'Dimensions of Organization Structure', *Administrative Science Quarterly*, 13: 65–105.

Punch, M. (1994), 'Politics and Ethics in Qualitative Research', in N. K. Denzin and Y. S. Lincoln (eds), *Handbook of Qualitative Research* (Thousand Oaks, Calif.: Sage).

Rafaeli, A., Dutton, J., Harquail, C. V., and Mackie-Lewis, S. (1997), 'Navigating by Attire: The Use of Dress by Female Administrative Employees', *Academy of Management Journal*, 40: 9–45.

Ragin, C. C., and Becker, H. S. (1989), 'How the Microcomputer is Changing our Analytic Habits', in G. Blank et al. (eds), *New Technology in Sociology: Practical Applications in Research and Work* (New Brunswick, NJ: Transaction Publishers).

Ram, M. (1994), *Managing to Survive: Working Lives in Small Firms* (Oxford: Blackwell).

——(1996), 'Uncovering the Management Process: An Ethnographic Approach', *British Journal of Management*, 7(1): 35–44.

Ramirez, I., and Bartunek, J. (1989), 'The Multiple Realities and Experiences of Internal Organization Development in Healthcare', *Journal of Organizational Change Management*, 2(1): 40–57.

Ranson, S., Hinings, B., and Greenwood, R. (1980), 'The Structuring of Organizational Structures', *Administrative Science Quarterly*, 25: 1–17.

Raz, A. E. (1999), *Riding the Black Ship: Japan and Tokyo Disneyland* (Cambridge, Mass.: Harvard University Press).

Reason, P. (1999), 'Integrating Action and Reflection through Cooperative Inquiry', *Management Learning*, 30(2): 207–26.

——and Marshall, J. (1987), 'Research as Personal Process', in D. Boud and V. Griffin (eds), *Appreciating Adult Learning* (London: Kogan Page).

——and Rowan, J. (1981) (eds), *Human Inquiry* (Chichester: John Wiley).

Reed, M. (1985), *Redirections in Organizational Analysis* (London: Tavistock).

Reed, M. I. (1997), 'In Praise of Duality and Dualism: Rethinking Agency and Structure in Organizational Analysis', *Organization Studies*, 18(1): 21–42.

——(2000), 'The Limits of Discourse Analysis in Organizational Analysis', *Organization*, 7: 524–30.

Reinharz, S. (1992), *Feminist Methods in Social Research* (New York: Oxford University Press).

Reiss, A. J. (1968), 'Stuff and Nonsense about Social Surveys and Participant Observation', in H. S. Becker, B. Geer, D. Riesman, and R. S. Weiss (eds), *Institutions and the Person: Papers in Memory of Everett C. Hughes* (Chicago: Aldine).

——(1976), 'Systematic Observation of Natural Phenomena', in H. W. Sinaiko and L. A. Broedling (eds), *Perspectives on Attitude Assessment: Surveys and their Alternatives* (Champaign, Ill.: Pendleton).

Richards, L., and Richards, T. (1994), 'From Filing Cabinet to Computer', in A. Bryman and R. G. Burgess (eds), *Analyzing Qualitative Data* (London: Routledge).

Richardson, L. (1990), 'Narrative and Sociology', *Journal of Contemporary Ethnography*, 19: 116–35.

——(1994), 'Writing: A Method of Inquiry', in N. K. Denzin and Y. S. Lincoln (eds), *Handbook of Qualitative Research* (Thousand Oaks, Calif.: Sage).

Riessman, C. K. (1993), *Narrative Analysis* (Newbury Park, Calif.: Sage).

Ring, P. S., and Van de Ven, A. (1994), 'Developmental Processes of Cooperative Interorganizational Relationships', *Academy of Management Review*, 19(1): 90–118.

Ritzer, G. (1975), 'Sociology: A Multiple Paradigm Science', *American Sociologist*, 10: 156–67.

Roberts, H. (1990), *Doing Feminist Research* (London: Routledge).

Robinson, W. S. (1951), 'The Logical Structure of Analytic Induction', *American Sociological Review*, 16: 812–18.

Roethlisberger, F. J., and Dickson, W. J. (1939), *Management and the Worker: An Account of a Research Programme Conducted by the Western Electric Company, Hawthorne Works, Chicago* (Cambridge, Mass: Harvard University Press).

Rosen, M. (1991), 'Coming to Terms with the Field: Understanding and Doing Organizational Ethnography', *Journal of Management Studies*, 28(1): 1–24.

Rosenau, P. M. (1992), *Post-Modernism and the Social Sciences: Insights, Inroads, and Intrusions* (Princeton: Princeton University Press).

Rosnow, R. L., and Rosenthal, R. (1997), *People Studying People: Artifacts and Ethics in Behaviorioral Research* (New York: W. H. Freeman).

Rousseau, D. (1985), 'Issues of Level in Organizational Research: Multi-Level and Cross-Level Perspectives', in L. Cummings and B. Staw (eds), *Research in Organizational Behaviour*, vol. 7 (London: JAI Press).

Roy, A., Walters, P., and Luk, S. (2001), 'Chinese Puzzles and Paradoxes: Conducting Business Research in China', *Journal of Business Research*, 52: 203–10.

Roy, D. (1958), 'Banana Time: Job Satisfaction and Informal Interaction', *Human Organisation*, 18: 156–68.

Rubin, H. J., and Rubin, I. S. (1995), *Qualitative Interviewing: The Art of Hearing Data* (Thousand Oaks, Calif.: Sage).

Saavedra, R., and Kwun, S. (2000), 'Affective States in Job Characteristics Theory', *Journal of Organizational Behavior*, 21: 131–46.

Sackmann, S. A. (1992), 'Culture and Subcultures: An Analysis of Organizational Knowledge', *Administrative Science Quarterly*, 37(3): 363–99.

Sacks, H., Schegloff, E. A., and Jefferson, G. (1974), 'A Simplest Systematics for the Organization of Turn-Taking in Conversation', *Language*, 50: 696–735.

Salancik, G. R. (1979), 'Field Stimulations for Organizational Behavior Research', *Administrative Science Quarterly*, 24: 638–49.

Samuel, R. (1976), 'Oral History and Local History', *History Workshop Journal*, 1: 191–208.

Sanjek, R. (1990), 'A Vocabulary for Fieldnotes', in R. Sanjek (ed.), *Fieldnotes: The Making of Anthropology* (Ithaca, NY: Cornell University Press).

Sarsby, J. (1984), 'The Fieldwork Experience', in R. F. Ellen (ed.), *Ethnographic Research: A Guide to General Conduct* (London: Academic Press).

Scandura, T. A. and Williams, E. A. (2000), 'Research Methodology in Management: Current Practices, Trends and Implications for Future Research', *Academy of Management Journal*, 43(6): 1248–64.

Scase, R., and Goffee, R. (1989), *Reluctant Managers: Their Work and Lifestyles* (London: Routledge).

Schaeffer, D. R., and Dillman, D. A. (1998), 'Development of a Standard E-Mail Methodology', *Public Opinion Quarterly*, 62: 378–97.

Schegloff, E. A. (1997), 'Whose Text? Whose Context?', *Discourse and Society*, 8: 165–87.

Schlesinger, P., Dobash, R. E., Dobash, R. P., and Weaver, C. K. (1992), *Women Viewing Violence* (London: British Film Institute).

Schoonhoven, C. B. (1981), 'Problems with Contingency Theory: Testing Assumptions Hidden within the Language of Contingency Theory', *Administrative Science Quarterly*, 26: 349–77.

Schrøder, K. C. (1999), 'The Best of Both Worlds? Media Audience Research between Rival Paradigms', in P. Alasuutari (ed.), *Rethinking the Media Audience* (London: Sage).

Schuman, H., and Converse, J. (1971), 'The Effects of Black and White Interviewers on Black Responses in 1968', *Public Opinion Quarterly*, 35: 44–68.

—— and Presser, S. (1981), *Questions and Answers in Attitude Surveys: Experiments on Question Form, Wording, and Context* (San Diego, Calif.: Academic Press).

Schutte, N., Toppinnen, S., Kalimo, R., and Schaufeli, W. (2000), 'The Factorial Validity of the Maslach Burnout Inventory—General Survey (MBI—GS) Across Occupational Groups and Nations', *Journal of Occupational and Organizational Psychology*, 73(1): 53–67.

Schutz, A. (1962), *Collected Papers, I. The Problem of Social Reality* (The Hague: Martinus Nijhof).

Schwartzman, H. B. (1993), *Ethnography in Organizations*, Qualitative Research Methods Series 27 (Newbury Park, Calif.: Sage).

Scott, A. (1994), *Willing Slaves?: British Workers under HRM* (Cambridge: Cambridge University Press).

Scott, A. M. (1994), *Gender Segregation and Social Change: Men and Women in Changing Labour Markets* (Oxford: Oxford University Press).

Scott, J. (1990), *A Matter of Record* (Cambridge: Polity).

Scott, W., Banks, J., Halsey, A., and Lupton, T. (1956), *Technical Change and Industrial Relations* (Liverpool: Liverpool University Press).

Seale, C. (1999), *The Quality of Qualitative Research* (London: Sage).

Shaffir, W. B., and Stebbins, R. A. (1991), *Experiencing Fieldwork: An Inside View of Qualitative Research* (Newbury Park: Sage).

Shapiro, M. (1985–6), 'Metaphor in the Philosophy of the Social Sciences', *Cultural Critique*, 2: 191–214.

Sharpe, D. (1997), 'Managerial Control Strategies and Subcultural Proccesses', in S. Sackmann (ed.), *Cultural Complexity in Organizations* (London: Sage).

Sheehan, K. (2001), 'E-Mail Survey Response Rates: A Review', *Journal of Computer-Mediated Communication*, 6, **www.ascusc.org/jcmc/vol6/issue2/sheehan.html**.

—— and Hoy, M.G. (1999), 'Using E-Mail to Survey Internet Users in the United States: Methodology and Assessment', *Journal of Computer-Mediated Communication*, 4, **www.ascusc.org/jcmc/vol4/issue3/sheehan.html**.

Shenoy, S. (1981), 'Organization Structure and Context: A Replication of the Aston Study in India', in D. J. Hickson and J. McMillan (eds), *Organization and Nation: The Aston Programme IV*. (Aldershot: Gower).

Shrivasta, P., Mitroff, I. I., Miller, D., and Miglani, A. (1988), 'Understanding Industrial Crises', *Journal of Management Studies*, 25: 283–304.

Silverman, D. (1984), 'Going Private: Ceremonial Forms in a Private Oncology Clinic', *Sociology*, 18: 191–204.

—— (1985), *Qualitative Methodology and Sociology: Describing the Social World* (Aldershot: Gower).

—— (1993), *Interpreting Qualitative Data: Methods for Analysing Qualitative Data* (London: Sage).

—— (2000), *Doing Qualitative Research: A Practical Handbook* (London: Sage).

Simon, H. (1960), *The New Science of Management Decision* (New York: Harper).

Skinner, B. (1953), *Science and Human Behaviour* (New York: Macmillan).

Smith, C. B. (1997), 'Casting the Net: Surveying an Internet Population', *Journal of Computer-Mediated Communication*, 3, **www.ascusc.org/jcmc/vol3/issue1/yun.html**.

Smith, J. K. (1983), 'Quantitative versus Qualitative Research: An Attempt to Clarify the Issue', *Educational Researcher*, 12: 6–13.

—— and Heshusius, L. (1986), 'Closing down the Conversation: The End of the Quantitative–Qualitative Debate among Educational Enquirers', *Educational Researcher*, 15: 4–12.

Smith, T. W. (1995), 'Trends in Non-Response Rates', *International Journal of Public Opinion Research*, 7: 157–71.

Snow, C. C., and Thomas, J. B. (1994), 'Field Research Methods in Strategic Management: Contributions to Theory Building and Testing', *Journal of Management Studies*, 31(4): 457–80.

Snyder, N., and Glueck, W. F. (1980), 'How Managers Plan—The Analysis of Managers' Activities', *Long Range Planning*, 13: 70–6.

Spender, J. (1989), *Industry Recipes: An Enquiry into the Nature and Sources of Managerial Judgement* (Oxford: Blackwell).

Spradley, J. P. (1979), *The Ethnographic Interview* (New York: Holt, Rinehart & Winston).

——and McCurdy, D. (1972), *The Cultural Experience.* (Chicago: Science Research Associates).

Sprokkereef, A., Larkin, E., Pole, C. J., and Burgess, R. G. (1995), 'The Data, the Team, and the Ethnograph', *Studies in Qualitative Methodology*, 5: 81–103.

Sprouse, M. (1992) (ed.), *Sabotage in the American Workplace* (San Francisco: Pressure Drop Press).

Stacey, J. (1988), 'Can there be a Feminist Ethnography?', *Women's International Studies Forum*, 11: 21–7.

Stacey, M. (1960), *Tradition and Change: A Study of Banbury* (London: Oxford University Press).

Stake, R. E. (1995), *The Art of Case Study Research* (Thousand Oaks, Calif.: Sage).

Stanley, L., and Temple, B. (1995), 'Doing the Business? Evaluating Software Packages to Aid the Analysis of Qualitative Data Sets', *Studies in Qualitative Methodology*, 5: 169–97.

Starbuck, W. H. (1981), 'A Trip to View the Elephants and Rattlesnakes in the Garden of Aston', in A. H. van de Ven and W. F. Joyce (eds), *Perspectives on Organization Design and Behaviour* (New York: Wiley).

Stewart, R. (1967), *Managers and their Jobs* (London: Macmillan).

Stiles, P. (2001), 'The Impact of the Board on Strategy: An Empirical Examination', *Journal of Management Studies*, 38(5): 627–50.

Storey, J., Quintas, P., Taylor, P., and Fowle, W. (2002), 'Flexible Employment Contracts and their Implications for Product and Process Innovation', *International Journal of Human Resource Management*, 13(1): 1–18.

Strauss, A. (1987), *Qualitative Analysis for Social Scientists* (New York: Cambridge University Press).

——and Corbin, J. M. (1990), *Basics of Qualitative Research: Grounded Theory Procedures and Techniques* (Newbury Park, Calif.: Sage).

——and Corbin, J. M. (1998), *Basics of Qualitative Research: Techniques and Procedures for Developing Grounded Theory* (Thousand Oaks, Calif.: Sage).

——Schatzman, L., Ehrlich, D., Bucher, R., and Sabshin, M. (1973), 'The Hospital and its Negotiated Order', in G. Salaman and K. Thompson (eds), *People and Organizations* (London: Longman).

Sudman, S., and Blair, E. (1999), 'Sampling in the Twenty-First Century', *Journal of the Academy of Marketing Science*, 27(2): 269–77.

——and Bradburn, N. M. (1982), *Asking Questions: A Practical Guide to Questionnaire Design* (San Francisco: Jossey-Bass).

Sutton, R. I. (1992), 'Feelings about a Disneyland Visit: Photography and the Reconstruction of Bygone Emotions', *Journal of Management Inquiry*, 1: 278–87.

——and Rafaeli, A. (1988), 'Untangling the Relationship between Displayed Emotions and Organizational Sales: The Case of Convenience Stores', *Academy of Management Journal*, 31: 461–87.

Sutton, R. I., and Rafaeli, A. (1992), 'How we Untangled the Relationship between Displayed Emotion and Organizational Sales: A Tale of Bickering and Optimism', in P. J. Frost and R. Stablein (eds), *Doing Exemplary Research* (Newbury Park, Calif.: Sage).

Swales, J. M., and Rogers, P. S. (1995), 'Discourse and the Projection of Corporate Culture: The Mission-Statement', *Discourse and Society*, 6(2): 223–42.

Sweet, C. (2001), 'Designing and Conducting Virtual Focus Groups', *Qualitative Market Research*, 4: 130–5.

Terkel, S. (1974), *Working* (Harmondsworth: Penguin).

Thomas, R., and Linstead, A. (2002), 'Losing the Plot? Middle Managers and Identity', *Organization*, 9(1): 71–93.

Thompson, E. P. (1968), *The Making of the English Working Class* (London: Pelican).

Thompson, P. (1989), *The Nature of Work*, 2nd edn. (London: Macmillan).

Tinsley, C. H., and Brett, J. M (2001), 'Managing Workplace Conflict in the United States and Hong Kong', *Organizational Behavior and Human Decision Processes*, 85(2): 360–81.

Tourangeau, R., and Smith, T. W. (1996), 'Asking Sensitive Questions: The Impact of Data Collection Mode, Question Format, and Question Context', *Public Opinion Quarterly*, 60: 275–304.

Tranfield, D., and Starkey, K. (1998), 'The Nature, Social Organisation and Promotion of Management Research: Towards Policy', *British Journal of Management*, 9: 341–53.

Trow, M. (1957), 'Comment on "Participant Observation and Interviewing: A Comparison"' *Human Organization*, 16: 33–5.

Truss, C. (2001), 'Complexities and Controversies in Linking HRM with Organizational Outcomes', *Journal of Management Studies*, 38(8): 1121–49.

Tse, A. C. B. (1998), 'Comparing the Response Rate, Response Speed and Response Quality of Two Methods of Sending Questionnaires: E-Mail vs. Mail', *Journal of the Market Research Society*, 40: 353–61.

——(1999), 'Conducting Electronic Focus Group Discussions among Chinese Respondents', *Journal of the Market Research Society*, 41: 407–15.

Turner, B. A. (1983), 'The Use of Grounded Theory for the Qualitative Analysis of Organizational Behaviour', *Journal of Management Studies*, 20(3): 321–48.

——(1994), 'Patterns of Crisis Behaviour: A Qualitative Inquiry', in A. Bryman and R. G. Burgess (eds), *Analyzing Qualitative Data* (London: Routledge).

Usunier, J. C. (1998), *International & Cross-Cultural Management Research* (London: Sage).

Van Maanen, J. (1978), 'On Watching the Watchers', in P. Manning and J. Van Maanen (eds), *Policing: The View from the Street* (Santa Monica, Calif.: Goodyear).

——(1988), *Tales of the Field: On Writing Ethnography* (Chicago: University of Chicago Press).

——(1991a), 'Playing Back the Tape: Early Days in the Field', in W. B. Shaffir and R. A. Stebbins (eds), *Experiencing Fieldwork: An Inside View of Qualitative Research* (Newbury Park, Calif.: Sage).

——(1991b), 'The Smile Factory: Work at Disneyland', in P. J. Frost, L. F. Moore, M. R. Louis, C. C. Lundberg, and J. Martin (eds), *Reframing Organizational Culture* (Newbury Park, Calif.: Sage).

——and Kolb, D. (1985), 'The Professional Apprentice: Observations on Fieldwork Roles in two Organizational Settings', *Research in the Sociology of Organizations*, 4: 1–33.

Vaughan, D. (1990), 'Autonomy, Independence and Social Control: NASA and the Space Shuttle *Challenger*', *Administrative Science Quarterly*, 35: 225–57.

Von Wright, G. H. (1971), *Explanation and Understanding* (London: Routledge).

Vroom, V. H. (1964), *Work and Motivation* (New York: Wiley).

Waddington, D. (1994), 'Participant Observation', in C. Cassell and G. Symon (eds), *Qualitative Methods in Organizational Research* (London: Sage).

Wajcman, J., and Martin, B. (2002), 'Narratives of Identity in Modern Management: The Corrosion of Identity Difference?', *Sociology*, 36: 985–1002.

Walsh, D. (1972), 'Sociology and the Social World', in P. Filmer, M. Phillipson, D. Silverman, and D. Walsh, *New Directions in Sociological Theory* (London: Collier-Macmillan).

Wasko, J., Phillips, M., and Meehan, E. R. (2001) (eds), *Dazzled by Disney: The Global Disney Audiences Project* (London: Leicester University Press).

Warren, C. (1988), *Gender Issues in Field Research* (London: Sage).

Wass, V. J., and Wells, P. E. (1994), *Principles and Practice in Business and Management Research* (Aldershot: Dartmouth).

Watson, T. (1994a), *In Search of Management: Culture, Chaos and Control in Managerial Work* (London: Routledge).

——(1994b), 'Managing, Crafting and Researching: Words, Skill and Imagination in Shaping Management Research', *British Journal of Management*, 5S: S77–87.

Weaver, A., and Atkinson, P. (1994), *Microcomputing and Qualitative Data Analysis* (Aldershot: Avebury).

Webb, E. J., Campbell, D. T., Schwartz, R. D., and Sechrest, L. (1966), *Unobtrusive Measures: Nonreactive Measures in the Social Sciences* (Chicago: Rand McNally).

Weber, M. (1947), *The Theory of Social and Economic Organization*, trans. A. M. Henderson and T. Parsons (New York: Free Press).

Weick, K. E. (1990), 'The Vulnerable System: An Analysis of the Tenerife Air Disaster', *Journal of Management*, 16: 571–93.

——(1995), *Sensemaking in Organizations* (Thousand Oaks, Calif.: Sage).

Weil, S. (1987), *Formative Writings 1929–1941* (London: Routledge).

Weinholtz, D., Kacer, B., and Rocklin, T. (1995), 'Salvaging Quantitative Research with Qualitative Data', *Qualitative Health Research*, 5: 388–97.

Weitzman, E. A., and Miles, M. B. (1995), *Computer Programs for Qualitative Data Analysis* (Thousand Oaks, Calif.: Sage).

Westwood, S. (1984), *All Day Every Day: Factory, Family, Women's Lives* (London: Pluto Press).

Wetherell, M. (1998), 'Positioning and Interpretative Repertoires: Conversation Analysis and Post-Structuralism in Dialogue', *Discourse and Society*, 9: 387–412.

Wharton, A. (1993), 'The Affective Consequences of Service Work', *Work and Occupations*, 20: 205–32.

Whitfield, K., and Strauss, G. (1998) (eds.), *Researching the World of Work: Strategies and Methods in Studying Industrial Relations* (Ithaca, NY: Cornell University Press).

Whittington, R. (1989), *Corporate Strategies in Recession and Recovery* (London: Unwin Hyman).

Whyte W. F. (1953), 'Interviewing for Organizational Research', *Human Organization*, 12(2): 15–22.

——(1955), *Street Corner Society*, 2nd edn. (Chicago: University of Chicago Press).

Widdicombe, S. (1993), 'Autobiography and Change: Rhetoric and Authenticity of "Gothic" Style', in E. Burman and I. Parker (eds), *Discourse Analytic Research: Readings and Repertoires of Text* (London: Routledge).

Wiersma, U. (1994), 'A Taxonomy of Behavioral Strategies for Coping with Work–Home Role Conflict', *Human Relations*, 47(2): 211–21.

Wilkinson, S. (1998), 'Focus Groups in Feminist Research: Power, Interaction, and the Co-Production of Meaning', *Women's Studies International Forum*, 21: 111–25.

——(1999a), 'Focus Group Methodology: A Review', *International Journal of Social Research Methodology*, 1: 181–203.

——(1999b), 'Focus Groups: A Feminist Method', *Psychology of Women Quarterly*, 23: 221–44.

Williams, R. (1976), 'Symbolic Interactionism: Fusion of Theory and Research', in D. C. Thorns (ed.), *New Directions in Sociology* (London: David & Charles).

Willman, P., Renton-O'Creevy, M., Nicholson, N., and Soane, E. (2002), 'Traders, Managers and Loss Aversion in Investment Banking: A Field Study', *Accounting, Organizations and Society*, 27: 85–98.

Willmott, H. (1990), 'Beyond Paradigmatic Closure in Organisational Enquiry', in J. Hassard and D. Pym (eds), *The Theory and Philosophy of Organizations*, (London: Routledge).

—— (1993), 'Breaking the Paradigm Mentality', *Organization Studies*, 14(5): 681–719.

Wilson, F. (1995), *Organizational Behaviour and Gender* (London: McGraw Hill).

Winch, P. (1958), *The Idea of a Social Science and its Relation to Philosophy* (London: Routledge & Kegan Paul).

Winter, R. (1989), *Learning from Experience: Principles and Practice in Action-Research* (Falmer: London).

Wolcott, H. F. (1990), *Writing up Qualitative Research* (Newbury Park, Calif.: Sage).

—— (1995), 'Making a Study More Ethnographic', in J. Van Maanen (ed.) *Representation in Ethnography* (London: Sage).

Woodward, J. (1965), *Industrial Organization: Theory and Practice* (Oxford: Oxford University Press).

Woolgar, S. (1988), *Science: The Very Idea* (Chichester: Ellis Horwood).

Yin, R. K. (1984), *Case Study Research: Design and Methods* (Beverly Hills, Calif.: Sage).

Yun, G. W., and Trumbo, C. W. (2000), 'Comparative Response to a Survey Executed by Post, E-Mail, and Web Form', *Journal of Computer-Mediated Communication*, 6, **www.ascusc.org/jcmc/vol6/issue1/yun.html**.

Zachary, G. P. (1994), *Showstopper: The Breakneck Race to Create Windows NT and the Next Generation at Microsoft* (New York: Free Press).

Zamanou, S., and Glaser, S. R. (1994), 'Moving toward Participation and Involvement', *Group and Organization Management*, 19(4): 475–502.

Zerubavel, E. (1981), *Hidden Rhythms: Schedules and Calendars in Social Life* (Chicago: University of Chicago Press).

Zimmerman, D. H., and Wieder, D. L. (1977), 'The Diary: Diary-Interview Method', *Urban Life*, 5: 479–98.

Zuber-Skerritt, O. (1996), *New Directions in Action Research* (London: Falmer).

Name Index

Subject Index

Page numbers in **bold** refer to expositions of subjects in boxes.